FREEMASONS

SOUTH DAKOTA TERRITORY

A - K

Freemasons South Dakota Territory – A - K - Compiled with graphics and edits by Darrell Jordan, Copyright ©
First Edition 2024. All rights reserved.

No part of this book may be reproduced in whole or in part without the written permission from the publisher, nor stored in any retrieval system or transmitted by any means, electronic, mechanical, photocopying, recording, or other, without the written consent of the publisher.

For bulk purchases, please contact the publisher.
Enquiry@Athenaia.Co

Library of Congress Cataloging-in Publication Data
Names: Jordan, Darrell
Freemasons South Dakota Territory – A – K, Darrell Jordan, MPS
Description: First U.S. edition. | Coeur D'Alene, Idaho: Athenaia [2024]
Identifiers: LCCN (pending) |
ISBN 979-8-88556-055-9 (First Edition hardcover)
Subjects: OCC012000: SOC038000: SOCIAL SCIENCE / Freemasonry & Secret Societies |
BODY, MIND & SPIRIT / Mysticism |
PHI013000: PHILOSOPHY / Metaphysics
LC record available at https://lccn. loc.gov

On the internet: Parallel47North.com/collections/esoteric-books
Managing Editor: Darrell Jordan
Original Author and Essay: Freemasons South Dakota Territory – A - K
Executive Producer: Yuka Jordan
Book Cover Design by Yuka Jordan
Book Cover Art and Illustrations: Jessica Naomi
Image Credits: Freemasons South Dakota Territory and Darrell Jordan's personal collection
Printed and bound in the United States

Publisher: Athenaia, LLC
2370 N Merritt Crk Lp, Ste 1
Coeur D'Alene, ID 83814
The United States

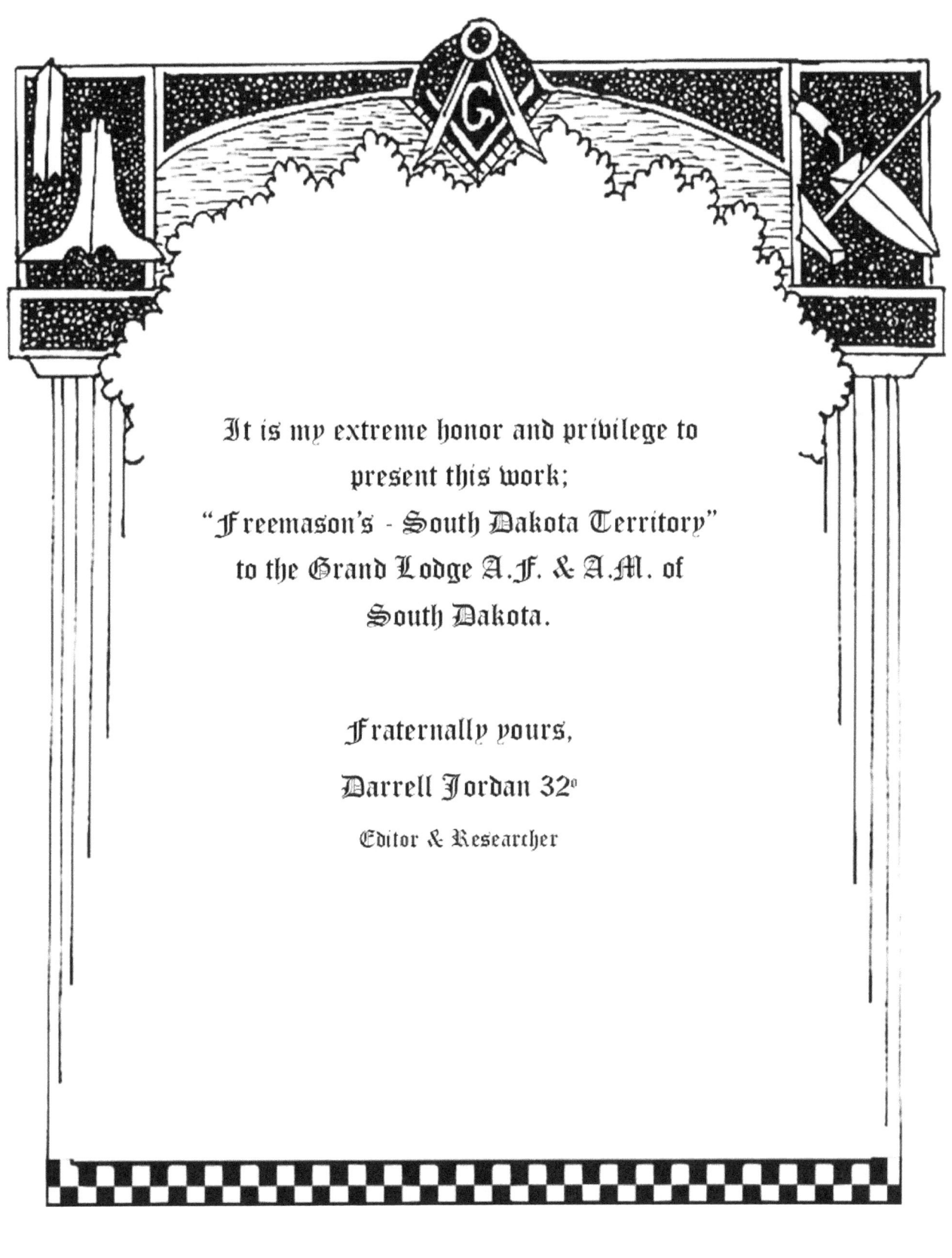

It is my extreme honor and privilege to
present this work;
"Freemason's - South Dakota Territory"
to the Grand Lodge A.F. & A.M. of
South Dakota.

Fraternally yours,
Darrell Jordan 32°
Editor & Researcher

Sources:

History of South Dakota Vol II; Robinson, Doane; 1904

History of Dakota Territory Vol. IV; Kingsbury, George W.; 1915

History of the great Northwest and its men of progress; Hyde, Cornelius William Gillam; 1901

SOUTH DAKOTA

Chronology

1609. Territory granted to Virginia by charter.

1628. Granted to John Endicott and other "Joint Adventurers."

1671. Spain took formal possession of all country west of Lake Michigan and the Mississippi River.

1681. Marquette's map, outlining principal features of state, known to exist.

1700. Mahas or Onakas occupies southeastern part of state.

Ree Indians known to be dwelling in Missouri River valley.

1703. On or before this date Charles Le Sueur published a map of the territory which is now South Dakota.

1712. French king granted the territory to Anthony Crozat for a period of twenty-five years.

1733. Reverted to king of France.

1743. Verendrye visited western part of state and took possession for France.

1750. Rees attacked by Sioux nation (date approximated) and after years of warfare are forced to retreat to the north.

1762. France ceded the territory to Spain.

1785. Pierre Dorion made an alliance with the Yankton Indians.

1790. Pierre Garreau resided with the Rees at Arikara at the mouth of the Grand River.

1796. Cedar Island, below Pierre, known to contain the trading house of Trudeau.

1800. Spain recedes the territory to France.

1803. Territory purchased of France by the United States.

1804. Attached to the Territory of Indiana, for judicial purposes.

Actual transfer of title and possession accomplished.

Lewis and Clark start on their expedition.

1805. The District of Louisiana becomes the Territory of Louisiana.

1806. Return trip of Lewis and Clark.

1807. First conflict with Indians.

1808. American Fur Company organized by Pierre Chouteau and Manuel Lisa.

1810. Loisel's post burned.

1811. Expedition of John Jacob Actor passes through state and touches the northern point of the Black Hills.

1812. Becomes part of Missouri Territory.

1816. Trudeau's trading house burns.

1817. American Fur Company construct a post on what is now

Goddard's Island. Two years later removed to Ft. Pierre.

1821. Missouri admitted to Union, and that part of the state west of the Missouri River left without government until 1854, while the part east of that river remained without government until 1834.

1822. Rocky Mountain Fur Company organized for trade along the Missouri River.

1823. General Ashley, head of the above company, routed in an attack by Rees, while attempting to go up the river. Colonel Henry Leavenworth leads an attack upon the Rees and punishes them, this being the first military invasion.

1828. Waneta removes from Elm to Missouri River.

1831. Steamboat Yellowstone makes first trip on Missouri.

1832. George Catlin, famous Indian portrait painter, visits the state and plies his art, securing many valuable portraits.

1834. South Dakota territory east of Missouri becomes part of Michigan.

1836. Michigan admitted as state and our state becomes a part of Wisconsin.

1837. Smallpox scourge practically destroys the Mandan Indian tribe and severely injures many other tribes.

1838. Becomes part of Iowa Territory.

1839. General John C. Fremont visits state in interest of science.

1840. Rev. Stephen R. Riggs, an eminent missionary to Indians, visits Fort Pierre.

1843. John J. Audubon, the renowned naturalist, and Edward Harris, a geologist of note, made a joint expedition to the territory.

1849. Minnesota Territory erected and made to include all of South Dakota east of the Missouri River.

1851. A second smallpox epidemic visits and despoils Indians.

1854. Territory west of Missouri River included in Nebraska.

1855. The fur trade practically over.

Fort Pierre fur station purchased by national government and 1200 troops stationed there during winter of 1855/56.

1856. Western Town Company, incorporated at Dubuque, Iowa, makes settlement at the Falls of the Sioux.

1857. Dakota Land Company, of St. Paul, organized and locates townsites at Falls of the Sioux, Flandreau, Medary, Estelline and other points in the Sioux valley.

Spirit Lake, Iowa, Massacre by Indians from Dakota.

Rescue of Abigail Gardner by Christian Indians, near Ashton.

1858. Minnesota admitted to Union and territory east of Missouri River left without any government until 1861.

General Harney makes treaty with Indians, which was never ratified.

A legislature elected which met at Sioux Falls and passed a memorial to Congress praying for the establishment of a Territorial government.

1859. A new election held at which Judge J. P. Kidder for Delegate to Congress, and a full quota of Territorial officers, including a new legislature, were elected. Congress ignored the movement.

Ratification of treaty opening land to settlement lying between the Sioux and Missouri rivers and extending as far north as a line between Pierre and Watertown.

Permanent settlements made at Elk Point, Yankton, Vermillion and Bon Homme.

Dakota "Democrat." a newspaper, established at Sioux Falls.

1860. Mass Convention held at Yankton praying Congress for Territorial government.

First schoolhouse built at Bon Homme.

1861. Territory erected, embracing what is now North and South Dakota, Montana and much of. Idaho and Wyoming. The "Dakotain" at Yankton and the "Republican" at Vermillion established.

1862. First Legislature meets at Yankton, which town becomes the capital of the Territory.

Territorial (now State) University located at Vermillion and the penitentiary located at Bon Homme.

A regiment recruited for service in the Civil War Minnesota Massacre occurs.

1863. Idaho Territory formed, leaving Dakota Territory practically as it remained until statehood.

Governor Jayne runs for Congress, seems to be elected, and resigns as governor.

Newton Edmunds of Yankton appointed governor.

First Masonic lodge established; St. John's, No. 166.

1865. Treaty signed at Fort Pierre which terminated the hostilities

resulting from the Minnesota Massacre.

1866. Andrew J. Faulk appointed governor.

Beginning of Red Cloud war which continued to 1868, and prevented the government from constructing roads through the state to the gold fields of Idaho and Montana.

1868. Red Cloud war ends. Sioux Reservation, west of Missouri River and including Black Hills, created.

1869. John A. Burbank appointed governor.

1872. First railroad in state, Sioux City to Vermillion.

1873. Above road continued to Yankton. Winona & St. Peter railroad built to Lake Kampeska.

1874. John L. Pennington appointed governor.

Custer expedition discovers gold in the Black Hills.

1875. Government attempts to secure treaty with the Indians

permitting mining in the Hills.

Miners rush to gold fields in violation of treaty rights.

A.F. & A.M. Grand Lodge established.

1876. Indians assemble for war on miners.

Battle of Little Big Horn and Custer Massacre.

Black Hills relinquished by treaty signed only by chiefs. Reservation Indians disarmed.

1878. William A. Howard made governor.

1879. Great boom begins.

Railroads start extensions.

1880 Governor Howard dies and N. G. Ordway is appointed governor.

Great October blizzard and continuous winter until middle of April, 1881.

1881. High waters in all rivers.

Springfield Normal established.

Small tract of land given to Nebraska.

Yankton College established.

Vermillion completely destroyed.

Capital removal commission appointed.

1882. Capital removed to Bismarck.

Division and statehood convention held at Canton. University buildings provided for by Clay County voting $10,000 bonds for buildings.

1883. First constitutional convention held at Sioux Falls. Brookings College established.

Madison Normal founded.

Presbyterian College opens at Pierre.

Sioux Falls College founded.

1884. Gilbert A. Pierce appointed governor and succeeds N. G. Ordway.

All Saints School founded at Sioux Falls.

1885. Law passed providing for a constitutional convention for part of Territory south of the forty-sixth parallel.

1887. Governor Pierce resigned and Louis K. Church was appointed by President Cleveland to the position.

Dakota Wesleyan founded.

School of mines founded.

Redfield College founded, and school opened in September.

1889. Territory divided and South Dakota admitted as a state.

A. C. Mellette succeeds Church as Territorial governor and later becomes first governor of the state.

Third constitutional convention meets in Sioux Falls. Beginning of new period of hard times.

Augustina College founded at Canton.

1890. The Messiah war and battle of Wounded Knee.

Death of Sitting Bull.

Lands between White and Cheyenne rivers opened to settlement.

1891. Governor Mellette enters upon second term.

W. W. Taylor becomes state treasurer.

Financial conditions somewhat improved.

1893. Charles H. Sheldon succeeds Mellette as governor.

Taylor succeeds himself.

Severe nation-wide financial panic.

1894. Financial conditions very unsatisfactory. Land values poor, many banks fail.

1895. Governor Sheldon continues as head of the state.

Treasurer Taylor, unable to settle with the state, absconds.

Later returns, is convicted and serves a term in the penitentiary.

Hard times continue.

1896. Andrew E. Lee, Populist, elected governor. Anti-prohibition amendment to constitution carries.

1897. James H. Kyle, Populist, elected senator.

1898. One regiment, the First South Dakota, and one battalion of cavalry, known as Grigsby's Cowboys, organized and mustered for service in Spanish war.

1899. First South Dakota arrives in Philippine Islands and sees service in subduing rebellion.

Governor Lee succeeds himself.

Initiative and referendum clauses added to Constitution. President McKinley visits state and welcomes First South Dakota regiment upon its return.

1900. Republicans returned to power. Charles N. Herreid elected governor.

1901. Robert J. Gamble elected senator in place of R. F. Pettigrew. Law school established at State University.

Department of History organized at Pierre, under state control.

Northern Normal and Industrial School opens.

1902. Governor Herreid reelected.

Senator Kyle dies and A. B. Kittredge is appointed to take his place.

The battleship South Dakota christened at San Francisco by Miss Grace Herreid, daughter of the governor.

1904. Rosebud Indian reservation opened to settlement by novel method of drawing for chance to file.

Mitchell-Pierre capital fight.

Period of free transportation.

Great era of settlement and abundant prosperity begins.

1905. Samuel H. Elrod becomes governor.

Legislature provides for a commission to construct a new capitol building and outlines method to finance same. Legislature refuses to place upon the ballot an initiated bill for a primary election law. Authorizes the construction of shirt and overall and twine factories at the state penitentiary.

New railroad construction both east and west of the river announced.

Plans for two, million-dollar bridges over the Missouri, drawn.

1906. Republican party split into factions. Coe I. Crawford elected governor.

1907. "Reform legislature" passes anti-pass, anti-lobby, primary election laws and also measures designed to control corporations.

1909. R. S. Vessey becomes governor. Coe I. Crawford succeeds A. B. Kittredge as senator.

1910. Governor Vessey succeeds himself.

1911. Ziebach County created.

Under census of 1910 state gets another congressman and legislature districts the state.

Return of hard times caused by almost complete failure of 1911 crops.

1912. Frank M. Byrne elected governor.

1913. Thomas Sterling elected senator.

Tax Commission created.

Bureau of Public Printing created.

Mothers' Pension Fund System established. Verendrye Plate found.

1914. Frank M. Byrne elected to succeed himself.

Peter Norbeck elected lieutenant governor.

Ed. M. Johnson, Democrat, elected senator.

1915. Capital punishment abolished.

Bank Guaranty of Deposits' Law enacted.

Haakon County created from part of Stanley. Jackson County created from part of Stanley.

1916. Peter Norbeck elected governor.

W. H. McMaster elected lieutenant governor. Constitutional prohibition of the liquor traffic enacted.

1917. Rural credit system started.

State sheriff and state constabulary provided for.

Code commission appointed.

Educational survey undertaken.

United States enters world war and South Dakota sends troops to front.

Highway appropriation made by state to match appropriations by congress.

Torrens system of land registration enacted. Workmen's Compensation Law passed.

Jones County created from part of Lyman.

EARLY SETTLEMENTS

Scarcely had the Indians removed from their old hunting grounds when settlers began to enter the territory and erect their western cabins.

In 1859 the first white families settled in the counties of Union. Clay, And Yankton. George Brown located at Vermillion in August, 1859, and erected the old "Miner Hotel." Miner Robinson, L. E. Phelps and P. H. Jewell, removed to Vermillion during the same season, and J. H. McHenry opened the first store at that town in September, 1859, and in the following spring the Van Metre ferry and Compton & Deuel's saw-mill were put in operation. In July J. Stanage selected his claim on James River, erected a house, opened a farm, and established a ferry for the crossing of the public travel. Thomas Frek and Henry Arend located near the upper ferry, which at that time was the old government crossing, and kept by J. M. Stone, to whom the settlers' mail matter once a week was delivered from Sioux City, by the driver of the Fort Randall express, enclosed in an old oilcloth satchel. During the same season D. T. Bramble erected the first frame building in Yankton, as a store, near the levee, on the newly surveyed townsite of the Upper Missouri Land Company, consisting of J. S. B. Todd, A. W. Hubbard, Enos Stutsman, and others. Captain Todd erected his little law-office on the corner of Broadway and Second streets during the same winter. M. K. Armstrong came as the first land surveyor in Dakota, in 1859, and on the cold, blue Christmas day, H. C. Ash and wife, at the head of the pioneer family of Yankton, entered the place, and opened a tavern in a rude log house on the west side of Broadway. During the following year the old log churches at Yankton and Vermillion were erected, in which the Revs. Hoyt, Ingham, and Martin, were the first to proclaim the word of God to the pioneers of Dakota. At this time Sioux Falls, owned by the Dubuque and St. Paul Town Companies, was the leading town in the territory, and the United States survey of lands had been extended to that place in September, 1859, and in the fall of 1860 the first tier of townships was surveyed along the Missouri river, in which year Vermillion commenced its rapid strides in growth and settlement, and outstripped all its competitors, while Yankton was ranked as the third town in Dakota. The three places were aspirants for the embryo capital. At Sioux Falls the Northwest Independent was published, elections had been held, provisional officers chosen, a delegate to congress elected, and legislatures convened in 1858-59 and 1859-60.

But government appears to have looked with more surprise than compassion on these early political freaks of Dakotans. The people who had settled on the western slope of Dakota, however, were more moderate in their demands, and more successful in their petitions to congress. These pioneers, on the 8th day of November, 1859, assembled in mass convention to petition congress for a territorial organization. A memorial was drafted and signed by the citizens of the territory, which was conveyed to Washington by J. B. S. Todd, calling the attention of the government to our situation. The session passed, congress adjourned, and amid the tumultuous preparations for a presidential election and the muttering thunders of a rising rebellion, Dakota was left ungoverned and unorganized.

Not to be discouraged by this partial failure, the pioneers assembled again in mass convention at Yankton, Dec. 27, 1860, and again on Jan. 15, 1861, and prepared an earnest and lengthy memorial to congress, which was signed by 578 citizens and forwarded to the speaker of the house and president of the senate. Again, a cloud hung dark over Dakota's prayer. A new president had been elected — the old power was retiring, a new one advancing; and the rebellion which, but the year before, was muttering in smothered tones, had now burst forth in all its fury, and was bearing upon its maddening waves seven revolted states of the Union. But through the gathering darkness a ray of light was seen. The old power could organize —

the new one appoint; and on the second day of March, 1861, President Buchanan approved the bill giving to Dakota a territorial government.

The news did not reach Yankton until the 13th of the month, and on that night hats, hurrahs and town lots "'went up," to greet the dawning future of the Great Northwest.

Under its new boundaries the territory comprised all of the present Territory of Montana and the eastern slope of Idaho, and contained about 350,000 square miles, which was bounded on the north by the British line, east by Minnesota and Iowa, south by the Iowa line, and the Missouri. Niobrara and Turtle Hill rivers, up to and along the forty-third parallel of latitude, to the Rocky Mountains, thence along their snowy range to British America. Some 70,000 square miles of this territory was situated east of the Missouri river, and constituted that country which had been trimmed off from the state boundaries of Minnesota in 1858, while a vast expanse of the new territory, reaching out from the Missouri to the Rocky Mountains, was carved out of the old Territory of Nebraska, as formed in 1854. Dakota, thus established, constituted the largest organized territory in the United States, and afforded a river navigation of not less than 2,000 miles. In June the following officials, appointed by the new administration, arrived and entered upon the discharge of their duties: Wm. Jayne of Illinois, governor; John Hutchinson of Minnesota, secretary; P. Bliss of Ohio, chief justice; L. P. Williston of Pennsylvania and J. L. Williams of Tennessee, associate justices; W. E. Gleason of Maryland, district attorney; G. D. Hill of Michigan, surveyor general; W. F. Shaffer, marshal; W. A. Burleigh of Pennsylvania, agent of Yanktons; H. A. Hoffman of New York, agent of Poncas. H. A. Kennedy was appointed register and Jesse Wherry receiver, of the Vermillion land office during the same season, both of Dakota Territory. On the 6th of June the Weekly Dakotan was issued at Yankton, under the head of the Dakotan Company. In the following month The Dakota Republican was started at Vermillion by Bedell and Clark.

A census was taken, showing the population of the territory to be 2,402, and on the 13th of July the first proclamation of the governor was issued, dividing the territory into judicial districts, and assigning the judges thereto. Chief Justice Bliss was assigned to the second district at Yankton; Assistant Justice Williston to the Vermillion district: and Judge Williams to the Bonhomme district. On the 29th of July a second proclamation was issued, dividing the territory into council and representative districts, and appointing the 16th of September for a general election.

ANCIENT FREE AND ACCEPTED MASONS

Among the very first settlers of South Dakota were several Masons, and as early as 1862, during the first session of the territorial legislature, consultation began looking to the organization of a lodge, but the Indian troubles of that season suspended operations in that line for a period. However, no sooner was safety to the community assured that the matter was again taken up and Melancthon Hoyt, Episcopal missionary; John Hutchinson, secretary of Dakota territory; Henry C. Ash, the pioneer hotelkeeper, of Yankton; Nelson Miner, captain of Company A, Dakota Volunteer Cavalry; Justus Townsend, physician, and auditor of Dakota territory; Downer T. Bramble, legislator and pioneer merchant; G. N. Propper; James M. Allen, who was secretary of the provisional government established at Sioux Falls, and Frank M. Ziebach, founder of the Dakotan newspaper, petitioned for a dispensation to establish a lodge of the Ancient Free and Accepted Masons at Yankton. The dispensation was duly granted and the lodge instituted with the petitioners above named as charter members, the charter bearing date June 3, 1863. The lodge was called St. John's, No. 166, of the jurisdiction of Iowa. For six years thereafter it was the only lodge in the territory.

The genealogy of Dakota Masonry is as follows: From England to North Carolina, from North Carolina to Tennessee, from Tennessee to Missouri, from Missouri to Iowa, from Iowa to Dakota territory, from Dakota territory to South Dakota. The first officers of St. John's lodge were as follows: Melanchton Hoyt, master; Downer T. Bramble, senior warden; John Hutchinson, junior warden; George W. Kingsbury, treasurer; Moses K. Armstrong, secretary; George N. Propper, senior deacon; F. M. Ziebach, junior deacon; Bligh E. Wood, tyler.

The next lodge to be instituted in Dakota territory was Incense No. 257, of Vermillion, chartered February 10, 1869. Alpheus G. Fuller, of Yankton, who had been elected delegate to congress by the Sioux Falls provisional government in 1858, was the instituting officer. A year later, April 16, 1870, Elk Point Lodge, No. 288, was instituted, with H. H. Blair as master; Elias Hyde, senior warden; E. H. Webb, junior warden; P. E. Maynard, treasurer; John Lawrence, secretary; C. W. Beggs, senior deacon; J. A. Wallace, junior deacon; Eli B. Wixson, tyler. On June 10th Minnehaha Lodge, No. 328, was chartered at Sioux Falls, with Thomas H. Brown, R. C. Hawkins, E. Sharpe, T. Pomeroy, G. B. Sammons, W. H. Holt, J. H. Moulton, and George Hill as charter members. On June 3, 1875, Silver Star Lodge, No. 345, was organized at Canton, and W. H. Miller, Sr., M. W. Bailey, S. H. Stafford Jr., W. M. Cuppett, D. H. Hawn and others were charter members.

Delegates from these five lodges met in the hall of Elk Point Lodge on June 22, 1875. These delegates were empowered to take such measures as were necessary in order to form a grand lodge of Freemasons within and for the territory of Dakota. This convention adopted a constitution and by-laws and elected officers for a grand lodge and petitioned the Iowa grand lodge, to which they were still subject, for an organization. Pursuant to this action and petition the Iowa grand lodge sent T. S. Parvin to Dakota and at Vermillion, on July 21, 1875, the grand lodge of Dakota was duly instituted by Mr. Parvin in the old Baptist church.

The delegates who met in the convention at Elk Point on June 22d and took the preliminary steps toward the organization of the grand lodge of Dakota were as follows: St. John's Lodge No. 166, Yankton, George H. Hand, L. M. Purdy, F. J. DeWitt; Incense No. 257, Vermillion, Horace J. Austin, A. H. Lathrop, Vernette E. Prentice; Elk Point No. 288, J. A. Wallace, H. H. Blair, D. W. Hassen; Minnehaha No. 328, Thomas H. Brown, J. W. Callendar, Richard A. Pettigrew; Silver Star No. 345, Canton, William H. Miller, Sr., Mark W. Bailey, S. H. Stafford, Jr.

The first officers of the grand lodge were as follows: T. H. Brown; master; Mark W. Bailey, secretary. The grand masters have been Henry H. Blair, 1876; George H. Hand, 1877 to 1880; Thomas H. Brown, 1881; Oscar S. Gifford, 1882 and 1883; John F. Schrader, 1884; William Blatt, 1885 and 1886; Henry M. Wheeler, 1887; John Q. A. Braden, 1888; George V. Ayers, 1889; Theodore D. Kanouse, 1890; George A. Johnston, 1891; Harvey J. Rice, 1892; Richard C. McAllister, 1893; William C. Allen, 1894; Frederick H. Files, 1895; James Lewis, 1896; Albert W. Coe, 1897; J. G. Bullen, 1898; Louis G. Levoy, 1899; W. H. Roddle, 1900; John A. Cleaver, 1901; Charles E. Hill, 1902; Frank A. Brown, 1903, and Byron P. Dague, 1904; Mark W. Bailey was secretary for two years until his death, in 1877; W. E. Caton succeeded him for one term and Charles T. McCoy was secretary from 1878 until 1893, when he was succeeded by George A. Pettigrew, who still serves in that capacity.

The meetings of the grand lodge have been held as follows: 1875, Elk Point and Vermillion; 1876, Yankton; 1877, Yankton; 1878, Sioux Falls; 1879, Yankton; 1880, Yankton; 1881, Sioux Falls; 1882, Watertown; 1883, Rapid City; 1884, Aberdeen; 1885, Fargo; 1886, Bismarck; 1887, Huron; 1888, Deadwood; 1889, Mitchell; 1890, Madison; 1891, Watertown, 1892, Sioux Falls; 1893, Yankton; 1894, Hot Springs; 1895, Pierre; 1896, Huron; 1897, Mitchell; 1898, Sioux Falls; 1899, Yankton; 1900, Aberdeen; 1901, Sioux Falls; 1902. Huron; 1903, Deadwood; 1904, Yankton. At the last report there were one hundred Blue Lodges in South Dakota, having a total of 5,444 members.

The institution of the York Rites in Dakota territory date from 1885, when, on the 25th of February, charters were issued to the following chapters: Yankton No. 1, Yankton; Sioux Falls No. 2, Sioux Falls; Dakota No. 3, Deadwood; Siroc No. 4, Canton; Huron No. 10, Huron; Watertown No. 12, Watertown; Aberdeen No. 14, Aberdeen; and on June 8th of that year Mitchell No. 15, Mitchell; Denver No. 17, Arlington; Brookings No. 18, Brookings; Orient No. 19, Flandreau, and Redfield No. 20, Redfield, were chartered. It will be observed that the above numbers do not run in regular order, this fact being due to the North Dakota chapters then in this jurisdiction.

The grand chapter was organized at Sioux Falls, July 8, 1885, the first fourteen chapters taking part in the organization. The meetings of the chapter since the first have been held at the same place and approximate time as the grand lodge. The grand high priests have been as follows: 1885 and 1886. William S. Blatt; 1887, Peter Picton; 1888, Collins D. Pratt; 1899, John F. Schrader; 1890, John Davidson; 1891. Henry S. Williams; 1891, Park Davis; 1892, William J. McMackin; 1893, Edward B. Bracy; 1894, Robert T. Sedam; 1895, Louis G. Levoy; 1896, Harvey T. Rice; 1897, George V. Ayers; 1898. Samuel J. Coyne; 1899, George A. West; 1900. P. F. Ives; 1901, Martin G. Carlisle; 1902. Samuel J. Moore; 1903, Ed S. Ames; 1904, Samuel H. Jumper. The grand secretaries: Thomas J. Wilder, from organization until statehood, when the jurisdiction was divided, and since that date George A. Pettigrew has held the position. There are now twenty-nine chapters, having at the last report 1,784 members.

The commandery preceded the chapter in this jurisdiction. There are now fourteen of these bodies, the first of which is Dakota No. 1, organized at Deadwood, August 19, 1880. The grand commandery was organized at Sioux Falls on May 14, 1884, by Theodore S. Parvin, of Iowa, under warrant of the grand commandery of the United States. The right eminent grand commanders since organization have been: 1884, Samuel Roy; 1885. Levi B. French: 1886, Daniel S. Glidden; 1887, Marc A. Brewer; 1888, Joseph A. Colcord: 1889, William D. Stites; 1890, John F. Schrader; 1891, Samuel H. Jumper; 1892, George W. Burnside; 1893, George H. Rathman; 1894, William J. McMackin; 1895, Frank A. Brown; 1896, J. J. Casselman; 1897, Joseph T. Morrow: 1898, William T. Doolittle; 1899, George V. Ayers; 1900, E. W. Coughran; 1901, Morris H. Kelly; 1902, Ed S. Lorimer; 1903, Fred A. Spafford. Edwin E, Sage was the first grand recorder, but was succeeded at the first election by Bruce M. Rowley, who held the office from

1885 until 1892. William H. Holt then held it for two years, when, in 1895, he was succeeded by George A. Pettigrew, who continues in the office.

For the history of the Scottish Rite bodies in South Dakota we are under obligation to T. W. Taubman, of Aberdeen, who writes: "I have had some difficulty in gathering the authentic history of the Rite in the territory of Dakota and the state of South Dakota. In 1874 Albert Pike, the sovereign grand commander, attached Dakota territory to the state of Minnesota and placed the same under the jurisdiction of A. T. C. Pearson, inspector general of that state, but it seems that he did not do any work within the territory. On January 6, 1883, the territory was annexed to Nebraska and was in charge of Robert Carrell Jordan, the inspector general of that state [and first grandmaster of Nebraska 1857-60], but prior thereto and on January 1, 1882, Arthur James Carrier, thirty-second degree, was appointed deputy for the territory of Dakota. He did the first work within the territory and established Alpha Lodge of Perfection No. I, in Yankton, on February 3, 1882, but I am informed that the date of its charter was February 8th of that year.

"Brother William Blatt writes me that Brother Carrier was an Indian trader and boarded with Mrs. Dawson on the southwest corner of Third and Linn streets in that city, where he occupied the parlor and there communicated to him and several others whose names he was unable to recall the degrees from the fourth to the fourteenth, who immediately thereafter applied for a charter, bought nine hundred dollars' worth of paraphernalia, and, in unison with the other Masonic bodies, leased the west half of the present hall, remodeled it at great expense and began work hopefully and energetically, but fearfully in debt. Brother Jordan inaugurated Mackey Chapter, Rose Croix, in Yankton, February 27, 1883, and Dr. D. Frank Etter was elected wise master, and Brother Fleming writes me that John B. Dennis was appointed deputy for Brother Jordon. About the last of July or the first of August of that year Brother Pike visited Yankton and Sioux Falls and he states in his allocution for that year that Brother Dennis accompanied him for the purpose of establishing bodies at Yankton and Sioux Falls. Brother Dennis was appointed deputy for the supreme council for the southern part of Dakota April 25, 1884. Robert B. Bruce Council of Kadosh No. I was not chartered until March 10, 1887, but I do not know by whom nor when it was inaugurated, but find that it is mentioned as paying dues in 1886. Brother Rufus E. Fleming, thirty-third degree, who had been deputy for the northern part of Dakota territory, was, on October 19, 1886, made an active inspector general for the entire territory, and Dr. Etter was his deputy until his death. He was succeeded by Brother Blatt and he by Brother Beadle. Oriental Consistory was chartered at the 1888 session of the supreme council and was instituted by Brother Fleming on December 10th of the same year, when George A. Archer was elected master of Kadosh. When first chartered it was known as No. 2, but Occidental Consistory No. I at Sioux Falls having forfeited its charter in 1889, the supreme council authorized Oriental to be known as No. I, which it now is. Other bodies of the Rite which have been instituted in the state are Webster Lodge of Perfection, June 13, 1887; Cyrus Lodge of Perfection, at Watertown, August I, 1887; Khurum Lodge of Perfection, at Sioux Falls, September 15, 1884; and Albert Pike Chapter, Rose Croix, at Sioux Falls, September 15, 1884. At the session of the supreme council in 1884 there was a petition for a consistory at Sioux Falls, but the same was rejected because there was no council of Kadosh, but one was subsequently established. The application for a consistory was again rejected in 1888, but a recess vote was taken and a charter granted and a consistory at Sioux Falls inaugurated by Brother Fleming on either the day before or after the one at Yankton. Their council of Kadosh was known as Cour DeLain No. 2 and was instituted by Brother Fleming May 2, 1888. The lodge and chapter at Deadwood was constituted May 21, 1892, the council May 23, 1892, and the consistory October 20, 1892. A lodge of perfection was located at Hot Springs in November, 1894; at Aberdeen a lodge and chapter was instituted April 6, 1894; the council February 21, 1895, and the consistory January 16, 1896, and the Albert Pike Lodge of Perfection at Eureka January 18, 1898, but the charters were never granted either to Watertown,

Hot Springs or Eureka and those at Sioux Falls were forfeited in 1892 or 1894, they never having done any work. At the present time the total membership in the state in about eight hundred."

After the division of Dakota territory, North and South Dakota remained one jurisdiction, under the supervision of Rufus Eberly Fleming, thirty-third degree, inspector general, until October, 1899, when the supreme council divided the territory and made South Dakota a separate jurisdiction and elected Edward Teare Taubman, thirty-third degree, of Aberdeen, the inspector general for the state.

There are thirty-six chapters of the auxiliary Order of the Eastern Star in South Dakota. The grand chapter was organized at Watertown July 10, 1889, delegates from the chapters at Watertown, Flandreau, Webster, St. Lawrence, Aberdeen and Madison taking part in the organization. The grand matrons have been; 1889, May H. Monks; 1890, Florence M. Mudgett; 1891, L. Leslie McBride; 1892, Lurancy W. Norton; 1893, Mary Brown; 1894, Sarah J. Clark; 1895, Hettie Downie; 1896, Fannie R. Roddle; 1897. Jennette E. Herreid; 1898, Jennie E. Bradley; 1899, Jennie Shirk; 1900. Margaret Y. Hitchcock; 1901, Eudora Z. Pettigrew; 1902, Annie Marston; 1903, Eva G. Davison, Mrs. A. C. McAllister has been secretary from the organization. At the last report there were 2,439 members.

Magnificent temples for the Masonic bodies have been erected at Yankton, Aberdeen and Deadwood. The Masonic bodies meeting at Chamberlain own a very commodious and well-arranged temple.

There are in South Dakota two temples of the dependent order of Ancient Arabic Order of the Nobles of the Mystic Shrine, El Riad Temple, at Sioux Falls, organized May 25, 1888, and Naja Temple, at Deadwood, founded September 19, 1892. An application for a charter has been made at Aberdeen for the establishment of a temple there.

* Past Grandmaster SD

‡ Past Grandmaster of another state

TABLE OF CONTENTS

A - 1
B - 26
C - 104
D - 160
E - 188
F - 208
G - 235
H - 273
I - 328
J - 332
K - 360

GEORGE W. ABBOTT

Since 1891 George W. Abbott has resided in Sioux Falls and throughout the entire period, covering almost a quarter of a century, has been prominently connected with its financial interests. He is also a leading figure in Masonic circles, few members of the order in the state being as widely known. His efforts have indeed been a tangible asset in the advancement of Masonry in South Dakota and his acquaintance among his brethren of the craft elsewhere is also extensive.

Mr. Abbott is a native of New England. He was born at Tamworth, Carroll County, New Hampshire, October 10, 1858, a son of Lyman and Shuah W. (Rowe) Abbott. Upon the homestead farm he was reared and in his native town acquired his education by attending the public schools. He also continued his studies in the high school and Phillips Academy at Exeter, New Hampshire, and thus liberally educated started out to make a place for himself in the world. At the age of twenty years, he went to Colorado as secretary to a mining expert and continued in that state until 1882, when he came to the territory of Dakota, settling in what is now Mcintosh county, North Dakota, which county he aided in organizing and which he also served as its first superintendent of schools. He engaged in general merchandising and also filled the position of postmaster of Hoskins, now Ashley. At the same time, he operated a cattle ranch and was thus closely associated with the early development of that section of the state. In 1887 he removed to Minneapolis, where the furniture and hardware business claimed his attention until 1891, when he removed to Sioux Falls and accepted the position of general manager of the Cooperative Loan & Savings Association, filling the position until 1894, when he resigned. Immediately afterward he organized the Union Savings Association and became general manager, secretary and treasurer. To his unfaltering exertion, his strong executive ability and keen insight is due the splendid success of what is today one of the city's most important financial institutions. In 1891 he was elected vice president of the International Building & Loan League, an organization representing over a half billion dollars of paid in capital, and he served until 1894 He has also figured prominently in connection with other financial interests. In 1902 he was one of the reorganizes of the Colton State Bank at Colton, South Dakota, and was chosen its first president, so remaining until he sold his interests in that institution in 1904. He remained in active connection with the Union Savings Association until 1912, when he disposed of his interests therein.

On the 1st of June, 1885, Mr. Abbott was united in marriage to Miss Mary G. Quinlan, of Cleveland, Ohio, and they have become the parents of four children: George L., now living in Des Moines; Gladys, who attended and graduated from All Saints school of Sioux Falls and continued her education at Lake Forest, Illinois; Ann Josephine, who became a student in Wellesley College of Wellesley, Massachusetts, and graduated therefrom in 1914; and John Marion, a student in the Shattuck Military Academy of Minnesota.

George W. Abbott is prominent in club life. For many years he has been a member of the Minnehaha Country Club, a member of the Dacota Club and for several years its president, and has served as director, vice president and president of the Commercial Club of the city. In Masonry he has attained high rank, belonging to Minnehaha Lodge, No. 5, A. F. & A. M.; Sioux Falls Chapter, No. 2, K. A. M.; Cyrene Commandery, No. 2, K. T., of which he is a past eminent commander; and El Riad Temple, A. A. O. N. M. S., of which he is past potentate and past representative to the imperial council. He is likewise a member of Occidental Consistory, No. 2, A. & A. S. R. He may justly be proud of his Masonic record, for few, if any, in the state have had higher honors conferred upon them by that organization than has Mr. Abbott. He is now the representative in the grand lodge of the grand lodge of Mississippi and also the representative of the grand commandery of the District of Columbia in South Dakota. He is also a member of the Elks and the Knights of Pythias organizations. His political allegiance has been given to the republican party where national issues and questions are involved but he has neither sought nor desired political office. He has served, however, as a member of the board of education for several years and is a stalwart champion of the cause of education. In fact, his influence is always on the side of progress and advancement. He is a member of the First Congregational church and he has served as a member of the board of trustees and as its chairman. He is a lover of outdoor life, greatly enjoying hunting and other sports which take him into the forest and bring him close to the heart of nature. His friends, and they are many, find him a most congenial companion, pleasant to meet at all times, and his fellow townsmen know him as a reliable man, thoroughly trustworthy under all circumstances and on all occasions, and in his entire record there is an absence of anything sinister or anything to conceal.

ORLIN A. ABEEL

O. A. ABEEL, cashier of the Alcester State Bank, in Alcester, Union County, is a native of the city of Albany, New York, where he was born on the 17th of August, 1849, being a son of Waldo and Maria Abeel, who were likewise born in that state. The Abeel family is one of the old and honored ones in the Empire state, and the records extant show that John Abeel, of whom the subject is a direct descendant, was mayor of Albany in 1694, and that he signed the charter for historic old Trinity church in New York City. Henry V. S. Abeel, grandfather of our subject, was a valiant soldier in the war of 1812. Orlin A. Abeel received an excellent common-school education, but his training has been most effectually rounded out under the discipline of that wise headmaster, experience. When he was three years of age his parents removed to Wisconsin, locating in Madison, and his father became superintendent of the Madison division of the Chicago & Northwestern Railroad, retaining the incumbency until his death. In 1865, at the age of sixteen years, our subject inaugurated his independent career, securing a position as clerk in the office of the Chicago & Northwestern Railroad at Madison, and later being promoted to the office of cashier for the same company in its office at Missouri Valley, Iowa. Later he was for three years in charge of the country department of the Bradstreet Mercantile Agency, in its Chicago office, and then became pool clerk for the Chicago & Northwestern Railroad, in the same city. In 1884 he became private secretary to Charles M. Hays, at St. Louis, Missouri, in the general manager's office of the Gould system, retaining this incumbency until 1884, in December of which year he came to what is now the state of South Dakota and located on a farm in Union County. In 1888 Mr. Abeel was elected cashier of the Bank of Centerville, Turner County, and was elected county treasurer in 1890. In 1896 he took up his residence in Alcester and here was publisher and editor of the Alcester Union from 1896 until January 1, 1903, when he was elected to his present position as cashier of the Alcester State Bank. He is a fine accountant and endowed with excellent executive ability, and the affairs of the institution are most consistently placed in his charge. He has disposed of his newspaper plant and business, having made the Union a true exponent of local affairs and interests and an able advocate of the principles of the Republican party, to which he has ever given an uncompromising allegiance.

He is identified with the Masonic fraternity, and was master of the lodge at Parker, South Dakota, for three years, while he served for three years in the same capacity in Alcester Lodge, No. 115, Ancient Free and Accepted Masons. He and his wife are members of the Methodist Episcopal church. On the 14th of December, 1888, Mr. Abeel was united in marriage to Miss Edith L. Hall, of Union County, Dakota territory, daughter of Samuel W. Hall, who served with distinction in the Civil war, as a member of a Missouri cavalry regiment. Mr. and Mrs. Abeel have five sons, whose names are here entered, with respective ages at time of this writing, in December, 1903: Charles Wallace, fourteen; Verne Waldo, twelve; Paul Jordan, six; Clyde Ambrose, four; and Orley, one.

EDWARD L. ABEL

E. L. ABEL, president of the First National Bank of Bridgewater, was born in Springfield, the capital city of Illinois, on the 19th of November, 1860, being the only child of Oramel H. and Mary (Moore) Abel, the former of whom was born near Buffalo, New York, June 19, 1833, while the latter was born in Springfield, Illinois, on the 17th of May, 1838. The father is now a resident of Murphysboro, Illinois, the mother having died at Springfield, Illinois. As a boy Oramel H. Abel accompanied his parents on their removal to Springfield, Illinois, and he was there reared and educated, becoming a successful railroad contractor. At the outbreak of the war of the Rebellion he enlisted as a private in an Illinois regiment, being made lieutenant of his company. Later he was appointed mustering officer and was stationed for some time at Camp Butler. He was then sent to the front, being first lieutenant in his company, which formed a part of the One Hundred and Forty-fourth Illinois Volunteer Infantry, of which he was eventually made adjutant general, serving until the close of the war. He then returned to Springfield, and for a number of years served as city clerk. In 1874 he removed to Carbondale, that state, where he engaged in the banking business and where he also held the position of city clerk for several terms, besides being called to other offices of local trust. About 1887 he removed to Murphysboro, Illinois, where he has since lived retired. He is a stanch Republican in politics and was a personal friend of Abraham Lincoln, their intimacy continuing from their boyhood days until the death of the martyred President, at whose personal request the subject of this sketch received his second name, Lincoln. The father of our subject is a member of the Independent Order of Odd Fellows and the Grand Army of the Republic, having been commander of his post in the latter organization.

Eward L. Abel received his early education in the public schools of his native city and supplemented this by a course of study in the Southern Illinois Normal University, at Carbondale, while he was engaged in teaching school for two winters after leaving college. In 1879 he began reading law under the preceptorship of Judge Andrew D. Duff, of Carbondale, one of the most eminent members of the Illinois bar, and while prosecuting his legal studies he worked at various occupations, being dependent upon his own resources. In February, 1884, Mr. Abel was admitted to the bar of his native state, and the same spring was elected city attorney of Carbondale, being chosen as his own successor, without opposition, in the spring of 1885. During these years he was associated with the banking business in Carbondale, accepting a clerkship in

1878 and shortly afterward being made cashier of the bank. In 1887 Mr. Abel came to Bridgewater, South Dakota, being admitted to the bar of the territory in the following year, though he has never devoted much attention to the work of his profession here. Upon his arrival in his new home, he purchased stock in the State Bank of Bridgewater, of which institution he was made cashier. In 1897 he was elected to the presidency of the same, and upon the reorganization of the institution as the First National Bank, in August, 1903, he was elected to the presidency of the same. In 1889 he was appointed, by Governor Mellette, a member of the board of trustees of the state penitentiary, at Sioux Falls: he has served with signal acceptability as mayor of Bridgewater, retaining this office three terms, and he is now serving his third term as a member of the board of education, of which he was president in 1902. He is a member at large and chairman of the Republican committee of the second circuit. In 1902 he was elected to represent his district in the state senate, in which he served with characteristic ability, proving a valuable member of the body. For two terms he was secretary of the South Dakota Bankers' Association, and in July, 1903, he was honored by his associates in that body by being chosen its president. He has been an active and efficient worker in the Republican party, having delivered many campaign addresses and being regarded as one of the party's most able and forceful speakers in the state. Mr. Abel is a member of Eureka Lodge, No. 72, Ancient Free and Accepted Masons; Salem Chapter, No. 34, Royal Arch Masons; Constantine Commandery, No. 17, Knights Templar, of Salem; El Riad Temple, Ancient Arabic Order of the Nobles of the Mystic Shrine, at Sioux Falls; Sioux Falls Lodge, No. 262, Benevolent and Protective Order of Elks; Bridgewater Lodge, No. 72, Ancient Order of United Workmen; and Bridgewater Lodge, No. 3790, Modern Woodmen of America. On the 25th of December, 1883, was solemnized the marriage of Mr. Abel to Miss Ella C. Smith, of DuQuoin, Illinois, and they have two children, Roy W. and Gertrude M.

FRANK L. ACKERMAN

Frank L. Ackerman, living in Rapid City, is numbered among the pioneers of western South Dakota, where he has lived since his boyhood days. He was born in Hastings, Nebraska, December 20, 1865, a son of Daniel C. and Elizabeth C. (Jellison) Ackerman, natives of Kansas and of Nebraska respectively. The father was a stockman and rancher, conducting important business interests and also taking a prominent part in democratic politics. His opinions carried weight in political circles and he served for two terms as a member of the Nebraska legislature. In 1879 he removed to the Black Hills country with his family and engaged extensively in ranching in Pennington County. He acquired landed interests which he had well stocked and at the time of his death, in 1891, he was one of the prominent stock-raisers, prosperous ranchers and a highly respected citizen of his community. His widow survives and now resides in Rapid City.

The educational advantages, which Frank L. Ackerman received were of the most limited character, for he was reared upon the frontier and, moreover, it was necessary for him to earn his own living from an early age. When a youth of fourteen he became a clerk in a general store in Deadwood, where he remained until his nineteenth year and then returned home. At that time, he engaged in cattle ranching in connection with his father and soon afterward he began in the same business on his own account, continuing successfully therein until 1896, when he sold his ranch and stock.

At that time Mr. Ackerman removed to Rapid City and through the succeeding eight years was connected with the Tom Sweeney Hardware Company. Still later he became a member of the hardware and implement firm of Duhamel Brothers & Ackerman, which was afterward reorganized under the name of the Duhamel Ackerman Company, while the business was developed into one of the most important enterprises of the kind in the state. Their trade covered a wide territory and their business constantly grew in volume and importance. In July, 1911, however, Mr. Ackerman sold out his entire mercantile interests to turn his attention to the insurance business, becoming one of the stockholders and directors of the First National Life & Accident Insurance Company. He assumed the office of general agent and district manager of all the territory in the state west of the Missouri river. He has since devoted his time with characteristic energy to the upbuilding of the business of this important and rapidly growing home company.

Mr. Ackerman is a democrat in politics, yet, while actively interested in political questions and issues and in obtaining success for his friends who are candidates for office, he has never sought nor accepted any political honors for himself.

On the 28th of March, 1894, Mr. Ackerman wedded Hattie A. Garlick, a daughter of Edward and Anna Garlick, and they have become the parents of three children: Esther, the wife of O. H. Borst, of Pierre, South Dakota; Frances Marguerite; and Frank L.

The family attend the Episcopal church, of which Mr. Ackerman has been a member since his boyhood days, and he is particularly interested in its charitable work. He is a Mason and in the York Rite has attained the Knight Templar degree in the commandery. He also holds membership with the Knights of Pythias, the Elks and the Odd Fellows. In everything pertaining to the upbuilding of his city, of the Black Hills country and his state he is interested. He is a progressive of the most ardent type and few men have given so large a portion of their time, energy and money to the furthering of the development of South Dakota. He is genial in manner, generous in disposition and very popular. An able business man, his activity is regarded as a distinct asset not only to the business ventures that engage his attention but to the community in which he lives. He was one of the pioneers in the good roads movement and did much to give that most worthy cause a decided impetus at a time when good roads were considered an expensive fad. Today, however, they are generally regarded as a necessary adjunct of progress and Mr. Ackerman has done much to bring about this accepted view. Few men have or deserve to have a wider circle of friends. The usefulness and unselfishness of his life are uniformly recognized and the high regard in which he is entertained is but the logical sequence of his well spent life.

JUDGE EZRA ADAMS

For six years Judge Ezra Adams ably served upon the county bench and is an attorney of prominence in Hazel, Hamlin County. He is also president of the Security Bank of Wallace, South Dakota, and the owner of a large tract of land. He was born in Ontario, Canada, on the 25th of May, 1851, a son of Elihu and Dienna (De Pencier) Adams, both natives of Ontario. The father farmed in that province until after the demise of his wife, which occurred in October, 1887. He subsequently came to South Dakota and lived for two years with the subject of this review. He then went to Los Angeles, California, and made his home with his son, Abel B. Adams, until his death, which occurred in 1902, when he had reached the advanced age of eighty-four years.

Judge Adams was reared at home and pursued his education in the public and high schools of Prescott, Ontario. After completing his studies, he secured a clerkship in a law office in Prescott and two years later was made deputy clerk of courts. In 1880 he came to the States and located in Watertown, South Dakota, on the 24th of February, of that year. On the 16th of the following May he filed on a preemption claim on section 20, Brantford township, Hamlin County, and proved up upon this within six months and then filed on a homestead adjoining. In November, 1883, he took up a tree claim adjacent to his other holdings and from time-to-time bought land until he now owns seven quarter sections in one body and also holds title to a half section in Stanley County, this state. The prices which he paid for the land that he bought at various periods indicate the advance in realty values. In 1887 or 1888 he purchased a quarter section for eight hundred and forty-five dollars, the following year he paid twelve hundred dollars for one hundred and sixty acres, five years later a quarter section cost him three thousand, two hundred and eighty dollars, and still later he had to pay sixty-four hundred dollars in order to buy one hundred and sixty acres. In 1909 he built a fine residence and set of farm buildings upon the place for which he paid eight hundred and forty-five dollars.

After coming to South Dakota Judge Adams was elected clerk of the circuit court of Hamlin County and served for two terms in that office, from 1892 to 1895. During this time, he continued his law studies and after the expiration of his second term as clerk he completed his preparation for the legal profession in the office of Judge Julian Bennett of Watertown. On the 5th of October, 1894, he passed the examination before the state board at Pierre and was admitted to the bar. He subsequently opened offices in Castlewood, where he successfully practiced his profession for four years. During this time, or in 1895, he was elected states attorney and acceptably discharged the duties of that office for two terms, his record winning him reelection. In his capacity as states attorney, he prosecuted the first murder case ever tried in that county, namely, the notorious Tom Hall case. The criminal in question was convicted and is now serving a life sentence in the state prison. From 1900 to 1906 Judge Adams served upon the county bench and his rulings and decisions were marked by a thorough knowledge of the law and a strict and equable application of its principles to the matters in question. Since coming to Hazel in 1906 he has become recognized as one of the leaders of the local bar and has a representative and remunerative practice. He is also president of the Security Bank of Wallace, Codington County, and is much interested in everything that subserves the interests of his section of the state.

Judge Adams was married in February, 1872, to Miss Esther L. Howe, of Kemptville, Ontario, and to this union nine children have been born, eight of whom survive. Morton A. resides in Pierre, and is chief clerk in the office of the commissioner of schools and public lands. Amos E. is cashier of the Security State Bank and a resident of Wallace. Dr. Burton A. lives in Bristol. William W. and Harold Hugh are farming the home place. Lulu B. is the wife of Andrew Melham, a banker of Hazel. Linnie M. is the wife of P. H. Setbacken, a farmer of Hamlin County. Myrtle M. is the wife of A. J. Buskrud, a hardware merchant of Hazel.

Judge Adams is a republican in politics and is loyal in his support of the policies of that organization. He is a member of the Episcopal church but attends the Methodist Episcopal church, to which his wife belongs. Fraternally he belongs to the Masons and the Modern Woodmen. Aside from his position as one of the leaders of the local bar, he is held in the highest esteem in Hazel, as all who know him recognize and value his integrity and his many other admirable personal qualities.

JUDGE JOHN E. ADAMS

Judge John E. Adams long occupied a central place on the stage of public activity in Brown County, which numbered him among its leading and valued citizens, for he rendered active aid in many public movements which resulted in benefit to the entire community. He was mayor of the city of Aberdeen, was county judge and was also receiver of the United States land office. His splendid service in these offices and his upright conduct in every relation of life gained for him the confidence, goodwill and high regard of all with whom he was associated.

His birth occurred in Patterson, New Jersey, May 13, 1857, his parents being John and Sarah J. Adams, both of whom were of Scotch-Irish extraction. In his childhood days his parents removed to Pennsylvania and it was there that he acquired his early education in the public schools, later supplementing his course in Allegheny College at Meadville. While there he took up the study of law, made rapid progress in his studies and was admitted to the bar of the state in 1880. For two years thereafter he practiced law in Pennsylvania, but in the spring of 1882 sought the opportunities offered in the west, making his way to Iowa. He first settled in the southwestern part of the state, where he followed the practice of law until the spring of 1883, when he removed to the territory of Dakota, opening a law office in Columbia, then the county seat of Brown County. His professional ability soon gained him recognition and won for him a liberal and growing practice.

Moreover, the active part which Judge Adams took in public affairs led to his selection for mayoralty honors in 1887 and for one term he administered the affairs of that city as its chief executive. He removed to Aberdeen when that city was made the county seat of Brown County and became as prominent in that community as he had been in Columbia. In 1890 he was elected county judge and the excellent record which he made upon the bench led to his reelection for a second term. He was also judge of the probate court for eight years and in 1900 he was elected mayor of Aberdeen, giving to the city a businesslike administration, characterized by many needed reforms and improvements. In 1905 he was made receiver of the United States land office in Aberdeen and served with satisfaction to the government, to the patrons of the office and to all concerned until the office was removed to Timber Lake in 1911. With many movements for the upbuilding and improvement of Aberdeen he was closely associated, and his counsel and cooperation were greatly valued in such connections.

Judge Adams was married August 12, 1888, to Miss Martha E. Wilkinson, a native of Kankakee, Illinois, born April 15, 1867, her parents being William H. and Mary Wilkinson. Judge and Mrs. Adams became the parents of six children, all but one of whom survive, namely: Maple F.; Merle E.; Constance M.; Bessie M., who died at the age of three years; Mildred and Doris L.

The family circle was again broken by the hand of death when, on the 18th of May, 1912, Judge Adams was called from this life. All who knew him deeply regretted his loss, for he had made for himself an honorable place in the community and his name was one which commanded respect and confidence. He was one of the prominent Masons of South Dakota, having attained the thirty-third degree, conferred only in recognition of high standing and of valued service rendered to the order. He likewise held membership with the Knights of the Maccabees, the Modern Woodmen of America and the Ancient Order of United

Workmen. His political allegiance was given the republican party and he always studied closely the problems and questions of the day, giving thereto careful consideration and ever supporting the measures and movements which he deemed of greatest value to the community.

OLIVER N. AINSWORTH, M. D.

Dr. Oliver N. Ainsworth, engaged in the practice of medicine in Spearfish, was born in Ogle County, Illinois, October 15, 1850, a son of Andrew and Mary (Hemmingway) Ainsworth, the former a native of New York and the latter of Pennsylvania. The father removed from the east to Illinois and in that state engaged in mercantile pursuits. Later he turned his attention to farming in northern Iowa, where he spent his remaining days, and in the community where he lived, he became a man of prominence and influence, his fellow townsmen calling him to a number of public offices, the duties of which he discharged with credit to himself and satisfaction to his constituents. His wife passed away in Illinois.

Dr. Ainsworth attended the common schools of Iowa and the Upper Iowa University at Fayette. His professional education was pursued in Rush Medical College of Chicago and in the College of Physicians & Surgeons at Keokuk, Iowa, now the medical department of Drake University. His practice for the profession of medicine, however, did not immediately follow his more specifically literary education, for at the age of nineteen years he joined a surveying party in New Mexico, continuing with them for about three years, his labors taking him to New Mexico, Arizona and the republic of Mexico in the survey of Mexican land grants and similar work. It was after this that he entered the medical school, in which he completed his course in 1878. He then engaged in practice in northwestern Iowa, being a member of the medical fraternity at Sloan, that state, for fifteen years. He then located in the Black Hills in 1893, settling at Spearfish, where he has practiced continuously since. He is now well known as an able physician and surgeon and is accorded a good practice. He is very careful in the diagnosis of his cases and seldom, if ever, at fault in determining the outcome of disease. He also is interested in mining claims and ranches in South Dakota and has thus made judicious investment of his funds.

In 1880 Dr. Ainsworth was united in marriage to Miss Ellen Ellis, a native of Clarke County, Iowa, while her parents were natives of Kentucky. Her father was a farmer by occupation and held the office of sheriff in Clarke County, Iowa. Both he and his wife have passed away. To Dr. Ainsworth and his wife have been born six children: Isabel, now the wife of A. O. Pemberton, a cattleman residing at Boise, Idaho; Archie, who is in the employ of an express company in Old Mexico; Loraine, the wife of Ernest Town, who is engaged in merchandising in Spearfish; Ellis, who is engaged in the cattle business at Boyes, Montana; and Ruth and Marion, both at home.

Dr. Ainsworth gives his political allegiance to the republican party and is a firm believer in its principles. He is a member of the Masonic lodge, the Knights of Pythias and the Ancient Order of United Workmen, while his strictly professional connections are with the Lawrence County Medical Society, the Black Hills Medical Society, and the South Dakota Medical Association. He concentrates pia energies upon his professional duties and at all times conforms his practice to the highest standards of professional ethics.

A. ALDER, one of the leading citizens and most progressive and highly esteemed business men of Volin, Yankton County, claims the Empire state of the Union as the place of his nativity, having been born in the city of Buffalo, New York, on the 29th of August, 1846, a son of John and Mary A. (Rosenbach) Alder, of whose seven children five are living at the present time, namely: John, who is chief clerk in the Indian school at Lawrence, Kansas; Eugene, who resides in Eastman, Minnesota; Louisa, who is the wife of James A. Dickson, of Oklahoma, who was for many years superintendent of schools of Yankton county; Jennie, who is the wife of Charles Campbell, of Eastman, Minnesota; and Alfred, who is the immediate subject of this sketch.

The father of the subject was born in the city of Berwick, on the Tweed, in England, in 1817, and was there reared to maturity, having learned the trade of millwright and become an expert in the line, while he also served seven years in the English army. In 1843 he came to the United States and immediately enlisted in the army, in which he served one year. He then returned to Buffalo, where he was engaged in the work of his trade until 1857, when he came to the west, locating in Crawford county, Wisconsin, where he continued to be actively engaged in the work of his trade until his death, which occurred in 1880, while in 1871 he became the owner of a grist mill at Eastman, that state, continuing to operate the same successfully until he was called from the scene of life's endeavors, in the fulness of years and well-earned honors. His wife was born in Germany, in the year 1811, and also is now deceased.

Alfred Alder, whose name introduces this sketch, secured his early educational discipline in the public schools of Buffalo, New York, being about ten years of age at the time when his parents removed thence to Wisconsin, where he was reared to manhood, learning the trade of millwright under the effective direction of his father and devoting his attention to that vocation until 1871, when he assumed a position in the mill owned by his father in Eastman. He continued to reside in Wisconsin until 1880, when he removed to Middle Branch, Nebraska, where he erected a flouring mill, successfully operating the same until 1886, when he disposed of the property and came to the city of Yankton, South Dakota, where he established himself in the mercantile business, carrying a general stock of goods. About two years later he came to Volin, and here he continued in the same line of enterprise until May, 1892, building up a large and prosperous business and being known as one of the most enterprising and reliable merchants in the county. In the month mentioned he sold out his mercantile interests and in the autumn of the same year he instituted the erection of the Volin flouring mill, which was completed the following summer, the same having proved of inestimable benefit to the people of this section, affording facilities for which there had been a recognized demand.

In politics Mr. Alder is a stalwart Republican, and it was his privilege to cast his first presidential vote for Abraham Lincoln, while serving in the Union army and before he had attained his legal majority, since he was but eighteen years of age at the time. In March, 1864, he enlisted as a private in Company K, First Illinois Light Artillery, with which he served until August of the following year, when he received his honorable discharge, victory having crowned the union arms and the rebellion been suppressed. His father also served with gallantry as a Union soldier, having enlisted, at the age of forty-seven years, in Company I, Fifth Wisconsin Volunteer Infantry, with which he served for three years and four months, while his son John W. served for three years as a member of Company I, Third Wisconsin Volunteer Cavalry. The subject is at the time of this writing incumbent of the office of treasurer of the village of Volin, but he has never been ambitious for public office, though ever ready to do his part in forwarding the civic and general interests of his home town and county, to which he is signally loyal. Fraternally he is identified with St. John's Lodge, No. I, Free and Accepted Masons, of Yankton.

On the 27th of November, 1873, Mr. Alder was united in marriage to Miss Mary A. Finney, of Eastman, Wisconsin, and of their ten children nine are still living, namely: John, who is employed in his father's mill, being an able young business man: Eunice, who remains at the parental home; Bertha, who is a teacher in the public schools at Estherville. Iowa: Ephraim; who is engaged in farming in Yankton County; Winifred, who is a teacher in the district schools of the county; and Alfred, Jr., Herbert, Bessie and Charles, who remain beneath the home roof.

WILLIAM F. ALDRED

William F. Aldred is proprietor of a lumberyard at Frankfort, which business he has conducted since 1904 — the year of his arrival in the state. He came from Iowa, where he had previously made his home through the greater part of his life, although he was born in Mount Vernon, Kentucky, on the 30th of September, 1859, his parents being Robert and Henrietta (Collett) Aldred. The family is of English lineage and was established in America many generations ago. The father was a farmer by occupation, following that pursuit throughout his entire life, which was terminated, however, in 1860, when he was but thirty-two years of age. He was laid to rest in the cemetery at Mount Vernon, Kentucky, and his wife, who long survived him, passed away in 1912 and was buried at Ocheyedan, Iowa.

William F. Aldred was a lad of seven years when he went to the Hawkeye state with his mother and brother and in the schools of Iowa he completed his education, continuing his studies to the age of twenty-one years through the winter seasons, while the summer months were devoted to farm work. On attaining his majority, he purchased a farm which he operated until he turned his attention to the lumber business, purchasing a yard at Ocheyedan. This was in 1894 and for ten years he conducted the business, building up a large trade which necessitated his handling an extensive amount of lumber each year. He also opened a private bank at Ocheyedan and conducted both interests up to the time of his removal to South Dakota, when he disposed of his business in Iowa. On removing to Frankfort, he opened a lumberyard and now does a large business in building materials, being accorded an extensive patronage which is well merited by reason of his honorable business methods, his indefatigable industry and his efforts to please. Many other. business interests have also profited by his cooperation, for he is a man of sound judgment and resourcefulness. He is now treasurer of the Frankfort Elevator Company and a director of the James River Bank, built the Farmers State Bank building and is engaged in the real-estate business, negotiating many important realty transfers. Whatever he undertakes he carries forward to successful completion and the course which he has followed is one which will bear close investigation and scrutiny.

On the 16th of March, 1886, at Sutherland, Iowa, Mr. Aldred was united in marriage to Miss Emma J. Osborne, a daughter of Page and Anna (Poizer) Osborne. The father, a pioneer agriculturist of Iowa, passed away at Ocheyedan in November, 1910, when seventy-two years of age, and was there buried. His widow still makes her home at Ocheyedan. To Mr. and Mrs. Aldred have been born five children, as follows: Adelbert, who died on the 21st of April 1900, when twelve years of age; Vesta A., who married C. W. Habicht, now conducting a general store at Wessington Springs, South Dakota; Viola E.; a high-school student; Lulu A., who also attends high school; and Herbert W., likewise pursuing his education.

Mr. Aldred has always been a stalwart republican since age conferred upon him the right of franchise and has done all in his power to further the interests of the party yet has never been an office seeker. He is an exemplary representative of Masonry and he also has membership with the Modern Woodmen of America. His life has been well spent and his entire career has been an active and useful one. Prompted by laudable ambition, he has gradually worked his way upward and he now controls important trade and financial interests that contribute to the prosperity of the community as well as to his individual success.

ALVA N. ALDRICH

A. N. ALDRICH, mayor of the city of Aberdeen, South Dakota, where he is also proprietor and manager of the Wisconsin House, one of the leading hotels of the city, was born at Ionia, Michigan, on August 29, 1866, the son of William E. Aldrich, who was born near Buffalo, New York, February 23, 1840, the son of Warren and Sarah Aldrich, both born near Buffalo, New York. William E. Aldrich went to Indiana in 1856, where he followed farming. He served ten months as a member of Company E, Thirtieth Regiment Indiana Infantry, as a private. He removed to Michigan in the fall of 1857, and his death occurred February 2, 1877. He married Amelia E. Stedman, who was born at Spencer, Medina County, Ohio, in 1848, the daughter of Nelson and Roxana (Parrent) Stedman, natives of New York state, the former born in 1809, the later in 1810.

The subject was reared to manhood in and about his native place, and attended the public schools. In 1887 he came to South Dakota and took up a homestead in Frederick, Brown County. which he at once proceeded to improve and upon which he resided for the following two years. Owing to the stringency of the times and the difficulty experienced in obtaining a livelihood from his land, he disposed of the same at the expiration of the above period, being obliged to sell at such a low figure as to cause the loss of nearly all of his labor and improvements. For some time after disposing of his homestead Mr. Aldrich clerked in a clothing store in Aberdeen, and it was while thus engaged that he decided to go into the hotel business, and in May, 1896, with borrowed capital, he purchased the Wisconsin House, which he at once remodeled and refurnished throughout, making of it one of the leading hotels of the city. The hotel contains forty commodious rooms, with accommodations for a hundred guests, is modern in its appointments, and supplied with all the comforts and conveniences found in any first-class hotel. Mr. Aldrich has proven a model landlord, his companionable and congenial nature having won him a host of friends among the traveling public. Not only is he popular with his guests, but he stands high with his fellow citizens who esteem him highly as a man and citizen, and have honored him in electing him to important places in the city government. In April, 1898, he was elected as a Republican to the board of aldermen at Aberdeen, and was re-elected to that body in 1900 and 1902. In 1898 he was made chairman of the committee on fire department, and remained at the head of that important committee as long as he was alderman. During that period the Gamewell fire alarm system was installed. In 1902 the board of aldermen honored him by electing him acting mayor. In March, 1904, Mr. Aldrich was nominated by the Republicans for the office of mayor, and in April, following, he was elected. His administration began with the inauguration of needed reforms, among which was the strict closing of all saloons on Sunday, and causing the proprietors to comply with the law forbidding them to obstruct the public view of their bars by the placing of palms, sign's, etc., in the front windows. He also closed all the gambling houses, and began the vigorous enforcement of other ordinances, among the same being the one forbidding spitting upon pavements and sidewalks. And those who know the mayor feel certain the public can rest assured that these reforms are not spasmodic, but will continue as long as he remains at the head of the city's government.

Mr. Aldrich is a member of the Masonic fraternity, belong to the blue lodge, the chapter and commandery at Aberdeen. He is also a member of the Knights of Pythias order. On June 5, 1895, Mayor Aldrich was married to Miss Louise Wylie, of Aberdeen, and to this union one son has been born: Louis Wylie, who is now in his sixth year.

CLARK B. ALFORD, M. D.

In April, 1907, Dr. Clark B. Alford retired from the practice of medicine after having been continuously connected with professional interests of Huron since 1886, winning prominence and distinction in this field. He is now in the second term of his able service as surveyor general of South Dakota. He was born near Plattsburg, New York, May 7, 1839, a son of Reuel and Sylvia (Chase) Alford. He acquired his early education in the schools of Beckman town and Plattsburg and when he was nearly eighteen years of age removed to Illinois. He studied medicine in the Louisville Medical College and after receiving his degree turned his attention to practice. In 1886 he came to South Dakota and located at Huron, where he has since resided. He soon built up a large and lucrative practice and became known as one of the leading physicians in the city and state, for he possesses a comprehensive and exact knowledge of the underlying principles of medicine, was capable and conscientious in the diagnosis of his cases and ever watchful over the interests of his patients. In 1907 Dr. Alford retired from the practice of medicine and on the 1st of January, 1908, by appointment by President Roosevelt assumed the duties of United States surveyor general for the district of South Dakota. He has since served in that capacity under reappointment by President Taft and has proven capable and efficient in the discharge of his responsible duties.

On the 14th of March, 1886, Dr. Alford was united in marriage to Miss Lucinda Carroll, of Morris, Illinois, and they have two sons. The Doctor is a member of the Methodist church and is connected with the Masonic fraternity, of which he has been a member for the past forty-eight years, belonging to the blue lodge, chapter, commandery and Shrine. He gives his political allegiance to the republican party and served for three terms as president and superintendent of the state board of health. He is widely and favorably known in Huron, where he has resided for over a quarter of a century.

CHARLES A. ALSETH

Charles A. Alseth has since 1911 been a factor in financial circles of Lake Preston. His birth occurred near Whitewood, South Dakota, on the 26th of November, 1883, his parents being John 0. and Martha Alseth, pioneers who settled in Yankton County, South Dakota, in 1869 and removed to Kingsbury County in 1878. He homesteaded on section 21, township 110, range 54, and also took up a tree claim, devoting his attention to general agricultural pursuits with excellent results for a number of years. At the present time he is living retired in Lake Preston, enjoying a rest which he has truly earned and richly deserves.

Charles A. Alseth pursued his early education in the public schools and subsequently entered Yankton College, which institution conferred upon him the degree of Bachelor of Arts in 1910. The following year he entered the Merchants Exchange Bank of Lake Preston as cashier, having purchased an interest in the institution, of which he remained a director and stockholder until January 1, 1915. In 1915 Mr. Alseth organized and became one of the incorporators of the Farmers National Bank of Lake Preston, which has a capital of twenty-five thousand dollars, and he is serving as cashier of that institution. In his capacity of cashier, he has contributed to the growth and success of the bank in no uncertain degree and enjoys an enviable reputation as a popular, courteous and able official. He was likewise one of the organizers of the Lake Preston Lumber Company.

In politics Mr. Alseth is a stanch republican, while fraternally he is identified with the Masons and the Yeomen. His religious faith is that of the Congregational church, the teachings of which he exemplifies in his daily life. He has gained a creditable measure of success in business and financial circles for one of his years, and South Dakota is proud to number him among her native sons.

JUDGE OLIVER H. AMES

Judge Oliver H. Ames, who is now serving for the fifth consecutive term on the bench of the county court of Clark County and makes his home in the city of Clark, was continuously engaged in the practice of law from 1898 until called to his present position, and comprehensive knowledge of the principles of jurisprudence is the basis of his success both as an attorney and a jurist. He was born in St. Paul, Minnesota, November 21, 1875, a son of Oliver and Emma B. (Benson) Ames, the former a farmer by occupation. Both parents are now deceased.

Spending his youthful days under the parental roof, Judge Ames attended the public schools of St. Paul and afterward entered the University of Minnesota, in which he prepared for the legal profession, and was graduated with the class of 1898. The same year he was admitted to the bar and entered upon practice in connection with J. B. and E. P. Sanborn at St. Paul, with whom he remained for six years. In 1904 he came to South Dakota, settling in Clark, where he won a liberal share of the public patronage in the field of law practice. While his attention to his clients' interests was proverbial, he never forgot that he owed a still higher allegiance to the majesty of the law. In the fall of 1906, he was elected county judge of Clark County, entering upon the duties of the position the following year, and he is now serving for the fifth consecutive term, his reelections coming to him in evidence of the confidence reposed in him by the public.

Judge Ames holds membership in the Episcopal church. His political allegiance is given to the republican party and he is a prominent figure in fraternal circles, holding membership with the Shriners, the Masons, the Odd Fellows, the Knights of Pythias, the Elks, the Modern Woodmen and the United Workmen. In Masonry he has taken the degrees of the royal arch chapter and has also attained the thirty-second degree of the Scottish Rite. He has social qualities and personal characteristics which render him popular and which have gained for him the high and enduring regard of all with whom he has been brought in contact. He never allows outside interests, however, to interfere with the faithful performance of his professional duties and his course upon the bench has been marked by a masterful grasp of every problem presented for solution.

ALBERT M. ANDERSON

Business activity at Sturgis finds a worthy representative in Albert M. Anderson, a hardware merchant, who in the conduct of his business interests carries forward to successful completion whatever he undertakes as the result of his unfaltering industry, keen sagacity and un aba ting enterprise. He was born at Neenah, Wisconsin, July 15, 1868, a son of Henry O. Anderson, mentioned elsewhere in this work. He attended school at Yankton as a kindergarten pupil and later continued his education in a log school building at South Bend, near Deadwood. He also studied at Gayville and at Central City for one winter and then walked from Central City to Deadwood, where he attended school in the basement of the Congregational church. He was then out of school until 1888, when he became a student in the Spearfish Normal school, from which he was graduated with the class of 1891.

After leaving the normal school he was sent by his father to eastern South Dakota to dispose of a band of horses and spent about six months in that work. The following year his father admitted him to partnership in the hardware business at Sturgis and the association between them has since been maintained. They have a well-appointed store, carrying a large and carefully selected stock of shelf and heavy hardware, and their honorable business methods and enterprise secure to them a liberal patronage. In connection with his father Mr. Anderson is also interested in ranch property and is a director and stockholder in the Bear Butte Valley Bank of Sturgis, but the major portion of his time and attention are devoted to the hardware trade.

On the 27th of September, 1898, Mr. Anderson was united in marriage to Miss Minnie Van Koughnet, who was born at Carthage, New York, a daughter of John and Ann (Spencer) Van Koughnet. The father's birth occurred in the Mohawk valley of New York, May 8, 1827, and the mother was born in the Empire state, April 6, 1839. Mr. Van Koughnet engaged in farming in the east until 1900, when he removed to Sturgis and again turned his attention to agricultural pursuits in that locality, remaining upon the farm until 1907, when he purchased a home in Sturgis, which he and his wife now occupy. At the present writing he is living retired from business, his former activity having brought to him capital sufficient to enable him to enjoy a well-earned rest. He is a member of the Masonic fraternity and is a highly respected resident of Sturgis. To him and his wife were born four children: William, a farmer residing on the old homestead in New York; Mary, who is with her parents; Charles, who is engaged in the drug business at Forest Grove, Oregon; and Mrs. Anderson, who by her marriage has become the mother of three children: Earl Henry, born September 15, 1901; Harold Oscar, October 4, 1905; and Wilma Mildred, November 1, 1909.

Mr. Anderson is a Scottish Rite Mason and a member of the Mystic Shrine at Deadwood. He is a prominent Odd Fellow and has passed through the chairs of that organization a number of times. He is also connected with the Ancient Order of United Workmen and his religious belief is indicated by his membership in the Presbyterian church. In politics he is a republican and has served as a member of the city council of Sturgis. The cause of education finds in him a stalwart champion. He has served on the school board of Sturgis, acting as its president until 1914, and he was president of the Spearfish Normal Alumni Association for three years. He has also been regent of education for the state of South Dakota since 1908 and does everything in his power to advance the standards of public instruction and make the schools of both the lower and more advanced grades of greater efficiency in preparation for life's practical and responsible duties.

C. J. ANDERSON

C. J. ANDERSON, of Plankinton, the capital of Aurora County, was born in the city of Zanesville, Muskingum County, Ohio. He secured his early educational discipline in the common schools and supplemented this by a course of study in the Ohio State Normal School, where he continued his discipline until he had attained the age of twenty-one years. In 1861 he enlisted as a private in the Nineteenth Ohio Volunteer Infantry, which was assigned to the Western Army and with which he continued in active service for four years and three months, representing practically the entire period of the war. He received his honorable discharge and then returned to his home in Zanesville, where he remained until he removed to Delavan, Illinois, where he maintained his home for a number of years, having been engaged in the hardware business for the major portion of the time. He then came to South Dakota, and located in Aurora County, taking up a homestead claim adjoining the site of the present city of Plankinton, and becoming one of the founders of the town, while he was also concerned in the organization of the county. Soon after his arrival he established the first mercantile business in the town, having a small building in which he installed a stock of general merchandise, while later he gave his attention entirely to the hardware business, in which he was engaged until he disposed of his interests in the line and established his present enterprise, having a well-appointed establishment, in which he carries a fine assortment of clothing and furnishing goods, while he controls a large and representative trade.

In politics Mr. Anderson has ever given a stanch support to the Republican party, taking an active part in the promotion of its cause, while he has been called upon to serve in various positions of public trust. He received from the board of county commissioners the appointment to the office of register of deeds, and became ex-officio county clerk, the two offices having been jointly administered for a number of years. He held the dual office under this appointment for a period, and then was elected to fill the same, and was chosen as his own successor at the expiration of his first regular term.

Fraternally he is affiliated with the Grand Army of the Republic, and the Ancient Free and Accepted Masons. Mr. Anderson was united in marriage to Miss Elizabeth Gates, of Delavan. Wisconsin, and they have three children.

NELS C. ANDREWS

Nels C. Andrews, who is now acting as manager for J. H. Queal & Company, of Minneapolis, his home being in Irene, was born on the 14th of August, 1868, in Racine, Wisconsin, and is a son of Christ and Marie (Nielsen) Christensen, natives of Denmark. Coming to America in 1868 the father first settled in Wisconsin, where he made his home until 1877, and then removed to Turner County. South Dakota. There he secured one hundred and sixty acres of government land and for several years devoted his time and energies to the improvement and cultivation of his place, though by trade he is a wagonmaker. having followed that occupation in the old country. He also worked with a brother at wagonmaking in Racine, Wisconsin, and to his own industry, perseverance and economy is due his success in life. In religious faith he is a Baptist and in politics is an ardent Republican. His family consists of six children, namely: Christine, now the wife of Nick Nielson, a farmer; Tillie; John, who married Minnie Olson; Mary, wife of C. F. Frederickson, a farmer of Turner County, South Dakota; Anton, who is operating the home place for his father; and Nels C, of this review.

Nels C. Andrews spent his early life upon a farm and had good educational advantages. After attending the public schools for some years, he entered Sioux Falls, College at Sioux Falls, in 1896, completing the scientific course and graduating with the class of 1899. For ten years he successfully engaged in teaching school in Turner County, being in charge of the city school at Viborg a part of the time, but as previously stated he now holds the position of manager for J. H. Queal & Company, at Irene, Yankton County.

In 1895 Mr. Andrews was united in marriage to Miss Christine Olson, a daughter of Christ and Marie (Nelson) Olson, who were born in Denmark and are now living in Turner County, South Dakota. Her father is a very up-to-date and prosperous farmer, being now the owner of eleven hundred and twenty acres of good farm land in this state. He has a family of five children, namely: Christine, Nels. Frank, Victor and Arthur. The sons are still at home. The children born to Mr. and Mrs. Andrews are Rubie v., Una Z., Pearl B. and Newell C.

Although comparatively a young man, Mr. Andrews has already met with fair success in life and is the owner of some town property in Irene. He is an honored member of several civic societies, belonging to the Masonic lodge at Centerville: Yankton Consistory, No. I; the Modern Woodmen Camp, No. 2323; the Danish Brotherhood, No. 141: and the Order of Home Guardians, No. 2. Politically he is a stalwart Democrat, and he has taken quite an active and influential part in local politics. His fellow citizens, recognizing his worth and ability, have called upon him to serve as justice of the peace, town clerk, alderman and mayor of Irene and his official duties have always been discharged in a commendable and satisfactory manner.

WELLINGTON J. ANDREWS

W. J. ANDREWS, one of the well-known and honored citizens of Sioux Falls, is a native of the dominion of Canada, having been born near the city of Ottawa, on the 14th of April, 1865, and being a son of William H. and Eliza Ann (Johnson) Andrews, who were likewise born in Canada, where they continued to maintain their home until 1874, when they came as pioneers to what is now the state of South Dakota, locating near Scotland, Bon Homme County, where the father took up government land and developed a good farm, becoming one of the representative citizens of that section of the state.

The subject of this review received his rudimentary education in the common schools of his native county, and was nine years of age at the time of his parents' removal to South Dakota. Here he was reared to manhood under the sturdy discipline of the pioneer farm, the while continuing to attend the public schools until 1885, when he entered the academy at Scotland, where he was graduated as a member of the class of 1886. Thereafter he continued to assist in the work and management of the home farm until 1886, when, at the age of twenty-one years, he went to Parkston, Hutchinson county, where he was engaged in the agricultural implement business and dealing in livestock until 1893, when he returned to Scotland, where he opened a general merchandise store, building up a successful business and there continuing operations in the line until 1898, when he sold out and came to Sioux Falls, where he established himself in the grocery business, in which he has ever since continued, catering to a large and representative trade and having a finely equipped store. His establishment is modern in all its appointments, and the stock carried is exceptionally comprehensive and select, while he is recognized as an energetic and progressive business man and as one well worthy of the uniform confidence and esteem in which he is held. In politics Mr. Andrews has ever given an uncompromising allegiance to the Democratic party, has taken an active part in the promotion of its cause, having been a delegate to various state and county conventions, and having been called to serve in a number of minor offices, though he has never sought personal preferment in the line.

Fraternally he is identified with Unity Lodge, No. 130, Ancient Free and Accepted Masons; Scotland Chapter, No. 31, Royal Arch Masons; Parkston Lodge, No. 99, Independent Order of Odd Fellows; and Sioux Falls Lodge, No. 262. Benevolent and Protective Order of Elks.

On the 8th of February, 1890. Mr. Andrews was united in marriage to Miss Persis U. Tyler, who was born in Des Moines, Iowa, being a daughter of L. S. Tyler, who has been a resident of Sioux Falls since 1892. Mr. and Mrs. Andrews have one daughter, Edith Alice.

JOHN W. ARTHUR

J. W. ARTHUR, one of the representative business men of Webster, Day County, is a native of the city of Philadelphia, Pennsylvania, where he was born on the 30th of June, 1858, being a son of Robert and Mary (Scott) Arthur, both of whom were born in Ireland. As a young man the father of our subject left his old home in the northern part of the Emerald Isle and came to America, settling in Philadelphia, where he was for many years engaged in the coal business, becoming successful in his endeavors and continuing to reside in the fair old City of Brotherly Love until his death, which occurred in 1902, his wife having passed away in 1871.

John W. Arthur, the immediate subject of this review, completed the curriculum of the public schools in his native city and then entered Crittenden College, in the same city, where he was graduated as a member of the class of 1875. He then learned the drug business, with which he there continued to be identified until 1884, when he came to South Dakota, bringing a number of car loads of livestock and settling in Day County, where he continued to be engaged in the raising of stock for a number of years, after which he became identified with newspaper work. He purchased an interest in the Reporter and Farmer, published in Webster, South Dakota, and continued to be associated in its editorial and business management until 1901, when he disposed of his interests in the line. In 1898 he was appointed postmaster of Webster, retaining this incumbency until 1902, and giving a most satisfactory administration. Since that time, he has been established in the real-estate business, controlling valuable farming and grazing lands in this section of the state, as well as improved and unimproved town property, and having at all times represented on his books many desirable investments. He is specially interested in realty in Webster, where he has built a large number of houses. In politics Mr. Arthur is a stanch and uncompromising advocate of the principles of the Republican party, and he has taken an active part in the promotion of its cause in the state of his adoption, having held membership on both the county and state central committees and been a delegate to the various conventions of his party.

He is affiliated with the lodge and chapter of the Masonic fraternity and also with the Independent Order of Odd Fellows and the Ancient Order of United Workmen. In 1885 Mr. Arthur was united in marriage to Miss Clara F. McDougall, who was born in Sparta, Wisconsin, being a daughter of Peter and Elizabeth (Farrington) McDougall, who were born and reared in Maine, being representatives of stanch old colonial stock, while the records establish the fact that members of the Farrington family were soldiers of the Continental line during the war of the Revolution. Mrs. Arthur was summoned into eternal rest on the 29th of December, 1897, and is survived by three children, Robert, Irene and Walter Scott. The elder son is now attending the United States Military Academy at West Point, being one of the youngest cadets in the institution. On the 30th of June, 1903, Mr. Arthur wedded Mrs. Mary Ella Whitemore, of Stillwater, Minnesota.

B. C. ASH

B. C. ASH, one of the prominent and successful stock growers of Hughes County and also incumbent of the office of sheriff of the county, is a native of the Hoosier state, having been born in White County, Indiana. When he was about five years of age, his parents removed from Indiana to Sioux City, Iowa. The subject received his preliminary educational training in the schools of Sioux City, and after the removal of the family to Yankton continued his studies in the common schools of that place as opportunity presented, while he early initiated his independent career. Mr. Ash was appointed deputy United States Marshal, and continued to serve in this capacity for varying intervals during a number of years. Subsequently he left Yankton and removed to the site of the present thriving and attractive city of Bismarck, and his is the distinction of having erected the first house in the town. He held the position of wagon master for General Custer, who was then making his first trip through this section of the northwest, where his life was later sacrificed. Later Mr. Ash located in Pierre, where he engaged in the livery business and also conducted a general store, becoming one of the leading and influential business men of the capital city. He identified himself with the stock business, to which he has since given much attention, raising cattle and horses upon an extensive scale and having a large and well-improved ranch, which is located one hundred and twenty-five miles northwest of Fort Pierre, in Stanley County. In politics he is a stanch advocate of the Democratic party and has been one of the active workers in the party ranks. In 1900 he was elected sheriff of Hughes County, giving a most able administration and being chosen to this office again in the spring of 1904, for a second term of four years. In 1896 he received from President Cleveland the appointment as Indian agent at the Lower Brule agency, retaining this incumbency four years and proving a most capable official.

He is identified with the Ancient Free and Accepted Masons, the Ancient Arabic Order of the Nobles of the Mystic Shrine, and the Benevolent and Protective Order of Elks. Mr. Ash was united in marriage to Miss Sarah A. Brisbine, and they have three children.

HENRY C. ASH

Henry C. Ash of Meade County, is a native of Allegany County, Maryland, and was born on Christmas day, 1827. He remained under the paternal rooftree in his native state until he reached the age of eleven, then moved with his parents to Tippecanoe County, Indiana, where the family engaged in farming in which he assisted, attending a little country school near the homestead in the winter months, thus supplementing in a small way the slender educational facilities he had enjoyed in his former home. In a short time, he entered actively on farm work in connection with his father, remaining so occupied until the death of the latter, when the son was but sixteen years old. Mr. Ash and his brother conducted the farm for a number of years under the supervision of their step-mother, then divided their interests and he went to White County and began farming on his own account, uniting stock raising to his other work. He developed a fine farm and built himself a comfortable residence, making his property one of the most desirable rural homes of the section in which it was located. In 1856, believing there were better opportunities for thrift and enterprise in the hardier west, he sold his Indiana home and came to Sioux City, arriving at that place on May 26th.

The town then consisted of a few tents and shacks and contained only one house with a shingle-roof. On July 4th he opened the first hotel ever conducted in the town and continued to conduct it until the fall of 1850, the building being built of logs. At the time last mentioned he moved his family to Dakota, arriving at Yankton on Christmas eve. There he built the furth house in the town, a log structure with a dirt roof and no floor but the earth, and here he again engaged in the hotel business, this being the second frontier town in which he ministered to the wants of the traveling public, and this enterprise being practically the first hotel within the present limits of the state. He continued in active control of it until 1876, when he sold it and went to the Black Hills, whither he had been ordered as United States deputy marshal, an office he had held continuously since 1862. His outfit was the first to cross the Missouri on the way to the Hills, and the party was obliged to make its own trail through the wilderness from the Missouri to Deadwood. They arrived at what is now Rapid City on March 25th and then pushed on to Deadwood.

Mr. Ash made a number of trips back and forth over this route in his official capacity, taking away the first prisoner ever taken out of Custer County, a man whom he had arrested for selling whiskey without a license. In 1877 he moved his family to Deadwood, and while on the passage up the Missouri the boat on which they were traveling caught fire and they lost all their possessions aboard of her. The climate at their new home not agreeing with Mrs. Ash, she returned to Yankton, but he remained in the territory and in August settled at Sturgis. The town was staked out on August 7th, and the next day he located on his present site, having taken up one hundred and sixty acres of land. Of this he still owns forty acres, but has sold the rest in town lots, the depot and St. Martin's Academy having been built on land which was originally in his farm. He built a log house on his tract and in the fall of 1878 his family joined him there. He engaged in the real-estate business and found it profitable. Sturgis was a thriving town in those days and there was ready sale for land in the vicinity.

He resigned as deputy marshal in the fall of 1878 and the next fall was elected justice of the peace, an office to which he was continuously re-elected for a period of seven years. While living at Yankton Mr. Ash represented Yankton County in the territorial legislature, serving two terms in that capacity. In 1894 his residence was destroyed by fire and he at once began the erection of a fine stone dwelling. The facilities for building were not first class and a long time was consumed in building this house, but when it was completed, it rewarded his patience and efforts, being the best residence in the town and beautifully located on the brow of a small hill about half a mile from the center of the place commanding a view of a wide extent of the surrounding country. It is in colonial style with a wide veranda around it, and is in the midst of a fruitful orchard and garden. The house is elegantly finished and furnished throughout, and the place is one of the finest homes in the west.

Mr. Ash belongs to the Masonic order, with membership in the lodge at Sturgis. In 1863, as a charter member, he helped to organize St. John's Lodge, No. I, at Yankton, the first Masonic body in the state, and he is one of its two surviving charter members.

On March 22, 1851, at Mount Jackson, White County, Indiana, Mr. Ash was married to Miss Mary Reynolds, a native of Ohio. They have five children, Ben C, Julia (Mrs. Bates), Harry C, William B. and Elizabeth (Mrs. Eccles).

HORACE J. AUSTIN

HORACE J. AUSTIN.   MRS. RACHEL M. R. AUSTIN.

Standing in the clear white light of a life and character such as denoted the late Horace J. Austin, we are moved to a feeling of admiration, respect and reverence, for he stood for all that signifies sane, well poised and noble manhood. He was one of the foremost citizens of the state of South Dakota, and in his home city of Vermillion, Clay County, his death came with a sense of personal bereavement to his fellow townsmen, who could not but appreciate his sterling worth and his value to the community. Tt is fitting that in this history be incorporated a memoir of this distinguished citizen.

Horace J. Austin was born in Washington County, New York, July 11, 1837, and when he was two years of age his parents removed thence to Essex County, that state, where he was reared to manhood, continuing to abide beneath the home roof until the fall of 1857, when, as a young man of twenty years, he set forth to seek his fortunes as a pioneer in the west, his educational advantages having been such as were afforded in the common schools. He proceeded as far as Dubuque, Iowa, where he secured employment with a company of surveyors, and there he made his home for two years save when absent on surveying expeditions. Twice within this period his business brought him within the confines of the territory of Dakota, and on the second trip he decided to here take up his permanent residence. Accordingly, he located in Yankton, the capital of the territory, where he was living at the time of the outbreak of the Civil war. In 1861 he enlisted in Company A, First Dakota Cavalry, which was stationed for some time in Vermillion, where it was mustered out on the 9th of May, 1865, having thus served during the entire period of the war, principally in repelling the ravages of hostile Indians, and the record of our subject as a soldier was one that will ever redound to his horror. After his military career he continued to reside in Vermillion until his death, which occurred on the 27th of February, 1891, as the result of an attack of pneumonia, which brought his life to a close in the zenith of its power and usefulness. From a previously published outline of his career, we enter the following excerpt:

Although he never had the advantages of what is technically designated as higher education, he was a man who had the power of gaining much through absorption, observation and personal application, and his knowledge of men and affairs was well rounded and symmetrical. His honesty, integrity and steadfastness of character won him a high place in the hearts of the people, and he was six times elected a member of the legislature. In 1868-9 he was president of the territorial council. As a civil engineer he secured government surveying contracts every year from 1866 until his death, and there are few if any counties in the state which do not bear some of his surveying stakes. In temporal affairs Mr. Austin was greatly prospered, but freely as he received, with equal freedom did he give to the poor and needy. His was a kindly, sympathetic nature and charity and tolerance abided with him as constant guests. The principles of diligence and faithfulness were early mastered by him and ever dominated his course in life. His name, too, was a synonym of honesty, and in writing to his sister, several years prior to his death, he said: "I am being prospered, but this much I can say, I have never taken an unjust penny from any man." In the political history of South Dakota, he bore an honorable part, and as a legislator was associated with such men of prominence as Moody, Brookings and a host of others, and was the acknowledged peer of all. As a citizen he believed in law and its obeyance, and as a man he was gentle, courteous and obliging. In truth, Horace J. Austin was well-nigh the embodiment of man's ideal. He was a sturdy pioneer, a patient soldier, a faithful legislator, a true citizen, a loyal friend, and, last but not least, a loving and indulgent husband.

On the occasion of his funeral the president of the State University spoke of him as follows: "With all his modesty and simplicity, he was a great, strong man and played a full man's part in the world. He could not be moved from the position which he believed to be right; he was true to his conscience. He was like a child in freedom from trickery or meanness or malice. He was every inch a man in the thick of life's struggles with evil and wrong. With a heart tender to suffering, he knew what it was to be righteously indignant against the evils that produce suffering. What a wide range of character these traits cover! A simple-hearted, strong-willed, generous, gentle man — what more can be said of character? And I call this life successful because, first, Mr. Austin won an honorable success in his chosen pursuit. He became an expert surveyor; he acquired reputation and a competence. His work was honest work. Successful, second, in that he was a loyal and loved citizen and an honored public servant. There was no public enterprise in which he was not interested. He could be counted on for everything that concerned the welfare of the people. And it was a matter of course that such a man should be chosen for public service. He was the model citizen. He never sought office; he was too distrustful of his own abilities, too modest for that. He shunned rather than courted responsibility, yet, like a true man, when the office sought him, he accepted it as a true citizen, with determination to do his best." Mr. Austin was a number of the lower house of the state legislature at the time of his death, and thus he died in the harness, faithful to the last and one of that noble band of pioneers who were associated in the founding and building of a great commonwealth. His political support was given to the Republican party and fraternally he was prominently identified with the Masonic order and he was one of the original delegates who met in the convention at Elk Point on June 22, 1875, and took the preliminary steps toward the organization of the grand lodge of Dakota. He was also with the Grand Army of the Republic. Though he never formally identified himself with any religious body he had the deepest reverence for the spiritual verities as exemplified in the Christian faith, and guided and guarded his life in accord with the teachings of the divine Master, whom he served with humility and reverence, his being the faith that makes faithful.

The home of Mr. Austin was ever to him a sacred spot, and here his ambitions and affections centered and shone most resplendently. To violate this sanctity by words of eulogy would be most flagrant abuse in this connection, but in conclusion of this memoir we enter a brief record concerning the domestic chapter in his life history. On the 21st of March, 1870, Mr. Austin was united in marriage to Miss Rachel M. Ross, who was born in Trumbull County, Ohio, on the 1st of June, 1838, being a daughter of Benjamin and Mary (Palm) Ross. The father died in Arkansas and Mrs. Ross later came to Vermillion Dakota, where she died on the 22d of January, 1876. Mrs. Austin, whose death occurred March 6, 1904, was a woman of gracious presence and noble character and proved a true helpmeet to her husband, their companionship being ideal in all its relations. Mr. and Mrs. Austin had no children, but their generous natures prompted them to provide a home for three children, all of whom were reared with utmost care and solicitude, namely: Leroy O. Stevens, who is now living at Victor, Colorado; Anna Ross, who is now at Silex, Missouri, and Helen P., who was legally adopted by them in infancy, being now of Vermillion.

GEORGE V. AYRES *

GEORGE V. AYRES

When the good roads movement commenced in western South Dakota about five years ago, George V. Ayres, then chairman of the board of county commissioners of Lawrence County, took an active part as a pioneer in modern highway progress. His activity and his well-known ability soon made him a leader in a movement that grew rapidly, and today Lawrence County has mountain highways that are the admiration of the west, while others are in course of construction throughout western South Dakota that are destined to mean the greatest prosperity for this region; and to George V. Ayres, more than to any other one man, is due the credit for this progress. He is justly proud of his achievement as a constructive designer and builder of good roads; probably more so than of any other success he has attained during his long and useful career.

Mr. Ayres has labored long and earnestly in behalf of the movement, recognizing clearly the relation between commercial development and good roads. He was a delegate to and chairman of the first and second good roads conventions which started the work west of the river on the Black and Yellow Trail (Chicago, Black Hills and Yellowstone Park highway, extending from Yellowstone Park to Chicago), and the Deadwood and Denver highway, from Deadwood, South Dakota, to Denver, Colorado.

In political belief, Mr. Ayres is a republican and has taken a prominent part in the affairs of the party in South Dakota. He was for four years chairman of the board of county commissioners and is still serving as a member of the board. Under President Harrison he served as receiver of public moneys at the United States land office at Rapid City for three and a half years, proving himself to be a capable and conscientious official. He was a member of the Deadwood city council for two years, and for six years served as chairman of the republican county committee. For four consecutive years the republican state committee enjoyed his services as vice chairman.

Mr. Ayres has for years been recognized as one of the very active members of the Society of Black Hills Pioneers of '76. He served as president of that body in 1900 and again in 1914 and 1915. He is a member of Deadwood Lodge, No. 508, B. P. O. E.

He is a stockholder and director in the Franklin Hotel; stockholder in the First National Bank; and an active member of the Deadwood Business Club, having served on the board of directors and as its president for several years. He is president of the Deadwood-Heidelberg Mining Company and is connected with a number of other local mining enterprises. He is also a member of the South Dakota Retail Hardware Association and one of the board of directors of the South Dakota Children's Home Society.

He has utilized wisely the opportunities that have presented themselves, and his busy life has not only won him individual success but has been decidedly instrumental in promoting the public welfare along many lines of endeavor, and all who know him give him the respect which true worth alone can command.

For forty-one years Mr. Ayres has been a Mason, and if he had done nothing else in his life than the service he has rendered to Masonry in unselfish loyalty and good hard work he could well be remembered for this alone. He joined the order in 1874 and has been one of the few men who has been prominent in Masonic circles of the state for many years. He served his lodge as master for three years, being first elected to that office in 1884. On June 13, 1888, he was elected deputy grand master of the Grand Lodge of Dakota, and on June 12, 1889, grand master of the Grand Lodge of South Dakota, serving one year. He was elected high priest January 10, 1894, and served for two years. On June 13, 1895, he was elected deputy grand high priest of the Grand Chapter of South Dakota, and grand high priest June 12, 1896, serving for one year. He has served as deputy master of Lakota Council U. D. Royal and Select Masters. After serving in minor offices of his commandery he was elected eminent commander in 1888 and later served as grand commander of South Dakota and in various other offices in the Grand Commandery.

Mr. Ayres has been a member of the Scottish Rite since 1893 and is now an honorary thirty-third degree and deputy of the S. G. Inspector General for South Dakota. He is registrar and secretary of the four bodies in the Black Hills Consistory. He crossed the burning sands of Naja Temple, A. A. O. N. M. S., at Deadwood in 1893 and served as potentate in 1897. He represented Naja Temple at the Imperial Council in 1898. He is also past worthy patron of Deadwood Chapter, No. 23, O. E. S.. During the term of his office as grand master of the State Grand Lodge, Mr. Ayres was very rigid in enforcing a resolution which had been adopted by the Grand Lodge and drove the so-called "Cerneau Rite" out of the state. He also established the "Grand Charity Fund."

[The following masonic data was extracted from the Robinson/Doane document]

Mr. Ayres is one of the prominent and honored Freemasons of the state, his record in the connection being a noteworthy one. He was raised to the sublime degree of Master Mason June 27, 1874, in Beatrice Lodge, No. 26, Ancient Free and Accepted Masons, at Beatrice, Nebraska, and later served the same as secretary and junior warden. On the 16th of April, 1882, he demitted from this lodge, and on the 7th of the following November affiliated with Deadwood Lodge, No. 7, of which he still remains a member. He served as junior and senior warden of this lodge in turn, and November 7, 1884, was elected worshipful master of the same, in which capacity he served three successive years, while he was again elected to the office December 2, 1902, and served one year. Never having previously held any office in the grand lodge, he was "taken from the floor" and elected deputy grand master of the grand lodge of Dakota, on the 13th of June, 1888, while on the 12th of June of the following year he was elected grand master of the grand lodge of the newly admitted state of South Dakota, having the distinction of being the first to hold the office and serving for one year. On the 13th of July, 1875, Mr. Ayres received the final degree in Livingston Chapter, No. 10, Royal Arch Masons, at Beatrice, Nebraska, of which he served as secretary in the same year. In 1880 he demitted from this chapter and affiliated with Dakota Chapter, No. 3, at Deadwood, on the 8th of that month, while on the 22d of the following December he was elected its treasurer, serving three years, after which he was secretary of the chapter for six successive years from December 12, 1883. January 10, 1904, he was elected high priest, for a term of two years. On the 13th of June, 1895, he was taken from the floor of the grand chapter of the state and elected deputy grand high priest, while on the 12th of June, 1896, he was elected grand high priest, serving one year. On the 9th of October, 1895, Mr. Ayres received the degrees in Lakotah Council, U. D., Royal and Select Masters, in Deadwood, of which he was appointed deputy master the same evening.

On the 1st of January, 1881, he received the orders of knighthood in Dakota Commandery, No. 1, Knights Templar, in Deadwood, of which he was elected recorder in 1883, while by subsequent elections in later years he held the office for a total of six years. In 1884 he was elected junior warden of the commandery, senior warden in 1885, generalissimo in 1887, and eminent commander in 1888, June 22, 1895, he was elected grand senior warden of the grand commandery of South Dakota, was made grand captain general the following year, grand generalissimo in 1897, deputy grand commander in 1898, and grand commander on the 16th of June, 1899, serving one year. In the grand council of anointed high priests of the state, on the nth of June, 1896, he was anointed a high priest, and is an active member of that body. In the Ancient Accepted Scottish Rite of the southern jurisdiction Mr. Ayres received the degrees in Golden Belt Lodge of Perfection, No. 5, on the nth of April, 1893; Robert Bruce Chapter, Rose Croix, No. 3, April 11, 1893; Deadwood Council of Kadosh, No. 3, April 12, 1893; and Black Hills Consistory, No. 3, July 14th. of the same year, and has been an active member ever since. On October 20, 1903, he was elected knight commander of the Court of Honor. In the Ancient Arabic Order of the Nobles of the Mystic Shrine Mr. Ayres crossed the burning sands in Naja Temple, located in Deadwood, on April 14, 1893. He was elected assistant rabban in 1894 and 1895, was chosen chief rabban the following year, and illustrious potentate in 1897, while in the following year he was representative to the imperial council. He was one of the organizers and is an active member of the Masonic Veterans' Association of the state.

[End Robinson/Doane extract]

George Vincent Ayres was born in Monroe township, Wyoming county, Pennsylvania, November 1, 1852, a son of James L. and Patience M. (Vincent) Ayres, both of whom were natives of the Empire state, the mother born in Beakman township, Dutchess County on the 9th of October, 1819, and the father in New York city on the 11th of May, 1810. In early life the latter engaged in the logging business but later turned his attention to farming. James Leonard Ayres and Patience Maria Vincent were married November 11, 1837, at Kingston, Luzerne County, Pennsylvania, by the Rev. Benjamin Bidlack. In 1857 the family emigrated from Pennsylvania to De Kalb county, Illinois, and resided in Illinois for over a year, moving from there to Buchanan county, Missouri, in the fall of 1858, and from there to Nemaha county, Kansas, in the spring of 1859, and thence to Gage county, Nebraska, in the spring of 1860 and located on a farm five miles east of Blue Springs, where the family resided until the spring of 1800, when they moved into Beatrice, Nebraska, in order to give the children school advantages. There the father engaged in the hotel business for a number of years but sold out and lived retired during the later years of his life. Both he and his wife passed away in that city, the father on the 11th of December, 1892, and the mother on the 12th of December, 1905.

George V. Ayres is the fifth in order of birth in the family of seven children born to his parents and received his schooling in Beatrice, Nebraska. When seventeen years of age he accepted a position as clerk in a drug store in Beatrice in order to learn the business and was so engaged until 1876, when he resigned and went to the Black Hills.

He left Beatrice, Nebraska, March 1, 1876, and proceeded to Cheyenne, Wyoming, by rail and there he and five others hired a team and driver to haul their provisions and outfit to Custer City, Black Hills, while they themselves walked. The party left Cheyenne, March 8, and arrived at Custer City March 25, 1876, having been on the road seventeen days, and although it snowed ten of those days and the weather was severe, they slept out of doors without even a tent to protect them from the weather. After prospecting in the vicinity of Custer City for a time, Mr. Ayres pushed on to Deadwood, arriving there May 26, and shortly after engaged in cutting saw logs near Deadwood for the firm of Thompson & Street. Rev. Henry Weston Smith, the "Pioneer Preacher of the Black Hills," who was killed by Indians on Sunday, August 20, 1876, was employed there at the same time, firing the boiler in the sawmill.

Mr. Ayres remained there until July 8, 1876, when he returned to Custer City and worked for a year in the general store of Harlow & Company, and the Cheyenne & Black Hills Stage Company's office. At the end of that time, he prospected for a few months on Spring creek, and in September, 1877, returned to Deadwood and secured employment in Richard C. Lake's hardware store, thoroughly familiarizing himself with all the aspects of that business. He saved his money and in 1882 purchased an interest in the business and is now its sole owner. He has a full stock of shelf and heavy hardware and specializes in mining supplies, carrying the largest stock in that line of any store in the Black Hulls. He conforms his business methods to the highest standard of commercial ethics, and his fair dealing and reasonable prices have been largely responsible for the increased patronage of his store.

Mr. Ayres was married on the 23d of April, 1885, to Miss Kate Towle, a native of Beatrice, Nebraska. She was born August 15, 1859, and was the first white child whose birth occurred in Gage County, Nebraska. Her parents were Albert and Catherine (Holt) Towle, the former a native of Russellville, Logan County, Kentucky, born May 13, 1822, and the latter of Warren County, New York, born January 6, 1817. The father was one of the founders of Beatrice and engaged in the hotel business there for a number of years. For nineteen years he served efficiently and conscientiously as postmaster of that city. His death occurred on the 8th of March, 1879, and his widow survived him for ten years, her death occurring on the 10th of March, 1889. Mrs. Ayres passed away at Rapid City on the 28th of March, 1892. She was the mother of two children: James Albert, who was born in Deadwood, March 29, 1886, and is now a Presbyterian minister at Lead, South Dakota; and Helen, who was born January 1, 1888, and died June 13th of the same year. Mr. Ayres was married at Omaha, Nebraska, on the 21st of December, 1898, to Miss Myrtle Coon, a native of Hebron, Nebraska, and a daughter of Mr. and Mrs. Charles B. Coon, who were early residents of Nebraska, the father serving as county treasurer for a number of years, also as member of the state legislature and is now government gauger, and still living in Omaha. Five children were born to the second marriage of Mr. Ayres, namely: George Vincent, Jr., born August 18, 1899; Frances Glenn, born August 11, 1900; Alice, born December 19, 1902; Albro Charles, born July 1, 1907; and Lloyd Richard, born December 7, 1909.

HOWARD BABCOCK

Howard BABCOCK, attorney-at-law, and for a number of years a leading member of the Sisseton bar, and the present mayor of Sisseton, was born in Waterloo, Wisconsin. December 21, 1867, being the son of Seth C. and Sarah C. (Cole) Babcock, both natives of New York. Seth C. Babcock, a farmer by occupation, was descended from old colonial stock, his family having been among the earliest settlers of York state, and not a few of the name participating in the struggle for independence. He was a veteran of the late Civil war, serving in Company H, Twenty-ninth Wisconsin Infantry, and made an honorable record as a brave and gallant soldier. The Coles also belong to an old family, the early history of which dates from a remote period in the time of the colonies, and the name is still familiar in New York, where they originally located. Seth and Sarah Babcock were the parents of four children who grew to maturity, three sons and one daughter, all living.

Howard Babcock remained in his native town until about eight years of age and in 1875 he moved with his parents to Racine, Mower County, Minnesota, where he worked on a farm and attended the public schools and the Spring Valley high school until his eighteenth year. After teaching two terms of school, he spent the ensuing three years in the Cedar Valley Seminary at Osage, Iowa, and at the expiration of that time began the study of law with Judge C. C. Willson, of Rochester, Minnesota, under whose instruction he continued until his admission to the bar in 1892. Mr. Babcock began the practice of his profession at Wilmot, South Dakota, in 1892, and two years later was elected state's attorney, which position he held the constitutional term of four years, proving an able, faithful and untiring official. Retiring from office, he resumed the general practice and when the county seat was moved to Sisseton he changed his residence to that place, and has built up a large and lucrative practice in the courts of Roberts and neighboring counties. Mr. Babcock is one of the leading lawyers of the Sisseton bar, stands high in the esteem of his professional associates and the public, and has earned an enviable reputation in his chosen calling. His success has been as pronounced financially as professionally and he is today one of the well-to-do men of his city and county, owning valuable real estate, besides his interests in the First National Bank and Reservation State Bank, of Sisseton, the First State Bank of Summit and the Citizens' Bank at White Rock. He helped to organize these institutions and has been a member of the directorate of each bank ever since, and at this time he is president of the First State Bank of Summit. He also organized the Sisseton Loan and Title Company and is heavily interested in the Roberts County Land and Loan Company, being president of both institutions. Mr. Babcock owns one of the finest residence properties in Sisseton and a half section in Roberts County, which is under a high state of cultivation and well improved in the way of buildings, fences, etc. He is essentially a self-made man, his professional success and financial prosperity being the result of his own untiring efforts and industry, and it is eminently fitting to claim for him a prominent place among the representative citizens of his adopted state.

Mr. Babcock is a member of the Masonic fraternity and at the present time holds the office of junior warden in Sisseton Lodge, No. 31, he is also identified with the Pythian brotherhood, belonging to Reservation Lodge, No. 66. Mr. Babcock, on January 22, 1895, contracted a matrimonial alliance with

Miss Ella Jones, of Mitchell, Iowa, and their union has been blessed by three children, Dana B., Gordon C. and Carroll H., who are sturdy examples of the boys they raise in South Dakota.

WEST BABCOCK

West Babcock, agent for the state of South Dakota for the Mutual Benefit Life Insurance Company of Newark, New Jersey, was born in Chickasaw county, Iowa, May 9, 1858, and is a son of Lemuel R. and Martha (Hodson) Babcock, the former a native of New York. The family is of English origin and was founded in America by the great-great-grandfather of our subject, who came from England to New York, where his son and grandson were born.

West Babcock acquired a limited education in the public schools of Dundas, Minnesota, whither his parents had moved in 1868. After laying aside his books he learned the cooper's trade and followed that occupation in connection with farming until 1886. In that year he removed to Northfield, Minnesota, and turned his attention to the livery business, conducting an enterprise of this character for four years. In 1890 he became connected with the Mutual Benefit Life Insurance Company of Newark, New Jersey, for which he acted as agent in Northfield until 1903. He was then made state agent with headquarters in Sioux Falls and has since held this responsible and important position. He does a large business and has accomplished a great deal in the interests of his company, being regarded as one of its most trusted and valued representatives.

On the 10th of January, 1882, at Northfield, Minnesota, Mr. Babcock was united in marriage to Miss Carrie F. Hibbard, a daughter of Culver Hibbard, who served in a Minnesota regiment during the Civil war. Mr. and Mrs. Babcock have become the parents of four children: Fannie L., the wife of A. V. Kelley, of Sioux Falls; Martha Maude, who married Arthur T. Fosdick; Earl H., who died at the age of six years; and Beatrice M., who died at eighteen months.

Mr. Babcock gives his political allegiance to the republican party. He holds membership in the Elks, the Country and the Dacotah Clubs and is a thirty-second degree Mason. In 1914 he was eminent commander of Cyrene Commandery, No. 2, and was grand scribe of the Grand Chapter of South Dakota in 1914-15. He is well known in Sioux Falls and his many friends esteem him highly for his business ability and his genuine personal worth.

CHRISTEN J. BACH

Christen J. BACH, a successful business man and representative citizen of Turner County, who is at present the state commissioner of school and public lands, and is president of the Bank of Hurley, at Hurley, is a native of Denmark, where he was born on the 10th of November, 1858, being a son of Jacob S. Bach, a pioneer of Yankton, South Dakota. The subject received his early education in the excellent schools of his native land, and there remained until 1873, when he came to Dakota territory, where he has availed himself of the opportunities presented and has won definite success through his own earnest and honorable endeavors. He located in Centerville, Turner County, in 1884, where he engaged in the hardware business, also establishing a store in Hurley. He built up a very profitable business in the line and continued operations in both towns until the 1st of October, 1892, when he established himself in the banking business in Hurley, and has since given the major portion of his attention to the supervision of the same. The bank is ably managed and established on a solid financial basis, while its popularity is indicated by the representative support accorded by the people of the section.

In politics Mr. Bach is a stalwart supporter of the principles of the Republican party, in whose cause he has been an active and valued worker, while his is the distinction of having been a member of the first and second general assemblies of the legislature of the state. In the fall of 1902, he was elected the state commissioner of school and public lands, and has since remained incumbent of this office. He and his wife are prominent and zealous members of the Lutheran church, and fraternally he has attained to the thirty-second degree of Ancient Accepted Scottish Rite Masonry, being identified with the consistory at Yankton, while he is also one of the influential members of the Independent Order of Odd Fellows, being past grand master of the grand lodge of the order in the state. On the 4th of October, 1878, the subject of this sketch was married to Carrie Franson, who was born in Norway, on the 28th of December, 1858, and they have six children, namely: Forest, Guerdon, Mae, Bernie, Etta and Ruth.

CHARLES OLIN BAILEY

Charles Olin Bailey was born in Freeport, Illinois, July 2, 1860. He is the oldest son of the late Judge Joseph Mead Bailey (former chief justice of Illinois) and Anna Olin Bailey. He comes of old New England stock and is in the ninth generation from James Bailey, who settled at Rowley, Massachusetts, about 1640. On his mother's side he is in the seventh generation from John Olin, who settled in East Greenwich, Rhode Island, about 1678. Among his ancestors are William Bradford, who came over in the Mayflower and was the second governor of Plymouth colony, and Captain John Mason, the noted Indian fighter and the hero of the Pequot war of 1637.

Mr. Bailey received his early education in the public schools of Freeport, Illinois. In the fall of 1876, he entered the University of Rochester, Rochester, New York, at which institution he graduated in June, 1880, with the degree of A. B. He was a member of the Alpha Delta Phi fraternity, of which his father, brother and two sons have also been members. In July, 1880, he entered upon the study of law in the office of Neff & Stearns at Freeport, and in March, 1881, he became a student in the office of Rosenthal & Pence in Chicago. In May, 1881, he entered the law department of the Chicago & Northwestern Railway Company as garnishee clerk, where he continued his legal studies under Burton C. Cook, the general solicitor and Augustus M. Herrington, the solicitor, of that company. He was admitted to the bar in 1882. He has been admitted to practice in the states of Illinois, Iowa, Nebraska, South Dakota and the territory of Dakota. On October 25, 1893, he was admitted to the bar of the supreme court of the United States, his admission being moved by General John M. Palmer, then a United States senator from Illinois.

In March, 1883, Mr. Bailey removed to Eagle Grove, Iowa, where he became a division attorney for the Chicago & Northwestern Railway Company on its Northern Iowa Division. In 1884 he was elected the member of the Iowa democratic state central committee for the tenth congressional district. Upon the election in that year of President Cleveland, he was placed in charge of the distribution of the federal patronage in the thirteen counties of his congressional district. In 1885, he was reelected a member of the state central committee. In the same year he was elected mayor of the city of Eagle Grove.

In January, 1886, Mr. Bailey removed to Chicago, where he formed a law partnership with Allan C. Story and William G. Witherell. This partnership was dissolved at the end of a year and Mr. Bailey came to the territory of Dakota, taking up his residence at Sioux Falls, April 1, 1887. His younger brother, the late Joseph Mead Bailey, Jr., had preceded him to Sioux Falls and was engaged there in the banking business.

After locating at Sioux Falls, Mr. Bailey opened a law office and practiced alone until July, 1887, when he formed a partnership with Herbert Taft Root, under the firm name of Bailey & Root. This partnership was dissolved in February, 1888. In the fall of 1888, Mr. Bailey was nominated as the democratic candidate for district attorney of Minnehaha County, Dakota. At the November election he was elected to that office by over five hundred majority, running over one thousand five hundred ahead of his ticket and being the only democrat elected in the county. In 1890, while he was serving as district attorney, a local option law went into effect in his county. Mr. Bailey at once applied to the board of county commissioners for an appropriation sufficient to enforce the law. His request being refused, Mr. Bailey promptly resigned his office. He did not propose to attempt, without adequate financial resources, to enforce a law upon which there was a strong division of public sentiment and, on the other hand, he was not willing to continue as the public prosecutor of his county and permit the laws to be violated. Since then, he has not held nor sought any public office. For some years he continued to take an active interest in politics and from 1894 to 1904 he was the chairman of the Minnehaha County democratic central committee. He declined a further reelection in 1904 and has ever since devoted himself to his profession.

In January, 1890, Mr. Bailey entered into a law partnership with the late Captain William H. Stoddard and William H. Wilson, under the firm name of Bailey, Stoddard & Wilson. In 1891, Mr. Wilson withdrew from this firm and the business was continued under the name of Bailey & Stoddard. In January, 1892, this firm was dissolved and Mr. Bailey formed a partnership with John Howard Voorhees, under the name of Bailey & Voorhees. In July, 1895, Judge Frank R. Aikens and Harry E. Judge joined the firm, the name being changed to Aikens, Bailey & Voorhees. In October, 1897, Judge Aikens and Mr. Judge withdrew and formed the firm of Aikens & Judge and the name of Bailey & Voorhees was resumed. Since that time there has been no change in the firm name, although the membership of the firm has several times changed by the admission and withdrawal of various partners. It is at present composed of Charles Olin Bailey, John Howard Voorhees, Peter G. Honegger and Theodore Mead Bailey.

The firm of Bailey & Voorhees enjoys the most extensive practice of any law firm in South Dakota, a practice not confined to Sioux Falls and Minnehaha County alone but extending throughout the entire state. The firm has a large corporation practice and also does an extensive commercial law business. It occupies practically the entire second floor of the Bailey-Glidden building for its offices and employs a large corps of clerks and stenographers. The law library of Mr. Bailey (the collection of which was commenced by his father, the late Judge Joseph Mead Bailey, in 1856) is the largest law library in the Dakotas and one of the largest private law libraries in the United States. It contains upwards of ten thousand volumes of textbooks and reports.

In June, 1887, shortly after coming to Sioux Falls, Mr. Bailey was appointed attorney for the mercantile agency of R. G. Dun & Company, a position which he has ever since held. He has been the attorney in South Dakota for the Illinois Central Railroad Company ever since that road was built into Sioux Falls in the fall of 1887. Since 1890, he has been the counsel in South Dakota for the Western Union Telegraph Company. He is also counsel for the American Surety Company, the American Express Company, Wells Fargo & Company, the Adams Express Company, the Sultzberger & Sons Company, and many other corporations. He is the local legal representative at Sioux Falls of the Chicago, Milwaukee & St. Paul Railway Company. In March, 1907, he was appointed receiver of the Missouri River & Northwestern Railway Company and held that position until the receiver's sale of that road in 1909. He has been employed in many important litigations during his residence in the state and of the thirty-three volumes of South Dakota reports which have been issued since the admission of the state there are but two volumes which do not contain reports of cases in which he has acted as counsel. His name also appears in the reports of the supreme courts of Illinois, Iowa and of the territory of Dakota, of the appellate court of Illinois, of the supreme court of the United States and of the United States circuit court of appeals.

Mr. Bailey has taken much interest in Masonry. He is a past master of Minnehaha Lodge, No. 5, A. F. & A. M.; past high priest of Sioux Falls Chapter, No. 2, R. A. M.; thrice illustrious master of Alpha Council, No. 1, R. & S. M.; past eminent commander of Cyrene Commandery, No. 2, K. T.; past venerable master of Khurum Lodge of Perfection, No. 3, A. & A. S. R. He is also a member of Albert Pike Chapter of Rose Croix, No. 2, A. & A. S. R.; Coeur de Leon Council of Kadosh, No. 2, A. & A. S. R.; Occidental Consistory, No. 2, A. & A. S.; Jasper Chapter, No. 8, O. E. S.; and El Riad Shrine, A. A. O. N. M. S. He received the thirty-third degree of the Scottish Rite at Washington in October, 1909. He was grand commander of Knights Templar of South Dakota, 1909-10. He is also a member of Granite Lodge, No. 8, Knights of Pythias; and of Sioux Falls Lodge, No. 9, I. O. O. F., and Royal Purple Encampment, No. I, I. O. O. F.

Mr. Bailey is a charter member of the Minnehaha County and the South Dakota Bar Associations and has been for many years a member of the American Bar Association, of which he has served as vice president for South Dakota. He is a member of the Dacotah and of the Minnehaha Country Clubs of Sioux Falls, of the Iroquois Club of Chicago, and of the Alpha Delta Phi Club of New York. He is a member of the Sons of the American Revolution and the vice president of the South Dakota Society of that organization. In religion he is an Episcopalian.

Mr. Bailey has taken great interest in horticulture and also in historical and genealogical researches. His private library of some five thousand volumes is rich in historical literature.

On March 28, 1887, Mr. Bailey was married in Chicago, Illinois, to Mary Emma Swan. They have had children, as follows: I. Theodore Mead Bailey, born at Sioux Falls, January 14, 1888, was educated at Dartmouth College and at the University of Michigan, at which latter institution he graduated in 1910. He attended the South Dakota State University Law School and was admitted to the bar in 1911. He married Miss Marguerite Wadsworth, September 3, 1912, and is now a member of the firm of Bailey & Voorhees. II. Charles Olin Bailey, Jr., born at Sioux Falls, April 19, 1890, graduated at Bowdoin College in 1912 and at the Law School of the South Dakota State University in 1914. He is now connected with the law office of Bailey & Voorhees. III. Anna Elida Bailey, born at Sioux Falls, December 24, 1892, is a member of the class of 1915 of Wells College, at Aurora, New York. IV. Joseph Mead Bailey III., born at Sioux Falls, July 27, 1895, died at Sioux Falls, April 28, 1898. (The above sketch is corrected to December 1, 1914.)

DANA REED BAILEY

Dana R. BAILEY, one of the distinguished members of the bar of Minnehaha County, and county judge, is a native of the old Green Mountain state, having been born in Montgomery, Franklin County, Vermont, on the 27th of April, 1833. He was reared to the sturdy discipline of the farm and after completing the curriculum of the district schools, he continued his studies in Leland Seminary, at Townshend, Vermont, and finally completed his education in Oberlin College, Oberlin, Ohio, in 1858. He taught three terms in the district schools, was for six months an instructor in a select school, and later was a teacher in the Beekman school, at Saratoga Springs, New York, for one year. In June, 1856, Judge Bailey began reading law and in the following year entered the office of the late Chief Justice Royce, of the supreme court of his native state, under whose preceptorship he continued his technical reading for some time. He then entered the Albany Law School, at Albany, New York, where he was graduated in April, 1859. In the following month he entered upon the practice of his chosen profession, locating in Highgate, Vermont, being there established in practice until the 1st of September, 1864. In that place he held for two years the office of town agent and for an equal period was trustee of the United States reserve fund. He was also deputy collector of the United States customs at Highgate, having charge of the office for three years and three months, while for six months he acted as special agent of the war department. In 1863 he was appointed secret aid of the United States treasury department, serving in this capacity for three years. On the 1st of September, 1865, Judge Bailey opened a law office in St. Albans, Vermont, and on the 3d of the following February he entered into a professional partnership with Park Davis, while a year later H. C. Adams became a member of the firm. The subject was a delegate to the Republican national convention in 1868, and was a member of the state central committee of the party in Vermont two years. He served two years as state's attorney of Franklin County, and in 1870 was elected a member of the state senate, being chosen as his own successor two years later and serving with marked ability and distinction, having been chairman of the judiciary committee, while by vote of the joint legislature he was appointed one of a committee of five to investigate the Vermont Central Railroad, which investigation was not concluded until July, 1873. He was for two years a member of the board of school directors of St. Albans.

In 1869 Judge Bailey became identified with the interests of the west, having, in 1871, laid out the town of Baldwin, St. Croix County, Wisconsin, of which he was the original proprietor. He there built the Matchless flouring mills and was the owner of three sawmills and half-owner of two grain elevators. He had in the meanwhile taken up his permanent abode in the town and for a decade was there engaged in the manufacture of flour and lumber and in farming and merchandising as well. For several years he maintained a large herd of high-grade shorthorn cattle, selling the same in 1877, in the Chicago market, for the highest average price offered for any herd in the United States in that year.

In 1874 Judge Bailey removed to Baldwin, St. Croix County, Wisconsin, where he served three years as president of the municipal council, as treasurer one year and as school director for seven years. In 1877, at the Republican district convention, he was nominated by acclamation for the state senate, as representative of the twenty-fourth senatorial district, comprising seven counties, and in the county in which he resided he received in the ensuing election all the votes cast, with the exception of fifty-seven, the total vote being three thousand one hundred and thirty-one, while the Republican nominee for the lower house of the legislature had only ninety-nine majority in the county. He was chairman of the judiciary committee in the senate during the session of 1879. In 1880 the Judge was elected a member of the board of county commissioners of St. Croix County, and was re-elected in each of the two succeeding years, resigning his position on the 19th of December, 1882, at which time he was also chairman of the board, and on the 21st of the same month he arrived in Sioux Falls, South Dakota, where he has ever since maintained his home. From the time of his arrival until March, 1884, he had charge of the Dakota business of the Northwestern Mutual Life Insurance Company, of Milwaukee, and on the 11th of the month last mentioned he opened a law office here, in the Masonic Temple, being the first tenant to occupy rooms in the new building, and here he actively resumed the practice of his profession. In January, 1886, he formed a co-partnership with Park Davis, who had been his professional colleague in Vermont many years previously, and in 1888 William H. Lyon became a member of the firm, which was known as Bailey,

Davis & Lyon, and which held a foremost position among the legal associations of the territory and state during the entire time of its existence. Judge Bailey served as city attorney of Sioux Falls from 1885 until 1889, and on the 21st of August, 1890, upon the resignation of Charles O. Bailey, he was appointed state's attorney for Minnehaha County, retaining this office, by subsequent re-elections, until 1895, when he resumed the private practice of his profession. In November, 1900, he was elected county judge of Minnehaha County, serving for a term of two years and being then re-elected, in 1902, for a second term of equal duration. In the territorial days the Judge was for two years a member of the Republican central committee of the territory, and in 1895-6 he was a member of the state agricultural board. In 1899 he edited and published a history of Minnehaha County, a valuable contribution to the histories of the territory and state in the field covered, and the work is considered authoritative, gaining distinctive commendation from those most capable of judging its true merits. Judge Bailey has ever been a stanch advocate of the principles of the Republican party and has been prominent in its councils in the three states in which he has lived and labored so effectively. Fraternally he is identified with the Masonic order.

GEORGE MYRON BAILEY

George M. Bailey, who is established in the real-estate and abstract business in Redfield, Spink County, claims the old Empire state as the place of his nativity, having been born in Middlebury, Wyoming County, New York, on the 27th of November, 1874, and being a son of Myron C. and Rosetta M. Bailey, both of whom were born in New Hampshire. The genealogy in the agnatic line is of English and Scotch derivation, and the original ancestors in America settled in Massachusetts in the colonial epoch of our national history. Later representatives of the name removed to New Hampshire, and from that state came the branch of the family which early settled in western New York. The parents of the subject removed to Iowa when he was about fourteen years of age and settled in Kossuth County, where the father turned his attention to mercantile business, and he and his wife are now residing in Lamberton, Minnesota. The subject completed the curriculum of the public schools, being graduated in the high school at Algona, Kossuth County, Iowa, and later taking a course of study in the Northern Iowa Normal School in that city. He was thereafter engaged in the real-estate and abstract business in the Hawkeye state until early in 1901, when he came to South Dakota and took up his residence in Redfield, where he is now in control of an excellent business in the handling of real estate, while he also has an excellent set of abstracts of title for Spink County, his records being in large demand by the residents and property owners of the county. He is enterprising and straightforward in his business methods, and is held in high esteem by all who know him. In politics Mr. Bailey is a stanch advocate of the principles and policies for which the Republican party stands sponsor, and fraternally is identified with the Masonic order, the Knights of Pythias and the Improved Order of Red Men.

NATHAN L. BAILEY, M. D.

Dr. Nathan L. Bailey is a well-known physician and surgeon of Lake Preston, where he has been successfully engaged in the practice of his profession during the past decade. His birth occurred in Boscobel, Wisconsin, on the 13th of September, 1860, his parents being Mark and Rebecca (Darland) Bailey, both of whom are deceased. Throughout his active business career, the father was engaged in general agricultural pursuits.

Nathan L. Bailey obtained his education in the graded and high schools of his native state and was subsequently engaged in farming in association with his brother in Wisconsin. In 1881, when a young man of twenty-one years, he came to South Dakota but a short time later returned to the state of his nativity. In 1887 he again came to South Dakota, locating at Lake Preston, where he entered the drug store of which his brother was proprietor, the latter being also a physician by profession. He remained in the store until 1890 and in that year became a student in the Keokuk Medical College of Iowa, being graduated from that institution with the degree of M. D. in 1892. During the next twelve years he was engaged in the practice of medicine in Wisconsin and then returned to Lake Preston, this state, which has since remained the scene of his professional labors. An extensive and well merited practice has been accorded him as he has demonstrated his skill and ability in the successful treatment of many difficult cases. With the steady progress of the profession, he keeps in close touch through his membership in the Third District Medical Society, the South Dakota State Medical Society and the American Medical Association. He has served as superintendent of the county board of health and is now acting in the capacity of county poor physician.

In January, 1890, Dr. Bailey was united in marriage to Miss Cora Chase, her father being Dudley L. Chase, who was a pioneer settler of South Dakota and broke the first five acres of ground in Kingsbury County. The Doctor and his wife have three children, namely: Ethelyn, who follows the profession of teaching in Kingsbury County; and Vena and Vera, twins, who are high-school students.

In politics Dr. Bailey is a stanch republican and he served as the second mayor of Lake Preston, giving the town a progressive and beneficial administration. He has also done valuable service as a member of the council for a number of years. His religious faith is that of the Congregational church and fraternally he is identified with the Masons, being a worthy exemplar of the craft. Hunting, fishing and motoring afford him pleasure and recreation and he is well known and popular in both professional and social circles of his adopted state, being widely recognized as an able physician, a public-spirited citizen and a trustworthy friend.

JOHN CRAIGON BAIRD

John C. BAIRD, is a native of Green Lake County, Wisconsin, the son of John and Mary (McAdam) Baird, and he dates his birth from the 8th day of February, 1858. Reared on a farm and early taught the lessons of industry and thrift which makes that pursuit successful, he grew up with a full appreciation of life and its responsibilities, and after acquiring a fair education in the common schools, he entered at the age of eighteen a store, where he spent three strenuous years, during which time he became familiar with the varied details of the mercantile business. Resigning his clerkship at the expiration of the period noted, he came to South Dakota and settling in Hanson County, spent some time as manager of a branch store belonging to William Van Epps, of Sioux Falls, South Dakota. Severing his connection with those gentlemen, he changed his abode to Douglas County and filed on a homestead, choosing for his location a fine tract of land about three and a half miles east of Armour, which he at once began to improve and for which in due season he acquired a title from the government. Shortly after selecting his homestead Mr. Baird revisited his native state, and while there was married, in 1879, to Miss Ella Whittemore, who was also born and reared in Wisconsin. Returning to South Dakota a little later, he took up, in 1880, his permanent abode on the land already referred to and since that time has greatly improved the same, besides adding at intervals to its area, until he now owns a fine tract of four hundred and eighty acres, one hundred and sixty of which are in a successful state of cultivation.

Mr. Baird is an up-to-date agriculturist, well acquainted with the nature of soils and their adaptability to different crops, and, employing modern methods and the latest and most approved implements and machinery, he realizes bountiful returns from the time and labor expended on his farm. He is also engaged quite largely in the live-stock business, raising large numbers of cattle, horses and hogs, from the sale of which is derived no small part of his income. He has made many valuable improvements on his place, has a substantial and attractive residence and good outbuildings and his home, situated in one of the finest sections of Douglas County, indicates the dwelling place of not only a man of enterprise and progressive ideas, but a gentleman of intelligence, sound judgment and excellent taste, as well. Personally, he enjoys great popularity among his neighbors and friends and as a citizen he is public-spirited and a leader in all laudable movements. He served eight or nine years as school clerk, also held the office of township supervisor for a considerable length of time and is now township treasurer.

Politically he is a pronounced Democrat, and fraternally is identified with the Masonic brotherhood, the order of Maccabees and the Ancient Order of United Workmen. Mr. and Mrs. Baird have a family of eight children, whose names in order of birth are as follows: Grace, Walter. John R., Maude, Robert. Agnes, Frank and Pearl, all living.

WILLIAM P. BAKEN

WILLIAM P. BAKEN

With scarcely an exception the county officials of Pennington County have been men of ability who have discharged their official duties efficiently and William P. Baken. the present sheriff of the county, is an excellent man for the place, fearless, capable and conscientious. He was born in Rossie, New York, on the 2d of May, 1868, and his parents were William P., and Catherine (McGreery) Baken, also natives of that state. Upon reaching years of maturity the father followed the trade of a carpenter and builder. He held a number of local offices in the Empire state and in 1872 removed to Park City, Utah, whence in 1889 he came to Hill City, Dakota. In the latter place he engaged in mining until his death, which occurred in 1892 when he was sixty-two years of age. His father, Alanson Baken, was also born in New York, although his father was a native of England, whence he emigrated to America previous to the Revolutionary war. Our subject's maternal grandfather, Hugh McGreery, was a native of Ireland. Mr. and Mrs. William P.

Baken, Sr., were the parents of seven children, of whom two survive.

Their son William P., is the third in order of birth. He attended successively the grammar and high schools of Salt Lake City and then worked in mines in Utah on the engineer's staff until 1886, in which year he removed to Idaho, where he was employed as a mining engineer until 1890, when he arrived in the Black Hills. He served as engineer at the tin mines of Hill City until 1893, when he removed to Keystone, where he held the position of engineer of mines for three years. For the next three years he was engaged in the drug business and in 1900 was elected clerk of court of Pennington County for two years. He resumed the drug business on the expiration of his term and was a member of the Baken-Davis Drug Company in Keystone until 1906, when he sold his share in the business. He was subsequently appointed game warden and deputy sheriff and in 1912 his excellent record in this connection was instrumental in winning him the election to the office of sheriff. In 1914 he was reelected to that position and is now serving his second term. He has proved very efficient in controlling the lawless element that is found in every community, and his record has gained him the approval of all good citizens.

On the 8th of January, 1906, Mr. Baken was united in marriage to Miss Nettie Oswald, a daughter of Charles and Augusta (Long) Oswald, of Rapid City. Mr. Baken is a Mason, an Elk and a Knight of Pythias. He enjoys shooting and fishing and spends not a little of his leisure time in that way. He still owns property in Keystone and is well-to-do. He has the respect of his fellow townsmen and his admirable traits of character have won him many warm personal friends.

J. C. BAKER, M. D.

The year 1906 witnessed the arrival of Dr. J. C. Baker in Ramona, where he has since continuously engaged in the practice of his profession, winning a gratifying measure of success. Iowa claims him as a native son, his birth having occurred in Rockford on the 26th of September, 1878, his parents being George H. and Mary E. (Cutler) Baker. The father has devoted his life to farming and merchandising and he and his wife now make their home in Minnesota. They are members of old-time pioneer families of eastern South Dakota, arriving in this state in 1882. They settled first at Mitchell, the father securing a homestead claim there, and later went to Woonsocket, where he filed on a tree claim. With the development of his section of the state he has been closely identified and his work has been an element in public progress.

At the usual age Dr. Baker became a public-school pupil and, passing through consecutive grades, was at length graduated from the high school of Madison, South Dakota. In the period of early manhood, he mentally reviewed the business situation, studying the various avenues open for activity, and at length reached the conclusion that he preferred medical practice as a life work. Accordingly, he entered upon a course of study in the Lincoln Medical College at Lincoln, Nebraska, and there won his professional degree upon graduation with the class of 1906. He put his theoretical knowledge to the practical test by a year's service in the city hospital and in the Lincoln Hospital, gaining thereby the broad knowledge and experience that come so readily in no other way. Removing to Ramona, he there entered upon the private practice of his profession and in the eight years which have since come and gone has been very successful, becoming well established as an able physician and surgeon, careful in the diagnosis of his cases and skillful in administering both medical and surgical aid. He is likewise a stockholder in the Electric Light Company of Ramona and, moreover, is deeply interested in horticulture, which he makes a source of recreation.

On the 26th of January, 1910, Dr. Baker was united in marriage to Mrs. Edith Louise Corliss. They are members of the Episcopal church and Dr. Baker holds to the principles of the socialist party. He has attained high rank in Masonry, belonging to the lodge, to the consistory at Yankton and to the Mystic Shrine at Sioux Falls. He also has membership in the local organization of Odd Fellows and in his life, he exemplifies the teachings of these organizations, which are based upon a recognition of the brotherhood of man. Advancement has ever been his watchword and has been manifest in all of his deeds. In his profession he has made progress through his wide reading and research, keeping in touch with the advanced thought and scientific investigations of the day.

GEORGE L. BAKER

George L. Baker is filling the position of postmaster at Britton, where he is also conducting a drug store. He was born in La Salle, Illinois, November 22, 1850, a son of Richard and Sarah (Raycraft) Baker, who were natives of Ireland, born in 1818 and 1823 respectively. About 1848 Richard Baker went to Canada and it was in that country that they were married. In 1849 they removed to La Salle, Illinois, and for a number of years he engaged in farming. In Canada he had conducted business as a brewer. The year 1880 witnessed his arrival in Dakota territory, at which time he homesteaded in Clark County, and he proved up on his claim and there resided until his death. The town of Elrod now stands upon his old homestead. His parents never left Ireland, but the maternal grandparents of George L. Baker came to the new world and died in Wisconsin. In his political faith Richard Baker was a democrat and both he and his wife were consistent and active members of the Methodist Episcopal church, in the faith of which they passed away, the former in 1901 and the latter in 1907. To them were born nine children, two of whom died in infancy, while five are yet living, as follows: George L., of this review; Esther, who is the widow of Frank Salter and makes her home in Chicago; John, who lives on the old homestead at Elrod, South Dakota; Mollie, who makes her home with her brother John; and William, who is engaged in the wholesale liquor business in Chicago.

George L. Baker attended both public and parochial schools in La Salle, Illinois. He started in life as a farm hand and afterward was connected with a meat market at Ohio, Illinois, for five years. Removing westward to Dakota territory, he secured a homestead claim in Spink County upon which he lived for about a year and then went to Groton, remaining there one year. In 1884 he located in Britton, where for a short time he conducted a hotel but later traded his interest in that business for a drug store. Afterward he disposed of that but again purchased a drug store and has since continued in this line of business, his son, George G. Baker, being an equal partner in the undertaking.

In 1878 Mr. Baker was united in marriage to Miss Kate Fagan, a native of Illinois, by whom he has three children, namely: Edward W., who lives with his father; George G., who is engaged in the drug business at Britton; and Claude C, who conducts a moving picture show in Britton.

Mrs. Baker belongs to the Presbyterian church and she presides with gracious hospitality over her home, making it a delightful resort for many friends. Mr. Baker is well known as an exemplary representative of the Masonic fraternity. He belongs to the lodge, the chapter, the commandery, the consistory and the Mystic Shrine and he is also a member of the United Workmen and the Maccabees. He has served as master of the lodge, was its secretary for twenty years and has been high priest of the chapter. His political views accord with the principles of the democracy and during President Cleveland's first term he was appointed to the position of postmaster and was again called to that office by President Wilson in

September, 1914. He also served as probate judge for one term during territorial days and at all times he has most ably and efficiently discharged the duties of the positions to which he has been called. At the same time, he has made a creditable record in business circles, for he came to Dakota a poor boy and is now numbered among the substantial residents of his district, owning town property to the value of twenty-five thousand dollars, together with a quarter section of land in Marshall County.

CORWIN B. BALDWIN

One of the successful merchants of Rapid City is Corwin B. Baldwin, who was born in Olivet, South Dakota, on the 28th of September, 1877, a son of William B. and Louise (Shaw) Baldwin, the former a native of Mentor, Ohio, and the latter of Chardon, that state. The father arrived in South Dakota in the days of its pioneer development, having traveled by rail and steamboat to Yankton and thence by ox team to Olivet. He settled upon a homestead near the latter place in 1872 and farmed for many years. He and his wife are still living upon the land which he entered from the government.

Corwin B. Baldwin is the third in order of birth in a family of seven children and in the acquirement of his early education attended the district schools near his father's farm. Desiring to prepare himself for his life work, he entered the school of pharmacy of the South Dakota State Agricultural College at Brookings and was graduated therefrom with the class of 1900. For a year he was employed at Parkston, and then removed to Yankton, where he spent two years. In 1903 he removed to Rapid City and for the succeeding five years was in the employ of others. However, by 1908 he had acquired sufficient capital to start in business on his own account and he purchased the drug store which he still owns. In the years that have since intervened he has managed his business so ably that it has grown steadily and rapidly and is now the largest exclusive retail drug establishment in western South Dakota. The greatest care is taken in the filling of prescriptions, his drugs are of full strength and of absolute purity and he carries an excellent line of druggists' sundries. He is also interested in the Western South Dakota Commission Company, of which he is the president, and in a number of other concerns.

On New Year's Day, 1903, Mr. Baldwin was united in marriage with Miss Helen M. Morrison, a daughter of Edward and Jessie (Miner) Morrison, of De Smet, South Dakota. Two children, Corwin E. and Donald, have been born to Mr. and Mrs. Baldwin. He is independent politically. Fraternally he is a Mason and has attained high rank in that order, belonging to the chapter, commandery and Shrine. He is also a member of the Knights of Pythias and of the Elks, being a charter member of the Rapid City Lodge of the latter organization. During his college days he took part in track athletics and continues to find much pleasure in outdoor sports, his chief recreations being fishing and hunting. His success is gratifying and well deserved and he is held in high esteem by his fellow citizens, who have found him alert, energetic, capable and thoroughly dependable.

GEORGE B. BALE

G. B. Bale, is a native of England and dates his birth from November 25, 1867. He first saw the light of day in Norfolk and spent his early life in that place, receiving a good education in the schools of the same, and remaining with his parents until eighteen years of age. Severing home ties in the spring of 1885, he came to the United States, making his way direct to Watertown, South Dakota, where he remained for a brief period, after which he traveled extensively over various western states and territories, going as far as the Pacific coast. Being pleased with Dakota, he finally returned to this state, and took up a pre-emption on the "Divide" near Battle creek, Custer County, where he engaged in farming, but the venture not proving successful, he left his place and for some time thereafter was employed by a horse dealer, to whom his services proved of great value. Later Mr. Bale began buying and selling horses upon his own responsibility, and in due time worked up an extensive and lucrative business in the vicinity of Battle creek. In 1890 he changed his location to the Cheyenne River, where he continued running horses until 1897, when he effected a co-partnership in the business with C. W. Arnold, the two greatly extending the scope of their operations, buying up all the outfits in a large area of territory and within a short time achieved the reputation of being the largest and most successful horse dealers in the western part of the state. The firm thus constituted lasted until 1902, in which year the subject withdrew from the partnership and purchased the ranch on Battle creek, twenty-three mines east of Hermosa, where he has since lived and prospered, as a cattle raiser, devoting considerable attention the meantime to the improvement of his place. In addition to the live-stock business, Mr. Bale also carries on farming, the greater part of his land being irrigated and easily susceptible to tillage. He raises abundant crops of grain, vegetables and fruits, which with the returns from his cattle sales yield him a handsome income every year.

He belongs to the Masonic lodge at Hermosa, and, like the majority of intelligent and progressive citizens, manifests an abiding interest in public and political affairs, giving his support to the Republican party. On November 11, 1901, Mr. Bale and Miss Nettie Bower, of South Dakota, were united in the holy bonds of wedlock, the marriage resulting in the birth of one child, a son who answers to the name of George J.

LEVI WILLIAM BALLARD

The name of Ballard figures prominently in connection with industrial and manufacturing interests in Sioux Falls, where Levi William Ballard is now managing an extensive marble business, conducted under the style of Ballard & Son. He was born upon a farm in Palo Alto County, Iowa, June 12, 1876, a son of Samuel William and Emily (LaBarr) Ballard. The family is of English lineage and was founded in America at the time of the Revolutionary war by four brothers of the name who came to the new world and served in the colonial army in behalf of the cause of independence. The original American ancestor in the maternal line came from France with La Fayette and both he and his brother, who crossed the Atlantic at the same time, were soldiers in the American revolution which brought about the independence of the nation. The patriotic spirit of the family was manifest again at the time of the Civil war, when Samuel W. Ballard offered his services to the government. He was first sergeant of Company A, Sixty-eighth Regiment of the New York National Guard, with which he was connected for thirty days and was then honorably discharged at Elmira, New York, on the 29th of July, 1863. He reenlisted for active duty at the front and ably defended the interests of the Union. He now resides in Mitchell, South Dakota, where he conducts business under the name of the Mitchell Granite & Marble Works. In his family are four living children, while one son died at the age of eighteen months. He is a thirty-second degree Mason and a member of the Mystic Shrine.

In the district schools of his native county Levi W. Ballard pursued his education to the age of fifteen years and afterward attended the public schools of Emmetsburg, Iowa, being graduated from the high school there with the class of 1896. He afterward pursued a commercial course in the Nora Springs (Ia.) Commercial College and in August, 1897, came to Sioux Falls, South Dakota, to be manager of a marble shop for the Emmetsburg (Ia.) firm of Godden & Ballard, of which his father was a member. In 1900 Levi W. Ballard purchased the interest of his father's partner and the firm then became Ballard & Son. Their business today covers South Dakota and parts of Iowa and Minnesota. The father is interested in a number of other concerns in this state and Iowa, and in 1908 a marble yard was established at Mitchell, South Dakota, of which he is sole proprietor. This company is the largest in the state manufacturing monuments from the rough marble and granite. The plant is operated with compressed air machinery, pneumatic tools doing the decorative and design work, and in Sioux Falls employment is furnished to ten people. Something of their fame in a business line is indicated by the fact that recently they were called upon to erect a mausoleum at Rochester, New York. The business has grown to extensive proportions and the trade of the firm indicates how commendable are its business methods.

On the 30th of April, 1903, at Sioux Falls, Levi W. Ballard was united in marriage to Miss Matie Eichmeier, whose parents were Charles L. and Louise Eichmeier, of Rockford, Iowa, where both died. They were natives of Germany.

Mr. Ballard holds membership in the Methodist Episcopal church and he gives his political allegiance to the republican party. He has never sought nor desired office, however, preferring to concentrate his energies upon his constantly increasing business interests. In Masonry he is well known, having taken the degrees of the York and Scottish Rites. He is also a Mystic Shriner and is a most worthy exemplar of the beneficent principles of the craft. He likewise belongs to the Knights of Pythias, the Independent Order of Odd Fellows, being a member of the lodge, encampment and canton, and to the Modern Woodmen of America. He is also known as an Elk and he has the confidence, goodwill and high regard of all of his brethren of these organizations. Success has attended his efforts since starting in the marble business and he is today one of the prosperous citizens of Sioux Falls. His own home is a splendid Vermont marble structure, built in attractive style of architecture and tastefully furnished, the only one of the kind west of Chicago. It is, moreover, the abode of warmhearted hospitality, which is greatly enjoyed by the many friends of Mr. and Mrs. Ballard.

JESSE A. BALLOU, M. D.

The medical fraternity has always been held in high esteem and its great work of curing disease and instructing the public in regard to the laws of health is of vital importance. Dr. Jesse A. Ballou, of Lead, is a worthy representative of his profession and has gained the confidence and regard of his fellow townsmen. He was born in Schuyler County, Illinois, July 4, 1878, a son of J. A. and Mary (Malcomson) Ballou. The father was born in Tennessee but removed to Illinois at an early day in the history of that commonwealth. He and his wife are now residents of Rushville, Illinois.

Dr. Jesse A. Ballou is the second in order of birth in a family of four children and was reared under the parental roof. He attended the common and high schools of Rushville and also Knox College at Galesburg, Illinois, where he was a student for four years. In 1901 he went to Chicago, where he matriculated in the medical department of the University of Illinois, and in 1905 was graduated from that institution with the degree of M. D. Immediately thereafter he removed to Lead, South Dakota, and entered the Homestake Hospital as a staff physician, where he remained for five years, but in 1910 began a general practice of medicine and surgery in Lead. In the intervening years he has gained a large practice which is constantly growing as his skill and conscientiousness become more widely known. He is still an earnest student of the profession, keeping abreast of the advancement that is constantly being made in medical knowledge by means of attendance at clinics and broad reading of medical and surgical literature. He also finds his membership in the Black Hills Medical Society, the South Dakota State Medical Society and the American Medical Association of great value to him in enabling him to familiarize himself with the discoveries made by other practitioners. In 1912 he was elected coroner of Lawrence County and was reelected to that office in 1914 for another two-year term.

On the 11th of January, 1906, Dr. Ballou was married to Miss Elizabeth Barnette, of Rushville, Illinois. The Doctor is an adherent of the republican party but has confined his political activity to the exercise of his right of franchise. Fraternally he belongs to Lead Lodge, No. 747, B. P. O. E.; Golden Star Lodge, No. 9, A. F. & A. M.; Golden Belt Chapter, No. 35, R. A. M.; Lead Commandery, No. 18, K. T.; and Naja Temple, A. A. O. N. M. S., of Deadwood. His professional ability has gained him a leading place among the physicians and surgeons of Lead, and his attractive personality has won for him many warm friends who greatly enjoy his company.

GEORGE E. BARKLEY

George E. Barkley, residing on section 6, Sioux Falls township, Minnehaha County, is widely known as a breeder of registered shorthorn cattle and Duroc-Jersey hogs and owns a tract of one hundred and twenty acres comprising one of the most fertile and most valuable farms in South Dakota. His birth occurred in Boone County, Iowa, on the 16th of February, 1879, his parents being M. C. and Mary E. (Smith) Barkley, the former a native of Iowa and the latter of Ohio. James Barkley, the paternal grandfather of our subject, removed to Iowa from Indiana in 1842, taking up a homestead in Linn County, Iowa, before Mount Vernon was laid out. He was a carpenter by trade and helped to erect the first building of Cornell College at Mount Vernon. In 1856 he removed to Boone County, where M. C. Barkley was reared and married and where three children were born to him and his wife. In the spring of 1887, he took up his abode in Sac county, Iowa, purchasing his present home farm of eighty acres for seventeen dollars an acre. The land is now worth two hundred dollars an acre. M. C. Barkley enjoys an enviable reputation as one of the substantial and esteemed citizens of Sac County and has served in the various township offices, being elected as a candidate of the republican party.

George E. Barkley was reared under the parental roof and in the acquirement of an education attended the common schools and also the high schools of Odebolt and Boone. On his twenty-first birthday he started out as an agriculturist on his own account by renting land and for about ten years followed farming in Sac county, Iowa. In 1910 he came to South Dakota and took up his abode on the southeast quarter of section 30, Split Rock township, Minnehaha County, having purchased this farm in the fall of 1909. At the end of a year, however, he disposed of the property and purchased one hundred and sixty acres of land where he now resides. Two years later he sold forty acres of this farm, which at present comprises one hundred and twenty acres and which is situated just outside the city limits of Sioux Falls, lying in the Bix Sioux bottoms and being therefore one of the most fertile and most valuable tracts in South Dakota. Mr. Barkley is engaged in the breeding of registered shorthorn cattle and Duroc-Jersey hogs, shipping his stock as far west as the Pacific coast. He is becoming widely known as a successful breeder and on the 23d of January, 1914, sold twenty-five head of hogs and sixteen head of cattle for four thousand one hundred and fifty-two dollars. He has almost his entire farm seeded to grass and rents outside land for farming purposes. His is one of the best improved properties of Minnehaha County and in its able management he has won prosperity.

In September, 1904, Mr. Barkley was united in marriage to Miss Caroline Hanson, of Sac County, Iowa, who is a native of Long Island, New York. They have three children: Ralph Wallace, Edna May and Flora Belle. Mr. Barkley gives his political allegiance to the republican party and is identified fraternally with the Masons, belonging to Unity Lodge, No. 130, of Sioux Falls. He is also connected with the Modern Woodmen of America, while his religious faith is indicated by his membership in the First Methodist Episcopal church of Sioux Falls, to which his wife likewise belongs. He is a young man of force, ambition and enterprise and he stands high in the esteem and confidence of his fellow citizens.

M. C. Barkley was reared and married and where three children were born to him and his wife. In the spring of 1887, he took up his abode in Sac County, Iowa, purchasing his present home farm of eighty acres for seventeen dollars an acre. The land is now worth two hundred dollars an acre. M. C. Barkley enjoys an enviable reputation as one of the substantial and esteemed citizens of Sac County and has served in the various township offices, being elected as a candidate of the republican party.

George E. Barkley was reared under the parental roof and in the acquirement of an education attended the common schools and also the high schools of Odebolt and Boone. On his twenty-first birthday he started out as an agriculturist on his own account by renting land and for about ten years followed farming in Sac County, Iowa. In 1910 he came to South Dakota and took up his abode on the southeast quarter of section 30, Split Rock township, Minnehaha County, having purchased this farm in the fall of 1909. At the end of a year, however, he disposed of the property and purchased one hundred and sixty acres of land where he now resides. Two years later he sold forty acres of this farm, which at present comprises one hundred and twenty acres and which is situated just outside the city limits of Sioux Falls, lying in the Big Sioux bottoms and being therefore one of the most fertile and most valuable tracts in South Dakota. Mr. Barkley is engaged in the breeding of registered shorthorn cattle and Duroc-Jersey hogs, shipping his stock as far west as the Pacific coast. He is becoming widely known as a successful breeder and on the 23d of January, 1914, sold twenty-five head of hogs and sixteen head of cattle for four thousand one hundred and fifty-two dollars. He has almost his entire farm seeded to grass and rents outside land for farming purposes. His is one of the best improved properties of Minnehaha County and in its able management he has won prosperity.

In September, 1904, Mr. Barkley was united in marriage to Miss Caroline Hanson, of Sac County, Iowa, who is a native of Long Island, New York. They have three children: Ralph Wallace, Edna May and Flora Belle. Mr. Barkley gives his political allegiance to the republican party and is identified fraternally with the Masons, belonging to Unity Lodge, No. 130, of Sioux Falls. He is also connected with the Modern Woodmen of America, while his religious faith is indicated by his membership in the First Methodist Episcopal church of Sioux Falls, to which his wife likewise belongs. He is a young man of force, ambition and enterprise and he stands high in the esteem and confidence of his fellow citizens.

EDMUND A. BARLOW

Edmund A. Barlow, who is register of deeds of Lyman County, is one of the honored pioneers of the state and is at the present time president of the Old Settlers' Association of the county. He was born in Eaton, province of Quebec. Canada, on the 14th of February, 1855, and is a son of George F. and Ann (Day) Barlow, both of whom were born in the state of New Hampshire, whence they removed to the province of Quebec in the same year in which their marriage was solemnized, passing the remainder of their lives in the dominion of Canada, the father being a carpenter and inventor. The subject received his early educational training in his native province, and at the age of seventeen years removed thence to Eau Claire, Wisconsin, where he continued to attend school as opportunity afforded, defraying his expenses for a time by clerking in mercantile establishments and later by teaching in the public schools. In 1879 he attended the Wisconsin State Normal School, at River Falls, and in the following, year came to what is now the state of South Dakota, locating in Flandreau, Moody County, where he secured a clerical position in the important mercantile house of the W. Jones Company. About three years later he purchased the business, which he successfully continued until 1887, when he disposed of the same and purchased the general merchandise business of Ross Whalen, in Artesian, Sanborn County, South Dakota. In the fall of 1880, he removed thence to Chamberlain, South Dakota, purchasing a stock of general merchandise and preparing to engage in business immediately upon the opening of the Sioux Indian reservation to settlement, this occurring the following spring. He then brought his stock of goods to Lyman, where he continued his mercantile business about eighteen months, at the expiration of which he sold out and engaged in ranching, to which line of enterprise he successfully gave his attention until June, 1903, when he disposed of his interests in that line, in order to assume the duties of his present office. He is a stanch adherent of the Democratic party, and in 1890 he was appointed postmaster at Lyman, serving about three years. He also served one term as county superintendent of schools and four years as justice of the peace, ever proving worthy of the confidence reposed in him by the people of the county. In November, 1902, Mr. Barlow was elected to his present office, that of register of deeds, for which he is specially well qualified.

He has ever taken a lively interest in educational affairs in the county and has done much to advance the cause. He is a member of Flandreau Lodge, No. II. Free and Accepted Masons; Pilgrim Chapter. No. 32, Royal Arch Masons: Cyrene Commandery. No. 2, Knights Templar, at Sioux Falls, and Lodge No. 9449, Modern Woodmen of America. He has served as president of the Old Settlers' Association of Lyman County since 1900, is well known throughout this section and is held in the highest esteem in business and social circles. On the 23d of November, 1883, Mr. Barlow was united in marriage to Miss Carrie Jones, of Flandreau, this state, no children having been born of this union.

C. BOYD BARRETT

C. B. BARRETT, of Aberdeen, South Dakota, is descended on the paternal side from one of the old families of Maryland, while on the maternal side from the old Carr family, of Virginia. His family experienced in full the vicissitudes and misfortunes which fell so heavily upon so many of the sterling old families of the south during the period of the Civil war, but they were willing to make all these sacrifices, though theirs was to become eventually the "lost cause."

Major Barrett was born on the ancestral plantation, in Loudoun County, Virginia, on the 23d of May, 1838, being a son of John F. and Caroline (Wade) Barrett, both representatives of prominent old families of that commonwealth. The father of the subject followed the vocation of a planter until he was summoned from the scene of life's labors and was a man of prominence and influence in the community, having been a captain in the state militia and having held various local offices of public trust. Both he and his wife were devoted members of the Presbyterian church, in which he served as elder for many years. Major Barrett was reared under the gracious influences of the old homestead and received a good academic education. As a youth he became a member of a cavalry company in the state militia, and was in active service with his command in guarding the Potomac at the time when John Brown made his famous raid. At the outbreak of the Civil war this company became a part of the Sixth Regiment of Confederate Cavalry, and later was assigned to the Thirty-fifth Virginia Battalion, under General K. V. White. It was the portion of our subject to take part in thirty-eight of the pitched battles incidental to the progress of the great internecine conflict, and he was in active service during practically the entire period of the war. His command was in service in northern Virginia, being for much of the time in the Shenandoah valley and the Piedmont region, under "Stonewall" Jackson. He also took part in the Pennsylvania campaign, participating in the battles of the Wilderness, Antietam, Sharpsburg and in the Gettysburg campaign, under command of the gallant General Wade Hampton, and he was with his regiment at Appomattox at the time of General Lee's surrender. For some time, he was assigned to detail duty on the staff of General Lawton, of Georgia. Major Barrett was three times wounded in action, and thrice had his horse killed from under him. He was captured in a skirmish in Clark County, Virginia, in 1862, and was confined for four months in the federal prison in the city of Washington, being one of the one hundred and thirty-five prisoners who were the last to be exchanged before the close of the war. His widowed mother, in the midst of alarms and menacing turbulence, had bravely remained on the old homestead, in company with one devoted old slave. The fortunes of the family fell to the lowest ebb and the beautiful old plantation was a scene of havoc at the time when our subject returned. He had been reported killed in the battle of the Wilderness, and his mother had been bowed under this additional sorrow, knowing not that he was still living until he put in his appearance at the old home. He devoted four years to endeavoring to restore the prestige and prosperity of the plantation, but was eventually compelled to abandon this devoted service. He removed to Alexandria, Virginia, where he was engaged in the hotel business for five years and then took up his residence in Washington, D. C. where he engaged in mercantile business, continuing this enterprise until 1883, when impaired health, resulting from the injury received in a wound through the right lung while in service, compelled him to seek a change of climate. He accordingly came to South Dakota and located in the village of Aberdeen, Brown County, where he continued in the hotel business until 1884, and he then purchased the Aberdeen Republican, now known as the Aberdeen Democrat. He retained the original name, but changed the political policy of the paper, making it an excellent advocate of the principle of the Democratic party, and he successfully conducted the paper until 1893, when President Cleveland conferred upon him the office of receiver of the United States land office in Aberdeen. He continued incumbent of this position four years, after which he again became editor of the Republican, having retained possession of the property. He sold the plant and the business in 1902, after having been closely identified with its fortunes for more than a decade and a half. He is a vigorous and able writer, and made the paper a force and power in the political affairs of the state. He has ever been a stalwart advocate of the principles of the Democracy and has been prominent in its councils and formed the acquaintanceship of its leading men. In 1894-5 he was a member of the Democratic congressional committee.

Mr. Barrett is an elder in the Presbyterian church and is a Mason. He married Mollie D. Fadeley, of the same county in Virginia, and they have two children: C. Boyd, Jr., and Caroline B. Mr. Barrett is also engaged in the real-estate and insurance business, the firm being Barrett & Son.

CHARLES HENRY BARRETT

As president of the Vermillion National Bank, Charles Henry Barrett is a prominent figure in financial circles of that city. He was born in Saratoga Springs, New York, April 5, 1859, a son of Artemus and Fidelia R. (Brown) Barrett. The father was a hatter and engaged in that business until he retired from active life. He died at Saratoga Springs in 1904 but his widow survives and makes her home in Bernardston, Massachusetts, with a daughter. Mr. Barrett was twice married, his first union being with Miss Lovisa Close, of New York, by whom he had three children: John R., a retired business man residing in Los Angeles, California; Beebe R., deceased; and Lovisa A., the widow of E. H. Potter, and a resident of Bayonne, New Jersey. To the second marriage four children were born: Addie P., who married Rev. Eugene Frary, a Congregational minister of Bernardston, Massachusetts; Charles Henry; Orie L., who is at home; and Frederic A., a linotype man of Newtonville, Massachusetts.

Charles H. Barrett passed his boyhood days in Saratoga Springs and there attended school, being graduated from the high school in 1875. For the following three years he taught school and worked in his father's hat store but at the end of that time removed to Manchester, Iowa. He arrived there in 1878 and taught school there for two years. In 1880 he took a position as bookkeeper with a large mercantile concern, with which he was connected for three years. He then entered the employ of Conger Brothers, bankers, as bookkeeper and teller, remaining in that capacity for four years, and in 1887 removed to Vermillion, South Dakota, in company with L. T. Swezey. They purchased the Clay County Bank, which they reorganized and conducted under that name until 1904, when they took out a national charter and changed the name to the Vermillion National Bank. Mr. Barrett was cashier of the institution until the death of Mr. Swezey in 1912, when he was elected president. He is thoroughly familiar with the practice and policies of the bank and is also well informed as to banking conditions in the country at large. He is very efficient as president of the bank and under his direction its continued growth is insured. The safety of funds on deposit is the first consideration of the officers of the institution but they extend credit to individuals and business houses, thus promoting the commercial development of Vermillion. The bank pays good dividends and enjoys the full confidence of the public. Mr. Barrett is not only president and a director of this bank but is also interested in the Bank of Wakonda, this state, he and his associates buying it in 1903 when it was in danger of collapse. They reorganized it and placed it upon a sound financial basis and it has since been a paying institution and has come to be regarded as one of the strong banks of this section. Mr. Barrett was one of the organizers of the Vermillion Hotel Company and is an executive officer of that corporation. His standing among the bankers of the state is indicated by his election in 1910 as president of the South Dakota State Bankers' Association.

Mr. Barrett was married, September 17, 1889, to Miss Laura E. Dunham, a native of Manchester, Iowa, and a daughter of Francis and Mary A. (Stark) Dunham, both natives of Vermont. The father, who was an educator, passed away in 1880, but the mother survives and makes her home in Manchester, Iowa. To Mr. and Mrs. Barrett five children were born: John F. and Ruth, both of whom died in infancy; George, who died in 1909, when fifteen years of age; Charles S., now twelve years of age; and Marjorie, who died in infancy.

Mr. Barrett is a progressive republican and for several years has served as city treasurer of Vermillion. For ten years he was a member of the city council. He has always taken an interest in politics but has not been a politician in the sense of office seeking. His connection with the Congregational church and the Masonic order indicates the principles that govern his life. In the latter organization he has taken high rank, belonging to all of the bodies from the blue lodge to the commandery in the York Rite and also to the

Shrine. He has served as worshipful master and has held other high offices in the lodge. He is now treasurer of the blue lodge and also of the chapter. His fraternal associations also include membership in the Modern Woodmen of America. He has done his full share in promoting the development of his city along all lines and takes great pride in its advancement and prosperity.

C. H. BARROW

C. H. BARROW was born in Schuylkill County, Pennsylvania, and received his education which he attended an academy, graduation in the public schools and the high school, therefrom. He went to Redwing, Minnesota, and read law, being in due time admitted to the bar. He began practice at Minneapolis, but soon afterwards located at Ipswich, South Dakota, where he has since been engaged, meeting with distinct and gratifying success. He has been honored by election to the state legislature and has served as state's attorney several terms. Fraternally he belongs to the Masons, Odd Fellows, Maccabees and United Workmen. Mr. Barrow was married to Effie L. Hawkins, and they have two children.

ARTHUR W. BARTELS

Arthur W. Bartels, an enterprising and progressive real-estate dealer of Gary, was born at Nora Springs, Iowa, November 29, 1878, a son of Fred and Mary Bartels, who in 1879 removed with their family to South Dakota, settling in the vicinity of Gary, the father securing a tree claim on section 6, Herrick township. In addition to developing his property according to the methods which won him ownership, he engaged in the grain business, in which he continued for a number of years. Later he established a hardware store which he successfully conducted for a time and then extended the scope of his activities by purchasing a stock of general merchandise. Thus, for a considerable period he was closely identified with the business development of his district. Eventually he and his wife removed to California, where his death occurred in 1907, while Mrs. Bartels is still living in that state.

Arthur W. Bartels was educated in the public schools and in the Mankato (Minn.) Commercial College, in which he continued his course for a year. After leaving school he worked with his father in the store and later became connected with the First National Bank at Canby as assistant cashier. He also held a similar position at a later date in Gary and eventually became manager of the Farmers Elevator, after which he was appointed postmaster in 1907 by President McKinley, at which time the office was of the fourth class. He was reappointed by President Roosevelt, at which time the office had risen to the third class. He retired from the position in August, 1913, and then joined his brother in the real-estate business, in which he has since continued with growing success. He is now thoroughly informed concerning property values and has gained a good clientage.

On the 25th of December, 1907, Mr. Bartels was united in marriage to Miss Ethel Asher, a daughter of Manlius and Carrie Asher, of Yellow Medicine County, Minnesota. They have one child, Paul Asher, who is in his first year. The parents hold membership in the Presbyterian church and Mr. Bartels is an exemplary representative of Gates City Lodge, No. 14, A. F. & A. M., and the Eastern Star, and also has membership with the Elks lodge at Watertown and with the Modern Woodmen. In politics he is a republican and has served on the board of trustees of the town of Gary and as town treasurer. In 1914 he was elected to the office of state representative for the fifty-ninth district. He is fond of all outdoor sports and exercises and is interested in everything pertaining to South Dakota and her welfare. The faith of the majority of South Dakota's citizens in the state cannot be shaken and Mr. Bartels is one who recognizes its natural resources, its advantages and its opportunities. In his business connections he has made substantial advancement and ranks with the leading real-estate dealers of Deuel County.

CLARENCE A. BARTLETT

Clarence A. BARTLETT, editor and publisher of the daily and weekly Capital Journal, at Pierre, was born in West Vienna, Oneida County, New York, on the 20th of June, 1859, and is a son of Aldis and Mary (Chisholm) Bartlett, the former of whom was born in Vermont, of English descent, while the latter is of Scotch ancestry and was born in the state of New York, where their marriage was solemnized. The Bartletts were numbered among the early Puritan settlers of the New England colonies, and the great-grandfather of the subject of this review was a soldier in the Continental line during the war of the Revolution and was a brother of Josiah Bartlett, one of the signers of the Declaration of Independence. The Chisholm family was established in America in the early part of the nineteenth century, the founders of the same in the new world having come hither from Scotland. In 1865 Aldis Bartlett removed with his family to Minnesota and located in Fillmore County, where he and his wife still maintain their home, being numbered among the honored pioneers of that section.

The subject of this sketch received his early educational training in the public schools of Fillmore County, having completed a course in the grammar school at Preston, and having thereafter been a student in Curtis College, in the city of Minneapolis. In 1880, when twenty-one years of age, he came to what is now the state of South Dakota and became ticket agent and cashier for the Chicago & Northwestern Railroad at Pierre, while in the same year, as deputy county treasurer, he opened the first set of books for Hughes County. In 1886 he was transferred to the city of Deadwood as agent for the Fremont & Elkhorn Railroad and the Northwestern Express, Stage & Transportation Company, remaining a resident of that city until 1890, and having in the meanwhile accumulated a nice sum through judicious speculations in mining properties. In the year last mentioned he returned to Pierre, and here made notable investments, having erected two substantial business blocks and also other buildings and thus identifying himself permanently with the capital city. In 1900 he effected the purchase of the Capital Journal, which was established in 1881, being the oldest paper in this section of the state, as previously noted, and of this he has ever since continued as owner, publisher and editor, both the daily and weekly editions being models in their line and exerting much influence in local and state affairs of a public nature. In politics Mr. Bartlett has ever been a radical adherent of the Republican party, in whose cause he has rendered most effective service in a personal way and through the medium of his paper. In January, 1893, he was appointed deputy county treasurer, in which capacity he continued to serve for eight consecutive years, while in November, 1900, he was elected treasurer, being chosen as his own successor in the election of November, 1902, so that at the time of this writing he has been consecutively identified with the administration of the fiscal affairs of the county for the long period of twelve years.

Fraternally he is a member in good standing of the local organizations of the Ancient Free and Accepted Masons and the Ancient Order of United Workmen. On the 15th of September, 1894, Mr. Bartlett was united in marriage with Miss Elsie M. Gleason, who was born in the city of Chicago, Illinois, on the 2d of December, 1871, being a daughter of Alonzo and Sarah Gleason. Mr. and Mrs. Bartlett have, six children, namely: Aldis, Eveline, Elsie, Elwin, Cora and Ella.

WILLIAM BARTLET

WILLIAM BARTLETT

William Bartlett, of Edgemont, gives by far the greater part of his time and energy to the management of the sulphur spring owned by the city of Edgemont, which he and Robert Calder have leased under a franchise and around which there promises to grow up a well-known health resort. He also owns a great deal of property in Lead, Edgemont and elsewhere and is a business man who has long been accustomed to direct enterprises of importance. He has an enviable reputation in the city as a builder and contractor and has erected some of the finest structures in various South Dakota cities.

A native of Bristol, Gloucestershire, England, he was born on the 10th of July, 1847, of the marriage of George and Sarah (Pointing) Bartlett. The father, who owned a large transfer business in Bristol and operated a number of vans, passed away when our subject was but fourteen months of age but was survived for many years by his widow. When William Bartlett attended school in Bristol, England, there were no free schools and each week he took the money to pay his tuition. When thirteen years of age he began working for others and for something over a year he was page to the Bishop of Bath and Wells. In the meantime, his mother had married a second time and her husband, a general contractor and builder, insisted that our subject should learn the carpenter's trade. He therefore devoted several years to the mastery of the trade and thereafter continued in business with his stepfather until 1870, when as a young man of twenty-three years he concluded to try his fortune in the United States and left his native land. After residing in Chicago for a short time he went to Madison, Wisconsin, where he secured the contract for the building of the Park Hotel. He remained there a year and then, having a contract for a building at Newton, Jasper County, Iowa, he went there and later removed to Avoca, that state. He next established a chain of brickyards, two at Avoca, one at Orland and one at Walnut. For about thirteen years he resided at Avoca and was very successful in the management of his business affairs.

At the end of that time Mr. Bartlett sold out and came to South Dakota, taking up government land in Hand County, where he resided until 1892. His energy, foresight and excellent management enabled him to succeed as well in ranching as he had in other lines of work. In 1802 he left the family living upon the ranch and went to Fargo, North Dakota, to engage in the rebuilding of that city after its destruction by fire. He secured many contracts and continued there for about two years. In the meantime, he took contracts in a number of other places, building the high school in Mitchell, South Dakota, and a number of important buildings in Minnesota and in 1875 he erected the first courthouse at Sioux City, Iowa. He was also the contractor for a number of structures at Marshall, Minnesota, and upon finishing his work there he received a telegram to go to Yankton to meet those who had charge of the letting of the contract on the high-school building at Lead, this state, and he made a bid. He secured the contract and erected the building, also the Smead Hotel and the First National Bank of that city and, moreover, superintended the construction of the recreation building there and of the library. For about nineteen years the family home was maintained at Lead and during part of that time he conducted a brickyard there. For a year he operated the Smead Hotel and proved very successful in its management. About 1907 he arrived in Edgemont and purchased the business of the Paine Lumber Company of that place, which he turned over to the direction of his son. Our subject next erected the store building which is now occupied by another son. Although he became closely identified with business interests of Edgemont in 1907 it was not until 1910 that he took up his residence there, having continued to live in Lead during the intervening period. He erected and owns the opera house, which is a credit to Edgemont, and since his first arrival in the city he has done much to secure its rapid development.

Mr. Bartlett was one of the first to recognize the value of the deep artesian well which is owned by the city of Edgemont, and he and Robert Calder are exploiting it under a fifteen-year franchise. The water has been analyzed by an expert chemist and has been pronounced to be superior to other mineral waters for the treatment of many chronic diseases by eminent medical authority, and Mr. Bartlett and Mr. Calder are preparing to accommodate the many patients who desire to take treatments there. Six bathrooms and cooling rooms, eight by ten feet each, are already built and decorated and are adequately furnished and equipped. The front part of the building is used as a reading and writing room, and the lessees of the spring intend doing everything possible to add to the comfort of their patients and make the spring rank with the very best in the country as a health resort. Although up to the present time there have been but poor facilities, for taking treatment, many people have already found that the spring water has cured them of chronic disorders and it already has a reputation as a therapeutic agency. Now that the building and equipment necessary to utilize the water to the best advantage have been added it is but a matter of time before the spring will be well known throughout the state and throughout this whole action of the country and many patients will come to profit from its curative properties. In developing the possibilities latent in the splendid artesian well of sulphur water of great medicinal value at Edgemont, Mr. Bartlett and Mr. Calder are performing a great service for the city as well as adding to their own individual prosperity. Mr. Bartlett's wide experience in varied lines of business combined with his characteristic initiative and aggressiveness, make him an especially valuable man for the place and he has already demonstrated his ability to carry the project through to success.

Mr. Bartlett is a member of the firm of Phillips & Bartlett, general contractors and brick manufacturers, well known throughout the state. He is also interested in the electric light plant at Sturgis, South Dakota, his partners in the ownership of the concern being Mr. Philips and Mr. Allison. He is also a stockholder in the First National Bank of Lead and a director in the Smead Hotel at Lead. He also has other extensive property interests in that city and owns much valuable read estate in Edgemont. He erected the Masonic temples at Deadwood and at Spearfish and since removing to Edgemont has built a number of the more important structures there. In addition to his extensive and varied interests already mentioned he has important mining properties in the Black Hills, including his holdings at Rockford, South Dakota, and likewise his interest in mines in the Rocky Mountains.

Mr. Bartlett was married in February, 1865, to Miss Emma Laura Ashman. She was born in Edford, England, a daughter of Richard and Ann Elizabeth (Webb) Ashman, who were lifelong residents of England. The father was a lumber dealer and was quite successful in his business undertakings. Mr. and Mrs. Bartlett have four children. Hubert William, who resides at Edgemont and is engaged in the hardware business, married Miss Grace Johnson, of Redfield, this state. John Frederick, who resides upon eight hundred acres of land in Hand County, is carrying on stock-raising very successfully. He married Miss Susie Kenyon, of that county. Anna Elizabeth, the widow of Samuel Bushong, resides upon eight hundred acres of land in Hand County and operates the ranch herself. Her husband died in 1911, at Rochester, Minnesota, where he had undergone an operation. Arthur Edward, who is a resident of Edgemont and is engaged in the lumber business, married Analbert Kenyon, a sister of the wife of his brother, John Frederick.

Mr. Bartlett is a republican and while he has taken a good citizen's interest in politics, he has always been too busy with his private affairs to think of accepting office. His religious faith is that of the Episcopal church and fraternally he is connected with the Masonic order and the Elks. In the former organization he belongs to the various bodies from the blue lodge to the Shrine, and he is a life member of the Elks.

He is prominent in fraternal circles of his part of the state and is always ready to do anything in his power to further the interests of the organizations to which he belongs. His son Hubert is past grand high priest in the Masonic order.

In whatever community Mr. Bartlett has resided he has become a prime factor in its growth and development, and he has many friends throughout the west who admire his seemingly limitless energy and unshakable resolution and hold him in warm regard for his large heartedness and capacity for friendship. He is a man to whom any pettiness is utterly foreign and the same power of seeing things in large that has been such an important factor in his success in the business world has made his advice in regard to matters of public concern of great value and Edgemont is fortunate in that he has identified his interests with those of the city.

JULIUS D. BARTOW

Julius D. BARTOW, one of the prominent and highly esteemed merchants of Plankinton, Aurora County, was born in Republic, Seneca county, Ohio, on Christmas day of the year 1851, being a son of Joel C. and Mary A. (Hosford) Bartow, the maternal ancestry tracing back to English origin. The name is of French derivation and was originally spelled Barteaux. Joel C. Bartow was born at Bartow's Ridge, in Erie County, Ohio, the name having been given to the locality by four brothers of his mother, they having been pioneers of that section, whither they emigrated from the state of New York in an early day. After his marriage the father of our subject removed to Seneca county, Ohio, where he was identified with farming, and also with merchandising and the hotel business in the town of Republic, where he died October 19, 1901, at the age of seventy-four years, having been one of the honored and influential citizens of that locality. He was a Democrat and a member of the Odd Fellows' fraternity. His devoted wife, who died on the 9th of March, 1891, at the age of sixty-seven years, was born in Dartmouth, England, whence she came to America with her parents when a child of six years. The subject of this sketch attended the common schools of his native place and then completed a four-years course in the academy at Republic. He then entered the employ of the firm of Hemmingway & Hensinger, dealers in groceries and drugs at Republic, where he remained one year. He was married in 1873 and for the following eight years had charge of his father-in-law's farm, in Seneca County, Ohio. On the 19th of February, 1883, he and his family arrived in Plankinton, South Dakota, having been out on a tour of inspection through the west during the preceding year. Shortly after locating in Plankinton Mr. Bartow purchased the general store of Conway Thompson, and from this modest nucleus has been built up the magnificent business now controlled by him, twenty-one thousand two hundred feet of floor space being demanded for the accommodation of the various departments of the enterprise, which is one of the most extensive of the sort in the county. In September, 1900, the business was incorporated and is now conducted under the title of the Aurora Lumber Company, while the mercantile house has well-equipped departments, including those devoted to dry goods, groceries, boots and shoes, harness and saddlery goods, agricultural implements, etc. Mr. Bartow is also the owner of valuable farming land in the county. He is now a stanch Republican in politics, but was formerly arrayed with the Democracy, as the candidate of which he was elected to the state legislature in 1890, serving one term. He was for several years a member of the board of education of Plankinton, which is celebrated for having one of the best schools in the state.

He is identified in a prominent way with the Masonic fraternity, being affiliated with the lodge in Plankinton, the chapter and commandery in Mitchell, the consistory of the Scottish Rite in Yankton and the temple of the Mystic Shrine in Sioux Falls, while he is also a member of the lodge of Elks in Sioux

Falls and of the Independent Order of Odd Fellows in his native town in Ohio. He and his family are members of the Congregational church. On the 7th of May, 1873, Mr. Bartow was united in marriage to Miss Clara A. Stearns, of Republic, Ohio, where she was reared and educated, being a daughter of John B. and Adaline H. Stearns. Of this union were born six children, of whom three survive, namely: Addie, who remains at the parental home; Nona, who is the wife of F. L. Snyder, of Plankinton, and John S., who is also at home.

BURTON D. BASCOMB

The history of a city save in a few rare instances is never merely an account of a single gigantic business enterprise, but is the outcome of the united efforts of various business men, each carefully and successfully controlling his own interests. Prominently connected with the industrial activity of Clark is B. D. Bascomb, who is now manager of the Clark Roller Mills. He was born in Oronoco, Minnesota, April 4, 1868, and is a son of D. J. and Maryette (Crowell) Bascomb, who in the year 1884 brought their family to South Dakota, although the father had previously located in this state in 1882. When he came to Clark, he removed his stock of general merchandise from Minnesota and opened the first store of the kind in Clark, conducting the business successfully until 1886. In 1887 he purchased an interest in the mill under the firm name of Bascomb & Wilson and was thus connected with the manufacture of flour for two years. In 1889 he purchased his partner's interest and his son Burton became active manager although the father continued his connection with the business until seven years ago, when he sold out to his son. He thereafter lived retired until his death, which occurred in September, 1912. His widow survives as do his children: Minnie L., now Mrs. Batson, of Clark; Millie, the wife of Hamlin H. McCray, who is in the lumber business in Pine Island, Minnesota, and by whom she has two sons; Burton; Tresa Aleath, at home; and Jay C, also at home.

Burton D. Bascomb, the elder of the sons, was educated in the public schools of Minnesota and when a youth of sixteen years came with his mother and the other children of the family to join the father in South Dakota. He afterward assisted his father in the milling business, in which he became owner of a half interest, and finally he purchased his father's interest in the business. He manufactures flour of superior grade according to the most modern and improved methods and the output finds a ready sale on the market. He also runs an elevator, doing a general grain business, and was engaged in the lumber business from 1890 until May, 1914, when he sold out to L. E. Foss. He now concentrates his energies upon his elevator and his milling interests and excellent results are attending his efforts.

On the 6th of September, 1905, Mr. Bascomb was united in marriage to Miss Nellie Kneen, of Bangor, Wisconsin, where her birth occurred, and they have a daughter, Marjorie, born November 30, 1913. Mr. Bascomb is an advocate of republican principles, believing the party platform to contain the best elements of good government. He has served as chairman of the town council and is interested in all matters affecting the political welfare of state and nation, but does not seek nor desire public office. He is identified with various fraternal organizations, including the blue lodge of Masons, the Knights of Pythias, the Modern Woodmen, the Knights of the Maccabees and the Fraternal Union, and his religious belief is that of the Congregational church. He has cooperated in all movements which have tended to advance the material, intellectual, social, political and moral welfare of his community and his influence has been a potent element for reform, progress and improvement.

Ormlle S. BASFORD is a native of the old Green Mountain state, having been born in Shelburne, Vermont, on the 29th of August, 1848, and being a son of Samuel and Henrietta (Kingsbury) Basford, the former of whom was a mechanic by vocation, while both passed their entire lives in New England. In the agnatic line the genealogy is traced back to four brothers who came to America from England in the latter part of the eighteenth century, having been originally from Wales, and their descendant in the new world are now numerous and found in the most diverse sections of the Union, while the orthography of the name has become varied, — Basford, Bassford, Bashford, etc. The subject received his early education in the common schools and then completed a four-years classical course in the University of Vermont, as a member of the class of 1876. Prior to his graduation he was regularly stationed as a licentiate of the Vermont conference of the Methodist Episcopal church, and later was duly ordained to elder's orders. After five years of successful work in the ministry of his church in Vermont, at Hilton, Hyde Park and Essex, he came to the territory of Dakota, in 1880, his prime object being to induce his brothers, who were merchants, to avail themselves of advantages offered in the securing of government lands. He was given a Methodist circuit embracing the south half of Spink County, and within the three years following he organized four societies and erected three churches, at Hitchcock, Crandon and Redfield. He then became concerned in political affairs and withdrew from the active work of the ministry. In 1894 he was chosen chairman of the Republican state central committee, maneuvered his forces with much ability during the campaign of that year, and in the spring of the following year resumed ministerial functions, removing to Missouri, where he was for four years pastor of a church at Wellsville, Montgomery County, and for three and one-half years incumbent of a charge at Linnens, Linn County. His health became impaired and he accordingly returned to South Dakota, where the invigorating climate soon enabled him to recuperate his energies. He is now associated with his two sons. Frank and Harry, and is manager and editor of the Redfield Press, which is published by the firm of Basford Brothers & Basford. He was postmaster of Redfield from 1890 to 1804, inclusive, and in 1887-8 was editor and publisher of the Dakota Methodist.

He has been an active worker in the cause of the Republican party, as has already been noted in this context, and fraternally he is identified with the Masonic order, the Knights of Pythias, the Modern Woodmen of America, the Good Templars and the Independent Order of Odd Fellows, of which last he was elected grand master of the grand lodge of the state, at Deadwood, in 1890, while in the following year he was elected grand representative at Yankton.

Mention should be made of the fact that Mr. Basford enlisted, in 1864, as a member of the Seventeenth Vermont Volunteer Infantry, but was rejected by reason of his youth and was thus unable to assist in the defense of the Union during the Civil war. He was a member of the board of commissioners of Spink County from 1884 to 1886, inclusive, and was a member ci the board of regents of the Mitchell University in 1887-8-9. On the 22d of August, 1871, at Geogia, Vermont, Mr. Basford was united in marriage to Miss Arminda M. Blake, and they are the parents of six children, namely: William B., Caroline A., Delta C, Frank W., Orville K. and Harrison D.

MARWOOD R. BASKERVILLE

Marwood R Baskerville, residing in Watertown, has gained for himself an enviable position in business circles through the possession of the qualities of industry, initiative and integrity. He has been identified with various enterprises and business concerns which have contributed largely to the upbuilding of the city and he is now the president of the Watertown Gas & Light Company. His birth occurred in Delaware county, Iowa, on the 16th of July, 1861, his parents being the Rev. Job and Grace (Caldwell) Baskerville, both of whom were natives of Devonshire, England, where they were reared and married. About 1848 they came to America, making their way at once to Delaware county, Iowa, where they settled upon a farm, the father there engaging in agricultural pursuits for a long period. He was also an ordained minister of the United Brethren church and occasionally filled the pulpit for other ministers, but never held any regular pastorate after coming to this country. He died in Delaware county at the advanced age of eighty-four years, while his wife passed away at the age of eighty-two years.

Marwood R. Baskerville was reared under the parental roof, with the usual experiences of the farm lad. His early education was obtained in the public and high schools of Earlville, Iowa, and later he attended the Western College of Cedar Rapids and Epworth Seminary at Epworth, Iowa. He also pursued a commercial course in Bayless Business College at Dubuque and following the completion of his student days he secured a position as bookkeeper in the Chamberlain Plow Works at Dubuque, in which capacity he continued for three years or more. He next went to Winona, Minnesota, as business manager of the Winona Plow Company and acted in that capacity for three years. On the 1st of May, 1888, he arrived in Watertown and has since been closely and prominently connected with the commercial and industrial development and upbuilding of the city. He established an implement business soon after his arrival and has since been prominently identified with that line, building up a trade of large and gratifying proportions. His business methods are thoroughly reliable, his energy unfaltering and his initiative has carried him beyond a point where a less venturesome man would go. In all things, however, his actions have been guided by sound judgment and a keen sagacity that has permitted no false steps.

In 1907 he was the principal factor in the organization of the Baskerville & Rowe Wholesale Grocery Company, which opened its doors for business on the 1st of January, 1908. For five years Mr. Baskerville remained as president of the company, which in 1913 sold out to the Winslow & Griffin Company, Mr. Baskerville then severing his connection with the business. In 1906 he was one of four who organized the Watertown Gas & Light Company, which was incorporated and which owns and controls the gas system of the city. He is president of that company and is also a stockholder and director of the Citizens National Bank. In connection with his sale of farm implements he does an extensive business in the sale of automobiles. He is today one of the prosperous residents of Watertown and what he has accomplished represents the fit utilization of the innate powers and business talents which are his. In addition to his other interests, he is a heavy investor in farm lands in Codington County.

In his political views Mr. Baskerville has long been a stalwart republican and for a number of years he has been recognized as one of the dominant factors in shaping the policy of the party in this locality. While never seeking public office, he has worked untiringly for his friends and for the adoption of party principles and he has served as a member of the republican state central committee and as chairman of the county central committee at different times. In fact, his opinions carry great weight in the councils of his party and he enjoys a state-wide reputation in connection with his political activity. While he has never been an aspirant for office, his fellow townsmen have urged upon him the duty of serving them in public positions and for two terms, beginning in 1904, he was mayor of Watertown. His administration was most businesslike and utility and progress were the dominant features of his official record.

On the 28th of November, 1895, Mr. Baskerville wedded Miss Harriett Lord Fahnestock, of Watertown, a native of Gettysburg, Pennsylvania, who in 1887 came to this state with her father, Henry Fahnestock, who is now deceased but for some years was widely and favorably known among the business men of the city. To Mr. and Mrs. Baskerville have been born two children, Henry Marwood and Walter Gregory.

In fraternal circles Mr. Baskerville is well known, holding membership in Watertown Lodge, No. 838, B. P. O. E., of which he has served as exalted ruler. He was the principal factor in bringing about the erection of the lodge building in 1908, Watertown now having one of the finest Elks homes of the state. In recognition of his part in this undertaking Mr. Baskerville was elected a life member of the lodge and presented with a beautiful gold card of life membership. In Masonry he is equally prominent, belonging to Kampeska Lodge, No. 13, A. F. & A. M.; Watertown Chapter, No. 12, R. A. M.; Watertown Commandery, No. 7, K. T.; Watertown Consistory, A. & A. S. R.; and Yelduz Temple, A. A. O. N. M. S., of Aberdeen. He also has membership in Trishocotyn Lodge, No. 17, K. P., in the Minneapolis Athletic Club and the Watertown Country Club—connections which indicate his social nature, while his geniality and cordiality have made him popular in those organizations. In the midst of a most active and busy life Mr. Baskerville has never neglected his religious duties and he and his wife are valued and zealous members of the Episcopal church. For the past three years he has served as superintendent of its Sunday school. His position is established by the consensus of public opinion, which places him in the foremost rank among the business men and citizens of Watertown.

JAMES H. BASKIN

James H. BASKIN, one of the best-known and most popular residents of Bon Homme County, and late mayor of the town of Scotland, was a native of the sunny south, having been born in the city of Atlanta, Georgia, on the 17th of February, 1845, a son of John and Elizabeth (Penton) Baskin, of whose seven children four are living at the present time, namely: Anna, who is the wife of a Mr. Harris, of Atlanta; Walter, who likewise continues to reside in that city, as does also Zachariah; and James H., the immediate subject of this sketch. The father of the subject came of stanch English lineage and was himself a native of the state of South Carolina, where he was reared to maturity. He finally removed thence to Atlanta, Georgia, where he established himself in the blacksmithing and wagon-making business, in which he continued to be actively engaged for many years, and in that city, he continued to reside until his death, at the age of seventy years, while his devoted wife passed away when the subject was quite young.

James H. Baskin was reared and educated in his native city and was a lad of sixteen years at the time of the outbreak of the Civil war. His sympathies were naturally with the section in which he had been reared, and he was among many others of the chivalrous and valiant young men of the south who tendered their services to the Confederate government. At the age of sixteen years he enlisted, in September, 1861, as a member of a Georgia regiment, heavy artillery, with which he continued in active service until November, 1864, when he was captured at Fisher Hill, Virginia, and taken to the Union prison at Point Lookout, Maryland, being released on parole two weeks later. He had participated in many of the important engagements of the war and had proved a valiant defender of the "lost cause." After his release from captivity, he passed a short interval in New York city and then drifted westward to St. Louis, Missouri, while in 1868 he came as a pioneer to the territory of Dakota, which was then on the frontier of civilization. For a year after his arrival, he was in the employ of the firm of Duett & Bogue, traders, at Fort Thompson. About this time the Indians were removed to the Santee agency, and our subject was sent to that point in the employ of the government, and there he continued in service until 1875, when he took up his residence in Springfield, Bon Homme County, where he established himself in the hotel business, in which he there continued for the long period of eleven years, gaining a wide acquaintanceship throughout what is now the state of South Dakota and becoming one of the most popular pioneer hotel men of the state. In 1886 he came to Scotland, where he conducted the Baskin hotel, which is a popular resort of the traveling public, no pains being spared to provide the best possible accommodations and cater to the comfort and pleasure of the guests of the house. That the subject was a man of versatility is shown when we state that for seven years after coming to Scotland, he was editor and publisher of the Scotland Journal, which he made an able exponent of local interests and a factor of importance in public and political affairs in this section. In 1890 he was elected mayor of the town, and served continuously as chief executive of the municipal government from that time to the date of his death, save for an interim of two years. He maintained a progressive policy and yet conserved economy in all departments, while his long retention in office was the best voucher of the popular appreciation accorded his well-directed efforts in the connection. In 1899 Mr. Baskin was elected a member of the lower house of the state legislature, and during his service of one term he proved an able and discriminating legislator, taking an active part in the work of the body, while he had the distinction of being chairman of the important committee on ways and means and also held membership on the committee on railroads and that on military affairs. He was originally an adherent of the Democratic party, but was a man who ever showed the courage of his convictions, and in harmony therewith he transferred his allegiance to the Republican party in 1896, during the campaign of which year he gave effective service in the support of the candidacy of President McKinley, and he afterward continued a stalwart advocate of the cause of the "grand old party."

He and his wife were communicants of the Protestant Episcopal church, and fraternally he was identified with Scotland Lodge, No. 52, Free and Accepted Masons, and Scotland Chapter, No. 31, Royal Arch Masons. On the 1st of December, 1888, was solemnized the marriage of Mr. Baskin to Miss Mary Kula, of this county, and they became the parents of two sons, James E. and Frederick R., both of whom remain at the parental home. Mr. Baskin departed this life on February 29, 1904.

JOHN C. BASSETT

J. C. BASSETT, president of the Aberdeen National Bank, and one of the well-known and successful bankers of South Dakota, was born in Killingly. Windham county, Connecticut, August 26, 1864, the son of Augustus and Sarah J. Bassett. The parents were born in Connecticut and their family names have been identified with New England for many generations.

John C. Bassett was educated in the public schools of Danielson, and began his business career in 1880 as secretary of a milling company at Danielson. In 1888 he came to South Dakota and located at Langford, Marshall County, where he engaged in the banking business. In 1900 he was elected cashier of the Aberdeen National Bank, and removed his residence to that city. In 1902 he was elected president of the above bank. Mr. Bassett's banking and financial interests are extensive, as besides holding the presidency of the Aberdeen National Bank, he is president of the Commercial Bank of Langford, South Dakota, president of the State Bank of Pierpont, South Dakota, vice-president of the First State Bank, of Aberdeen, and a stockholder in other banking institutions.

In politics Mr. Bassett is a Republican, and he belongs to the different Masonic bodies and to the Ancient Order of United Workmen. He and his wife are members of the Presbyterian church. On June 29, 1892, Mr. Bassett was married to Harriet Galbraith, who was born in Minneapolis, Minnesota, on November 12, 1864. Mr. and Mrs. Bassett are the parents of the following children: Ruth, Hellene, Margery and Clarke.

DAVID K. BATCHELOR

David K. Batchelor, who is filling the position of county auditor of Fall River County and has also for a number of years been a well-known contractor of Hot Springs, was born in Forfarshire, Scotland, August 31, 1876, and of that place his parents, Alexander and Ella (Kidd) Batchelor, were also natives, there spending their entire lives. The father was a tailor by trade. Their family numbered six children, of whom David K. was the second, and he attended school in his native country to the age of about sixteen years. He then learned the stonemason's trade, which he followed in Scotland until 1900, when he crossed the broad Atlantic and settled at Pittsburgh, Pennsylvania. There he followed his trade for about nine months, after which he removed to Kansas City, Missouri, where he also worked as a stonemason for nine months. He next went to Texas, where he followed his trade for about four or five months. In Colorado he continued in the same business for about six or eight months, and thence went to Arizona, New Mexico and again to Texas. In the spring of 1902, he arrived in Hot Springs, South Dakota, and was engaged in the construction of the Battle Mountain Sanatorium for about four or five years. He then engaged in contracting and building as a mason and has since been identified with building operations in Hot Springs and Fall River County. He is now in partnership with Stuart Hill, who looks after the business of the firm, while Mr. Batchelor is giving much of his attention to his official duties as county auditor.

In politics Mr. Batchelor has always been a stalwart democrat since becoming a naturalized American citizen. He has never been a politician in the usually accepted sense of office seeking, but was called to the position of county auditor and discharged his duties so creditably that he has been reelected for a second term.

In January, 1904, Mr. Batchelor was married to Miss Delia Keyes, who was born at Springfield, Illinois, of which state her parents were also natives. They occupy a pleasant home in Hot Springs and Mr. Batchelor is also the owner of landed interests in Fall River County. He is identified with several fraternal organizations, including the Independent Order of Odd Fellows, the Modern Brotherhood of America and while in Scotland joined the Masonic fraternity, but never demitted from the old lodge. He has never had occasion to regret his determination to come to the new world, for here he has found and improved good business opportunities and has gradually worked his way upward, winning a creditable measure of success through his close application and capability.

JOHN N. BEACH

John N. BEACH, farmer and stock raiser, was born in Lesueur County, Minnesota, June 10, 1857. He was reared and educated in his native state, grew to the years of manhood on a farm, and on attaining his majority left home for the Black Hills, coming via Pierre to Boulder Park. He came empty-handed, and for two years worked on a milk ranch for wages, then he rented the place and conducted it during the winter of 1881. In the following spring he returned to Minnesota where he purchased a large number of cattle which he drove to the Black Hills, selling them at good prices in Sturgis, Deadwood and Rapid City.

Mr. Beach continued these trips between Minnesota and South Dakota for two years, and did a thriving business, buying and selling cattle, but in 1884 he turned his attention to mining in the tin district near Hill City, following the same until the spring of the succeeding year. On June 7, 1885, he was united in marriage to Miss Ettie M. Robinson, of Minnesota, and immediately thereafter moved to his wife's ranch on Squaw creek, four miles south of Hermosa, where he engaged in the live-stock business, raising cattle and horses, in addition to which he also bought a large number of these animals, becoming in due time one of the most extensive livestock dealers in Custer County. Mr. Beach resided on Squaw creek until July, 1902, when he moved to his homestead on Spring creek, purchasing the same year a large tract of land adjoining, on which he has since pastured his cattle and horses, his business the meanwhile continuing to grow in magnitude, until he now ranks with the leading live-stock men of western Dakota. His ranch contains seven hundred and twenty acres of land, under irrigation, and the improvements on the same are among the best in the country, consisting of a comfortable and attractive residence and substantial outbuildings, which with the fine condition of the place in general indicate the home of a man of progress and thrift, as well as of public spirit and good taste. It is worthy of note that at one time Mr. Beach could have traded a single cow for one hundred and sixty acres of the land on which Pierre now stands.

His fraternal relations are represented by the Masonic brotherhood, and the Knights of the Maccabees, belonging to the lodges at Hermosa and Black Hills Chapter, No. 25, Royal Arch Masons, at Rapid City. Mr. and Mrs. Reach move in the best social circles of the community and are active in promoting every good work, being interested in public and private charities, and their influence has always been exercised on the right side of every moral issue. They have a family of two children whose names are Troy C. and William W.

WILL A. BEACH

The position which Will A. Beach, president of the Will A. Beach Printing Company, has obtained among the prominent and representative men of Sioux Falls is visible evidence of the value of industry, ability and business insight in the development of a successful career. Starting in a small way, he has built up by his efforts one of the largest blank book and general office supply concerns in this state and because of his able and intelligent management of his interests is meeting with constantly increasing prosperity. He was born on a farm in Sullivan County, Pennsylvania, May 2, 1862, and is a son of George H. and Mary E. (Black) Beach, the former a native of Staffordshire, England. He came to America with his parents in boyhood and died in Emmetsburg, Iowa, in 1911. He had located there in 1872, and during the later years of his residence was a building contractor.

Will A. Beach acquired his education in the public schools of Des Moines and of Palo Alto County, Iowa, and in a business college at Milwaukee, graduating from the latter institution in 1881. Two years later he located in Sioux Falls and entered the employ of F. W. Taylor as bookkeeper in his hardware establishment. At the end of five years, he formed a partnership with a Mr. Sutton under the firm name of Sutton & Beach and established a small job printing office which was the nucleus of his present large enterprise. Soon afterward he bought out the interest of Mr. Sutton and continued the business under the name of Will A. Beach, printer and binder, until 1905, when it was organized into the Will A. Beach Printing Company, with Will A. Beach, president; A. H. Beach, vice president; J. D. Beach, treasurer: and W. G. George, secretary. In 1907 Charles H. Parshall, the present secretary and superintendent, purchased the interest of W. G. George in the business.

The Will A. Beach Printing Company has had a rapid and steady growth since its organization and it controls today one of the largest and best equipped printing, binding, stationery and office-supply establishments in the northwest. It is state agent for numerous office devices, among them the Herring-Hall-Marvin line of safes and vault doors, the Safe Cabinet Company's fireproof safe cabinets, the Elliott-Fisher book typewriter, the Yawman & Erbe line of steel vault fixtures, and the Yawman & Erbe and the Weis lines of wood filing devices. The company has a large and increasing business in all of these lines. When the business was started the equipment consisted of two job presses without any power attachments, whereas there are now in the press room five job presses, four cylinders and one auto press, with electric motor equipment, in the composing room one of the latest model linotype type-setting machines and full equipment of the very best job fonts. The binding department, which has been under the supervision of J. W. Olson since its beginning, is fully equipped with all of the most improved machinery in the binding line, consisting of two ruling machines, power cutters, rotary perforators, electric punching machines, a folding machine and everything contained in the modern, up-to-date eastern binderies. The blank book and office-supply department recently installed by the Will A. Beach Printing Company is one of the finest in this part of the state and no other city of the size of Sioux Falls contains so well equipped an establishment. The firm gives employment to from thirty-five to fifty people according to the seasons of the year, the payroll being in 1914 over thirty-five thousand dollars. They have a large and modern plant equipped with everything necessary to supply the demands of an extensive and increasing business and the outside territory is taken care of by three traveling salesmen, covering all of the state of South Dakota, eastern Wyoming and Montana, parts of North Dakota, southwestern Minnesota and northwestern Iowa. In the mail order department, the company counts its customers from all parts of the northwest.

At Canton, South Dakota, November 6, 1883, Mr. Beach was united in marriage to Miss Lida Alice Barber and they have two daughters, Hazel M. and Maude Barbara. Mr. Beach is a member of the Episcopal church and gives his political allegiance to the republican party. He is a thirty-second degree Mason, holding membership in the commandery and Shrine, belongs to the Knights of Pythias and has been through all of the chairs in the Independent Order of Odd Fellows, being past chief patriarch of the encampment. He is past chancellor of Granite Lodge, No. 18, K. P., and past exalted ruler of Sioux Falls Lodge, No. 262, B. P. 0. E. He is recognized as one of the prominent and able business men of Sioux Falls, a position which he has earned by many years of rightly directed effort.

HON. JOHN S. BEAN

John S. BEAN is a native of the old Granite state, having been born in Warner, Merrimac County. New Hampshire, on the 16th of February, 1839, a son of James and Marinda (Stewart) Bean, and the old homestead in which he first saw the light of day was likewise the birthplace of his honored father, who there, passed his entire life, which was devoted to agricultural pursuits. He lived to attain the venerable age of eighty-two years and traced his lineage back to one of two brothers, John and David Bean, who were born in Scotland, whence they went to England, from which "tight little isle" they emigrated to America in 1668, settling near historic old Plymouth, in the colony of Massachusetts, whence their descendants later scattered through various parts of New England. The mother of the subject was likewise born in New Hampshire, whither her parental grandparents came from Ireland. She died at the age of thirty years, and of her three children the subject is the only one living at the present time. James Bean became a member of the Know-nothing party at the time of its organization and later became a radical Republican, and while he never sought official preferment, he was called upon to serve on the town board for many years and also held other offices of local trust.

John S. Bean was reared to the sturdy discipline of the New England farm and his early educational training was secured in the common schools, and supplemented by a two-years course in the New Hampton Academy. It was his desire to be graduated in this institution but his financial resources reached so low an ebb that he was compelled to withdraw at the end of two years, and he then, at the age of nineteen, began teaching in the schools of his native state, devoting his attention to the pedagogic profession for three winters. In March, 1861, he left the ancestral home and set forth upon his independent career, being dependent upon his own resources in facing the battle of life. He came west to Wisconsin, where he called upon his uncle, C. K. Stewart, whom he found confined to his bed with an illness which promised to be protracted, and under these conditions he was pressed into service and took charge of his uncle's farm. The Civil war commenced in April of that year and the subject was most anxious to at once tender his services in defense of the Union, but he was not able to leave his uncle until the 22d of October, 1862, when he enlisted as a private in Company D, Sixteenth Wisconsin Volunteer Infantry, with which he proceeded to the front, the regiment being assigned to the Army of the Tennessee. The regiment was in Prentice's division at the memorable battle of Shiloh, and this division was captured by the enemy, our subject having escaped this fate by reason of the fact that he had been wounded on the morning of the same day and thus incapacitated for service. He was in the hospital at Savannah. Georgia, and Mount Vernon, Indiana, about three months, after which he returned to Wisconsin and was detailed to recruiting service, being located in turn at Columbus, Beaver Dam and Madison. In February, 1863, Mr. Bean rejoined his regiment, at Lake Providence, Louisiana, but the effects of the wound in his arm were such that he could not handle a gun, and he was thus detailed as clerk of courts martial and the quartermaster's department, serving in this capacity for three months, at the expiration of which the court was disbanded and he was then detailed to the quartermaster's department alone. He was finally made chief clerk under the contraband bureau. After serving three months he went with his regiment to Vicksburg, but did not take part in the engagement there, and the winter was passed in Redbone, Mississippi, whence they returned to Vicksburg in the spring, Mr. Bean's company at this time reorganized and Mr. Bean was commissioned as second lieutenant in a colored company, with which he later took part in the tendays siege before Blakely and the fourteen-days siege of Mobile. Still later the regiment embarked on a transport for Selma, Alabama, and while enroute learned of Lee's surrender. The subject was thereafter on provost duty for several months, and the command was finally sent to Baton Rouge, where they received honorable discharge on the 4th of January, 1866. Before this he had been promoted to first lieutenant. Mr. Bean then visited his old home in New Hampshire, and shortly afterward went again to Wisconsin. At the time of his discharge, he was importuned to remain in the south as a member of a regiment which there continued in service two years after the close of the war, and though he was offered a commission as captain he did not deem it expedient to accept the overtures.

After his return to Wisconsin Mr. Bean engaged in farming, in Dodge County, becoming the owner of a good property, and there he remained until May, 1882, when he came to Douglas County, South Dakota, taking up a preemption claim four miles northeast of the present village of Armour, the county seat, where he continued to devote his attention to the improvement and cultivation of his farm until the autumn of 1890, when he took up his residence in Armour. In November of the same year he was elected a member of the state senate, serving; one term, and in the fall election of 1892 he was chosen to represent his district in the lower house of the Legislature, in which he likewise served one term. He then engaged in the real-estate and insurance business in Armour and later also became identified with the undertaking business here, having been retired from the two former enterprises. He served one year as township treasurer and three years as township clerk, while his was the distinction of having been elected the first county clerk and register of deeds after the reorganization of the county. He was incumbent of the office of justice of the peace for several years and since 1895 he has held the office of weighmaster at Armour. At the present time he is a member of the board of county commissioners. His religious faith is that of the Freewill Baptist church, but as there is no organization of this denomination in Armour he attends the services of the Baptist church. He is a charter member of Arcania Lodge, No. 97, Free and Accepted Masons, of which he was the first worshipful master, serving three years, and he is an honored member of O. P. Morton Post, No. 51, Grand Army of the Republic, of which he is now serving for the sixth consecutive year as commander.

On the 26th of October, 1864, was solemnized the marriage of Mr. Bean to Miss Ellen C. Eastman, of Warner, New Hampshire, who proved to him a devoted wife and helpmeet until she was summoned into eternal rest, on the 19th of August, 1899. They became the parents of two children. Mabel died at the age of twenty-two years, and Jennie, the wife of George E. Sanders, of Armour, with whom the subject now makes his home.

JOHN BELL

John BELL, postmaster of Spearfish, and one of the old and worthy citizens of Lawrence County. South Dakota, is a native of England, born in Yorkshire on the 13th day of December, 1849. Deprived of a father's guidance and loving care at the early age of three years, the childhood and youth of young Bell was beset with many vicissitudes and not a few hardships, by reason of which his educational advantages were exceedingly limited. While still a mere lad he was apprenticed to the blacksmith trade and after serving his time and becoming an efficient workman he followed his calling at different places in Lancashire, where he was reared until his twentieth year. In 1870 Mr. Bell came to the United States and after working at his trade in various towns and cities, finally located in Pittsburg, Pennsylvania, where he operated a shop until 1876, when, by reason of the excitement caused by gold in the Black Hills, he joined the tide of fortune hunters and made his way to Dakota, reaching the mining district in the spring of the year noted. Immediately after his arrival in the Black Hills he started a blacksmith shop, the first one in the place, his only shelter being a large tree on the bank of White Wood creek. There was much more work than he could do and frequently he would be kept busy far into the night attending to the needs of his numerous customers. Later in the summer of 1876 he pushed on to Central City, where he started a shop and worked at his trade continually until 1883, when he closed his establishment and, removing to Spearfish, engaged in the livestock business. He moved his family to the latter place in 1886 and has since made it his home, the meantime continuing to raise, buy and sell cattle, until 1902, when he sold out his live-stock interests, the better to attend to his duties as postmaster, to which office he was appointed by President McKinley in 1898. He was reappointed in 1902 by President Roosevelt and still holds the position, proving a most capable, painstaking and obliging official.

Mr. Bell is a Republican in politics and a zealous party worker. Fraternally he is a member of the Masonic order, belonging to Blue Lodge, No. 18, and Lookout Chapter, No. 36, Royal Arch Masons at Spearfish. He was married, January 20, 1872, at Pittsburg, Pennsylvania, to Miss Mary A. Perrett, a native of England, who has borne him nine children, of whom the following are living: Maggie E., Lula M., Rosa, Maud S. and Thomas A. the deceased are Bertha, Kate and two that died in infancy.

Mr. Bell has been quite successful in the raising and handling of livestock, from which and his trade he realized sufficient means to retire in comfort, being now the possessor of an ample competence for his declining years. Being still in the prime of life, however, with a liberal income from the post office, he keeps abreast of the times in all matters pertaining to the material welfare of the city of his residence, being interested in its various enterprises, and co-operating with every laudable undertaking for the social and moral good of the community.

CLAUDE A. BENNETT

Claude A. Bennett, judge of the county court of Stanley County, who since 1908 has been an active representative of the South Dakota bar, was born on the 18th of April, 1882, six miles west of the city of Canton, in this state, his parents being Millard and Mary Bennett, who settled on a homestead in Lincoln County in 1874. The father was a native of New York born of English parentage and the mother a native of Illinois and of Welsh descent. Both are residents of Canton at the present time. They were pioneers in the development of the great west, recognizing its possibilities and aiding in the work of reclaiming the broad acres for the purposes of cultivation and improvement.

Judge Bennett mastered the elementary branches of learning and qualified for entrance into the Canton high school from which he was graduated in 1898. He subsequently became a student in the Yankton College from which he won the Bachelor of Science degree upon graduation with the class of 1904. Subsequently he became a student in Chicago University, completing the course there in 1907 and in 1913 Yankton College conferred upon him the Master of Arts degree. He closely applied himself to his law studies and his careful preparation has constituted the foundation of his success at the bar. He settled at Philip, South Dakota, on the 11th of May, 1908, and there entered upon the active practice of law, winning a large clientage that connected him with much of the important litigation tried in the courts of his district. His ability in handling intricate and involved legal problems led to his selection for the office of county judge of Stanley County and following his election he removed to Fort Pierre on the 1st of January, 1913. He is now upon the bench and his decisions are strictly fair and impartial, being based upon a comprehensive knowledge of the law and the equity of the case.

On the 28th of August, 1912, at McLaughlin, South Dakota, Mr. Bennett was united in marriage to Miss Irene M. Harris, who is a daughter of Mrs. Anna Harris of McLaughlin, and who was born in Beadle County, South Dakota, in 1885. Judge and Mrs. Bennett attend the Congregational church in which she holds membership and he belongs to the Masonic fraternity, being affiliated with Philip Lodge, No. 153, A. F. & A. M.; Pierre Chapter No. 22, R. A. M.; and Capital Commandery, No. 21, K. T. He has always been an earnest republican in his political views, believing firmly in party principles, yet he has never allowed partisanship to interfere with the faithful performance of his judicial duties.

FRANK BENNETT

Frank Bennett, who since 1906 has been identified with the transfer and storage business in Watertown, is now classed among the city's representative and substantial citizens. He claims the state of Wisconsin as the place of his nativity, his birth having occurred in Osceola on the 30th of March, 1868. His parents, James G. and Susan A. Bennett, were born in the east, the father in Pennsylvania, and the mother in Maine. They were married, however, in Stillwater, Minnesota, and directly afterward located in Osceola, Wisconsin, where the father was engaged for a number of years in the milling business. He subsequently removed to Luverne, Minnesota, and still later to Pipestone, that state. In 1889 he again made a change in his residence, this time removing to Seattle, Washington, where in his later life he engaged in the painting and decorating business. His death occurred in the coast city on the 27th of December, 1913, while his wife, surviving for only a few months, was called to the home beyond on the 22d of April, 1914.

Frank Bennett was reared in his parents' home and accompanied them on their various removals during the period of his boyhood and early manhood. He acquired his education in the public schools of Luverne and Pipestone, Minnesota, and on reaching mature years engaged in farming, operating a tract of rented land near Pipestone for about five years. On the expiration of that period, he engaged in the livery business in Pipestone but at the end of two years his barn was destroyed by fire, which was a total loss to Mr. Bennett, as he carried no insurance on his property. This left him practically penniless but he bravely met his misfortune and secured work by the day. For about three years he was employed by a produce house in Pipestone and in May, 1897, came to Watertown, where he found employment in a similar capacity. He remained in that position for nine years, during which time he worked earnestly in the hope he might some day retrieve his lost possessions and be able to engage in business on his own account. To this end in 1906 he formed a partnership with Frank E. Munger in the establishment of a general drayage business, the concern operating under the style of Munger & Bennett. In December, 1908, the death of Mr. Munger occurred, since which time Mr. Bennett has been sole owner of the business. On the 14th of February, 1914, he removed the business to his present commodious building and added to the draying and transfer business a storage department. He is well equipped for carrying on his work and is quick to respond to a call for his services, while his warehouse ensures safety to any goods that may be stored therein. He has built up a splendid trade in his line and his success is well deserved.

Mr. Bennett was married on the 26th of April, 1887, to Miss Ethelyn Bernard, of Pipestone, Minnesota, and to this union two daughters have been born. Camille is the wife of Frank Smith, of Osceola, Wisconsin, by whom she has one son, Robert. The younger daughter, Marjorie, is the wife of George G. Briggs, a resident of Minneapolis, Minnesota, by whom she has a daughter, June. The mother and daughters belong to the Congregational church.

In his political views and affiliations Mr. Bennett is a democrat and dots his duty as a private citizen. He is a Mason, being identified with Kampeska Lodge, No. 13, A. F. A, A. M.; Watertown Chapter, No. 12, R. A. M.; and Watertown Commandery. No. 7, K. T. He likewise holds membership relations with Watertown Lodge, No. 838, B. P. O. E.; the Modern Woodmen of America; Watertown Council, No. 291, U. C. T. and Kampeska Aerie, No. 1381, Order of Eagles. He keeps in touch with the progress and advancement of public movements through his membership in the Commercial Club. He is entirely a self-made man, his prosperity being the reward of his energy and intelligently directed efforts.

FRANKLIN E. BENNETT

Among the prominent citizens of Belle Fourche is Franklin E. Bennett, who has many business interests in that part of the state and is engaged in breeding pure bred stock on an Urge scale. He was born in La Salle, Illinois, January 20, 1865, the eldest of five children whose parents were William C. and Florence (De Merritt) Bennett. The father was born in Brownsville, Pennsylvania, August 10, 1836, and the mother in Portland, Maine, in 1845. William C. Bennett engaged in steam boating in early life and in the '50s emigrated from eastern Pennsylvania to Illinois, where he was employed on the river during the Civil war and afterward until 1868. In that year he entered the employ of Deere & Company at Moline, with whom he remained until 1871. He then became connected with the Barnard & Las Manufacturing Company of that city, and is still president of that company and an important factor in the industrial interests of his locality. He served as mayor of Moline for one term and the affairs of the city were managed in an efficient, businesslike manner during his administration. His wife passed away in 1881.

Franklin L. Bennett attended high school at Moline and for a short time was a student in a business college at Davenport, Iowa. When fifteen years of age he went west and worked for others, herding cattle in central Nebraska for a time, after which he returned home. When twenty years of age he entered the employ of the Deere & Mansure Company at Moline as stenographer and paymaster and was connected with that concern until 1887. In August of that year, he went to Minneapolis, Minnesota, and was employed as office man by the Wilford & Northway Manufacturing Company until the spring of 1891, when he came to Belle Fourehe and in association with a Mr. Teall erected a flour mill. He was engaged in the milling business until 1903 or 1904 and from 1893 to 1906 also dealt in lumber. These connections were not his only interests as he was identified with the waterworks and also with the Belle Fourehe Electric Light & Power Company, which is now the Belle Fourehe Consolidated Power & Light Company. He is now president of the company which publishes the Belle Fouche Bee, a wide-awake and enterprising weekly newspaper. His attention at present, however, is mainly given to the breeding and raising of pure bred Rambouillets as a member of the firm of Cock & Bennett, which owns extensive grazing lands in Butte County.

Mr. Bennett was married on the 15th of October, 1890, to Miss Gertrude Teall. She was born in Eau Claire, Wisconsin, of the marriage of Benjamin F. and Julia (Van Cleef) Teall, both of whom were born in the vicinity of Seneca, New York. Mr. Teall engaged in mercantile business and in 1891 came with his family to Belle Fouche. He formed a partnership with Mr. Bennett and the firm built a mill with which he was connected until his death in 1902. His widow is still living in Belle Fourehe. To their union were born three children, of whom Mrs. Bennett is the eldest. Mr. and Mrs. Bennett have two children: Franklin Teall, whose birth occurred July 25, 1892; and Sara L., born June 3, 1894. Both are attending the University of Minnesota.

Mr. Bennett is a republican and was county auditor of Butte County from March 1, 1913 to March 1, 1915. For two terms he was county treasurer and that his record in that connection was satisfactory to his constituents is proven by his being chosen county auditor. He likewise served for two terms as trustee of the township board. He is a member. of the Masonic blue lodge and chapter and served as master for two terms and is at present secretary. He likewise holds membership in the Ancient Order of United Workmen. Strict attention to business, conformity to high standards of morality and the exercise of sound judgment have brought him to his present position as one of the well-to-do men of his county, and he possesses the goodwill and esteem of those who have been brought in contact with him.

JAMES L. BENTLEY

James L. Bentley, general agent at Deadwood for the Chicago, Burlington & Quincy Railroad, was born in Wyoming, Ontario, Canada, December 28, 1863, a son of Joseph L. and Jane (Williams) Bentley. The mother was born in Wyoming, Ontario, December 25, 1841, and the father was a native of Middlesex County, Ontario, born July 3, 1837. He learned the trade of shoemaking in early life and also engaged in farming. About 1801 he removed across the border into Michigan, settling at Grindstone City, where he carried on general agricultural pursuits. He died in 1905 while visiting a son in Lead, South Dakota, in which place his widow now resides.

James L. Bentley was the first born in a family of ten children. He attended school in Newbury, Canada, and when about sixteen years of age began earning his own living, working at various occupations both in Canada and in Michigan. On the 27th of December, 1883, when a young man of twenty years, he went to Hubbell, Nebraska, where he entered the employ of the Chicago, Burlington & Quincy Railroad Company as night operator. After about six months he was transferred to Wymore, Nebraska, where he had charge of the freight department as clerk for about two years. On the expiration of that period, he removed to Hardy, Nebraska, where he spent eighteen months as agent, and then for a year and a half or two years he acted as extra man. He was agent at Pawnee, Nebraska, for two and a half years, after which he was made traveling freight and passenger agent at Beatrice, Nebraska, continuing in that position for about three years. He came to Deadwood on the 26th of October, 1894, as general agent for the company and has since acted in that capacity. For almost a third of a century he has been continuously in the employ of the Chicago, Burlington & Quincy Railroad Company and is one of their most trusted and efficient representatives.

In May, 1889, Mr. Bentley was united in marriage to Miss Sarah L. Hawkins, who was born at White Sulphur Springs, Virginia, a daughter of Thomas J. and Rebecca (Ervine) Hawkins, both of whom were natives of Virginia and at an early period in the development of Nebraska went to that state, settling at Pawnee, where the father engaged in general merchandising. Both he and his wife died in that state. To Mr. and Mrs. Bentley has been born a son, James Marvin, who is still with his parents in Deadwood.

Fraternally Mr. Bentley is connected with the Masons, holding membership in the blue lodge, commandery and shrine. He is also a member of the Benevolent Protective Order of Elks. In politics he is an independent republican, but has never aspired to office, preferring to concentrate his energies upon his business affairs, his close application, energy and reliability having won for him the advancement which has come to him. He is now well known in Deadwood, where he has so long resided, and he enjoys the high regard, confidence and goodwill of his fellow townsmen.

OTTO C. BERG

O. C. Berg, who is now serving his second term as secretary of state of South Dakota, is one of the prominent and influential citizens of the commonwealth and has here maintained his home for more than a score of years, so that he is entitled to the distinction of being classed among the pioneers of this favored section of our great national domain. Mr. Berg comes of stanch Norseland lineage and is himself a native of Norway, having been born in Brottum, Ringsager, on the loth of September, 1849, and being a son of Christian T. and Christence Berg, who are both now dead. The subject secured his educational training in the excellent national schools of his native land and instituted his independent career by securing a clerkship in a general store at Lillehammer, later becoming bookkeeper in a wholesale establishment at Drammen. In 1873 he came to America and located in Wisconsin, becoming one of the prominent citizens of Norwalk, Monroe County, where he served as postmaster and also held the office of county clerk. In 1883 he came to what is now the state of South Dakota and took up his abode in Northville, Spink County, where he engaged in the general merchandise business, building up a prosperous enterprise in the line. For six years he served as clerk of the circuit and county courts, manifesting an active concern in public affairs and early becoming one of the leaders in the ranks of the Republican party of the state. In 1900 he was elected secretary of state and was chosen as his own successor in 1902, so that he is incumbent of this responsible and exacting office at the time of this writing. He is a leading Republican and takes a deep interest in the furtherance of the principles and policies of the party. His religious faith is that of the Lutheran church, while Mrs. Berg and family are devoted members of the Congregational church.

Fraternally he is affiliated with Redfield Lodge, No. 34, Ancient Free and Accepted Masons, at Redfield; Redfield Chapter, No. 20, Royal Arch Masons; South Dakota Consistory, Ancient Accepted Scottish Rite Masons, in Aberdeen; and Northville Lodge, No. 36, Ancient Order of United Workmen, at Northville.

On the 1st of May, 1879, was solemnized the marriage of Mr. Berg to Miss Edith O. Rowe, who was born at Coldspring, Jefferson County, Wisconsin, being a daughter of David R. Rowe, an influential citizen of that place. Of this union have been born three children, Edna Mathea, who died January 8, 1904, at the age of twenty-three years; Christine, who died in infancy, and Paul B., who is sixteen years of age at the time of this writing, in 1904.

ALEXANDER BERTRAND

Alexander Bertrand is superintendent of the Lawrence County poor farm at Deadwood. He was born in Bordeaux, France, October 18, 1855, a son of Marcell and Marcelle (Levis) Bertrand, the former a native of Bordeaux, while the latter was born in northern Italy. The father was a farmer by occupation and in the year 1864 he left France and with his family sailed for the new world, making his way to Montreal, Canada. He conducted a farm on the Ottawa river near Point Fortune to the time of his death, which occurred in 1893. For a number of years, he had survived his wife, who died in 1880.

Alexander Bertrand was brought to America at the age of nine years and was reared upon the home farm to the age of fourteen years, when he left the parental roof and began steam boating on the St. Lawrence River, being connected with the steward's department. He worked there for three summers and then went to Michigan, operating a blacksmith shop in partnership with an old friend, Mr. Bouillian. On leaving that state in 1876 he went to Aspen, Colorado, where he engaged in prospecting for a short time, when with some companions he started on foot for the Black Hills of South Dakota. En route he remained at Cheyenne, Wyoming, for a year and a half and arrived in the Black Hills in the spring of 1879. He then secured employment as a cook in the old Merchants Hotel at Deadwood for a short time, after which he obtained a position in the Gilmore Hotel and in the fall of 1880 became proprietor of a boarding house in Blacktail Gulch, where he remained until 1882. He afterward conducted the Overland Hotel in Deadwood until 1883 and subsequently conducted a summer hotel at Hudson, Quebec, for two years. In 1885 he returned to the Black, Hills and became a cook in a restaurant at Lead for a year. He afterward conducted a restaurant in Galena, South Dakota, until 1890, when he entered the employ of Lawrence County as the jailer in Deadwood, remaining in that capacity until 1906, when he was appointed county superintendent of the poor farm. He has since occupied this position, covering a period of about nine years, and has made an excellent record in the office.

In 1905 Mr. Bertrand was married to Mrs. Mabel Lindscott, of Deadwood. He is a republican in his political views and is well known in fraternal connections, being a prominent Mason. He holds membership in Central City Lodge, No. 22, A. F. & A. M.; Dakota Chapter, No. 3, R, A. M.; Dakota Commandery, No. 1, K. T.; and Black Hills Consistory, No. 3, S. P. R. S., having thus attained the thirty-second degree of the Scottish Rite. He is likewise a member of Naja Temple of the Nobles of the Mystic Shrine at Deadwood and he belongs to Eureka Lodge, No. 3, 1. O. 0. F., of Deadwood. Starting out in life on his own account when but fourteen years of age, he has since been dependent entirely upon his own resources and has led a busy life, there being few idle hours in all the years that have since come and gone.

WILLIAM BERTOLERO

William Bertolero, of Lead, has by dint of intense and well directed activity and wise investment accumulated enough capital to enable him to devote almost his entire time to the management of his financial interests. He was born in the city of Borgiallo, province of Torino, Italy, in 1859. His parents, John and Veronica Bertolero, are both deceased, the mother passing away in Lead. The father was a laborer and was known as a steady and efficient worker.

William Bertolero attended school in his native land and at the age of thirteen years began working upon a railroad. He was employed on the famous tunnel between Como and Switzerland, packing tools for one year. At the age of fourteen he went to the island of Sardinia, where he was employed in the silver mines for four years, and next worked in the iron mines of France for a time. He also engaged in railroad work in France and was employed in the silver mines, spending in all about a year in that country. He then went to Algiers, in northern Africa, where he was engaged in railroad work but after four years was recalled to Italy to do military service. At the age of twenty-one years, he was mustered in, January 3, 1880, but on his way to the barracks his leg was broken and he spent six months in a hospital, being then discharged from the service because of physical disability due to the before mentioned accident. On the 2d of August, 1881, he sailed for America, and on the 21st of that month landed in New York City. He went to Collinsville, Illinois, where he was employed in the coal mines for some time. He worked in various mines in southern Illinois until February 25, 1883, when he removed to the Black Hills, arriving in Deadwood on the 3d of March, 1883. Three days later he became an employe of the Homestake Mining Company and remained connected with that concern for twenty-six years. In 1907 he was appointed Italian consul and held that office for four years, resigning in 1911. During the time that he was working in the Homestake Mine he and his wife conducted a boarding house but in 1912 discontinued it. He is now a director and vice president of the Miners & Merchants Bank of Lead and gives the greater part of his time to the supervision of his investments as by economy and careful management he has accumulated a considerable fortune. He is financially interested in several mining projects of a promising character and is one of the most prosperous residents of Lead. In 1900 he returned for a visit to his old home in Italy and again in 1912 visited his native land.

Mr. Bertolero was married in 1889 to Miss Rosa Caffaro, who was born in Italy, where her parents passed their entire lives. To Mr. and Mrs. Bertolero have been born two children: Leo, a resident of Lead; and John, who is a student in the State University of South Dakota.

Mr. Bertolero is a republican and has taken quite an active part in local politics although he has never been a candidate for office. His fraternal associations include membership in Lodge No. 747, B. P. O. E.; Universal Liberty Lodge, No. 342, A. F. & U. R., an Italian lodge, of which he is past master; Chapter No. 43, R. A. M., of Red Lodge, Montana; the local lodge of the Society of Christopher Columbus, being the first president of the local lodge; the encampment of Odd Fellows; the Knights of Pythias; and the Ancient Order of United Workmen. He is also a member of the Homestake Veterans Association, an organization composed of those who have been for many years in the service of the Homestake Mining Company. For some time, he was a volunteer fireman, belonging to Hose Company No. 2, and he has ever been willing to do anything within his power to increase the prosperity and add to the prestige of his adopted city. He is very progressive in his views and believes that the best is none too good and that the old order should give way to the new whenever it is apparent that a change would be conducive to real advancement.

ALBERT C. BIERNATZKI

Albert C. Biernatzki, a prominent and successful member of the bar of McCook County, being actively engaged in the practice of his profession in Salem, was born in Webster City, Iowa, on the 3d of December, 1860, being a son of Charles and Margaret (Noland) Biernatzki, the former of whom was born in Poland and the latter in Ireland. The father of our subject was reared to maturity in his native land, and secured his educational training in the military academy in St. Petersburg. He was thereafter commissioned a colonel in the Russian army, but as his mother was strenuously opposed to his continuing in the military service, he resigned his office and was appointed a member of the government engineering corps, with the rank of colonel. He became involved in the revolution of 1847, manifesting that distinctive loyalty which was one of his dominating characteristics, and his patriotism placed his life in jeopardy, so that in that year he left his native land and came to America, locating in Oswego, New York, where he became identified with the shipping trade, owning and operating two or more vessels. In 1857 he removed to Webster City, Iowa, where he engaged in farming and live-stock enterprises, becoming one of the prominent and influential citizens of that section and being signally prospered in his business operations. He died in 1899, at the venerable age of eighty-two years, honored by all who knew him and recognized as a man of fine intellectuality and sterling character. He was a stanch Republican, and while never ambitious for office he was an influential factor in the councils of his party. His wife is still living.

Albert C. Biernatzki secured his early educational discipline in the public schools of his native place and then entered the University of Des Moines, Iowa, where he continued his studies for two years, while in 1881 he was matriculated in the Iowa State University, at Iowa City, where he had simultaneously prosecuted a technical course in the law department of the university, in which he was graduated in 1884, with the degree of Bachelor of Laws. In March of the following year, he took up his residence in Salem, South Dakota, being one of the early members of the bar of the county, and here he has ever since been established in the active practice of his profession, having built up an excellent business and retaining a representative clientage, while he has high standing at the bar of the state. He continued to be a close and appreciative student, and is considered one of the best-read lawyers in this section. He is a stalwart advocate of the principles and policies of the Republican party, in whose cause he has been an effective worker, and he served as county judge from 1889, until 1903, with the exception of one term, his rulings being signally impartial, indicating not only the possession of an intrinsically judicial mind but also a wide and intimate knowledge of the science of jurisprudence.

The Judge is a member of Fortitude Lodge, No. 72, Free and Accepted Masons: Salem Chapter, No. 34, Royal Arch Masons; Constantine Commandery, No. 17, Knights Templar, and El Riad Temple of the Ancient Arabic Order of the Nobles of the Mystic Shrine, at Sioux Falls. On the 7th of June, 1887, was solemnized the marriage of Judge Biernatzki to Miss Emma Sibley, of State Center, Iowa, and they are the parents of one son and two daughters, Charles, Margaret and Helen.

JAMES E. BIRD

James E. Bird, conducting a real-estate, loan and insurance agency in Watertown, where he has made his home since the spring of 1901, was born in Iowa on the 18th of December, 1869, his parents being William and Mary Bird, the former a farmer by occupation. Having mastered the branches of learning taught in the public schools, he assisted his father for a time, then took up the profession of teaching, which he followed for three years, afterwards holding a position with a general mercantile establishment at Marcus, Iowa, and at the outbreak of the war with Spain he joined the army as a member of Company M, Fifty-second Iowa Volunteer Infantry, and served for eight months. Upon his return to his native state, he engaged in the implement business at Sibley, Iowa. In the spring of 1901 he arrived in Watertown, where he engaged in the real-estate business, first in partnership with Keogan & Bird, but for the past eight years he has been alone, conducting an important real-estate, loan and insurance agency. He is well known in this connection and has handled many important realty transfers. His business interests are carefully managed and his indefatigable energy and ability have gained for him a creditable measure of success.

In September, 1906, Mr. Bird was united in marriage to Addie I. Brooks, a daughter of Jacob Brooks, a representative of an old-time family of Sibley, Iowa. Mr. Bird has membership relations with Masonic and Elk lodges in Watertown, and he gives his political allegiance to the democratic party. That he is one of its leaders in South Dakota is indicated in the fact that in the 1914 election he was its candidate for the office of secretary of state. He is fond of athletics, including baseball and tennis and along those lines seeks his recreation. His wife is active in work connected with charity organizations and is chairman of the relief committee of the Sunshine Society of Watertown. After being a student at Cornell College of Iowa, she engaged in teaching, and all through her life has been a student not only of books but of people and events, learning many valuable lessons from life. Her interests are broad and her helpful spirit is manifest in most practical aid.

SAMUEL CROCKETT BLACK

S. C. BLACK, secretary of the South Dakota & Iowa Land & Loan Company, with headquarters in Mellette, was born on a farm in Champaign County, Ohio, on the 23d of September, 1849, and is a scion of one of the old and honored families of the Buckeye state, where his grandfather, Alexander H. Black, who was a native of Kentucky and of Scotch lineage, took up his residence in 1809, taking part in the early Indian wars and serving as captain of a company in the command of General Wayne, known to history as "Mad Anthony Wayne," by reason of his intrepid daring. In this connection Captain Black accompanied his doughty general on the march to the lakes and saw not a little of active service in conflict with the Indians. He became possessed of a large tract of land in Champaign County, and there passed the closing years of his life, while his son Samuel C. Sr., the father of the subject, also lived on this ancestral homestead and became a prominent and influential farmer and stock grower. He likewise was a native of Kentucky and died in Ohio, as did also his devoted wife, whose maiden name was Mary Ann Grant. They became the parents of nine children, while of the number five are living at the time of this writing.

Mr. Black was reared on the home farm and received his early educational training in the common schools, after which he continued his studies in Wittemberg College, in Springfield, Ohio. He then resumed his association with agricultural pursuits, and also took up the study of medicine, to which he devoted his attention for a short time. After the death of his father, he took charge of the homestead farm and in connection with its operation also continued to deal in livestock until 1882, when he came to the present state of South Dakota and purchased land in Spink County, where he became the owner of three-quarter sections of land eleven and a half miles northeast of Mellette. He removed his family to South Dakota in 1886, and there continued to be engaged in farming and stock growing until 1898, when he took up his residence in Mellette and turned his attention to the handling of grain and livestock, with which important line of enterprise he has since been prominently identified, controlling a large business, while in 1902 he associated himself with the South Dakota & Iowa Land & Loan Company, with headquarters in Mellette, and he has since been secretary of said company, which controls a large real-estate and loan business throughout North and South Dakota. He served for two terms as mayor of Mellette, giving a most satisfactory administration of municipal affairs.

He has passed the commandery, Scottish Rite and Shrine degrees in the Masonic fraternity, being secretary of his lodge at the time of this writing. He is also a member of the Ancient Order of United Workmen. On the 18th of March, 1884, was solemnized the marriage of Mr. Black to Miss Frances Miller, who was born and reared in Ohio, and they have two daughters, Jessie, who is a graduate of the Holy Angels Academy, in Minneapolis, and Lola.

THOMAS C. BLAIR

Thomas C. BLAIR, of Keystone, is a native of Nova Scotia, born on June 5, 1854, and the son of Duncan B. and Mary (McLean) Blair, who were born and reared in Scotland. The father was a Presbyterian clergyman at Pictou. Nova Scotia, and there the son grew to manhood and received his education. When he was sixteen years of age he went into a mercantile house as a salesman and bookkeeper, continuing so employed until the spring of 1879, when he started for the Black Hills. After a long drawn-out and tedious journey, he reached Deadwood in July of that year and soon afterward removed to Terry, where he worked in the mines until the spring of 1880. He then located at Rockerville and engaged in placer mining for a year, after which he took up his residence at Keystone as it is now, and helped to construct the Harney hydraulic flume, which was then building. Since then, he has been continuously occupied in prospecting and mining in this section, and has discovered several famous mines. He was one of the locators of the old Keystone mine, his partners in this being William B. Franklin and Jacob S. Reed. They located the mine in 1890 and sold it to the Keystone Mining Company in 1892. That same year the town of Keystone was started, Mr. Blair being one of its founders, owning a considerable portion of the land on which it is built. He is also one of the original locators of the Holy Terror mine, William Franklin. J. A. Fayel and A. L. Ausbury being associated with him in this. They located this property in 1894 and before the end of the year they built a five-stamp mill on it, which they operated until May, 1895, when they sold the whole property to eastern capitalists who formed and incorporated the Holy Terror Mining Company, which has since then absorbed all the Keystone properties. From that time to the present Mr. Blair has been prospecting most of the time and has located several good claims.

He is a zealous Freemason, being one of the founders and a charter member of the lodge at Keystone. On January 30, 1884, at Rapid City. Mr. Blair was united in marriage with Miss Anna L. Reed, a native of Pennsylvania, who died on May 17, 1896, leaving four children, Etta B., Alice, Grace and Mary S.

CHARLES A. BLAKE

Charles A. BLAKE, register of the United States land office at Huron, is a native of Port Washington, Wisconsin, where he was born August 20, 1854. He is the son of Barnum and Christine Blake. He was educated in the Port Washington common schools, attended the Racine College and graduated from the academy at Winnetka, Illinois, and from Drew's Business College. He was a partner in the People's Bank of Chicago and also engaged in the coal business until 1878, when he became the Chicago correspondent of the New York Commercial Review, continuing in this position until he came to Dakota in 1882 and located at Wessington in the real-estate and insurance business. In 1890 he purchased the Wessington Times, which he still conducts. In 1898 he was appointed by President McKinley to his present position. Mr. Blake was always a Republican and has been prominent in party affairs during his long residence in South Dakota.

He is a prominent Mason, belonging to the commandery and the Shrine, and is also a member of the Huron lodge of the Benevolent and Protective Order of Elks. Mr. Blake was married, December 16, 1884, to Miss Minnie M. Barnes. They have four children, all excellent students in the Huron schools, George B., Ambrose B., Elma B. and Nellie M. The prominence which Mr. Blake has attained in the community is but a recognition of his integrity, ability and public spirit.

GEORGE W. BLISS, M. D.

Dr. George W. Bliss, a well-known physician and surgeon of Valley Springs, South Dakota, has there followed his profession continuously for almost two decades and is widely recognized as one of the successful practitioners of Minnehaha County. His birth occurred in Cambria, Wisconsin, on the 27th of March, 1868, his parents being John and Emily (Hodkinson) Bliss, the former a native of New York City and the latter of Staffordshire, England. Emily Hodkinson came to the United States when a child of seven years in company with her parents, who were among the pioneer settlers of Wisconsin. John Bliss removed to the Badger state as a lad of twelve years, the paternal grandparents of our subject being also numbered among the early residents of Columbia County, Wisconsin. There he grew to manhood, was married and located on a farm. In 1880 he came west to Dakota territory, settling in Minnehaha County and purchasing a farm six miles north of Sioux Falls. On that place both he and his wife spent the remainder of their lives, Mr. Bliss passing away in 1906, at the age of sixty-three years, and Mrs. Bliss in 1912, when she had attained the age of seventy. They were well known and highly esteemed as people of genuine personal worth and gained many friends during the long period of their residence in the community. The old home farm is still in the possession of the family.

George W. Bliss was reared at home and began his education in the district schools, while subsequently he attended Sioux Falls College, where he completed a philosophical course by graduation in 1890. After finishing his more specifically literary education he made further preparation for a professional career by taking up the study of medicine under the preceptorship of Drs. Brown and Tufts, of Sioux Falls, and in the fall of 1892, he entered the College of Physicians & Surgeons of Minneapolis, Minnesota, from which institution he was graduated with the class of 1895. Subsequently he served for six months as house physician in the Minneapolis City Hospital and in the fall of 1895 located for practice at Valley Springs, which is a half mile from the Minnesota state line and five miles from the Iowa state line. He took the examination before these state boards and is registered to practice in South Dakota, Minnesota and Iowa. Dr. Bliss has been very successful and has built up an extensive and remunerative practice. He is a member of the Seventh District Medical Society of South Dakota, a charter member of the Sioux Valley Medical Society, an honorary member of the Southwestern Minnesota Medical Society, a member of the South Dakota State Medical Society and a fellow of the American Medical Association.

On the 24th of March, 1897, Dr. Bliss was united in marriage to Miss Lucy E. Udell, of Sioux Falls, by whom he has a daughter, Rowena Udell. Fraternally he is identified with the following organizations: Unity Lodge, No. 130, A. F. & A. M., of Sioux Falls, enjoying the distinction of being the first candidate ever raised in that lodge; Occidental Consistory, No. 2, A. & A. S. R.; El Riad Temple, A. A. O. N. M. S., of Sioux Falls; Crystal Lodge, No. 29, K. P., of Valley Springs; the Modern Woodmen; and Sioux Falls Lodge, No. 503, Loyal Order of Moose. Few men conform their practice so closely to a high standard of professional ethics and there are few who enjoy in greater degree the confidence and respect of both their fellow practitioners and the general public.

EARL V. BOBB, M. D.

E. V. BOBB, was born August 2, 1873, in Richland, Wisconsin, and is the son of Martin L. and Mary (Wailing) Bobb, the father a native of Pennsylvania, the mother of Wisconsin. Martin Bobb came to Dakota a number of years ago and settled in Davison County, with the public affairs of which part of the state he became quite actively identified; he served six years as clerk of the county court, took a prominent part in advancing the material interests of his community, and was a man of intelligence and wide influence and withal a most excellent and praiseworthy citizen. As a leader of the Republican party, he became prominent in state as well as in local affairs and in the private walks of life enjoyed the esteem of all classes. He died in Davison County, in October, 1902, at the age of sixty years, leaving to mourn his loss a widow, who is still living, and six children of whom the subject of this review is the second in order of birth. Dr. B. A. Bobb, the oldest of the sons of Martin and Mary Bobb, is a distinguished physician of South Dakota, practicing his profession in the city of Mitchell and at the present time he is president of the State Medical Association.

Dr. Earl V. Bobb was about nine years old when his parents moved from Wisconsin to South Dakota and since 1882 his life has been closely identified with the latter state. After attending the public schools for some years, he entered the University of South Dakota, where he finished his literary education, and then became a student of the Northwestern University at Evanston, from the medical department of which he was graduated with high honors in 1899. Preparatory to the general practice of his profession, the Doctor did a large amount of hospital work under the direction of some of the most distinguished medical talent of the day, after which he opened an office in Sisseton, South Dakota, where he has since built up a very extensive professional business, commanding at this time a patronage second in magnitude and importance to that of no other physician in the city or county.

Dr. Robb prepared himself for his life work by careful study and critical research, and being a close student, he keeps in touch with the trend of modern professional thought, is familiar with the latest investigations and discoveries in the profession and possesses the discernment and tact to select what is most valuable of this knowledge and use it in his practice.

In addition to his professional labors, Dr. Robb since coming west, has been actively identified with the public and business affairs of Sisseton and Roberts counties, and at the present time is holding the office of coroner. He is stanchly Republican in his political views, manifests a deep and abiding interest in his party and has contributed not a little to its success in the county, district and state. In the fall of 1902 Dr. Bobb purchased the leading drug store in Sisseton and is now conducting the same in connection with his practice and doing a very lucrative business. He is a member of the State Medical Society, the Aberdeen District Medical Society, and other organizations whose object is to promote a higher standard of efficiency in the medical ranks of South Dakota.

He is also interested in secret fraternal and benevolent work, belonging to the Masonic lodge at Sisseton and the Knights of Pythias, in both of which orders he is recognized as an influential member and a zealous worker.

On September 25, 1900, Dr. Bobb and Miss Elizabeth Morton, of Chicago, Illinois, daughter of John Morton, of that city, were united in the bonds of wedlock. Dr. and Mrs. Bobbs have a beautiful and attractive home in Sisseton which is well known to the best society circles of the city, and both are popular with the people and have many warm friends and admirers, here and elsewhere.

JOHN R. BONNER

J. R. BONNER, who has a well-improved and valuable farm of three hundred and twenty acres, eligibly located five miles northeast of Pierpont, Day County, was born on a farm in DuPage County, Illinois, on the 13th of August, 1859, the old homestead being within sight of the city of Chicago. He is a son of Charles and Sarah (Rooke) Bonner, both of whom were born and reared in Lincolnshire, England, while their marriage was solemnized in March, 1855. Upon coming to America Charles Bonner settled in DuPage County, Illinois, being numbered among its pioneer farmers, and there he continued to resides until 1884, when he removed to Remington, Indiana, where he and his devoted wife now maintain their home, being venerable in years, but in excellent health and spirits. They became the parents of eight children, of whom five are living, the subject of this sketch having been the third in order of birth.

John R. Bonner was reared on the old homestead farm and early became inured to the labors involved in the cultivation, while in the connection he gained that intimate knowledge of the practical details of the great basic art of agriculture which has so signally conserved his success in the line during the years of his residence in South Dakota. He initiated his independent career in 1881, having received his educational training in the public schools of his native county. He there remained two years subsequently to starting out for himself, and then, in 1883, came as a pioneer to the present state of South Dakota, where he secured homestead and tree claims, the two constituting his present fine farm, which has been his home during the long intervening years, within which he has contributed his share to the work of developing the county and its resources, taking a proper interest in public affairs and ever standing ready to do his part in pushing forward the work of progress and material and social advancement, while his efforts have been so ably directed that he has not been denied a full measure of success. His farm is improved with good buildings and practically the entire tract is under cultivation, yielding large crops of wheat and other grains. Mr. Bonner has not had a crop failure in the past twenty years, and the productive integrity of the soil of his farm seems not in the least impaired. He has an excellent supply of water on the place and in addition to diversified agriculture makes somewhat of a specialty of raising an excellent grade of swine. He is a stanch adherent of the Republican party and has served in the various township offices, having been chosen to such preferment soon after locating in the county.

Fraternally he is a master Mason and identified with the Ancient Order of United Workmen and the Knights of the Maccabees. On the 14th of September, 1889, Mr. Bonner led to the hymeneal alter Miss Stella Burt, who was born in the state of Michigan, and who has proved a devout wife and helpmeet. They have five children, James, Sarah, Joseph, Susan and Helen.

JOSEPH H. BOTTUM

Joseph H. BOTTUM, state senator from Faulk County, comes of sterling old colonial stock in both the paternal and maternal lines and both families are of stanch English extraction. Records extant show that two of the maternal ancestors were valiant soldiers in the Continental line during the war of the Revolution, having been participants in the historic battle of Bunker Hill. The original patronymic in the agnatic line was Longbottom, the initial syllable having been dropped after the establishment of the family in America.

The subject of this sketch is a native of the Empire state, having been born in West Bloomfield, Ontario County, New York, on the 26th of September, 1853, and being of the eldest of the eight children of Henry

C. and Helen M. (Burnham) Bottum, both of whom were born and reared in Vermont, as was also the paternal grandfather of our subject. Roswell Bottum, who was a man of prominence and influence in the old Green Mountain state, having served for a number of terms as a member of its legislature and also held other offices of distinctive public trust and responsibility. The original American progenitors settled in the Massachusetts colony and the name has been long and honorably identified with the annals of New England. As a young man the father of the subject removed to the state of New York, locating in Ontario County, where he was engaged in the mercantile business until 1854, when he came west to Wisconsin, settling in Fond du Lac County, and became one of the pioneers of that section. He was prospered in his efforts and developed a large and valuable farm, which he still owns. He has always taken a prominent part in the politics of the county and state and was for three years a member of the Wisconsin legislature. He has attained the age of nearly eighty years and is admirably preserved in mind and body, while he is honored as one of the venerable pioneers of the Badger state.

Joseph H. Bottum passed his boyhood days on the homestead farm in Wisconsin, having been an infant in arms at the time of his parent's removal to that state, and his early educational discipline was secured in the public schools, after which he completed a course of study in Ripon College, in the town of that name, being there graduated as a member of the class of 1877 with the degree of Bachelor of Science. Shortly afterward he entered the law office of the firm of Shepherd & Shepherd, of Fond du Lac, the interested principals being leading members of the bar of Wisconsin, and under their able preceptorship he continued his technical study of the law until 1880. when he was duly admitted to the bar. He immediately came to what is now the state of South Dakota, locating in the city of Sioux Falls, where he remained until the spring of 1882, when he removed to Spink County, where he was engaged in newspaper work until March, 1883, when he located in the village of La Foon, five miles east of the present county seat, and was there engaged in the practice of his profession until January, 1887, when the railroad was completed through Faulkton, whereupon he removed to this point, where he has ever since been prominent in professional work and public and civic affairs, being one of the most successful members of the county bar and being held in the highest regard in the community, as is evident from the dignified official position which he has been called upon to fill, in the gift of the people. The county was organized in 1883, and Mr. Bottum had the distinction of being its first register of deeds, La Foon being then the county seat, while he served as state's attorney for the county from 1890 to 1894, inclusive, making an enviable record as a public prosecutor. In 1898 he was elected to represent his county in the state senate, serving during the sixth general assembly, and in 1902 he was again chosen for this responsible preferment, being a member of the assembly at the time of this writing and having gained a reputation as a conservative and conscientious legislator and as one thoroughly devoted to the interests of the people of the state.

Fraternally he is a Royal Arch Mason, and is also identified with the Knights of Pythias and the Ancient Order of United Workmen. Senator Bottum has taken a deep interest in local affairs, particularly in the cause of popular education, and at the present time he is president of the board of education. In June, 1885, Senator Bottum was united in marriage to Miss Sylvia G. Smith, who was born and reared in Missouri, and who is a daughter of Judge Darius S. Smith. Of this union have been born seven children, namely: Nellie, Fannie, Dora, Emily, Julia, Roswell and Joseph H.. Both parents are members of the Congregational church.

ROSWELL BOTTUM

Roswell BOTTUM, one of the leading real-estate men of Aberdeen, was born in Fond du Lac County, Wisconsin, on the 3d day of August, 1857. He spent his boyhood and youth in his native state and attended for a number of years the public schools, supplementing the training thus received by a course in Ripon College. Leaving that institution, he engaged in teaching, which profession he followed in Wisconsin for a period of three years, and at the expiration of that time came to South Dakota, locating in Spink County in 1879, and took up a homestead near the town of Redfield. When that county was set apart as an independent jurisdiction, Mr. Bottum took an active part in its organization, which being affected, he was appointed county treasurer, holding the office one term. He discharged his official functions in an eminently satisfactory manner, in addition to which he also exercised a potent influence in shaping county affairs generally, the meanwhile devoting all of his leisure to the improvement of his homestead, which increased greatly in value as the country became more thickly populated. After living on his place for about six years, he removed to Faulkton, Faulk County, where, in partnership with his brother. J. H. Bottum, he established the Citizens Bank, of which he was cashier during the four years of the institution's existence. Disposing of his interests in Faulkton, Mr. Bottum, in 1892, changed his residence to Watertown, where he was engaged in the real-estate business until 1896, when he found a larger and more favorable field in the city of Aberdeen. Since the latter year Mr. Bottum has built up a large and prosperous business, which includes the handling of all kinds of city and country real estate in many of the best counties of South Dakota, besides acting as agent for F. R. Clement, of Minneapolis, whose extensive landed interests in this state are subject to his management. He has consummated a number of large deals, for which liberal commissions were received, and his patronage has steadily grown, until in magnitude and importance his business now compares favorably with that of the most successful agencies of the kind in the state.

Mr. Bottum is a thirty-second-degree Scottish Rite Mason, and has been honored with a number of high official positions in the brotherhood; he is an active worker in the lodge at Aberdeen and like all true members of the mystic tie, endeavors to square his life and control his conduct according to its precepts. Mr. Bottum is a married man and the father of two children, a son, Frank, and a daughter by the name of Margaret. His wife was formerly Miss Alia A. Beardsley, of Redfield. South Dakota, and the ceremony by which her name was changed to the one she now so worthily wears took place in that town on the 23d of August, 1887.

ADELBERT H. BOWMAN, M. D.

Adelbert H. Bowman, one of the popular and able physicians and surgeons of the city of Deadwood, is a native of Rock County, Wisconsin, where he was born on the 27th of October, 1851, being a son of William P. and Charlotte L. (Boynton) Bowman, both of whom were born and reared in the state of New York, the former being a son of Thaddeus Bowman, who was born in Vermont, of old colonial stock, while the maternal grandfather of the Doctor was Ephraim Boynton, who was born in Massachusetts, being a descendant of one of the valiant minutemen of that state who gave so material service in the cause of independence during the war of the Revolution. This honored ancestor was Captain John Poynton, who was born in Rowley, Massachusetts, on the 8th of September, 1736, and he held the rank noted during his service in the Continental line. The original American progenitor in the line was John Boynton, who settled in Rowley, Massachustts, in 1638, and Captain John mentioned was of the fifth generation, having been a son of Joseph, who was a son of Joseph, who was a son of Ephraim, who was a son of the original settler in Rowley. The father of the Doctor manifested the same intrinsic patriotism and loyalty during the war of the Rebellion, in which he served as a member of the First Wisconsin Heavy Artillery during the latter part of the great civil conflict. In the spring of 1866, he removed with his family to Osage, Iowa, and he and his devoted wife now reside in Spencer, that state, where they celebrated their golden wedding in 1897, while both are well preserved in mental and physical vigor, the father, at the venerable age of eighty years, being still actively engaged in the mercantile business. Of their eleven children eight are still living, the subject of this sketch having been the third in order of birth.

Dr. Bowman received his early educational discipline in the public schools of Wisconsin, and was about fifteen years of age at the time of the family removal to Iowa, where he continued to attend the public schools until 1869, when he entered the Cedar Valley Seminary, at Osage, that state, where he pursued his studies during the winter months until 1872. Later he took up the study of medicine under Dr. McAlister, of Spencer, Iowa, and in 1876 entered the renowned Rush Medical College, in the city of Chicago, where he completed the prescribed course and was graduated on the 25th of February, 1879, receiving his well-earned degree of Doctor of Medicine and coming forth admirably equipped for the work of his chosen profession. He initiated his professional career in his home town of Spencer, Iowa, where he continued in successful practice until 1887, when he came to Deadwood, where he met with success from the start and where he now controls a large general practice as a physician and surgeon. The Doctor is a member of the American Medical Association, the Iowa State Medical Society, the South Dakota State Medical Society and the Black Hills Medical Association, of which he is president.

In politics the Doctor is arrayed as an intelligent and loyal supporter of the principles and policies of the Republican party and fraternally he is identified with Central City Lodge, No. 22, Ancient Free and Accepted Masons; Dakota Chapter, No. 3, Royal Arch Masons; Dakota Commandery. No. 1, Knights Templar; and Naja Temple, Ancient Arabic Order of the Nobles of the Mystic Shrine. At the time of the Spanish-American war the Doctor enlisted as assistant surgeon in the First South Dakota Volunteer Infantry, with which he served ten months in the Philippines, returning to his home in March, 1899. On the 16th of October, 1886, was solemnized the marriage of Dr. Bowman to Miss Ida Potter, who was born in West Springfield, Pennsylvania, being a daughter of Riley and Hulda (Austin) Potter, the former of whom was engaged in merchandizing at West Springfield at the time of his death, which occurred in 1884, while his wife passed away in 1900. Dr. and Mrs. Bowman are the parents of three children, namely: Laura L., Potter and Dorothy.

WILLIAM BENJAMIN BOSWELL

"Ben" Boswell is the editor and proprietor of the Hamlin County Republican of Castlewood and he has long been a leading factor in molding public thought and opinion in connection with affairs of vital significance in his part of the state. He was born in Menominee, Michigan, April 16, 1864, and is a son of Albert W. and Ellen (Hannan) Boswell, the former a native of New Hampshire and a representative of one of the old New England families, tracing his ancestry back to the Mayflower Pilgrims. The mother was born in Peterboro, Canada, and her parents were from Ulster, Ireland. Albert W. Boswell and Ellen Hannan were married in De Pere, Wisconsin, and settled in Menominee, Michigan, where the father was identified with the lumber industry for many years. In September, 1880, he came west to South Dakota on a tour of inspection and when on that trip took up a homestead of one hundred and sixty acres in Estelline township, Hamlin County. On his return to Michigan for his family he stopped off at Marshall, Minnesota, to buy one hundred and sixty acres of railroad land adjoining his homestead. The father and his son Ben took up their abode on the homestead in the spring of 1881 and kept bachelor's hall until the fall of 1882, when they were joined by the others of the family. Upon the farm which he there developed Mr. Boswell still remains and own his original holdings of three hundred and twenty acres.

Ben Boswell was reared under the parental roof and was a youth of seventeen years when he accompanied his father to South Dakota. He acquired his education in the high school of Menominee, Michigan, in the South Dakota State College at Brookings and in the Curtiss Business College at Minneapolis, Minnesota, and was thus well qualified for life's practical and responsible duties. He accompanied his father to this state on his trip of inspection in 1880 and again in the spring of 1881 returned with him and aided in making the initial improvements upon the home farm. He continued under the parental roof until 1893 but during that period, or in 1884, took up the vocation of teaching and for seven years was identified with educational work. He was the first teacher of the Bryant schools, which he helped to organize, continuing as an instructor there for three years, during which time he built up the school system to a high state of efficiency. In 1892 he was elected auditor of the county and served for two terms, retiring from the position as he had entered it — with the confidence and goodwill of all concerned. On the expiration of his second term in that office, in 1897, he purchased the Hamlin County Republican of Castlewood, which he has since published, and he is today a well-known figure in journalistic circles in his part of the state. The paper which he publishes is thoroughly up-to-date in its methods of securing and handling news and in its workmanship. In 1885 Mr. Boswell purchased a quarter section of land in Estelline township, which he still owns.

He has been active in the public life of the community along many lines. In 1890 he was a candidate for county superintendent of schools but owing to the populist landslide of that year he was defeated by nine votes. In 1900 he was elected county treasurer of Hamlin County, serving in that position for two terms, and in the fall of 1912, he was elected a member of the board of county commissioners, in which position he is now serving. There is perhaps no resident of the county to whom the public owes a greater debt of gratitude for efforts to promote the interests and improve the conditions of the schools. He has served for seventeen years as secretary of the board of education in Castlewood and has recently been elected for another three years' term. During these years he has worked indefatigably for higher education and better schools and has lived to see the fruition of his hopes and his aims. Today Castlewood has a twenty-five-thousand-dollar school building, with an approved full four years' high school course, which includes manual training and domestic science, each department being fully equipped, seven teachers being employed to care for the high-school work. Mr. Boswell was also president of the board of trustees of the town of Castlewood from 1901 until 1905 and again from 1909 until 1914.

On the 22d of June, 1892, Mr. Boswell was united in marriage to Miss Minnie E. Shepherd, of Brantford township, Hamlin County, South Dakota. To them have been born seven children, six of whom survive, namely: Edith Pearl, Ellen Mildred, Benjamin George, Theodore Roosevelt, Catherine Louise and Paul.

In addition to his home property in Castlewood, Mr. Boswell is the owner of a fruit ranch in the Bitter Root valley of Montana. He and his wife are members of the Presbyterian church and he is identified with the Masonic fraternity as a member of Sioux Valley Lodge, No. 125, A. F. & A. M., and of Watertown Chapter, No. 12, R. A. M. His life has indeed been a potent force for good in his section of the state. He has worked diligently and persistently to advance the public welfare and has ever used the columns of his paper to further the interests of the community wherein are involved the questions of civic advancement.

While his ideals have been high, his methods have been practical and he never gives up until his aim is accomplished.

DOWNER TENNY BRAMBLE

In every community there are men who can rightfully be termed the leaders in business in the sections in which they reside and to whose efforts the material advancement and prosperity of the district can be attributed; but there are few men who can be rightfully called the upbuilders of a great commonwealth. The press of South Dakota, however, unite in saying that but one or two other men did as much for Dakota in its territorial days as did Downer Tenny Bramble. He indeed left the impress of his individuality and ability for good upon the history of the state and no work of this character would be complete without extended reference to him.

Mr. Bramble was born in Hartland, Vermont, February 28, 1832, a son of Charles Francis and Matilda (Jackman) Bramble. He attended school in his native village and when but sixteen years of age left the home farm, going to Nashville, Tennessee, where he clerked in a drug store owned by his two elder brothers, Gilman and George Francis Bramble. At a later date he went to New Orleans in the employ of the same brothers and after clerking in the drug store he turned his attention to general merchandising, trading from a wagon with the Yankton Indians. It was in the year 1856 that he arrived in the northwest, when this vast stretch of territory was largely uninhabited save by the red men. He located at Ponca, Nebraska, on the Missouri river, but in 1859 removed to Yankton, South Dakota. About 1862 he built a small store building, hauling the lumber from Sioux City, but the roads were in such condition that he could bring only a small amount at one time. He also hauled the stock of goods, which he sold to the Indians or traded to them in Yankton. His business career was marked by struggle yet also by steady advance, and at all times, whether dealing with the representatives of the red race or the white, he was thoroughly honorable, reliable and upright. For twenty-five years his name stood at the head of the firm of Bramble, Miner & Company of Yankton and was known throughout the territory. As the years went by there was a great change in the character of his patrons as the district became more and more thickly settled with a population from the east. His business affairs were carefully conducted and in time prosperity came to reward his labors.

As the country became settled and there was opportunity for the establishment of other business interests, Mr. Bramble became a prominent factor in promoting the material development of city and county and in laying broad and deep the foundation upon which has been built the present progress and prosperity of the state. He became a stockholder in the First National Bank of Yankton, was president of the Excelsior Mill Company and held the ferry franchise permitting the operation of a ferry from Yankton to the Nebraska side of the Missouri river. He also organized, stocked and operated a freight line from Yankton through to all available points in the Black Hills the year following the massacre of General Custer and his troops. Four years afterward he opened another freighting line from eastern points through to Boise City and other points in Idaho and Montana. He was prominent in the work for the building of the Dakota Southern Railroad from Sioux City to Yankton. He seemed to readily recognize every possibility and took advantage of it and his efforts were of a character that ever contributed largely to the upbuilding and development of the state.

Mr. Bramble was a member of the first military organization formed for defense against the Indians at Yankton in 1862, and served until the need for defense was over and the company, under Captain Tripp, was honorably discharged and disbanded. Mr. Bramble was equally well known in political circles. Throughout his entire life he gave unfaltering allegiance to the democratic party and always worked faithfully for the furtherance of all true democratic principles, feeling that in the party platform were found the best elements of good government. In 1861 he became a member of the council of the first territorial legislature, served as a member of the council of the second legislature in 1862, was a member of the house of the sixth legislature in 1866 and a member of the council of the tenth legislature in 1873.

On the loth of January, 1865, at Yankton, Mr. Bramble was married to Miss Virginia L. Vanderhule, the second daughter of Jesse D. and Hannah Woodward (Wicks) Vanderhule. The family of Jesse D. Vanderhule found a home at Yankton in the early '60s and he was the first proprietor of an exclusive drug store in the territory. To Mr. and Mrs. Bramble were born two sons: Harry Jesse, who passed away and was laid to rest in the Fort William McKinley cemetery near Manila, Philippine Islands; and Frank Litchfield Bramble, now living in Watertown.

Mr. Bramble became a member of the Masonic fraternity in early life, was one of the nine original organizers of St. John's Lodge, No. I, at Yankton, in 1863, and was master of that lodge in 1867. He held membership in the Episcopal church and guided his life by its teachings. It would be impossible to overestimate the worth of his work. He was among those who blazed out the paths that others have since trod in the settlement of the territory and in the development of the state and his name will ever deserve to be honored as that of one of the empire builders in South Dakota.

CHRISTOPHER S. BRAKKE

Christopher S. Brakke, president of the Farmers State Bank at Flandreau, belongs to that class of self-educated and self-made men to whom opportunity has constituted the threshold of the door through which they have passed to success. It is true that his opportunities were only such as come to every individual, but he had the persistency of purpose to utilize them to the best advantage. His difficulties and obstacles seemed to serve rather as an impetus than a bar to prosperity, calling forth his latent energies, his determination and his ambition. Like many another now prominent citizen of South Dakota, Mr. Brakke claims Norway as the land of his nativity. He was born September 12, 1865, a son of Severt and Martha (Hopperstad) Brakke, who came to the United States in 1878, making their way direct to South Dakota, with Moody County as their destination. There the father secured a homestead, on which he resided to the time of the death of his wife in 1902, and since then he has lived with a daughter in Minnesota.

Christopher S. Brakke was a lad of thirteen years when the family came to the United States. Previously he had attended the public schools of his native country, but after reaching the new world it was necessary that he give his services to his father in the development of the farm, as did hundreds of other Norwegian boys. The family was in limited financial circumstances and it was incumbent that all the members of the household should put forth their best efforts toward the rapid development of a farm which would meet their needs. At a later date, however, Mr. Brakke was able to pursue a three months' course of study in the Sioux Falls (S. D.) Business College. He early became a wage earner, working for neighboring farmers when any employment could be secured. He continued at farm work until 1884 and then secured a position in a general store in Flandreau. The following ten years were devoted alternately to clerking, to grain buying and to farming. In the meantime, his worth and ability were recognized by his fellow townsmen and appreciation on their part was indicated in their generous support of him when he became a candidate for the office of county treasurer of Moody County in 1894. He was elected and by reelection served for almost three terms. Subsequently he established himself in the mercantile business in the small town of Airlie, just over the Minnesota state line, and there remained for five years in active connection with commercial pursuits. On the expiration of that period, he was offered and accepted the position of cashier of the Farmers Exchange Bank at Toronto, South Dakota, with which he was thus connected for three years.

In 1909 Mr. Brakke came to Flandreau and that year was one of the active spirits in the organization of the Flandreau Elevator Company, of which he was made manager. He wisely directed the interests of the new undertaking and continued in that capacity until 1911, when he organized the Farmers State Bank of Flandreau and was made its president. He then resigned the management of the elevator company to give his undivided attention to the newly organized financial institution. His efforts in this direction have been a most effective force in promoting its rapid growth. He is familiar with every phase of the banking business and is now in control of an institution which is of notable worth to the community. In addition to his bank stock and financial interests Mr. Brakke owns two hundred acres of the original homestead of the family, situated seven miles northeast of Flandreau.

On the 25th of October, 1892, Mr. Brakke was married to Miss Minnie Berge, of Flandreau, a native of Iowa, and to this marriage three daughters have been born, Esther L., Gladys V. and Ruby M. They are giving their children excellent educational opportunities and the first two are graduates of the Flandreau high School and are now attending Wesleyan College at Mitchell, South Dakota.

Politically Mr. Brakke is a democrat and his opinions carry weight in the local councils of his party, as is indicated in the fact that he is now secretary and treasurer of the democratic county central committee. He belongs to Flandreau Lodge, No. 11, F. & A. M.; to Orient Chapter, No. 19, R. A. M.; to the Modern Woodmen of America; and the Ancient Order of United Workmen. He is not only well known, but is favorably known and wherever he has gone he has made friends. The substantial traits of his character are many and he possesses in large measure those qualities which are most admired and commended in every land and clime.

FRANK LITCHFIELD BRAMBLE

Frank Litchfield Bramble, of Watertown, was one of the organizers of the Dakota Mutual Life Insurance Company and for the past seven years has been its secretary. He was born in Yankton, South Dakota, May 23, 1872, a son of Downer T. Bramble, a pioneer of Yankton and one of the first settlers of the territory. Extended mention of him and the great work which he has done for the state is made elsewhere in this work.

In the pursuit of his education Frank L. Bramble attended the public schools of Yankton and also Yankton College and in early life became a clerk in the post office at Watertown. Later he was otherwise connected with public office, serving for four years as county auditor of Codington County and for a year and a half as deputy public examiner. Later he was made public examiner for South Dakota, continuing in the position for two years and four months, and the knowledge which he gained of the insurance business during his incumbency in that office led to his cooperation in organizing the Dakota Mutual Life Insurance Company, which was formed August 22, 1906, and began writing business in May, 1907. This was reorganized as a stock company on the 26th of February, 1909, by John B. Hanten, Fred B. Smith, H. M. Finnerud, D. M. Bannister, John W. Martin and F. L. Bramble. The company was capitalized for two hundred thousand dollars and is now licensed to do business in the states of North and South Dakota and Minnesota. During the eight years of its organized existence the company has written and had in force on January 1, 1915, eight million, six hundred thousand, thirty dollars of business, with an asset of nine hundred and fifty-six thousand dollars. The growth of the company has been very marked in the face of as strong competition as any company ever had to contend with. The officers of the company are with one exception the same as those originally elected. The company writes participating and non-participating business and will in all probability write only non-participating business after January 1, 1916. Throughout the existence of the company Mr. Bramble has been secretary and has contributed much to the success of the business through his thorough understanding of insurance conditions, through his close application and systematic methods.

On the 12th of January, 1903, in Minneapolis, occurred the marriage of Mr. Bramble and Miss Dana Lewis, a daughter of Elmer Lewis, a pioneer of Roscoe, Edmunds County, South Dakota. They have one child, Jeanette, who was born February 8, 1912.

The parents hold membership in the Episcopal church and Mr. Bramble is identified with various fraternal and club interests, belonging to Watertown Lodge, No. 13, A. F. & A. M., of which he was treasurer for three years: Watertown, Chapter, No. 12, R. A. M.; Watertown Council, No. 7, R & S. M.; and Watertown Commandery, No. 7, K. T., of which he was recorder in 1912. He also holds membership in Oriental Consistory No. 1, Yankton, and El Riad Shrine, Sioux Falls. He was the secretary of Watertown Lodge, No. 291, U. C. T., from 1903 until 1909, inclusive; was secretary of Watertown Lodge, No. 838, B. P. O. E., throughout the same period; and in 1910 became exalted ruler of the Elks. He is likewise a member of the Watertown Country Club and of Sioux Falls Chapter of the Sons of the American Revolution. In politics he is a republican of the old school. At the present writing he is serving as a member of the board of education of Watertown. His military history covers three years' service with Company H, First Regiment, S. D. N. G., and six years with Troop C of the First Cavalry. Wide-awake and enterprising, thoroughly alert and energetic, he is in close touch with the leading movements of the times affecting the welfare of city and state, cooperating heartily in all plans and projects for the public good and thus carrying forward under present-day conditions and amidst present-day environments the work begun by his father in pioneer times.

CHRISTEN C. BRATRUD

Christen C. BRATRUD was born on a farm on Root prairie, Fillmore County, Minnesota, on the 27th of December, 1855, and was thus reared amid the scenes of pioneer life in that state, being a son of Ole C. and Ambjor Bratrud, the former of whom was born in Sigdal and the latter in Eggedal, Norway, from which fair Norseland they came to America and became pioneers of Fillmore County, Minnesota, where by industry and honesty the father attained a position of independence, becoming one of the successful and highly honored farmers of that section. The subject was reared on the homestead farm and early began to assist in its work, while his educational advantages were such as were afforded in the common schools of the locality and period. In 1883 he came to South Dakota and located in Estelline. Hamlin county, where he was engaged in the buying and shipping of grain for the ensuing four years. In the autumn of 1887 he removed to Bryant, in the same county, where he became identified with mercantile pursuits, having an interest in a general store. In the following year he effected the organization of the Merchants' Bank, of that place, and had the supervision of its affairs until 1893. In 1894 he closed out his interests in Bryant and came to Sioux Falls, where he has since been successfully engaged in the real-estate and loan business, his books at all times showing most desirable investments, particularly in choice lands in the southeastern part of the state and residence and business property in the city of Sioux Falls. He is a loyal citizen and takes an active interest in all that makes for the progress and material prosperity of the state of his adoption, the state in which he has attained success through his own well-directed efforts, while he has so ordered his life in all its relations as to merit and receive the unqualified esteem of his fellow men.

In politics he exercises his franchise in support of the Republican party and its principles; he is an appreciative member of the Masonic fraternity and both he and his wife are prominent and valued members of the Norwegian Evangelical Lutheran church in their home city. On the 20th of November, 1897, Mr. Bratrud was united in marriage to Miss Ellen Marie Strom, who was born in the beautiful old city of Christiania, Norway, on the 1st of January, 1873, being a daughter of Feodor and Elizabeth Strom.

GEORGE C. BRIGGS

G. C. BRIGGS, who is presiding with marked ability and distinction as judge of the court of Hand County, is a native of the old Granite state, having been born in Hinsdale, Cheshire County. New Hampshire, on the 15th of June, 1857, and being a son of Erastus and Sylvia (Chamberlain) Briggs, both representatives of old and honored families of New England, where was cradled so much of our national history. The father of the subject was a clergyman of the Baptist church, and was born in Michigan, whither his parents emigrated from New England, while his devoted wife was a native of New Hampshire.

Judge Briggs received his elementary education in the common schools of Vermont, and later continued his studies in Powers Institute, at Bernardston, Massachusetts, and the Kimball Union Academy, at Meriden, New Hampshire, in which latter institution he was graduated as a member of the class of 1877. He then began reading law in the office of his uncle, Benjamin F. Briggs, one of the leading members of the bar of the city of Boston, and completed his technical studies under the preceptorship of Hosea W. Brigham, of Whitingham, Vermont, being duly admitted to the bar of the old Green Mountain state in the year 1880. He was thereafter engaged in the practice of his profession at Whitingham, that state, for one year, and in August, 1883, he removed to Cropsey, McLean County, Illinois, where he was engaged in teaching in the public schools until April, 1884, when he came to Miller, South Dakota, where he has ever since been identified with the active work of his profession. He is thoroughly grounded in the science of jurisprudence and has marked facility in the proper application of his knowledge in the handling of cases coming before him. The Judge is a man of positive character and has never lacked the courage of his convictions, while his personality is such as to command to him the respect of even those who differ with him or even resent his adjudications of litigations in which they are involved. In politics he is a stalwart advocate of the principles and policies of the Republican party and has ever taken an active interest in public affairs. In 1898 he was elected county judge, and was chosen as his own successor in 1900 and again in 1902, so that he is now serving his third consecutive term on the bench, a fact which indicates the proper estimate placed upon his services. He also served for several years as justice of the peace and held other local offices.

He and his wife are prominent and valued members of the Baptist church, and fraternally he is identified with the Masonic order and the Ancient Order of United Workmen. On the 29th of September, 1886, Judge Briggs was united in marriage to Miss Gertrude S. Sherman, who was born and reared in Dover, Windham County, Vermont, being a daughter of Edwin F. and Sophia (Menifield) Sherman.

HIRAM ELLSWORTH BRISBINE

Hiram Ellsworth Brisbine, a merchant of Yankton and also identified as a stockholder or officer with other important business concerns, has throughout his entire life closely studied the possibilities of any situation and using his opportunities to good advantage, has made steady advancement. His course has never been actuated by the spirit of vaulting ambition but he has followed the path that favoring opportunity has pointed out and the simple weight of his character and ability has carried him into important relations.

A native of Wisconsin, Mr. Brisbine was born in Fremont, November 11, 1860, his parents being Thornton Whiteker and Mary Ann (Unkefer) Brisbine. The family comes of English origin and was established on American soil in the early part of the eighteenth century. Thornton W. Brisbine was born at New Lisbon, Ohio, on the 27th of November, 1821, and died on the 21st of June, 1911. Had he lived a few more months he would have reached the age of ninety years. At the time of the Civil War, he joined the army as a member of a Wisconsin cavalry regiment and served throughout the period of hostilities, participating in a number of hotly contested engagements. After the war he returned home but decided to again go to the south, thinking to make a location there. On the way, however, he met members of the pioneer families of Dakota of Judge G. C. Moody and Dr. Burleigh and they persuaded him to locate in Yankton. He listened to their counsel and arrived in that city on the 4th of August, 1866. From that time forward he remained a valued and honored resident of the northwest and his ability led to his early selection for public office. He served as judge of the probate court and also filled other county offices. Like most of the early settlers of the state he also took a claim, opening up the first farm which was developed west of Yankton. During his long residence there he enjoyed the esteem of the old settlers of Yankton County in a marked degree, for his life justly commanded the goodwill and confidence of all with whom he was brought in contact. His death was the occasion of deep and widespread regret, when on the 21st of June, 1911, he passed away. His wife, who was born at New Franklin, Ohio, in 1827, had departed this life long before, being called to the home beyond in 1889.

Mr. and Mrs. Thornton W. Brisbine were the parents of eight children, six sons and two daughters: Harvey, a veteran of the Civil war, who came to Yankton in 1866 and there died in 1874; J. Milton, who is in the treasury department at Washington, D. C; William Albert, who died in the Black Hills of South Dakota in 1902; Sarah A., the wife of Ben C. Ash, of Minneapolis; Thomas Moore, who is living retired at Artesian, South Dakota; Frank R., a resident of Minneapolis; Hiram Ellsworth; and Ada. B., the wife of George W. Greene, proprietor of the Landour Hotel of Minneapolis.

Hiram E. Brisbine was a little lad of six years when in 1866 the family came to the northwest. At that time Dennison was the terminus of the western railroads and from that point the family proceeded to Yankton with ox teams. That district today bears little resemblance to the region in which they settled almost a half century ago. All around was the wild, unbroken prairie and Yankton was the very outpost upon the western frontier. There were many hardships and privations to be borne and many difficulties to be encountered before the seeds of civilization had taken root and the settlers were able to secure the conveniences and advantages which they had enjoyed in the older east. They were of a class of men, however, who accomplish results because of determination and enterprise. Hiram E. Brisbine became a pupil in the public schools of Yankton and was graduated from the high school in June, 1878. He then became a dry-goods clerk at a salary of twelve dollars per month. Twelve years later he was being paid a salary of two thousand dollars per year. He speaks five languages, which he has acquired in thirty-six years spent behind the counters of Yankton's dry-goods stores. He entered the firm of Cox, Brisbine & Stone in 1890 but sold his interests in that firm in 1892 and a month later opened a new store in partnership with Ward L.

Stone. This relationship continued for five years, but Mr. Brisbine bought out his partner in 1897 and has since conducted the business independently, remaining at his present location, where he carries a large and well selected line of dry goods. His patronage is liberal and is well merited because he conforms his interests to a high standard of commercial ethics.

In 1884 Mr. Brisbine was married at Michigan City, Indiana, to Margaret Cowdin and they had two sons: Dawes E., an attorney practicing at Isabel, South Dakota; and Hiram C., at home. The Wife and mother died in 1897 and on the 21st of June, 1899, at Mitchell, South Dakota, Mr. Brisbine was married to Miss Mina C. Van Tassel, a daughter of Clarence H. Van Tassel, who for many years was United States internal revenue collector for Dakota territory. To Mr. and Mrs. Brisbine have been born three daughters, Margaret M., Evelyn and Catherine, all in Yankton with their parents.

The family attend the Congregational church and Mr. Brisbine belongs to the Yankton Commercial Club. He is also affiliated with the Elks and is a Mason of high degree, having been elected knight commander of the Court of Honor and thirty-third degree honorary by the supreme council of the Ancient and Accepted Scottish Rite at Washington, D. C.. His political allegiance is given to the republican party and in 1886-7 he was alderman of Yankton from the third ward, but he has no political ambitions and prefers to concentrate his energies upon his business affairs rather than seek public office. He is loyal to the best interests of city and state, however, and he makes a ready response when he is called upon to aid in any project for the public good.

N. J. BROCKMAN

N. J. BROCKMAN, vice-president and manager of the State Bank of Spencer, is a native of Germany, where he was born on the 26th of April, 1853, being a son of Claus and Aple (Stuhr) Brockman, both of whom passed their entire lives in Germany.

The subject of this review was reared to manhood in his native land and was given the advantages of a collegiate education. He came to America in 1871, with but little financial reinforcement, and located in the city of Davenport, Iowa, where he was variously employed for several months. He then went to Tama county, that state, where he was identified with agricultural pursuits until 1877, when he took up his residence in the town of Traer, Iowa, where he engaged in the mercantile business, in which he was very successful, there laying the foundation for the distinctive prosperity which he today enjoys. In 1881 he engaged in the same line of enterprise in Gradbrook, Iowa, where he remained two years, at the expiration of which he disposed of his interests there and engaged in the lumber trade at Kingsley, that state, also buying and shipping grain. There he continued to make his home until 1901, when he sold his prosperous business and removed to Sac City, Iowa, where he resided until January 1, 1903, when he became associated with M. D. Gates in the purchase of the State Bank of Spencer, South Dakota, Mr. Gates being made president of the corporation, while the subject assumed his present office of vice-president and general manager.

Mr. Brockman is a Republican in his political proclivities, while he and his wife are members of the German Lutheran church, and fraternally he is identified with the lodge, chapter and commandery of the Masonic order, and also with the Ancient Arabic Order of the Nobles of the Mystic Shrine. In 1883 Mr. Brockman was united in marriage to Miss Bertha E. Gebauer, of Lyons, Iowa. One son has been born of this union, Ray, who is now a student in the Iowa State Agricultural College, at Ames.

GEORGE HOLMES BRONTE

George Holmes Bronte, a capitalist and pioneer resident of Pierre, has been connected with the capital city for almost a third of a century, having taken up his abode there in 1882. England claims him as a native son, his birth having occurred in Yorkshire, December 18, 1851, his parents being Robert and Maria (Holmes) Bronte. The father, who was a saddlery and harness manufacturer, died when his son George H. was but a year and a half old. The latter attended the common schools of his native county and at the age of seventeen years ran away from home, taking passage to New Zealand, where he remained for about a year and a half at Christ Church. He later went to New South Wales, Australia, where through the succeeding three or four years he followed the business of a trader among the sheep camps. In 1874 he returned to England on a visit but again he heard and heeded the call of the west and the following year came to America, intending to cross the country on a return trip to Australia, thus completing a journey around the world. However, while visiting an aunt he formed the acquaintance of Miss Jennie E. Daubner, and this circumstance led to his becoming an American citizen. He sought the lady's hand in marriage and in October, 1875, the wedding ceremony was celebrated at the home of her parents, Joseph and Rebecca (Holmes) Daubner, of Brookfield, Wisconsin.

Not long afterward Mr. Bronte purchased a farm near Toledo, Ohio, where he resided until 1882, when he came to Dakota territory, locating at Pierre. The following year he returned to Ohio for his family. He began investing and dealing in city property and his keen sagacity was displayed in the success which attended his undertakings in that direction. His ability also led to his selection for various public offices, and he served as commissioner of streets, city marshal, justice of the peace and member of the board of education. In all of these different capacities he rendered valuable service and his effective efforts were seen in the city's progress and improvement. He was one of the most prominent and efficient workers in the entire campaign for the location of the capital at Pierre and to him no small credit is due for the fact that that city became the center of state government. He was one of the first to select the north side as a place in which to build a home and has lived to see this become the finest residence district of the city.

In 1893 he removed to Chicago, where he entered the real-estate business and later, he became interested in the manufacture and sale of duplicating machines. He was appointed western sales manager of the Neostyle Company, having the sales management for a large group of western states. In connection with his son, Loron H. Bronte, he became a large stockholder and was elected one of the directors of the South Side Savings Bank of Chicago. He is still interested to a considerable extent in real estate in that city, but in 1907 he retired from active business and returned to Pierre to reside permanently, devoting his time to the care of his various private interests.

In 1907 Mr. Bronte was called upon to mourn the loss of his wife, who passed away on the 17th of March, of that year, and their only son, Loron H., met a tragic death by drowning on the 17th of October, 1913. On the 1st of January, 1914, Mr. Bronte wedded Mrs. Florence J. Daubner, of Waukesha, Wisconsin. Mr. and Mrs. Bronte recently purchased a home in Pierre, beautifully located on the heights on the north side of the city.

Mr. Bronte belongs to Pierre Lodge, No. 27, A. F. & A. M.; to Pierre Chapter, No. 22, R. A. M., to which he demitted from Normal Park Chapter, No. 210, of Chicago; and Pierre Commandery, No. 21, K. T. Motoring and travel, both in America and abroad, constitute his chief recreation. Although largely deprived of educational advantages in his youth, extensive reading, travel and contact with the world have made him an exceptionally well-informed man with broad and enlightened views of life, its opportunities, possibilities and purposes. Industry, conservation of his resources, good business judgment and a close conformity to the highest ethics of commercial transactions have been the salient factors in his growing success and prosperity, while his individual worth has made him one of Pierre's most prominent citizens.

JOHN H. BROOKS

J. H. BROOKS, the popular and capable proprietor of the Commercial Hotel in Britton, Marshall County, comes of stanch old Quaker stock, the original American ancestors, in both the paternal and maternal lines, having first settled in Vermont, while later they removed to Pennsylvania, where the respective families have resided for several generations. The subject was born in York County, Pennsylvania, on the 11th of June, 1852, and was reared to manhood in the famous old Keystone state of the Union. His father, John Brooks, was born in that state, on the 1st of January, 1812, and there both he and his wife, whose maiden name was Eliza Harry, passed their entire lives, being persons of sterling character and ever commanding uniform respect and esteem. They became the parents of five children, of whom three are living, the subject of this review being the youngest. Mr. Brooks received his educational training in York, the capital of his native county, where he attended the public schools until he had attained the age of eighteen years. In 1870 he went to the city of Baltimore, Maryland, where he learned the machine-molder's trade, continuing his residence in the "Monument City" until 1875, when he removed to Ogle County, Illinois, where he remained for three years, engaged in farming and also teaching school for a time. He thence went to Wichita, Kansas, where he was engaged in the buying and selling of cattle about three years, making trips to Texas and other points for the purpose of securing stock for shipment. In 1881 he went to Pierce City, Missouri, where he remained until the spring of 1883, when he came to the present state of South Dakota and numbered himself among the pioneers of Marshall County. In May of that year, he filed entry on a pre-emption claim in the immediate vicinity of the present village of Newark, being one of the first settlers in that locality and remaining on his claim one year, duly perfecting his title. He also took up a homestead and a tree claim after proving on his original claim, and to the two latter tracts he proved title in 1886. In that year he engaged in the livery and draying business in Newark, successfully continuing operations in the line until 1893, when he was elected sheriff of the county and forthwith removed to Britton, the county seat, in the meanwhile disposing of his business interests in Newark. After the expiration of his official term, he engaged in farming and trading, thus continuing until November, 1899, when he purchased the Commercial Hotel, which he has since conducted most successfully, having doubled the capacity of the house and made it modern and attractive in all respects. The building is three stories in height and has forty sleeping rooms, while its appointments are first-class throughout and its cuisine exceptionally excellent. He spares no pains in catering to the wants of his patrons, and is ably seconded by his wife, both being genial and hospitable and having the esteem of all who know them. It may be stated at this point that Mrs. Brooks also has the distinction of being a pioneer of the county, having been the first woman to permanently settle in Newark township. In politics Mr. Brooks is a stalwart Republican, and has taken an active part in public affairs, though he has not held other important official preferment than that of sheriff, in which capacity he made a most creditable record.

He is a member of Benevolent Lodge, No. 98, Ancient Free and Accepted Masons. On the 21st of December, 1880, Mr. Brooks was united in marriage to Miss Adella Tarbert, who was born and reared in Maryland, as were also her parents, Andrew and Amelia Tarbert. Mr. and Mrs. Brooks have no children.

CHARLES A. BROWN, M. D.

C. A. BROWN, who is successfully engaged in the practice of his profession at Armour, Douglas County, was born on a farm in Tama county, Iowa, on the 22d of January, 1868, and is a son of George and Sarah (Phillips) Brown, both of whom were born and reared in the state of Pennsylvania, where they were married. Soon afterward they removed to Iowa, locating in Iowa City, and later removing to Tama county, where Mr. Brown took up a homestead claim, to whose improvement and cultivation he continued to devote his attention until the early eighties, when he retired from active labor, taking up his residence in Waterloo, that state, where he now maintains his home, giving a general supervision to his landed and capitalistic interests. He is a Republican in politics but is a stanch advocate of the prohibition of the liquor traffic, which result he believes must be accomplished through the interposition of one of the dominating political parties. He and his wife are zealous members of the Baptist church. Dr. Brown was reared on the homestead farm and after attending the district schools he entered the high school in Waterloo, where he was graduated. While still a student in the high school he began teaching, having been thus engaged three winter terms, and he simultaneously prosecuted his medical studies, under the preceptorship of Dr. A. L. Martin, of Clinton, Iowa, under who.sc direction he later continued to prosecute his technical study during his college vacations. In the autumn of 1888, the subject was matriculated in the medical department of the Iowa State University, at Iowa City, where he was graduated in the spring of 1891, receiving his coveted degree of Doctor of Medicine. For a few months after his graduation the Doctor was associated in practice with Dr. William Woodburn, of Spencer, Iowa, and he then established himself in practice at Lamont, that state, where he built up an excellent practice, remaining for a number of years. In January, 1898, he sold his practice in Spencer and came to Armour, South Dakota, and here he has gained prestige as one of the thoroughly skilled and discriminating members of his profession in the state. He is a stanch Republican in his political proclivities, and he is at the present time incumbent of the office of superintendent of the Douglas County board of health, according no nominal service but making it a point to insure the best possible sanitary conditions throughout his jurisdiction.

He is a member of Arcania Lodge. No. 91, Free and Accepted Masons; Armour Lodge, No. 25, Knights of Pythias, in whose affairs he takes a particularly active interest; Armour Camp, No. 2475, Modem Woodmen of America, and Armour Tent, No. 18, Knights of the Maccabees. He is medical examiner for the two lodges last mentioned and also for several of the old-line insurance companies having local representation. On the 19th of August, 1893, Dr. Brown was united in marriage to Miss Helen M. Stewart, of Lamont, Iowa, and they have four sons, George L., Charles E., Otho S. and Leland.

PROFESSOR GEORGE LINCOLN BROWN

Professor George Lincoln Brown, dean of the faculty and vice president of the South Dakota State College at Brookings, was born in Bates County, Missouri, January 25, 1869. His father, John Brown, was of Ohio parentage, while his mother, who bore the maiden name of Elizabeth Seavers, was a native of Illinois. The family numbered four sons, of whom George L. is the second. He was reared to farm life and his early education was acquired in a country school.

In 1884 he entered the preparatory department of the University of Missouri and after an irregular attendance was graduated in 1892 with the degree of Bachelor of Science. At the end of his junior year, he received the Rollins fellowship of fifty dollars, awarded to the best junior in the science course, and during his senior year he held a teaching fellowship in German. He returned to the same institution for post-graduate work in mathematics during the next two years, holding a teaching fellowship in mathematics and receiving the degree of Master of Science in Mathematics in 1893. Having been awarded a fellowship in mathematics in the Chicago University in 1894, he pursued post-graduate- work in that institution through the succeeding two years, completing the work for the degree of Doctor of Philosophy, which he holds from that institution. In the fall of 1896, he obtained a position as teacher of mathematics in the high school of Rock Island, Illinois, but resigned on the 1st of February, 1897, to accept the chair of mathematics in the South Dakota Agricultural College, which name has since been changed to the South Dakota State College of Agriculture and Mechanic Arts.

In the summer and fall of 1908, during the absence of the president, Professor Brown was acting president of that institution. He was made dean of the faculty in 1910 and was made vice president in 1913. Upon the transfer of President R. L. Slagle to the presidency of the South Dakota State University on the 1st of February, 1914, Professor Brown became acting president of the South Dakota State College, in which capacity he continued until August 1st of the same year, when President Ellwood C. Perisho took up the duties of that office.

In June, 1898, Professor Brown was married to Miss Winifred Geraldine Loucks, a daughter of H. L. Loucks, at that time a resident of Deuel County but now of Watertown, South Dakota. In April, 1908, Mrs. Brown passed away, leaving three children: Cecil Langford, aged fifteen years; Elizabeth Louise, aged twelve; and Florence Margaret, nine years of age. In 1910 Professor Brown was united in marriage to Anna York Loucks, and they have one child, a daughter, Winifred York Loucks.

Professor Brown is a member of Phi Beta Kappa, a college fraternity, whose membership is based upon scholarship. He is also a Mason, belonging to Brookings Lodge, A. F. & A. M., and to Brookings Chapter, No. 18, R. A. M. While a man of scholarly attainments, his ambition and opportunities carrying him beyond the point that many men have reached, there is nothing in him of the pedantic; on the contrary, he has that touch of human sympathy and interest which has enabled him to understand and inspire not only students but also those with whom he has come in contact in other relations. He exemplifies in his life the teachings of Masonry, recognizing the brotherhood of man.

HOMER B. BROWN

Homer B. Brown, filling the office of postmaster at Clark, was born in Morrison, Illinois, on the 27th of June, 1875, a son of Samuel N. and Mary (Baird) Brown, who with their family came to South Dakota, settling in Clark County, where the father secured a homestead. They experienced many of the hardships and privations of pioneer life while making an attempt to bring their land under cultivation, but as time passed on the labors of Mr. Brown wrought the desired change and his claim became a valuable farm property. In the early '80s he established a hardware store in Clark, but later turned over to his sons the active management of the business. Both he and his wife are still living upon the farm and have an extensive circle of warm friends throughout the community.

Homer B. Brown was educated in the public schools and made his initial step in the business world in connection with the hardware store of his father. He succeeded to the business in 1895 and was identified with it for about twenty years and became well known through his mercantile connections. In 1900 the business became Brown Brothers and Max R. Brown is now the active manager. In July, 1913, Homer B.

Brown was appointed postmaster of Clark by President Wilson for a term of four years and is the incumbent in the position.

Mr. Brown was united in marriage to Miss Loa Yeamans, daughter of Merton and Carrie Yeamans, of Clark, on the 6th of October, 1897, and they have become the parents of three children: Ralph, Katharine and Carolyn. Mr. and Mrs. Brown hold membership in the Congregational church and he is a popular member of several fraternal organizations, including the blue lodge of Masons, the Benevolent Protective Order of Elks and the Knights of Pythias. The political allegiance is given to the democratic party and he does everything in his power to promote its growth and ensure its success. Everything pertaining to South Dakota's welfare is of interest to him and he stands for progress and improvement along all lines. In Clark County he has a wide acquaintance and a circle of friends almost coextensive therewith.

JAMES M. BROWN

J. M. BROWN, judge of the county courts of McPherson County, comes of stanch old colonial stock, the genealogy in the paternal line showing that the family was founded in America in 1500. The ancestors were driven out of England during the persecution of those identified with the Society of Friends, or Quakers, and they filed to Holland and thence to America at the opening of the sixteenth century, as previously noted, the original settlement having been made either in New England or Rhode Island, while the name was for many generations more particularly identified with agricultural pursuits than any other vocation. Judge Brown was born on a farm in Oneida County, New York, on the 10th of January, 1861, and is a son of John and Hannah (Mitchell) Brown, both of whom were born and reared in that same county, and both of whom are now deceased. The paternal grandfather of the subject likewise bore the name of John, and he likewise was born in the state of New York, whither his father, Thomas J. Brown, removed from Rhode Island, the place of the latter's nativity. Thomas J. was an active participant in the war of the Revolution, and this implies that he must, in a sense, have deviated from the principles of his ancestral faith, since the Quakers are opposed to warfare. The father of our subject became a successful farmer of Oneida County, was public-spirited, his integrity was beyond question and he wielded no little influence in his community, having been called upon to serve in various county offices. In his family were two children, James M., the subject of this sketch, and Minnie B., a resident of Chicago, Illinois. The parents were consistent and devoted members of the Friends church.

Judge Brown received his early educational training in the public schools of his native county, and then entered Hamilton College, in the same county, in which famous old institution he continued his studies until his health became so impaired as to compel him to abandon his course and seek a change of climate. Accordingly, he went to the south, and at Galveston, Texas, in 1876, he joined the engineer department of the government and was identified with its field work for the ensuing six years, in various portions of the south and west. In 1883 he came to South Dakota and located in La Grace, Campbell County, where he remained three years, at the expiration of which he removed to Eureka, McPherson County, where he has since maintained his home, having been one of the early settlers of the town and having been closely identified with its material, civic and political development and progress. In the meanwhile, he had taken up the study of law and so thoroughly covered the field of jurisprudence as to secure admission to the bar of the territory of Dakota in 1887, while he has ever since continued to be identified with legal affairs in this section of the state, either as a general practitioner, public prosecutor or as judge. He was state's attorney of the county for several years, and has served on the bench of the county court for a total of three terms, though not absolutely in a consecutive way, while he is incumbent of this responsible office at the time of this writing and has made a record for fair and impartial rulings, based upon the law and evidence, so that he has had few reversals of his decisions by the higher tribunals. In 1901 he was appointed by Governor Herreid as one of the three code commissioners to revise and codify the laws of the state of South Dakota, the other two commissioners being Judge Bartlett Tripp and the late Judge Gideon C. Moody.

The Judge is a Knight Templar Mason and identified with the Order of the Eastern Star, the Knights of Pythias and the Modern Woodmen of America. On the 9th of January, 1895, Judge Brown was united in marriage to Miss Hattie A. Van Gorder, who was born and reared in Prairie du Guen, Wisconsin.

RICHARD F. BROWN, M. D.

Dr. Richard F. Brown, president of the Brown Drug Company of Sioux Falls and thus active in the management of one of the more important and extensive commercial enterprises of the northwest, was born in Seneca, Ohio, on the 9th of March, 1858, a son of Abram G. and Lucretia (Gray) Brown. In the public schools of Ohio, he pursued his education, and in 1879, when a young man of twenty-one years, entered the Starling Medical College at Columbus, that state. Upon his graduation with the class of 1882, he won his professional degree and in February of that year made his way westward to Dakota, settling at Plankinton, where he was successfully engaged in the general practice of medicine and surgery until 1891. He then removed to Sioux Falls and engaged in the retail drug business. In 1901 the wholesale drug house conducted under the name of the Brown Drug Company was organized with Dr. Brown as the president. The business met with splendid success and was developed along progressive lines, becoming the largest wholesale drug business in the state and one of the most important in the west. In May, 1913, their establishment was entirely destroyed by fire, but immediately a new structure was begun with the result that their present fireproof building is not only one of the city's finest commercial blocks, but is undoubtedly the finest building in point of modern equipment devoted to the wholesale drug trade in the west. Dr. Brown has demonstrated the fact that he possesses the unusual combination of successful medical practice with ability to manage with equal success important and extensive commercial interests.

In 1884 occurred the marriage of Dr. Richard F. Brown and Miss Minnesota Cook, who died December 8, 1893, leaving two children, Mary R. and Rush A. Dr. Brown is a republican in his political views. He is in hearty sympathy with the teachings and tenets of Masonry and has attained the Knight Templar degree of the York Rite. He also has membership with the Elks and is a member of the Minnehaha County Country Club, the Dacotah Club and the Commercial Club. He enjoys shooting, fishing, golf, motoring and all manly athletics and outdoor sports and his record proves the truth of the statement that almost equally important to working well is the ability to play well, thus maintaining an even balance in the physical and mental development.

SAMUEL AUGUSTINE BROWN, M. D. *

DR. SAMUEL A. BROWN

Samuel Augustine Brown, M. D., a graduate of Jefferson Medical College of Philadelphia, has since 1871 devoted his attention to the practice of medicine and surgery and is regarded as one of the ablest representatives of the profession in Sioux Falls. Moreover, he is prominent in Masonic and church circles and his life along many lines has been one of beneficence to those with whom he has come in contact.

He was born at North Cove, North Carolina, June 25, 1848, a son of John S. and Rebecca (Burnett) Brown. The family is of English lineage. The first representative of the name in America came from England with William Penn and the great-grandfather of Dr. Brown in the maternal line was killed at the battle of Kings Mountain.

After attending the public schools to the age of thirteen years, Dr. Brown received private instruction for four years and in 1867 entered upon the study of medicine at Marion, North Carolina. Two years later, or in 1869, he matriculated in Jefferson Medical College at Philadelphia and was graduated therefrom with the class of 1871. In that summer he pursued several special courses, after which he applied to the navy department at Washington for permission to appear before the board of examiners for the medical corps. This led to his appointment as assistant surgeon in the United States navy, with the relative rank of ensign. After a short service at the naval hospital in Norfolk, Virginia, he was detailed to the old sloop of war Marion. Congress had then decided to build no more war ships, being willing to grant money only for repairs. Under the designation "repairs" it was decided to make a new ship out of the Marion, which was notoriously unseaworthy but which, according to orders, must report at the navy yard at Kittery, Maine, which had been selected as the place where the new ship should be built. A crew of seasoned seamen and experienced naval officers was detailed to take the Marion to Kittery, but the officers as far as possible obtained a leave of absence and thus it was that Dr. Brown was detailed as surgeon. On the trip north the Marion encountered severe weather such as even a sailor seldom sees in the course of a lifetime, and it was only with the greatest difficulty that the ship was finally towed into Kittery. In the meantime, she had been given up as lost and Dr. Brown found his obituary with those of other officers on board in the New York Herald. Later he returned to Norfolk, made a cruise to Elizabeth City by way of the Dismal Swamp and was then ordered to the United States steamship Powhatan at Philadelphia, an old-time frigate with side-wheel paddle propellers, which after various needed repairs was sent to Norfolk to get the monitor Canonicus and tow her to Key West, Florida, to take the place of the Terror, which was ordered back for repairs. The Canonicus, however, was in such condition that it must be repaired before the trip could be made and in the meantime the Powhatan made trips to Kittery, Portland and other points. In early winter it was learned that the trip was to be made to Key West with the Canonicus as originally planned. Upon the return trip the retiring commander-in-chief of the North Atlantic station, Rear Admiral Joseph Greene, went aboard the Powhatan and his flag was raised to the mizzenmast head. Moreover, many sick soldiers from the hospital ship were sent to the north and upon Dr. Brown devolved the duty of acting as surgeon in the absence of his superior officer. There were sixty-five sick on board and this made life strenuous for him, as the report was supposed to be handed over to the captain by ten o'clock in the morning after a visit to every one who was ill.

There were many pleasurable events as well as hardships connected with the service, however. After a few weeks spent in port the Powhatan went to sea for drill and target practice and then to Halifax, Nova Scotia, where society entertained the officers. At the time the Countess of Dufferin, wife of the governor general, was sojourning in Canada, and Prince Louis of Battenberg was in port as a midshipman aboard the Royal Alfred, a British flagship. Dr. Brown had the distinguished pleasure of presenting Prince Louis to the wife of Captain Beaumont. After the return of the ship to New York the news was received of the threatened outbreak of war with Spain. The United States steamship Kansas was immediately put into commission and Dr. Brown found himself aboard as the only surgeon and caterer of the ward room mess. Experience was not called into play in loading the ship and order had not been brought out of chaos when the Kansas became enveloped in a hurricane so severe that she could neither steer her course by steam nor sail. To keep afloat she must run before the wind. This kept up for five days and nights before the storm abated and after a long time the vessel crept into Bermuda Islands. Then all on board wrote home, but the day before their letters reached their intended destination the obituaries of the officers had appeared, that of Dr. Brown a second time. In course of time the Kansas reached Santiago and anchored in the bay with guns loaded. She remained in tropical waters a part of the summer of 1873, making soundings and surveys on the south side of Haiti, but the sick list grew to such serious proportions that she was taken to Key West, Florida, and a large part of her crew was invalided home. On the 25th of September there was trouble in New Orleans and the Kansas was ordered to that city, but the trouble proved to be but a comparatively slight incident. The cruise of the Kansas was ended soon afterward and Dr. Brown spent a few days at home, being then assigned to duty at the Philadelphia Naval Hospital, which is situated in the grounds of the Naval Asylum where the superannuated seamen dwell. Therefore, among his patients were mariners who had been in the service from twenty to forty years and one or another had participated in most of the important naval events in American history. Promotion came and Dr. Brown was transferred to California, to the United States receiving ship Independence, at Mare Island. This was an ancient craft — a salting ship of the line — that had never been out of port since steam was discovered. It was used for recruiting and training enlisted men. When it was his turn to make a cruise Dr. Brown was detailed to the United States Flagship Pensacola, which was sent to South Pacific waters to care for American interests at the outbreak of the war between Chile on the one side and Peru and Bolivia on the other. The Pensacola was present at no battles, but lingered for some time in southern waters and after eighteen months cruising departed for the Sandwich islands, reaching Hilo, Hawaii, after a voyage of six weeks. These various cruises brought to Dr. Brown many interesting experiences. While in the Sandwich islands he saw the native women, garbed in a haloku, drop into the water above a cascade some forty feet in height, glide down the rock channel, shoot out into the air with the water, drop into the turbulent basin below, disappear for a time as if lost, to be seen at the edge of the pool again when one had given them up for drowned. He also saw the surf riding, where the native would go out a mile or two into the sea to ride back on the surf on a board a foot wide and eight feet in length, at first lying upon the board, then crouching and finally standing, and sometimes the surf rider would come in with the speed of a toboggan upon the steepest hillside. At Honolulu the officers on the Pensacola were royally entertained by members of the court, including the representatives of the reigning house, King Kalakaua, the Princess Likiliki and the Princess Liliuokilani, besides the chancellors, chamberlains and equerries in plenty. On leaving the Sandwich islands it was decided that the ship should pay a visit to Alaska, but a broken crank-shaft prevented this plan being carried out. Altogether, however, the experience of Dr. Brown in the navy enriched his life with pleasant and attractive memories never to be forgotten.

He continued in the navy until 1884, when he resigned and came to Sioux Falls, where he has now made his home for more than three decades. He at once entered upon the practice of medicine and surgery in this city and it was not long before his ability had established here a reputation which makes him one of the foremost physicians and surgeons of the city. He has ever been a close student of the profession, keeping abreast with the advancement of the times along medical lines, while his skill in surgery has its root in his comprehensive knowledge of the component parts of the human body, his thorough understanding of the onslaughts made by disease and his entire lack of a nervous condition in an emergency. It is in such a crisis that he seems to have the best mastery of himself, being thoroughly ready to meet the demand of the hour. A number of years ago he served as health officer of the city of Sioux Falls, also of Minnehaha County, South Dakota, and is now a member of the pension board.

In 1876 Dr. Brown was married in Portland, Maine, to Miss Clara K. Cross, who died in 1889, and in 1896 he wedded Miss Susan Ward, of Wayland, Massachusetts. Dr. Brown has no children of his own, but two nieces of his first wife have shared his home, while Charles R. Brown, aged seven years, and Elizabeth R. Brown, aged four, orphan children of his brother, Rev. John C. Brown, of North Carolina, came into his family in 1908.

In his religious faith Dr. Brown is an Episcopalian, active, earnest and helpful in the church work. He is now serving as senior warden of Calvary church and was for some years a member of its board of trustees and of the bishop's council of advice. His political allegiance is given to the democratic party, but he has never sought nor desired office outside Ihe strict path of his profession. He is a very prominent representative of Masonry, having taken all of the degrees of the York and Scottish Rites, while upon him has been conferred the honorary thirty-third degree. He was the real factor in founding Unity Lodge, F. & A. M., of Sioux Falls, which is now the largest in membership in the state, and he is recognized as the best posted man on Masonry in South Dakota. A Masonic publication has given his record as follows: "He commenced his Masonic career in Minnehaha Lodge No. 5 at Sioux Falls, being initiated February 14, 1887; passed March 10, 1887, and raised June 21, 1887. He received the capitular degrees in Sioux Falls Chapter No. 2, October 17, 23 and November 2 and 3, 1888; was made a member of Alpha Council No. 1, Royal and Select Masters, in 1891; became a member of the Order of High Priesthood June 16, 1898; was knighted in Cyrene Commandery No. 2, at Sioux Falls, December 14, 1888. He is a member of the Masonic Veterans Association. He has served in all of the offices of the subordinate bodies and as grand royal arch captain, grand principal sojourner and grand captain of the Host in the Grand Chapter, R. A. M., of South Dakota. In 1906 he was elected junior grand warden of the grand lodge, in 1907 senior grand warden, in 1908 deputy grand master and in 1909 most worshipful grand master. He is grand representative of the grand lodge of Ireland. He is a charter member of Occidental Consistory No. 2, A. A. S. R., at Sioux Falls and is its registrar, last October receiving the honorary degree at Washington of Knight Commander Court of Honor. He is also a member of El Riad Temple, A. A. O. N. M. S., at Sioux Falls. For ten years, up to the time of assuming the gavel of grand master, he was chairman of committee on foreign correspondence and his reports are among the best, exhibiting a thorough knowledge of Masonic history and subjects. He is versed in standard and current literature and has wielded a trenchant and ready pen; he has ever hewed to the line of his own inherent convictions of right, no matter on which side stood his confreres."

That Dr. Brown has the respect, honor and admiration of his fellow practitioners is indicated in the fact that he has been president of the Minnehaha County Medical Society and of its successor, the Seventh District Medical Society. He was also the first president of the Sioux Valley Medical Association and has been honored with the presidency of the South Dakota Medical Association. An excellent characterization has been given of him, as follows: "A man kind of heart, of a genial and lovable disposition, even in the most heated debate no one ever heard him speak an acrimonious word. Studious for the welfare of all enterprises in which he has been engaged, his life has been studded with results which make for the betterment of mankind in general."

HON. CHARLES HENRY BURKE

Hon. Charles Henry Burke, who as a member of the fifty-sixth, fifty-seventh, fifty-eighth, fifty-ninth, sixty-first, sixty-second and sixty-third congresses represented South Dakota in the national house of representatives for fourteen years, makes his home in Pierre, where he will later engage in active business. The Burke family of which he is a representative is of Norman origin and with the Butlers and Fitzgeralds is ranked with the most distinguished of the Norman Irish. The ancestor of the Irish Burkes was William Fitz-Aldelm-de-Burgo, who accompanied King Henry II to Ireland as his steward in 1171 A. D. The family was related by the ties of blood to that of William the Conqueror. Two of them, Robert de Burgo and his brother William, were with the Norman conqueror at the invasion of England, and the former was afterward created Earl of Cornwall. In the reign of King John the Burkes obtained large possessions in Connaught through rivalry and quarrels with the O'Connors. Becoming powerful, they subsequently renounced their allegiance to the kings of England and adopted the Irish language, dress and customs and compelled all other families of Norman origin in Connaught to do likewise. Two of them became Irish chiefs and settled in what is now embraced in the present County Mayo. Other branches settled in Limerick, Clare and Tipperary. Many members of the family attained distinction in military achievements, while others won fame along literary lines. Edmund Burke, "one of the greatest sons of men," was of this family. John Burke, the celebrated genealogist who established "Burke's Peerage," was also of this family. Thomas Burke, of Revolutionary war fame as a writer and patriot, was a native of Galway, Ireland, and became governor of North Carolina. Robert O'Hara Burke, the celebrated Australian explorer, was a native of Galway and also of this family. Joseph Burke, an uncle of Charles Henry Burke, acquired renown both in Europe and America as an actor and violinist and almost in his infancy was a histrionic and musical prodigy. He played in Great Britain and the United States before immense audiences, his ability being accounted the most astounding instance of precocious talent the musical world has ever known. Constant study and practice continually developed his talent and his standing as an artist is indicated in the fact that he was chosen to accompany Jenny Lind on her tour of the United States in 1850 in the role of violinist. He afterward became her treasurer and private secretary as well as her musical director. He was born in Galway, Ireland, in 1817, and died in Batavia, New York, in 1902.

Dr. Miles Burke, the grandfather of Charles H. Burke and a native of Galway, Ireland, was a physician and surgeon of wide repute who was graduated from a famous school of surgery of London, England, in 1809 and afterward practiced in Ireland for a number of years. He emigrated to America in 1830, taking up his abode in New York city, where he resided for a number of years. Subsequently he removed to Troy, New York, and finally to Canada, near Niagara Falls, where his demise occurred in 1845.

Walter Burke, his son and the father of Charles H. Burke, was also a native of County Galway, born November 10, 1820. He came to America in 1830 with his father. Following the death of his father he located, in 1846, in Genesee County, New York, purchasing and settling upon Summerville Farm, where he continued to live and carry-on agricultural pursuits the remainder of his life, passing away in 1911 at the venerable age of ninety-one years. He was married in 1856 to Miss Sarah T. Beckwith, who was born in Connecticut, October 17, 1828. While Mr. Burke is a representative of an old and noted Irish family on the paternal side, his ancestral record in the maternal line is traced back through the history of one of the prominent old New England families. The maternal grandfather of Mrs. Burke was Nathan Tinker, a Revolutionary soldier and pensioner, and her father, Josiah Beckwith, was a soldier in the War of 1812. Mrs. Burke, the mother of Charles H. Burke, was a school teacher in her younger days, being a lady of liberal education and wide culture. She died in 1907. Mr. and Mrs. Walter Burke became the parents of five children who lived to maturity, as follows: Catherine Elizabeth, who is the wife of C. J. Harris, of Genesee County, New York; Joseph W., residing on Summerville Farm, the old homestead in Genesee County, New York; Charles Henry, of this review; Lulu J., who is the wife of John G. Torrance, of Batavia, New York; and Grace, a resident of Batavia, New York.

Charles Henry Burke was born on Summerville Farm April 1, 1861, and there his boyhood days were passed, his early education being acquired in the rural schools of the neighborhood. At one period in his life, he drove five miles to and from school each day while doing the ordinary farm chores morning and evening. During the summer seasons he worked as other farm boys usually do, assisting more and more largely in the labors of the fields as his years increased until he was making a full "hand" upon the place. When he was still in his teens, he secured a teacher's certificate and taught for four months in the year, covering the winter season, while the remainder of his time was devoted to active farm work. Immediately after attaining his majority, on the 6th of May, 1882, he started for the west with capital only sufficient to take him to his destination — Moorhead, Minnesota. There he secured employment at the carpenter's trade in the midst of a building boom. He faced life with courage and determination and each day saw him farther advanced because of the good use he made of his time and opportunities and the lessons which he learned from experience. In the summer of the same year, he joined a former New York friend of about his own age in a mercantile venture at Broadland, Beadle County, South Dakota, and at the same time homesteaded. After a year he removed to Blunt, Hughes County, and in 1887 he became a resident of Pierre, where he has since made his home. When he took up his abode at Blunt in the spring of 1883 he entered into partnership with Caldwell & Smith, of Huron, in the land and real-estate business, and while negotiating property transfers, he devoted the hours which are usually termed leisure to the study of law and was admitted to the bar in 1886. He then entered upon active practice, which he followed in connection with the conduct of his real-estate business at Blunt until September, 1887, when he removed to Pierre and entered the employ of the Security Mortgage & Investment Company, in which connection advancement brought him to the position of manager. He continued in that capacity until he closed up the company's business and subsequently, he became a member of the law firm of Burke & Goodner of Pierre, which connection was dissolved when Mr. Burke was elected to congress.

Previous to his congressional experience, however, he took an active part in local and state affairs. In 1890 he was secretary of the Pierre capital committee, in which capacity he devoted eight months almost exclusively to campaign work, his labors proving most effective and winning him high appreciation. From the beginning of his public service, he has been very forceful in political circles and in 1894 was elected on the republican ticket to the state legislature, in which he served for two terms. His ability as a lawmaker was quickly recognized, for his course showed that he readily grasped the various phases of the different questions which came up for settlement and that in all of his legislative work he was actuated by a desire to further the public good.

Accordingly in 1898, appreciative of his worth in the general assembly, Mr. Burke was nominated by the republicans as a candidate for one of two congressmen at large and elected in November of the same year. During his first term in congress his course met the highest expectations of his constituents so well that in the three succeeding nominating conventions, in 1900, 1902 and 1904, he was nominated by acclamation and elected in each succeeding election. In 1906 he was defeated in convention but was again nominated in June, 1908, in a statewide primary and elected to the sixty-first congress, and reelected to the sixty second and sixty-third congresses. Mr. Burke's congressional career is one which reflects honor and credit upon the state which honored him, his service being most useful to his district, to his commonwealth and to the nation. During the sixty-first congress he was chairman of the important committee on Indian affairs, succeeding Vice President Sherman in that capacity, and during the sixty-second and sixty-third congresses he was the ranking minority member of that committee. He was also a member of the committee on interstate and foreign commerce in the fifty-eighth and fifty-ninth congresses, which committee had charge of the famous Hepburn rate bill. During the sixty-third congress he was the "republican whip," an indication of his standing among his colleagues. During the sixty-first congress he was chairman of the special committee that investigated the Gore charges in Oklahoma and he was a member during the sixty-third congress of the joint Indian commission from the house and senate, of which Senator Robinson was chairman, this commission having full investigating powers on all general Indian affairs. At the same time, he was a member of the special commission to- investigate and report on the Yakima Indian reservation irrigation project of Washington and the New Mexico Indian tubercular sanitarium, of which subject the commission made an exhaustive study and reported fully to congress. In 1913 Mr. Burke announced his retirement to private life, owing to three severe surgical operations which he had undergone. In January, 1914, in spite of Mr. Burke's firm opposition and without his sanction, his friends proposed him as a republican nominee for United States senatorial honors as the opponent of Senator Crawford, a representative of another faction of the republican party. Mr. Burke was nominated over Crawford in the primaries, carrying forty-one of the sixty-one counties, but was defeated at the general election of November, 1914, by the democratic candidate, Ed S. Johnson of Yankton.

On the 14th of January, 1886, Mr. Burke was united in marriage to Miss Caroline Schlosser, a native of Lodi, Wisconsin, by whom he has four children, as follows: Grace, who is the wife of Milton P. Goodner, of Seattle, Washington; Elizabeth, at home; Walter H., a resident of Chicago; and Josephine L., who was born in Washington, D. C, and is also at home.

Mr. Burke is now living retired temporarily save for the supervision which he gives to his personal property interests and investments. He is a director of the Pierre National Bank but otherwise is not before the public in any business connection. During territorial days he was a member of the militia of South Dakota. Fraternally he is identified with the following organizations: Pierre Lodge, No. 27, A. F. & A. M.; Pierre Chapter, No. 22, R. A. M.; Pierre Commandery, No. 21, K. T.; the Ancient Order of United Workmen; and the Benevolent Protective Order of Elks. The religious faith of Mr. Burke is that of the Episcopal church. He holds membership in Trinity church at Pierre, in which he is serving as vestryman and treasurer. He is most popular among his fellow townsmen and the sterling traits of his character are indicated by the fact that he is most highly esteemed where best known.

It would be an incomplete and unsatisfactory record of Charles H. Burke if there was no mention made of the opinions which have been expressed concerning him by his colleagues in public life, for it has been through his congressional service that he has become best known to the country. When it was known that he would retire from congress, in March, 1907, Hon. William P. Hepburn of Iowa, chairman of the committee on interstate and foreign commerce, appointed from that committee a committee which made the following report: "That the committee on interstate and foreign commerce, upon which the Honorable Charles H. Burke has served for two congresses, hereby express its sincere regrets that our colleague will no longer be a member of the house after March 4th next, and that his membership on this committee will end. It is the unanimous opinion of this committee, made known in regular committee meeting, at which every member was present, that by the retirement of Mr. Burke from the house this" committee loses an able and most efficient and faithful representative, one who at all times has devoted his time, ability and attention to the public business, and by his courtesy, kindness, and gentlemanly bearing, has endeared himself to all who knew him, but more particularly to the members of this committee." On the same occasion Mr. Hepburn said: "Your comrades on the committee are not willing that this connection should be terminated without many an expression as to their regrets, and they have deputed me to strive to express to you, in part, their feelings. You have been a member of the committee for many years. Your industry, your punctuality, the interest you have always shown when on the duties with which it has been charged, and the high order of ability you have brought to bear upon all questions it has considered, have marked you as one of its most valued members. These qualities could not have been exhibited as they have without doing something more than winning our respect. They call for our admiration, in largest measure our confidence. As a slight mark of our high appreciation of your personal and valued qualities, the committee have procured this service which I am directed to present to you as coming from all the members. It is an expression of affection and admiration for your splendid virtues of courage, fortitude, intelligence, and gentleness, which are marked essentials in your character, and in part the qualities that make us love you. In this parting our regrets are very many and lasting, but wherever you go you may be assured that you carry with you our best and kindliest wishes for your well-being — that the future may have in store for you only the choicest of blessings."

James R. Mann, in his characteristic and vigorous way, spoke of Mr. Burke as follows: "We know him to be great. He has made good on this committee, he has made good as a public servant. Men come and go in public life; they appear and disappear from the halls of congress. The world goes on much the same, but I venture to believe that few men have made so great an impression in the present house of representatives during his term of service as has Charles H. Burke. He has established himself in the absolute confidence of this committee, which, in my opinion, is the greatest committee in the house. Our committee deals with more subjects covering a greater variety in interests than any other committee of congress. It takes hard work and long experience to become of the greatest value in this committee. By his assiduous devotion to his public work, by his conscientious efforts to study the work coming before our committee, Mr. Burke has made himself so valuable to us that we who remain will miss him more than we can tell."

"I have had peculiar opportunity to learn of Congressman Burke's personal qualities," said Congressman Esch of Wisconsin. "I have been impressed with his industry, his good judgment, his attention to duty and his high ideals." With genuine warmth, Congressman Townsend, of Michigan, spoke in part as follows: "I have learned to respect and admire Mr. Burke for his modest, earnest and effectual work on this committee. He is differently constituted from myself, and I have profited by his example. I have known him outside of this committee room. It is said that one must 'summer and winter with a man' in order to know him well. Since I came to Washington I have lived at the same hotel with our colleague and in his modest, unassuming manner there, the same as here, he won his way into the hearts of all. I trust and believe that the same qualities of heart and head which have made his congressional life so great a success, will enable him to render even greater service to his state and this during what I hope will be the many years to come."

One of Mr. Burke's democratic colleagues in congress, Mr. Adamson of Georgia, said: "In my association with Charles H. Burke here as man, member of committee and congressman, I have admired in him the highest merit, exercised with the most beautiful modesty. Patient, industrious and wise, polite and considerate of his opponents, vigilant with adversaries, he stands a splendid example of a great, useful congressman. His sincere and genial disposition, constantly doing kindnesses, make all love him. He gives the most complete, exhibition of generous unselfishness I have ever observed in the conduct of any man. He never loses his temper. He uses intellect in transacting business. He analyzes the issue with his mind and is convinced by his reason. He will rank with the greatest and with the best and brightest who have served mankind in these halls."

At the conclusion of the consideration of the Indian appropriation bill in the house of representatives on January 9, 1915 (See Cong. Rec, p. 1364), the chairman of the committee, Mr. Stephens, yielded to the republican leader, Mr. Mann of Illinois, who said: "Mr. Speaker, I think it is quite appropriate for me to say a word, under the circumstances, conveying at least the best wishes of the House to those members of the Committee on Indian Affairs who will not be with us in the next House.

"There are eight of them who go off the committee. On this side of the House two of the oldest members in point of service upon the committee will retire. Two of the ablest Members on this side of the House will go out of the House and off the Committee on Indian Affairs. The gentleman from South Dakota (MR. BURKE) has shown that he is one of the most capable men who ever sat in this Hall and one of the men who had the most intimate knowledge of the intricacies of Indian affairs. While we on this side of the House had hoped still to have his services in another body, we sincerely regret that we are to part with his services. Mr. Burke, in my opinion, has at different times, both as chairman and as member of the Committee on Indian Affairs, saved to this Government and to the Indians many millions of dollars, and we could well have afforded, so far as money considerations are concerned, to have paid him a pension for life in order that he might give us his knowledge and his sound judgment of Indian affairs.

"I say the same kind words to the gentleman from Oklahoma (MR. McGUIRE), and I extend the best wishes of this side of the House to the Members on the other side of the House who are going off this great Committee on Indian Affairs, where more service is rendered that is not of a personal interest to Members, probably, than on any other committee of the House."

JOHN L. BURKE

John L. Burke, register of the United States land, office at Rapid City, was born in Millville, Butler County, Ohio, December 12, 1856. His father, Addison Milton Burke, followed the profession of teaching but died when his son John was but two years of age. The mother, who in her maidenhood was Dorcas Lewis, was born in Ohio and has also passed away.

John L. Burke is the elder of two children. He attended the public schools of Millville and the Dayton Business College at Dayton, Ohio. He entered upon his business career as a bookkeeper for the Variety Iron Works at Hamilton, Ohio, remaining in that connection for two years. He next entered the auditing department of the Clover Leaf Railway at Dayton, Ohio, and subsequently was with the same company at Toledo, that state, where he was promoted to the position of chief clerk and later to that of traveling auditor. In 1885 failing health made it necessary that he resign and, hoping to be benefited by a change of climate, he came west to the Black Hills, settling at Hot Springs, where he took up a homestead. Subsequently he became connected with the Dakota Hot Springs Company, serving as its secretary. In 1890 he organized the Burke Stone Company, of which he was president and manager. It is his nature to concentrate his energies with effect upon anything that he undertakes and carry it forward to successful completion and in his business life his interests have ever been most carefully managed and directed.

In 1892 Mr. Burke was called to public office in his election to the state legislature and in 1894 he was chosen treasurer of Fall River County, to which office he was reelected with very little opposition in 1896. In 1900 he was chosen to represent his district in the state senate, serving from 1901 until 1903, and on the 1st of April, of the latter year, he was appointed receiver of the United States land office at Rapid City, where he has since resided. In April, 1908, he received the appointment of register of United States lands and except for a brief period, when ill health compelled a years' absence, he has filled this important position continuously and with ability to the present time, covering six years. He also has other important interests, being president of the Western South Dakota Alfalfa Growers Association, one of the state's most useful organizations from a development standpoint, for it is largely through the efforts of its members that this part of the state has been brought to a position of leadership as an alfalfa growing district, placing the state first in seed production in 1914. Mr. Burke owns two valuable ranches devoted largely to the growing of alfalfa. In addition to his activities already mentioned Mr. Burke served in 1900 as supervisor of the United States census for the western district of South Dakota and during his residence in Hot Springs he was for years a member of the school board.

On the 21st of September, 1893, Mr. Burke was married to Miss Mattie Spangler, a daughter of Elijah and Ellen (Farr) Spangler. They have four children, A. Milton, J. Timon, Allan L., and Alice. Mrs. Burke is prominent in the social, charitable, church and club work of the city.

Mr. Burke holds membership in various fraternal organizations, the Masons, the Elks, the Knights of Pythias and Modern Woodmen of America and he has always given his political allegiance to the republican party. His is a long and creditable record of public service, in which he has displayed a conscientious devotion to duty and a close application of his energies and business ability, with the result that his present office ranks among the highest in efficiency in the government service. He finds recreation in farming, which might be termed his hobby, and of it he has made a close study along modern scientific lines. He is one of the city's deservingly prominent and successful citizens and public officials.

GEORGE H. BURLEIGH, M. D., C. M.

Dr. George H. Burleigh has won for himself a prominent position among the practitioners of Estelline and he displays particular ability in surgery and has also specialized to a large extent in the treatment of diseases of the eye, ear, nose and throat. He was born in Cambray, Canada, County Victoria, Ontario, on the 11th of October, 1870, and is a son of William Spencer and Delia Ann Burleigh. The father was a carriage builder, devoting the greater part of his life to that business, but both he and his wife have passed away.

After attending the public schools Dr. Burleigh became a student in Trinity University and afterward in the medical school, now the Toronto Medical College, from which he was graduated on the 1st of June, 1900. He then entered the Toronto General Hospital as an interne, there remaining for twelve months, during which time he gained the broad knowledge and experience that only hospital practice can bring. After leaving Toronto Hospital he attended Chicago Clinical School and then located at Emerson, Nebraska. In 1903 he returned to Chicago for six months' study in the Chicago Eye, Ear, Nose and Throat College. He then returned to Toronto for a short while, but on account of ill health again came west. He located first at Lane, South Dakota, where he was first president of the town board. Soon after he removed to Estelline, where he has since remained. In 1913 he attended the Polyclinic Post Graduate School of Chicago and each year he goes to Chicago for further post-graduate work in the leading medical colleges of that city. He now has an extensive practice in Estelline and throughout the surrounding country and the nature of his business is of a most important character. He practices surgery in the Volga Hospital at Volga, in the Brookings Hospital, and does nearly all of the surgery for the neighboring country. Even in his surgical work he specializes in the surgical treatment of the eye, ear, nose and throat. His study and investigations along those lines have given him particular ability and power and his efforts have been attended with excellent results. In addition to his other professional work, he is health officer for Estelline.

On the 24th of March, 1896, Dr. Burleigh was united in marriage to Miss Carrie Long, daughter of Benjamin and Mary Ann Long of Melbourne, Ontario. Dr. and Mrs. Burleigh have a daughter, Ruby Adelaide, born June 30, 1898. Motoring is a favorite source of enjoyment with the family and when opportunity offers Dr. Burleigh turns from his professional activities to attend the meetings of the Masonic, Eastern Star, Odd Fellows, Workmen and Woodmen societies. Mrs. Burleigh is past matron of the Eastern Star Chapter and past noble grand of the Rebekahs. The Doctor was worshipful master in 1914 of Kurhum Lodge, No. 96, A. F. & A. M., also belongs to the chapter and has passed through all of the chairs in the Odd Fellows lodge. He is most loyal to the teachings and tenets of the craft and he utilizes in his profession the many opportunities offered to exemplify its principles. Along strictly professional lines his membership is with the Third District Medical Society, the South Dakota State Medical Society, the Sioux Valley Medical Society and the American Medical Association. He recognizes fully the duties and obligations that devolve upon him and as the years go by the increases his efficiency by broad reading and study, his ability winning for him high rank in his chosen field.

GEORGE W. BURNSIDE

GEORGE W. BURNSIDE, the able chief executive of the municipal government of the beautiful city of Sioux Falls, is one of the representative business men of the place and a progressive and public-spirited citizen. Sioux Falls owes to him a perpetual debt of gratitude and approval for what he has accomplished in her behalf, and as mayor of the city his course has been that of a broad-minded, liberal and independent executive, — one whose policy has been dictated by consummate tact and good judgment.

GEORGE W. BURNSIDE.

George Washington Burnside was born in Delaware county, New York, on the 3d of November, 1858, being a son of Thomas and Mary (Walley) Burnside, the former of whom died in August, 1892, while the latter was summoned into eternal rest in June, 1902, the father having been a carpenter by trade and vocation. The subject received limited educational advantages, having attended the public schools of his native county during his boyhood, while he was a student in night schools in Iowa for a short time. At the age of thirteen years Mr. Burnside left the parental roof and went to Linn County, Iowa, where he lived in the home of his uncle for the ensuing two years, at the expiration of which, when fifteen years of age, he located in Cedar Rapids, that county, and initiated his independent career. He there learned the mason's trade, becoming a skilled artisan in the line, and he continued to follow his trade in Iowa until 1883. On the 28th of April of which year, he arrived in Sioux Falls, where he established himself in business as a contractor and builder, continuing operations in this line for the ensuing three years. In 1888 he established himself in the omnibus and general transfer business, and in the following year also added a livery department to his enterprise, while another feature of the business was the undertaking department, the equipment being of the best throughout. His became the leading concern of the sort in the city and he successfully continued operations until August, 1903, when he disposed of the livery and transfer business, still retaining the undertaking branch, which he continues to conduct. Mr. Burnside was one of the promoters and organizers of the Citizens' Telephone Company, which was incorporated on the 1st of January, 1902, and which inaugurated business in July of the following year, with a thoroughly complete and modern plant. He was made vice-president of the company at the time of its organization, and in September, 1903, was chosen general manager, of which office he has since been incumbent, giving his attention to the duties involved and also to the superintendence of his undertaking business.

In the spring of 1886 Mr. Burnside was elected city marshal, serving two years. In 1893 he was elected to represent the fifth ward on the board of aldermen, being retained in this position five successive terms and making a most creditable official record. In 1898 he was the Republican nominee for the mayoralty and was defeated by only ten votes, and in 1900 he again became the nominee of his party for this office and was victorious at the polls, giving so able an administration as to gain to him distinctive popular confidence and endorsement, as was shown in his re-election as his own successor in 1902, the consensus of opinion being that the city has never had a more discriminating, independent, conscientious and public-spirited executive. It was in natural sequence that he should receive the nomination of his party for a third term, on the 12th of April, 1904, and in the ensuing election he again demonstrated his hold upon popular confidence and esteem, the result being his re-election by about six hundred majority. It should be noted in this connection that he has been from the start an uncompromising advocate of the municipal ownership of such public utilities as the water-works and the electric lighting system, and it is principally due to his indefatigable efforts that Sioux Falls now controls both its fine water and electric systems, the water-works being practically completed at the time of this writing. Through this system will be afforded the city a far superior supply of water than that given by the old system, controlled by eastern capital. While he met with much opposition in his plans for the installing of the new plant, he had the courage of his convictions and the determined spirit which enabled him to bring them to consummation, and citizens in general will have cause to commend him for his action for many years to come. The original water company was bonded for four hundred and thirty thousand dollars, while the city has installed a much better plant at a cost of only two hundred and ten thousand dollars. Under Mayor Burnside's administration the city also put in its own electric-lighting plant, which is modern in all respects and gives the best of service at a minimum cost, while he has infused vitality and business-like methods into all other departments of the municipal service, keeping all details under his personal attention and sparing neither time nor effort in his labors to protect and promote the general welfare. He is known as a most liberal and unostentatious supporter of charitable objects and enterprises, and in these lines his aid and influence are ever freely and graciously given.

In politics Mr. Burnside was affiliated with the Democracy until 1896, when he gave his support to the late lamented President McKinley, and since that time he has given a stanch allegiance to the Republican party, in whose cause he is a most zealous and enthusiastic worker. Fraternally the Mayor is identified with Minnehaha Lodge, No. 5, Ancient Free and Accepted Masons; Sioux Falls Chapter, No. 2, Royal Arch Masons; and Cyrene Commandery, No. 2, Knights Templar. He is one of the prominent and influential members of the time-honored fraternity in the state, and is past grand commander of the grand commandery of Knights Templar of South Dakota. He is a charter member of El Riad Temple, Ancient Arabic Order of the Nobles of the Mystic Shrine, and of Sioux Falls Lodge. No. 262, Benevolent and Protective Order of Elks.

SILAS BURTON

SILAS BURTON, one of the honored and esteemed residents of Yankton County, was born in Litchfield County, Connecticut, on the 22d of December, 1837, his parents being James and Harriet Burton, in whose family were nine children, namely: Silas, Malvina, Lewis, Diadama, Almoure (who died in the United States army), Charles, Mary, Elizabeth, Florence, Ruth and George. All but five have passed away, these being Silas, Malvina, Charles, Diadama and Ruth, and with the exception of the subject and Ruth these are residents of New Haven, Connecticut.

The public schools of Litchfield County. Connecticut, afforded to Silas Burton his educational privileges and he continued his studies until nineteen or twenty years of age, thus gaining a broad practical knowledge in order to fit him for the responsible duties of a business career. When he put aside his text-books he worked at the butcher's trade at Kent Corners, Connecticut, being thus employed until 1863, when his patriotic spirit was aroused and he enlisted in the Second Heavy Artillery of Connecticut, being with the army for twenty months. He participated in the battles of the Wilderness and afterward became ill and has never yet fully recovered his health. Before starting to the front, he was married on the 6th of December, 1862, to Miss Ellen Stewart, who was born in Hunter, New York, a daughter of Alonzo and Mary (Tate) Stewart. In her parents' family were six children: Edgar, Herman, Ellen, Charles, William and George, of whom Edgar and Charles are now deceased. The living brothers of Mrs. Burton are yet residents of Connecticut.

Following the Civil War Mr. Burton removed from Connecticut to New York, where he remained for two years and then came west with his family. In 1868 he settled in Yankton County, South Dakota, having traveled by stage from Sioux City to his destination. The government afforded good facilities for purchasing land and Mr. Burton secured a pre-emption claim of one hundred and sixty acres. Subsequently he purchased an additional tract of one hundred and sixty acres and he now farms two hundred and eighty acres, raising grain and stock. In 1881, by reason of the flood caused by the ice gorges in the Missouri, he lost all of his cattle, his house and his barns, in fact, his entire personal property was destroyed save one team of horses. Thus, he has met with discouragements in what would seem to be a prosperous career. He has ever persevered in his work, however, and as the years have gone by, he has accumulated a comfortable competence and has become one of the very successful farmers of South Dakota. Unto Mr. and Mrs. Burton have been born eight children: Mary, who became the wife of W. R. Smith, died at the age of twenty-three years, leaving two children, Edgar and George, but the latter was drowned in the Missouri river at the age of thirteen years and Edgar is now living with his grandfather, the subject of this review; Edgar, the second child of Mr. Burton, has passed away; Hattie is the wife of Mr. Anderson, a farmer of Yankton county; Jennie is the wife of M. C. Nelson, a resident farmer of this county; Arthur is living at home at the age of fourteen years; Theodore has departed this life and two of the children died in infancy. For the past thirty-five years Mr. Burton has been connected with the schools of Dakota and the cause of education finds in him a warm and helpful friend.

In politics he is a stanch Democrat and fraternally he is connected with the Masonic lodge. His wife and children are members of the Congregational church and the family is one of prominence in the community, the members of the Burton household occupying an enviable position in social circles and in the regard of their many friends.

JOHN A. BUSHFIELD

J. A. BUSHFIELD, editor and publisher of the Pioneer Press, at Miller, Hand County, is a native of the old Buckeye state, having been born in Cambridge, Guernsey county, Ohio, on the 9th of August, 1856, and being a son of John M. and Sarah E. (Moore) Bushfield. He received his early educational discipline in the public schools of his native town, and there served an apprenticeship at the printer's trade, gaining a thorough knowledge of the mysteries of the "art preservative of all arts," and securing incidentally that training which has been well said to be equivalent to a literal education — the discipline of a newspaper office. He continued his residence in Ohio until 1878, when he located in Atlantic, Cass County, Iowa, where he was identified with newspaper work until 1883, when he came to the present state of South Dakota and cast in his lot with the early settlers of Miller, which was then but a small and primitive frontier village. Here he purchased a half interest in the Pioneer Press, which, had been established the preceding year, and in 1889 he purchased his partner's interest in the enterprise, which he has since individually conducted, the paper being a model country journal and wielding much influence in the local field, both in a political and civic way. The Pioneer Press is issued on Thursday of each week, is a six-column quarto and is the official paper of the city and county in which it is published. Mr. Bushfield is a member of the State Press Association and is popular in the circles of the newspaper fraternity of the state, as is he also in business and social circles in his home city. In politics he has ever accorded an unequivocal allegiance to the Republican party, and both in a personal way and through the columns of his paper he has done much to further its interests in a local way. In January, 1899, the late lamented President McKinley appointed him postmaster of Miller, and in January, 1903, he was reappointed, by President Roosevelt, so that he is incumbent of the office at the time of this writing.

He is identified with the local lodge of the Ancient Free and Accepted Masons. On the 9th of November, 1880. Mr. Bushfield was united in marriage to Miss Cora E. Pearson, of Atlantic, Iowa, and they have three children, Harley J., Laura D. and Anna M.

MILTON WALLACE BUTTS

One of the prominent and successful business men of Belle Fourche is Milton Wallace Butts, who is a dealer in ice, coal and fuel and also conducts a livery and transfer business. He was born in Linn County, Kansas, October 2, 1861, a son of Milton Wallace and Cynthia A. (Dunham) Butts, natives of New York and Ohio respectively. The father emigrated from New York to Illinois and thence to Indiana, where his marriage occurred. He later removed to Kansas and in 1862 went to Cerro Gordo County, Iowa, where he followed agricultural pursuits during the remainder of his life, passing away in 1902, eight years after the death of his wife, who died in 1894.

Milton Wallace Butts was the fourth in order of birth in a family of five children and his educational opportunities were those afforded by the schools of Cerro Gordo County, Iowa. When but seventeen years of age he began farming rented land in Iowa, being so occupied until twenty-one, when he removed to St. Onge, South Dakota. He worked for others for a few years upon farms and was then employed in Belle Fourche for a year. Following that he was on the range for two years and then engaged in the transfer business in Belle Fourche until 1896. In that year he was elected sheriff, but after serving for a year joined the rush to the Alaskan gold fields, spending two years at Dawson City and three years at Cape Nome. Although his mining ventures did not prove a financial success, he has never regretted going and can never forget his many experiences in the far north. He went from Dawson City to Cape Nome, a distance by trail of over eighteen hundred miles, with a dog team, leaving the former place on the 16th of February and arriving at Cape Nome on the 2d of April.

Upon leaving Alaska Mr. Butts returned to Belle Fourche and engaged in the transfer and livery business. For some time, he had from fifteen to twenty-five driving teams but of later years has kept but six driving teams, while he uses from six to eight teams in the transfer business. He also deals in ice, coal and fuel, which is proving a profitable venture. Mr. Butts and his partner own a whole block of valuable city property, including their livery and transfer barns, but the ice houses, storehouses, coal sheds, etc., are located elsewhere.

Mr. Butts was married in June, 1904, to Miss Pearl Helm, a native of Mitchell County, Iowa. Her parents, William and Keziah (Davis) Helm, were both born in Wisconsin, whence they removed to Iowa, spending the remainder of their lives in that state. The mother died in 1903 and the father in 1914. Mr. and Mrs. Butts have a son, Wallace, whose natal day was June 20, 1908.

Mr. Butts is a democrat and, as before stated, was elected sheriff of Butte County in 1896 but resigned in 1897 to go to Alaska. For three terms he has been a member of the city council of Belle Fourche and casts his vote for many measures that have proved of value to his municipality. He belongs to the Masonic order, holding membership in all of the Scottish Rite bodies from the blue lodge to the consistory and having also crossed the sands of the desert with the Nobles of the Mystic Shrine. He is likewise identified with the Benevolent Protective Order of Elks and not only in the organizations named but also in business and social circles is highly respected and esteemed.

CHARLES A. CADWELL

Charles A. Cadwell, a well-known resident of Sioux Falls, was born in Griggsville, Pike County, Illinois, March 7, 1860, a son of Addison and Martha S. (Burns) Cadwell. The father was born in Kentucky in 1831 and died in Pittsfield, Illinois, in 1910. He was married in 1855 and had three sons and two daughters, all of whom survive, the subject of this review being the second in order of birth and the oldest son. Addison Cadwell was treasurer of Pike County, Illinois, for one term.

Charles A. Cadwell acquired his education in the public schools of Griggsville and New Salem, Illinois, and later attended Chaddock College at Quincy and was also a student in the Wesleyan University at Bloomington. In 1881 he went to Maryville, Missouri, where a relative was engaged in the implement business, and one year later accepted a position as traveling salesman for several implement concerns in Illinois. In this capacity he acted until January 1, 1886, when he moved to Kansas City, Missouri, establishing himself in the real-estate business there. In October, 1889, he went to Neponset, Illinois, where for three years he conducted a retail implement business, afterward working for several years on the road as a buggy salesman. In July, 1899, he entered the employ of the Moline Plow Company and was identified with that corporation until the first of August, 1915, being one of its most reliable and trusted representatives. On the 1st of September, 1905, he came to Sioux Falls as manager of the branch here, conducted under the name of the Dakota Moline Plow Company. He gave practically all of his time to the affairs of this business, which he managed intelligently and capably under a policy which made it one of the important institutions of its kind in this section of the state.

On the 27th of December, 1887, at Bloomington, Indiana, Mr. Cadwell married Miss Martha O. Wallingford and they have become the parents of a daughter, Margaret. Mr. Cadwell is a member of the Methodist Episcopal church, belongs to the Dacotah Club and the blue lodge in Masonry and gives his political allegiance to the republican party. He is an able and farsighted business man, broad in his views and progressive in his ideas, and upon these qualifications has built a success which places him among the substantial and representative men of Sioux Falls.

CHARLES VERTNER CALDWELL

Charles Vertner Caldwell, state's attorney of Minnehaha County and a prominent and popular resident of Sioux Falls, the consensus of public opinion establishing him high in the regard of his fellow townsmen, was born on the old Caldwell homestead near Hartford, South Dakota, October 18, 1878. He attended the public schools and afterward studied in the Sioux Falls high school, from which he was graduated with the class of 1898. He subsequently spent two years as a student in the Sioux Falls College and later entered the government mail service, becoming a carrier in Sioux Falls. He secured that position in order that he might earn the necessary sum that would enable him to continue his education. He worked by the day and studied law at night, continuing thus for six years — a fact which indicates the elemental strength of his character and the resolute purpose which has been one of the salient features in his success. At length he retired from the mail service and entered the University of South Dakota in the law department. He there completed his course and was graduated with the class of 1909.

For a year thereafter Mr. Caldwell practiced his profession in Hartford and in 1910 entered into partnership with C. J. Morris under the firm style of Morris & Caldwell, a connection that has since been maintained with mutual pleasure and profit. The firm ranks high at the bar of Sioux Falls and eastern South Dakota and has been accorded a large and distinctively representative clientage connecting it with much important litigation tried in the courts of the district. In the fall of 1914 Mr. Caldwell was elected state's attorney of Minnehaha County for a term of two years and entered upon the duties of the position on the 1st of January, 1915.

On the 1st of November, 1899, Mr. Caldwell was united in marriage to Miss Cora E. Kiltz, a daughter of Barney and Chloe Kiltz, of Lincoln County, South Dakota. Her father was a farmer of that county but is now living retired, making his home in Sioux Falls. Mr. Caldwell is a member of Unity Lodge, A. F. & A. M., of Sioux Falls, and the principles which govern his conduct are further indicated in the fact that he has membership in the Methodist church. His political allegiance is given to the republican party and he keeps well informed on the questions and issues of the day arid is ever ready to support his position by intelligent argument, preferring always to concentrate his energies upon his professional duties which have been of growing importance.

DYER H. CAMPBELL

Dyer H. CAMPBELL, the able and popular sheriff of Brookings county, is a native of the old Keystone state of the Union, having been born in the town of Edinboro, Erie county, Pennsylvania, on the 28th of November, 1858, a son of John W. and .Susan (Walker) Campbell, the former of whom was likewise born in that county, in 1817, being a son of John and Mary (Laughrey) Campbell, who were natives of Scotland, the grandfather having emigrated thence to America in the early part of the seventeenth century. He located in Pennsylvania, where he devoted the remainder of his life to agricultural pursuits. The father of the subject was likewise identified with the great basic art of agriculture and was also engaged in the mercantile business in Edinboro, while he served two terms as a member of the Pennsylvania legislature. In 1865 he removed with his family to Olmstead County. Minnesota, where he was engaged in farming for the ensuing three years. In 1869 he removed to the town of Rochester, that county, where he was for six years an attaché of the office of register of deeds. He served as justice of the peace and held other offices of local trust and responsibility, his death occurring in Rochester in 1887, while his widow was summoned into eternal rest in 1892, at Moorhead, Minnesota. Of their three children we enter the following brief record: John V. is a resident of Erie, Pennsylvania; Martha J. became the wife of Arthur G. Lewis, of Moorhead, Minnesota, and is now deceased, and Dyer H. is the immediate subject of this sketch.

Dyer H. Campbell was seven years of age at the time of his parents' removal from Pennsylvania to Minnesota, and there he attended the district schools until the family located in Rochester, where he continued his studies in the public schools for two or three years. At the age of fifteen years, he initiated his independent career, securing a position in a meat market in Rochester, and being thereafter employed in the same and in a grocery about three years. He then secured a position in an abstract insurance office, in which he remained until 1881, when he came to Brookings, Dakota, having been married about two years previously. Upon arriving in Brookings, he secured a position in what was then the Brookings County Bank, but is now the First National Bank, where he held the office of assistant cashier until the institution was reorganized, as the First National Bank, in 1883, from which time forward he continued to retain the position of assistant cashier until the 1st of January, 1903, when he resigned his office to assume the duties of the shrievalty, having been elected sheriff of the county in November of the preceding year, as the candidate of the Republican party. Sheriff Campbell served for fifteen terms as city treasurer of Brookings, while for seventeen years he was secretary of the Brookings Building and Loan Association.

For the past twenty years he has been identified with the Independent Order of Odd Fellows, and is one of its prominent representatives in the state, being at the present time grand master of the grand lodge in South Dakota. He is also a member of Brookings Lodge, No. 24, Free and Accepted Masons, as well as of the Modern Woodmen of America and other fraternal bodies of auxiliary character. He has served four years as chief of the fire department of Brookings, and has been chosen as incumbent for another term of two years. He is one of the wheelhorses of the Republican party in the county, and is chairman of the county central committee at the time of this writing, while he has been a delegate to various state and county conventions of the party. He and his family attend the Presbyterian church. On the 9th of November, 1879, Mr. Campbell was united in marriage to Miss Emma Haber, a daughter of George and Melissa Haber, the former of whom was born in Germany and the latter in the state of Ohio, and of this union have been born six children, namely: Walter, who is serving as deputy sheriff: Bertha is the wife of E. F. McCarl; Arthur, Martha and Horace, who remain at the parental home; and Harriet, who died at the age of one year.

ABRAM E. VAN CAMP

Abram E. Van Camp has devoted his life to various business interests, most of which have brought him substantial success. He is now giving his attention almost exclusively to the selling of farm implements and machinery in Highmore and to the insurance business, but in previous years was active in real-estate dealing and also owned and conducted a farm located within the city limits, devoted principally to stock-raising.

Mr. Van Camp was born in Muscatine County, Iowa, September 29, 1852, a son of Kiple and Ann Maria (Little) Van Camp, who were natives of Sussex County, New Jersey. The father, who always followed farming as a life work, removed to Iowa in 1850, securing a farm, upon which he continued to reside until his death. He held various local offices, making a creditable record in such connections, and his sterling worth won for him the high regard of all with whom he came in contact. His widow still spends the summer months at the old home, which is yet a part of the estate, and passes the winter months with a son in western Iowa.

Abram E. Van Camp was the second in order of birth in a family of ten children, eight of whom are living. He supplemented his public-school education by a term of three months in an academy at Iowa City and through the period of his boyhood and youth aided more and more largely in the work of the home farm as his age and strength increased. He remained at home until about twenty-two and then began farming on his own account in Iowa, where he remained for seven years. In June, 1882, he came to South Dakota and took up his abode on a quarter section of land, on which a part of the town of Highmore now stands. In that year he platted the town and began selling lots. In fact, he conducted a general real-estate business for some time. In the spring of 1884, he shipped the first carload of farm machinery to the town and with the exception of a few years has been continuously engaged in that business to the present time. He also carried on general farming and stock-raising for a number of years and to some extent he still engages in raising the crops best adapted to soil and climate. He has one hundred acres within the corporation limits of the town but at the present time he devotes the major part of his attention to the implement trade and to the insurance business.

On the 5th of May, 1874, Mr. Van Camp was married to Miss Louisa C. Sherfey, a native of Muscatine County, Iowa, and a daughter of John and Patience A. Sherfey. Her grandparents were natives of Germany and the grandfather on coming to America was bound out so that his wages might pay his fare. Her father was a farmer by occupation and in 1837 removed westward to Iowa, settling in Muscatine County, where he secured land and developed a homestead farm, upon which he and his wife spent their remaining days. Their family numbered six children, of whom Mrs. Van Camp was the fifth. She died on the 19th of October, 1899, leaving one son, Shreve, who was born June 1, 1875, and is now associated with his father in business. He married Emma Bottcher, of Highmore, who was born in New York state and came with her parents to South Dakota in 1883. After the death of his first wife Mr. Van Camp of this review married Miss Florence E. Walker, a native of Illinois, who was brought by her parents to South Dakota in 1883, the family locating in Sully County, seven miles north of Harrold.

In his political views Mr. Van Camp has always been a stalwart republican since age conferred upon him the right of franchise. He served as one of the first county commissioners of Hyde County and was postmaster of Highmore under appointment of President Harrison for four and a half years and again under appointment of President Roosevelt for seven and a half years. He is a prominent Mason, belonging to the Ree Valley Lodge, No. 70, A. F. & A. M., at Highmore, of which he served as master for six years; to the chapter at Miller; to the council at Salem; to the Capital City Commandery, No. 21, K. T., at Pierre; and to the Mystic Shrine at Sioux Falls. He is an ex-president of the Masonic Veterans Association of South Dakota and is a charter member of the Eastern Star chapter at Highmore. He is likewise a charter member of the Ancient Order United Workmen, and of the Degree of Honor at Highmore. The city in which he lives is largely a monument to his enterprise and progressive spirit. Laying out the town, he has cooperated in every movement and measure for its upbuilding and development, and his work has brought excellent results, largely promoting the public welfare and at the same time advancing his individual interests. He planted a whole block of trees and also many others.

ANDREW NELSON VAN CAMP

Andrew Nelson Van Camp is now devoting the greater part of his time and attention to the management of the business of the telephone company at Highmore, South Dakota, but has been a prominent figure in political circles of the state, his opinions carrying weight in republican councils, while his efforts have been productive of beneficial results along political lines. Mr. Van Camp is a native of the neighboring state of Iowa, his birth having occurred in Muscatine County, December 18, 1850. Mention of his family is made in connection with the sketch of A. E. Van Camp, which appears on another page of this work.

After attending the public schools of his native state Andrew N. Van Camp continued his education in the Wilton (Ia.) Academy and in the Iowa State University at Iowa City, in which he pursued his law course, being graduated in 1871. He also pursued a commercial course before he entered upon preparation for the bar. He had completed his education before he attained his majority and had tried some cases before, he reached the age of twenty-one years. Following his admission to the bar he practiced in Iowa until 1882, when he came to Dakota territory, settling on government land which at that time had not been surveyed. His place was a mile from the present site of Highmore and he still owns the land. He resumed the practice of law in Highmore and continued the cultivation of his farm until 1903, when he removed his family from the farm to the town. In 1907 he erected the Telephone Exchange building, which would be a credit to a city of much larger size. It is a brick veneer, two-story structure with basement and its dimensions are forty by forty-eight feet. In 1902 he organized the Hyde County Telephone Company, of which he is now a stockholder and the secretary and general manager. He rents his farm lands and is devoting the greater part of his attention to the telephone business.

On the 22d of July, 1873, Mr. Van Camp was married to Miss Kate Allen, a native of County Tipperary, Ireland. Her father came to America in early manhood and died in Boston before the arrival of his family in the new world. Mrs. Van Camp with her mother removed from the east to Rock Island, Illinois, and later came to South Dakota, Mrs. Allen spending her last days at the home of her daughter, where she passed away in 1895.

To Mr. and Mrs. Van Camp have been born nine children: James K., who is district agent at Yankton for the De Laval Separator Company, married Marguerite Mulvey, by whom he has two children, Cyril and Marguerite. William N., residing in Highmore, is engaged in educational work in Hyde County and for two terms was county superintendent of schools. He was a member of the lower house of the state legislature for one term and secretary of the state senate during the sessions of 1913 and 1915. During the last three or four years he has been special traveling salesman for the American Book Company, having charge of the territory of North and South Dakota. He married Marie Quirk, of Highmore, and their children are Fred, Florence, Howard and Royal. Francis Joseph, the third of the family, died in Wilton, Iowa, in infancy. Harry Theodore died in 1895, at the age of fifteen years. John Edgar, residing at Fort Dodge, Iowa, is district agent for the Free Sewing Machine Company, having charge of several counties. He married Miss Georgia Thompson, of Canton, South Dakota, and they have five children. Allen A., born in Hyde County, is now residing in Highmore and is assisting his father in the telephone business. He married Edith McKillip and they have one child, Philip. Ella Ann is the wife of J. H. Quirk, a stockman and real-estate dealer of Highmore. George is now in the moving picture business at Los Angeles, California. For a number of years, he was connected with the Sioux City Journal and was secretary of the senate in 1911. Kathryn B. completes the family.

Mr. Van Camp is a member of the Masonic lodge at Highmore and of the Ancient Order of United Workmen and holds membership in the Methodist Episcopal church. His political indorsement has always been given to the republican party, which recognizes in him one of its prominent supporters in this state. He served as the first county superintendent of schools of Hyde County, was district attorney in territorial days, was states attorney for two terms and was assistant chief clerk of the house during the session of 1893. He also served on the board of education in Bramhall township, Hyde County, for about fifteen years. At the convening of the special session of the first state legislature under the constitution October 15, 1889, in the transition from territorial to state government, at which time the first state officers were sworn in and the first United States senators were elected, he acted as assistant to Secretary of the Senate F. A. Burdick and for him wrote the records of the session in the great book in the office of the secretary of state, and also at the dictation of State Senator A. B. Kittredge, afterward United States senator from this state, wrote the certificate of election of one of the newly elected United States senators, Moody and Pettigrew, to the United States senate. During the regular session which convened January 7, 1890, Mr. Van Camp acted as legislative reporter for the Sioux Falls Daily Press and The Deadwood Pioneer-Times and made what is termed a newspaper scoop by discovering and exposing a movement on the part of some of the members to dissipate and waste the large patrimony given the state by congress for educational, charitable and other general state purposes, to accomplish which purposes and to boost favored localities, as well as to draw away as much opposition as possible from a permanent location of the capital at Pierre, the combination sought to locate an additional agricultural college at Aberdeen, another state university at Huron, another reform school at Watertown, another normal school at Forest City and various other institutions at different places in the state. His early exposure of the plot in the columns of the Press resulted in arousing the friends of the institutions already located to action and caused the bills, which had been referred to a special committee, composed of friends of Mr. Van Camp, named by Lieutenant-Governor Fletcher, to never be reported for action. The value of the services thus rendered can never be estimated. With him patriotism has ever been before partisanship and the public good before personal aggrandizement. He has worked earnestly and effectively to advance the best interests of the state along many lines and the value of his services places him among the substantial and honored residents of South Dakota.

STEPHEN CAPPA

Stephen Cappa is the owner of a men's furnishing store in Lead which enjoys a large and profitable trade, drawing its patronage from the representative people of that city and district. He was born in Villa Castelnuovo, near Turin, Italy, in June, 1878, a son of Lawrence and Margaret Cappa, who were also natives of that place. The father, who was a farmer by occupation, has passed to his reward, as has also the mother, they were the parents of four children, of whom the subject of this review is the youngest.

Stephen Cappa attended the public schools until the age of thirteen years and later a private night school for three years, working during the daytime. He assisted in the cultivation of the home farm until he was twenty years of age and then entered the Italian army, in which he served for two years. He advanced to the rank of corporal and for about fifteen months had charge of the books of his post. At the end of two years, he received his honorable discharge and then went to Germany, but only remained there for a short period, after which he worked in Switzerland as timekeeper for a railroad construction company. He returned home for two weeks and then sailed for America. Crossing the country to Lead, South Dakota, he arrived there in December, 1901, and entered the employ of the Homestake Mining Company, working as a miner for six years. He then entered the retail shoe and men's furnishings business as a member of the Cappa-Rosio Company, but in February, 1912, bought out his partner and has since conducted the business alone. He carries a large stock which is well selected to meet the demands of his customers and his trade is increasing from year to year as his enterprise and honorable business methods become more widely known. In 1912 he was made Italian consular agent for North and South Dakota and is now the incumbent in that office.

Mr. Cappa was married in 1905 to Miss Frances Civretto, a native of Terraville, South Dakota, and to them have been born four sons, Lawrence, Peter, Arthur and an infant as yet unnamed. Mr. Cappa is a republican and takes a keen interest in everything relating to governmental affairs. He is a member of the council of Universal Liberty, Lodge No. 342, of the American Federation of Human Rights, belongs to the Ancient Free & Accepted Masons under the Paris jurisdiction, to the Christopher Columbus Society, the Fraternal Order of Eagles and to the Ancient Order of United Workmen. He is the fortunate possessor of a personality that wins friends easily and there is no more popular man in Lead than Stephen Cappa. He is also highly respected and all concede that his success is due entirely to his industry, wise management and fair dealing.

ALBERT N. CARLISLE

Albert N. Carlisle is now living retired at Woonsocket, enjoying a rest which he has truly earned and richly deserves. For many years he was extensively engaged in the grain trade in that part of the state and his capably conducted business affairs brought to him the substantial competence that now enables him to rest from further labors. He was born in Chautauqua County, New York, on the 11th of May, 1855. His father, John Carlisle, was a farmer by occupation and in 1880 removed to Miner County, Dakota territory, where he remained for a short time. He then returned to Minnesota, where he had settled in 1867, making his home in Fillmore County for about thirty-seven years, his death there occurring on the 11th of May, 1903 when he had reached the age of seventy-six. He married Ann Spratt and they became the parents of eight children, of whom Albert N. was the third in order of birth. Both parents were natives of the north of Ireland and it was in the year 1854 that they came to the new world. Both passed away in 1903, the mother's death occurring in the month of January, when she was seventy-three years of age.

Albert N. Carlisle attended the district schools in New York, Wisconsin and Minnesota and was also a high-school pupil at Spring Valley, Minnesota. He started in the business world as an apprentice to the harness maker's trade, which he followed for nine years. In 1880 he removed to Lake Herman, Dakota territory, where he established a harness shop which he conducted for a short time. He then turned his attention to the grain business in connection with an elevator company and in 1884 he came to Woonsocket, representing the grain company until 1900. He then purchased a line of elevators of his own at Woonsocket and at Lane and remained as one of the foremost grain merchants of his part of the state until 1912, when he retired from active business. He had handled a large amount of grain annually, his business reaching extensive proportions. He also owns a farm of six hundred and forty acres north of Woonsocket devoted to the raising of grain, and the place is splendidly improved and presents a most attractive appearance.

On the 14th of December, 1887, Mr. Carlisle was united in marriage to Miss Louisa Seekatz, of Waverly, Iowa, her parents being August and Mary (Schlund) Seekatz, the former a native of Germany and the latter of Wisconsin. Our subject and his wife have one child, Rachael, who is a graduate of the Woonsocket high school and the Dakota Wesleyan University.

Mr. Carlisle is the owner of an automobile and makes motoring his chief source of recreation. Politically he is a republican with independent tendencies, and when his judgment dictates an independent course in the exercise of his right of franchise, he does not hesitate to follow it. He was a member of the Woonsocket school board for six years and has also served on the city council and at all times labors for the welfare of the community.

Fraternally he is connected with the Masons and the Odd Fellows. He is a champion of the cause of temperance, is an advocate of good roads and a stalwart supporter of many plans and measures for civic progress and improvement. He now has leisure to more thoroughly investigate those subjects which are of significant interest to his community and the people at large and his influence is always on the side of right and progress. In his business career the capable direction of his affairs has led to prosperity. He has ever followed constructive methods in his business and his path has never been strewn with the wreck of other men's fortunes. He is noted for his integrity as well as for his industry, for his justice as well as for his enterprise, and thus it is that he is numbered among the honored and representative residents of his city.

DENIS CARRIGAN

Denis Carrigan is connected with various public and private interests in Custer County, where he is filling the office of member of the board of county commissioners and is also president of the First National Bank of Custer and the owner of large landed holdings in that locality. A native of Montreal, Canada, he was born on the 31st of October, 1845, of the marriage of Stephen and Ellen (Core) Carrigan, both natives of Ireland. However, they were married in Montreal and the father there followed his trade, being a stone mason. Much of his life, however, was devoted to the stock business and he bought and shipped heavily. He resided in the United States but a very short time and both he and his wife passed away in Montreal. They were the parents of three children, of whom the subject of this review is the eldest.

Denis Carrigan attended school in his native city and when about fifteen years old became associated with his father in buying and shipping cattle. Five years later, when a young man of twenty years, he came to the states and made his way to Chicago, where he resided until the winter of 1865-6. At that time, he removed to Iowa and for about three months was in the employ of others. He

then went to Omaha and entered the service of the Union Pacific Railroad Company, with which he remained until 1867. In that year he became connected with the business interests of Sidney, Nebraska, where he engaged in merchandising until 1879. He then turned his attention to cattle-raising, conducting a ranch thirty-two miles west of Sidney. Two years later he sold that property and made his way to Custer, South Dakota, and not long after his arrival established the Bank of Custer. In 1890 the First National Bank succeeded the Bank of Custer and from that time until the present Mr. Carrigan has been president of the institution, which is in a prosperous condition. It owns the bank building, which was erected in 1911 and was designed especially for banking purposes. Mr. Carrigan is not only a leader in financial circles in Custer but he also owns considerable land in the state and likewise some excellent city property. His duties as president of the bank require the greater part of his time and he keeps a firm grasp upon all of the affairs of the institution.

Mr. Carrigan was married in July, 1871, to Miss Louisa McWhinney, a native of Quincy, Illinois and a daughter of Newton and Frances (Pell) McWhinney. The father, who was a farmer and stock-raiser by occupation, was born in Ohio, and passed away in California. The mother, a native of Kentucky, died in Custer.

Mr. Carrigan is a democrat but is somewhat independent in the exercise of his franchise, believing that the welfare of the people is of more importance than the close following of party leaders. While living in Cheyenne County, Nebraska, he was one of the first county commissioners and also the first county judge. In the early '90s he was a member of the board of commissioners of Custer County and is also serving in that body at the present time. For over twenty years he served as school treasurer and in all of his official connections he has proved faithful to the best interests of the community and able in the discharge of his duties. He is well known in Masonic circles as he is a thirty-second degree Mason and has also crossed the sands of the desert with the Nobles of the Mystic Shrine, he indorses the principles of the order most enthusiastically and his daily life bears witness to his loyalty to the ideal of human brotherhood. He has been a resident of Custer for over a third of a century and in that time his fellow citizens have learned to know him intimately and those who know him best are his most sincere friends, a fact which is indubitable proof of the sterling worth of his character.

DAVID JAMES CARSON, M. D.

Dr. David James Carson, a successful medical practitioner of Faulkton, was born at Ottawa, Canada, November 16, 1866, his parents being Archibald and Charlotte (Gehan) Carson, the former born in Ireland about 1820 and the latter in Scotland about 1828. They became farming people of Canada but never removed to the United States.

Dr. Carson attended school in Canada, where he mastered the general branches of learning, and in preparation for a professional career entered the Jefferson Medical College of Philadelphia, from which he was graduated in the class of 1894. He also attended other medical schools and did hospital work, spending some time in the general hospital at Bridgeport, Connecticut, while for three months he was a student in Tulane University at New Orleans, Louisiana. His broad study and early hospital experience well qualified him to enter upon the private practice of medicine. His professional course, however, did not immediately follow his public-school training, for in the meantime he had provided for his own support, beginning work at the age of fifteen years in the employ of a railroad company. He also taught school for a number of terms before he left Canada and came to the United States. In 1888 he traveled through Montana, working for others, and in 1890 he returned to the east to take up the study of medicine, to which he devoted the years of 1891, 1892, 1893 and 1894. Having completed his course in the Jefferson Medical College, he spent a number of years in hospital work in the eastern states, gaining the broad experience and varied practice that only hospital work can bring. In 1897 he arrived in South Dakota, settling in Faulkton, where he practiced for three years. He then returned to Michigan, where he followed his profession until 1906, when he once more located in Faulkton, where he has since remained in general practice. He is also a landowner and operates a large farm near the town devoted to the cultivation of cereals best adapted to soil and climate and also to stock-raising. The major portion of his time and attention, however, is given to his practice, which was increasing so rapidly that when Dr. L. J. Cook of Chicago came to Faulkton, he was admitted to a partnership by Dr. Carson. The latter is now a member of the South Dakota State Medical Society and also of the American Medical Association.

On the 2d of July, 1910, Dr. Carson was united in marriage to Miss Ida Knapp, a native of Bay City, Michigan, and a daughter of William Knapp. Mr. Knapp still survives, having now attained the age of eighty years.

In politics Dr. Carson is a democrat but has never aspired to office and in fact has refused to accept political positions. He is a member of the Presbyterian church and is a well-known Mason, holding membership in the lodge and chapter at Faulkton, the Knight Templar commandery at Redfield and in the Mystic Shrine at Aberdeen. In his practice he rinds ample opportunity to exemplify the principles of the craft and again and again he extends a helping hand where it is needed. He has never regarded lightly his obligations to his fellows nor the work of his profession and is deeply interested in everything which tends to bring to man the key to the complex mystery which we call life.

JOSEPH WALTERS CATLETT

Joseph W. CATLETT, cashier of the Bank of Estelline, Hamlin County, was born in Monroe County, Missouri. He was reared on the home farm and assisted in its work during the summer seasons, while during three or four months each winter he pursued his studies in the public schools, so continuing until he had attained years of maturity, after which he taught one term of district school and then attended the normal school at Kirksville, Missouri. Thereafter he returned to the homestead farm, and for the following five years taught during the winter terms in the country schools, while for the major portion of the intervening period he was employed as bookkeeper in the office of a lumber firm at Centralia, Missouri. He then obtained a state certificate to teach and applied for the principalship of a city school, but was defeated by one vote, the only objection entered being that he was not a married man. He then came to the territory of Dakota and arrived in Estelline on his birthday anniversary. Here he established himself in the lumber business, becoming one of the pioneers of the town, and later added a hardware department to his enterprise, which he successfully conducted for a number of years, while he is still the owner of the lumber business which he established more than a score of years ago, having disposed of his hardware business. Upon the organization and incorporation of the Bank of Estelline. Mr. Catlett was elected its president, in which capacity he continued to serve until the stockholders felt that the prestige and success of the enterprise would be furthered if he were placed in active charge of its affairs, and he was accordingly elected cashier and has since remained incumbent of this position, while under his direct management the bank has gained a place among the most popular and substantial financial institutions in this section of the state. He is a stalwart advocate of the principles and policies for which the Democratic party stands sponsor, and was prominent in effecting the party organization in Hamlin County, while for the past twelve years he has represented said county as a member of the South Dakota delegation to the national convention of the party in 1900, at Kansas City.

He is a member of the Ancient Free and Accepted Masons, and he was reared in the faith of the Christian church, but is not formally identified with any religious body, Mrs. Catlett being a member of the Baptist church. Mr. Catlett was united in marriage to Miss Elizabeth Bland, who was born in Paris, and they have three children.

HARRY D. CHAMBERLAIN

Harry D. CHAMBERLAIN, the efficient and popular Indian agent at the Crow Creek reservation, was born in Boone county, Illinois, on the 3d of September, 1856, and is a son of Joseph and Sally (Hovey) Chamberlain, of whose eleven children five are still living, namely: Helen, who is the widow of O. C. Brown, is a resident of Sterling, Nebraska; Eliza J. is the wife of Eugene Reeves, of Burr, that state; Leroy E. is a resident of Capron, Illinois; Harry D. is the immediate subject of this sketch; and Horace resides in Belvidere, Illinois. The parents of the subject were born in New York. Joseph Chamberlain removed with his mother to Boone County, Illinois, in 1832, his father having died in Brattleboro, Vermont, and a few years later the parents of his future wife also took up abode in the same county, which was then practically an unbroken wilderness. The paternal grandmother of the subject was one of the first settlers in that section, where she lived to attain the venerable age of ninety-eight years, while the maternal grandparents had nearly attained the age of ninety at time of death. Joseph Chamberlain became one of the pioneer farmers of Illinois, and his death occurred on the land which he secured from the government fifty-nine years prior to his demise, which occurred in 1891. After his death his widow removed into the town of Capron, where she has since maintained her home, being eighty-one years of age at the time of this writing, in 1903. The father was originally a Whig and later a Republican, and though he held various local positions of trust he was never an office seeker.

The subject of this review was reared on the old homestead farm and his early educational advantages were those afforded in the common schools. He was married at the age of twenty years and then took charge of the home farm, where he remained until the spring of 1883, when he came to the territory of Dakota and located in the village of Lafoon, which was later made the county seat of Faulk County. South Dakota. In 1886 the line of the Chicago & Northwestern Railroad was completed through Faulkton. and the same year the subject was elected sheriff of the county. The county seat was removed to Faulkton in the following year, and Mr. Chamberlain naturally transferred his residence to that place. In 1888 he was re-elected to the shrievalty, thus serving for two consecutive terms. After retiring from office, he was engaged in contracting for one year, and in 1892 engaged in the general merchandise business in Faulkton. Two years later he closed out his interests in this line, and he was thereafter engaged in the hotel business in the town until June 1, 1901, when he rented his hotel property to enter upon the duties of his present office. He has been one of the leading figures in the Republican party councils in the state, having served two terms as a member of the state central committee, and in May, 1902, he was appointed to his present office as government agent at the Crow Creek Indian reservation, where he is rendering most satisfactory service.

He is a member of Faulkton Lodge, No. 95, Free and Accepted Masons; Faulkton Chapter, No. 30, Royal Arch Masons; Lacotah Commandery, No. 6. Knights Templar; and El Riad Temple, Ancient Arabic Order of the Nobles of the Mystic Shrine, at Sioux Falls. On the 29th of November, 1876, Mr. Chamberlain was married to Miss Ada S. Marvin, of Union Center, Wisconsin, and of their seven children three are living, namely: Iva, who is the wife of Rude H. Sands, of Belvidere, Illinois; and Josie F. and Vera, who remain at the parental home.

M. J. CHANEY

M. J. Chaney is one of the leading citizens of Vermillion and has been connected with the development of his city and section along a number of lines of activity. He is president of the Citizens Bank & Trust Company of Vermillion and also of the Bank of Wakonda, and is the owner of much South Dakota land. He has taken active part in public affairs, having represented his district in the state legislature for a number of terms and serving as speaker of the house during two terms.

Mr. Chaney was born in Ogle County, Illinois, October 1, 1858, a son of Osborn and Amanda (Rice) Chaney, the former a native of Virginia. In 1836 the parents traveled overland to Ogle County, Illinois, and there the father followed agricultural pursuits for a number of years although he at length turned his attention to the lumber business. Both he and his wife are deceased.

M. J. Chaney attended the public schools of Rock ford, Illinois, and thus acquired a good education. In 1880 he went to Newell, Buena Vista County, Iowa, and there purchased a farm, upon which he remained for thirteen years. In 1893 he sold that place and came to South Dakota, locating at Wakonda, Clay County. He soon became identified with the banking interests of that place, as cashier and later president of the Bank of Wakonda, and in 1914 he organized the Citizens Bank & Trust Company of Vermillion, which opened, its doors for business on the 1st of September, 1914. Mr. Chaney has been president of the institution since its establishment and is also still president of the Bank of Wakonda. He is highly respected in financial circles and his knowledge of the banking business, acumen and sound judgment are generally recognized. He has unbounded faith in the future of South Dakota and owns about thirteen hundred acres of fine farm land in Clay County, ten hundred and thirty-five acres thereof being the old Tee & Prentiss ranch.

Mr. Chaney was married in 1886 to Miss Helen McFarline, a daughter of Alexander and Cynthia McFarline, both natives of New York. To Mr. and Mrs. Chaney have been born three children, Florence, Dorothy and Morris.

Mr. Chaney is a prominent republican and from 1903 to 1909 represented his district in the state legislature and during his last two terms was made speaker of the house. As a legislator he proved efficient and public spirited and as speaker he gained the commendation of men of both parties for his capable and impartial discharge of his duties. He is a Knight Templar Mason, belonging to the commandery at Vermillion. His religious faith is that of the Congregational church and he is one of the active members of the local organization. He has not used his ability and knowledge for his own advancement alone but has always given freely of his time and thought as well as his means to movements which have as their object the betterment of his city, county or state. The high respect in which he is generally held is richly deserved and the warm personal regard entertained for him by many is a just tribute to the worth of his character.

CHARLES W. CHAPMAN

Charles W. Chapman, member of the board of county commissioners of Hamlin County and a resident of Bryant, was born in Jefferson County, Wisconsin, on the 24th of September, 1857, a son of Richard and Mary (Cannon) Chapman, both natives of England, the former born in Cornwall and the latter in London. They were married, however, in Wisconsin, to which state the father had emigrated as a young man, while in girlhood the mother had gone to that state with her parents. After their marriage they settled on a farm in Jefferson County, Wisconsin, where they resided until the fall of 1862, when they removed westward to Iowa, taking up their abode in Benton County, where they lived for two decades. In 1882 they came to South Dakota and on arriving in this state, then a territory, Mr. Chapman homesteaded a quarter section in Garfield township, Hamlin County, on which he resided up to the time of his death, which occurred about 1895, when he was seventy-two years of age. His wife died on the 8th of January, 1888.

Charles W. Chapman was reared at home and devoted much of his youth to the acquirement of a public-school education and to farm work. He was early trained to the best methods of plowing, planting and harvesting and continued to assist his father until he attained his majority. For two years thereafter he worked as a farm hand in the employ of neighboring farmers and on the 22d of December, 1880, he was married. The following spring, he began farming on his own account as a renter in Cherokee county, Iowa, and continued to engage in agricultural pursuits there for four years. In 1885 he arrived in Dakota Territory and the following spring took up a homestead of one hundred and sixty acres in Garfield township, Hamlin County. He at once began to till and develop the place and year by year saw a greater amount of the land under cultivation until his farm became one of the productive places of the county.

He resided thereon until the spring of 1911, when he took up his abode in Bryant, where he has since been engaged in the grain and coal business, becoming a member of the firm of Rice & Chapman. They operate a grain elevator at Bryant and also conduct a coal yard, their sales of both products being quite extensive.

As a companion and helpmate on the journey of life Mr. Chapman chose Miss Lizzie Jeffrey, of Benton County, Iowa, who was called to her final reward January 29, 1913. Mr. and Mrs. Chapman became the parents of four children, two of whom survive, namely: Charles H., who is employed in his father's elevator; and Eva Belle, at home. Charles married Esther Solberg, of Minneapolis, who, however, is a native of Bryant, and they have one daughter, Marcia Edrey, born February 17, 1915.

Mr. Chapman votes with the republican party, which he has stanchly indorsed since age conferred upon him the right of franchise. He has served at two different periods or for seven years as a member of the board of county commissioners, acting in that capacity from 1901 until 1905. In May, 1911, he was appointed a member of the board to fill out an unexpired term, and in 1912 was regularly elected to the office, so that he is now acting in that capacity. His long continuance in the position is indicative of the ability which he displays and the confidence reposed in him by his fellow townsmen.

Fraternally he is identified with the following organizations: Bryant Lodge, No. 118, A. F. & A. M.; Fern Leaf Chapter, No. 45, O. E. S.; and the Modern Woodmen. Mr. Chapman is recognized as a citizen whose life work has contributed to the welfare and upbuilding of county and state. He started out in life empty-handed, but he early recognized the eternal principle that industry wins, so that industry became the beacon light of his life and has been the force which has brought him to his present creditable position as a successful business man.

H. N. CHAPMAN

H. N. CHAPMAN, was born in the province of Quebec, Canada, and was reared and educated in his native land. At the age of twenty-one he went to Boston, Massachusetts, and passed a year in the employ of a wholesale house, then returned to Quebec, where he remained until 1871. In March of that year, he came to South Dakota, and settled at Yankton, taking contracts on the construction of the Dakota & Southern Railroad. Later he engaged in butchering at Yankton. In 1876 he arrived at Deadwood with two wagon loads of window glass, the first brought to that point, and sold it at a great profit, getting his own price. Here he devoted his time to mining, doing placer work for the most part, and making his home at Deadwood, where he remained until he came to Rapid City and located land on Spring creek twelve miles from the town, but still retaining his mining claims, of which he yet has a number. Settling on his place, he engaged in raising stock, beginning with sheep and following with cattle and horses. In politics he is an earnest and ardent working Republican, taking an active part in all the campaigns of the party, but without desire or effort to secure office for himself. In 1895 he moved his family to Rapid City, and since then he has maintained his home there, having a fine modern residence, but he is still engaged in the stock industry and his interests in it are large.

The Masonic order awakened his interest many years ago and since then he has been active and earnest in devotion to its welfare. At Yankton Mr. Chapman was united in marriage with Miss Sarah A. Davis, a native of Canada, and they have four children.

MOSES H. CLAGETT, M. D.

Moses H. CLAGETT, Hutchinson County, is a native of the fine old Blue-grass state of Kentucky, having been born in Grayson County, on the 16th of March, 1861, and being a scion of stanch old southern stock. To his parents, John G. and Mary J. (Harrold) Clagett, were born eight children, and of the six surviving we enter the following brief record: Charles W. is sheriff of Grayson County, Kentucky; John H. is a successful teacher in Bowling Green, that state; Mary A. is a missionary of the Baptist church in Japan, where she has been stationed for the past fifteen years; Martha J. is the wife of Hon. W. O. Jones, of Litchfield, Kentucky; Emma is the wife of W. P. Adams, of Pleasure Ridge Park, that state; and Moses H. is the subject of this sketch. The father was born in Maryland, in 1818, the family having early been established in the state and being of English extraction. As a young man he removed to that portion of Virginia which later became a portion of Grayson County, Kentucky, and there he continued to reside until his death, having been a successful farmer and a man who commanded unqualified respect and esteem. He was a Democrat and served about eight years as sheriff of his county, being incumbent of this office at the time of the Civil war. He was summoned to his reward on the 28th of December, 1899, in the fulness of years and honors, at the home of his eldest son; the widow is still living.

Dr. Clagett was reared on the old homestead and after completing the curriculum of the common schools he entered Center College, at Danville, Kentucky, where he continued his studies for four years. In 1885 he began reading medicine, his preceptor being Dr. A. J. Slayton, a prominent physician and surgeon then of Milwood, Kentucky, and now of Litchfield, that state. In the fall of the same year our subject was matriculated in the medical department of the University of Louisville, where he was graduated in March, 1887, receiving his degree of Doctor of Medicine and coming forth well equipped for the active and responsible duties of his chosen profession. He entered practice by establishing an office at Caneyville, Kentucky, where he remained two years, and in September, 1889, he came to Menno, South Dakota, where he has ever since retained his home, having built up a large and representative professional business. In 1893 Dr. Clagett established a telephone system in Menno, and two years later extended its usefulness by constructing a line to Olivet, while in 1898 he disposed of the latter line to the Western Electric Company, still retaining and operating the Menno exchange, which includes about fifty telephones in the village and several in the surrounding country.

He is a member of the State Medical Society, in politics holds to the faith in which he was reared, being a stanch Democrat, and fraternally he is identified with Scotland Lodge, No. 52, Free and Accepted Masons; Scotland Chapter, No. 31, Royal Arch Masons, both of Scotland, Bon Homme County; and with Menno Camp, No. 3071, Modern Woodmen of America. He is held in high esteem in professional and social circles and is one of the leading physicians and surgeons of this section of the state. In October, 1888, Dr. Clagett was united in marriage to Miss Suda Frances Porter, of Caneyville, Kentucky, daughter of George E. Porter, whose parents brought him to Kentucky from Virginia when but a child. Her mother's maiden name was May Hulda Kennedy, of Kentucky. Mrs. Clagett was born in Kentucky and was educated in the public schools there. She has become the mother of four children, all of whom are deceased but one, Mary, who was born July 16, 1889, and is now attending the public schools.

ARTHUR E. CLARK

Arthur E. CLARK, cashier of the Bank of Hecla, is a native of the old Empire state, having been born in Onondaga county. New York, on the 2d of April, 1863, and being a son of Fayette and Priscilla (Spaulding) Clark, both of whom were likewise born and reared in that county, while Chester Clark, the paternal grandfather, was a native of Connecticut, whence he removed to New York state, in an early day. The family is of English extraction and was founded in New England in the colonial epoch of our history, while it is interesting to note that our subject is in the sixth generation of direct descent from Joseph McCoy, who married Jerusha Sawyer, the latter being a member of one of the Puritan families that came over in the historic Mayflower. In 1875 the parents of Mr. Clark removed to Michigan and settled in Ionia County, where the father died in 1878, having been a farmer by vocation. His wife passed away in 1901, and of their three children all are living. Arthur E. Clark, the second of the three children, secured his early educational discipline in the public schools of his native county, and continued his studies in the schools of Michigan, having been twelve years of age at the time of the family removal to the Wolverine state. In his youth he learned the art of telegraphing, which he followed for some time in Michigan, and in 1885 he came to the present state of South Dakota, first locating in Roscoe, Edmunds County, and being thereafter engaged in farming for a short interval. In October, 1885, he became a telegraph operator in the office of the Chicago & Northwestern Railroad at Aberdeen, working at several points as relief agent and operator, until September of the following year, when he located in Hecla, as station agent and operator on the same line of railroad. From an interesting brochure issued by the bank of which he is cashier, we make the following excerpts, as apropos in connection: "In September, 1886, our present cashier, Mr. A. E. Clark, came to this town and opened the station, taking charge as agent and operator. He participated in some of the luxuries of pioneering, to the extent, at least, of sleeping in a pile of straw with a few boards laid on to make it feel like bedding. On December 9, 1887, he opened the books of the State Bank of Dakota, but waited until January 21, 1888, for its first depositor, who was John Quickborner, the agent for Stokes Brothers. In the fall of 1888, when the First National Bank of Columbia, Dakota territory, surrendered its charter, Mr. Charles A. Baker, a man of wealth, induced us to associate our interests and organize the Bank of Hecla, which was chartered December 7, 1888, with an authorized capital of thirty-five thousand dollars. With Charles A. Baker as president and A. E. Clark as cashier, the Bank of Hecla opened its doors in its new building, in which it is still located, on the 28th of May, 1889, with a paid-up capital of fourteen thousand dollars. The Russian thistle and hot winds of the season caused Mr. Baker to long for a more congenial atmosphere and society, and on December 27th of the same year he sold his interests in the bank to James Holborn, who was elected president. At this time the paid-in capital was reduced to ten thousand dollars, and January 1, 1891, a further reduction was affected, to the amount of five thousand dollars. On the 21st of October, 1892, Mr. Holborn resigned the presidency of the bank and P. C. Wright was elected his successor.

"Then followed the 'times that tried men's souls,' the whole country suffering from short crops and the effect of the panic of 1893, until we struck our low point on the 8th of June, 1895. Acknowledgment should be made of the true worth and work of B. S. Clark, who was elected vice-president on the 31st of August, 1893, and who has contributed no small share toward keeping and making the Bank of Hecla an institution of which to be proud."

The management of the bank has at all times been conservative and discriminating, and it is known as a solid and well conducted concern. From its statement rendered on March 2, 1904, we find that its capital is retained at five thousand dollars, while its individual deposits are in excess of seventeen thousand dollars; above thirteen thousand dollars are represented in certificates of deposits, while the undivided profits show an aggregate of nine hundred and three dollars and twenty-three cents. The banking office is a modern and attractive one, with the best of appointments and facilities, and the funds are protected by a Hall fire and burglar-proof safe.

Mr. Clark continued to be more or less identified with the management of the local railway station until 1893, since which time he has given his undivided attention to his banking and other interests. He has been for a number of years prominently concerned in the real-estate business, and has owned much valuable farming and grazing land, having at the present time three quarter sections under effective cultivation and supplied with fine artesian wells, while he also owns a large tract of grazing land. In politics he allies himself with the Socialistic party and is one of its wheelhorses in the state, while his name has appeared on its ticket in connection with nomination for important offices. He is the party candidate for the office of state treasurer at the time of this writing, the election to be held in November, 1904. He is in all senses a most eligible candidate, and his personal popularity is such that he will certainly receive a good endorsement at the polls.

He is affiliated with the Masonic fraternity and the Ancient Order of United Workmen, as well as with the auxiliary branch of the latter, the Degree of Honor. On the 22d of January, 1888, Mr. Clark was united in marriage to Miss Bertha Wilmsen, who was born in Wisconsin. They have no children.

JAMES B. CLARK

James B. CLARK, member of the firm of Clark & Sparling, dealers in general merchandise in Gettysburg, was born on a farm in Harrison County, Ohio, on the 1st of December, 1846, being a son of Joseph and Sarah (Dunlap) Clark, both of whom were born in Pennsylvania, while both died in Ohio, where the father gave his attention to agricultural pursuits until the time of his demise. His grandfather was of English lineage and came to America prior to the war of the Revolution, in which he served as a loyal soldier in the Continental line.

The subject was reared on the homestead farm and was afforded the advantages of the common schools. He continued to be associated in the work and management of the home farm until 1878, when he removed to Nebraska, becoming a pioneer farmer of Pawnee County, where he remained until April, 1883, when he came to South Dakota to repeat his pioneer experiences in Potter County. He filed entry on one hundred and sixty acres of government land, twelve miles southwest of the present attractive village of Gettysburg, and there improved a valuable farm, on which he was actively engaged in diversified agriculture and stock raising until 1890, when he was elected to the office of register of deeds, while at the expiration of his term he was re-elected as his own successor, thus serving four consecutive years and giving a most acceptable administration. Upon retiring from office, he established himself in the general merchandise business in Gettysburg, and has ever since been prominently and successfully identified with this line of enterprise. He continued the business individually until March, 1903, when he admitted John E. Sparling to partnership, under the firm name indicated in the opening paragraph of this sketch, Mr. Sparling being the husband of his eldest daughter and the subject of a personal sketch on another page of this work.

In politics Mr. Clark is a stanch adherent of the Republican party; and fraternally he is identified with the Masonic order, in which he has attained the thirty-second degree of the Ancient Accepted Scottish Rite, being affiliated with Aberdeen Consistory. On the 26th of April, 1876, Mr. Clark was united in marriage to Miss Mary J. Jameson, who was born and reared in Harrison county, Ohio, being a daughter of William and Sarah Jameson, and they are the parents of three daughters, namely: Maud C, who is the wife of John E. Sparling, associated in business with the subject; Nellie, who is a clerical employe in the Potter County Bank, of which her father is a stockholder; and Elizabeth, who is at the time of this writing assistant principal of the public schools at Redfield, Spink County.

JAMES K. CLARK

James K. Clark, vice president of the Lemmon State Bank, a well-organized and carefully managed institution of the town of Lemmon, was born in Polo, Missouri, August 26, 1881, a son of Robert J. and Sallie A. (Moore) Clark, natives of Tennessee and Missouri respectively. In the latter state they were married, the father having removed to that district when a young man. For twenty-five years he was active in financial circles as the cashier of the Lawson Bank of Lawson, Missouri. Further mention of him is made in connection with the sketch of his son, Orson Clark, on another page of this work.

James K. Clark was educated in the public schools of Lawson and in the Presbyterian College of Upper Missouri, from which he was graduated with the class of 1899. He then entered his father's bank, acting in the capacity of bookkeeper for nine months. On the expiration of that period, he went to Oklahoma where he entered into partnership with R. P. Nickelson in the cattle business near Bristow, continuing his activities along that line for two years. Later he was associated with the civil engineering department of the Frisco Railroad, operating in southern Missouri, Tennessee and Arkansas. He worked for the railroad for about a year and in December, 1903, he located at Evarts, South Dakota, where he was made cashier of the Evarts State Bank, acting in that capacity until 1906, when he removed to Seim, this state, and organized the Grand River State Bank, of which he remained cashier until June, 1907. At that date the bank was removed to Lemmon, was subsequently nationalized and merged into the First National Bank. In March, 1911, Mr. Clark sold his interest in that institution and for six months thereafter engaged in the real-estate business in partnership with B. R. Watt. He then removed to Morristown, South Dakota, and purchased an interest in the Morristown State Bank, with which he was identified until October 1, 1912, when he disposed of his interests there and returned to Lemmon, becoming one of the stockholders of the Lemmon State Bank, of which he was elected vice president. He is now active in control of this institution and is regarded as one of the safe and conservative financiers of his part of the state. He also has some land holdings in Perkins County and also in Adams County, North Dakota.

In November, 1910, Mr. Clark was united in marriage to Miss Donna Tripp, of Eyota, Minnesota, by whom he has one child, Floyd O. Fraternally he is identified with the Masons, belonging to Lemmon Lodge, No. 151, A. F. & A. M., of which he has served for two terms as master; Lemmon Chapter, No. 44, R. A. M., of which he served as high priest; and the local chapter of the Order of the Eastern Star, of which he is the present worthy patron. He is a worthy exemplar of the teachings and principles of the craft and is regarded, moreover, as a representative business man and valued citizen whose work has been a directly beneficial force in bringing about the material progress and upbuilding of the city in which he lives.

ORSON CLARK

Orson Clark, vice president of the First National Bank of Mobridge, has devoted practically his entire life to the banking business, starting out in a clerical capacity. He was born in Lawson, Ray County, Missouri,

May 31, 1873, and is a son of Robert J. and Sallie A. (Moore) Clark, the former a native of Tennessee and the latter of Missouri. In young manhood Robert J. Clark toured the western country, covering many of the middle western and coast states looking for a permanent location. However, after his marriage, which was celebrated in Missouri, he settled in Lawson and for many years was prominently identified with its mercantile interests. Subsequently he became associated with the banking business and for twenty-six years was cashier of the Lawson Bank, becoming well known among the loading financiers of the state, remaining in active connection with the bank until he retired from business life, his home being now in Richmond, Missouri. He was formerly a prominent figure in democratic circles but while he had marked influence in party councils, he was ever an aspirant for public preferment although he served for some years as public administrator in Ray County, Missouri. He and his wife are consistent members of the Methodist Church, South, and he belongs to the Masonic lodge, of which he was secretary for thirty years.

After his graduation from the Lawson high school Mr. Clark entered the Presbyterian College of Upper Missouri but toward the close of his first year the college was destroyed by fire and his educational work was never resumed. He then entered a mercantile establishment in Lawson and for seven years gave his attention to clerical work in the different stores of the town. Still later he entered the Lawson Bank as assistant cashier of that institution, serving under his father for seven years. In July, 1907, he arrived in South Dakota, making his way to Lemmon, where he became assistant cashier of the Grand River State Bank. That bank was afterward nationalized and merged into the First National Bank, of which Mr. Clark became the vice president, continuing in that capacity until March, 1910, when he sold his interest and returned to Missouri. For two years thereafter he engaged in the hardware business in Maryville and in the spring of 1912, he returned to South Dakota, settling at Mobridge, where he acquired an interest in the Mobridge State Bank, which was later converted into a national bank and merged into the First National Bank, of which Mr. Clark is now the vice president. Thorough training along banking lines with broadening experiences throughout his entire business career has well qualified him for the discharge of the duties which devolve upon him and for the solution of the intricate problems connected with the banking business.

On the 19th of September, 1899, Mr. Clark was married to Miss Emma Campbell, of Lawson, Missouri, and to them have been born two children, Ernestine Frances and Dorothy Virginia. Mr. Clark votes with the democratic party and is active in public affairs, serving as police commissioner and as member of the school board of Mobridge, acting as treasurer of the board at the present time. His fraternal connections are with Mobridge Lodge, No. 164, A. F. & A. M., and Lemmon Chapter, R. A. M., while he and his wife are members of the Order of the Eastern Star at Mobridge. He is also identified with the Mobridge Lodge of the Knights of Pythias, the Elks, the Modern Woodmen of America and the Owls. He and his wife hold membership in the Congregational church and the varied phases of public life are to him matters of interest. He never neglects his obligations of citizenship nor his opportunities to aid in promoting public progress.

S. WESLEY CLARK

S. WESLEY CLARK.

S. W. CLARK, a representative and successful member of the bar of Spink County, was born at Platteville, Grant County, Wisconsin, on the 28th of December, 1873, and is a son of Samuel P. and Elizabeth (Huntington) Clark, who now maintain their home in San Jose, California. Samuel P. Clark was born on a farm near the city of Rutland, Vermont, in the year 1838, and in 1847 he accompanied his parents on their removal thence to Wisconsin. His father, Pliny Clark, was one of the early pioneers of the Badger state, where he reclaimed a good farm, being compelled in the early epoch to haul his produce by wagon to Milwaukee, eighty miles distant. The Clark genealogy is traced back to pure English extraction and family tradition indicates, that the original representatives in America were Puritans who came over on the historic Mayflower, either on its first or second voyage. Abraham Clark, one of the signers of the Declaration of Independence, was of this family. The father of the subject was reared in Dane county, Wisconsin, where he was educated in the common schools of the pioneer era and the state university, at Madison, where he completed a partial course, withdrawing from that institution in order to assist his parents, by teaching. In 1862 he was united in marriage to Miss Elizabeth Huntington, who was born in Liverpool, England, in 1842. In 1849 her father, Thomas Huntington, came with his family to the United States and settled in Dane county, Wisconsin, becoming one of the prominent farmers near the town of Mazomanie, where the mother of the subject received her early education in the common schools, supplementing this discipline by a course of study in a seminary at Evansville, that state. She and her husband are communicants of the Episcopal church. Thomas Huntington was a prominent architect and builder in Liverpool, after coming to America abandoned his profession and lived quietly on his farm in Wisconsin until summoned to his reward.

In July, 1882, the parents of the subject came to South Dakota and located in Faulk County, within whose confines the father took up a considerable tract of government land and engaged in farming and stock growing, while in 1883 he established the post office of Wesley, named in honor of the subject of this sketch, who was the youngest white boy in the county, having been eight years of age when the family located in Faulk County. During the early years he watched his father's cattle on the prairies and assisted in trapping many wolves and foxes during the winter months, while in August, 1882, he espied a single buffalo, not far distant from the primitive home, and wished to take his father's rifle and shoot the animal, but was forbidden to do so by his anxious mother, her husband being absent at the time. Mr. Clark stated to the writer that he had ever retained a sincere regret that he had failed to shoot at that buffalo. He early manifested a distinctive predilection for the reading of good books and while still a boy expressed a wish to become a lawyer. When but thirteen years of age he began to read with absorbing interest such books as he could obtain as touching both ancient and modern history, as well as scientific works, and the while secured such educational advantages as were offered in the pioneer common schools of Faulk and Spink counties. When but nine years of age he met on his father's farm near Athol, Spink County, Thomas Sterling, now dean of law at the state university, and through a conversation with him determined to take up the study of law as soon as he could secure the necessary books, while it may be said that in the passing years, he has not abated in the least his enthusiasm in the study of the science of jurisprudence in its various branches. He herded cattle for fifteen dollars a month and thus secured the money which enabled him to begin his collegiate work. He studied out on the prairies while keeping watch and ward over the cattle, and at times became so immured in his reading that his charges took unkind advantage of his abstraction and wandered away from their prescribed province. After completing the curriculum of the public schools Mr. Clark entered Redfield College, in which he was graduated as a member of the class of 1894, having taught school to aid in defraying his college expenses and having held a first-grade teacher's certificate when but eighteen years of age. Immediately after his graduation he entered the law office of Sterling & Morris, at Redfield, and devoted himself assiduously to his legal duties until February, 1897, when he was admitted to the bar of the state, upon examination before the supreme court. He then remained with his preceptors for two years, on salary, and at the expiration of this interval, in 1899, entered into a professional partnership with E. B. Korns, at Doland, Spink County, this alliance continuing until the removal of Mr. Korns to Tracy, Minnesota. In 1900, upon his election to the office of state's attorney of Spink County. Mr. Clark returned to Redfield and here entered into partnership with his honored preceptor and friend, Thomas Sterling, and they have since continued to be associated in practice, under the firm name of Sterling & Clark, while they control the leading law business in Spink and adjoining counties. At the time of his election to the office of state's attorney Mr. Clark was but twenty-seven years of age, being at the time the youngest incumbent of such office in the state. At the expiration of his two years' term, in 1902, he was re-elected, receiving the largest majority ever accorded a candidate for public office in the county. His second term will expire in January, 1905, while it should be stated that he has made a most admirable record as a public prosecutor. In politics he gives an uncompromising allegiance to the Republican party.

His religious faith is that of the Congregational church, with which he united while attending college; and fraternally he is identified with the Masonic order, the Knights of Pythias, the Ancient Order of United Workmen, and the Modern Woodmen of America, being at the time of this writing chancellor commander of Ivy Lodge, No. 23, Knights of Pythias. He has ever taken an interest in military affairs, and has been a member of the National Guard since he was sixteen years of age. He enlisted at the time of the Spanish-American war, at Sioux Falls, but was in poor health at the time and thus unable to pass the required physical examination and was not accepted as a volunteer. He is at the present time captain of Company G, Second Regiment, South Dakota, National Guard, at Redfield. Mr. Clark is of sanguine temperament and genial personality, and has a host of loyal friends, his only enemies being malefactors whom he has hard pressed in his various prosecutions. He went to California in 1890, with the intention of permanently locating, but became homesick for the prairies and the invigorating climate of South Dakota, to which state he returned after six months, convinced that this is the ideal place for young men.

On the 7th of February, 1900, at Doland, this county, was solemnized the marriage of Mr. Clark to Miss Daisy Gertrude Labrie, who was born in the state of Illinois but who has resided in South Dakota since infancy, being here reared and educated. She is a daughter of Joseph E. Labrie, who came to this county in 1879, becoming a member of the first board of county commissioners and being one of the most prominent pioneers and influential citizens of Spink County; he is now postmaster at Doland. Mr. and Mrs. Clark have twin sons. Sterling and Stanton, who were born at the home of his parents, in San Jose, California, on the 1st of June, 1902, and when they were but six weeks of age the two lively youngsters were brought to their South Dakota home snugly ensconced in a basket.

WILLIAM R. CLARKE

W. R. CLARKE, one of the prominent and representative farmers and honored citizens of Spink county, has the distinction of being a native of the great western metropolis, the city of Chicago, where he was born on the 2d of November, 1859, being a son of Richard and Fanny Clarke, both of whom were born and reared in Manchester, England, where they continued to reside until 1850, when they came to America and made their way directly to Chicago, where they took up their residence on the 20th of August of that year. The father of the subject is a landscape gardener and florist by vocation, and was long and prominently identified with work along these lines in Chicago, where he is now living practically retired, having attained the venerable age of eighty-four years and still enjoying good health and marked mental vigor.

The subject of this sketch was reared to the age of sixteen years in his native city, where he was afforded the advantages of the public schools. At the age noted he moved to Alden, Minnesota, in which state he passed five years, devoting his attention principally to farming, and he then, in 1881, came to the present state of South Dakota, locating in Spink County on the loth of May of that year. Three and one-half miles south of the present thriving village of Northville be entered pre-emption and homestead claims, which constitute an integral portion of his present fine landed estate, which comprises eight hundred acres. He has been very successful in his operations and has accumulated a valuable property, his farming being improved with high-grade buildings and other modern accessories and conveniences, while the place is especially favored in its supply of water, being one of marked fertility and yielding large crops of grain and other products, while Mr. Clarke also devotes considerable attention to the raising of livestock of good grade.

In politics he accords a stalwart allegiance to the Republican party, but has never been an aspirant for public office. He is prominently identified with the Masonic fraternity, in which he has attained to the thirty-second degree of the Ancient Accepted Scottish Rite, being identified with the consistory at Aberdeen, South Dakota, and with El Riad Temple of the Ancient Arabic Order of the Nobles of the Mystic Shrine, at Sioux Falls, while he is also affiliated with the Ancient Order of United 'Workmen and the Modern Woodmen of America. On the 16th of November, 1887, Mr. Clarke was united in marriage to Miss Nellie Stewart, who was born at Fond du Lac, Wisconsin, on the 8th of October, 1866, and whose death occurred on the 14th of October, 1900. She is survived by two children, Fanny Marguerite and Richard Stewart.

GEORGE ALVIN CLAUSER, M. D.

Dr. George Alvin Clauser has been actively engaged in the practice of medicine and surgery at Bridgewater since 1900 and has won and maintained an enviable reputation as a leading and able representative of the profession in McCook County and South Dakota. His birth occurred in Rossville, Indiana, on the 3d of January, 1865, his parents being William and Carrie (Kuhns) Clauser, both of whom have passed away. Throughout his active business career, the father was successfully identified with general agricultural pursuits.

George Alvin Clauser began his education in the graded schools and later continued his studies in the high school of Logansport, Indiana, while subsequently he was graduated from the Northern Indiana Normal School at Valparaiso, winning the degree of Bachelor of Science in 1891. He then took up the profession of teaching and for three years was identified with educational interests as school principal at Ladora, Iowa. On the expiration of that period, he entered the College of Medicine of the State University of Iowa at Iowa City, which institution conferred upon him the degree of M. D. in 1897. During the following two and a half years he did his initial work as a medical practitioner at Rossville, Indiana, and in 1900 came to Bridgewater, South Dakota, where he has since remained and has been very successful, enjoying a gratifying and well merited practice. His standing in the profession is high and he is now serving as president of the Mitchell District Medical Society, holds the position of city health officer and is vice president of the county board of health. He likewise belongs to the South Dakota State Medical Society and the American Medical Association.

On the 6th of October, 1893, Dr. Clauser was united in marriage to Miss Carrie Warren, of Iowa, a daughter of Calvin and Julia (Back) Warren. To this union have been born three children, namely: Clarence Francis, Zula Mae and Alvin Robinson. The religious faith of the family is that of the Presbyterian church, and in politics Dr. Clauser is a stanch republican. His fraternal relations are with the Masons, the Benevolent Protective Order of Elks and the Independent Order of Odd Fellows. He possesses the personality, acute mental powers and skill in diagnosis which are so essential to the practitioner. Of studious habits, he is constantly striving to improve the standard of his own work and that of the profession in general, readily adapting in his practice every new method the efficacy of which he feels is above question.

JOHN ALBERT CLEAVER *

John A. Cleaver, a representative business man and popular citizen of Huron, Beadle County, was born in Havana, Mason County, Illinois, on the 28th of October, 1860, being a son of Hiram R. and Isabelle (Wilburn) Cleaver, the father being a druggist by vocation and being long one of the prominent business men of Havana. The subject received his early educational training in the public schools of his native town and later continued his studies in the Presbyterian College, at Lincoln, Illinois. Upon leaving school he initiated his business career by securing a position as bookkeeper for a firm of retail implement dealers, in Havana, Illinois, and in 1881 he engaged in the same line of enterprise on his own responsibility, in his native town of Havana. In 1884 he entered the employ of the A. J. Hedges Header Company, in the capacity of traveling representative, and he came to the territory of Dakota in the interest of the company, and, as he states the case, he "managed to get mixed up in the Highmore cyclone in 1885 and was scared out of a year's growth." He passed the winter of 1886-7 in South America, as a representative of the same company, which was succeeded by the Acme Harvester Company in 1891, and Mr. Cleaver facetiously remarked to the writer that he "went with the assets," passing the years 1891 and 1892 in Lincoln, Nebraska, as the local representative of the company, while during the ensuing two years he was in the home office of the company, at Pekin, Illinois, while in 1895 he returned to South Dakota and took up his residence in Huron, where he has since maintained his home, being the general agent of the same company for this state.

In 1898 Mr. Cleaver was elected mayor of Huron, his administration proving so acceptable that he has ever since been retained at the head of the municipal government, by successive yearly elections. Fraternally he is identified with Huron Lodge, No. 26, Ancient Free and Accepted Masons, of which he is past master; Huron Chapter. No. 10, Royal Arch Masons, of which he is past high priest; Lacottah Commandery, No. 6, Knights Templar, in which he is captain of the guard at the present time; South Dakota Consistory, No. 4, Ancient Accepted Scottish Rite; and El Riad Temple, Ancient Arabic Order of the Nobles of the Mystic Shrine, at Sioux Falls. He is one of the prominent and popular members of the time-honored fraternity, and in 1901 served as the grand master of the Masonic grand lodge of the state. He also is affiliated with Huron Lodge, No. 17, Ancient Order of United Workmen, of which he is past master workman. He and his wife are members of the Presbyterian church in Huron. While a resident of Illinois Mr. Cleaver was for five years a member of the National Guard of the state.

On the 27th of December, 1882, Mr. Cleaver was united in marriage to Miss Effie Pierce, of Havana, Illinois, she being a daughter of John and Mary Pierce.

ALONZO E. CLOUGH, M. D.

Alonzo E. CLOUGH, was born in St. Lawrence County, New York, and received his rudimentary educational discipline in the public schools of his native state. After the family removal to the west, he continued his studies in the common schools and at Cresco Academy, while later he was matriculated in the Upper Iowa University, at Fayette. Subsequently he entered the College of Physicians and Surgeons at Keokuk, Iowa, where he completed his technical course, being graduated and receiving his coveted degree of Doctor of Medicine. Later he took a special course in the New York Polyclinic, and he has also taken several special postgraduate courses in the leading medical schools of the city of Chicago.

Shortly after receiving his degree Dr. Clough came to South Dakota and located in Madison, Lake County, where he has ever since maintained his home and where he has built up a large and representative practice, and he is to be noted as one of the pioneer physicians of the state. The Doctor is a stanch Republican in his political proclivities, and has been one of the leaders in the party councils in the state, having had the distinction of serving as chairman of the state central committee in 1892-3, though he has never sought official preferment of a personal nature.

He is affiliated with the Masonic fraternity and also with the Independent Order of Odd Fellows. He and his family are communicants of the Protestant Episcopal church. Dr. Clough was united in marriage to Miss Mary P. Matheny, who was born and reared in Wauseon, Ohio, and of this union have been born three children.

LOUIS H. CLYBORNE

L. H. Clyborne, one of the representatives and highly honored citizens of Herreid, Campbell County, is a native of the state of Illinois, having been born in Cameron, Warren County on the 5th of October, 1861, and being a son of Archibald and Jennie E. (Leeder) Clyborne, the former of whom is now a resident of the city of Chicago. The original representatives of the Clyborne family in America were numbered among the first settlers of the patrician old state of Virginia, where the family became one of prominence and influence, the lineage of our subject being traced back to William Clyborne, who established his home in the Old Dominion state in the early colonial epoch of our national history. William L. Clyborne, the grandfather of the subject, was one of the early settlers in Cass County, Michigan, in which state Archibald Clyborne was born and reared. In 1860 he removed to Illinois and located near Galesburg, where he continued to reside until 1876, when he removed to the city of Chicago, where he has ever since maintained his home and where he is engaged in the live-stock commission business. Of the four children the subject of this sketch is the eldest.

Mr. Clyborne was reared in Illinois and secured his education in the public schools of Gales burg and Chicago. He continued to reside in Illinois until 1883, when he came to South Dakota, arriving in Aberdeen, Brown County, on the 27th of March. After passing a few months in Aberdeen he removed to Lagrace, Campbell County, in which locality he was engaged in farming and stock growing until 1890, having been very successful in his efforts and having contributed materially to the development of the industrial resources of this attractive section of the state. In the year mentioned he was elected register of deeds of the county, and took up his residence in Mound City, the county seat. He was re-elected in 1892, and thus remained incumbent of this office for four successive years. Upon retiring from office Mr. Clyborne engaged in the real-estate and abstract business in Mound City, and in 1895 formed a partnership with C. E. Eckert, which association has ever since continued. In 1897 they purchased the bank of Campbell & Johnston, in Mound City, which they conducted until 1903, when they moved to Herreid, and on the 1st of May, 1903, they purchased the Herreid State Bank, which they reorganized as the Campbell County State Bank, of which they still remain in control. The bank is capitalized for twenty thousand dollars, has deposits of fifty thousand dollars. The institution is a solid and reliable one, being ably and carefully managed and controlling an excellent business. Mr. Clayborne has extensive real-estate interests in the county, being associated with Mr. Eckert in the ownership of five thousand acres of valuable farming lands, while he is also interested in various manufacturing and industrial enterprises. He has an attractive modern residence in Herreid, and the same is a center of gracious hospitality.

In politics the subject accords a stanch allegiance to the Republican party, and fraternally he is identified with Acacia Lodge, No. 108, Ancient Free and Accepted Masons. He has been an earnest and zealous factor in church and Sunday school and is one of the prominent and valued members of the Methodist Episcopal church in his home town. He was for thirteen years superintendent of a Sunday school in Mound City. On the 19th of November, 1889, Mr. Clyborne was united in marriage to Miss Elizabeth N, Stuart, who was born in Fillmore County, Minnesota, being a daughter of Charles Stuart, who there, continued to reside until his death. Mr. and Mrs. Clyborne have four children, namely: Helen V., Robert A., Gladys Ramona and children, Ruth.

CLARK GILBERT COATS

On the pages of pioneer history of Sioux Falls appears the name of Clark G. Coats, and the worth of his work as a factor in the upbuilding and development of the city is widely acknowledged. His death, therefore, was not simply a private bereavement but a public misfortune when he passed away in a Chicago hospital on the 8th of August, 1915. He was born in Mecca, Ohio, March 14, 1844. The ancestry of the family is traced back to Spain to the Cortes family, so well-known in connection with the history of that country. Members of the Cortes family went to Holland during the thirty years' war as soldiers of the Spanish king. They remained in that country, settling on land granted to them by the Spanish king for their services in the wars which their monarchy carried on with the Netherlands. In time the family emigrated to England and settled there. Three brothers, sons of the first English settler of the Cortes family, separated. One brother went to Scotland and established the Coats family, known throughout the world as the famous thread makers. The second brother came to America in the seventeenth century and established his home near Amsterdam, New York City. Soon the other brother followed him to America and settled in the southeastern part of New York state. The Scotland brother and his descendants have always spelled their name Coats and so it was with the second brother and his children, but the youngest brother and his children have always spelled their name Coates. Thus, it is that the families go by different names.

Gilbert N. Coats, the father of our subject, was a very active man and kept the record of the family traditions to the last. He was one of the early settlers of the Buckeye state, to which he removed from Connecticut. He made farming his chief occupation in early life and afterward turned his attention to merchandising, which he followed in Mecca, Ohio, until 1847. He then failed in business and was largely involved financially, but although he had a chance to settle with his creditors at twenty-five cents on the dollar, he refused. He felt a moral obligation that demanded the payment in full of his debts, notwithstanding that the legal requirement was but twenty-five per cent. He turned his attention to novelty wood working and though it required a severe sacrifice and took him fifteen years to accomplish it, he paid his creditors in full — one hundred cents on the dollar. This principle of honor greatly impressed his son Clark G., whose youthful mind so clearly retained the remembrance of this character-forming incident that he was prepared for a similar trial and similar result in his later life as indicated further on in this sketch. At the time of his death Gilbert N. Coats was a resident of Cortland, Ohio, four miles distant from his old home at Mecca. He was prominent in public affairs and left the impress of his individuality upon the welfare of his community. He married Sarah Ann Lake, also a native of Connecticut, and they became the parents of six children, of whom Clark G. was the second in order of birth. A brother, Charles Coats, is now a resident of Fort Dodge, Iowa.

In the common schools of Mecca, Ohio, Clark G. Coats pursued his education and until eighteen years of age remained an active assistant of his father, who was conducting novelty wood works at that place. In the meantime, he learned the cooper's trade and in 1862 went to Cleveland, Ohio, where he remained until 1869, when, attracted by the opportunities of the growing west, he started for the territory of Dakota, establishing his home in the little settlement of Fort Dakota, a military reservation situated upon the western frontier. At that place there was then but one white woman outside the fort, and this was the nucleus of what is now Sioux Falls. Here Mr. Coats began business as an Indian trader, making his headquarters at Flandreau, but in 1870 he took up a homestead three miles south of Sioux Falls and began the development of a farm. The country was practically a wild, unbroken, houseless prairie, and for a time his home was in a part of the old army barracks which the government had abandoned. Laborious effort enabled him in time to break the sod and bring his fields under cultivation and he continued to engage actively and successfully in general agricultural pursuits until 1904, when he retired from business save for the supervision which he gave to his private interests and investments.

Mr. Coats was a man of resolution and determined action, ever ready to take a chance on any investment which gave fair promise and thus he readily extended his holdings. He was the owner of extensive property interests adjoining the city limits. At its inception he was connected as a stockholder with the Dakota National Bank. He was also known for many years as a breeder of fast harness horses and was a well-known driver on the race track, owning at different times many valuable standard bred horses which he drove himself. He was one of the prominent and wealthy pioneers, whose investments in land became valuable owing to the improvements which he made upon his property and the natural rise in realty values owing to the increased population. Mr. Coats started the first frame house ever built in Sioux Falls, its location being at the northwest corner of Phillips and Twelfth streets. He hauled the lumber from Sioux City when it took a week to make the trip. He occupied the house for several years before removing to the farm, and the building is still standing, although it has been removed to Third avenue. The original well on the property was dug by three of Sioux Falls' prominent men – Mr. Coats, ex-Senator R. F. Pettigrew and N. L. Phillips. The well was thirty-five feet deep and was dug by throwing the dirt from scaffold to scaffold. From the late '80s until about 1900 South Dakota suffered a reaction in its activities and a partial financial panic brought heavy losses to many, among them Mr. Coats, who Jost properties valued at about a half million dollars, but he weathered the storm, honorably meeting all of his obligations, and again became financially strong. The example of his father had never been forgotten. It had left an indelible impress upon the mind of the son and he felt that no other course was honorable than that of paying all debts in full. He refused, as did his father, to take advantage of any legal technicalities to escape doing so and in course of years he could honestly say that he could look any man squarely in the face, knowing that he did not owe him a single cent.

On the 4th of June, 1870, Mr. Coats was united in marriage to Miss Ella Pierson, a daughter of D. J. Pierson, of Kalamazoo, Michigan, and they became the parents of two children: Maud, now the wife of Will L. Bruce, of Yankton; and Mark D., who is living in Sioux City, Iowa. While Mr. and Mrs. Coats were on a trip, the latter was taken ill at Athens, Ohio, and gradually grew weaker until she was confined to her bed. A stroke of paralysis followed and three weeks later she died, in March, 1915. Her remains were brought back to Sioux Falls for interment and the Masonic fraternity furnished the pallbearers. She was always patient and uncomplaining, a most lovable, charitable and Christian character who ever thought of others, how she might aid them, and remained such to the last. Mrs. Coats was for many years very active in church and charitable work and was the organizer of the first Sunday school in the territory, serving as its superintendent. Her efforts were a potent force in advancing moral progress in this section of South Dakota. She was also a member of the Eastern Star. A lady of innate culture and refinement, she also possessed notable talent and ability. In her earlier life she was well known as an artist in oils. Her work was of high character and was eagerly sought by art critics, while flattering offers were made by collectors. Many fine specimens of her paintings of portraits, animals, fruit and landscape adorned their home. Two especially noteworthy oil paintings by Mrs. Coats are one of the Indian maid Pocahontas in complete Indian costume, and the other a very large picture of Pharaoh's Horses.

In politics Mr. Coats was a republican with independent tendencies. For six years he served as a member of the city council of Sioux Falls and was made a member of the constitutional convention which framed the present organic law of the state. He attained the Knights Templar degree in Masonry and was one of the organizers of the order in Sioux Falls. He joined the fraternity in Bloomfield, Ohio, and his identification therewith extended over a half century. He was also affiliated with the Eagles. He enjoyed his automobile and motoring was his chief source of recreation, his financial condition giving him leisure in which to enjoy this phase of outdoor life.

Forty-six years were added to the cycle of the centuries from the time that Mr. Coats arrived in Dakota until he was called to his final rest and great were the changes which were made during that period. He was ever an interested witness of the events which occurred to bring about present-day progress and prosperity and at all times bore his share in the work of general improvement. As he possessed only four hundred dollars when he came to the west, he may truly be called a self-made man, deserving of all the honor and trust which the term implies. He made what may be termed a double financial success, for while he prospered during the earlier years of his residence in South Dakota, the panic swept away his fortune and forced him to start in business life anew. Again, he won with honor, becoming one of the substantial citizens of his part of the state. He will be remembered for many years to come as a kind-hearted man, fair and just to all, his career constituting an example well worthy of emulation, for his life displayed all that is admirable in conduct and character.

FRANK R. COCK

Frank R. Cock is a prominent rancher living at Belle Fourche and has made a most creditable record as a state official, serving as a member of the South Dakota live-stock sanitary board. Perhaps no resident of the state is better qualified for this office and none could display greater loyalty in the discharge of duty. He was born in Davenport, Iowa, April 30, 1867. His father, Charles C. Cock, was a native of Ohio, and in 1862 removed westward to Iowa, where he turned his attention to the manufacture of farm implements for a time and later to the sale of implements, remaining actively and successfully in that business until his death, which occurred in Cedar Rapids, Iowa, in 1899. He took an active and helpful interest in local affairs and was for many years a member of the city council of Davenport during his residence there. He married Rebecca Raff, a native of Ohio, who still survives and makes her home in St. Joseph, Missouri. She is of Holland Dutch ancestry, tracing her lineage back to the settlement of New Amsterdam. The ancestors of the Cock family were associates of William Penn in the early settlement of Pennsylvania and were devout adherents of the Quaker faith.

Frank R. Cock was the second in a family of four children and spending his youthful days in Davenport, Iowa, he pursued his education in its public schools, passing through consecutive grades to the high school. In 1884 he went to Central City, Nebraska, and there had his first experience in the live-stock business as an employe on his uncle's ranch. At the end of a year, he removed to Lincoln County, Nebraska, where he began ranching on his own account and in 1889, he came to South Dakota, settling in Belle Fourche valley, where he has since been largely interested in the conduct of a ranch, meeting with excellent success in his undertakings. At the present time he is operating a ranch of twelve hundred acres in Butte County, employing the latest improved and approved methods in the conduct of his business. He has been for many years a persistent and discriminating student of the diseases of farm animals and their eradication, or better still, their prevention, and his valuable work in that direction made him one of the logical appointees when the state department of live-stock sanitation was created in 1909. He has served continuously since on the live-stock sanitary board, also acting as its secretary. In 1913 when the department was thoroughly reorganized, he was the only member reappointed, a fact which is highly complementary and indicates in no uncertain terms the ability which he displayed and the fidelity with which he discharged the duties devolving upon him. The administration of his duties has been marked by an intelligent, earnest zeal in behalf of the stock-growing interests of the state and his activities have proven a distinct asset to the industry. Largely through his efforts the department has been brought to a high working efficiency and has eliminated the hardship of frequent federal quarantines characteristic of the earlier days.

Mr. Cock was married April 17, 1895, to Miss Louise C. Teall, a daughter of B. F. and Julia Phelps (Van Cleef) Teall, of Eau Claire, Wisconsin. They have had two children but the son, Charles C, is deceased. The only living child is Dorothy G.

The family attend the Congregational church and Mr. Cock holds membership in the Masonic fraternity. In politics he has always been a stalwart republican but not an office seeker in the usually accepted sense of the term. He served for a number of years as a member of the Belle Fourche school board and for several years was its president, wisely directing the interests of the schools along the lines of progress, making the system one of thorough preparation for life's practical and responsible duties. He finds his recreation in big game hunting and has secured various trophies of the chase.

ALBERT WELLS COE *

Albert W. Coe, one of the honored pioneers and prominent business men of the city of Deadwood, is a native of Madison County, New York, where he was born on the 14th of August, 1833, being a son of Albert E. and Mary (Bridge) Coe, both of whom were likewise natives of that county, the former having been born in the same ancestral homestead as was the subject. The grandfather, who bore the name of David Coe, was a native of Middletown, Connecticut, while the name has been prominently identified with the annals of New England from the early colonial epoch. The ancestry is traced back in direct line to Roger Coe, who was burned at the stake in England, during the reign of Queen Mary, so commonly known as "Bloody Mary." The original progenitor in America was Robert Coe, who emigrated from the "tight little isle" to this country in 1634. From one of his three sons the subject of this review is directly descended. A number of representatives of the family rendered valiant service in the cause of independence during the war of the Revolution, and the subject's daughter. Miss Clara D., is thus entitled to and maintains membership in the Daughters of the Revolution. David Coe was a lad of twelve years at the time of his parents' removal from Connecticut to Oneida county. New York, where he was reared to manhood. He married at the age of twenty-one years and thereafter removed to Madison County, that state, where he engaged in agricultural pursuits and where he passed the remainder of his life. The father of the subject passed his entire life in that county; he died in 1887, and his wife passed away in 1844. They became the parents of six sons and three daughters, of whom one of the sons and one of the daughters are still living.

Albert W. Coe, who was the third child in order of birth, was reared to the study discipline of the home farm and secured his education in the common schools of the locality and period. Upon attaining his legal majority, he set forth to seek his fortunes in the west. He located in what is now the city of Chicago, where he remained until 1856, when he removed to Milwaukee, Wisconsin, as one of the pioneers of the Cream City, and there continued to make his home for nearly thirty years — until the time of his removal to what is now the state of South Dakota. It may be consistently noted in the connection that a brother of his present wife was the third white child born in that city. Mr. Coe was one of the charter members of the Milwaukee board of trade and was for a number of years prominently identified with the commission business, after which he engaged in the hardware business, in which he there continued until 1883, when he came to South Dakota and located in Deadwood, where he has since maintained his home. Here he became associated with J. K. P. Miller in the grocery business, of which they continued for some time, then disposing of the enterprise and engaging in the real-estate business, of which the subject assumed control upon the death of his honored partner. He has since been identified with this line of enterprise and has been concerned in many important transactions and assisted materially in the developing of the great resources of this section of the state. Mr. Miller, with whom he was so long associated, was the promoter and builder of the Deadwood Central Railroad and the Deadwood Street railway, while Mr. Coe was secretary of both companies during the building of both systems, while after their completion he held the office of manager until the properties were sold. Mr. Coe is at the present time a member of the Business Men's Club, of Deadwood, and also the Mining Men's Association, while he is a member of the directorate of the Franklin Hotel Company and the Masonic Benevolent Association.

He is one of the prominent and honored members of the Masonic fraternity in the state, and is at the present time treasurer of the lodge, chapter and commandery with which he has affiliated, while he has attained the thirty-second degree in the Ancient Accepted Scottish Rite and is also affiliated with the Ancient Arabic Order of the Nobles of the Mystic Shrine. In 1897 he had the distinction of serving as grand master of the Masonic grand lodge of the state, and he is at the present time president of the South Dakota Masonic Veteran Association, having been a Mason for more than forty years.

On the 13th of July, 1854, Mr. Coe was united in marriage to Miss Emeline Gregg, who, like himself, was born and reared in Madison County, New York, and she died in Milwaukee, Wisconsin, in 1857, leaving no children. On the 31st of March, 1859, was solemnized the marriage of Mr. Coe to Miss Sarah D. Gregg, a daughter of Hendrick Gregg, who removed from Madison County, New York, to Milwaukee, Wisconsin, in 1836, being numbered among the early settlers in that locality and being one of the honored pioneer farmers of the Badger state. Mr. and Mrs. Coe have one son, Albert G., and a daughter, Clara D. The former was born in Milwaukee, Wisconsin, on the 18th of April, 1860, and is now associated with his father in business. On the 18th of September, 1883, he was united in marriage to Miss Agnes L. Foster, who was born in Racine, Wisconsin, being a daughter of Alfred Foster, who removed thence to Milwaukee when she was a child, so that she was reared and educated in the latter city. Of this union was born one child, Alberta, who died in infancy. Albert G. is a member of the Olympian Club, and, like his honored father, has attained the thirty-second degree of Scottish Rite Masonry, while his political faith is that of the Democratic party. The daughter, Clara D., also assists in the management of the business interests of the Coe establishment. She has been active in the affairs of the Order of the Eastern Star and has officiated as worthy matron of the local lodge.

HOWARD W. COLE

Howard W. Cole was serving for the second term as sheriff of his county when death called him on the 5th of June, 1905. He made his home in Aberdeen from the 1st of January, 1903, and bore an unassailable reputation for faithfulness in office. He had previously been engaged in agricultural pursuits in Brown County, in which connection he was also well known. Michigan numbered him among her native sons, his birth having occurred in Eureka, Montcalm County, on the 29th of March, 1857, his parents being Leander T. and Sarah Jane (Stout) Cole. His father was a native of New York but at the age of fourteen years left that state with his parents, who removed with their family to Jackson County, Michigan. In 1851 Leander T. Cole became a resident of Greenville, Michigan, and it was there that he became acquainted with and married Miss Sarah J. Stout. They began their domestic life on a farm in Eureka township, Montcalm County. In 1881 they removed to Brown County, South Dakota, and later located six miles north of Groton, this state, where Mr. Cole passed away January 17, 1900. He was for two years a member of the Twenty-first Regiment of Michigan Volunteer Infantry during the Civil war and participated in a number of the hotly contested battles which led up to the final victory that crowned the Union arms.

Howard W. Cole was the eldest in a family of four children and spent his youthful days on the home farm, being early trained to habits of industry and economy. He continued to assist his father in the work of the old homestead until he was married in 1880, at the age of twenty-three years. Not long afterward he removed to South Dakota, taking up his abode in Brown County, August 9, 1881, at which time he secured a preemption claim about ten miles north of the present town of Groton. In 1882 he disposed of that property and secured a homestead claim in what is now Claremont township, covering the southeast quarter of section 25, township 125, range 60. Soon afterward he became foreman on the farm of H. M. Fuller and in the spring of 1884, he formed a partnership with S. W. Weber, F. D. Adams and H. C. Sessions for the purchase of the Fuller farm, to which they added from time to time until the place comprised twelve hundred and eighty acres. The partnership was continued until the death of Mr. Adams in 1898 and Mr. Cole retained his interest in the property until in 1903, when the partners sold their interests. He retained three hundred and twenty acres, however, but sold this before coming to Aberdeen. Mr. Cole continued to reside on the ranch until the autumn of 1902, when he was elected sheriff of the county, and on the 1st of January, 1903, removed to Aberdeen to enter upon the active discharge of his duties. That he was loyal, capable and faithful during his first term is indicated in his reelection. He only served for five months of the second term, however, for death called him on the 5th of June, 1905. He was prominent in connection with a number on public affairs. He aided in the organization of Claremont township and served, on its board of supervisors for a number of years. For nine years he filled the office of school treasurer in his district and he represented his township in nearly all of the county and state republican conventions, the party recognizing in him one of its stalwart and effective champions. For two terms he acted as postmaster of Huffton.

As previously stated, Mr. Cole was married on the 9th of December, 1880, the lady of his choice being Miss Theresa M. Howell, who was born in the province of Ontario, Canada, a daughter of Gideon and

Nancy A. (Longstreet) Howell. Her father was a native of Oxford County, Ontario, and in 1865 he took his family to Michigan, where he followed the blacksmith's trade until 1884. He then removed to Detroit township, Brown County, South Dakota, opening the first blacksmith shop in that township. After living there for a time, he removed to Claremont and conducted a general blacksmithing business at that place until his life's labors were ended in death in 1901, when he was seventy-four years of age. He was married in Canada in 1854 to Nancy Ann Longstreet, and they were the parents of five children, of whom three are yet living, Henry Casper, Lawrence Richard and Mrs. Cole. Mr. Howell was a republican in his political views, always strongly indorsing the principles of the party. His religious faith was that of the Baptist church and his fraternal relations were with the Masons. Mrs. Howell now makes her home with her daughter Mrs. Cole in Aberdeen.

To Mr. and Mrs. Cole were born five children, of whom Charles Henry died at the age of four years and three months. Arthur Maxwell, who attended high school and later graduated from Granger Business College, is now cashier of the Naragan Investment Company. Mildred Nancy, now a teacher in the public schools, attended the Aberdeen high school and took a post-graduate course at the Northern Normal Industrial School. Mary Jeannette, who also pursued a post-graduate course at the Northern Normal School, is now the wife of Frank E. Guline, cashier in the freight department of the Northwestern Railroad office. Walter Gideon is attending high school.

Mr. Cole was well known in Masonic circles, holding membership in Cement Lodge, No. 103, A. F. & A. M., at Claremont; Aberdeen Chapter, No. 14, R. A. M.; Damascus Commandery, No. 10, K. T., of Aberdeen; Adah Chapter, No. 52, O. E. S., at Claremont; and was also a Scottish Rite Mason, belonging to James C. Bachelor Lodge of Perfection, No. 6; Aberdeen Chapter, No. 4, Rose Croix; Albert Pike Council, No. 4, Knights of Kodosh; South Dakota Consistory, No. 4, S. P. R. S.; and Yelduz Temple of the Mystic Shrine. He was identified with Claremont Lodge, No. 5, A. O. U. W.; Claremont Tent, No. 25, K. O. T. M.; and Claremont Camp, No. 6199, M. W. A. He was ever loyal to the teachings of these organizations and in his life exemplified the beneficent spirit which underlies them. He never sought to figure prominently in any public connection, but his genuine worth and strength of character made him a leading factor in local affairs and caused his death to be deeply regretted among those who knew him. He was a most upright man, was recognized as the soul of honor and was loved by all who knew him.

EDWIN GRANT COLEMAN

Edwin G. COLEMAN, of Flandreau, one of the able and representative members of the bar of the state and at the present time serving as state's attorney for Moody County, is a native of the state of Illinois, having been born in Pilot Grove township, Hancock County, on the 6th of March, 1867, a son of Charles B. and Nancy (Huckins) Coleman, who are now deceased, the father having been a farmer by vocation. Both the parental and maternal grandparents of the subject were numbered among the earliest settlers in Hancock County, whither the former came from Zanesville, Ohio, and the latter from Concord, New Hampshire, while both families trace the ancestral line back to stanch Puritan stock, having been founded in New England in the early colonial epoch.

The subject received excellent educational advantages in his early youth. After completing the curriculum of the common schools, he continued his studies in turn in the La Harpe Academy and the Giddings Academy, at La Harpe, Illinois; later attended the Northern Illinois Normal School, at Dixon; and in 1889 was matriculated in the law department of the University of Michigan, where he completed the prescribed course and was graduated on the 28th of June, 1892, having been admitted to the bar of that state on the 3d of the same month. He was admitted to practice before the supreme court of Illinois on the 11th of June, of the same year; and on the 15th of June, 1898, was admitted to practice before the supreme court of South Dakota. In the autumn of 1892 Mr. Coleman formed a professional alliance with J. F. Hamilton and engaged in the practice of law in Galesburg, Illinois, where he remained until the spring of 1898, when he came to South Dakota, locating in Flandreau on the 29th of April and here opening an office. He has since been actively and successfully engaged in the practice of his profession here, retaining a representative clientage and being known as a safe and conservative counselor and as an able trial lawyer. On the 1st of November, 1901, he entered into a professional partnership with John O. Adams, under the firm name of Adams & Coleman, and this association has since obtained, the firm holding a very high standing at the bar of the state and having the confidence and esteem of the community.

In politics Mr. Coleman is a stanch advocate of the principles and policies of the Republican party, in whose cause he takes an active interest, and he has served since 1902 as state's attorney for Moody county, proving a discriminating and faithful prosecutor, while for the past five years he has been a member of the village council of Flandreau. He was for six years a member of the Sixth Regiment of the Illinois National Guard, with which he was in active service during the labor strikes in Chicago, Pekin, Spring Valley and other places in the state, in 1894.

Fraternally he is a Master Mason and also identified with the Modern Woodmen of America, the Order of the Eastern Star, the Royal Neighbors, the Knights of the Maccabees and the Benevolent and Protective Order of Elks. On the 12th of June, 1902, Mr. Coleman was united in marriage to Miss Lucy M. Vance, a daughter of Nathan Vance, of Flandreau, she being a native of Minnesota and at the time of her marriage with Mr. Coleman a resident of Flandreau, North Dakota.

R. E. CONE

R. E. Cone is a prominent representative of financial interests in Huron as president of the James Valley Bank, of which institution he has served as the chief executive officer since 1911. His birth occurred in Iowa in 1881, his parents being James W. and Emily (Staples) Cone, who came to Brule County, South Dakota, in 1883. The father, an attorney by profession, was engaged in the abstract business at Sioux Falls. He died October 10, 1913.

R. E. Cone acquired his early education in the public schools and subsequently attended the Baptist College. After putting aside his textbooks he secured a position as stenographer and in January, 1902, became identified with the banking business at Mitchell, entering the service of the Commercial & Savings Bank, with which he remained for nine years and eight months, acting as cashier of the institution for several years. In September, 1911, he came to Huron to take up his duties as president of the James Valley Bank, in which important capacity he has served to the present time. The bank was incorporated on the 15th of May, 1902, with the following officers: George S. Hutchinson, president; C. H. Bonesteel, vice president; John J. Greene, M. L. Tobin and William Waibel, directors; and Frank J. Sauer, cashier. On the 13th of July, 1911, R. E. Cone bought out Mr. Hutchinson and succeeded the latter as president of the institution, which owns a handsome structure at the corner of Dakota and Third streets. Its present officers are as follows: R. E. Cone, president; C. H. Bonesteel, vice president; V. C. Bonesteel, cashier; C. C. Smith, assistant cashier. The directors are R. E. Cone, John J. Greene, C. H. Bonesteel, M. L. Tobin and William Waibel. Following is the statement made to the public examiner for the close of business on August 9, 1913.

The James Valley Bank pays four per cent compound interest on savings accounts, receives deposits subject to check, loans money on personal security, makes farm loans at lowest rates, giving quick service, and rents safety deposit boxes for valuable papers at one dollar per year. As the head of this institution Mr. Cone has contributed in large measure to its continued growth and success and is widely recognized as a prominent and respected citizen of Huron.

In 1903 Mr. Cone was united in marriage to Miss Frances Haney, of Newton, Kansas, by whom he has three children. His political allegiance is given to the republican party, while his religious faith is that of the Episcopal church. Fraternally he is identified with the Benevolent and Protective Order of Elks and the Masons, being past master of Resurgam Lodge, No. 31, A. F. & A. M., and a member of the chapter, council and commandery at Huron. Though still a young man, he has already won an enviable position in financial and social circles of the state in which practically his entire life has been spent.

CHARLES A. CONKLIN

Charles A. Conklin was born in Greenwood, Steuben County, New York, on the 1st of August, 1853, and is a son of Hon. S. J. and Maria Conklin, who came to the west in 1857 and located in Waterloo, Wisconsin, where the father became prominent in the pioneer history of the state, being successfully identified with agricultural enterprises and also becoming one of the distinguished members of the bar of that commonwealth. He served as quartermaster in the Forty-eighth Wisconsin Regiment and was adjutant general for South Dakota for four years. He died in South Dakota in November, 1872, while his wife died at Clark. The subject has one brother, who lives in Chicago, and a sister, who lives in Hammond, Indiana.

Charles A. Conklin was a lad of five years at the time of his parents' removal to Wisconsin, where he was reared to maturity, securing such advantages as were afforded in the excellent public schools of Waterloo, that state, and remaining at the parental home until 1873, when he went to Freeborn County, Minnesota, where he engaged in farming until 1876, when he disposed of his interests there and came as a pioneer to South Dakota. He proceeded by railroad as far as Watertown, which was then the terminus of the line, and then located in the village of Clark, in the county of the same name, where he engaged in buying grain for the Porter Milling Company, of Winona, and there he continued to make his headquarters, continuously connected with the line of enterprise noted, until 1892, when he removed to Cherry creek and was there engaged in the capacity of government farmer on the Cheyenne Indian reservation for the ensuing two years, at the expiration of which he opened up his present fine stock ranch, on the Cheyenne river, fifty miles from Fort Pierre and two miles distant from Lindsey, which is his post office address. He has here been since engaged in the raising of cattle and horses, carrying forward the enterprise with characteristic energy and discrimination and having an ample range, well-watered by the river as well as a number of natural springs of pure water. He gives his preference to the Hereford breed of cattle and to Morgan horses, and on his ranch may be usually found about three hundred fine specimens of the former and one hundred and fifty or more of the latter. In politics Mr. Conklin has ever given an unfaltering allegiance to the Republican party, but he has refused to permit the use of his name in connection with political office of any description.

He is a member of the Masonic and Pythian fraternities. On the 28th of April, 1876, Mr. Conklin was united in marriage to Miss Martha Austin, who was born and reared in Wisconsin, being a daughter of

Samuel Austin, and she was summoned into eternal rest in April, 1888, and is survived by four children, namely: Roy, Rena, Samuel and Clyde. On the 2d of October, 1890, Mr. Conklin was united in marriage to Miss Ida Geyer, who was born in the state of Illinois, being a sister of Isaac M. Geyer, who is the subject of an individual sketch on another page of this work. To said article reference may be made for data concerning the family. Of this union has been born one child, Wanita, who was born in Clark, Clark County, South Dakota, July 21, 1891, and is now twelve years old and has been attending school at Pierre for the last four years.

HON. SYLVESTER JONES CONKLIN

Sylvester J. CONKLIN was born in Penn Yan, Yates County, New York, May 5, 1829, and is of Holland-Dutch descent on his father's side and Welch and French on the side of his mother. His father died when he was but four years of age, leaving the widow without other means than her own labor to support three children, of which the subject was the eldest. At the age of twelve years, he was apprenticed to a shoemaker and tanner; at the age of sixteen years, he had mastered both trades and worked as a journeyman until he was eighteen years of age, when he went into the business of tanning and shoemaking for himself. In 1856 he left the shoe bench and took the stump for John C. Fremont, then the first Republican candidate for the presidency. The defeat of Fremont nearly broke his heart and in January, 1857, he disposed of his business and settled in Waterloo, Wisconsin. There he studied law and was admitted to practice in the circuit and supreme courts of that state, and also in the district, circuit and supreme courts of the United States. In 1859 he was elected to the Wisconsin state legislature and served one term. He enlisted for service during the Civil war and served in the several capacities of regimental quartermaster, post quartermaster, post commissary, and judge advocate of a general court martial. He was mustered out at Leavenworth in December, 1865, and at once resumed the practice of his profession, being again elected to the Wisconsin legislature in 1869. He accepted an appointment in the United States revenue service, in which he served over four years, and then engaged in journalism in Waterloo, Wisconsin, until the spring of 1879. In April of that year, he removed to Watertown, South Dakota, and established the Dakota News. Five years later he sold that paper to Hon. A. C. Mellette, and established Conklin's Dakotan, also at Watertown, for which he obtained a large circulation in both South and North Dakota. He continued its publication until 1896, when he was so severely injured in a railroad accident in Sioux Falls that for a year and a half, he was unable to attend to his paper and was compelled to suspend its publication. His recovery was slow, but eventually he regained in a measure his former health and usefulness. At the first organization of the South Dakota Press Association, he was chosen its president and was twice thereafter reelected to the same position, and, although the demand was almost unanimous, he declined further election.

During his long residence in South Dakota, Mr. Conklin has persistently refused to hold office, but he has ever taken a deep pride in the military affairs of his state, and, seeing that they were at a low ebb and that the state militia had practically ceased to exist, he accepted the appointment he now holds, being commissioned adjutant general of the state by Governor Herreid on the 9th of March, 1901. He was induced to undertake these duties because he firmly believed that he could organize a militia that would compare favorably with other states possessing like opportunities and means. Since that time, he has recruited a state guard composed of twenty-nine companies, and has held two battalion encampments, one at Yankton and the other at Aberdeen, and three annual encampments of all arms. During this time, he has, as required by law, discharged the duties of adjutant general, quartermaster general and chief of ordnance and commissary. Governor Herreid, in his biennial message to the legislature of 1903, speaking of the reorganization of the militia, said: "For this work selected a man whom I knew, from a long personal acquaintance, to be pre-eminently qualified by education, experience and individual force of character for the manifold duties devolving upon the adjutant general. On March 9, 1901, thoroughly aware of the difficulties to be encountered, Hon. S. J. Conklin accepted the appointment, and from that day until this hour he has, with singular energy and enthusiasm, devoted all his time to the service of the state. How well he has succeeded, even beyond the most sanguine expectations of his friends who prevailed upon him to undertake the work and who expected success, will be manifested by a careful perusal of the report of his department."

Now, at the age of seventy-five years, General Conklin is possessed in a remarkable degree of the energy and executive ability which has characterized his entire history. He is manifestly a self-educated and self-made man, for while the record of his life shows that he had little opportunity for schooling, his ability as a writer and speaker tells the story of toiling hours in manhood's years while others slept, to acquire the store of knowledge with which he has been armored for every occasion and every duty he has undertaken to perform.

General Conklin was married in 1848, to Miss Mary Wait, and three children were born to this union, namely: Alice, Emmet F. and Charles A. Mr. Conklin was again married, in 1884, to Miss Mattie Greenslate, and again, in 1895, to Mrs. Anna Duff. Fraternally the General is a Mason, having attained to the thirty-second degree in the Ancient Accepted Scottish Rite.

EDMUND COOK

Edmund COOK, was born in the province of Saxony, Germany, on the 20th of March, 1847. After receiving a thorough academic training he entered a commercial establishment and later became a bookkeeper until entering the Prussian army in 1865. In common with all able-bodied young men of Germany, he was obliged to devote a certain number of years to military service, and it so happened that shortly after entering the army the war between Prussia and Austria broke out and it fell to him to take an active and by no means unimportant part in that celebrated struggle. He went through the one campaign of the war, that of 1866, during the greater part of which he was on the staff of General Von Barneco, commanding the Twelfth Regiment of Hussars, and saw much active service. When hostilities ceased Mr. Cook was honorably discharged, after which he re-entered mercantile life and continued to give it his attention as long as he remained in the fatherland. According to the custom which requires every soldier to report for duty at certain times, young Cook, at the age of twenty, was thus called upon and in due time presented himself at the proper place. To the great surprise and astonishment of the officers, however, the young man came into their presence decorated with the cross of honor, won for brave and meritorious conduct, and with a discharge in his pocket, which fact exempted him from further military duty. Shortly after this he came to the United States, intending to be absent but one year, but after spending some months in this country he became so attached to it and so pleased with the advantages it held out to young men with ambition to rise in the world, that he concluded not to return to Germany. Mr. Cook reached America in 1868 and some time afterwards located at Milwaukee, Wisconsin, where he accepted the position of traveling salesman for a wholesale house. He later represented a St. Paul firm on the road for several years. In 1882 he came to Wilmot, South Dakota, and established the general store which he has conducted with success and financial profit to the present time. Recently he began closing out this establishment, the better to devote his attention to his other business enterprises, being vice-president of the First State Bank of Wilmot and a director of the Wilmot Land and Loan Company, besides having large landed interests in various parts of Roberts County.

For several years Mr. Cook devoted considerable attention to live stock and farming and achieved quite a reputation as an importer and breeder of Oxford-down sheep and other high-grade domestic animals. While not so much interested in stock raising as formerly, he now farms quite extensively and to this vocation he proposes to devote the greater part of his time hereafter, finding it not only greatly to his taste, but quite profitable as a source of income. Among his lands is a fine farm of three hundred and thirty acres, contiguous to Wilmot, ten acres within the city limits, and on this place, he has made many valuable improvements, including one of the handsomest modern residences m the county, which, surrounded by beautiful grounds, tastefully laid out in gardens, shade trees, walks, smooth lawns, interspersed with flowers, etc., bespeaks the home of a man of wealth, elegant leisure, refined taste and decidedly progressive ideas.

Mr. Cook was married in Plainview, Minnesota, June 1, 1875, to Miss Martha Brooks, daughter of Reuben Brooks, a pioneer of that state and for many years a leading citizen of his community. Mr. and Mrs. Cook have one child, a son by the name of Arthur W.. They are among the most highly esteemed people of Wilmot, take an active interest in everything pertaining to the growth and development of the city, are alive to all charitable and benevolent enterprises, and the hospitality of their beautiful home is unbounded.

In his political affiliations Mr. Cook is a prominent Democrat and has perhaps as much influence in his party as any man in northeastern Dakota. He has been a delegate to nearly every county, district and state convention in the last twenty years, and in 1896 was a delegate to the Chicago national convention, in addition to which he has also been nominated for a number of important offices, his election being made impossible by reason of normally overwhelming Republican majorities. Mr. Cook is a thirty-second degree Scottish Rite Mason, also a Knight Templar, besides belonging to various other branches of the order and he has long been a familiar figure at all the meetings of the grand lodge.

HUGO H. COOK

Hugo H. Cook, a successful and enterprising young representative of financial interests in Turner County, has since 1911 been cashier of the Marion Bank, of which his twin brother, Herman H., is the president. His birth occurred in Cedar County, Iowa, on the 24th of April, 1884, his parents being Fritz and Sophie Cook, of German lineage. The father, who was formerly engaged in business as an agriculturist and hotel proprietor, is now living retired.

Hugo H. Cook attended the public schools in the acquirement of an education and assisted his father in the operation of the home place until he started out as an agriculturist on his own account, successfully carrying on farming in Iowa for four years. On the expiration of that period, he accepted a position as assistant cashier of the Farmers & Merchants Bank of Verdon, South Dakota, remaining in that capacity for a year and a half, while subsequently he served as vice president of the Bank of Bowdle for fifteen months. In 1911 he came to Marion as cashier of the Marion Bank, which had been purchased by Herman H. Cook and which has since steadily prospered under the able management and direction of the twin brothers. Hugo H. Cook enjoys an enviable reputation as a capable and popular official of the institution and his efforts have contributed in no small degree to its success. He has likewise built up a profitable business in real estate, insurance and farm loans and is the owner of considerable real estate in South Dakota.

On the 14th of February, 1906, Mr. Cook was united in marriage to Miss Vera Walter, by whom he has one child, Darline C. He exercises his right of franchise in support of the men and measures of the democracy and has been active in local and state politics, being widely recognized as a most public- spirited and progressive citizen who takes a helpful interest in the public welfare. His religious faith is that of the Lutheran church, while fraternally he is identified with the Knights of Pythias at Sunbury, Iowa, and Parker Lodge, A. F. & A. M. His personal characteristics render him popular with many friends and he is much esteemed in social and business circles of the community.

FLOYD J. COOPER

Floyd J. Cooper is an able young attorney of Canton who has practiced his profession successfully for the past eight years and is also associated with his father in the abstract, real-estate and insurance business. His birth occurred in Canton, this state, on the 30th of June, 1887, his parents being Henry N. and Mary Cooper. The father took up his abode in Canton among its earliest residents and is still engaged in business there, being now associated with our subject in the conduct of an abstract, real-estate and insurance concern.

Floyd J. Cooper acquired his education in the public schools and was graduated from the Canton high school in 1904. Having determined to become a representative of the legal profession, he entered the law department of the University of South Dakota, from which institution he was graduated in 1907, being admitted to the bar in the same year. He immediately returned to his home town and began the practice of law, in which he has been engaged continuously to the present time, also assisting in the conduct of his father's business. In no profession is there a career more open to talent than in that of the law, and in no field of endeavor is there demanded a more careful preparation, a more thorough appreciation of the absolute ethics of life, or of the underlying principles which form the basis of all human rights and privileges. Unflagging application, intuitive wisdom and a determination to fully utilize the means at hand, are the concomitants which ensure personal success and prestige in this great profession, which stands as the stern conservator of justice; and it is one into which none should enter without a recognition of the obstacles to be overcome and the battles to be won, for success does not reward all, but comes only as the result of unmistakable ability and close application. Possessing all the requisite qualities of the able lawyer, Mr. Cooper has been accorded a gratifying clientage which he well merits.

His political views are in accord with the principles of the republican party, and he is a member of the Commercial Club and other civic organizations. Fraternally he is identified with the Masons, belonging to Silver Star Lodge, No. 4, A. F. & A. M., and Siroc Chapter, No. 4, R. A. M., while his religious faith is indicated by his membership in the Congregational church. He is very fond of all outdoor sports and in these finds needed recreation. Mr. Cooper is popular in both professional and social circles of his home town and has readily made and retained friends.

HENRY T. COOPER

Henry T. Cooper, of Whitewood, has been for a number of years actively connected with the business development of his part of the state and has also served for four terms as state senator. He is cashier of the Whitewood Bank and for a long period was extensively interested in cattle-raising in this state but has now transferred most of his interests in that line to Louisiana. He was born in Warwickshire, England, June 25, 1850, and his parents were Fred and Emma Cooper, likewise natives of that country. The father became a merchant in early manhood and continued to follow that business until his demise, which occurred then his son, Henry T., was but seven years of age.

The latter attended public school in England and continued to reside in that country until he was twenty-seven years of age, when he crossed the Atlantic and located in New York City. He followed the Union Pacific Railroad to Bismarck, North Dakota, in the employ of the Northwestern Freight & Transportation Company, remaining there until 1880, and then removed to Pierre, South Dakota, with the same company, continuing at Pierre for five years. At the end of that time, he went to Chadron, Nebraska, and engaged in the freighting business for himself for a short time. He then removed successively to Buffalo Gap, Rapid City, Sturgis and Whitewood, arriving in the latter place in the fall of 1887. He continued there until 1890, when he disposed of his interests in the freight and transportation business, gradually selling his wagons, horses and mules. Subsequently he became bookkeeper in the Merchants National Bank of Deadwood although he continued to make his home in Whitewood. In 1895 he was elected county treasurer and during his term of office discharged his duties to the satisfaction of his constituents. In 1890 he put in a waterworks system in Whitewood, which he sold to the city a number- of years later, and in 1900 became cashier of the Whitewood Bank, in which capacity he is still serving. He understands well the minutiae of banking and also the larger monetary and financial problems that so closely affect all banks, and under his direction the institution has prospered. He is president of the Whitewood Electric Light & Power Company and for a number of years operated a large cattle ranch north of Whitewood. However, he recently abandoned the raising of stock in South Dakota and became interested in the cattle business in Louisiana, where he owns a large ranch and where he considers climatic conditions more favorable than in this state. He still owns considerable land in South Dakota, however.

Mr. Cooper was married in April, 1888, to Miss Kate Grimshaw and to that marriage were born two children: Henry Grimshaw, who died at Grinnell College in 1911, when twenty-one years of age; and Ellwood, a resident of Chicago. The wife and mother died in 1901 and in April, 1904, Mr. Cooper was married to Miss Dollie Pray, a native of Omaha, Nebraska, and a daughter of John Pray. Her father was an early settler of Omaha and was for a number of years a master mechanic in the employ of the Union Pacific Railroad Company. He now draws a pension from the railroad for long service and also is on the pension list of the government, as he was a soldier in the Union army during the Civil war. He lives part of the time with Mr. and Mrs. Cooper in Whitewood, spends part of each year upon the ranch in Louisiana of which Mr. Cooper is one of the owners, and the remainder of the time with a son in Omaha.

Mr. Cooper is a republican and for one term served as county treasurer and for four terms, in 1899, 19&1, 1905 and 1907, represented his district in the state legislature, where he made an enviable record for efficiency and devotion to the public good. His religious belief is that of the Presbyterian church and he takes a helpful part in the work of that organization. Fraternally he is a member of the Masonic order. The ranch in Louisiana which Mr. Cooper owns together with a partner is situated north of Baton Rouge and comprises twenty-eight hundred acres of land, which is devoted to the raising of high-grade beef cattle. He finds conditions more favorable there to successful ranching than in South Dakota and has great faith in the success of his venture. He has been connected with the west for many years, coming here when the railroads had just begun to open up the country, and as a freighter learned much of pioneer conditions, as he continued in that business until the extension of the railroads made it no longer profitable. As the country became more thickly settled and as towns and cities sprang up, he adapted himself to the changing conditions of life and took advantage of opportunities as they arose. He has gained financial prosperity and has also the satisfaction of knowing that he has had a part in the development of his adopted state.

MILES M. COOPER

Miles M. COOPER farmer, stock raiser and also ex-member of the South Dakota house of representatives, is a native of Jennings County, Indiana, and dates his birth from November 16, 1845. Like the majority of country lads, he was reared on the farm, early became familiar with the rugged duties and wholesome discipline of the same, and of winter seasons attended the public schools of his neighborhood, acquiring a fair knowledge of the branches constituting the usual course of study. When a youth of sixteen he left home and after spending several years in the northern part of the state, yielded to a desire of long standing by making an extensive trip through the west. Young Cooper started on this journey in the spring of 1864, crossing the plains to Montana, thence to Virginia City, where he engaged in placer mining, operating for some time in Alder Gulch and various other places and meeting with reasonably fair success as a gold seeker. He spent the greater part of three years in the above section of country, but in 1867 went to Wyoming and entered the employ of the Union Pacific Railroad Company, whose main line was then in process of construction.

After devoting the ensuing three years to railroad work, Mr. Cooper severed his connection with the company and from 1871 to 1873 inclusive was engaged in the live-stock business, buying cattle in Kansas and shipping them to various eastern markets, also selling to different parties in that and other states. Discontinuing this line of business, he spent the succeeding three years at and in the vicinity of Fort Bridger, Wyoming, devoting his attention the meanwhile to prospecting and mining, in addition to which he also took a number of contracts for various kinds of government work north of the fort, completing the same in due time with credit to himself and to the satisfaction of his employers. In the spring of 1877, he joined a party at Cheyenne and started for the Black Hills country, arriving in Deadwood the following April, and immediately thereafter engaged in farming in Boulder Park, east of the city. In connection with agriculture, he did considerable freighting at odd times, between Deadwood and Pierre, and to these lines of work he gave his time until the spring of 1883, when he disposed of his interests in the Black Hills and came to Meade County, taking up a fine tract of land about six miles east of Sturgis, on which he has since lived and prospered as a farmer and stock raiser.

Mr. Cooper exercised excellent judgment in the selecting of his ranch, his place being admirably situated for agricultural and live-stock purposes, and by his labors and judicious management it has become one of the most productive and valuable farms in the county of Meade. He has added a number of substantial improvements, including among others a fine modern residence, supplied with all the latest comforts and conveniences calculated to make country life desirable, and his business affairs have so prospered that he is now in comparatively independent circumstances, with a liberal competence laid up against possible adversity and for his declining years.

Politically Mr. Cooper wields a strong influence for the Democratic party, of which he has been a zealous supporter since old enough to exercise the rights of citizenship, and for a number of years past he has been a prominent factor, not only in local affairs, but in public matters of district and state import. In the fall of 1889, he was elected to represent Meade County in the general assembly, and his record as a lawmaker proved so satisfactory to his constituents that he was again chosen in 1891. While in the legislature he was untiring in his efforts to promote the interests of his county and state, serving on several important committees, taking an active part in the general deliberations of the. house and earning the reputation of one of the hardest workers in the body, as well as winning recognition as a leader on the Democratic side, his party, however, being in the minority.

Mr. Cooper is a man of great energy and has done much to advance the material prosperity of Meade County, giving his encouragement and support to all enterprises with this end in view. Public-spirited in all the term implies, he has frequently lost sight of self in his endeavors to promote the public welfare and today there are few men in western Dakota as widely known or who in a greater degree enjoy the esteem and confidence of the people regardless of party ties.

He is a member of the Masonic fraternity, belonging to the lodge at Sturgis, and is also identified with the local lodge of the Ancient Order of United Workmen at the same place, having been honored with high official station in both organizations. On March 9, 1881, occurred the marriage of Mr. Cooper, his wife having formerly been Miss Mary P. Ranft, who was born and reared in the state of Ohio. The union has resulted in an interesting family of eight children, whose names are as follows: Otto P., Allyn R., Harold M., Lawrence, Edith, Jefferson, Edna and Bryan.

JUDGE JAMES ALFRED COPELAND

Judge James Alfred Copeland, of Clay County, was born in Winnebago County, Illinois, September 21, 1852, a son of Alfred William and Hannah (Brewster) Copeland, the latter a descendant of Elder Brewster, who came over in the Mayflower. The father was of Scotch-Irish descent, although members of the family have lived in this country for many generations. He was a farmer by occupation and was well known in his locality, his demise, which occurred in 1876, being the occasion of sincere regret. His widow survived for only a few years. They were the parents of three children. George, who when last heard from was living in the mountains of California and was a great hunter, was for several years United States commissioner at Tobacco, Montana. Caroline, the only daughter, is deceased. The subject of this review is the youngest of the family.

Judge Copeland grew to manhood upon his father's farm and attended the district school until he was sixteen years of age. He then entered Wheaton College at Wheaton, Illinois, and remained a student in that institution for two years. He then returned to the homestead and following his father's death engaged in buying stock for one season. He then went to Fairmont, Nebraska, and for two years farmed there, cultivating land which he had purchased with money that he had earned. From Nebraska he returned to Iowa and engaged in the stock business for two years, after which he removed to Dakota territory and entered the real-estate field in Vermillion, dealing in realty for three years. He then entered the employ of a machine company, maintaining his connection with that concern for seven years. During that time, he studied law and in 1890 was admitted to the bar of South Dakota. However, he held his position with the machine company for some time after his admission to the practice of law. After following his profession for a time, he was elected clerk of the court of Clay County and faithfully discharged the duties of that office during a term of four years. At the end of that time, he resumed the practice of law and two years later was elected county judge, which office he has held ever since, with the exception of two years, during which time he was engaged in private practice. The county judge has probate and limited civil and criminal jurisdiction. Judge Copeland is well fitted for the bench as he adds to the necessary legal training and experience an openness of mind and fine sense of justice that enables him to make the impartiality of the bench a fact and not merely a theory.

Judge Copeland married Miss Estella E. Hays, a native of Illinois, who, however, was taken by her parents to Sioux Falls, South Dakota, when that region was just being opened up by white settlers. The marriage of Judge and Mrs. Copeland was celebrated at Rockford, Illinois, on the 27th of December, 1880, and they have had eight children: Jay W., who died in infancy; Flora E., the wife of LeRoy Cowles, a farmer of Hamburg, Iowa; Winfield O., a painter residing in Vermillion, South Dakota; Nettie and Jamie, both deceased; Laurel H., an expert produce man, who is still living at home; and Doris and Susan, who are high-school students.

Judge Copeland is a republican and his religious affiliation is with the Baptist church. He is widely known in local Masonic circles, being a member of the blue lodge, chapter, commandery and the Eastern Star. He has held offices in the bodies of which he is a member and in twenty out of the last twenty-one years has been in office. His connection with the Masonic fraternity extends over three decades, as he was taken into the order in 1884. He is the author of an authoritative and excellently written history of Incense Lodge, No. 2, A. F. & A. M., and in many ways has done much for the good of the order. He is also a member of the Modern Woodmen of America and has been clerk of the local lodge for seven or eight years. The record of Judge Copeland as a man and jurist is one that will bear the closest investigation and scrutiny, as he has in all of life's relations been guided by high ethical principles.

GEORGE D. CORD

G. D. Cord, one of the founders and builders of the attractive and thriving town of Delmont. Douglas county, and the president of the Security State Bank of Delmont, was born in Kaukauna. Outagamie county, Wisconsin, on the 8th of September, 1866, being a son of Charles and Mary (Knapp) Cord, of whose five children we enter the following brief record: Catherine A. is the wife of William Dyke, of Effingham, Illinois; Mary died March 24, 1904, and was the wife of Howard Parmelee, of Lincoln, Nebraska, Dr. Charles E. is a practicing physician at Chicago Heights, Illinois; Mark D. is a resident of Danbury, Iowa, having been engaged in the real-estate business, but being now retired; and George D. is the immediate subject of this sketch. The honored father was born in Lincolnshire. England, about the year 1835, and was there reared and educated, learning the trade of millwright. In 1854 he came to the United States, locating in Milwaukee, Wisconsin, where he was employed as a miller for a number of years, in different mills. Later he became the owner of a mill at Barton, that state, operating the same for several years, and while there residing his marriage was solemnized. He finally removed to Kaukauna, where he built a flouring mill, operating the same about five years, this being at the time of the Civil War. He had a large stock of flour on hand and at the time of Lee's surrender there was so great a depreciation in the value of this commodity that he met with great financial loss, being forced into bankruptcy. He then removed to Madison, Wisconsin, where he secured employment in the mills, continuing to be thus engaged until he had to a degree recouped his financial resources. He then removed to Anamosa, Iowa, where he erected mills, and in 1881 he located in Oakland, Nebraska, where he operated a mill about four years, and there he met his death as the result of an accident. He was preparing to clean a revolver, and in taking the same from a trunk the lid fell in such a way as to discharge the weapon, the shot causing his death within ten minutes. He was at the time preparing to come to the Black Hills district of Dakota, to take charge of milling properties. He was a man of excellent business ability and sterling character, was a Republican in politics, a communicant of the Protestant Episcopal church and a member of the Masonic fraternity. His widow, who was born in the state of New York, now resides in the home of her elder daughter, in Effingham, Illinois, she likewise being a devoted communicant of the Episcopal church.

George D. Cord, the immediate subject of this sketch, was reared under the grateful influences of a refined and cultured home, and secured his educational discipline in the public schools, completing his studies in the high school at Anamosa, Iowa. At the age of sixteen years, he secured a position in a job-printing office in Milwaukee, Wisconsin, where he remained one year, gaining an excellent knowledge of the "art preservative." He then entered the service of the Chicago. St. Paul, Minneapolis & Omaha Railroad, in the capacity of station agent, remaining in the employ of this company for a period of about sixteen years, within which was located at various points on the line of the system, having been for thirteen years the agent at Coleridge, Nebraska. In 1899, at which time he was agent at Harrington, Nebraska, he resigned his position and forthwith came to South Dakota, locating in Delmont, Douglas County, the town having at the time a population of only eighty persons, and here he engaged in the real-estate business, bringing to bear in his operations the characteristic push and energy with which he is so eminently endowed. Mr. Cord has bought and sold much of the village property and also the major portion of the land for miles around, having been largely instrumental in bringing here a desirable class of settlers, who have developed rich and productive farms and have been signally prospered. It may be safely said that to him more than to any other one man is due this gratifying development of this section, while he has so ordered his course as to gain and retain the highest confidence and esteem of all. In January, 1903, he effected the organization of the Security State Bank, in which he owns the controlling stock, and he is president of this institution, which is ably conducted and which is accorded an appreciative support in the community. In politics he is a stalwart advocate of the principles and policies of the Republican party, in whose cause he has been an active and valued worker, and during the campaign of 1902 he was a member of the state executive committee of his party, while at the time of this writing he is a member of the county executive committee.

His religious faith is that of the Episcopal church, and fraternally he is prominently identified with the Masonic order, being affiliated with Arcania Lodge, No. 97, Free and Accepted Masons, at Armour; Scotland Chapter, No. 31, Royal Arch Masons, at Scotland; St. Bernard Commandery, No. 11, Knights Templar, at Mitchell; Oriental Consistory, No. 1, Ancient and Accepted Scottish Rite, at Yankton, and El Riad Temple, Ancient Arabic Order of the Nobles of the Mystic Shrine, at Sioux Falls.

On the 20th of January, 1886, was solemnized the marriage of Mr. Cord to Miss Carrie F. Jones, of Milwaukee, Wisconsin, and they have two sons. Charles B. and Arthur E.

WILLIAM FRANCIS CORRIGAN

William F. Corrigan was born at Prior Lake, Scott County, Minnesota, on the 22d of January, 1865, and is a son of Peter Corrigan, a native of Ireland, who came to the United States in his youth and who won success through his own indefatigable efforts, having the respect and esteem of his fellow men. The subject secured his early educational training in the public schools of Scott County, Minnesota, and at the age of seventeen years began reading law, having decided to adopt its practice as his vocation in life. He took up his residence in Mellette. South Dakota, on the 2d of August, 1895, and at the October term of the supreme court of the state he was admitted to the bar in that year. He at once established himself in practice in Mellette, and by his devotion to his work and his excellent technical knowledge and his power of applying the same he has built up a representative general practice in the state and federal courts and is one of the highly honored members of the bar of his county. He is general attorney for South Dakota of the St. Croix Lumber Company, of Minnesota, and is also similarly retained by other important corporations.

In politics Mr. Corrigan is stanchly arrayed as a supporter of the principles and policies of the Republican party, and fraternally he is identified with the local lodge of the Ancient Free and Accepted Masons, and with the chapter of the Order of the Eastern Star. On the Toth of October, 1891, Mr. Corrigan was united in marriage to Miss Hattie B. Skinner, who was born in Delphis, Ohio. They have no children.

ALONZO A. COTTON, M. D.

A. A. COTTON, who is successfully engaged in the practice of medicine and surgery at Vermillion, Clay County, is a native of the state of Iowa, having been born in Cedar County, on the 28th of October, 1861, and being a son of Luzerne and Mary A. (Dwigans) Cotton, the former of whom is now engaged in the real-estate business at Jennings, Louisiana, while the latter died at Jennings in 1889. The Doctor received his early educational training in the public schools of Iowa City, and then entered the state university, in the same city, where he completed the scientific course and was graduated as a member of the class of 1884, receiving the degree of Bachelor of Science. He was then matriculated in the homeopathic medical department of the same great institution, where he completed the prescribed technical course and was graduated in 1886, with the degree of Doctor of Medicine. In January of the following year, he engaged in the active practice of his profession in Sioux City, Iowa, where he remained for the ensuing five years, after which he was in practice at Dixon, Nebraska, for one year, removing thence to Vermillion, South Dakota, in 1893, and having here been especially successful in the upbuilding of a large and representative practice. In politics the Doctor is a stanch Republican, but so exigent are the demands placed upon his time and attention by his professional duties that he has not found it expedient to take an active part in political affairs, though he is essentially loyal and public-spirited in his attitude. He is a member of the lodge and chapter of the Masonic fraternity in his home city of Vermillion, and both he and his wife are valued members of the Methodist Episcopal church.

At Newton, Iowa, on the 17th of September, 1886, Dr. Cotton was united in marriage to Miss May E. Lyon, who was born and reared in that state, and they are the parents of six children, namely: Earl L., Carl, Schuyler, Daniel L., Alonzo and Cornelia M. Mrs. Cotton is a graduate of the class of April, 1886, of Drake University (medical department), Des Moines, Iowa, and she and Mr. Cotton combine the practice of medicine. Dr. Cotton is a member of the Homeopathic Medical Society of South Dakota, and the Quadri-state Homeopathic Society, the headquarters being at Sioux City; also, the American Institute of Homeopathy, it being the national society. Mrs. Cotton is a member of the Order of the Eastern Star, Ladies of the Maccabees and the Degree of Honor. Mr. Cotton is also a member of the Ancient Order of United Workmen, the Woodmen of the World, Modern Brotherhood of America, Yeomen and other kindred societies.

FRANK H. CRAIG

Frank H. CRAIG, supervising mechanic in connection with the Indian school maintained at Greenwood, Charles Mix County, is a native of the domain of Canada, having been born near the city of Toronto, on the 28th of December, 1845, and being a son of Davis C. and Mary J. (Witherel) Craig, both of whom were born and reared in the state of New York, whence they removed to Canada, where they maintained their home about eleven years, the father having been a farmer and mechanic. In 1854 the family removed to Elliota, Minnesota, locating in Fillmore County, where the parents continued to reside until 1881, when they came to South Dakota, where the father of our subject took up government land, in Fillmore County, there passing the remainder of his life. He died in June, 1901, his devoted wife having passed away in September of the preceding year. They became the parents of seven children, of whom four are living, all being residents of South Dakota. In early life Davis C. Craig was a Whig in politics, but he identified himself with the Republican party at the time of its organization and was ever afterward a supporter of its cause. He enlisted as a member of Company C, Third Minnesota Volunteer Infantry, at the outbreak of the Civil War, and was in active service about four years. It may also be noted in the connection that the subject of this sketch enlisted in Company A, Second Minnesota Cavalry, with which he served about two and one-half years, principally under General Sully and in connection with the Indian warfare in the northwest. He received his honorable discharge on the 4th of April, 1866, having made an excellent record as a valiant and loyal soldier.

Frank H. Craig received a common-school education and was about nine years of age at the time of his parents' removal to Minnesota, where he was variously employed for a number of years, finally becoming identified with railroad work, in which he was engaged up to the time of coming to South Dakota, from Chicago, in 1879. He took up a homestead claim in Spink County, on the 16th of June of that year, and there continued to reside until 1891, having been one of the early settlers of the county and one of its popular and influential citizens. He erected the first frame house in the county, and the same was used for some time as a court house. He served for five years as a member of the board of county commissioners and held other local offices of trust, including those of justice of the peace, while he was for many years a school official.

In politics he gives an unwavering allegiance to the Republican party and has been an active worker in its cause. Fraternally he is identified with Frankfort Lodge, No. 77, Ancient Free and Accepted Masons; Redfield Chapter, No. 20, Royal Arch Masons; Frankfort Lodge, No. 83, Independent Order of Odd Fellows, and to Sol Meredith Post, Grand Army of the Republic.

In 1891 Mr. Craig disposed of his interests in Spink County and took up his residence in Greenwood, where he has since held the position of government mechanic at the Indian school, in which connection he has accomplished a most satisfactory work. He is the owner of a fine ranch of five hundred and eighty-five acres in Boyd County, Nebraska, and he is also the owner of a fine herd of cattle on his ranch in Nebraska. He has attained success since coming to Dakota and is one of the loyal and public-spirited citizens of the state.

On the 4th of July, 1868, at Harmony, Fillmore County, Minnesota, Mr. Craig was married to Miss Eliza M. Craig, who was born and reared in Canada, being a daughter of John and Elizabeth Craig, the former being a farmer by vocation. Of this union were born eight children, namely: Leslie, Herbert, Claud and Neva, who are deceased; Harold, who remains at the parental home, as do also James E., Bessie and Earl F.

WILLIAM D. CRAIG

William D. CRAIG, cashier of the James River Bank, at Frankfort, Spink County, is a native of the province of Ontario, Canada, where he was born on the 26th of August, 1849, being a son of David C. and Mary J. Craig, both of whom were born in the state of New York. In 1855 they removed from Canada to Winneshiek County, Iowa, remaining but a short time, since within the same year they removed to Fillmore County, Minnesota, where Mr. Craig became one of the early settlers and pioneer farmers, being duly successful in his efforts and being one of the influential citizens of his section. The parents came to Spink County, near Frankfort, in 1882, and here died, the mother dying in the summer of 1899, and the father dying in the summer of 1901. During the war of the Rebellion the father served three years and ten months as a member of the Third Minnesota Volunteer Infantry. The subject of this sketch was reared on the home farm, in Fillmore County, Minnesota, and received his early educational training in its common schools. He continued to assist his father in the work and management of the home place, until he married, when he engaged in farming on his own responsibility, continuing his residence in Minnesota until 1884, when he came to South Dakota and located in Spink County, where he secured a farm of three hundred and twenty acres and engaged in farming and stock growing. In the autumn of 1888, he was elected sheriff of the county and was reelected in 1890, while in 1892 he was elected to represent his district in the state senate, succeeding himself in the election of 1894, and proving himself a valuable working member of the general assembly of the newly admitted commonwealth, while in 1902 he was elected a member of the lower house of the legislature, as a representative of Spink County. He is still the owner of valuable farming land in the county and is also engaged in the buying and shipping of grain, in addition to his banking interests, while he has shown a helpful interest in all that has tended to conserve the advancement and material prosperity of his home town and county.

In politics he has ever been stanchly arrayed in support of the principles and policies of the Republican party, and fraternally he is identified with Frankfort Lodge, No. 77, Ancient Free and Accepted Masons, and Frankfort Lodge, No. 303, Ancient Order of United Workmen, being recorder of each of these organizations at the time of this writing. For the past quarter of a century, he has been a member of the Methodist Episcopal church, and of the same Mrs. Craig also is a member. On the 25th of May, 1873, at Harmony. Fillmore county, Minnesota, was solemnized the marriage of Mr. Craig to Miss Addie R. Elliott, who was born in St. Lawrence County, New York, in March, 1852, her parents having likewise been born in the old Empire state, whence they removed to Minnesota in the pioneer days. Mr. and Mrs. Craig have two children, John D., who was born on the 26th of April, 1874, and Edith J., who was born on the 23d of February, 1879, and who married Oscar Blain, of Frankfort, South Dakota.

JUDGE GEORGE W. CRANE

George W. Crane, judge of the municipal court at Aberdeen and one of the leading members of the legal profession in the city, was born at Hoxie, Kansas, October 6, 1884, a son of George W. and Mary (White) Crane. The mother has passed away, and the father now makes his home in Washington, D. C, where he is connected with the census bureau.

George W. Crane was reared in Washington and there acquired a public-school education. He afterward entered Georgetown University and was graduated from the law department in June, 1909, spending part of his time during that year in the law office of J. S. Easby-Smith. In the same year he came to Aberdeen, where he engaged in professional practice, winning rapidly a large clientage and becoming recognized as a strong, forceful and able lawyer. His ability received suitable recognition in 1911, when at the non-partisan election he was made judge of the municipal court for a term of four years and was reelected for a second term in April, 1915. He is the present incumbent of that office and discharges its responsible duties with promptness, dispatch and impartiality and in a manner which reflects credit upon his sincerity of purpose and his public spirit.

On the 11th of October, 1911, Judge Crane was united in marriage to Miss Edith Lane Coombs, of Washington, D. C, and they had one son, Vinton C, who died July 23, 1914. Judge Crane joined the Masonic lodge at Washington and is connected also with the Benevolent Protective Order of Elks. He is a member of the Baptist church and gives his political allegiance to the republican party, taking an active interest in community affairs. He fills his present office with credit and distinction and has won wide recognition in professional, official and social circles.

CORIE ISSAC CRAWFORD

The bustling events of a young state cannot fail to test the mettle of the men who are active in its construction. There is a sifting process always in force in such a community which eventually winnows the chaff from the grain, the adventurer and charlatan from the men of substantial merit and serious purpose. Those who survive this ordeal, proving their stability of character, worth and ability, are the men who — as a painter would say — give tone and color to the institutions of the embryo commonwealth, and a definite trend to its pi-ogress. Among the men of South Dakota who are typical of this character, Corie — usually contracted to "Coe" — I. Crawford, the subject of this sketch, must ever stand prominent by his sturdy qualities and notable achievements. He was born upon his father's farm in Allamakee County, Iowa, in 1858. He is Scotch-Irish on his father's side, and Irish English on his mother's, both of Presbyterian faith. Grandfather and Grandmother Crawford were Scotch, whose ancestors emigrated to the north of Ireland and were connected with the Ramseys, Funston's and McConnel's, who came from the north of Ireland and settled in western Pennsylvania and eastern Ohio immediately after the war of 1812. General Funston of Kansas, and of Philippine fame, is one of this family. Coe I. Crawford's father, Robert Crawford, was a wagon maker and farmer, born in Ohio in 1828. He moved to Allamakee County, Iowa, in 1853 and opened up a farm. He was in comfortable circumstances and raised a large family. He died in 1896. He was a sturdy man of unflinching integrity, and a member of the Presbyterian church. In politics he was a staunch Republican, and a leading man in his county. He was for a number of years chairman of the Board of County Commissioners. His wife, Coe I. Crawford's mother, was born in Ohio in 1830. Her maiden name was Sarah Shannon. Governor Shannon, so well-known in the early history of Kansas, was of the same family.

Mr. Crawford's opportunity for education in early life was very meager, consisting of three months of schooling in the winter and occasionally a summer term of three months; these were ungraded, common country schools. When fifteen years of age he was permitted to attend the village school for one year, and thus made such progress that he was prepared to teach. When he began to teach it was in the country district schools. For this he received twenty dollars a month in summer and thirty-three dollars a month in winter, out of which he had to pay his board. He did the janitor work besides, gratis. He taught three years in Iowa and two in Ohio. In the meantime, he studied hard in a private way, and read very extensively. He was assisted very materially in his study of Latin, Geometry and Literature by an educated physician in whose family he lived for two years. After he quit teaching, he secured a position as a field agent for a subscription book publishing house of Chicago, and traveled extensively through New York, Ohio and West Virginia, for two years. The work was not congenial; in fact, he detested it, although it was not without its value in after life. He left it to enter the law department of the University of Iowa in 1881, from which he graduated in 1882. His proficiency may be judged from the fact that he was made president of the Law Literary society, and was one of the speakers chosen for the commencement exercises. He also was awarded a share of a dividend prize for his written thesis. In 1883 he formed a partnership with Hon. W. H. Holman, for the practice of law at Independence, Iowa, where he remained for one year. He then removed to Pierre, where he met with immediate success. His first case of any importance was the defense of a poor German, charged with murder. Three men had come to his corral not far from Pierre, and engaged with him in a quarrel over some cattle. A light followed in which he resorted to a gun, killing one man and wounding the other two. Mr., Fawcett of Pierre, lately deceased, was Mr. Crawford's associate. They convinced the committing magistrate that their client acted in self-defense and lie was discharged. The next suit was a personal Injury case which he prosecuted, asking $5,000 for his client. It arose from the negligence of a telephone company in leaving a wire obstruction in the street. The first trial resulted in a compromise verdict, awarding his client only fifty dollars. A new trial resulted in a verdict of over three thousand dollars. On appeal to the supreme court the judgment was affirmed.

In 1885 Mr. Crawford formed a partnership with Mr. C. E. Deland, under the firm name of Crawford & Deland, which continued for twelve years, during which time the practice was large and lucrative. Mr. Crawford was a leading counsel on one side or the other in nearly one hundred cases in the supreme court. The wide range and profound character of these suits may be seen in the Sixth South Dakota Territorial Report, and in the first ten volumes of the South Dakota Supreme Court Reports. Mr. Crawford was attorney general of the state of South Dakota from 1893 to 1897. He was admitted to practice in the supreme court of the United States in 1893. During the years 1895 and 1896 it became his duty to prosecute the state treasurer and his bonds men and others charged with conspiracy to defraud the state. The suits were both civil and criminal; also, to prosecute the commissioner of schools and public lands for failure to distribute school funds. These cases were complicated with habeas corpus and extradition proceedings, writs of error and other intricate litigation, involving the most specious pleas that could be devised by the defense, supported by ample means. The cases were historic and among the most exciting events in the history of the young state. The parties so successfully prosecuted were, many of them, personal friends and associates of Mr. Crawford in fraternal orders. He has been strongly commended for his unswerving fidelity to the interests of the people of the state in these arduous and prolonged litigations. The prodigious labors connected with them nearly ruined his health. In 1897 he accepted the position of attorney for the Chicago & Northwestern railway for the entire state, and moved to Huron, where he now resides, still engaging in the general practice of law, although the railway is his principal client.

He was president of the State Bar association of South Dakota during the year 1899. Mr. Crawford has no military record, for he was too young for the Civil war and too old to enlist for the Spanish war. He has, however, a brother, Robert T. Crawford, a first lieutenant of the 42d Regiment U. S. Volunteers, now in the Philippines. He has always been a Republican. He was state attorney for Hughes County from 1886 to 1888; member of the last legislature of the territory of Dakota, that which convened at Bismark in 1889; member of the first South Dakota state senate, 1889 and 1890 at Pierre, the new capital; in 1892 elected attorney general of the state, and reelected in 1894: by the largest majority of any candidate on the ticket. He was nominated for congress in 1896, but the wave of free silver and populism rose to high tide that year, and the Republican electors, members of congress and candidate for governor were defeated by small pluralities ranging from fifty to three hundred and fifty. He made in that, the greatest political conflict in the history of the state, one hundred and three speeches.

Since then, he has withdrawn from active work in politics, although still staunch in the faith. He is a Mason and a Knight Templar, and a member of the Presbyterian church. He was married in 1884 to Miss May Robinson, daughter of Levi Robinson, a lawyer of Iowa City, Iowa. She died in 1894, leaving two children: Miriam, now fourteen years of age, and Irving, eight years old. In 1896 he was married to Lavinia Robinson, of the same family, at Iowa City. They have also a child, Robert, now two years old.

JUDGE LOUIS W. CROFOOT

One of the leading and able representatives of the bar of South Dakota is Judge Louis W. Crofoot, former associate judge of Dakota territory and since 1911 city attorney of Aberdeen. He was born in Pontiac, Michigan, February 4, 1857, and is a son of M. E. and Annie E. Crofoot. He acquired his early education in the public schools of his native city and in June, 1874, entered West Point Military Academy, resigning from that institution in 1876. He afterward read law with his father and was admitted to the bar in 1878. He was engaged in practice in Pontiac, Michigan, in partnership with his father until 1882, and on the 28th of February, that year, he came to South Dakota, locating at Huron, where he remained until October 7, 1888, when he was appointed associate judge of the territory. He served in that position until November, 1889, and his record upon the bench was one of important, capable and progressive work.

Judge Crofoot came to Aberdeen in 1888 and following his retirement from the bench engaged in the general practice of law here, building up a large and representative patronage which connected him with the conduct of important litigated interests. In 1911 he was appointed city attorney of Aberdeen and he still holds that position, the duties of which his legal ability, impartiality and keen mental powers eminently well qualify him to fill.

On the 2d of October, 1884, Judge Crofoot was united in marriage to Miss Carrie E. Rerr, of Huron, South Dakota, a native of Ohio, and they have become the parents of three children, one of whom has passed away. The Judge is a member of the Congregational church and a democrat in his political beliefs. He is connected fraternally with the Masonic lodge and with the Independent Order of Odd Fellows, and has gained a place among the substantial and representative men of Aberdeen. In personal, professional and official relations he commands widespread respect and esteem.

GREGOR CRUICKSHANK

Gregor CRUICKSHANK was born in Inverness-shire, Scotland, on the 15th of November, 1852. He was reared in the schools of the same, and when a youth in his teens entered upon an apprenticeship to learn the stone-mason's trade, completing his term of service in his twentieth year. In 1873 he came to the United States and for some time thereafter followed his trade in St. Paul, Minnesota, later doing considerable masonry work in the cities of Minneapolis, Stillwater and Huron, besides spending the greater part of two years in the timber region of Minnesota. Mr. Cruickshank, in 1873, went to New York and after working for some time in that state, returned to his native land for the purpose of revisiting his home and the scenes of his childhood. After spending several months with relatives and friends he went to Glasgow, where he found employment at his trade, but later left that city for Liverpool, England, at which place he spent one year on the police force. Resigning his position at the expiration of the time noted, he again returned to Scotland where he was engaged for two years as foreman on a railroad and after severing his connections with that line of work, he went to Inverness-shire, his native place, and took up the pursuit of agriculture on the home farm. His experience as a tiller of the soil covered a period of two years, at the end of which time he made his second voyage to the United States, sailing in September, 1883. On arriving at his destination, he came direct to South Dakota, locating in the Black Hills, where his brother Alexander was then living, and accepted a position with the Homestake Mining Company, at Lead City. His first work with this great corporation was in the ditches, but after some months he resumed his trade and did considerable stone and brick laying in Spearfish, including the state normal school building, one of the finest structures in the state. Later he re-engaged with the Homestake Mining Company, as foreman of masonry work, which responsible position he still holds, being one of the company's faithful and trusted employes.

Meantime, 1885, Mr. Cruickshank took up land on Alkali creek, fifteen miles from Sturgis, which he converted into a fine ranch, and since that date he has devoted a great deal of attention to stock raising, in connection with his duties at the mine. His ranch, which contains about three thousand acres of rich grazing land, is in excellent condition and fully answers the purpose for which intended, being well improved with good buildings, fences and other accessories necessary to the successful prosecution of live-stock raising. Mr. Cruickshank, in 1896, purchased for his brother Alexander a ranch three and a half miles east of Sturgis, on Bear Butte creek, where the latter has since lived and prospered as a stock man, the two working to each other's mutual interests, and their efforts have been crowned with the most encouraging success.

While exercising personal supervision over his ranch and his large and constantly growing live-stock interests, Mr. Cruickshank spends the greater part of his time in Lead City, where, as already indicated, much of his attention is required to attend to the duties of his position with the Homestake Company. His various enterprises have resulted greatly to his financial advantage, and he is now in independent circumstances, owning, in addition to his ranch and livestock, considerable real estate in Lead City, also valuable mining interests in various parts of the country, besides a large amount of capital invested in different business and industrial enterprises. His success since coming west has been remarkable, and his career bespeaks for him a soundness of judgment, a fertility of resource and executive ability of an order far higher than those with which the great majority of his fellow men are endowed.

Mr. Cruickshank has been actively identified with the material interests and public affairs of the city and county in which he lives, and is also a politician of more than local reputation, being one of the staunch Republicans of his part of the state and an aggressive party worker. Like the majority of wide-awake, enterprising men of every community, he manifests a decided interest in secret benevolence work, holding membership with the Masonic fraternity of Lead City, the Mystic Shrine, at Deadwood, the Benevolent and Protective Order of Elks, and the Master Workmen of America, at the former place, besides being a leading spirit in the order of Scottish Clans of America, an organization composed of his fellow countrymen throughout the United States. Mr. Cruickshank was married in Glasgow, Scotland, June 18, 1878, to Miss Annie McLennan, a native of that country, and has a family of six children, whose names are as follows: John M., Robert, Donald M., Jessie A., Roderick A. and Edwin W.

THOMAS CRUICKSHANK, M. D.

Dr. Thomas Cruickshank is one of the leading and learned representatives of the medical fraternity in Clay County, South Dakota, who for the past fifteen years has practiced successfully in Vermillion. His birth occurred in Norway on the 17th of June, 1866, his parents being John and Anna (Olson) Cruickshank, the former a native of Scotland. Professor Thomas Cruickshank, the paternal grandfather of our subject, had removed to Norway as a member of the faculty of an agricultural college of that country. John Cruickshank and a brother, Alexander, who is now living in Wisconsin, were graduates of this institution. The former was a scientific farmer and at one period of his life a man of means who devoted much time and money to experiments along agricultural lines, for he loved the soil and was interested in developing its possibilities. In 1894, after having lost two sons and also his fortune, he left Norway and came to the United States, spending the first six years of his residence in this country at Larchwood, Iowa. In 1900 he located in Vermillion, South Dakota, and there made his home with our subject until the time of his demise in 1905. His widow still resides with her son Thomas and has now reached the age of eighty-six years.

Thomas Cruickshank spent the first twenty years of his life in the land of his nativity and attended the common schools in the acquirement of an education. His father, who had lost his fortune, advised him to emigrate to America, and thus it was that he came to this country in 1886. He made his way to Canton, South Dakota, and during the first winter worked for his board and attended the country schools in order to learn the English language. Mr., Cruickshank subsequently worked his way through Augustana College and afterward attended the Northern Illinois Normal College at Dixon, Illinois, from which institution he was graduated with the degree of B. S. in the class of 1894. In that year he went to Beloit, Iowa, and was there identified with the Lutheran Orphanage Asylum for two years, instituting the movement which resulted in securing the farm given tb the institution by a Mr. Nelson. In 1896 he went to St. Louis and took up the study of medicine in the medical department of Barnes University, being graduated therefrom with the class of 1899. During the following three months he was located in Woodlawn, Illinois, but did not find the prospects alluring there and consequently removed to Vermillion, South Dakota, where he has remained in practice continuously since. The success and reputation which he now enjoys have come in recognition of his ability to cope with the intricate problems testing the powers of the physician and surgeon. He is a member of the Yankton District Medical Society, of which he has served as vice president and censor, the South Dakota State Medical Society and the American Medical Association. For the past thirteen years he has been a member of the board of insanity examiners of Clay County, and since the establishment of the medical department of the University of South Dakota has been a lecturer in that institution.

Fraternally Dr. Cruickshank is identified with the Masons, belonging to the following organizations: Incense Lodge, No. 2, A. F. & A. M.; Vermillion Chapter, No. 21, R. A. M.; Vermillion Commandery, No. 16, K. T.; and El Riad Temple, A. A. O. N. M. S.. He has likewise been a member of the Vermillion Commercial Club since its organization and is widely recognized as one of the progressive and enterprising residents of the city. In professional and social circles, he holds to high standards and enjoys in large measure the confidence and trust of those with whom he is brought in contact in every relation of life.

CHARLES F. CULVER, M. D.

Dr. Charles F. Culver, a successful representative of the medical profession in Sioux Falls, has built up an extensive practice since locating here in January, 1903. His birth occurred in Deer field, Iowa, on the 3d of April, 1872, his parents being Cyrus Heman and Sarah A. (Pettit) Culver, the former a son of Heman Culver, a native of New York. Cyrus H. Culver was born in the Empire state, June 5, 1839, while his wife was a native of Pennsylvania. He enlisted at Oil City, Venango County, Pennsylvania, August 12, 1862, and was soon sent to Harrisburg, where his company was made Company I, of the One Hundred and Forty-second Pennsylvania Volunteer Infantry. The troops were then sent on to Washington, where they arrived about the 1st of September, 1862. From there they were sent to join McClellan's army at Antietam and South Mountain and from that time on Mr. Culver participated in all the battles with the Potomac army until Lee's surrender at Appomattox, except Gettysburg, at which time he was in the hospital, ill with typhoid fever. In this engagement his regiment was very nearly annihilated, only thirty escaping death or injury. He was several times hit but not seriously injured, although his left ear drum was ruptured at the battle of Cold Harbor. It has been noted that his regiment was quite a remarkable one, standing number three in the fighting four hundred, there being but two other regiments that saw harder service and lost more men in proportion to the numbers engaged, than the One Hundred and Forty-second Pennsylvania. His regiment served in the old first corps, in the new, Bucktail, brigade of all Pennsylvania regiments. The old first corps was so nearly wiped out at Gettysburg that it was made one division and assigned to the fifth corps, where they served until the close of the war. Mr. Culver was at the surrender at Appomattox and in the Grand Review in Washington, where as senior captain of the regiment, he had the honor of commanding the color, or leading platoon of the regiment. He was discharged May 29, 1865. He was promoted from the ranks to fourth sergeant soon after the company was organized, later to first sergeant, commissioned first lieutenant October 6, 1863, and to captain on April 22, 1864, and was elected by the regiment as major, but the regiment was so reduced that they were not allowed another field officer, so he was not commissioned. In 1882 Mr. Culver moved from Mendon, Michigan, to Foster County, Dakota territory, and settled on a homestead which is still in his possession, but the county having been divided he at present is living in Eddy County, North Dakota. He has been an active factor in local and state politics, wielding a wide influence for good.

Charles F. Culver acquired his education by attendance at the schools of Iowa, Illinois, Pennsylvania and North Dakota. Having determined upon the practice of medicine as a life work, he prepared for that profession as a student in the medical department of the University of Minnesota, which institution conferred upon him the degree of M. D. in 1899. He then put his theoretical training to the practical test during a year's internship in the St. Paul Hospital and subsequently opened an office at Chetek, Wisconsin. In January, 1903, he removed to Sioux Falls, South Dakota, and has there remained throughout the intervening years, an extensive practice having been accorded him in recognition of his skill and ability. He has held numerous appointive offices in connection with his profession and has proved an able incumbent in all.

On the 2d of September, 1903, in St. Paul, Dr. Culver was united in marriage to Miss Grace I. Cameron, her father being Thomas Cameron, a native of Canada, now living in St. Paul, and the owner and manager of the Valley Iron Works. They have two children: Gladys Marie, born in 1905; and Margaret Cameron, whose natal year was 1908.

In politics Dr. Culver is a stanch republican, while his religious faith is indicated by his membership in the Congregational church. He has attained the thirty-second degree of the Scottish Rite in Masonry, also belongs to the Mystic Shrine, and in 1910 became master of Unity Lodge, No. 130, F. & A. M., of Sioux Falls. He maintains the strictest conformity to the highest professional ethics and enjoys in full measure the confidence and respect of his professional brethren as well as of the general public.

L. E. Cummings, receiver of the United States land office at Pierre, to which position he was appointed in 1913, has throughout his entire life been identified with the west, and the spirit of progress and enterprise which has ever characterized this section of the country has been a dominant element in his life. He was born in Independence, Iowa, February 22, 1857, a son of William G. and Elizabeth (Wright) Cummings. The father was one of the early merchants of Iowa and at the time of the Civil war responded to the country's call for troops, doing active service on southern battlefields. Following the close of hostilities, he became a traveling salesman and to that vocation devoted the remainder of his active business career.

L. E. Cummings was the second in a family of five children and was educated in the public schools of Independence, Iowa, and of Yankton, South Dakota, his parents having removed with their family to the latter place in the year 1873. He was next appointed to the United States Naval Academy at Annapolis, Maryland, and after attending school there for two years resigned. He then turned his attention to the study of law in the offices and under the direction of the firm of Pendleton & Wakefield at Sioux City, Iowa. Subsequently he was associated as a law student with E. E. Hasner of Independence and was admitted to the Iowa bar in 1878. For a time, he engaged in active practice in Independence and then entered the insurance business, in which he continued until 1893, when he returned to South Dakota, settling at Yankton, where he conducted the Windsor Hotel. Subsequently he was manager of the Chandler Hotel at Vermillion, where he remained until 1903, when he removed to High more, South Dakota, where he engaged in the real-estate business. There he continued until 1913, when he was appointed receiver of the United States land office at Pierre, where he now resides.

Mr. Cummings is a democrat and has always taken an active interest in political questions and issues and a helpful part in advancing the interests of democracy, being recognized as one of the party leaders in the state. He holds membership in the Episcopal church and in Masonry has attained the thirty-second degree of the Scottish Rite and become a member of the Mystic Shrine. He is also a Knight of Pythias and a member of the Benevolent Protective Order of Elks. In everything pertaining to the work of general development and public improvement he is an out and out progressive. Among other beneficial movements that have claimed his attention and cooperation is that of the agitation for improved public highways. He furthers every practical movement for advancing the good roads system, his sagacity enabling him to recognize the advantages that will accrue therefrom, and at the same time he looks beyond the exigencies of the moment to the needs and opportunities of the future. His office is being conducted in a highly efficient manner and he ever fully meets the obligations which devolve upon him in this connection.

BURTON ALBERT CUMMINS

Burton Albert Cummins, whose high position in financial circles in South Dakota is indicated by the fact that he has been honored with the presidency of the State Bankers' Association, makes his home in Pierre, where, since July, 1890, he has been connected with the First National Bank, of which he is now the vice president. He has other important financial and business interests which have won him place with the leading representative citizens of the capital. He was born April 3, 1869, in Montpelier, Vermont, a son of Albert Oren and Mary Frances (Ellis) Cummins. The father, who was born August 3, 1829, died April 28, 1912, and the mother, who was born April 14, 1846, is still living. The ancestry of the family can be traced back to Isaac Cummings, of Ipswich, Connecticut, who was born in 1601 and died in 1677. Albert

O. Cummins spent six years and thousands of dollars in compiling the genealogy of the Cummins family. During the latter years of his life, he was a member of a firm conducting a large tannery at Montpelier, Vermont. Mrs. Mary Frances Cummins is a well-known author and a leading member of the Science church in Vermont.

In his student days Burton Albert Cummins attended the Washington county grammar school at Montpelier from which he was graduated on the 17th of June, 1887. Later he became a student in the Bryant and Stratton Business College of Boston, of which he was a graduate of the class of June, 1888. He began work in July of the same year as an employe in the Sioux National Bank of Sioux City, Iowa, and left there to enter the First National Bank of Pierre, South Dakota, in July, 1890. He has since worked his way upward through intermediate positions until he is now vice president of this bank, which is one of the strong financial institutions of the state. He occupies a prominent position in financial circles, his opinions carrying weight among the bankers of the state. In 1892 he occupied the presidency of the South Dakota Bankers' Association and has been a member of its executive committee almost continuously since. He has also been vice president of the American Bankers' Association and he has a wide acquaintance among leading financiers.

Aside from owning one half of the stock in the First National Bank of Pierre, he is a stockholder in the First National Life Insurance Company of Pierre and he has large property interests in California. He is treasurer of the Chicago, Black Hills & Yellowstone Park Highway Association.

On the 3d of April, 1890, in Sioux City, Iowa, Mr. Cummins was united in marriage to Miss Clara Belle Merrick, a daughter of F. L. and Nancy (Chapman) Merrick, of Kankakee, Illinois. Mrs. Cummins possesses considerable musical talent and is greatly interested in theatricals, having played many parts in amateur theatricals. Mr. and Mrs. Cummins have a daughter, Aline, who was born February 19, 1897, and they lost a son, Albert Oren, who died in 1896, when three years of age.

Mr. Cummins has always refused to become a candidate for office and has used his political influence only for his friends and in support of the principles in which he believes. He is a stalwart republican and has been a member of the state central committee at various times. He was United States disbursing agent when the Federal building was being erected in Pierre. He has held honorary office as a member of the staff of Governor Herreid with the rank of colonel. He supports the Episcopal church and holds membership in various fraternal and social organizations. He is now treasurer in Pierre Lodge, A. F. & A. M., which office he has filled since 1897. He has also taken the degrees of the chapter and commandery and is a member of the Mystic Shrine. The Sioux City Boat Club numbers him among its charter members and he also belongs to the Pierre Commercial Club. He was likewise chairman of the Pierre Capital Committee for two years, during the intense contest over the location of the capital. In 1914 he served as president of the South Dakota State Historical Society and is now one of its trustees.

For a quarter of a century, he has lived in this state and has been an interested witness of its growth and development, taking active and helpful part in the support of many projects for the general good. None occupy a more enviable position in public regard or in financial and business circles, not only on account of the success he has achieved but also owing to the straightforward and honorable business policy that he has ever followed.

DAILY MARTIN CURL

A growing district always offers an excellent field to the enterprising real-estate man and the efforts of Daily Martin Curl in this direction have been a potent force in bringing success to the Western Land Security Company since he became its secretary and treasurer in 1911. He had a good collegiate training and broad practical experience in business life ere entering upon his present connection and he has made creditable success for one of his years.

Mr. Curl was born upon a farm in Shelby County, Iowa, March 6, 1880, and is a son of Martin Luther and Abigail (Barbee) Curl, both of whom were natives of Ohio. Both the father and the grandfather served as privates in the Civil war, being members of the same company. In the country schools of Shelby County, the son began his education which was supplemented by a year's study in the Normal School at Logan, Iowa, and two years in the Iowa State College. He studied mechanical engineering while in college and afterward followed the profession for eight years, but in 1911 withdrew from that field of activity. He had been a resident, of Sioux Falls since 1909 and realizing that there were excellent opportunities for the real-estate man, owing to the rapid and substantial growth of the city, he embarked in the real-estate business in 1911, becoming secretary and treasurer of the Western Land Security Company. He has thoroughly acquainted himself with realty values, knows the property that is upon the market and through his enterprising methods and close connection with the business has been able to negotiate many important realty transfers.

On the 19th of March, 1907, in Omaha, Nebraska, Mr. Curl was united in marriage to Miss Jennie Ann Wilson, a daughter of Andrew W. Wilson, and they have one child, Dorothy Mildred, born November 25, 1910.

Mr. Curl holds membership with the Methodist Episcopal church and honorable principles actuate him in every relation of life. His political allegiance is given to the republican party and fraternally he is connected with the Masons and the Odd Fellows. In the York Rite of Masonry, he has attained the Knight Templar degree and he has also crossed the sands of the desert with the nobles of the Mystic Shrine. His life exemplifies his Christian belief and the beneficent teachings of the Masonic fraternity which are based upon the principles of mutual helpfulness and brotherly kindness. He has gained many friends during his residence in Sioux Falls and high respect is everywhere accorded him by those who know him.

JOHN EDWARD CURTIS, M. D.

Dr. John Edward Curtis, engaged in the practice of medicine and surgery at Lemmon, was born in Grant County, Wisconsin, February 17, 1876, his parents being William B. and Sarah (Dennis) Curtis, the former a native of Pennsylvania and the latter of England. The mother came to the United States when a maiden of sixteen summers with her mother, her father having died in England.

Dr. Curtis completed his literary education in the high school at Fennimore, Wisconsin, and when seventeen years of age began work on the Fennimore Times in the capacity of printer's devil. He rose through successive promotions to the position of foreman on the paper in eighteen months, becoming an expert workman with comprehensive knowledge of the printing business and also of the editorial department. The paper was owned by Henry E. Roethe, who was candidate for governor in 1914.

In the year 1899 Dr. Curtis was married in Fennimore to Miss Minnie Dempsey and the following year removed to Lone Rock, Wisconsin, where he opened a barber shop, conducting business along that line for five years. In 1905 he went to Louisville, Kentucky, and became a student in the medical department of the University of Louisville, from which he was graduated in 1909. After completing his course, he located for practice in Haynes, North Dakota, where he continued for four years, and in 1913 he went to Lemmon, South Dakota, where he has since remained, gaining a creditable position in the foremost rank of the medical profession in that part of the state.

The Doctor and his wife have four children, namely: Dennis Dempsey, Stanton Clark, Camilla Irene and Aldene Elizabeth. Fraternally Dr. Curtis is identified with the Masons, belonging to Palestine Lodge, No. 114, of Lone Rock, Wisconsin, and he is likewise a member of the Modern Woodmen of America, the Mystic Workers and the Beavers. His political allegiance is given to the republican party but the honors and emoluments of office have no attraction for him. Along strictly professional lines his membership connection is with the Aberdeen District Medical Society and the State Medical Society and through broad reading and conference with his colleagues he keeps in touch with the most advanced thought of the profession. He is conscientious in the discharge of his duties, accurate in analysis, careful in diagnosis and by reason of his ability has gained a place among the most able representatives of medical science in Perkins County.

FREDERIC T. CUTHBERT

Frederic T. CUTHBERT, of Canton, the present incumbent of the office of county judge of Lincoln County, was born in Whiting, Monona County, Iowa, on the 2d of April, 1876, being a son of Rev. Thomas and Emily J. (Denham) Cuthbert, the former being a clergyman of the Methodist Episcopal church. While the subject was a mere child his parents removed to Mapleton, Iowa, where they resided a number of years, thence removing to Rolfe, that state, and there remaining about two years. When Frederic was fifteen years of age he accompanied his parents to England, their native land, and the family continued to abide in the "tight little isle" about four years, during the major portion of which time our subject continued his educational discipline in a private school. In 1883 the family home was established in Sioux Falls, South Dakota, and the father soon afterward located on a farm near this city, our subject attending the public schools here until the removal to England, as noted. The subject returned to the United States in 1895, and located in Canton, South Dakota.

In 1895 Mr. Cuthbert took up the study of law in the office of A. R. Brown, of Canton, and he was admitted to the bar of the state on the 13th of May, 1897. He forthwith established himself in practice in this place, entering into partnership with M. E. Rudolph. A few months later he formed a professional alliance with L. J. Jones, with whom he was associated until May, 1901, in the meanwhile gaining a reputation as an able advocate and counsellor. Upon the dissolution of this partnership Mr. Cuthbert formed a partnership with A. B. Carlson, under the firm name of Cuthbert & Carlson, and this association has since obtained, the firm controlling a representative business.

Judge Cuthbert has always been a stanch advocate of the principles and policies of the Republican party, and he took a particularly active part in the campaign of 1896, doing effective work in the party cause, as has he also done in subsequent campaigns. In 1900 he delivered more than twenty speeches in advocacy of the Republican principles, and he is known as one of the most able young public speakers in the state. In the spring of 1898, he was elected justice of the peace in Canton, retaining this incumbency one year, and in 1900 he was elected city attorney, serving one term. In the autumn of that year still more distinguished preferment came to him in his election to the office of county judge, in which judicial capacity his services met with so marked popular approval that he was chosen as his own successor in the election of 1902, being thus in tenure of the office at the time of this writing.

Fraternally, Judge Cuthbert is identified with Silver Star Lodge, No. 4, Free and Accepted Masons, Siroc Chapter, No. 4, Royal Arch Masons, and with Canton Lodge, No. 52, Knights of Pythias, all of Canton.

RUEL E. DANA

Ruel E. Dana, secretary and treasurer of the corporation of Wait & Dana, editors and publishers of the Armour Herald, was born in Fairmount, Minnesota, on the 23d of May, 1872, being a son of Charles T. and Lucinda (Gilman) Dana, of whose five children he is the eldest of the three now living, the others being Frank N., who is a resident of St. Paul, Nebraska, and Myrtie L., who is the wife of William A. Torbert, of Deavertown, Ohio. The father of the subject came of stanch New England stock, of English extraction. He was born in the state of Vermont, in 1820, and as a young man he set forth to seek his fortunes in the west, becoming one of the pioneers of the state of Wisconsin, where he remained for a few years and then repeated his pioneer experiences in Minnesota, where he resided many years. His death occurred in St. Paul, Nebraska, August 4, 1893, at the age of seventy-three years. In his youth he learned the trade of carpenter, becoming a skilled artisan in the line, and he was for many years successfully engaged in contracting and building, while he also was prospered in his operations as a farmer. In 1887 he removed to Howard County, Nebraska, and later to Thomas County, in the same state, where he remained about three years. He identified himself with the Republican party at the time of its organization in Wisconsin and continued to support its cause for many years, but finally identified himself with the People's party, of whose principles he continued a stanch advocate until his death, at which time he was incumbent of the office of county commissioner of Thomas County. In earlier years he held, at various times, practically all the county offices in the section where he resided, having never been defeated for any office for which he was a candidate, and having been a power in local affairs, showing much ability in the marshalling of political forces and being an influential factor in his party councils. His wife, who was born in the province of Quebec, Canada, July 20, 1842, is now sixty-two years old. Mr. Dana held membership in the Methodist Episcopal church in his earlier life, while his widow is a member of the Baptist denomination. Ruel E. Dana, the immediate subject of this sketch, remained at the parental home until he had attained the age of sixteen years, his educational advantages having been such as were afforded in the public schools during a portion of the winter periods, his time during the summer months being taken up with work on the farm. At the age noted he initiated his independent career, having, in the summer of 1887, entered the office of the Advance, a weekly paper then published at Worthington, Minnesota, under the editorial direction of A. P. Miller, a prominent journalist and a poet of considerable reputation. There Mr. Dana gained his initiation into the mysteries of the "art preservative," remaining until the autumn of the same year, when he accompanied his parents on their removal to Nebraska, where he secured employment in the office of the St. Paul Phonograph and later was an employe of the Greeley Herald, at Greeley Center, that state. In October, 1892, Mr. Dana came to Howard, South Dakota, arriving here without funds, since the proceeds of his former labors had largely been devoted to assisting in the support of the family. Previous to his arrival he had been offered employment in the office of the Miner County Democrat, in Howard, resigning his position with the Greeley (Nebraska) Herald to accept the South Dakota position, and less than two months later, on the 1st of December, 1892, he formed a partnership with Levi D. Wait, his present associate, and purchased the plant of the Democrat "on tick," which they continued to publish under the same title, the enterprise proving a financial success, as is evident when we revert to the fact that the young men were able to pay for their plant within eleven months after its purchase, while they advanced the paper to a position among the best and most widely quoted in that section of the state. In 1898 Mr. Dana purchased his partner's interest and individually continued the publication about one year, when he sold the plant and business to Mr. Wait, and he then secured employment in a local mercantile establishment, his impaired health having necessitated this change of vocation. In the autumn of 1900 Mr. Dana went to Seneca, Missouri, where he took a working interest in the Seneca Dispatch, with an ultimate view of purchasing the property if satisfied with the business outlook and climatic conditions. After a six-months residence in the Missouri town he was not satisfied, however, and thereafter made a trip through Oklahoma, Indian Territory and Texas, returning to Howard, South Dakota, in April, 1901, and there rejoining his family. Within the period of his absence Mr. Wait had sold the Democrat and in May, 1901, had come to Armour and contracted for the purchase of the Armour Herald, publishing the first copy under his name. One-week later Mr. Dana joined his old partner here and purchased a half interest in the business, which has since been continued under the firm name of Wait & Dana, merged into a corporation January 5, 1904, all the stock being owned by the subject and his partner.

In politics Mr. Dana is a zealous advocate of the principles of the Democratic party, in whose work he has taken an active part. While a resident of Howard he held the office of village recorder for two terms. In the fall of 1902, yielding to the importunities of his party friends, he became a candidate for the office of auditor of Douglas County, and he was elected to this office, notwithstanding the fact that the normal political complexion of the county is strongly Republican and that he had been a resident of the county only eighteen months at the time of his election. He received a majority of thirty-one votes, and was appreciative of the honor conferred upon him by the voters of the county, while his service has proved the wisdom of their confidence and support.

Fraternally, Mr. Dana is a Mason and a member of Washington Lodge, No. 104, Independent Order of Odd Fellows, of Armour. He passed through all the chairs of Lodge No. 48, Independent Order of Odd Fellows, at Howard and has been a representative to the grand lodge of the state. He is also identified with the encampment of the order and with the Daughters of Rebekah, while he is affiliated with Armour Camp, No. 2746, Modern Woodmen of America. He and his wife are communicants of the Protestant Episcopal church. Mrs. Dana is at present noble grand of Pleiades Lodge, No. 86, of Armour, and is the representative to the state assembly, of South Dakota, for 1904. On the 15th of August, 1894, was solemnized the marriage of Mr. Dana to Miss Ellen Moore, of Howard, this state, and they are the parents of three children, Florian Alice, Charles M. and Clarence E.

GEORGE JONATHAN DANFORTH

George Jonathan Danforth, a member of the well-known firm of Wagner & Danforth, prominent and successful attorneys of Sioux Falls, was born near Meeme, Manitowoc County, Wisconsin, November 21, 1875. He is a son of Quincy Aimes and Gertrude (Silbernagel) Danforth, the former of whom served for three years and six months in Company C, Fourth Wisconsin Volunteer Infantry, rising from private to the rank of sergeant. The family is an old American one having been founded in this country by Nicholas Danforth, who came from England in 1638. The grandfather of the subject of this review, Jonathan Danforth, was born in Vermont in 1802 and died in 1879, at the age of seventy-seven years.

In the acquirement of an education George J. Danforth attended the public schools at Meeme and later was a student in the State Normal School at Oshkosh, Wisconsin. He afterward enrolled in the law department of the University of Wisconsin at Madison and was graduated with the degree of LL. B. in 1903. In the same year he came to Sioux Falls and began the practice of his profession, in which he has since made rapid and steady advancement. In 1913 he became a member of the firm of Wagner & Danforth, which controls today a representative patronage connecting them with a great deal of important litigation and they occupy a prominent place among the leading representatives of the bar in the community. In 1909 Mr. Danforth was appointed state's attorney and served in that capacity for two years, discharging his duties in a capable and conscientious manner. He is a director in the Sioux Life and Casualty Company of Sioux Falls and acts also as attorney for this corporation. In December, 1914, he was elected president of the Minnehaha County Bar Association, which indicates his high standing among his professional brethren.

In Manitowoc, Wisconsin, August 21, 1907, Mr. Danforth was united in marriage to Miss Nora Isabel Tollefson, a daughter of Iver Tollefson, a veteran of the Civil War. Mr. and Mrs. Danforth have become the parents of three children: George Jonathan, Jr., born July 7, 1909; Edward Aimes, born June 7, 1912; and Marie Gertrude, born August 4, 1914.

Mr. Danforth is a member of the Congregational church, in which he served as trustee, and is connected fraternally with the Masonic blue lodge. He gives his political allegiance to the republican party and served for two years as secretary and treasurer of the Sioux Falls library board. His interests are, however, largely concentrated upon the duties of his profession, in which he has met with that success which always rewards unusual merit and ability.

ERIE S. DANFORTH

As owner and editor of the Republican, an excellent newspaper published at Vermillion, Erie S. Danforth is a man of influence in his part of the state. He was born in Wisconsin on the 6th of January, 1873, a son of William and Ann is (Ormsbee) Danforth, natives of Vermont and New York respectively. The father, who was a farmer, passed away in December, 1880, in Wisconsin. To him and his wife were born three children, of whom our subject is the youngest, the others being: Halbert, who died when five years old; and Nettie, who passed away in 1912.

Erie S. Danforth was reared in his native state and was graduated from the high school at Waldo in 1888. In June of that year, he removed to Vermillion, South Dakota, coming with an aunt and her husband, E. H. Willey. Mr. Danforth lost his father when about seven years of age and was largely reared by his aunt. Mr. Willey purchased the Republican at Vermillion and our subject learned the printer's trade in the office of that paper. In 1895 he purchased a half interest in the publication and has since retained his connection therewith. The Republican was started in 1860 by Bedell & Clark and has always gone under that name. The circulation of the paper is large and its subscribers are the representative people of Vermillion and its vicinity, as they are assured of reliable news, clearly written, and as the editorial policy of the paper is one to win commendation. The extensive circulation of the paper makes it valuable as an advertising medium and the local merchants patronize it as such.

Mr. Danforth is a republican and for four years, or two terms, has been a member of the city council. He served as police judge for more than a year and then resigned that position in order to take up a homestead. His social nature finds expression in his membership in the Masonic order and he has attained high rank in that organization, belonging to all of the bodies thereof with the exception of the consistory. He has held all of the chairs in the blue lodge and chapter. He is a member of the Independent Order of Odd

Fellows and was secretary for one term, and his fraternal connections also extend to the Knights of Pythias, in which he has held all of the chairs, the Benevolent Protective Order of Elks and the Modern Woodmen of America.

ANDREW D. DARLING, D. D. S.

A. D. DARLING, one of the representative dental practitioners of South Dakota, maintaining his residence in the thriving town of Tyndall, is a native of the state of Illinois, having been born in Princeton, Beaver County, on the 19th of September, 1862, a son of William D. and Clara O. (Smith) Darling, and the younger of their two children, his sister, Alice C. being the wife of James McCartney, of Wyncote, Wyoming. The father of the Doctor was born in the state of New York, of stanch Scotch extraction, and when he was a boy his parents removed thence to Illinois, where he was reared to the sturdy discipline of the farm, receiving his education in the public schools.

At the outbreak of the war of the Rebellion he tendered his services in defense of the Union, enlisting as a private in the Ninety-third Illinois Volunteer Infantry. At the battle of Lookout Mountain, he was suffering an attack of measles but insisted upon taking his place in the ranks and participating in the engagement. When the retreat was made, he was too ill to keep in line with his regiment and was captured by the enemy and incarcerated in Andersonville prison, where he died shortly afterward. His widow subsequently became the wife of John Vanderley, and they became the parents of one daughter, Nellie, who is the wife of Edward W. Carrell, residing near Piano, Illinois. The devoted mother entered into eternal rest in 1873.

Dr. Darling was reared in the home of his maternal grandparents, in Marion County, Iowa, and his early educational advantages were such as were afforded in the public schools of that locality, while he began to depend upon his own resources prior to attaining his fifteenth year, having thus been the architect of his own fortunes. For four years he worked as a clerk and general utility boy in a grocery at Pella, Iowa, and at the expiration of this period his employer failed in business and a local buyer offered to purchase the stock and place our subject in charge of the enterprise, but he considered it expedient to refuse the overtures thus made and went to Des Moines, that state, where he secured a clerical position in a leading dry-goods establishment. The sedentary occupation finally made serious inroads on his health and he accordingly determined to remove farther to the west. In the spring of 1892, therefore, he resigned his position and proceeded to western Nebraska, where for the first few months he worked on a ranch, receiving his board in compensation for his services but having in view the recuperation of his energies by the outdoor life. Later he secured a position as bookkeeper for an irrigating company, receiving a nominal salary. In July, 1893, he went to Denver, Colorado, arriving in that city in the midst of the severe financial panic of that year, and there he remained for a period of six weeks, by which time his available financial resources had reached a low ebb, being represented in the sum of twelve dollars, with this capital he purchased a ticket for Omaha, Nebraska, and thence went to Pacific Junction, Iowa, where his elder sister was then living. Shortly afterward he secured a position in an abstract office in Plattsmouth, Nebraska, where he remained until the 1st of March, 1894, when he came to Huron, South Dakota, and entered the dental office of his uncle, Dr. William H. Barker, under whose direction he made a careful study of operative and laboratory dentistry, continuing to be thus engaged for one year, at the expiration of which he went to Austin, Minnesota, in company with a Huron merchant, whom he assisted in establishing his business in the town mentioned. He remained in Austin until October, 1895, when he was matriculated in the American College of Dental Surgery, in the city of Chicago, the institution being now a department of the Northwestern University, of Evanston, Illinois. Dr. Darling continued his studies in this college for two years and then opened an office in South Chicago, and in 1899 he resumed his studies in the same college, where he was graduated in the spring of 1900. During the last year of his college course, he worked at night in his little office in South Chicago, often remaining until the morning hours, and while he was thus able to gain financial success in his chosen profession the dual strain caused a distinct impairment of his health, and he was compelled to remain for a short time in a local hospital, after which he returned to his home in South Chicago for a short rest. The exigencies of his business, however, did not permit him to secure the needed quiet and he accordingly removed to South Dakota, taking up his residence in DeSmet, where he passed the winter of 1901, and in the following spring he came to Tyndall, where he has since been actively engaged in the practice of his chosen profession, having built up a large and representative business and being known as one of the able members of his profession in the state. Dentistry implies both a science and a mechanic art, and in all phases of the same Dr. Darling is amply fortified for the highest order of work, so that his success has come as a natural sequel, while he has attained distinctive personal popularity in his chosen field of endeavor. He gives his allegiance to the Republican party and he is a communicant of the Protestant Episcopal church.

Fraternally the Doctor is identified with Capital Lodge, No. 110, Free and Accepted Masons, Des Moines, Iowa, and Des Moines Lodge, No. 68, Knights of Pythias. On the 11th of July, 1898, Dr. Darling was united in marriage to Miss Hattie Sturgeon, of DeSmet, this state, and of their three children two are living, namely: Stephen Foster and Paul Eugene, both of whom remain at the parental home. Mrs. Darling is a communicant of the Catholic church.

FLOYD C. DARLING

Floyd C. DARLING, deceased, was a native of the great Buckeye state, having been born in Warren, Trumbull County, Ohio, on the 18th of February, 1853, and being a son of Russell and Mary (Laraway) Darling. He received his educational training in the public schools of Ohio, and as a youth became identified with the great railroading industry. At the age of twenty-two years, he engaged as locomotive fireman on the line of the Erie Railroad, between Cleveland and Youngstown, Ohio. He was faithful and capable and in due time advancement came, and in 1879 he was placed in charge of an engine. In 1883 he came to Aberdeen, and was given an engine on the Chicago, Milwaukee & St. Paul Railroad, which he continued to run until his death. He was punctilious and careful in the discharge of his responsible duties and to this fact was due the excellent record he made, no serious accidents having marred his experience as an engineer.

In politics Mr. Darling was a member of the Republican party, and he held the Knights Templar degree in the York Rite of the Masonic fraternity, and also the thirty-second degree in the Ancient Accepted Scottish Rite, being a popular member of the various bodies of the order in Aberdeen, including the temple of the Ancient Arabic Order of the Nobles of the Mystic Shrine. He was also a knight commander of the Court of Honor and was also a member of the Brotherhood of Locomotive Engineers.

In Titusville, Pennsylvania, on the 20th of June, 1873, was solemnized the marriage of Mr. Darling to Miss Margaret McCauley, who was born in Pennsylvania. Of this union were born six children, concerning whom we enter the following brief record: Viola is the wife of Arthur W. Oliver, of Victor, Colorado; Etta is the wife of Orville Card, of Aberdeen; Nellie is the wife of John Clawson, of Aurora, Illinois; Margaret is employed in one of the leading mercantile establishments in Aberdeen, and Ruby is a member of the class of 1906 in the high school. Flora, the fourth child of Mr. and Mrs. Darling, died in Cleveland, Ohio. The eldest daughter was formerly the wife of the late Eugene A. Lamb, who was proprietor of the Aberdeen marble works and brick yard, and three children were born of this union, Gertrude, Francis and Marie. Mrs. Darling is a member of the Catholic church. Mr. Darling died April 3, 1904.

JOSEPH J. DAVENPORT *

Joseph J. Davenport is the president of the waterworks company of Sturgis and formerly was actively and successfully engaged in the banking business. His efforts have ever been of a character that have contributed to public progress as well as to individual success and his spirit of enterprise has constituted a factor in the upbuilding and development of the city in which he makes his home. To such men the northwest owes much, for they have been the real builders of the state's progress and prosperity. Mr. Davenport was born in Woodford County, Illinois, January 23, 1850, a son of John J. and Lucy A. (Bullock) Davenport, both natives of Woodford County, Kentucky, the former born in 1814 and the latter in September, 1825. They were married in Illinois, where John J. Davenport settled in pioneer times, becoming one of the early residents of Woodford County. In fact, both the paternal and maternal grandparents of Joseph J. Davenport took up their abode in that district in an early day and named the county in honor of the old home county in Kentucky. John J. Davenport devoted his life to farming until he passed away in 1852 during the cholera epidemic, his father, who was a minister, bringing the disease from Peoria, where he had been preaching. Mrs. Davenport long survived her husband, departing this life in Danville, Illinois, in October, 1914, after residing there with her daughter for thirty years. In the family were six children, of whom Joseph J. and a twin sister were next to the youngest and are the only ones now living. The sister, Maria M., is the wife of Benjamin F. Siner, a retired molder, living in Danville.

Joseph J. Davenport attended school at Minonk, Illinois, after having previously spent three months at a private school in Metamora. He was eighteen years of age before he entered school but he has made up for his lack of early opportunities in that direction and in the school of experience has learned many valuable lessons of life. In the fall of 1871, when twenty-one years of age, he entered the State University of Illinois at Champaign, where he continued his studies for three years. His life has been one of earnest and unremitting toil and at the time when most boys are in school and surrounded by parental care, he was forced to earn his own living, being but eight years of age when he was employed at herding sheep and similar work. He spent five years in the service of Isaac Boys, three miles north of Metamora, Illinois, and for two years he was a light weight rider for William Brady, of Peoria, the owner of fine racing stock. He then accepted a position under the station agent at Eureka, Illinois, for a year, during which time he studied telegraphy, and afterward was employed as a newsboy on trains for three years. He next accepted the position of brakeman, running between Peoria and Chenoa for about two years and during part of that time was in charge of a freight train. Up to that time he had never attended school and when he sustained an injury to his hand, he went to the road superintendent to show him his condition. The superintendent advised him, because of the injury, which would compel him to lay off for a time, to go back to his home and attend school.

Mr. Davenport followed the advice, walking from Peoria to Metamora. After a year spent in school at Minonk, he obtained a certificate and engaged in teaching school for a year. In 1871, as previously stated, he entered the University of Illinois at Champaign, where he remained until 1874, when his money was exhausted and he opened a news stand in Urbana. In 1875 he went to New York in the employ of the Chicago Feather Duster Company, opening a branch office in the eastern metropolis. He sold the first split feather turkey duster ever sold in New York city and continued in that business for three years. He then obtained a position in the Marine National Bank at No. 84 Wall Street, New York, and continued there until the failure of the bank in 1884. He remained with the receiver for one month, at the end of which time he started for the northwest with Sturgis as his destination, arriving there in June, 1884. He then accepted the position of cashier in the Lawrence County Bank, which he organized with a capital of twenty-five thousand dollars. Subsequently this was consolidated with the Fox & Stebbins Bank and Mr. Davenport organized the First National Bank of Sturgis, with which he was connected until he disposed of his banking interests in 1896. Four years before he had established the Sturgis water plant, turning on the water on the 9th of March, 1893, having obtained a twenty years' franchise. In 1896 he disposed of his banking interests to the organizers of the Meade County Bank and since that time he has concentrated his efforts upon the management of the waterworks, being president of the company, which is a close corporation, the family owning the entire stock, worth one hundred thousand dollars. Mr. Davenport has also engaged in the real-estate business continuously through the period of his residence in Sturgis and is still an extensive landowner in South Dakota.

On the 14th of October, 1885, was celebrated the marriage of Mr. Davenport and Miss Sara E. Jarvis, who was born in Brooklyn, New York, a daughter of Daniel and Amelia (Robinson) Jarvis, natives of the Empire state, born in 1835 and 1840 respectively. They were married in 1855. The father was reared on Long Island and became a sea captain, following the sea for thirty years or more. In 1892 he removed to the west, settling in Sturgis, where he engaged in ranching until his death, in February, 1908. For about thirteen years he had survived his wife, who died March 9, 1895. Mrs. Davenport was their only child. By her marriage she has become the mother of four children. Alice J., the eldest, is the wife of Albert L. Bodley, of the Security Land & Abstract Company of Sturgis, and they have one child, Virginia Jarvis. Florence Agnes, who is a graduate of Columbia University of New York, where she specialized in physical education, is now in charge of that work in a school for girls at Highland Hall, Hollidaysburg, Pennsylvania. She is also a graduate of All Saints school at Sioux Falls, South Dakota, spent one year in the Cumnock school at Los Angeles, California, and for two years was a teacher in All Saints at Sioux Falls. John J., the third of the family, died in February, 1909, at the age of fifteen years. Jarvis Daniel, the fourth of the family, is now attending the Shattuck Military Academy at Faribault, Minnesota, where he is preparing to take up the study of mechanical engineering and expects to enter Throop College, a technical school of California.

The family attend the Presbyterian church, of which Mr. and Mrs. Davenport are member, and he belongs also to the Masonic fraternity, holding membership in Olive Branch Lodge, No. 47, A. F. & A. M., of Sturgis; Black Hills Chapter, No. 25, R. A. M., of Rapid City; Dakota Commandery, No. 1, K. T., of Deadwood; Deadwood Consistory, No. 3, S. P. R. S.; and Naja Temple of the Mystic Shrine of Deadwood. He is very prominent in the organization, has passed through all of the chairs in the blue lodge, is a past potentate of the Shrine and was grand master of South Dakota in 1908 and 1909. Mr. Davenport is a member of the Masonic Veterans Association and was its president during 1904 and 1905. He is grand representative of the grand lodge of Australia, and he was one of the distinguished grand masters specially invited to attend the unusual ceremonies when ex-President Taft was made "a Master Mason at sight" in Cincinnati in February, 1909. He laid the corner stone of the new state capitol at Pierre in June, 1908, when the grand lodge assembled there especially for that purpose, and in October, 1908, he laid the corner stone of the new Masonic Temple at Redfield, South Dakota. He is known everywhere as a most eloquent speaker and his different addresses in the Masonic lodges as well as elsewhere are masterpieces of logic and show a remarkable fund of knowledge on all subjects.

His political allegiance has always been given to the republican party, which was the defense of the Union during the dark days of the Civil war, when he served as drummer boy for Company E, One Hundred and Eighth Illinois Volunteer Infantry. He was refused enlistment three times on account of his youth and size but remained with his company for over a year or until sent home with typhoid fever. Mr. Davenport is truly a self-made man and his life indicates that no matter how much may be done for the individual in the way of giving him the advantages which are sought in the schools and in other connections, he must essentially formulate, determine and give shape to his own character. He has persevered in the pursuit of a persistent purpose and has gained a most satisfactory reward. A man of great natural ability, his success in business from the beginning of his residence in Sturgis has been uniform and rapid. He thoroughly enjoys home life, takes great pleasure in the society of his family and friends, is always courteous, kindly and affable, and his life in many respects is most exemplary. He has ever supported those interests which are calculated to uplift and benefit humanity, while his own high moral worth is deserving of the warmest commendation.

LESTER M. DAVIS

Lester M. Davis, who was elected to the office of treasurer of Marshall County in 1914, was born in Waseca, county, Minnesota, December 23, 1881, being one of the two children of David and Clara (Hinkley) Davis. The father was born in Wisconsin in 1853 and the mother in Minnesota in 1857. They were married in the latter state and he has devoted his attention to farming, whereby he has provided a comfortable living for his family. In 1883 he removed to Marshall County, where he took up a homestead on which he lived for a number of years. He now resides upon an eighty-acre tract of land near Britton, and although he had only two dollars and sixty cents when he reached South Dakota, he is now in possession of a comfortable competence. His political support is given to the republican party. James Davis, the paternal grandfather of Lester M. Davis, was born in New York and at an early period in the settlement of Wisconsin took up his abode in that state. At the time of the Civil War, he put aside all business and personal considerations to aid his country in the defense of the Union. The maternal grandfather, Henry Hinkley, was born in Maine and after living for a time in Wisconsin removed to Minnesota, where he was living at the time of the Indian troubles. He afterward came to South Dakota, where he took up land and, in this state, spent his remaining days. It was his daughter Clara who became the wife of David Davis and they had a daughter, May, who is now the wife of O. C. Sherburn, a farmer living at Britton.

The other child of that marriage is Lester M. Davis, who was in his second year when brought to Marshall County. His education was acquired in the schools of Britton and he devoted his time and energies to general agricultural pursuits until he was elected to office. He has three hundred and fifty-four acres of valuable land in this county, upon which he has made excellent improvements, transforming it into one of the fine farms of the district. In 1903 Mr. Davis was united in marriage to Miss Olive Russell, her father being Edward Russell, an agriculturist of Marshall County. They have one child, Dorothy, who is in school.

Mr. Davis is a well-known representative of the Masonic fraternity in Marshall County, belonging to both the lodge and the chapter. He votes with the republican party and keeps well informed on the questions and issues of the day. In the fall of 1914, he became his party's candidate for the office of county treasurer and the election proved that he had the support of the majority, so that he is now the incumbent in that position, in which he is proving most capable. He has been familiar with the history of this county for about a third of a century and is an interested witness of the changes which have occurred and of the progress which has been wrought. At all times he has been in sympathy with movements for the general good and his labors have been resultant factors in the upbuilding of the community.

PARK DAVIS ‡

PARK DAVIS, of Sioux Falls, South Dakota, one of the leading lawyers of South Dakota, was born in Athens, Windham County, Vermont, September 24, 1837, son of Elijah and Miriam Davis. His father died when the subject was quite young and left him largely dependent on his own resources for advancement. He attended Leland Seminary at Townshend, Vermont, and in 1862 was graduated from Middlebury College. He read law under Butler & Wheeler, prominent attorneys of Jamaica, Vermont; was admitted to the bar in Windham County in 1864; and in February, 1865, commenced the practice of his profession at St. Albans, Vermont, with Dana R. Bailey, under the firm name of Bailey & Davis. Later he was admitted to the supreme court, the circuit court of the United States, and the supreme court of the United States. He prospered as a general practitioner of law at St. Albans until 1879, when he removed to St. Paul, Minnesota, and, in connection with Hiram F. Stevens, of that city, successfully practiced his profession until September 1, 1881. Then he temporarily withdrew from the law and engaged with his brother-in-law in a mercantile venture at Albany, New York, under the firm name of Gray & Davis. In October, 1885, he went to Sioux Falls, South Dakota, formed a partnership with his old friend and former partner, Dana R. Bailey, and since has ranked as one of the leading lawyers of his state. In 1874 he represented St. Albans in the general assembly of Vermont and was a prominent and influential member of that body.

Mr. Davis is highly distinguished in Masonic circles. He served three terms as grand master of Masons of Vermont. His record in this important office was a brilliant one. Since coming to South Dakota, he has been honored with the office of grand high priest and many other positions of honor and trust by the Masonic fraternity. He is the author of a treatise on Masonic trials and forms for procedure which have been incorporated into a monitor published by the grand lodge of Vermont.

Mr. Davis was married at Townshend, Vermont. October 27, 1863, to Delia S. Gray and they have two children, Henry P. and May L. Mr. Davis is one of Sioux Falls' leading citizens and is favorably known throughout the state. He is an able lawyer, a genial gentleman and his record as a man is without reproach.

EDGAR DEAN

Edgar Dean, secretary and manager of the Farmers Lumber Company at Canton, is a business man who has worked his way upward through close application and energy, making at all times wise use of his talents and his opportunities. Public honors of an important character have also come to him and in various relations of life his worth as a man and citizen is widely acknowledged. He was born in Sullivan County, New York, on the 26th of May, 1851, and is a son of George and Sarah (Tompkins) Dean. In early life the father followed lumbering, but afterward turned his attention to general agricultural pursuits. He served in the One Hundred and Twentieth New York Volunteer Infantry in the Civil war and participated in the battle of Gettysburg. He is still living at the very advanced age of ninety-one years, but the mother has passed away.

In the public schools Edgar Dean pursued his education and in the school of experience he has learned many valuable lessons. In early manhood he followed farming and also did some factory work for about two years, remaining in the east until 1874, when he determined to try his fortune in the northwest. Accordingly, he made his way to South Dakota, where he arrived on the 1st of May. He filed on a homestead and timber claim on the 14th of May, 1874, and with characteristic energy began the development and improvement of a farm, which he carefully and systematically operated for about fourteen years, when he put aside the active work of the fields, although he still owns the original property.

Mr. Dean's fellow townsmen have long recognized his worth and ability and his fitness for public office. Before leaving the farm, he was called to the position of county commissioner, in which he served for two terms. He left the farm when elected county treasurer, which position he filled for four years, proving a most capable custodian of the public funds. He then returned to the farm, upon which he spent the succeeding two years. He was again elected to office as he was chosen to represent his district in the state senate and he served in that capacity for two years. While thus engaged he purchased an interest in the lumber business, with which he has since been connected, and as secretary and manager of the Farmers Lumber Company he is now at the head of a large trade, which has been greatly promoted through his efforts. His energy and enterprise are a stimulus to the business and his carefully formulated plans are carefully but promptly executed, with the result that a substantial income accrues.

In 1871, Mr. Dean was united in marriage to Miss Lovina Parker, a daughter of Parley Parker, of southern Indiana, and their children are: Ralph P.; George H.; Effie, now the wife of C. H. Fitch, of Lincoln County; Edna J., the wife of Dr. C. L. Wendt, of Canton; Ella J., who became the wife of Hudson Baker and died in 1907; and Edgar Merle.

The religious faith of the family is that of the Methodist Episcopal church, to the support of which Mr. Dean contributes liberally. His political allegiance is given to the republican party and he is unfaltering in his advocacy of its principles. His fraternal relations are with the Masons and the Odd Fellows. He belongs to Silver Star Lodge, No. 4, F. & A. M., and Siroc Chapter, No. 4, R. A. M. He is also prominent in Odd Fellowship, holding membership in Centennial Lodge and in the encampment. He is now department commander, with the rank of colonel of the Patriarchs Militant. His life exemplifies the beneficent spirit upon which those organizations rest, for he is always loyal to their teachings. His opinions carry weight in political and business circles, for he is recognized as a man of sound judgment and keen discrimination. No one questions his devotion to the public good in the discharge of his official duties and none have doubt as to his integrity and his enterprise in the management of business affairs.

JOHN D. DEETS

John D. Deets, who since 1911 has been commissioner of immigration with office in Pierre, South Dakota, was born in Oil City, Pennsylvania, on the 9th of March, 1865, a son of Joseph and Margaret (Hayes) Deets, both representatives of old families noted for their loyalty to everything American. The mother belonged to the well-known Hayes family of western Pennsylvania. Her father, who came from County Antrim, Ireland, was of Scotch-Irish descent and was the first of the family to settle in the western part of the Keystone state. He was soon followed, however, by his brothers, some of whom settled in western Pennsylvania and others in eastern Ohio. The Deets family comes of German ancestry. Joseph Deets died in 1871, while Mrs. Deets, long surviving him, passed away in 1906.

Pursuing his education in the public schools at Parker, Pennsylvania, John D. Deets there mastered the common branches of learning and afterward entered Allegheny College at Meadville, Pennsylvania, being graduated from that institution on the completion of the classical course in 1888 with the Bachelor of Arts degree. Following his graduation from the high school he engaged in teaching and also worked in shops as a machinist until he had acquired a sum sufficient to enable him to defray the expenses of his college training. After leaving college he entered the ministry of the Methodist Episcopal church and devoted sixteen years of his life to that work. He has been continuously in the government service since 1906 in which year he became a United States special agent in charge of allotment work for the Indians. Five years later he was made commissioner of immigration and has filled the office continuously and acceptably since 1911.

On the 16th of April, 1896, at Jackson, Minnesota, Mr. Deets was united in marriage to Mrs. Villa Belle Boehl, a daughter of Joseph and Esther Dunham. The father was an extensive farmer and stock-raiser and was very successful. Mrs. Deets was born in Illinois and by her marriage has become the mother of five children: Margaret, Katherine, Emma, June and Deaver.

The parents hold membership in the Methodist Episcopal church and Mr. Deets is also a member of the Masonic fraternity and the Knights of Pythias. In politics he is a progressive republican and he is ever loyal to any cause which he espouses. It is well known that he stands fearless in defense of his honest convictions and neither fear nor favor can swerve him from a course which he believes to be right. He is therefore a very acceptable public officer and his record through the past seven years in office is an untarnished one.

ALEXANDER R. DEMPSTER

Sioux Falls with its pulsing industrial and commercial activities is continually drawing to itself men of enterprise who recognize the opportunities found in the great and growing northwest. Prompted by laudable ambition and impelled by enterprise and sound judgment, Alexander R. Dempster came to this city to establish a wholesale distributing house for the products made by the pump and windmill factory at Beatrice, Nebraska, in which he is interested.

His entire life has been passed in the Mississippi valley. His birth occurred in Dundee, Illinois, January 28, 1848, his parents being Alexander R. and Jane Blythe (Whittaker) Dempster. The former was a native of Aberdeen, Scotland, born May 15, 1811, and in 1832, about the time he attained his majority, he came to the new world. He first located in New York City, where he worked at his trade of quill making, but soon after his marriage went to Chicago, Illinois, subsequently settling on a farm near Dundee, Kane County, that state, where he devoted the remainder of his life to agricultural pursuits. There he passed away in 1893, having attained the venerable age of eighty-two years. His wife was born July 4, 1816, in New York state but her father was of Scotch birth. To Mr. and Mrs. Alexander R. Dempster, Sr., were born ten children, equally divided as to sex, of whom three sons and three daughters yet survive.

Alexander R. Dempster of this review acquired his early education in the public schools of Carpenterville, Illinois, and afterward attended the Elgin Academy at Elgin, that state, being graduated on the completion of several courses. He left Elgin in 1877 and went to Chicago, where he was in the employ of Field, Leiter & Company and subsequently with Marshall Field & Company until 1884. In that year he went to Beatrice, Nebraska, where he became connected with the manufacture of pumps and windmills. In 1895 he removed to Des Moines, Iowa, where he established a similar business, while still retaining his interests at Beatrice. Fifteen years were passed in Des Moines and in 1910 he came to Sioux Falls, South Dakota, to open a wholesale distributing house in order to handle the products made in the factories at Beatrice. This brings him into closer connection with the trade of the northwest. The sales now cover a wide territory in this section of the country and the business is a growing and profitable one. Mr. Dempster has already become recognized as one of the representative business men of the city, belonging to that class who, while promoting individual interests also contribute to public prosperity.

On the 20th of July, 1871, at Dundee, Illinois, Mr. Dempster was united in marriage to Miss Jennie Crichton and to them have been born several children: Grace Ethel; Jennie; Mabel, the wife of Roswell R. Marsh of Fort Pierre, South Dakota; Edna Alexandria, the wife of Lee A. Lumbard, of Des Moines, Iowa; and Arthur Ruben Dempster, who was married November 26, 1914, at Mankato, Minnesota, to Veva Churchill, and is now conducting a cattle ranch at Fort Bennett, South Dakota.

The religious faith of the family is that of the Congregational church and Mr. Dempster belongs also to the Masonic lodge. His political allegiance is given to the republican party, but he has never been an aspirant for office, preferring to concentrate his energies upon his business affairs which are growing in volume and importance. In youth he made good use of his educational opportunities, in manhood he has made equally good use of the possibilities for business advancement, and his determination and laudable ambition have carried him into important relations.

CHALKLEY H. DERR

Chalkley H. DERR, has the distinction of having been elected the first judge of the courts of Faulk County, while he continued on the bench for the long period of twelve successive years, and is still engaged in the practice of his profession in Faulkton. He is a native of the old Buckeye state and a scion of one of its pioneer families. He was born near the village of Salem, Columbiana County, Ohio, on the 14th of April, 1840, and is a son of Charles and Rebecca (Elliott) Derr, both of whom were likewise native of that state. The paternal great great-grandfather of the Judge was a patriot soldier in the Continental line during the war of the Revolution, and his great-grandfather took part in the war of 1812, while the subject himself upheld the military prestige of the name by his valiant service in the Civil war. Frederick Derr, grandfather of the Judge, was born in Pennsylvania, whither his father had come from Germany prior to the war of the Revolution. He removed to Ohio when a young man and located four miles south of Salem, Columbiana County, being one of the early settlers in that section of the state, where he engaged in farming and also in the work of his trade, that of cooler, while he and his good wife there made their home until they were called from the scenes of life's activities. The father of the subject was a millwright by trade and also owned a good farm in Columbiana County, his death occurring when the future judge was but thirteen years of age, so that the latter was soon thrown on his own resources, having been in the fullest sense the artificer of his own fortunes and having accumulated a competency through his own efforts.

Judge Derr secured his early educational discipline in the district and select schools of his native county, where he was reared to maturity. In September, 1861, as a young man of twenty-one years, he gave significant evidence of his patriotism by enlisting in defense of the Union, in response to President Lincoln's first call. He became a private in Company I, Nineteenth Ohio Volunteer Infantry, commanded by Colonel Samuel Bailey, and was mustered in at Alliance, Ohio, as orderly sergeant, whence he proceeded with his regiment to Cincinnati, where they were equipped, and went forward to Louisville and then to Columbia, Kentucky, where they passed the winter. The regiment thence proceeded into Tennessee in the spring and was actively engaged in the battle of Shiloh, in April, as well as the battle of Perryville. Kentucky, and the siege of Corinth, from, which city it went to Holly Springs, Mississippi, and to Florence and to Battle Creek, and thence over the mountains with General Buell's forces, reaching Louisville after having had daily skirmishes with General Bragg's forces. Thence they went to Stone river, where, owing to a severe attack of rheumatism and the results of an injury received in the battle of Shiloh, the subject became incapacitated for active service and was given a three month sick furlough, passing the time in Ohio and then being assigned to the quartermaster's department and being stationed at Nashville, Tennessee, for two years, having taken part in the last battle in that city, and having been honorably discharged, on the 1st of June, 1865, so that he served during practically the entire period of the war. He returned home in July and was shortly afterward married, after which he removed to Jones County, Iowa, where he purchased a large tract of land and became also interested in a large grain, stock and hardware business, with which he was identified for two years. In the meanwhile, he had continued to devote much attention to a careful study of the law, and had served six years in the office of justice of the peace. Owing to impaired health he came to Faulk County, South Dakota, in 1882, taking up his residence here before the county was organized, and here he has ever since maintained his home, having taken a prominent part in public affairs and in the upbuilding of the city of Faulkton, while he was admitted to the bar of the district court in 1888 and to the supreme court in 1899. He was elected the first judge of the courts of the county upon its organization, in 1884, and was retained in the office, by successive re-elections, for the consecutive period of twelve years, making a most admirable record for his fair and impartial rulings, based on the law and the evidence in the various cases, while it should be noted in the connection that he never had one of his decisions reversed by the higher tribunals.

In politics the Judge is a stalwart Republican, and is thoroughly well fortified in his convictions as to governmental policies, and fraternally he is identified with the Grand Army of the Republic and the Masonic order, in which latter he has attained the Knights Templar degrees and also become a member of Ancient Arabic Order of the Nobles of the Mystic Shrine. He is one of the strong, true, public-spirited men of Faulk County, and is held in the utmost confidence and esteem in the community. On the 23d of August, 1865, was solemnized the marriage of Judge Derr to Miss Eliza J. Camp, who was born and reared in Ohio, being a daughter of Levi Camp. She was summoned into eternal rest on the 31st of April, 1891, and is survived by three children, namely: Kate May, who is the wife of I. Allen Cornwell, of Faulkton; C. W., who is a resident of Turton, Spink County; and Inez, who is the wife of J. F. Armstrong, of Faulkton.

On the 21st of December, 1898, Judge Derr was united in marriage to Mrs. V. C. (Stewart) Coffee, who was born in Beaver, Pennsylvania, being a daughter of Samuel Stewart and the widow of Dr. T. L. Coffee.

CHALKLEY W. DERR

Chalkley W. Derr, a representative business man of Turton, Spink County, is a son of Judge Chalkley H. Derr, one of the distinguished and honored citizens of Faulkton, Faulk County, of whom specific mention is made on other pages of this compilation. The subject of this sketch was born in Jones County, Iowa, on the 27th of August, 1868, and he was there reared to the age of fourteen years, having received his educational discipline in the public schools of Olin, that county. He accompanied his parents on their removal to Faulkton, this state, where, in 1887, he engaged in the buying and shipping of wheat, with which important line of enterprise he has ever since been identified. In 1888, he removed from Faulkton to Turton, with whose business interests he became closely identified. In 1890 he established a lumber business here, and in 1900 opened a hardware store and warehouse for the sale and storage of agricultural implements and machinery, and he has since continued to successfully conduct the three enterprises, showing marked executive ability and facility in the management of his affairs, which are of wide scope and importance, while he is recognized as one of the most progressive and public-spirited men of the county, contributing to the general prosperity through the individual business activities with which he is identified. He has a well-equipped hardware store, and his business in all lines is constantly increasing, while he commands the uniform confidence and esteem of all with whom he comes in contact, his genial nature and unvarying courtesy doing much to conserve his personal popularity, while both he and his wife are leaders in the social life of the community.

In politics Mr. Derr is a stanch advocate of the principles of the Republican party, but has never sought official preferment, and fraternally he is identified with the following named organizations: Lodge No. 134, Ancient Free and Accepted Masons, at Conde, South Dakota; the chapter, Royal Arch Masons, at Clark, South Dakota; Damascus Commandery, No. 10, Knights Templar; Aberdeen Consistory, No. 4, Ancient Accepted Scottish Rite, at Aberdeen, and El Riad Temple, Ancient Arabic Order of the Nobles of the Mystic Shrine, at Sioux Falls, while he is also affiliated with Turton Lodge, No. 96, Ancient Order of United Workmen, and Turton Camp, No. 6067, Modern Woodmen of America, in his home town. Religiously he is affiliated with the Congregational church.

SAMUEL GRANT DEWELL

S. G. DEWELL, editor and publisher of the Free Press, at Pierre, was born in Shelby County, Iowa, on the 17th of April, 1864, being a son of Samuel and Harriet (Spicer) Dewell, the former of whom was a native of Ohio and the latter of the state of New York. In the agnatic line the genealogy is traced back to John Dewell, who was one of the valiant soldiers of General Lafayette, whom he accompanied from France to America at the time of the war of the Revolution. After the close of the great conflict which determined American independence he located near the city of Annapolis, Maryland, and later his descendants settled in the states of New York and Virginia, the branch of which the subject is a scion having been that which traces back to the Old Dominion. The mother of the subject was descended from Obediah Gore, who, with his brother John, was numbered among the Pilgrim fathers of New England. Samuel Dewell took up his residence in Shelby County, Iowa, in the year 1859, and there passed the residue of his life, engaged in surveying, his death occurring in 1889, while his devoted wife was summoned into eternal rest in 1897. They became the parents of eight children, of whom five are living.

Samuel G. Dewell was reared on the homestead farm in Iowa, and received his early educational training in the public schools, while at the age of twelve years he entered upon an apprenticeship at the printer's trade, in the office of the Sun at Magnolia, Iowa, he continued to be identified with newspaper work in Iowa until 1883, when, at the age of nineteen years, he came to South Dakota, and located in Norfolk, Sully County, where he became the publisher and editor of the Norfolk Spy, in 1884. In 1887 he became the publisher of the Nonpareil, at Blunt, Hughes County, where he remained until 1887, when he came to Pierre, where he has ever since maintained his home, having been for a time an employe in the office of the Signal, and later the Free Press, of which he is now proprietor and publisher, having secured control of the property in 1890. This is one of the leading papers of the state and exercises much influence in public affairs, its political policy being uncompromisingly Republican. The statement just entered indicates, as a matter of course, the political predilections of Mr. Dewell, who is one of the active and valued workers in the ranks of the "grand old party" in the state. On the 2d of March, 1898, he entered upon the discharge of his duties as postmaster of Pierre, having received the appointment under the administration of the lamented President McKinly, while at the expiration of his term, in 1902, he was re-appointed under President Roosevelt, so that he is in tenure of the office at the time of this writing.

Mr. Dewell has been identified with the South Dakota National Guard since 1897, having originally been a member of Company A. First Infantry, with which he started for the Philippines in 1898, but was rejected at the time the regiment was mustered into the United States service. He is at the present time quartermaster of the Second Regiment, South Dakota National Guard.

Fraternally he is affiliated with Pierre Lodge, No. 27, Ancient Free and Accepted Masons; Pierre Chapter, No. 22, Royal Arch Masons; Capital City Chapter, No. 39, Order of the Eastern Star; and also, with several mutual benefit associations. On the 3d of August, 1890, Mr. Dewell was united in marriage to Miss Alice Geltz, who was born in Port Hope, Huron County, Michigan, on the 14th of March, 1871, being a daughter of John and Julia (Moran) Geltz, who are now residents of Pierre. Of the three sons of Mr. and Mrs. Dewell we enter the following record: Perley Geltz, who was born July 11, 1891, died on the 14th of January, 1903; Paul Samuel was born December 14, 1893: and Julian, April 3, 1900.

STANLEY B. DICKINSON, M. D.

S. B. DICKINSON, is one of the able and popular young members of the medical profession in the state, being successfully engaged in practice in Watertown, and being held in high regard in professional, business and social circles. The Doctor is a native of the state of Michigan, having been born in Benton Harbor, Berrien County, on the 16th of April, 1871. He is a son of Joseph and Hannah A. (Davis) Dickinson, the former of whom was born in the state of Michigan and the latter in New York. Joseph Dickinson became one of the successful fruit growers in the famous peach belt of Michigan, was a man who commanded unequivocal confidence and esteem, and died at his home in Benton Harbor in 1888, at the age of fifty-five years, his wife being still a resident of that place. The paternal grandfather of the subject was Robert Dickinson, who was born in England, whence he came to America as a young man.

Dr. Dickinson received his early educational training in the public schools of his native place and then entered the Northern Indiana Business Institute, in Valparaiso, Indiana, where he was graduated as a member of the class of 1890. The following three years he was engaged in managing a fruit farm in his native county, and at the expiration of this period entered the medical department of the State University of Illinois, established in the city of Chicago, where he completed the prescribed course and was graduated as a member of the class of 1897, having passed the intervening summers in further technical study, under the preceptorship of Dr. John Bell, of Benton Harbor. After his graduation, with the degree of Doctor of Medicine, he held for a short time a position as interne in West Side Hospital, in Chicago, thus gaining farther and valuable clinical experience. He was thereafter engaged in the practice of his profession in Chicago for four years, at the expiration of which, in 1901, he came to South Dakota and opened an office in Watertown. where by his energy, ability, devotion to his profession and gracious personality he has built up a most gratifying and successful practice. While in Chicago he was for three years clinical instructor on diseases of children in the College of Physicians and Surgeons, while he also acted as medical examiner for the New York Mutual Life Insurance Company, the Prudential, of Newark, New Jersey, and other leading companies, as well as fraternal insurance orders. In politics the Doctor is an uncompromising Republican, taking a lively interest in the questions and issues of the hour.

He is a member of the Methodist Episcopal church, and fraternally is identified with the Masonic and Pythian orders, and belongs to the District, State and American Medical Associations. On the 26th of September, 1900, Dr. Dickinson was united in marriage, in the city of Chicago, to Miss Nellie C. Shurtleff, who was born and reared in that city, being a daughter of Barzella M. and Mary Ellen (Sibley) Shurtleff, the former of whom was born in Illinois and the latter in Vermont. Mr. Shurtleff has been for many years a prominent commission merchant in Chicago. The Sibley's are of a prominent old family of New England, and related to that redoubtable Revolutionary hero, General Israel Putnam. Laura Bridgeman, the famous blind mute, is also a relative of the family. Mrs. Dickinson is a member of the Woman's Club and is prominent in local social circles, being an accomplished musician and a woman of gracious refinement. They have one son, Robert Sibley Dickinson.

CHARLES HALL DILLON

Charles Hall Dillon, member of congress from the first congressional district of South Dakota and a resident of Yankton, has left and is leaving the impress of his individuality upon the history of his state, where he has become widely known both as a lawyer ana lawmaker. He is imbued with the spirit of enterprise which has ever characterized the development of the west. He was born three miles west of Jasper, in Dubois County, Indiana, on the 18th of December, 1853, and is a son of Matthew B. and Mary A. (Stewart) Dillon.

Liberal advantages were accorded Charles H. Dillon. He was graduated from the Indiana State University at Bloomington in June, 1874, and, having completed the scientific course, the B. S. degree was conferred upon him. His choice of a life work fell upon the law and in the same university he pursued his law course, winning his LL. B. degree upon graduation with the class of June, 1876. He entered upon the general practice of his chosen profession at Jasper, Indiana, where he remained for about five years, and then came to South Dakota in January, 1882, settling at Mitchell. He there formed a partnership with Harrison C. Preston, practicing under the firm style of Dillon & Preston for about twelve years, or until 1894, when he removed to Yankton, South Dakota, where he entered into a partnership with Hon. Robert J. Gamble under the firm name of Gamble & Dillon. That partnership was continued for five years, after which Mr. Dillon followed the practice of law independently until elected to congress. His ability at the bar was recognized in a large clientage that constantly grew in volume and importance, connecting him with much of the notable litigation tried in the courts of his state. His preparation of cases has always been thorough and exhaustive and in the presentation of a cause his logical reasoning has been a potent force in winning verdicts favorable to his clients. Aside from his law practice he became connected with business interests of Yankton as a director of the Dakota National Bank.

On the 28th of August, 1889, in Yankton, Mr. Dillon was united in marriage to Miss Maude B. Tripp, a daughter of Bartlett Tripp. She died November 6, 1894, and on the 26th of September, 1900, Mr. Dillon was joined in wedlock to Miss Frances D. Jolley, a daughter of Colonel John L. Jolley, of Vermillion, South Dakota.

Mr. Dillon is well known in fraternal circles. He was elected the second exalted ruler of the Elks lodge of Yankton and was appointed district deputy of the state of South Dakota by the grand exalted ruler of the Elks for the year 1910. He is a member of the Independent Order of Old Fellows, of which he is a past grand, and he also has membership in the Masonic lodge. Outside of his profession he is perhaps best known through his political activity. Before his election to congress he served as a member of the state senate from Yankton County through the sessions of 1903, 1905, 1907 and 1909.

He gave careful consideration to each question which came up for settlement and that the decisions which he made found favor with the general public is indicated in the fact that he was the successful candidate for congress in 1912 in the first congressional district of South Dakota. Again, he labored untiringly for the best interests of his district, his state and the country at large and in 1914 was reelected. In the sixty-third congress he served on the committee on coinage, weights and measures, the committee on revision of the laws and the committee on claims. He enjoys the high regard and confidence of his colleagues and even those who oppose his views speak of him in terms of high regard, recognizing the honesty of his opinions and his loyalty to his convictions. His integrity is one of his most marked characteristics and the ideals and principles which govern his life are found in the teachings of Christianity. He holds membership in the Yankton Congregational church and takes a great interest in its work. All movements seeking the betterment of his community and state receive his hearty support and he is an especially stalwart friend of institutions of higher education and as a member of the board of trustees of Yankton College has for the past twenty years done much for the welfare of that school.

WARREN DIMOCK

Warren DIMOCK, of Menno, Hutchinson County, was born in Iowa county, Wisconsin, on the 14th of September, 1859, a son of Warren S. and Lucy J. (Munson) Dimock, of whose seven children the following named five are yet living: Harry A., a druggist of Muscoda, Wisconsin: Almena, the wife of E. G. Schwingle, of Avoca, that state: Asa B., who is likewise a resident of that place, being a farmer and manufacturer; Bertha R., wife of Oscar Spicer, of Mason City, Iowa; and Warren, subject of this sketch, who is eldest of the number.

The father of the subject was born in Susquehanna, Pennsylvania, in 1819, and was there reared and educated, removing thence to Wisconsin in 1855 and settling on a farm near Avoca, Iowa county, where he was engaged in agricultural pursuits until the spring of 1903, when he received to the village mentioned, where he is now living retired, having attained the venerable age of eighty-four years, and being well preserved in mind and physical powers. He is one of the pioneers of the Badger state, where he purchased government land soon after his arrival within its borders, and he resided continuously on the one farm for forty-eight years. He is a Democrat in politics and is a man who has ever commanded the unqualified esteem of all who know him. His wife, who was born in the same town as was he, is still by his side, being sixty-eight years of age at the time of this writing (1903).

The subject of this review was reared on the homestead farm and after completing the curriculum of the public schools he continued his studies at the Plattville Normal school, at Plattville, Wisconsin. He taught school for three winter terms, working on the farm during the summer seasons. He continued to be identified with the operation of the home farm until 1886, but in the meanwhile had devoted careful attention to the reading of law. In the year mentioned he located in Muscoda, Wisconsin, where he was engaged in the real-estate and insurance business until 1889, when he came to Hutchinson County, South Dakota, locating in Menno, where he was employed for the ensuing year as assistant cashier in the Menno State Bank. In March, 1890, he was admitted to the bar and forthwith began the practice of his profession in Menno, where he has since resided, having secured a representative clientele and established a high reputation as an able advocate and safe and conservative counsel. He is a stalwart adherent of the Republican party, and in the fall of 1890, he was elected state's attorney for his county, serving one term, while in 1898 he was again called to this office, serving two consecutive terms and making a most excellent record as prosecutor.

He is a member of Muscoda Lodge, No. 70, Free and Accepted Masons, at Muscoda, Wisconsin; of Scotland Chapter. No. 31. Royal Arch Masons, at Scotland, South Dakota; and of Menno Camp, No. 3071, Modern Woodmen of America. On the 15th of December, 1886, Mr. Dimock was united in marriage to Miss Clara A. Stevens, of Monfort, Wisconsin, and they became the parents of two children: Murray S., who died at the age of fifteen months: and Lucy N., who remains at the parental home.

JOHN H. DOBSON

John H. Dobson postmaster at Alexandria, Hanson County, was born in the city of Beloit, Wisconsin, on the 26th of July, 1872, being a son of James and Anna L. (McCullough) Dobson, the former of whom was born in Lincolnshire, England, in 1844, and the latter in 1851. They are the parents of three children, David B., who is manager of the agricultural implement business of W. S. Hill, in Alexandria; Nettie, who remains at the parental home: and John H., who is the subject of this sketch. When the father was a lad of eleven years he accompanied his parents on their removal from England to the United States, the family locating in Rockford, Illinois, near which place he was reared to farm life, his three brothers being apprenticed to learn the trade of paper-making. James continued to devote his attention to agricultural pursuits, removing from Illinois to Rock County, Wisconsin, about 1871, and being there engaged in farming until 1885, when he came to South Dakota and located on a farm site adjoining the present thriving village of Alexandria, where he continued to reside until his death, which occurred in 1890. He was a stanch Republican, but never sought office, and his religious faith was that of the Baptist church. The mother of the subject was born on a farm near Durand, Winnebago county, Illinois, her parents having been born and reared in Scotland. She still resides in the homestead, Alexandria, having the affectionate regard of all who know her and being a devoted member of the Methodist Episcopal church, with which she affiliated after coming to this state, there having been no Baptist church in Alexandria.

The subject of this review secured his early education in the public schools of his native county, being about thirteen years of age at the time of the family removal to South Dakota, where he was reared to manhood on the home farm and in the meanwhile continuing his studies in the public schools of Alexandria, where he completed a high-school course, later supplementing this by a course in the commercial department of the university at Mitchell. In 1893 Mr. Dobson assumed a clerical position in the furniture and undertaking establishment of G. H. Montgomery, of Alexandria, and in the meanwhile gave special attention to acquiring a thorough knowledge of embalming and funeral directing, while in 1896 he took a special course of instruction in embalming under the direction of Professor Barnes, of Chicago, an authority in this art. In 1897 Mr. Dobson engaged in business upon his own responsibility, opening a piano, organ and sewing-machine house in Alexandria, and this enterprise he has since successfully conducted, also carrying a general line of musical merchandise. In 1898 he was appointed postmaster of Alexandria, under President McKinley, while in 1903 he was reappointed, under the administration of President Roosevelt. He is a zealous and uncompromising advocate of the principles of the Republican party, and he is at the present time a member of the board of education of Alexandria. He is a member of the board of trustees of the Methodist Episcopal church, and was also a member of the building committee under whose supervision the attractive new church edifice was completed in June, 1903.

Mr. Dobson has risen to high rank in the Masonic fraternity, being a member of Celestial Lodge, No. 36, Free and Accepted Masons; Eastern Star Chapter; Oriental Consistory, No. 1, Ancient Accepted Scottish Rite, of Yankton, in which he has passed the thirty-second degree; and El Riad Temple, Ancient Arabic Order of the Nobles of the Mystic Shrine, in Sioux Falls. He is also identified with Cypress Lodge, No. 24, Knights of Pythias, and Alexandria Camp, No. 2956, Modern Woodmen of America. On the 15th of June, 1897, Mr. Dobson was united in marriage to Miss Mary Durkee, of Alexandria, who was for several years a successful and popular teacher in the high school of this place, and of this union has been born two children, Burdette, the date of whose nativity was June 16, 1898, and Merrial Bertha, born September 11, 1903.

WILLIAM T. DOOLITTLE

William T. Doolittle was born in Loudonville, Ohio, March 30, 1849. He attended school until he was fourteen years of age, and then entered a railroad machine shop as an apprentice. When nineteen years old he became an engineer, and since March, 1873, has been engineer on passenger trains. He was in charge of the first passenger engine that ran into Sioux Falls, and, except for a little more than a year, has been the engineer on the passenger train between Sioux Falls and Worthington, Minnesota, since then.

In 1879, an incident occurred which gave him an unexpected vacation for thirty days. He was the engineer of the train which during that year started out from Worthington with R. F. Pettigrew and a Mr. Bottineau on board, each of them having in his pocket a deed which he was particularly anxious to get on record in Sioux Falls first, and was induced by Mr. Pettigrew to detach the engine at Brandon east of the city and bring Mr. Pettigrew in on the engine. Mr. Pettigrew explained to Mr. Doolittle that the attorneys on the other side were on the train with a snap judgment and were making every effort to get it on record before his, and that if they succeeded in doing so it would work a hardship on the people of Sioux Falls who had bought their homes, as they would be compelled to relinquish them without recompense. Mr. Doolittle replied that he would do nothing of the kind for Mr. Pettigrew, but he would do it for the people of Sioux Falls. Mr. Bottineau made complaint to the superintendent of the road, John F. Lincoln, stating the facts and demanding fifty thousand dollars damages. Superintendent Lincoln sent for Engineer Doolittle, and when he appeared the following colloquy took place: "William, if what is told is true, I am afraid you have gotten the company into trouble. I am told you detached your engine and took a party into Sioux Falls that he might get a deed on record before another passenger who had a deed to the same property, could do so. Is this true?" Mr. Doolittle replied, "It is." Mr. Lincoln then said: "I could not believe you would do such an act. The party having the other deed says he is damaged fifty thousand dollars by the transaction, and demands your dismissal, and threatens to sue the company for damages." Mr. Doolittle replied, "If my dismissal will appease the wrath of the gentleman, it is a small matter; but as to the damages, that is another thing." Here Mr. Doolittle, who had had been advised of all the facts in the case, related them to the superintendent, and told him it was simply a robbing scheme and so satisfied the superintendent that it was true, that he ended the interview by bringing his fist down on his desk, saying: "Let him sue; he can't recover a cent; but William, you need a rest of thirty or sixty days; take a vacation; I will see that your pay goes right along."

Mr. Doolittle resides with his family in Sioux Falls, where he has one of the finest homes in the city, and where for a number of years he has been prominent in the public and civic affairs of the municipality. He was elected alderman from the first ward in 1896, re-elected two years later, and since May, 1897, he has served as president of the council. In 1879 he organized the first division of Locomotive Engineers in Sioux City, Iowa, was chief of the organization for several years, and much of its success is directly attributable to his able and untiring efforts.

Mr. Doolittle has been identified with a number of undertakings since coming to Sioux Falls, notably among which are the Citizens' Telephone Company and the Interstate Telephone Company of Sioux Falls, being superintendent of the first named enterprise and president of the other two. Mr. Dolittle has always had the good of the community at heart, and, as an enterprising, progressive citizen, gives his influence and generous support to all measures calculated to promote the general welfare.

He is prominent in Masonic circles, has served as grand commander of the grand commandery. Knights Templar, of South Dakota, besides filling the honorable position of potentate of El Riad Temple, Nobles of the Mystic Shrine. Socially and as a citizen he stands well, numbers his friends by the score among all classes and conditions of people, and enjoys to a marked degree the esteem and confidence of the public. Mr. Doolittle's family consists of a wife and two children, the former before her marriage having been Miss Catherine Strock, of Galveston, Indiana. The only son, who resides at Sioux Falls, is Walter S., a locomotive engineer.

ROBERT T. DOTT, M. D.

R. T. DOTT, who is successfully engaged in the practice of his profession in Salem, McCook County, was born in Jones County, Iowa, on the 26th of October, 1859, and is a son of Robert and Sarah J. (Peters) Dott, of whose three children he was the second in order of birth. His elder brother, Richard M., is a resident of Sioux City, Iowa, and is a prominent member of the bar of the state; and George M. is a successful dental practitioner in Salem, South Dakota. The father of the Doctor was born in Cupar, Fifeshire, Scotland, on the 10th of September, 1824, and there was reared and educated, learning the trade of tailor in his youth. In 1843, at the age of nineteen years, he came to America, and after residing about five years in Illinois he removed thence to Anamosa, Iowa, where he engaged in business, also serving as justice of the peace for several years, while for three terms he held the office of auditor of Jones County. In 1883 he came to what is now the state of South Dakota and took up his residence in Sanborn County, where he had taken up a tract of government land the preceding year. He gave his attention to the improvement and cultivation of his farm for about four years and then removed to the village of Alexandria, where he has since maintained his home, being at the present time county judge of Hanson County, in which office he has served several terms, being one of the influential and highly honored citizens of the county. In politics he is a stanch Republican, and his religious faith is that of the Presbyterian church, of which he and his wife are devoted and active members.

He was a member of the territorial legislature just prior to the admission of South Dakota to the Union. Fraternally he is identified with the lodge, chapter and commandery of the Masonic order. Judge Dott manifested his loyalty to his adopted country at the time of the war of the Rebellion, having enlisted in Company H, Fourteenth Iowa Volunteer Infantry, and being made commissary sergeant of his regiment. In the battle of Shiloh his zeal led him into the thick of the fray. He borrowed a musket from one of his comrades and made his way to the front with his regiment, which was captured by the enemy, resulting in his being imprisoned at Macon, Georgia, for several months.

Dr. Robert T. Dott secured his early education in the public schools of Anamosa, Iowa, completing the high-school course, after which he served under his father as deputy county auditor for four years. Within this time, he took up the study of medicine, having as his preceptor Dr. E. W. Gawley, of Anamosa, and in the autumn of 1881, he entered that celebrated institution, Rush Medical College, in Chicago, where he completed a thorough course in medicine and surgery and was graduated on the 20th of February, 1883, with the degree of Doctor of Medicine. He then rejoined his parents in South Dakota, passing the summer on the homestead farm and also "holding down" a claim which he had entered in Aurora County. During the ensuing winter he was engaged in the practice of his profession in Shelby County, Iowa, and in the fall of 1884, he went to New York City and entered the Bellevue Hospital Medical College, of whose unexcelled advantages he availed himself by taking a post-graduate course, being graduated in this institution in the spring of 1885. He then took up his residence in Alexandria, South Dakota, where he was successfully engaged in the practice of his profession until the fall of 1888, when he removed to Mount Vernon, where he was established in practice two years, then returning to Alexandria. In 1897 the Doctor located in Sioux Falls, where he was in practice one year, coming thence to Salem in the latter part of

October, 1898, and having since established in a large and remunerative practice in the community, where his friends are in number as his acquaintances, his genial personality and high professional attainments having gained to him unqualified confidence and esteem. In politics Mr. Dott gives a stanch allegiance to the Republican party, and he served as coroner of Hanson County two terms, and as superintendent of the county board of health for four years. While a resident of Alexandria he served as village clerk and alderman, occupying the respective offices one year each. He is secretary of the board of pension examiners of McCook County, and is at the present time superintendent of both county and city boards of health.

The Doctor is affiliated with Fortitude Lodge, No. 73, Free and Accepted Masons, in which he was elected and installed worshipful master to serve during the year 1904; and is also identified with Pythias Lodge, No. 60, Knights of Pythias; the Modern Woodmen of America; the Modern Brotherhood of America and the Union Veterans' Union. He is examining physician for several of the leading I life-insurance companies, and professionally is one of the valued and appreciative members of the South Dakota Medical Society. On the 12th of April, 1885, Dr. Dott was united in marriage to Miss Olive Booth, of Sanborn County, this state, and they became the parents of one child, Bertram T. On the 13th of December, 1892, the Doctor consummated a second marriage, being then united to Miss Maud E. Foote, of Hanson County, this state, and they are the parents of two children, Delia M. and Robert O.

WESLEY DOUGLASS

Wesley DOUGLASS, engaged in the drug business in Menno, is a native of the province of Ontario, Canada, where he was born on the 30th of January, 1851, being a son of Robert and Jane (McGill) Douglass, of whose nine children only four are now living, namely: Alexander, who is engaged in the real-estate business in Winnipeg, Canada; Elizabeth, who is the widow of John Sproat and resides in Ontario, Canada; John, who is a physician in the city of Chicago; and Wesley, who is the subject of this review. Robert Douglass was born in the state of New York, where he was reared on a farm, and as a young man he removed to the province of Ontario, Canada, where the later years of his life were passed in agricultural pursuits, his death there occurring in 1888, at the age of eighty-four years. He was a man of strong individuality and well-fortified opinions, and loyal to his native land. He was a zealous advocate of the principles of the Whig party and an advocate of reform measures in the land of his adoption, while his religious faith was that of the Wesleyan Methodist church. He was of stanch old Scottish ancestry, his grandfather having come to the United States from Scotland during the war of the Revolution, arriving about the time of the historic "Boston tea party." The mother of the subject died in 1895, aged eighty-seven years.

Wesley Douglass received his educational training in the common schools of his native province, remaining at the parental home during the major portion of the time until he had attained the age of twenty years, prior to which he had been employed for a time in a drug store and in the office of his brother Robert, who was then engaged in the practice of medicine in Canada. In 1871, at the age noted, our subject came over "into the states," making his way to Kansas where he remained about two years, having been engaged in teaching school and in working in the office of the Atchison, Topeka & Santa Fe Railroad. He then returned to Canada, where he tarried one year, operating for the Grand Trunk Railroad, and in the spring of 1874, he became numbered among the pioneers of what is now the state of South Dakota, coming to Hutchinson County and entering homestead and timber claims a few miles northwest of the present town of Scotland. He resided on his farm about four years, in the meanwhile doing some freighting to the Black Hills and teaching school during the winter terms for two years. In the fall of 1878 Mr. Douglass was elected sheriff of Hutchinson County, being chosen as his own successor in 1880, and thus serving four consecutive years. After the expiration of his second term, he removed to the village of Scotland, where he was employed during the ensuing year as operator in the telegraph office of the Chicago, Milwaukee & St. Paul Railroad. In January, 1884, he came to Menno, where he has since resided. Shortly after locating here, he established himself in the drug business, being one of the pioneer merchants of the town, and this enterprise he has since successfully conducted, having a representative patronage.

He is a Democrat in his political allegiance, and fraternally is a member of Scotland Lodge, No. 53, Free and Accepted Masons. On the 3d of February, 1878, Mr. Douglass was united in marriage to Mrs. Caroline (Church) Johnson, who was born in Ontario, Canada. She had one child by her first marriage, Minnie, who is the wife of E. J. Swanton, of Menno, and of the second union have been born two children, Agnes J. and Gerald R., both at the parental home.

FREDERICK P. DRAYER

Frederick P. Drayer, proprietor of a general mercantile store at Frankfort, is actuated in his business dealings by a spirit of strong determination, indefatigable industry and unfaltering enterprise. He has conducted the business since 1894. Six years prior to that time he arrived in South Dakota, having come from Manteno, Illinois, where he was born May 27, 1869, his parents being Peter and Mary (Zepp) Drayer. The family is of German descent. The father was a farmer of Manteno and in the year 1888 brought his family to South Dakota, settling near Doland, where he engaged in farming until his death, which occurred in 1907, when he was sixty-eight years of age. His wife survived him until 1909, and was then laid by his side in the cemetery in their old home town, Manteno, Illinois.

It was in the schools of that place that Frederick P. Drayer acquired the greater part of his education, although he attended school to a limited extent after removing to Spink County, this state. Through vacation periods he assisted his father in the farm work, and in his later teens he secured employment in a store, where he acquainted himself with commercial methods. When twenty-one years of age he attended the Metropolitan Business College at Chicago, spending a year as a student in mastering branches of learning which would qualify him for life's practical and responsible duties in the business world. He then went to Doland, where he was employed as a clerk, and later he established a store at Turton, South Dakota, where he carried on business for nine months. He then removed his stock to Frankfort and has since been actively identified with the commercial interests of that place. He remained alone in business until 1911, when he admitted John D. Craig to a partnership. The stock of goods is a large one for a town the size of Frankfort, and is well selected. The business methods employed are those which commend the house to a liberal patronage, for Mr. Drayer is ever fair and honorable in his dealings.

In November, 1894, at Doland, South Dakota, Mr. Drayer was united in marriage to Miss Mamie Woodring, her parents being John and Marie (Runkle) Woodring, both of whom survive. The father was a pioneer agriculturist of this state. Mr. and Mrs. Drayer have two children, namely: Raymond, who is attending college at Brookings, South Dakota; and Phyllis, a high-school student.

In his political views Mr. Drayer is a republican, but without desire for office. He has taken the degrees of Masonry in the blue lodge and in the chapter and is loyal to the teachings of the craft. In Frankfort he has erected his store and residence and has thus contributed to the material improvement of the town. His life has ever been a busy one and his success is the direct reward of his labor. He ranks today among the representative merchants of Spink County.

FRED. W. DRICKEN

F. W. DRICKEN, an able and representative member of the bar of South Dakota, being now engaged in the practice of his profession in White, Brookings County, is a native of the state of Wisconsin, having been born in West Bend, Washington county, on the 2d of September, 1875, and being a son of William and Caroline (Seibert) Dricken. William Dricken came to South Dakota and located in Brookings County, as a pioneer.

Judge Dricken was a child of about three years at the time of his parents' removal to this state, and he passed his boyhood days on the homestead farm, in Afton township, where he secured his preliminary educational discipline in the district schools, later continuing his studies in the public schools of White, which he attended until he had attained the age of sixteen years. In 1893 he entered the Northern Indiana Normal School, at Valparaiso, Indiana, from which institution he received the degree of Bachelor of Science.

He was educated in the law, in the law department of the celebrated University of Michigan, at Ann Arbor, and was admitted to the bar of South Dakota, September, 1897, and forthwith established himself in the practice of his profession in White. His intrinsic loyalty and patriotism, however, soon led him to lay aside for a time the work of his profession, for in the spring of the following year he enlisted as a private in Company G, First South Dakota Volunteer Infantry, with which he shortly afterward proceeded to the Philippine Islands, where he remained in service for the following eighteen months. He was twice promoted for bravery and meritorious service and was recommended for a third promotion, having been mustered out with the rank of sergeant. He participated in all the engagements in which his regiment took part, and with the others of his command made a record which reflects lasting honor upon his state. He returned to his home in the autumn of 1809 and the next day after his arrival reopened his office in White and resumed the work of his profession, in which he has been eminently successful, gaining a prestige which many an older practitioner might well envy. He now practices before the United States district and circuit courts and has presented not a few important cases in the former. In 1900 he was elected county judge, and so ably exercised his functions on the bench that he was chosen as his successor in the fall of 1902, for a term of two years, so that he remains in tenure of the dignified and responsible office at the time of this writing. Politically the judge was reared in the faith of the Republican party, and he has never wavered in his allegiance to the same, while he has taken an active part in furthering the party cause and has been a delegate to various state, congressional and county conventions.

He is affiliated with the Masonic order and with the Order of the Eastern Star, of which last his wife likewise is a member. On the 29th of July, 1902, Judge Dricken was united in marriage to Miss Mabelle A. Brown, who was born in Chicago, and who is a daughter of Dexter G. Brown, a prominent citizen of Aberdeen, South Dakota, Mrs. Dricken is a communicant of the Episcopal church.

GEORGE C. DUNTON

George C. Dunton, cashier of the First National Bank at Webster, was born in Naples, New York, February 8, 1865, and is a representative of one of the old families of the Empire state, his ancestors having come from England to the new world. His grandfather, John Dunton, born in New York, was a successful farmer of that state for many years and there occurred the birth of his son, Lemuel M., in the year 1834. He was reared and educated at the place of his nativity and after attaining his majority wedded Harriett E. Oliver, who was born in New York in 1834, a daughter of George Culver, also a native of that state, who traced his ancestry back to the early Puritans who settled New England. Mr. and Mrs. Lemuel M. Dunton continued their residence in the east until 1870, when they removed to Missouri and afterward to Kansas, Mr. Dunton devoting his attention to sheep raising in both states. While in New York he had handled both sheep and cattle. He won a very gratifying measure of success and was well-to-do at the time of his demise. He was well educated and well-read and, in his community, exercised considerable influence over public thought and action. He died in the year 1910, having for a decade survived his wife, who passed away in 1900. She was a consistent member of the Presbyterian church. Mr. Dunton held membership with the Masons and belonged to both the blue lodge and chapter. His political allegiance was given to the republican party. To him and his wife were born two children, George C. and Harry I., the latter a resident of Canandaigua, New York.

George C. Dunton completed his education by graduation from the Canandaigua Academy of New York with the class of 1884 and for two years thereafter devoted his attention to merchandising in the Empire state. In 1886 he arrived in South Dakota, where he engaged in clerking for a time, and later established a store of his own at Langford. On disposing of that he lived retired for a short period and afterward purchased a hardware store. During his residence in Marshall County, he served as treasurer for four years and was a prominent and influential resident of that community. In 1902 he removed to Webster and organized the First National Bank, which from the beginning has been a substantial and paying institution. It is capitalized for twenty-five thousand dollars, has a surplus of fifteen thousand dollars and its average deposits amount to one hundred and sixty-five thousand dollars. A general banking business is conducted and as its cashier Mr. Dunton has practically managed its affairs and contributed in a very large measure to its success. He also has farming interests in this state and is a representative business man, alert and enterprising.

In December, 1898, occurred the marriage of Mr. Dunton and Miss Clara M. Deerson, a native of Illinois and a daughter of John Deerson, who was born in Germany but in early life came to the new world, settling in Illinois, where he followed the cabinetmaking trade. His daughter, Mrs. Dunton, is a member of the Episcopal church and occupies an enviable position in social circles of the city.

Mr. Dunton is a prominent Mason, having taken the degrees of the Scottish Rite and of the Mystic Shrine. A republican in his political views, he has been active in the work of the party yet never sought office as a reward for party fealty. He has a strong attachment for the west, which has given him his opportunity, and he possesses the enterprising spirit which has ever characterized the development of this section of the country.

FRANK E. DUBA

As cashier of the Belle Fourche State Bank, Frank E. Duba occupies an important position for one of his years. He has just completed his third decade, his birth occurring in Brule County, South Dakota, December 16, 1884. His parents, John A. and Annie (Vasicek) Duba, were both natives of Bohemia, where they were reared and married. The father in early manhood followed general farming but after removing to Sioux City, Iowa, was in the employ of the street railway company for about six years. In the winter of 1896, he returned to his farm, where he still remains, although he leaves its operation to others. He has three hundred and twenty acres in the home place and is also the owner of other valuable land in South Dakota.

Frank E. Duba is the fourth in order of birth in a family of five children and attended both the Sioux City schools and the country schools near the homestead, walking five miles each way. He did not think that a hardship, however, and maintains that he received more benefit from the district schools than from any other. He also attended the Kimball high school. When not yet sixteen years of age he found employment as messenger boy in a bank conducted by A. C. Whitbeck. He soon demonstrated his ability to do more important work and was given a chance to help in the bookkeeping. As his knowledge increased, he was given more and more responsibility and in a comparatively short time had charge of the books of the bank. Later he was made bookkeeper in another bank opened by Mr. Whitbeck, with which institution he remained for about four years. In that time, he had won still further promotion and by the time that he left the bank he held the position of assistant cashier. He next entered the Chamberlain State Bank as assistant cashier and a year later purchased stock in the Bank of Bijou Hills and became its cashier. When he assumed charge of its affairs the deposits were thirty-eight hundred dollars and in 1910, when he severed his connection with the institution, the deposits had grown to the sum of sixty-four thousand dollars, which increase is the best proof of his capability as cashier and manager. He had also bought more stock until at the time of leaving he owned a controlling interest which, however, he sold. His next removal was to Belle Fourche and in connection with his brother-in-law, C. A. Quarnberg, he established the Belle Fourche State Bank, of which he became cashier. Mr. Duba still holds that position and the solidity of the institution and the confidence that the people of the surrounding country have in it is largely to be ascribed to his knowledge of banking and his wise management. He is also a stockholder in the Alfalfa Mill and owns one hundred and sixty acres of well improved irrigated land near Vale, South Dakota, which he rents. His own time is completely taken up as cashier and he allows nothing to interfere with the discharge of his duties.

Mr. Duba was married on the 1st of May, 1907, to Miss Lillian Quarnberg, who was born at Centerville, South Dakota, a daughter of Hans and Minnie Quarnberg, both of whom were natives of Sweden, where their marriage occurred. Mr. Quarnberg is engaged at present in the milling business at Belle Fourche, to which place he removed in 1913. Mr. and Mrs. Duba have four children: Maurice, who was born in February, 1908; Dorothy, whose birth occurred in December, 1909; Rex, born in September, 1911; and John, born in April, 1914.

Mr. Duba is a democrat and has been content to perform his citizens' duties in a private capacity, leaving to others the holding of office. He is a loyal member of the Masonic order and belongs to the blue lodge, chapter and consistory and to the Eastern Star. He is also affiliated with the Knights of Pythias. He is a young man of marked ability and is distinguished by scrupulous honesty and a willingness to subordinate private interests to community welfare.

RICHARD DUNLOP

R. Dunlop, one of the pioneer mining men of the Black Hills, and now in charge of the Mineral Point stamp mill, of the Homestake Mining Company, at Central City, is a native of the city of Belfast, Ireland, where he was born on the 15th of February, 1855, being a son of James and Mary (Clark) Dunlop, who were likewise born and reared in that city, where their marriage was solemnized. In 1857 they came to America and after passing a short period of time in the state of New York came west to Iowa, locating in Scott County, where Mr. Dunlop continued to be engaged in agricultural pursuits until his death, which occurred in 1877, while his devoted wife passed away in 1892. They were folk of sterling character and commanded unqualified regard in the community which was so long their home. Their religious faith was that of the Presbyterian church, and in politics Mr. Dunlop was a Republican. Of the six children in the family all are yet living, the subject of this review having been the fifth in order of birth.

Richard Dunlop was reared on the homestead farm in Iowa and received his educational discipline in the public schools of his locality. In 1872 he went to Colorado, where he remained for a few years, devoting his attention principally to mining. In 1877 he came to the Black Hills, being numbered among the venturesome spirits who braved the dangers incidental to making the trip to this section, then isolated from civilization by many leagues of plains, infested by the warlike and implacable Indians whose originally was the domain. From Cheyenne, Wyoming, he came through by team to the Hills, in company with a party of other men, and they had little trouble with the Indians while enroute, reaching their destination in Deadwood, in March. There Mr. Dunlop engaged in placer mining for the Whitewood Flume Company, about five miles below Deadwood, a portion of the time working for himself, and he was successful in his efforts in both directions. In 1879 he entered the employ of the Homestake Mining Company, working as amalgamator and in other positions of responsibility, and in 1887 he was given charge of the Father DeSmet mill, owned by the company and named in honor of one of the heroic missionary priests of the Catholic church in the pioneer days in the northwest. He has since been the superintendent of this mill, which is now known as the Mineral Point, which is equipped with one hundred stamps and which is running to its full capacity since the completion of the auxiliary cyanide plant, in 1902. Since coming to the Hills Mr. Dunlop has given more or less attention to prospecting and has become interested in a number of promising properties. In 1892 he made a trip through Central America for the purpose, primarily, of looking over the mining properties in that section, and he has in his possession some fine specimens of gold-bearing quartz which he secured there. In politics he gives his allegiance to the Republican party, and fraternally he has attained the capitular degrees in the Masonic order and is identified with the Modern Woodmen of America.

On the 18th of October, 1882, Mr. Dunlop married Miss Jennie Baker, who was born and reared in Michigan and who died in April, 1884, leaving one son, Richard F., who is now attending St. John's Military Academy at Delafield, Wisconsin. On the 26th of March, 1890, Mr. Dunlop was united in marriage to Miss Laura Davidson, who was born in Johnson County, Indiana, and who was a resident of Lead City at the time of her marriage. No children have been born of this union.

HON. THEODORE WILLIAM DWIGHT

Hon. Theodore William Dwight, conducting a real-estate, loan and insurance business as a member of the firm of Knowles, Dwight & Toohey, has achieved a creditable measure of success in business circles and at the same time has become a prominent representative of political interests and activity in the state, being one of the recognized leaders of the republican party in South Dakota. He makes his home in Sioux Falls, to which city he removed in 1901. Wisconsin claims him as a native son, his birth having occurred in the town of Oregon, Dane county, March 12, 1865. His parents were Edward Wolsey and Elizabeth (Footed Dwight, both of whom were natives of New York and representatives of prominent old American families. The grandfather, Benjamin Dwight, was likewise a native of New York and the direct descendant of Rev. Timothy Dwight, D. D., one of the early presidents of Yale College, and of Rev. Jonathan Edwards, the eminent divine of New England in colonial days.

The common schools afforded Theodore W. Dwight his early educational opportunities. He attended the high school at Evansville, Wisconsin, and afterward entered the high school at Red Wing, Minnesota, from which he was graduated with the class of 1885.

He then went to Brooklyn, Wisconsin, where he secured a clerkship in a general store, thus receiving his initial business training, and in 1888, when twenty-three years of age, he came to South Dakota, settling at Bridgewater, McCook County, where he opened a general store. He was not long in building up a good trade and there he continued in active business until 1901, when he removed to Sioux Falls. His stock of goods, however, was removed to Emery, South Dakota, and Mr. Dwight took in a partner, who has charge of the business there. On moving to Sioux Falls Mr. Dwight embarked in the wholesale confectionery business, in which he continued for three years as secretary and treasurer of the Anthony-Dwight Company, which was incorporated under the laws of the state. This business also grew and developed along substantial lines, becoming one of the important commercial enterprises of the city. After three years Mr. Dwight sold out and turned his attention to the insurance, real-estate and loan business, forming a partnership with E. F. Knowles, while later C. T. Toohey was admitted under the present firm style of Knowles, Dwight & Toohey. Mr. Dwight is a man of determined spirit, carrying forward to successful completion whatever he undertakes, and his well formulated plans have brought him a substantial measure of prosperity.

On the 20th of August, 1889, at Red Wing, Minnesota, Mr. Dwight was united in marriage to Miss Jennie M. Brink, a daughter pf Charles R. Brink, who was a soldier of the Civil war. They have two children: Helen, born February 6, 1895; and Edward Brink, born November 24, 1899.

The parents hold membership in the Presbyterian church and Mr. Dwight is connected with several fraternal and social organizations. He is a Royal Arch Mason, a member of the Ancient Order of United Workmen and the Benevolent Protective Order of Elks. He is secretary of the Sons of the American Revolution of South Dakota and he belongs to the Country Club. His political allegiance has always been given the republican party since age conferred upon him the right of franchise and he is an active worker in party ranks. Appreciation of his service and capability came to him in 1899 in his election to the state legislature and he is now a member and vice president of the state board of regents, his term to continue to 1915. He was treasurer of the republican state central committee during the campaigns of 1908 and 1910 and his powers of organization came into good play in this connection. In 1913 he was president of the Commercial Club and he has been an interested and helpful factor in all that pertains to municipal welfare as well as general progress. He looks at life from the standpoint of an enterprising, progressive man who recognizes the duties and obligations as well as the privileges of citizenship.

CHARLES LEMUEL EAKIN

C. L. EAKIN, the owner of a finely improved ranch of sixteen hundred acres, near Blunt, Hughes County, is a native of Illinois, having been born in Indianola, Vermillion County, on the 2d of August, 1865, and being a son of Edmond W, and Ellen M. Eakin. He was afforded the advantages of the excellent public schools of his native state, completing his specific scholastic discipline in the high school at Danville. He continued to reside in Illinois until 1883, when he came to what was then the territory of Dakota, and here he has achieved prosperity and independence and gained prestige as one of the able business men and influential citizens of his home county, where he is held in high esteem by all who know him.

In politics Mr. Eakin is a stalwart adherent of the Republican party, and in a social way he is affiliated with the Masonic fraternity, the Ancient Order of United Workmen and the Knights of the Maccabees. On the 11th of November, 1891, Mr. Eakin was united in marriage to Miss Etta J. Sheldon, who was born in Eyota, Olmsted County, Minnesota, in 1865, and whose death occurred on the 14th of May, 1892. She was a daughter of Porter G. and Caroline Sheldon, who were numbered among the pioneers of Minnesota. On the 8th of July, 1895, the subject consummated a second marriage, being then united to Miss Lelia Bailey, who was born in Rochester, Illinois, on the 8th of March, 1870, being a daughter of Emory and Lucinda Bailey. Mr. Eakin has three children, one of whom was born of the first marriage, and two of the second, namely: Etta S., Russell L. and Muriel.

MARCUS D. EDGERTON

Marcus D. Edgerton, the proprietor of a well-known men's furnishings store in Spearfish, was born in Granville, Washington county, New York, January 19, 1859, a son of John and Charlotte (Wyman) Edgerton, both natives of Vermont. The father was born in Rutland County, his father, Captain Simeon Edgerton, being a pioneer of that county. John Edgerton was a farmer throughout his active life and never left the east. He died in 1885 but his widow survived until 1892. He was highly esteemed in his community and held a number of local offices.

Marcus D. Edgerton is the youngest in a family of five children. His educational opportunities were those afforded by the public schools of New York state. At the age of sixteen years, he began his business career, working for others in New York and also in Pennsylvania. When about twenty-one years of age he removed to Kansas City, Missouri, where he was employed as a hotel clerk for a short time, and afterward held a similar position in Lawrence, Kansas. Upon leaving that place he removed to Mitchell, South Dakota, and after engaging for a time in the laundry business entered a one hundred and sixty acre claim in Aurora County and resided thereon until he had proved up. He went to the Black Hills in 1884 and worked in Deadwood for the telephone company for one year. Going to Buffalo Gap, he was there employed in a grocery store for a year, and the following year he removed to Sundance, Wyoming, where he remained for about six months. His next removal was to Spearfish, South Dakota, where he worked in a grocery store for about three years, and then went to Minnesota, where he was connected with the confectionery and news business for two years. On his return to Spearfish, he purchased a stock of clothing and men's furnishings, boots and shoes and is still in that business, which has proved a distinct success. He carries a large and well selected stock and as his customers are sure of receiving full value for their money many of his patrons have traded with him for a number of years. He is interested in mining properties in the vicinity of Spearfish, the Break of Day and Castle Rock being two of the mines in which he has invested. He is also the owner of valuable real estate, including the building in which his store is located.

Mr. Edgerton was married on the 10th of September, 1889, to Miss Maud E. Daggett, who was born in Nebraska, a daughter of David and Julia (Leppler) Daggett, the former a native of Wisconsin. Her father engaged in farming in early life but later was connected with the drug business in Sloan, Iowa. He also lived in Nebraska for a time but in 1885 removed to the Black Hills and located in Spearfish, where he conducted a drug business until his death, which occurred in May, 1898. He had five children, of whom Mrs. Edgerton is the fourth in order of birth. She has become the mother of a son, Leroy D., who was born August 4, 1890, and is assisting his father in the tatter's business.

Mr. Edgerton of this review is a republican and for some time was a member of the city council and for two years held the office of city treasurer. He has not aspired to other offices, however, as his business demands his undivided attention and as he believes that in building up a prosperous mercantile enterprise, he also serves his city. Fraternally he is a member of the Masonic order, belonging to the blue lodge, chapter, commandery and Shrine, and is prelate in the commandery. He is also affiliated with the Modern Woodmen of America. His success in the business world has been founded upon industry, a keen sense of right and a readiness to see and utilize opportunities. Through adherence to high standards of conduct he has won the sincere respect of all who have had business dealings with him or have come in contact with him in the social relations of life and his activities are a factor in the development of Spearfish.

HERBERT L. EGGERS, D. D. S.

Dr. Herbert L. Eggers is a successful young dental practitioner of Tripp, where he has followed his profession for the past six years or since 1909. His birth occurred in Avon, South Dakota, on the 8th of November, 1888, his parents being Louis and Paulina Eggers, who came to this state about thirty-one years ago and still reside on a farm here. The father took up a homestead claim and successfully followed agricultural pursuits for many years but is now living retired in the enjoyment of well-earned rest.

Herbert L. Eggers attended the graded and high schools in the acquirement of an education and subsequently prepared for a professional career as a student in the Northwestern University Dental School of Chicago, from which institution he was graduated with the degree of D. D. S. in 1909. Returning to his native state, he opened an office in Tripp, where he has since remained and has built up a liberal and lucrative practice, having gained a reputation as a skilled and able exponent of modern dentistry. He belongs to the State Dental Association and acts as president of the Yankton district.

On the 1st of September, 1910, Dr. Eggers was united in marriage to Miss Faye Sadler, a daughter of Leonard Sadler. He gives his political allegiance to the democracy and is a Methodist in religious faith, while fraternally he is identified with the Masons, the Eastern Star, the Benevolent Protective Order of Elks and the Independent Order of Odd Fellows. Fishing, hunting and motoring afford him necessary recreation as well as pleasure. Dr. Eggers takes a deep interest in the development of South Dakota and does everything in his power to promote measures instituted to accomplish that end.

JOHN EISNACH

On the roster of county officials in Hamlin County appears the name of John Eisnach, who is now serving on the board of commissioners. The county on the whole has been signally favored with the class of men who have occupied its offices — men who are interested in the welfare of the community and who always subordinate personal interest to public good. Such is the record of John Eisnach, who in addition to holding public office is a blacksmith and dealer in farm implements at Estelline. He was born in Washington County, Ohio, January 25, 1856, and in the paternal line comes of German descent. His father, Phillip Eisnach, was born in Saxony, Germany, and served as a soldier in the German army. After his military experience was over, he came to the United States and for a brief period was a resident of Pennsylvania, in which state he met and married Caroline Wagner, who was there born and reared. A little later they removed westward to Washington county, Ohio, settling on a farm, and as the years went by Mr. Eisnach prospered in his undertakings. He had built his second home upon the place when the Civil War broke out and, feeling that his first duty was to his adopted country, he enlisted for active service in the Union army and was killed at the battle of Bull Run. His widow passed away about two years ago in West Virginia.

John Eisnach was a little lad of but six summers, when his father's death occurred. He remained upon the home farm with his mother up to his seventeenth year, at which time he was apprenticed to the blacksmith's trade in Lowell, Ohio, where he remained as an apprentice for two and a half years. He then went to Wheeling, West Virginia, where he worked in the rolling mills for three months, when he became a victim of the western fever and took a boat down the river to Cairo, proceeding from that point up the Mississippi to St. Louis, working on the boat in order to pay his passage. When he reached St. Louis, the captain expressed a wish that he should remain as a member of the crew, but this did not suit his plans and he left the boat and for a short time worked as a harvest hand in the grain fields of Illinois. Subsequently he took a boat up the river to Winona, Minnesota, where he worked in the wheat fields and in the winter, seasons was employed in the pineries, securing work at his trade. He spent two winters in the pineries and his employer, being unable to pay him for his work, gave him a relinquishment on a homestead in Hamlin County, South Dakota. It was this that made him a resident of the state, in which he has since been deeply interested and which has found in him a valued citizen.

It was in the spring of 1879 that Mr. Eisnach arrived in Dakota territory, making his way to his claim, on which he located, there residing until the fall of 1882, when the town of Estelline was laid out. He then took up his abode in the village, built a little blacksmith shop, sixteen by twenty feet, and before he could get the roof on, he was forced to go to work because of the demand for services in his line. This was the first commercial blacksmith shop opened in Hamlin County. About 1890 he began in a small way to deal in farm implements and in the intervening years has built up one of the largest trades in that line in Hamlin County. He has carried farm machinery of excellent makes, has been thoroughly reliable in his dealings and has put forth every possible effort to accommodate and please his patrons.

In 1884 Mr. Eisnach was united in marriage to Miss Marian Dubois, who came from Wisconsin, her native state, to South Dakota in the same spring that witnessed the arrival of Mr. Eisnach. They became the parents of six children, five of whom are yet living: Ernest P., who is employed by his father; Wallace

T., a grain buyer of Lothair, Montana; Bessie, the wife of C. A. Docken, a merchant of Estelline; and Willard and Lucille, who are yet at home.

Mr. Eisnach is an earnest believer in the principles and platform of the republican party, and served as a member of the first town board after the incorporation of the town of Estelline. Later he was again called to the same position and he has served for several years as a member of the school board, while in 1911 he was elected to the board of county commissioners and was reelected in 1914. He is the only living charter member of Khurm Lodge, No. 96, A. F. & A. M., and he belongs to Arlington Chapter, R. A. M. Estelline numbers him among her foremost citizens and his life record indicates what may be accomplished when energy and determination point out the way. He had no special advantages at the outset of his career and, in fact, his youth was a period of earnest and unremitting toil, but he was not afraid of work and as time passed on his industry overcame difficulties and obstacles and he advanced steadily until he is now one of the substantial citizens of Hamlin County, controlling a business of large and profitable proportions and at the same time figuring prominently in control of public affairs.

JOHN N. ELLERMAN

John N. Ellerman is vice president of the First National Bank of Fairfax and is one of the prominent factors in financial circles in Gregory County and that part of the state. He has the love of a native son for South Dakota, his birth having occurred in Jamesville, Yankton County, his parents being Herman and Emilie (Rudolph) Ellerman, who came to Dakota territory in the early '70s. The father homesteaded land and was actively identified with the pioneer development of Yankton County, where he was called to public office, serving as county treasurer and as county assessor. He is still living at Yankton but his wife has passed away.

John N. Ellerman early became a public-school pupil and continued his studies in successive grades until he was graduated from the high school. He afterward spent two years as a student in the University of Michigan at Ann Arbor and then accepted a position in the office of the county treasurer at Yankton, serving in that capacity for two years. He next became manager of the advertising department of the Dakota Freie Presse and when two years had passed, he severed that connection and came to Gregory County, settling at Fairfax, where he engaged in the real-estate business. His capability and public spirit won him recognition in an election to the office of county treasurer, which position he filled for four years. Still higher honors awaited him, however, for in 1907 he was chosen to represent his district in the state legislature and again was called to that office by popular suffrage in 1909.

After retiring from office Mr. Ellerman went to California for the benefit of his health, spending five years on the Pacific coast. He afterward returned to his old position and in 1904 entered, the bank as vice president, since which time he has bent his energies toward the upbuilding of the business and has been an effective force in increasing its clientage. He is likewise the secretary of the Johnson Farm Loan Company, which is a big institution, controlling an extensive business of that character.

On the 10th of June, 1908, Mr. Ellerman was united in marriage to Miss Lena M. Garrett, a daughter of James M. Garrett, of Caldwell, Idaho. They now have one child, Garrett Herman. The religious faith of the family is that of the Congregational church, while in his political belief Mr. Ellerman is a republican. He belongs to the Masonic fraternity, his membership being at Yankton, where he has attained the thirty-second degree of the Scottish Rite and has crossed the sands of the desert with the Nobles of the Mystic Shrine. He also belongs to the Odd Fellows lodge at Fairfax. He is interested in gardening, in fishing, hunting and motoring and along those lines finds his recreation. Opportunity has with him ever been a call to action and, utilizing the advantages which have come to him, he has not only steadily progressed in the business world in gaining substantial rewards for his labor but has also won the regard of his fellowmen by an active and well spent life.

JAMES D. ELLIOTT

Through a period of forty-two years James D. Elliott has been a resident of South Dakota and in a profession where advancement depends solely upon individual merit and ability, he has worked his way steadily upward until he stands as one of the eminent members of the South Dakota bar. In June, 1911, he was appointed United States district judge and in the same year removed to Sioux Falls, where he has since made his home. He has had other business interests, which indicate his ability and which have been features in winning for him his present substantial success, but he has disposed of these in order to give undivided attention to his judicial duties, which he discharges with a most marked sense of conscientious obligation.

A native of Illinois, Judge Elliott was born in Mount Sterling, Brown County, October 7, 1859, and is the eldest son of William and Mary (McPhail) Elliott. The father, a native of England, was born in 1833 and in his youthful days accompanied his parents to the United States, the family home being established in Pittsburgh, Pennsylvania, where the grandfather, who is an expert mechanic, served for many years as superintendent of the Sligo Iron Works. About 1850 the family removed to Brown County, Illinois, where the grandfather purchased land and devoted the remainder of his life to farming, dying at an advanced age.

William Elliott was educated in the schools of Pittsburgh and also began the study of law before removing to Illinois, where he continued his legal studies and was admitted to the bar. Later he removed to Mount Ayr, Iowa, where he entered upon the active practice of his profession, but soon after the outbreak of the Civil war he enlisted for active service in a Missouri regiment and was on active duty throughout the period of hostilities, being mustered out with the rank of captain. When the military chapter in his life history was ended, he returned to Mount Ayr and resumed the practice of law, becoming one of the leaders of the Iowa bar, his pronounced ability gaining him eminence in the field of his chosen profession. He also served as a member of the Iowa legislature and left the impress of his ability and individuality upon the statute books of the state. In 1872 he came to the territory of Dakota, settling in Clay County, where he remained until 1883, when he removed to Hurley, Turner County, where he continued in the practice of his profession. In 1891 he was elected county judge of Turner County and accordingly removed his residence to Parker, the county seat. He made an excellent record upon the bench, his decisions being characterized by the utmost impartiality and a masterful grasp of all the problems presented for solution. He likewise served as a member of the constitutional convention and took an active part in the work preliminary to the division of the territory and its admission into the Union as the two states of North and South Dakota. Originally a democrat, his allegiance following the Civil war was transferred to the republican party and for many years he has been a prominent figure in its councils. His life has indeed been one of far-reaching influence and benefit in the various states in which he has made his home. He belongs to the Grand Army of the Republic and progress and patriotism might well be termed the keynote of his character.

His son, James D. Elliott, spent his boyhood in Iowa and attended the schools of Mount Ayr and Panora. After the removal of the family to Dakota he continued his studies in the public schools of Vermillion and also pursued a two years' special course under Professor Culver, superintendent of schools of that place. Before his education was completed, he pursued various tasks in order to defray his expenses, and after his more specifically literary course was finished, he took up the profession of teaching, which he followed for three years. In the meantime, he invested his savings in cattle, which he placed on his father's farm with the purpose in view of gaining sufficient funds to enable him to pursue a course of study in the University of Michigan. However, the memorable flood of 1881 carried away and drowned all his stock. A short time afterward he started with a team for the Black Hills, where he spent the following summer. In the fall of that year, he returned home and became a teacher in the public schools of Lakeport, Yankton County, and later at Meckling, Clay County. On account of the havoc wrought by the flood he felt it necessary to return home and aid in retrieving the family fortunes. He entered upon the study of law under the direction of Colonel John L. Jolley and in 1883 entered the offices of Gamble Brothers of Yankton, with whom he continued his reading until his admission to the bar in April, 1884. He remained in the offices of Gamble Brothers until October of that year and then went to Springfield, Bon Homme County, where he entered upon the active practice of law. In 1885 he removed to Tyndall subsequent to the removal of the county seat from Springfield, and in 1887 he was elected state's attorney, which position he filled acceptably for four years. In 1897 he was appointed by President McKinley United States district attorney, serving continuously through both the McKinley and Roosevelt administrations. He continued as United States district attorney for the district of South Dakota for almost ten years, during which time he maintained his residence at Tyndall and practiced there, while his practice also extended to other parts of the state.

In January, 1910, Mr. Elliott was appointed by the Chicago, Milwaukee & St. Paul Railroad and the Puget Sound Railroad as solicitor for the states of North and South Dakota and made his headquarters at Aberdeen. He continued thus, organizing the work, until June, 1911, at which time he was appointed United States district judge by President Taft and on the 14th of June he qualified for the bench. His labors as a jurist have been of the highest class. In the fall of 1911, he removed to Sioux Falls. He holds court at Deadwood, Pierre, Sioux Falls and Aberdeen — two terms each year, and he has also done special work outside of his district through assignment of the presiding judge of the circuit. On his appointment to the bench, he disposed of his various other interests, putting aside all business relations of a different character in order to devote his time and attention unhampered to his judicial duties. His opinions have won high encomiums from the bar, from the public and from his fellow members on the bench in other sections of the state. Devotedly attached to his profession, systematic and methodical in habit, sober and discreet in judgment, calm in temper, diligent in research, conscientious in the discharge of every duty, courteous and kind in demeanor and inflexibly just on all occasions, these qualities have enabled Judge Elliott to take first rank among those who have held the highest judicial office in the state, and have made him the conservator of that justice wherein is the safeguard of individual liberty and happiness and the defense of our national institutions. His reported opinions are monuments to his profound legal learning and superior ability, more lasting than bronze or marble and more honorable than battles fought and won. They show a thorough mastery of the questions involved, a rare simplicity of style and an admirable terseness and clearness in the statement of the principles upon which the opinions rest.

Judge Elliott has been a member of the lower house of the state legislature, having been called to that office in 1885, and he nominated Judge A. G. Edgerton for the office of United States senator when South Dakota became a state. He has always been a stalwart republican, active and prominent as a leader of the party in this state, and in 1896 he served as chairman of the republican state committee. He is well known to the party leaders throughout South Dakota and his word carries weight in all party councils. Outside of his professional activities he had large land and stock-raising interests and for several years was the president of the Security Bank of Tyndall. He now concentrates his energies entirely, however, upon his judicial duties and ranks with the ablest jurists of South Dakota. His mind is naturally analytical, logical and inductive in its trend and as a lawyer he proved sound, clear-minded and well trained. In his practice he prepared for defense as well as attack and was, therefore, seldom surprised by a statement of the opposing counsel. In the application of a legal principle, he was seldom, if ever, at fault and there are few who are so careful to conform their practice to the highest standards of professional ethics.

On the 29th of May, 1890, Mr. Elliott was united in marriage to Miss Agnes Stilwell, a daughter of Charles H. Stilwell, a leading citizen of Tyndall. Their children are Marion A., Douglas S., Hiram McPhail and Mary H. Mr. Elliott is prominently known in fraternal circles. In Masonry he has taken the degrees of Bon Homme Lodge, No. 101, A. F. & A. M.; Scotland Chapter, R. A. M.; Yankton Commandery, K. T.; Yankton Consistory, A. & A. S. R.; and El Riad Temple, A. A. O. N. M. S. He also has membership with the Knights of Pythias and the Ancient Order of United Workmen and belongs to Sioux Falls Lodge, No. 262, B. P. O. E. From the age of thirteen years, he has resided in Dakota and for forty-two years, therefore, has been an interested witness of the growth and development of the state. His own life is typical of the progress of the northwest. He passed through the period of hardship and difficulties in his own career equivalent to the pioneer experiences of the state. Then came the time when he gained a financial foothold as the result of his persistent and determined efforts, and gradually he has worked his way upward until he is now numbered among the men of affluence in Sioux Falls, while his position as a leading jurist of South Dakota is a most enviable one.

JOHN W. ELLIS, M. D.

Dr. John W. Ellis, a physician and surgeon living at Elk Point, South Dakota, has continuously practiced his profession in that city since his graduation from Hahnemann Medical College of Chicago. He was born at West Avon, Livingston County, New York, on the 19th of August, 1852, a son of William W. and Helen M. (Blankenship) Ellis, the former a native of Canada and the latter of New York. The father was a farmer by occupation and spent the greater part of his life in Ontario, Canada. The Ellis farm was given to his father, John Ellis, by Captain Brent, an old Oneida chief, who had secured the land from the English government, and the place is situated near Brantford, Canada. Crossing the border into the United States, William W. Ellis took up his abode in New York, where he was married, but soon afterward he returned to Canada, where his death occurred. His widow then again became a resident of the Empire state, where she passed away ten years later, each being thirty-nine years of age at the time of their demise.

Dr. John W. Ellis lived with his mother until her death, but has maintained himself since his father's death, at which time he was but ten years of age. In his youthful days he mastered the branches of learning taught in successive grades in the public schools and continued his education in the high school of Lowell, Michigan, whither he had gone as a boy. He worked for his board while attending school and in his desire and efforts to secure an education he displayed the elemental strength of his character, giving promise of advancement and the attainment of success in later years. After reaching manhood he worked in the lumber woods of Michigan. The year 1875 witnessed his arrival in Elk Point, South Dakota, and he has since been familiar with its history, its upbuilding and its progress, although his residence here has not been continuous. For some time, he was employed as collector by the firm of Cole Brothers and by the Hart Company, dealers in machinery and lightning rods at Council Bluffs. In that connection he traveled through Nebraska and the southeastern part of South Dakota. In 1877, however, he returned to Elk Point and accepted a situation in the general store of C. W. Biggs, with whom he continued until he was married. He then went to the Black Hills, locating in Central City, where he worked in the mines. In August, 1880, he again became a resident of Elk Point and secured employment with Freeman Brothers, merchants, with whom he remained for five years. In 1885 he was made the census enumerator for Elk Point and Brule townships and in the fall of that year he was elected assessor of Union County and also served as deputy clerk of the courts. After a year, however, he resigned the position of assessor and was elected registrar of deeds and ex-officio county clerk. In 1892 he went to Chicago and took up the study of medicine, entering the Hahnemann Medical College. While pursuing his course there he acted as gatekeeper at the fairgrounds of the World's Columbian Exposition. He was graduated from Hahnemann on the 13th of April, 1895, and at once returned to Elk Point, where he opened an office and has since been engaged in successful practice.

Dr. Ellis was married to Miss Laura M. Steckman, of Elk Point, in 1878, and they became the parents of two children: Ray W., who is a graduate of Yankton College and of the National Law School of Washington, D. C, and is now state's attorney at Elk Point; and Lillian June, who is voice instructor at Parsons College in Fairfield, Iowa. The family is prominent in the social circles of the city and the hospitality of the best homes is freely accorded them.

In the Masonic fraternity Dr. Ellis is well known, belonging to Elk Point Lodge, No. 3, A. F. & A. M.; Vermillion Chapter, No. 21, R. A. M.; Vermillion Commandery; Oriental Consistory, No. I, A. & A. S. R., of Yankton; and El Riad Temple, A. A. O. N. M. S., of Sioux Falls. He is also a member of the Elk Point Commercial Club. In politics he has always been an earnest republican, giving unfaltering support to the party since age conferred upon him the right of franchise. He has served as a member of the school board at Elk Point and for several years was its secretary, doing effective work for the benefit of the schools and the improvement of the educational system. He served for several years as president of the state board of health and is the present superintendent of the county board of health. He is a member of the South Dakota Homeopathic Medical Society and profits from the discussion in its meetings of the most advanced methods of practice. He has always kept in touch with the scientific research that is continually shedding light upon the laws of health and, while never hasty in discarding the old and time-tried methods of practice, he is ever ready to take up any new idea that his judgment indorses as of benefit in the alleviation of pain or in checking the ravages of disease.

WILLIAM T. ELLIS

W. T. ELLIS, postmaster at Salem, McCook County, is a native of the Badger state, having been born in Rock County, Wisconsin, on the 2d of August, 1852, a son of Thomas and Mary (Davis) Ellis, of whose six children he is the third and the eldest of the three surviving. Of his brothers it may be noted that Allen B. is engaged in the grain business at Winnipeg, Manitoba, and that Edgar A., is engaged in the same line of enterprise in Assiniboine, Canada. The parents of the subject were born in Cardiganshire, South Wales, whence the father came to America when a young man, his marriage being solemnized in Ohio, where his wife had come with her parents when a girl. Thomas Ellis was a tailor by trade, but the sedentary employment made serious inroads on his health and he was thus led to abandon this vocation and turn his attention to agricultural pursuits. About 1850 he removed from the Buckeye state to Wisconsin, where he resided until 1855, when he removed to Freeborn County, Minnesota, where he initiated his operations as a farmer, becoming one of the prosperous men of that county, where he continued to reside until his death, which occurred on the 13th of September, 1874, since which time his loved and devoted wife has made her home with the subject of this review. Thomas Ellis was a Republican in politics and his religious faith was that of the Methodist Episcopal church, of which his widow is likewise a devoted member.

William T. Ellis was reared on the homestead farm in Minnesota, and after completing the curriculum of the district school he continued his studies in the high school at Albert Lea, that state. At the age of twenty-one years, he engaged in teaching in the public schools, and to this vocation he continued to give his attention at intervals for about twelve years, in Minnesota and South Dakota. In May, 1880, he came to Salem, this state, and within the same year entered a homestead claim in McCook County, at a point four miles west of Salem. He proved on this property and there continued to reside for a period of six years, developing a valuable farm. In 1888 he became associated with his brother Allen in the erection of a store building in Salem, and in the same they engaged in the hardware business, in which they continued to be associated until May, 1901. In 1897 the subject was appointed postmaster at Salem, taking charge of the office on the 1st of June, and he has ever since remained in tenure of the position. At the initiation of his regime the office was one of the fourth class, but in 1899 its business had so increased that it was brought into the class of presidential offices, so that Mr. Ellis received in that year his reappointment directly from President McKinley. It is needless to say that he is an uncompromising Republican, and in the connection, he has done effective service in behalf of the party cause in this section of the state. He served three years as a member of the board of county commissioners, having been incumbent of the office at the time of the erection of the present court house.

Fraternally Mr. Ellis is identified with Fortitude Lodge, No. 73, Free and Accepted Masons; Salem Chapter, No. 34, Royal Arch Masons; Omega Council, No. 2, Royal and Select Masters; Constantine Commandery, No. 2, Knights Templar, and El Riad Temple of the Mystic Shrine, in Sioux Falls. He is also affiliated with the local organizations of the Knights of the Maccabees. He was the first eminent commander of the Constantine Commandery, Knights Templar, of Salem, and has ever manifested a deep interest in the noble fraternity of Freemasonry.

HON. SAMUEL HARRISON ELROD

Hon. Samuel Harrison Elrod is one of the most modest but most popular men of South Dakota. If he has opponents, it is those who do not share his political opinions and who believe in machine rule rather than in the voice of the people. Those who know him, and he has a wide acquaintance throughout the state, usually call him Sam. It is an indication of his democratic spirit and manner and it is well known that there is no one more appreciative of individual worth in another. Business classification places him with the leading lawyers not only of Clark County but of the state, for he has comprehensive knowledge of the principles of jurisprudence and is accurate in his application of these principles to the points in litigation.

A native of Indiana, he was born near Coatesville on the 1st of May, 1856, and is a son of Jesse F. and Lydia (Pursel) Elrod. The father was a farmer by occupation, following that pursuit until his death. The mother has also passed away. Samuel H. Elrod pursued his early education in the public schools and afterward attended De Pauw University of Greencastle, Indiana, being graduated on the 22d of June, 1882. Eight days later he arrived in Dakota territory, coming to Clark County on a construction train on the 3d of July. The same day he was admitted to the bar by Judge Kidder at Watertown and he opened a little office in Clark. He has since been actively engaged in the practice of his profession save when busy with the duties of political office. There was not a dwelling in Clark at the time of his arrival and he built a little house or shanty before he could really enter actively upon his chosen life work. His life has been an extremely busy and useful one. His work in the fields in boyhood days was followed by close application to his studies.

Through the period of his college course and since coming to Dakota he has never known an idle day. The Daily Tribune of Salt Lake City, Utah, said of him: "A few days after arriving in Clark, where he opened a law office and located a preemption, Mr. Elrod made a Fourth of July speech to a crowd of settlers on the open prairies (there were no public buildings in the town then), and he has been getting acquainted with the people of the state ever since." Today there are few residents of South Dakota better known and it would be difficult to find one who has the confidence and regard of the people in general to a greater degree. As the population increased his law business grew and for ten years, he filled the office of states attorney. He was also called to the city council and aided in shaping the policy of the municipality. He became a recognized leader in republican circles and advanced continuously in that connection until he was made a standard bearer of his party in 1904. He received a good majority which put him in the gubernatorial chair, where he remained through 1905 and 1906. During his term as governor, he was chairman of the first capitol building committee and dictated the contract for plans for the capitol.

While he was a candidate a leading paper of South Dakota said: "S. H. Elrod, of Clark County, is a plain, unassuming South Dakotan. He is absolutely without pretense. There is a tinge of the Lincoln character in him, that free mingling with the common people and that everyday plainness that so endeared Lincoln to the masses. Elrod possesses a great deal of that same quality. One immediately feels a friendly feeling for him. He is warm-hearted, yet conservative; plain and unassuming, yet possessing quiet dignity; a man of clean, wholesome character, yet a man wise in the ways of the political world; and he is honest and sincere." His administration was characterized by various needed reforms and improvements and many tangible evidences of his public spirit and devotion to the best interests of the commonwealth can be cited. The legislature of North Carolina passed a resolution formally thanking him for the position he took in his message declaring in favor of returning to North Carolina the money forced out of that state on some repudiated bonds which were a gift to South Dakota. From the standpoint of fairness and decency his position was certainly right.

The Dakota Farmer paid the following tribute to Governor Elrod for his efforts in behalf of the agricultural interests of South Dakota. "From the moment Governor S. H. Elrod was sworn in as the chief executive of South Dakota up to the present time, in season and out of season, he has stood by every measure that would possibly benefit the agricultural interests of his state. Before in these columns we enumerated not less than half a dozen distinctly agricultural and live-stock measures that had his constant support during the last session of the legislature, a number of which, we believe, could never have become laws without it, and now we must record one more and in our estimation among his crowning achievements in this line. We refer to the securing of what was known as the Fishback quarter of one hundred and sixty acres of splendid land for the agricultural college and experiment station at Brookings. This splendid piece of land, as many know, was literally located in the very heart of the farm school grounds. It came up to the very doors of the college buildings on two sides, and was not only in every way perfectly adapted to the work and needs of the school but was fast advancing in price and being clamored for by many farsighted investors to be laid out in building lots. Much more than the price given could have been had for it for this purpose. The troubles relating to getting title to this land are too complicated to explain. It is enough to say that repeatedly, during the long drawn-out time this title was in jeopardy, the timely and personal interference of the governor saved it from going from the state forever."

On his retirement from the position of governor, Mr. Elrod returned to his home in Clark and resumed the private practice of law, in which he has since continued. The position which he occupies in the opinion of his fellow townsmen of Clark County is indicated in the fact that the township and village of Elrod were named in his honor.

Fraternally he is a Mason and has attained the Knights Templar degree of the York Rite. He also has membership with the Modern Woodmen, the Workmen and the Knights of Pythias. On the 11th of November, 1884, Mr. Elrod was united in marriage to Miss Mary E. Masten, a daughter of Matthias and Eliza Masten. They have become, parents of two children: Barbara, at home; and Arthur, who is attending the high school. Such in brief is the life history of one whom South Dakota has honored with the highest office within the gift of the state. He has ever worn his honors with most becoming modesty and at all times he has regarded a public office as a public trust — and no trust reposed in Samuel Harrison Elrod has ever been betrayed.

JAMES L. ELLIOTT

James L. Elliott, secretary and treasurer of Brown & Saenger, Incorporated, controlling an office supply and bindery business, is by virtue of this position one of the prominent men in the commercial life of Sioux Falls. He was born at Osage, Iowa, September 8, 1878, and is a son of John Logan and Emma (Abbott) Elliott, the former a native of Pennsylvania and the latter of New York. The paternal grandfather of the subject of this review was also born in the Keystone state.

James L. Elliott acquired his education in the public schools of Jesup, Iowa. He began his independent career as a salesman, continuing thus until February, 1908, when he entered the firm of Brown & Saenger, Incorporated, as secretary and treasurer, becoming interested in this business following the retirement of Colonel Brown. Brown & Saenger, Incorporated, control a large bindery and they are also extensive dealers in office supplies, the business being one of the largest of its kind in that city. Since he has been connected with it, Mr. Elliott has aided greatly in the development of the concern and in his capacity as secretary and treasurer has proven himself a man of insight, ability and intelligence.

On the 28th of May, 1906, at Lake Okoboji, Iowa, Mr. Elliott was united in marriage to Miss Isabel Givin, a daughter of William and Matilda Givin. Mr. and Mrs. Elliott have three children, Lois, Margaret and Eleanor. Mr. Elliott is a thirty-second degree Mason, and belongs to El Riad Temple, A. A. O. N. M. S.. He is a veteran of the Spanish-American war, having served six months in Cuba as a private in Company E, Forty-ninth Iowa Regiment. He gives his political allegiance to the republican party and as an intelligent and progressive citizen takes a great interest in public affairs, although he is not active as an office seeker. He is one of the representative and able men of Sioux Falls and is held in high regard in business circles.

CAPTAIN EDWARD T. ENEBOE

Captain Edward T. Eneboe is well known in eastern South Dakota as manager of the Sioux Valley News and also as captain of Company E of the Fourth Regiment of the South Dakota National Guard — the oldest military company in the state. He was born in Madelia, Minnesota, on the 30th of May, 1882, his parents being Tobias and Mary Eneboe, both of whom were natives of Norway, where they were reared and married. In the '70s they bade adieu to friends and native land and sailed for the United States, making their way into the interior of the country until they reached Madelia, where they established their home. The father, however, was permitted to enjoy his new home for but a comparatively brief period, his death occurring when his son, Captain Eneboe, was an infant of but six months. The mother survives and now makes her home with her son, Edward T.

Captain Eneboe was reared by his mother and at a very early age started out not only to earn his own living but to assist in the support of the family. When but a boy he became a wage earner. He apprenticed himself to the printer's trade even in his school days, working mornings, evenings, Saturdays and during the school holidays. About 1896 the mother removed with her family to Canton, South Dakota, and their Captain Eneboe began to work in the office of the Leader, where he remained for two years. At the end of that time, he left the Leader office and accepted a position on the Sioux Valley News, beginning work on that paper on the 1st of June, 1898. Soon afterward the foreman, Robert Hart man, resigned to attend college and Captain Eneboe was installed as foreman of the plant. Published articles of that date quote him as the youngest newspaper foreman in South Dakota. From 1898 until 1912 he continued to act in that capacity and in the latter year was made business manager of the paper, which position he still holds. The News presents an attractive appearance, is well assembled and is a paper creditable to the town and county.

In 1901 Captain Eneboe became associated with the state militia, enlisting in Company E of the First Regiment of the South Dakota National Guard. From a private in the ranks, he rose through the various promotions of corporal, sergeant, first sergeant, second lieutenant and first lieutenant to the captaincy, receiving his commission on the 18th of October, 1909. He has since remained at the head of the company. On the reorganization of the National Guard of the state the regiment to which he belongs became the Fourth South Dakota National Guard, and in this connection, he still commands his company, whose respect and affection he has in high measure.

Mr. Eneboe is a member of Silver Star Lodge, No. 4, A. F. & A. M., and of Siroc Chapter, No. 4, R. A. M. He also belongs to Centennial Lodge, I. O. O. F., and to the encampment, and he is a member of the Canton Commercial Club. He is numbered among the representative young men of his city and state — alert, enterprising and progressive and active in furthering all those interests which he deems of public benefit.

JULIUS ENGEL

Yankton county has been signally favored in the class of men who have occupied her public offices, for on the whole they have been loyal to duty, fully recognizing the obligations that devolve upon them and the opportunity afforded them for valuable public service. Such a one is Julius Engel, who in 1911 was elected county auditor for a four years' term. He is also identified with the Yankton Realty Company, Inc., as its secretary and treasurer.

Mr. Engel was born November 19, 1887, in the county which is still his home. The family is of German origin and his great-grandfather was among the number of German people who were invited by the Russian government to settle in southern Russia, many concessions being offered them to induce them to colonize that section of the country, such as release from military duty. They and their descendants became a wealthy, prosperous colony, but when the Russians sought to rescind the original agreement, they left that country and after some investigation as to opportunities offered in the new world, they settled in South Dakota about 1873. They have rapidly adapted themselves to the conditions of the country and have become splendid citizens. John G. Engel, father of Julius Engel, was among the number of the descendants of the German colony that went to Russia who left that country in 1873 and became residents of Yankton County, South Dakota. He still resides within the borders of the county, but after about twenty years' active connection with agricultural pursuits retired from his farm in 1893. Soon afterward he became postmaster at Lesterville, filling that office until 1911. He then removed to Scotland, Bon Homme County, South Dakota, where he is engaged in the real-estate business. He married Rosina Sayler, who was also born in southern Russia and in 1873 made the voyage across the Atlantic to the new world. They became the parents of thirteen children, of whom eight are yet living.

Julius Engel, who is the fifth in order of birth, was a little lad of about six years when his parents removed to Lesterville, where he spent his youthful days and there largely pursued his education in the public schools. Later, however, he attended the commercial college at Sioux City, Iowa, from which he was graduated. At the age of seventeen he became connected with the office of county clerk of Yankton County and has been continuously connected with county offices since 1905. His long experience has made him thoroughly familiar with the duties of the position of auditor and thus he was well qualified to take the management and control of the office when, in 1911, he was elected county auditor for a four years' term, and he is now discharging the duties devolving upon him in a manner most creditable to himself and satisfactory to his constituents. The only business in which he has been engaged outside of his official duties is fiat of insurance and real estate, being now secretary and treasurer of the Yankton Realty Company, which was incorporated in May, 1914.

On the 17th of June, 1908, at Wausau, Wisconsin, Mr. Engel was united in marriage to Miss Violet E. Benedict. In social circles of the city, they are well known and have many warm friends. In politics Mr. Engel has always been a stalwart republican, working earnestly for the party. He belongs to St. John's Lodge, No. I, A. F. & A. M., of Yankton, and has attained the thirty-second degree of the Scottish Rite in Oriental Consistory. He also has membership with the Elks lodge No. 994 and is true to the teachings of these organizations, exemplifying in his life their beneficent spirit.

GENERAL C. H. ENGLESBY

General G. H. Englesby, of Watertown, formerly adjutant general of the state, has a splendid record as soldier and legislator and is one of the men who are widely known throughout the confines of South Dakota. He was born in Brown County, Minnesota, in 1869, a son of Philo F. Englesby, of Minnesota and Dakota, a pioneer and a veteran of the Civil War. The military spirit characterized the family for many generations and the subject of this review is a direct descendant of an officer of the Revolutionary war.

The General came with his parents to Watertown, South Dakota, in 1879 and was educated in the public schools in that town and in the State College at Brookings. After leaving school he entered the field of journalism and became the editor and publisher of the Watertown Kampeskian, a weekly newspaper which he conducted successfully for five years, from 1893 to 1898. Upon the outbreak of the Spanish-American war he became captain of Company H, First South Dakota Volunteers, and for a year served with his regiment in the Philippines. During the Philippine insurrection he participated in twenty-two engagements with the natives and commanded a battalion throughout the campaign. He was slightly wounded in one of the engagements during the American advance on Malolos.

After the close of his service in the army General Englesby returned to South Dakota and in 1901 took his seat as a member of the state senate, serving as such until 1905. In 1909 he was honored by election to the lower house of the state legislature. He did much valuable work both in the committee room and upon the floor of the house and aided in securing the enactment of a number of laws that have proved of great value to the people of the state. In 1905 he was appointed adjutant general of the state, being reappointed three times and serving in that capacity until March, 1912.

General Englesby was married in 1895 to Miss Julia E. Parker, a daughter of the Rev. G. H. Parker, a Baptist clergyman of Watertown. Four children have been born to this union, of whom three are living: Adaline, now sixteen years of age; Ruth, twelve years of age; and Charles P., eight years old. One son, Hugh, died in infancy.

General Englesby has been active in the Masons, the Elks, the Knights of Pythias and the Ancient Order of United Workmen and is widely known in fraternal circles of the state. He has served his country with unselfish devotion as a soldier in time of war and his state as a legislator in the time of peace, and his life record is a credit to himself and to the family name.

JOHN P. EVERETT

John P. Everett, of Sturgis, member of the bar and county judge of Meade County, was born at Lyons, Nebraska, February 18, 1879, a son of Ben W. and Elise (Graut) Everett. The father, who was born in Maine in September, 1838, devoted his entire life to farming. His wife was born in New York in August,

1838, and in 1861 they removed westward to Iowa, while in 1866 they became residents of Nebraska, securing a homestead claim at Lyons. Mr. Everett still resides upon part of that claim, but turned his attention from agricultural pursuits to banking, in which he was engaged, for many years. He is now practically living retired, although he is still a landowner in that state, his previous success being sufficient to enable him to rest from further business labors. He has become recognized as a man of prominence and influence in his community, has held various local and county offices, and in 1886 served in the Nebraska legislature.

In a family of six children Judge Everett was the fifth in order of birth, and his home training developed in him traits of character which throughout his later years have awakened high regard and respect. He attended the high school of Lyons, Nebraska, and prepared for a professional career as a student in the law department of the State University, from which he was graduated in 1903. In the meantime, however, other business interests had claimed his attention. At the age of twenty-three he engaged in railroad contracting in southern Mexico and spent some time in Guatemala, devoting his time to railroad contracting for four years. After removing to Sturgis, he took up the business of ranching. He still owns six hundred and forty acres of land, conducting a general ranching business and also dealing largely in livestock. His place is sixty miles northeast of Sturgis, at Chalkbutte. He had engaged in law practice for two or three years before going to the south and he was admitted to practice in South Dakota in 1914. He was then elected county judge on the democratic ticket and is now filling that position in an acceptable and creditable manner. He had previously served for six years as county commissioner of Meade County, and his fellow townsmen recognized in him one who is always loyal and faithful.

In August, 1910, Judge Everett was married to Miss Leila M. Barber, who was born in Juneau, Wisconsin, a daughter of David and Lugene (Arnold) Barber, natives of New York and Wisconsin respectively. The father was born in 1820, while the mother was some years his junior. She now makes her home with Judge and Mrs. Everett at the age of seventy-seven years.

Judge Everett is a member of Phi Delta Phi and also of the Masonic fraternity, and exemplifies in his life the beneficent spirit of the craft, at all times recognizing the brotherhood of mankind and the obligations of every individual toward his fellows. His business experiences have been varied and the wide range of his travels and residence has brought to him broad knowledge, enabling him to place a correct valuation upon life, its opportunities and its advantages.

FREDRICK TAFT EVANS

The name of Fredrick Taft Evans has been indelibly inscribed upon the pages of the history of the Black Hills, for he was connected with many events which promoted its progress and development and shaped its annals. He particularly contributed to the improvement of Hot Springs and throughout that section of the state his name is well known and honored. He was born at Parkman, Ohio, not far from Cleveland, on the 28th of November, 1835, and his life record covered the intervening period to the 11th of October, 1902, when death called him.

Mr. Evans attended the public schools of his native state and also studied for a time in Hiram College when James A. Garfield, afterward president of the United States, was one of the teachers there. He was eighteen years of age when he went to the pineries of northern Wisconsin, working for others at Big Bull Falls. In 1856 he proceeded to De Soto, Nebraska, from which point he made a trip across the plains with a party to Walla Walla, Washington. The trip was fraught with many interesting incidents such as went to make up the experiences of the pioneer travelers to the coast. He remained in Washington for three years and then returned to Nebraska, where he became the owner of a large stock ranch. The whole town of Grand Island, Nebraska, now stands upon that ranch. He engaged extensively in the stock business, furnishing stock under contract to the United States government and to the Union Pacific Railroad until the completion of the line across the continent. Because of the depredations of the Indians he removed to Iowa, taking up his abode at Sioux City, where he built the first street railroad. He resided there until 1876, in which year he embarked in the transportation business, opening the trail from old Fort Pierre to the Hills. He continued actively in the freighting business until the Northwestern Railroad was completed, making Deadwood his freighting headquarters. For a time, he was in partnership with John Hornick under the firm style of Evans & Hornick. Terminal points were constantly changing as the country became settled. Freight was first carried by boat to Yankton, thence overland to Pierre and on to the Black Hills, Mr. Evans becoming the first settler of Pierre. As the different railroads were extended into the country routes were changed but new roads were opened up and the freighters pursued their interests. Mr. Evans hauled into the country much of the heavy machinery used in the early mines and in so doing overcame obstacles which would seem utterly insurmountable to men of less determination and resourcefulness. On the extension of the railroad from Rapid City to Whitewood he retired permanently from the freighting business. He related that at the time of his retirement there was owing him one hundred and twenty-one thousand dollars, part of which was protected by unendorsed notes and some of it only by verbal promises, but such was the honor among the early settlers that eventually every cent was paid. At the time of his retirement Mr. Evans had in actual service fifteen hundred oxen, one hundred and fifty mules and a force of from two to three hundred men, while in every town in the Black Hills warehouses had been established. In the meantime, he purchased a number of mining properties, several of which he never developed. After closing out the transfer business about 1889 he became interested in Hot Springs and erected the first hotel and also the first bathing house at that place. He believed that the village had natural advantages which would make it the largest city of the Black Hills country if properly handled. He erected the Minnehaha Hotel on the site where the Evans now stands and he also built the Minnehaha block. He built and sold to the county the edifice used as a courthouse in Deadwood and he gave to the county the ground for the State Soldiers' Home, which he built under contract. He also donated the ground upon which all of the churches of Hot Springs have been built and he was connected with practically every enterprise of the city. He built the present water, light and power system and he was also connected with the first bank of Hot Springs and at the same time was the owner of the stock of a bank at Pierre. He embraced every opportunity for furthering the interests and promoting the upbuilding of Hot Springs and he recognized opportunities that others passed heedlessly by.

On the 25th of April, 1863, Mr. Evans was united in marriage to Miss Theresa Beall, who was born in Fremont, Steuben County, Indiana, in 1844, a daughter of Enos and Hannah (Rowe) Beall, the former a native of Montgomery' county, Maryland, and the latter of New York city. The father, who was a prominent attorney and jurist, served on the supreme bench of Indiana for a number of years. He was a pioneer resident of that state and became one of the early settlers in Michigan, but after a brief period removed to Wisconsin and in 1861 cast in his lot with the early settlers of Nebraska, taking up his abode where Grand Island now stands. There he engaged in merchandising for a time but because of failing health retired and passed away there in 1873. His widow and her family afterward removed to Sioux City, Iowa, where her death occurred in 1889. Mr. Beall served in the Nebraska state legislature for a number of terms and left the impress of his individuality upon the laws enacted during that period. To him and his wife were born two children, of whom Mrs. Evans is the elder. Her brother, Rev. Byron Beall, is a Presbyterian minister now residing at Lincoln, Nebraska. Being in poor health he has been compelled to retire from the active work of the ministry. Mrs. Evans was educated at Hillsdale College in Hillsdale, Michigan. By her marriage she has become the mother of four children: Fredrick T., who is a county official residing at Seattle, Washington; Frank, who resides on a fruit and chicken ranch near Seattle; Ella, the wife of H. D. Clark, who is developing a large fruit ranch at San Fernando, California; and John, who resides on a large fruit ranch near Hot Springs.

Mr. Evans was a member of the Masonic fraternity and took all of the degrees, from the blue lodge to the shrine, exemplifying in his life the beneficent spirit of the craft, which is based upon a recognition of the brotherhood of mankind. Mrs. Evans is a member of the order of the Eastern Star and is prominently known in club and literary circles of Hot Springs. She belongs to the Travelers Club and the Mothers Club and she organized the society which erected the library building at Hot Springs and is now a member of the library board. Her influence has ever been on the side of integrity after moral progress and along those lines she fully sustained the efforts of her husband and, like him, held membership in the Methodist Episcopal church. In politics Mr. Evans was a republican and for one term represented Hall County, Nebraska, in the state legislature. After coming to Hat Springs, he was mayor of the city and did all in his power to further its interests and upbuilding, indorsing every plan and measure that tended to foster civic virtue and civic pride. He was always deeply interested in the development of the northwest and did everything in his power to promote work along that line. His name was indeed well known in pioneer times and in later days and his upright life made him honored and esteemed by all with whom he came in contact.

WILLIAM H. EVERHARD, M. D.

William H. Everhard, M. D., one of the representative members of the medical fraternity in Volga, Brookings County, was born in Ripon, Fond du Lac County, Wisconsin, on the 4th of May, 1857, and is a son of Dr. Aaron and Ann V. (Venett) Everhard, the former of whom was born in Doylestown, Wayne County, Ohio, and the latter in the state of Massachusetts. The father of our subject was graduated in the medical department of the Western Reserve University, one of the oldest educational institutions in the Buckeye state, and was a thoroughly skilled physician and surgeon, having been engaged in the active practice of his profession for full half a century. He located in Ripon, Wisconsin, in 1856, being one of the pioneer physicians of that section, and there continued in practice until his death, in 1892, at which time he was sixty-nine years of age. His widow is still living and makes her home with her children, who accord her the utmost filial care and solicitude. The father of our subject was mayor of Ripon for fourteen years and was one of the most honored citizens of the community in which he so long lived and labored. Of his seven children six are living, namely: Andrew T., who is a resident of Bryant, South Dakota: Kendrick M., who is engaged in Bryant, Hamlin County, South Dakota; Frank A., who is a practicing physician in Ripon, Wisconsin; Ella S., who is likewise a medical practitioner, engaged in the work of her profession in Dayton, Ohio; Mary, who is a resident of the city of Boston, and William H., who is the immediate subject of this review.

Dr. William H. Everhard was reared to maturity in his native town, and after completing the curriculum of the public schools be entered Ripon College for two years, being twenty-one years of age at the time. He was matriculated in Rush Medical College, in the city of Chicago, in 1878, and there completed the prescribed course, being graduated in this celebrated institution in February, 1880, and receiving his degree of Doctor of Medicine. It should be stated that he had previously taken up the study of medicine under the effective direction of his honored father. Almost immediately after his graduation the Doctor started for South Dakota, having determined to follow the advice of Horace Greeley by coming west and growing up with the country. He arrived in Volga on the 9th of April, 1880, the line of the Chicago & Northwestern Railroad having been completed to this point only a few months previously. The Doctor at once displayed his professional "shingle" in the new town, and that it was essential for him to find someone to "practice" upon may be well understood when we state that his cash capital was reduced to the sum of fifty cents the day succeeding his arrival. It was his good fortune, however, to find his services in demand that same morning, twenty-one patients coming to him for treatment. He is distinctively the pioneer physician of the town, and for many years labored with unabating zeal and self-abnegation in the relieving of suffering and distress in the community, driving to great distances, often through blinding snowstorms over the trackless prairies, and ever responding to the call of duty, no matter how great the personal discomfort or even hazard. He was very successful in his professional work and continued in active practice until 1901, when he sold out his professional business to Dr. D. L. Scanlan, in order that he might have more time to devote to his various capitalistic interests, while he gives special attention to dealing in real estate, being the owner of much valuable property in the county and elsewhere in the state. He is a member of the National Association of Railroad Surgeons.

Dr. Everhard is the owner of two thousand acres of land in the state, and the greater portion of this is in Brookings County, and he has shown marked discrimination in the handling of realty since coming here. He is associated with Messrs. John L. Hall and Robert Henry in the ownership of the First State Bank of Volga, which was organized and incorporated in 1900. He was the first single individual to raise a carload of hogs west of the Sioux river in Brookings County, and since 1893 he has had under effective cultivation in the county about fifteen hundred acres of land. He has paid out more than any other one man in the section of the county west of the Sioux river in the way of farm improvements, including labor, and has thus materially aided in the development of the resources of this section.

Dr. Everhard was aligned with the Democratic party until 1896, when he felt convinced that the platform of the party did not represent the organic principles which the name should imply, and he therefore transferred his allegiance to the Republican party, to which he has since given his support, having been a delegate to one of its state conventions. He was the first treasurer of the village of Volga, was county coroner for a number of years and also a valued member of the board of health. He served as surgeon for the Chicago & Northwestern Railroad Company from the time of coming here until he retired from practice, and he is now frequently called in consultation and emergency work.

Fraternally the Doctor is identified with the lodge, chapter and council of the Masonic order, having passed the official chairs in the lodge, and is also affiliated with the Benevolent and Protective Order of Elks, the Modern Woodmen of America and the Ancient Order of United Workmen. On the 19th of March, 1882, Dr. Everhard was united in marriage to Miss T. Ella Taggart, who was born in Meadville, Pennsylvania, being a daughter of George and Elizabeth Taggart, who settled in Brookings, in 1881, being numbered among the pioneers of this section of the state. Mr. Taggart served with distinction during the war of the Rebellion and he and his wife are now dead. Dr. and Mrs. Everhard have three children, namely: Frank T., who was graduated in Ripon high school, Wisconsin, in 1901, and who thereafter continued his studies for one year in the Wisconsin State University, at Madison, and is now in the University of Minnesota: Bertha M., who completed the course in the Volga graded school, later attended the college at Yankton for two years, and is now at the parental home; and Raymond is a student in the East high school at Minneapolis, Minnesota.

JAMES H. EXON

James H. EXON, one of the prominent and honored citizens of Charles Mix County, formerly incumbent of the office of county judge, as well as that of county auditor, and the principal figure in the County Seat State Bank, at Wheeler, is a native of the "right little, tight little isle" of England, having been born in Somersetshire, on the 11th of July, 1858, being a son of Henry and Sarah Exon, both of whom were likewise burn in Somersetshire, of stanch old English stuck. Both secured excellent educational advantages and both received life certificates as teachers in England, where both gained distinction and prominence in educational circles, the father having devoted the major portion of his active career to the pedagogic profession, while his wife also devoted herself to teaching for several years. The former was for nine years superintendent of the Ripleyville British schools and for eighteen years was principal of the schools at Wookey, Somersetshire, where the subject of this sketch was born. The mother of the Judge was likewise a teacher in the schools at that place. In 1882 the parents left their native land and came to the United States, our subject having come to Canada in the preceding year, and from New York City they proceeded to Iowa, where they resided about six months, after which they came to South Dakota, and secured claims in Charles Mix County, the property being located in what is now Forbes township.

In the month of May, 1881, Judge Exon bade adieu to home and native land and emigrated to America, landing in Quebec, and remaining in Canada about one year, at the expiration of which he joined his parents, who had located temporarily in Iowa, as has just been noted. In the autumn of 1882, he preceded them into what is now the state of South Dakota and selected the land for his father and for the four children who had attained years of maturity, the members of the family thus eventually being able to prove up on the five quarter sections which he had selected in Charles Mix County, of which they were pioneer settlers. Later three of these quarter sections were sold and the parents of the subject then removed to Gage County, Nebraska, where they now reside, the father having retired from active labors and being now sixty-eight years of age, while his devoted wife has attained the age of seventy years. Both are members of the Episcopal church and are folk of sterling character and high intellectual attainments.

Judge Exon attended the Ripleyville schools for a period of five years, during which time lie prepared himself for his collegiate course. He then entered Cullom College, near famed old Oxford, where he was graduated in 1879, after which he was for two years an assistant master in the schools at Ripleyville, Bradford and Yorkshire. It was the wish of his father that he should follow the profession of teaching, in which the former had attained so gratifying success, but the Judge early manifested a desire to turn his attention to agricultural pursuits and it was in harmony with this ambition that he was led to emigrate to America. After his location in South Dakota, he taught in the district schools during the winter months, and during the balance of the year devoted his time to the improving and cultivation of his farming land. In the autumn of 1890, he was elected to the office of county auditor, and in the following January he removed from his farm to the village of Wheeler, the county seat, to enter upon the active discharge of his official duties. He gave a most capable and satisfactory administration, and at the expiration of his term of two years he engaged in the abstract business, while in July of the same year he was appointed state's attorney, to fill the unexpired term of the regular incumbent. A. L. Hoppaugh, who removed from the state. In the following October Judge Exon was one of the leading spirits in bringing about the organization of the People's party in this section of the state, and, in company with seven other prominent workers in the movement, he purchased the Wheeler Courier, the weekly newspaper published in the capital town of the county, and this was thereafter made an effective exponent of the cause of the party. Our subject's appointment to the office of state's attorney, for which he was well qualified in an abstract way, led him to make a careful study of the technical branches of the science of jurisprudence, and he was admitted to the bar of the state, upon examination before the supreme court, at Pierre, on the 3d of October, 1893. From time to time, he continued to acquire the interests of other stockholders in the Wheeler Courier, of which he became sole owner in 1901, while the paper has been under his editorial charge and his general direction from the time it was purchased by him and others, as previously mentioned. In the autumn of 1898, he was elected to the office of county judge, serving one term, and in January, 1902, he again received the appointment of state's attorney to fill a vacancy caused by the resignation of T. J. Remington, and he served in this capacity until the expiration of the term, in January, 1903. In March, 1903, was effected the organization of the County Seat State Bank, and Judge Exon was made president of the institution at that time and still continues as chief executive. He still continues in the active practice of the law and is also engaged in the real-estate and abstract business. He now gives his allegiance to the Democratic party, of whose principles he is a stanch advocate, and his religious faith is that of the Protestant Episcopal church, of which he is a communicant, but as there is no church organization in Wheeler, he and his family attend the Congregational church services.

Fraternally he is identified with Doric Lodge, Free and Accepted Masons, at Platte, this state. On the 26th of June, 1886, Judge Exon was united in marriage to Miss Emma Smith, of Mitchell, South Dakota, and they became the parents of three sons, Arthur R., Walter E. and John J.. In 1896 Mrs. Exon's health had become so seriously impaired that he deemed it advisable to take her for an ocean voyage, in the hope that she might recuperate her energies, and they accordingly visited his old home in England, where she received treatment without avail, since her death there occurred four months later, on the 5th of August, 1896. On the 20th of April, 1898, at Paris, Kentucky, was solemnized the marriage of Judge Exon to Miss Marian Smith, a native of England and a sister of his former wife, and they are the parents of one child, Dorothy J.

CHARLES FANTLE

The name of Charles Fantle has come to be regarded as a synonym for progress and development in Sioux Falls, for during the period of over nineteen years that he has been connected with business interests there his influence has been a powerful force in community advancement. From a small beginning he and his brother Sam, comprising the firm of Fantle Brothers, have developed one of the leading dry-goods stores in the state and in consequence of this have taken their places among the substantial and able men of the city.

Charles Fantle was born in Ann Arbor, Michigan, November 18, 1862, and is a son of Charles and Regina (Gregor) Fantle. He acquired his education in the public schools of his native state and since laying aside his textbooks has been engaged in business. He and his brother Sam located in Sioux Falls in May, 1896, and opened up a dry-goods store in a single storeroom twenty-two feet wide, near their present location. A year later a building forty-four by one hundred and twenty-five feet was erected especially for the firm and at the end of another year a second store was added. Some years later the adjoining lot was purchased by Fantle Brothers and the store was enlarged to occupy these three fronts, sixty-six feet each, the business taking up both floors and the entire basement. In 1910 Fantle Brothers rebuilt the store and added a third story. They have modernized the entire property and the store is today ideal in its appointment, modern in detail and beautiful from every view. It has the advantage of elevators, rest rooms and writing rooms and free telephones for the customers.

When the Fantles opened their store in Sioux Falls it was a small dry-goods establishment but it has grown step by step with the advancement and development of the northwest. Not content with keeping pace with the growth of the city, Fantle Brothers have looked beyond the present, foreseeing the certain development of the northwest, and they planned the business and built the store for the future. Because of this attitude Fantle Brothers have always been reckoned with when predictions have been made of what Sioux Falls is yet to be. They have done more than build additions to their store, add new lines and increase their stock. They have built a name that counts for more than the magnitude of the business. To mention Fantle Brothers means to call to mind clean and honest merchandising, fair and honorable business methods, a policy of giving a dollar's worth of value for every dollar received. It has always been a custom for these merchants to keep in close personal touch with their customers and they employ only clerks who make friends with their patrons. They not only study how to sell merchandise but they strive to meet the wishes of the people and to completely satisfy their customers. This has been a dominating characteristic of Fantle Brothers. They do not permit their clerks to make extravagant claims to their merchandise when endeavoring to make a sale and their advertisements contain no untruthful or misleading statements. On the great first floor is found a varied stock comparable to that seen in great department stores of the largest cities. The ladies' ready-made suits and coats, the millinery, the muslin underwear and the furs are on the second floor. The third, floor has the carpets, draperies, linoleums, crockery and chinaware and house furnishing goods. The dressmaking department, which has been instituted in recent years and where the alterations in suits and cloaks are made, is in a building adjoining the main store. The basement is used for a stock room.

At St. Paul, Minnesota, in 1892, Charles Fantle married Miss Lillie Plechner and the children of this union are Bernice and Benjamin. Mr. Fantle belongs to the Elks and to the Country Club, is a blue lodge Mason and is identified also with the Knights of Pythias. He is a director in the State Bank and Trust Company of Sioux Falls. His career furnishes many splendid examples of the value of energy, perseverance and enterprise in the development of success, for his present great prosperity has been won solely by his own efforts.

WILLIAM JOEL FANTLE

William Joel Fantle scarcely needs an introduction to the readers of this volume beyond the statement that he is one of the partners in the firm of Fantle Brothers, dry goods merchants of Yankton, for this house in which he is interested is one of the foremost mercantile enterprises of the state and its policy is largely accepted as the standard of activity in that field. He bends every energy to the further upbuilding and development of the business and he comes of a family of merchants, so that his inherited tendency is in the line of his chosen vocation.

Mr. Fantle was born in Ann Arbor, Michigan, on the 1st of March, 1870, and was educated in the schools of that city and of St. Paul, Minnesota, the family having removed to the latter place when he was in his twelfth year. After leaving school he was employed in a wholesale millinery house for one year and then entered his father's store, in which he was employed through the succeeding nine years, thoroughly acquainting himself with every phase of the business and gaining intimate and accurate knowledge of modern commercial methods. He recognized the fact that close application and unremitting energy are necessary to meet the competition of the present day and he has always cultivated those qualities. In 1893 he located in Yankton and entered the dry-goods business in partnership with his brother, Moses Fantle, of whom mention is made elsewhere in this work. The venture was immediately successful, for their business methods at once won for them the confidence and patronage of the general public. Soon afterward they purchased the store of John McElroy, which they conducted until February, 1902, when the building with its contents was entirely destroyed by fire. The new store, however, rose Phoenix-like from the ashes, for they immediately began rebuilding and in February, 1903, their present store was opened to the public. Their business today constitutes one of the finest mercantile establishments of the state and is a monument to the genius, enterprise and progressiveness of the owners. The brothers constitute a strong combination, the efforts and ability of one ably supplementing and rounding out the labors of the other.

On the 12th of July, 1898, Mr. Fantle was united in marriage to Miss Carrie E. Eiseman, a daughter of Charles and Seba (Lehman) Eiseman, who were pioneer settlers of Yankton, and the father was one of the city's earliest merchants, continuing active in business there for a number of years. He is deceased but his wife now resides in Sioux City, Iowa. Mr. and Mrs. Fantle are the parents of four children, namely: Larena May, Willard Eiseman, Karl S. and Marion Belle.

Mr. Fantle holds membership in the Commercial Club and is in hearty sympathy with its purposes and its efforts to upbuild the city and extend its business connections. For five years he served as its president and under his administration the club accomplished substantial results. In politics he is independent. In Masonry he has attained the thirty-second degree of the Scottish Rite and he also has membership with the Benevolent Protective Order of Elks. He indulges in hunting, fishing and motoring when business leaves him time for recreation and he is a devotee of all healthful outdoor sports. He also greatly enjoys travel and has made extensive trips both in America and abroad. Genial, generous, and with well-earned and well-deserved prosperity, he is one of Yankton's solid citizens.

LUMAN B. FARLEY

L. B. FARLEY, proprietor of the leading drug house in Garretson, South Dakota, and a gentleman of high standing in social, as well as in the commercial and professional circles, is a native of South Dakota, and has spent all his life within its borders. His parents, L. T. and Carrie A. (Warner) Farley, came to South Dakota in 1868 from Rock County, Wisconsin, and settled in Lincoln County, where, entering land, the father engaged in farming and stock raising.

Luman B. was born on the homestead in Lincoln County, August 19, 1870, and grew up in close touch with nature, receiving his educational training in the public schools. In 1885, when a youth of fifteen, he took up the study of pharmacy and in due time, by close application and critical research, succeeded in mastering the profession, after which, in August, 1898, he engaged in business at Garretson, where, as already stated, he now owns a large and thoroughly stocked establishment, with a patronage second to that of no other drug store in the city. Mr. Farley's business career has been eminently creditable, prosecuting from the beginning a series of advancements which demonstrate not only a business ability of high order and superior professional training, but also a personal worth that has won him the confidence of the public.

Mr. Farley is a man of excellent habits, stands well with all classes of people and, being public-spirited and enterprising, gives his influence and, when necessary, his material assistance to encourage the growth and development of the city in which he resides. Fraternally he is a member of the Masonic brotherhood, also belongs to the Knights of Pythias, and in politics supports the Republican party. Mr. Farley is a married man and the father of two bright and interesting children, whose names are Wava and Roy. Mrs. Farley, formerly Miss Laura Christiansen, a native of Iowa, lived for some years in Canton, South Dakota, at which place her marriage was solemnized.

ALEXANDER O. FASSER, M. D.

Although Dr. Alexander O. Fasser, of Belle Fourche, engages to some extent in the general practice of medicine he gives the greater part of his attention to surgery and is already recognized as one of the leading surgeons of his part of the state. His birth occurred at Karlsruhe, Baden, Germany, October 9, 1878. His parents, Leonard and Mary Fasser, were both born in the same country, where the father was employed as an engineer in a gas works upon reaching years of maturity. In 1880 Mr. and Mrs. Fasser came with their family to America and settled at New Haven, Connecticut, where the father was a stationary engineer until 1913, when he retired. Both he and his wife still live in that city. He served with distinction in the Franco-Prussian war and while at the front was wounded in the leg by a cannon ball. However, he fought throughout the whole war and displayed such marked gallantry that he was awarded the iron cross and also bronze, silver and gold medals. As a further testimonial to his bravery, he has an autographed letter from Emperor William I.. To him and his wife were born seven children, of whom the subject of this review is the fourth in order of birth.

Dr. Andrew O. Fasser attended the public schools of New Haven, Connecticut, and after being engaged as a pharmacist there for eight years he prepared for Yale University at the Hopkins grammar school and later entered Yale Medical School, from which he was graduated with the degree of M. D. in 1905. His connection with the drug business began when he was fifteen years of age, when he found employment in a drug store in connection with the New Haven Hospital. He learned the business thoroughly and at the age of eighteen was licensed as a pharmacist in Connecticut. He left the New Haven Hospital at that time and for three or four years worked in the wholesale drug house of the C. W. Wittlesey Company, a New Haven concern. He then entered the employ of William Hull, a retail druggist of New Haven and remained with him for four years, after which he again entered school, as before stated. After graduating from Yale Medical School in 1905 he was appointed house surgeon of the New Haven Hospital and served in that capacity for twenty-two months and then was for six months connected with the Lying-in Hospital of New York and subsequently was house officer for two seasons at the Boston Floating Hospital. He then returned to New Haven and practiced medicine for six months, at the end of which time he was seized with the western fever and removed to the Black Hills, practicing for two years in Sturgis. At the end of that time, he settled in Vale, where he remained for two years and then removed to Belle Fourche, arriving there in 1909. In the years that have since come and gone he has built up an enviable reputation, especially as a surgeon. He is intensely interested in the development of modern surgery and the wonderful discoveries along that line which are constantly being made and which open up new possibilities in the restoration of health and the saving of life. He not only keeps in touch with the results of the experiments of investigators in the field of surgery but is also scrupulously conscientious in the care of his patients, giving them the benefit of his closest attention and best knowledge. Dr. Fasser has thoroughly identified himself with the Black Hills country and owns a stock ranch five miles south of Vale, which he devotes to the raising of sheep and hogs. It comprises three hundred and twenty acres and is well irrigated.

Dr. Fasser was married on the 1st of June, 1911, to Miss Inez Goddard, who was born near Hot Springs, this state, a daughter of Lon and Inez (Moses) Goddard, both natives of Texas. They were among the early settlers in Dakota territory and the father served in the first territorial legislature and also held various other offices of trust and responsibility. He passed away at Hot Springs following an operation for appendicitis and his widow now resides with Dr. and Mrs. Fasser.

The Doctor is independent politically, his religious affiliation is that of the Protestant Episcopal church and he is a member of the Masonic order. Along professional lines he belongs to the Black Hills Medical Society and the American Medical Association. He is a man of that progressive and energetic type that is so rapidly building up the state of South Dakota along all lines and is recognized as one of the valued and useful citizens of Belle Fourche.

WILLIAM EDWARD FEHLIMAN, M. D.

Among the up-to-date and successful physicians and surgeons of Lead is Dr. William Edward Fehliman, who has gained a high place in local circles of his profession. He was born near Goshen, Indiana, on the 16th of September, 1880, a son of Robert and Amanda (Gonzer) Fehliman. The father was born in Berne, Switzerland, and as he was early left an orphan, came to America with two brothers when but a child of eight years. They settled in Ohio in 1857 but shortly afterward went to De Kalb County, Indiana, where Robert Fehliman learned the carpenter's trade. In 1861 he enlisted in the Twenty-ninth Indiana Volunteer Infantry and served for four years and three months as a private. He later followed his trade in the United States Army for one year, but at the end of that time returned to De Kalb County, Indiana, and in 1867 removed to the vicinity of South Omaha, Nebraska. In 1868 he homesteaded in the Elkhorn valley there. He and his wife both survive and make their home in Cuming County, Nebraska. He is living retired, as his former labor enabled him to accumulate more than a competence, and the evening of his life is being spent in well-earned ease.

Dr. Fehliman is the fifth in order of birth in a family of nine children. He was reared in Cuming County, Nebraska, and his elementary education was acquired in a log schoolhouse. He subsequently attended the high school of Beemer, Nebraska, from which he was graduated. After leaving school he became a railway telegraph operator, working in that capacity for the Chicago & Northwestern, the Chicago, Burlington & Quincy, the Northern Pacific and the Oregon Short Line Railroads. Owing to operator's paralysis he gave up this work and entered the Fremont Normal School at Fremont, Nebraska, where he prepared himself for the study of medicine. After a year spent there, he matriculated in 1902 in Rush Medical College, the medical department of the University of Chicago. In 1906 he received his degree of M. D. and completed his professional preparation by two years spent as an interne. For six months of that time, he was in the Milwaukee General Hospital and for eighteen months was interne of the Cook County (Ill.) Hospital. In July, 1908, he came to Lead, South Dakota, and opened an office for the practice of his profession. In the intervening years he has built up a reputation as a successful physician and surgeon, being an able diagnostician and using the most approved methods of treatment. He keeps in touch with the latest developments in the fields of medical and surgical research and gives his patients the benefit of the constantly increasing knowledge of the medical fraternity. He is a member of the Black Hills Medical Society and the South Dakota State Medical Society and takes a great interest in their proceedings.

In January, 1911, Dr. Fehliman was united in marriage with Miss Lola Shackleford, of Lead. The Doctor is a member of Beemer (Nebr.) Lodge, No. 253, A. F. & A. M.; Golden Belt Chapter, No. 35, R. A. M., of Lead; and Lead Commandery, No. 18, K. T.. He affiliates with the republican party but has not been active in politics. Since 1909 he has been superintendent of the Lawrence County board of health and has done able work in that connection, paying especial attention to public hygiene. He is fond of outdoor life and finds much of his recreation in hunting. Professionally he holds the respect of his colleagues and of the public, and as a man and citizen is held in high esteem by all who know him, as in all relations of life he conforms his conduct to high ethical standards.

E. W. FEIGE., M. D.

E. W. FEIGE, one of the successful young physicians and surgeons of the state, established in the practice of his profession at Woonsocket, Sanborn County, was born on a farm near the city of St. Joseph, Missouri, on the 9th of August, 1871, and is a son of William and Frieda (Werner) Feige. He accompanied his parents upon their removal to the territory of Dakota, and he completed a course in the high school at Huron, South Dakota, being graduated as a member of the class of 1891, and he then took up the study of medicine. In the fall of 1892, the subject was matriculated in the Chicago Homeopathic Medical College, where he completed the prescribed course, being graduated with the degree of Doctor of Medicine. After his graduation he located in Hawarden, Iowa, where he was engaged in practice until December, 1896, when he located in Alpena, South Dakota, where he continued his professional work until he established himself in practice at Woonsocket, where he has since resided and where he has secured a most gratifying support. The Doctor is a stanch supporter of the principles of the Republican party, is a member of the Presbyterian church in his home town and has become affiliated with the Masonic fraternity.

ALLEN R. FELLOWS

Wide experience, keen insight and business discrimination have formed the basis of the success of Allen R. Fellows, one of the leading and valued business men of Sioux Falls. He is vice president and general manager of the Brown Drug Company and he holds a position of prominence and importance in business circles of the city. He was born on a farm in Cook County, Illinois, April 21, 1866, and is a son of Jonathan and Charlotte Augusta (Rich) Fellows. The father was a native of New York state, as was also the grandfather of the subject of this review, Samuel Fellows. The family came from England and is of Scotch-Irish descent.

Allen R. Fellows acquired his education in the public schools of Dunton, now Arlington Heights, Cook County, Illinois, and in the public schools of Chicago, completing the grammar-school course in 1879. He began his business career as clerk in a wholesale drug house in Chicago at three dollars a week and remained with this concern for eleven years, rising by the force of his ability and energy to be city buyer, a position in which his salary was thirty-five dollars per week. Following this Mr. Fellows was for eight years salesman for Lord, Owen & Company, wholesale druggists of Chicago, whom he represented in Dakota territory. In 1898 he resigned that position and entered the employ of Humeston, Keeling & Company, owners of another Chicago wholesale drug house, becoming their stock buyer. At the end of four years, he bought an interest in a manufacturing drug house in Chicago and at the end of a similar period of time disposed of his interests in that concern and located in Sioux Falls, buying an interest in the Brown Drug Company, of which he has since been vice president and general manager. He understands the drug business in all of its departments and his energetic and well-directed efforts are important factors in the growth of the concern with which he is connected.

On the 1st of January, 1888, in Chicago, Illinois, Mr. Fellows married Miss Harriet E. Le Fever and they have become the parents of three children: Lulu Augusta, a graduate of Carleton College of Northfield, Minnesota, and now a teacher in the high school at Princeton, Minnesota; Harriet Lindwood, who was graduated from Beloit College in 1912; and Agnes Edna, a student in Carleton College at Northfield, Minnesota.

Mr. Fellows belongs to the Masonic order, holding membership in the Shrine, and is also a member of the Elks and of the Dacotah and the Commercial Clubs. He is president of the Sioux Falls Country Club and president of the Credit Men's Association of Sioux Falls. His political allegiance is given to the republican party. Throughout his business career he has manifested an aptitude for successful management and his labors have resulted in the attainment of a prosperity which now places him among the men of affluence in this city.

ROBERT FERRIS

Extensive and important are the business interests which Robert Ferris controls as a member of the firm of Ferris Brothers of Yankton, South Dakota. He was born October 11, 1870, at Burnfoot Hill in Ayrshire, Scotland, his parents being Moses and Margaret (Barris) Ferris, who were natives of the north of Ireland and were there reared and married. They removed from the Emerald Isle to Ayrshire, Scotland, and in 1879 came to the United States, settling in Lowell, Massachusetts. Their family included the following named: W. J., now a resident of La Crosse, Wisconsin; Thomas, who is located at Osage, Iowa; James W., living at Watertown, South Dakota; Mrs. William L. True, of Dells Dam at Columbia, Wisconsin; and Robert.

The last-named attended school in Scotland until nine years of age. Afterward he pursued a course of study in the grammar schools of Lowell, Massachusetts, and in the night schools of that city. In early life he learned and followed the machinist's trade and gradually advanced in that connection from a machinist in the shops to a position where he was given charge of the erection of electrical equipment on the road: He was afterward made salesman of electrical machinery and in 1901 became associate director of the Electric Light and Power properties, of which he has been one of the owners. He is a member of the firm of Ferris Brothers, owners of electric light and power properties, having had properties at Monmouth, Illinois; Franklin and Union City, Indiana; Osage and Eldora, Iowa; and Yankton and Watertown, South Dakota. In addition to being president of the Watertown Light & Power Company he is secretary of the Osage Light, Heat & Power Company and secretary treasurer of the Yankton Light, Heat & Power Company.

On the 10th of October, 1906, at Yankton, Mr. Ferris was united in marriage to Miss Helen S. Donaldson, a daughter of Fred Donaldson, of Yankton, and a graduate of Yankton College. Her people were early pioneer settlers of this part of the state. The children of this marriage are Elinor Roberta, Edmund Arthur and Robert Martin.

In his political views Mr. Ferris has always been a stalwart republican. He has an interesting military chapter in his life record inasmuch as he was a member of Company O, Sixth Massachusetts Volunteer Infantry, and a member of the Massachusetts Ambulance Corps in 1908. Fraternally he is connected with the Elks and in Masonry has attained the Knights Templar degree and the thirty-second degree of the Scottish Rite in the Consistory. He is a past president of the Yankton Commercial Association and was formerly a member of the Union League Club of Chicago.

Mr. Ferris has always carried large responsibilities and is a keen student of commercial affairs. It was this which led to his nomination by the local banks for the position of class B, director in group I of district 9 of the Federal Reserve Bank of Minneapolis. The Dakota Herald in a comment upon the nomination said: "Mr. Ferris is not only a man of methodical, analytical mind, but is possessed of the powers of business initiative to an unusual degree. The testimony of his abilities is the steady and consistent expansion of his own business projects. 'A great many make money' because of fortunate speculations or strict economy, of whom it cannot be said they are good business men. They gain results from the magnitude or fortuitous placing of their investments, rather than from the logical planning of their enterprises, and a conservation of its every possibility by strict attention to detail. It can be written of Robert Ferris that he is a 'good business man' under the strict interpretation of that expression, and if the honor which is being sought for him should be accorded, Yankton will never be called upon to apologize for its representation on the reserve board." Another paper wrote: "Mr. Ferris is eminently fitted for the duties of the position. He has a clear, analytical mind, is a close and accurate reasoner and is fitted in mental powers and temperament for the exacting duties of the office. He has for many years been connected with large business and his uniform success on conservative lines in the handling of public utilities has brought him in touch with the financiers of that part of the country within the district he would represent if chosen. He has enjoyed liberal credit and has built up some splendid enterprises. His chances for success seem extremely good and it is certain that no better man for the position could be found in the whole district."

Mr. Ferris is a typical business man of the present day. He is alert, ready to meet any emergency and equally ready to grasp any opportunity, and thus it is that he has become firmly established in the public regard as one of the representative citizens and business men of Yankton.

NELSON LEE FINCH

Nelson L. FINCH, resident of the Citizens' State Bank of Andover, Andover, Day County, is a native of the Empire state of the Union, having been born in Broadalbin, Fulton County, New York, on the 12th of January, 1873, a son of William W. and Carrie (Lee) Finch, both of whom were likewise born in the state of New York, being of English and English-French lineage respectively. The subject of this sketch attended the public schools of his native town until he had attained the age of ten years, when, in 1883, he accompanied his parents on their removal to South Dakota, the family locating in Andover, Day County, where the father engaged in the mercantile business. Here Nelson continued to attend the public schools until 1889, during which year and that following he was a student in the South Dakota State Agricultural College, at Brookings, as a member of the class of 1893. In 1890 he continued his educational discipline in the Curtiss Commercial College, in Minneapolis, Minnesota, being graduated in July of that year. He then returned to his home in Andover and was thereafter associated with his father in the management of his business affairs until 1895. In January of that year his parents removed to New York state, our subject purchasing at that time his father's general merchandise business in Andover. This enterprise he successfully conducted until June, 1897, when he sold the same to E. C. Toy and soon afterward effected the organization of the Citizens' Bank, of which he continued proprietor and manager until July, 1902, when the institution was reorganized and incorporated as the Citizens' State Bank, and Mr. Finch has been its president from its inception, while Wallace Finch, of Gloversville, New York, is vice-president, and J. W. Krueger, cashier. The bank has a capital and surplus of twenty-five thousand dollars and is one of the solid and well-managed financial concerns of the state. The bank building is a substantial and attractive brick structure and the counting rooms are modern in their equipment and facilities, a portion of the building being utilized for the offices of the Day County Land Company. Of this latter corporation Mr. Finch was one of the organizers, in 1898, and when it was incorporated, in 1902, he was elected secretary and treasurer, which dual office he held until November 1, 1903. In December of the same year Mr. Finch disposed of his stock and retired from the institution.

Mr. Finch was the first president of the Andover Hotel Company, owners of the magnificent Hotel Waldorf, recently erected in Andover, and for several years was a director and executive officer in two other corporations there. He is president of the board of education, and has ever taken a deep and helpful interest in educational affairs and in all else that makes for the well-being of his home town, county and state.

Mr. Finch is a member of the Baptist church, and fraternally is a Knight Templar, a thirty-second-degree Mason and a Noble of the Mystic Shrine. In politics he is a stanch Republican, and while he has taken an active part in the promotion of the party cause he has never sought or held official preferment, except that of city treasurer, of which he has been continuously incumbent since 1897. He enjoys the highest popularity in business and social circles and is one of the progressive and able young business men of South Dakota. Mr. Finch is a bachelor.

WILLIAM H. FINCH

William H. Finch, who for a number of years was the popular and efficient steward of the Commercial Club at Aberdeen, was born at Windham, Greene County, New York, in 1839, a son of Rubel and Catherine (Bliss) Finch, the former a stock-dealer in the state of New York. The son spent his youthful days in the Empire state, acquiring a public-school education, and following the outbreak of the Civil war he joined the army, enlisting as a member of the One Hundred and Forty-fourth New York Regiment, of which he became quartermaster sergeant. He served throughout the period of hostilities, participating in a number of hotly contested engagements and on every battlefield proving his loyalty to the old flag and the cause which it represented.

At the close of the war Mr. Finch returned to New York, but in early manhood removed to Wisconsin, where he resided for a considerable period. In March, 1886, he arrived in Aberdeen, South Dakota, and for a year was proprietor of the Artesian Hotel. On the expiration of that period, he purchased a harness store, which he conducted for several years. When the Commercial Club started, he was chosen its steward and continued in that position for seven years, or until he was obliged to retire on account of ill health. He was a most popular steward, giving to the club splendid service in every particular and winning many friends among, its membership.

In 1868 Mr. Finch was united in marriage, at Reedsburg, Wisconsin, to Miss Mary Dwinnell, and they became the parents of five children, of whom four are living: Eva, now the wife of G. B. Kimberly, of Beresford, South Dakota; Essie, the wife of W. S. Gilmor, of Aberdeen; Marion, who is a teacher in a deaf-mute school at Salem, Oregon; and Lela H., who is a teacher of voice in the Normal School at Aberdeen. The family circle was broken by the hand of death when on the 24th of October, 1912, the husband and father was called from this life.

He had ever been a public-spirited citizen and one whose value and worth were greatly appreciated by all who knew him in Aberdeen. He served as justice of the peace and his decisions were strictly fair and impartial. His political allegiance was given to the republican party and his fraternal relations were with the Masons. In that order he attained high rank, becoming a member of the Mystic Shrine. He exemplified in his life its beneficent spirit and his entire career was characterized by fidelity to duty whether upon the battlefield, in public office or in connection with the duties that came to him in a business way. He left behind him many friends, who sincerely mourn his loss.

JOHN H. FIREY

J. H. FIREY, one of the representative business men of the city of Aberdeen, is a native of the state of Illinois, having been born in Edinburg, Christian County, on the 13th of November, 1859, and being a son of Henry and Minerva (Lord) Firey, the former of whom was born in Maryland and the latter in Ohio, the paternal grandfather, Joseph F. Firey, having been likewise born in Maryland. Joseph Tilden Lord, the maternal grandfather, who was an early pioneer in Ohio, was born in Vermont, and migrated to Ohio, and was a soldier in the war of 1812, in which connection he served under General William Henry Harrison, having been present at the battle of Tippecanoe, and also that of the Thames, where the famous Indian warrior, Tecumseh, met his death. Joseph F. Firey was a pioneer of Illinois. He removed to Sangamon County, and settled near the site of the present city of Springfield, the capital of that state. The old homestead still remains in the possession of the family, and there the grandfather died when seventy years of age. The maternal grandfather of the subject likewise became a pioneer of Illinois, and was there accidentally killed shortly after locating in the state, in the later thirties. The father of the subject of this sketch continued to follow the vocation to which he had been reared, becoming a successful and influential farmer of Sangamon County, where both he and his wife passed the closing years of their lives. Of their eight children seven are living, John H. having been the youngest of the family.

John H. Firey was reared on the old homestead farm and received his preliminary educational training in the district schools, after which he continued his studies in Carthage College, at Carthage, Illinois, where he was graduated as a member of the class of 1882. On the 17th of August of that year, he made his advent in what is now the city of Aberdeen, South Dakota, the place having been at that time scarcely more than a frontier village. He had previously become a registered pharmacist in Illinois and upon locating in Aberdeen he at once established himself in the retail drug business. His enterprise proved successful from its initiation and with the rapid settling of the surrounding country and the development and substantial upbuilding of Aberdeen tile business rapidly increased in scope and importance, so that he gradually developed a manufacturing and jobbing department, and it was this feature that led to his becoming one of the organizers and incorporators of the Jewett Drug Company, in 1903, while he is one of the stockholders in the concern and in the same holds the office manager. The company utilize a fine building, one hundred by one hundred and fifty feet in dimensions, four stories in height, besides basement, and constructed of light-colored pressed brick, with granite trimmings, and the wholesale and jobbing business already built up far surpasses the most sanguinary expectations of the interested principals, while the enterprise is a distinctive acquisition to the jobbing interests of the city. Mr. Firey is the general manager of the business and is handling its affairs with marked discrimination, being straightforward in his methods, forming his plans readily and carrying them to proper execution, and thus proving an able administrative officer and a business man who commands unqualified confidence and esteem.

In politics he gives his allegiance to the Democratic party, and he has held various local offices, including that of postmaster of Aberdeen, to which position he was appointed in 1885, serving four years. Fraternally he is identified with the lodge, chapter and commandery of the Masonic order and also with the Ancient Order of United Workmen. On the 25th of January, 1883, Mr. Firey was united in marriage to Miss Sue A. Mack, of Carthage, Illinois, she being a daughter of David Mack, a leading member of the bar of that section and president of the Hancock National Bank of Carthage. Of this union have been born two children, Carl R., who is an assistant in the drug establishment of which his father is manager, and Margaret, who is still attending school.

LEWIS L. FLEEGER

L. L. FLEEGER, an able and representative member of the legal profession in Turner County, is a native of the old Keystone state, having been born in Butler County, Pennsylvania, on the 12th of December, 1864, and being a son of Samuel L. and Mary A. (Pierce) Fleeger. When he was but two years of age his parents removed to Missouri and located in Cooper County, where his father engaged in farming, and in that county the subject secured his early educational discipline in the public schools, while he was reared to the sturdy life of the homestead farm. He continued his studies for some time in Clarksburg College, at Clarksburg, Missouri, and then entered Waynesburg College, at Waynesburg, Pennsylvania, where he was graduated as a member of the class of 1889, receiving the degree of Bachelor of Arts. After his graduation he took up the reading of law in the office of his cousin, George Fleeger, of Butler, Pennsylvania, one of the representative members of the bar of that section, and under this preceptorship continued his technical studies for two years, at the expiration of which, in the autumn of 1891, he returned to Missouri, and for the following years was engaged as instructor in mathematics in Clarksburg College, in which institution he had previously been a student, as has been noted in this context. In the autumn of 1892, he came to South Dakota and located in the city of Yankton, where he was shortly afterward admitted to the bar of the state, and there he was for a short interval engaged in the practice of his profession. In the spring of 1893, he came to Turner County and located in the village of Centerville, where he was engaged in practice about eighteen months, at the expiration of which he took up his residence in Parker, the judicial center of the county, where he has since been successfully established in practice, controlling a large and representative clientage. In politics Mr. Fleeger is a stalwart advocate of the principles and policies of the Republican party and he is one of its wheelhorses in Turner County, having served for the past four years as chairman of the Republican central committee of the county and having handled his forces with marked skill and discrimination in the furtherance of the interests of his party. In the autumn of 1893, he was elected state's attorney of the county and served in this capacity for two terms, or four consecutive years, making an admirable record as prosecutor.

Fraternally he is affiliated with Parker Lodge, No. 30, Ancient Free and Accepted Masons. On the 5th of November, 1899, Mr. Fleeger was united in marriage to Miss Cliffie M. Elliott, daughter of Judge W. Elliott, of Parker, and of this union has been born one son, Samuel Boyd.

JOHN K. FORMIS, M. D.

Dr. John K. Formis, an able and successful young physician and surgeon of Lennox, South Dakota, has practiced in that city since 1910 and has won an enviable reputation as a representative of the profession. His birth occurred in Germany on the 3d of July, 1880, his parents being Oscar and Mary (Cassilly) Formis. The father is deceased, but the mother survives and now makes her home in Florence, Italy.

John K. Formis acquired his education in the Real Gymnasium of his native country and subsequently studied chemistry for two years. Having determined upon a professional career and desiring to enjoy the greater opportunities of the new world, he crossed the Atlantic to the United States and matriculated in the Northwestern University Medical School of Chicago, Illinois, from which institution he was graduated in 1909. He began practice in that city but at the end of a year came to Lennox, South Dakota, which has since remained the scene of his professional labors. His practice has steadily grown with the increase of population, for he has demonstrated his skill and ability in successfully coping with the Intricate problems that continually confront the physician in his efforts to restore health and prolong life. He writes the "Department of Health" for the local paper and has made it a valuable and instructive feature of the journal.

In August, 1907, Dr. Formis was united in marriage to Miss Avis Thompson, a daughter of Thomas Thompson, of Utah. He is a Protestant in religious faith and politically a progressive republican. Fraternally he is identified with Lennox Lodge, No. 35, A. F. & A. M., and the Modern Woodmen of America, acting as examining physician for the local organization of the latter order. Dr. Formis is popular in both professional and social circles of his community and has many friends who esteem him highly.

JAMES H. FONGER, M. D.

Each community has in it men who are recognized as leaders in their special line of activity, and among the representatives of medical practice in Deuel County is James H. Fonger, whose ability places him with the leading physicians and surgeons of Gary. Early in his career he recognized that thorough study must constitute the foundation of his success, and close application, wide reading and conscientious performance of all his duties have since been salient features in his professional career. He was born in Bangor, Michigan, May 14, 1875, the only child of James R. and Flora Fonger. The father was a druggist, conducting business in Michigan until the fall of 1879, when he brought his family to South Dakota, settling at Gary, where he opened the first drug store of the town. Later the business was purchased by Mr. Rowland, who in turn resold it to Mr. Fonger, and the father is still actively engaged in its management. Both he and his wife are well known in Gary, their many sterling traits of character having gained for them warm friendship and high regard.

James H. Fonger supplemented a public-school education by a business course in Watertown and afterward entered Hamline University, from which he was graduated on the completion of a course in medicine with the class of 1900. He then returned to Gary and entered upon active practice there. He has since taken post-graduate work in the College of Physicians and Surgeons at Chicago and for one year was assistant bacteriologist for the city of Minneapolis. He has since practiced in Gary and has the major part of the surgical work. He has a hospital and has performed many difficult operations which indicate his expert skill and ability in this direction. He is also physician at the state school for the blind located at Gary and he has an extensive private practice.

Dr. Fonger holds membership in the Presbyterian church and he is connected with various fraternal organizations, belonging to Gates City Lodge, No. 14, A. F. & A. M., the Odd Fellows society, the Benevolent Protective Order of Elks at Watertown and the Royal Neighbors. He held the commission of captain of Company H, Third Regiment South Dakota National Guard until the disbanding of the company when he was transferred to the medical staff. He enjoys hunting, fishing and motoring and has an especially fine collection of relics in the shape of guns of various age and workmanship. His political allegiance is given to the democratic party, but while he believes in its principles, he has neither time nor inclination to seek office. Anything which tends to bring to man the key to the complex mystery which we call life is of interest to him. He is conscientious in his practice and broad reading kept him thoroughly informed concerning modern methods and standards.

CHARLES BOYD FONCANON

C. B. Foncanon, who is engaged in the real-estate and loan business in Eureka, and who is a member of the board of commissioners of McPherson County, was born in Millard, Missouri, on the 22d of April, 1869, being a son of Michael B. and Julia S. (Beatty) Foncanon, both of whom were born in Fairfield County, Ohio, the former tracing his lineage to the sturdy Holland Dutch stock which settled in the state of New York in the colonial epoch of our national history, while the maternal ancestry is of Scotch-Irish extraction, the original progenitors in America having come hither in the middle of the eighteenth century and having served with the Pennsylvania troops in the war of the Revolution. The parents of the subject removed to Missouri prior to the war of the Rebellion, having been a resident of the state during the days when it was the center of the border warfare, while the father served as a valiant soldier in defense of the Union, having been a member of the Seventh Missouri Volunteer Cavalry during the war. Charles B. Foncanon received his early education in the public schools of his native place, later attended the North Missouri State Normal School, at Kirksville. in which he was graduated as a member of the class of 1890.

and thereafter he took a special course in the Missouri State University. After leaving college he was for two years superintendent of the public schools at La Plata, Missouri, and in 1894 he came to Eureka, South Dakota, where he was for four years principal of the schools, and in 1898 he was elected superintendent of schools for McPherson County, retaining this incumbency four years, at the expiration of which he established himself in his present line of enterprise, noted in the initial paragraph, being one of the successful real-estate dealers of this section of the state and also making a specialty of financial loans on real-estate security of approved order. Mr. Foncanon is a stanch advocate of the principles of the Republican party, and in the fall of 1902, he was elected county commissioner from the fifth district of McPherson County, in which capacity he is now serving.

He is identified with the National Guard of the state, being adjutant of the First Battalion of the First Regiment, with the rank of first lieutenant. Fraternally he is identified with Eureka Lodge, No. 58, Knights of Pythias; Acacia Lodge, No. 108, Ancient Free and Accepted Masons: Batchelder Lodge of Perfection, No. 6, South Dakota Consistory No. 4, Ancient Accepted Scottish Rite, at Aberdeen, and El Riad Temple of the Mystic Shrine, at Sioux Falls. On the 18th of June, 1900 was solemnized the marriage of Mr. Foncanon to Miss Ottilia M. Hinz, who was born in Manchester, Wisconsin. November 12, 1879, being a daughter of Louis and Minerva Hinz. Mr. and Mrs. Foncanon have a winsome little daughter, Vivian Maurine, born May 4, 1901.

SAMUEL EDGAR FOREST

Samuel E. FOREST, cashier of the First National Bank of Britton, Marshall County, is a native of the city of Brooklyn, New York, where he was born on the 23d of April, 1865, being a son of Samuel A. and Lydia E. (Mortimer) Forest, the former of whom was born in England and the latter in the state of New York, while they are now living in St. Paul, Minnesota, moving there from Brooklyn in 1886, the father being a merchant by vocation. The subject of this sketch was reared to manhood in his native city, in whose public schools he secured his early educational discipline, while in 1880 he entered the celebrated Polytechnic Institute of that city, where he completed the collegiate course and was graduated as a member of the class of 1884. He initiated his business career in 1884, when he entered the employ of the Standard Oil Company, in New York City. He remained with that company for three years. In 1887 he came west to St. Paul, and in 1889 to Britton, South Dakota, and engaged in the lumber and coal business in the firm of Hamilton & Forest. He served as county treasurer of Marshall County in 1896. He was one of the organizers of the Citizens' Bank, of which he was cashier, but when the Citizens' was succeeded by the First National Bank he continued as cashier of the latter.

In politics Mr. Forest is a member of the Republican party. Fraternally he is affiliated with the Ancient Free and Accepted Masons, belonging to the chapter and commandery, and the Ancient Arabic Order of the Nobles of the Mystic Shrine; also, to the Ancient Order of United Workmen and the local organization of the Mutual Benefit Association.

On the 24th of January, 1900, Mr. Forest was united in marriage to Miss Frances C. Hall, who was born in Canandaigua, New York, being a daughter of S. P. and Mary Hall. They have one daughter, Margaret Elizabeth.

A. W. FOSSUM, D. D. S.

Dr. A. W. Fossum, who since 1898 has engaged in the practice of dentistry at Aberdeen, winning a place among the leading representatives of his profession in the city, was born in Lansing, Iowa, June 22, 1874. He is a son of A. C. and Walborg (Engobrefsen) Fossum, the former a pioneer in South Dakota. He came to this state in 1881 and was joined by his wife and children in the following year, the family making their home for some time in a sod shanty on a tract of government land which the father had taken up. He afterward engaged in the building and contracting business and became widely and favorably known in this locality.

After acquiring a public-school education Dr. Fossum entered the Chicago College of Dental Surgery, from which he received his degree of D. D. S. in 1898. In the same year he came to Aberdeen and opened an office. Here he has since engaged in the practice of his profession. His patronage has increased yearly and has now reached extensive proportions, being an excellent evidence of Dr. Fossum's skill and ability and of his standing in the eyes of the community.

On the 9th of August, 1899, Dr. Fossum was united in marriage to Miss Nellie Louise Wilson, a daughter of F. D. Wilson, of Aberdeen, and they have become the parents of two daughters. Dr. Fossum is a member of the Masonic lodge, chapter, commandery and Shrine and belongs also to the Benevolent Protective Order of Elks and the Knights of Pythias, of which he is the keeper of records and seals of Aberdeen Lodge, No. 55. He is a member of the Presbyterian church and gives his political allegiance to the republican party. He keeps in close touch with the advancement of his profession along all lines and his ability in his chosen field is pronounced.

CARVELL O. FOSSUM, D. D. S.

Dr. Carvell O. Fossum, engaged in the practice of dentistry in Aberdeen in partnership with his brother, Dr. A. W. Fossum, was born in Chicago in 1878, and is a son of A. C. and Walborg (Engobretsen) Fossum, of whom further mention is made elsewhere in this work. In the family were eight children: Dr. A. W., a partner of the subject of this review; Mrs. Nels Johnson, of Aberdeen; Dr. Carvell O.; George, who follows the profession of architecture; Thor, practicing dentistry in Groton, South Dakota; Andrew, Jr.; Louise, who holds the position of department clerk of courts; and Harry, who died at the age of seventeen.

Dr. Carvell O. Fossum spent his boyhood upon a farm and acquired his early education in the district school. Following this he entered the Chicago College of Dental Surgery, from which he was graduated with the degree of D. D. S. in 1901. He immediately located in Aberdeen, where he has since engaged in practice in partnership with his brother. He is a worthy exponent of the most advanced methods of dental practice and his ability is widely recognized and has brought him a large and growing patronage.

On the 13th of December, 1903, Dr. Fossum was united in marriage to Miss Daisy M. Shaft, a daughter of Fred S. Shaft, and they have become the parents of two children, a son and a daughter. Dr. Fossum is a member of the Masonic lodge, the Knights of Pythias and the Benevolent Protective Order of Elks, and he belongs to the Presbyterian church. His political allegiance is given to the republican party and he is now serving capably and conscientiously as a member of the city park board. He enjoys a large practice, is a progressive citizen and one whose position in the community is enviable, as the expression of public opinion regarding him is altogether favorable.

JESS W. FOSTER, M. D.

Dr. Jess W. Foster, engaged in the practice of medicine and surgery in Aurora, is one of the younger representatives of the profession, yet already has displayed ability and attained a professional position that many an older man might well envy. He was born in Fayette County, Iowa, on the 14th of September, 1886, and is a son of John A. and Jessie (McNaught) Foster, both of whom were natives of Scotland. They came to the United States in childhood with their respective parents and settled in McKeesport, Pennsylvania, where they were reared and eventually married. From early manhood the father worked in the coal mines of Pennsylvania until his removal to Iowa about 1870. He was a veteran of the Civil war, being among the first to respond to the call for troops following the outbreak of hostilities in 1861. He enlisted as a member of Company E, Fourth Pennsylvania Cavalry, and served with that command throughout the war, participating in a number of hotly contested engagements. When peace was restored, he returned to Pennsylvania, after which he continued work in the coal mines until 1870, when he came to the west, settling in Fayette County, Iowa, where he took up a homestead and began farming. For some time, he carried on general agricultural pursuits but in his later years he retired from farm work and removed to Arlington, where his death occurred in January, 1913, while his widow still resides there.

Dr. Foster spent his youthful days under the parental roof and after attending the district schools continued his education in Arlington, passing through consecutive grades until he became a high-school pupil. Later he took up the study of medicine, for he believed that he would enjoy the practice of that profession, and in 1906 he entered the medical department of the State University of Iowa at Iowa City, spending a year as a student in that institution. He next entered the medical department of the Northwestern University at Chicago and was graduated therefrom with the class of 1910. Immediately after the completion of his course he located for practice at Lake Preston, South Dakota, where he successfully followed his profession for three years. In August, 1913, he went to Brookings, where he remained until he removed to Aurora, where he is enjoying a fine practice.

Dr. Foster recently erected in Brookings a handsome residence, which is supplied with all modern improvements, equipment and conveniences and which he sold advantageously. In 1911 he was united in marriage to Miss Blanche Welch of Arlington, Iowa, and they have gained many friends. Dr. Foster belongs to the Brookings Commercial Club and has membership in Brookings Lodge, No. 24, F. & A. M. He is a member of the Third District Medical Society of South Dakota, of the State Medical Society and the American Medical Association. He has built up a remunerative practice and undoubtedly has a bright professional career before him. He and his wife are members of the Methodist Episcopal church and their sterling traits of character have established them in the high regard of their fellow townsmen.

JOHN R. FOSTER

John R. Foster, who has been a resident of Minnehaha County for more than four decades, was long and successfully identified with agricultural pursuits here and still owns four hundred acres of productive land in Benton township. He is now living retired at Sioux Falls, enjoying the fruits of his former labor in well-earned ease. His birth occurred in Stormont County, Ontario, Canada, on the 23d of January, 1851, his parents being Robert and Lilly Foster, of Irish descent. In 1865 they crossed the border into the United States, took up their abode in Wisconsin and there remained until 1872, when they came to South Dakota with horses and oxen, arriving in this state on the 3d of October. Robert Foster homesteaded a tract of land in Benton township, Minnehaha County, and continued its cultivation successfully until he passed away in 1886 at the age of sixty-seven years. The demise of his wife occurred in 1911, when she had attained the age of ninety-one years. They were among the early pioneer residents of the state. On the 7th of January, 1873, a brother and sister of our subject, aged respectively fourteen and twelve years, went a short distance from home and soon afterward a blizzard came up suddenly. The children wandered in the storm to an old sod house which stood out on the prairie and there sought shelter from the driving snow. However, as the house was roofless it afforded but poor protection against the blizzard and the children perished, their bodies being buried in the snow. Our subject and the father were absent from home at the time. Weeks passed and in spite of continued searching the bodies of the children were not found, but in March a neighbor dreamed that the children were in the old house and on the 16th of that month their bodies were found there.

John R. Foster acquired his education in the common schools and early became familiar with the work of the fields by assisting his father in the operation of the home farm. He homesteaded a tract of land in Benton township which is still in his possession and has extended the boundaries of the place by purchase until it now comprises four hundred acres. Success has attended his undertakings as an agriculturist in gratifying degree. His sole possessions at the time of his arrival in this state consisted of a yoke of cattle and sixty-two and a half dollars in cash. He did not own a wagon. By dint of industry, perseverance and energy he gradually accumulated a competence and at length, finding it increasingly difficult to secure competent help, he retired from the farm. He and his wife and daughter then removed to California but soon returned to South Dakota and in 1914 he purchased a residence on Covell avenue, where he has since made his home.

In 1886 at Hartford Mr. Foster was united in marriage to Miss Jennie Forney, who was born in Pennsylvania but who, when seventeen years old, came to South Dakota with her parents, Mr. and Mrs. P. J. Forney, pioneers of the state. In their family were seven children. Mr. and Mrs. Foster have three children: Harold E., a farmer of Benton township; Goldie M., who is the wife of C. G. Hall, of Wayne township, Minnehaha County; and Vina I., at home.

In politics Mr. Foster is independent, preferring not to be bound by party ties in performing his duties of citizenship. The cause of education finds in him a stanch champion and he has served as a member of the school board for many years. His religious faith is that of the Methodist church, while fraternally he is identified with the Masons, belonging to Hartford Lodge, A. F. & A. M. Throughout the entire period of his residence in Minnehaha County and South Dakota he has contributed in substantial measure to community growth and upbuilding, and his leisure is the reward of many years of earnest and faithful labor.

CHARLES ARTHUR FOUNTAIN

Charles Arthur Fountain, cashier of the Commercial Bank of Watertown, was born in Nashua, Iowa, on the 7th of November, 1858, a son of George H. and Dolly A. (Brown) Fountain, the former a native of the state of New York and the latter of Illinois, where they were married, the father having gone to that state when a young man. Immediately following their marriage, they removed to New Hampton, Iowa, where Mr. Fountain opened a hotel, and subsequently he removed with his family to Nashua, Iowa, where he also conducted a hotel for a time. He afterward embarked in merchandising and was thus prominently and successfully identified with commercial pursuits for many years, but eventually disposed of his store and for some years represented the house of G. Becker, wholesale clothiers of Chicago. In 1880, while still with that house, he came to South Dakota and homesteaded one hundred and sixty acres of land, also taking up a tree claim of one hundred and sixty acres and preempting a quarter section near the present county seat of Clark County. While he made his home there, he continued his work as a commercial salesman up to the time of his death. His widow survives and now makes her home with her children.

Charles A. Fountain spent his youthful days with his parents, acquiring his education in the public schools of Nashua, Iowa, with an evening commercial course in a business college in Minneapolis, Minnesota. In early manhood he spent a period of several months as an employe in a lumberyard in that city and later engaged in clerking in a grocery store there.

In 1880 Mr. Fountain came to South Dakota with his father and on his arrival here he availed himself, as did the father, of the opportunity to secure land in this state free. He homesteaded a quarter section, took up a tree claim of one hundred and sixty acres and also preempted another quarter section adjoining the present county seat of Clark County. At that time, however, there was no town there and not for two years thereafter was a railroad built into the county. He turned his attention to general agricultural pursuits, which he carried on for four or five years and then entered the county courthouse, where for several years he served as clerk in the office of the recorder of deeds and in the county treasurer's office. In 1890 he was appointed chief clerk of the Crow Creek Indian reservation under President Harrison and served in that position until after the election of President Cleveland, when he was removed to make way for a democratic successor. Mr. Fountain was then called to Lakota, North Dakota, to assist in the management of a company store being operated by the Minneapolis Elevator people. He managed the business for two years and then returned to Clark, South Dakota. He was afterward made assistant cashier in the Clark

County Bank and remained in that position for three years. While serving in the bank he was elected county auditor of Clark County and filled that position through two terms. On the expiration of his second term, he was appointed state bank examiner for South Dakota and remained in that important position for seven years or for a longer period than any other incumbent. In November, 1911, however, he resigned and came to Watertown to accept his present position as cashier of the Commercial Bank. As the years have gone on his activities have been of increasing importance, connecting him more and more largely with interests bearing upon the welfare, upbuilding and progress of the different communities with which he has been associated.

In 1882 Mr. Fountain was united in marriage to Miss Mira A. Hager, of St. Paul, Minnesota, by whom he has a daughter, Nellie, now the wife of Frank H. Cannon, a real-estate dealer of Watertown, South Dakota. Mr. and Mrs. Cannon have two sons, Frank Fountain and Robert Cassius.

In fraternal circles Mr. Fountain is widely known, having membership in Watertown Lodge, A. F. & A. M.; Watertown Chapter, No. 12, R. A. M.; Myrtle Lodge, No. 43, K. P., of Clark, South Dakota; Watertown Lodge, No. 838, B. P. O. E.; the Ancient Order of United Workmen of Clark; and the Modern Brotherhood of America at Clark. He is a charter member of four of these organizations, and is a prominent figure in fraternal circles, exemplifying in his life the basic principles of brotherhood and mutual helpfulness upon which these different orders are founded. He is also a member of the Watertown Country Club and his wife is a member of the Congregational church. Both are highly esteemed and in their section of the state they are widely and favorably known, their many good traits of heart and mind endearing them to all with whom they have been brought in contact.

REV. FRANK FOX, D. D.

Rev. Frank Fox is pastor of the First Congregational church at Sioux Falls, the largest church of the city. He is a well-known and prominent representative of the Congregational clergy and in his chosen life work his efforts have been of no restricted order or influence. He is also widely known as an educator, lecturer and traveler and from each experience of life he draws the lessons which it contains or gathers therefrom knowledge, anecdote, or illustration for his sermons and his lectures. He is a broad-minded man in the truest and best sense of the term, realizing fully the duties and obligations that rest upon the individual and appreciating as well the countless opportunities for improvement, progress and the development of Christian character.

A native of Ohio, Mr. Fox was born in Oxford, January 28, 1859, his parents being Michael and Elizabeth (Hampton) Fox, the former a native of County Fermanagh, Ireland, and the latter of Virginia. Broad educational advantages were accorded him and constituted his preparation for the holy calling to which he has concentrated his life. He won the Master of Arts degree at Valparaiso University of Valparaiso, Indiana, while the Chicago Theological Seminary conferred upon him the degree of Bachelor of Divinity when he had completed his regular course of study there in preparation for the ministry. The University of Kansas City, Kansas, bestowed upon him the honorary degree of Doctor of Divinity. In early manhood Rev. Fox studied law for some time but following his graduation from the Chicago Theological Seminary in 1895, he at once entered actively upon the work of the ministry, accepting the pastorate of the Congregational church at Three Oaks, Michigan, where he remained for four and one-half years. He then went to Kansas City, Kansas, where he continued for about six and one-half years. On the 1st of February, 1905, Dr. Fox accepted a call from the First Congregational church at Sioux Falls, where he has since remained. The Congregational church was organized almost a quarter of a century before but during the twenty-five years which had elapsed its growth had not kept pace with the growth of the city and the original church building was an unattractive edifice. With the arrival of Dr. Fox, however, the church took on new life and activity. He infused into it much of his own zeal and energy, manifesting from the first a consecrated devotion to his work that was felt by all. He sought out those who had become indifferent to their church duties, made the acquaintance of the students of the town, and his gifts of oratory and sound reasoning were factors in producing increased, attendance at the church services. It was not long before he formulated the plan of erecting a new house of worship and a meeting was called to consider the question on the 17th of January, 1906. In April, 1907, the erection of the present edifice was begun, the cornerstone being laid on the 5th of October of the same year. On the 28th of March, 1909, the church was formally opened to the public and the day was devoted to the raising of funds to make the final payment. On the 4th of April following Dr. Fox delivered the dedicatory sermon and turned over the keys of the new church to the trustees. Today the First Congregational church owns the finest ecclesiastical edifice in the city — a structure of which they have every reason to be proud. It is built in an attractive style of architecture and is splendidly equipped for the purposes used. In the spring of 1910 Dr. Fox was presented by his church with a purse of six hundred dollars and was given a leave of absence that he might travel in Syria, Palestine, Egypt and Europe. He was absent four months and during that period the present parsonage was built. Under his pastorate three hundred and sixty members have been added to the church and the work has been thoroughly organized in all of its departments, being productive of splendid results as a factor in the moral development of Sioux Falls and the surrounding country.

On the 16th of August, 1888, at Vandalia, Michigan, Dr. Fox was united in marriage to Miss Florence A. Thomas, a daughter of Silas and Elvira Thomas, and their children are Florence A., Harold W., Clement S., Mary H. and Rachel Inez.

During the summer of 1913 Dr. and Mrs. Fox traveled in Africa, Palestine, Syria, Greece, Turkey and most of the countries of Europe and were delegates to the World's Seventh Sunday School Convention in Zurich, Switzerland. Rev. Fox is a republican in politics and he is a member of the Commercial Club. He believes that no citizen is exempt from the duties of citizenship but owes an allegiance to his home town which should be manifest in active efforts for its upbuilding and substantial development. He is a prominent figure in Masonry, is a past master of Unity Lodge, No. 130, F. & A. M., has taken the degrees of the York and Scottish Rites and of the Mystic Shrine, and in October, 1913, was raised to the Court of Honor degree by the Scottish Rite Consistory at their meeting in Washington, D. C., thus receiving the last degree preceding the supreme degree, the thirty-third. He is well known upon the lecture platform and his lectures partake of the nature of instruction as well as entertainment. Expressions of the highest appreciation thereof have been received from various sections of the country. He is spoken of as a "cultured gentleman, a scholar, a clear thinker, an eloquent, convincing speaker and a man of deep convictions and of high purpose."

MARION L. FOX

Marion L. FOX, who was the organizer of the Security Trust Company, of Sioux Falls, and who has been its secretary and manager from the time of inception, is one of the able newspaper men of the state, having been prominently identified with several enterprises of this line in South Dakota. He is a native of Buncombe County, North Carolina, where he was born on the 25th of October, 1865, being a son of John Jacob and Elizabeth (Roberts) Fox, native of North Carolina and both of whom are dead, the former having been for many years engaged in agriculture and having served in the senate of North Carolina from 1884 to 1888. After completing the curriculum of the public schools, the subject entered Greenville and Tusculum College, at Tusculum, Tennessee, where he completed the scientific course and was graduated as a member of the class of 1889. Thereafter he was identified with the newspaper business in Asheville, North Carolina, until he was appointed to a clerkship in the department of the interior in the national capital. He retained this incumbency until 1893, when he resigned to accept a position on the staff of the Washington News, then recently established, and he afterward held a reportorial position in Washington with the United Press Association, and later was employed on the Washington Post. In 1895 Mr. Fox came to South Dakota and became editor of the Sioux Falls Daily Press in the fall of the following year. He retained this position until August, 1898, when he accepted the editorial charge of the Deadwood Independent. In 1900 he again became editor of the Sioux Falls Press and continued in tenure of the position until the paper was sold to its present proprietors, the firm of Dotson & Bowen. In January, 1901, he organized the Security Trust Company, of Sioux Falls, for the purchase and sale of cheap lands, and since that time has been actively and successfully identified with the real-estate business, the company mentioned controlling extensive and valuable landed interests in various sections of the state.

He is a Democrat in politics, a member of the Masonic order and is identified with the Presbyterian church. On the 7th of June, 1900, Mr. Fox was united in marriage to Miss Jessamine Lee, the only child of Governor Andrew E. Lee, of South Dakota.

NATHAN E. FRANKLIN

A community owes much to those men who direct and control its financial institutions and Nathan E. Franklin as president of the First National Bank of Deadwood has done a great deal to further the development of the city and its vicinity, making the bank of which he is the executive head of great service to the community. The first care of the institution has been the safety of the deposits, but it has been so wisely directed that this end has been attained and worthy business enterprises have also been fostered through the judicious extension of credit. The Consolidated Power & Light Company of Deadwood and Lead also owes much of its prosperity to Mr. Franklin, as he is its president. Although he has business interests which occupy much of his time and attention, he has been prominent in public affairs and is the present mayor of Deadwood.

Mr. Franklin was born in Burlington, Iowa, on the 15th of December, 1870, a son of Harris and Anna (Steiner) Franklin, both of whom were born in Hanover, Germany, in March, 1849. They came to America in childhood and their marriage occurred in Burlington, Iowa. The father came to this country when hardly nine years of age and resided in New York for some time but later removed to Iowa, eventually locating at Burlington. After being employed for some time at various things he became a traveling salesman for a Council Bluffs house and continued in that connection until 1875, when he went to Laramie, Wyoming. In that year he made a business trip to Custer, South Dakota, but returned to Wyoming and engaged in mercantile business in Cheyenne until 1878, when he came to Deadwood and established himself in business. In 1908 he retired from the cares and responsibilities of active life and now resides in New York City. He was one of the men who did much for the early development of the locality around Deadwood. He was among the first to mine in the flat formation here and was an organizer of the Golden Reward, one of the famous mines of the Black Hills, but later disposed of this mine to E. H. Harriman and his associates. He was the organizer of the American National Bank at Deadwood, which was afterward merged with the First National Bank; is the principal stockholder of the Franklin

Hotel and organized the Franklin Live Stock Company, which did an extensive business until the open ranges were taken up by settlers. He is a man of unusual public spirit and was always willing to give of his ability and money to assist in any project that would promote the advancement of Deadwood and its vicinity. His generosity is well known and no worthy cause ever sought his assistance in vain. Although he did so much for the public good outside of the political field, he always refused to hold office. His wife passed away January 10, 1902.

Nathan E. Franklin is an only child and received the best educational advantages. After graduating from the Deadwood high school in 1887, he entered Notre Dame University and was graduated therefrom with the class of 1890. In 1887, while still attending school, he served an apprenticeship in a drug store belonging to Kirk G. Phillips in the summer and in 1890 was employed by that gentleman as clerk. In 1891 he embarked in the drug business for himself at Deadwood, so continuing until 1902, when he disposed of his store and was cashier of the American National Bank for three years. At the end of that time the bank consolidated with the First National, and Mr. Franklin became president of the institution, in which capacity he is still serving. He has executive talent of a high order and under his direction all the departments work in harmony and the bank as a whole is growing steadily in assets and in the confidence of the community. Mr. Franklin not only thoroughly understands both the detail of banking routine and the underlying principles of banking and currency, but he is also an excellent judge of men and surrounds himself with those who are unusually competent for the discharge of their duties. He organized the Consolidated Power & light Company of Deadwood and Lead, which furnishes light and power to all of the mining companies in the locality and to a number of cities, including Whitewood, Sturgis, Belle Fourche, Portland, Terry and Central City. It is one of the largest power and light companies in the west and as its president Mr. Franklin has many important questions to decide and heavy responsibilities to bear, but his powers of administration are equal to the demands made upon them. He is prominent in the association of bankers and represents the state of South Dakota upon the executive council of the American Bankers' Association and is in addition vice president of the South Dakota State Bankers' Association.

Mr. Franklin was married on the 14th of September, 1893, to Miss Ada F. Keller, who was born in Cheyenne, Wyoming, a daughter of Frank and Minnie Keller. Mr. and Mrs. Franklin have one daughter, Anna Mildred, the wife of D. S. Traitel, a resident of New York City, who is engaged in the marble importing business and also takes contracts for marble work in the erection of new buildings. The Traitel Marble Company of Long Island is well known to the trade.

Mr. Franklin gives his political allegiance to the republican party and is the present mayor of Deadwood, giving to the municipality a vigorous and clean administration. He has been a director of the Deadwood Business Men's Club for eight years and its president for three years and under his direction the organization has accomplished much good for the city. He is also president of the local humane society. Fraternally he belongs to the Benevolent Protective Order of Elks and the Masonic order, in which he has attained the thirty-second degree. He is one of the commanding figures in business and financial circles of Deadwood and all concede that his position is due solely to his marked executive and business ability and to his proven probity.

JOHN S. FRAZEE, A. M., B. D.

J. S. Frazee, president of the State Normal School at Springfield. Bon Homme county, is a native of the old Buckeye state, having been born in Neville, Clermont County, Ohio, and being a son of Richard and Docia (Boggess) Frazee, the former having been a jeweler and civil engineer by avocation. The subject of this review passed his boyhood days in Ohio, and secured his preliminary educational discipline in the public schools, while in 1871 he was matriculated in the State University of Iowa, where he completed the classical course and was graduated as a member of the class of 1878, receiving the degree of Bachelor of Arts, while later his alma mater conferred upon him the degree of Master of Arts. He also received from the same institution the degree of Bachelor of Didactics. Mr. Frazee began teaching in his youth and has been identified with educational work to a greater or less extent ever since. He was for several years professor of mathematics at the State University at Vermillion. He was called to his present position in 1897 and has accomplished much for the advancement of the interests of the school of which he is the executive head, amplifying and systematizing its work and showing himself to be imbued with a spirit of utmost loyalty and enthusiasm, so that he naturally gains the earnest co-operation of those who labor under his direction, infuses vigor and effectiveness into all departments of the school work. He is honored by both teachers and students, has the faculty of gaining confidence and is a man of scholarly attainments and much initiative force, so that he is especially well qualified for the important office which he holds.

Fraternally he is identified with the Masonic order, the Independent Order of Odd Fellows and the Modern Woodmen of America. In 1882 Professor Frazee was united in marriage to Miss Margaret Emma Rankin, who is likewise a graduate of the Iowa State University.

FULTON FREASE

Fulton Frease, was born in Luzerne County, Pennsylvania, on January 27, 1846, and in that county was reared and educated, remaining there until he was twenty years old. In 1866 he moved to Ohio, where he remained five months, then went to work on the Northwestern Railroad in Iowa. After working on that enterprise for a period he went into the service of the government, teaming to Fort McPherson and Fort Sedgwick. In 1867 he accepted employment on the Union Pacific Railroad, which was then building through Nebraska. Two years later he returned to Colorado and until 1876 was engaged in herding and riding the range in the neighborhood of Denver. At the end of this time, he went to southwestern Nebraska and started a cattle industry for himself, remaining there four years. In the spring of 1880, he brought his cattle to the Black Hills and placed them at the mouth of Elk creek and on the Belle Fourche River, making his home at Rapid City. In 1888 he took up the ranch he now occupies on Box Elder creek eighteen miles from Rapid, and in 1890 he moved his family to the place where they have since made their home. He has been continuously engaged in the cattle business since his arrival in the state and has a fine ranch which is devoted exclusively to the use of his stock and raising hay for their support. In political affiliation he is an ardent Republican, and to the welfare of his party he is zealously devoted, being county commissioner in 1883 and county treasurer in 1884.

For a number of years, he was also a stockholder in the First National Bank of Rapid City. He is a member of the Masonic order, belonging to the lodge of the order at his home town. On September 5, 1886, he was married at Rapid City to Miss Hattie S. Ryan, a native of Indiana. They have four children, Paul, Hazel, Kate and Helen.

JOHN W. FREEMAN, M. D.

Dr. John W. Freeman, chief surgeon of the hospital department of the Homestake Mining Company of Lead, has achieved distinction in his profession and is very popular socially. He was born on his father's farm near Virden, Illinois, on the 13th of December, 1853, a son of Peter S. and Elizabeth Pierce (Warriner) Freeman. The father was born in New Jersey and was one of the pioneers of Illinois, where he followed farming for many years. He passed away in 1874 and his friends long cherished the memory of his well spent life. The mother of Dr. Freeman was born in Kentucky and died in 1886, having survived her husband for twelve years.

Dr. John W. Freeman was the eighth in order of birth in a family of eleven children. At the usual age he entered the Virden public schools and passed from grade to grade until he was graduated from the high school at that place. He subsequently attended Blackburn University at Carlinville, Illinois, for one year, after which he took a course at the Quincy Business College of Quincy, Illinois. In 1875 he began the study of medicine under the instruction of Dr. David Prince, of Jacksonville, Illinois. During the summers he was thus occupied, and in the winters attended the medical school of the New York University, from which he was graduated with the M. D. degree in 1879. He was then for two years the assistant of Dr. Prince, after which he entered the United States government service in 1881, acting as assistant surgeon in the regular army stationed at Fort Meade, South Dakota, with the rank of first lieutenant. He remained at Fort Meade for two years and in January, 1884, came to Lead as surgeon for the Homestake Mining Company. In 1903 he was made chief surgeon of the hospital department of this company and in the intervening eleven years has performed with marked ability the onerous duties devolving upon him in that capacity. He has the hospital maintained by the company under his charge and has proven not only an expert surgeon but also an able executive and the affairs of the institution have run smoothly under his management. The cooperation of doctors, nurses and all others connected with the work of the hospital has been secured and the institution has a fine record and has proved of inestimable value to the mining community whose needs it serves. Dr. Freeman is one of the eminent surgeons of the state and is widely known in professional circles here, his skillful work commanding the respect of his colleagues. He has successfully performed many difficult operations and his opinion upon any condition requiring surgical treatment is highly valued. Although he has achieved much, he is not content to rest upon his laurels, but is constantly seeking to increase his knowledge and efficiency, attending clinics for a month every year, either in this country or abroad. He also maintains membership in a number of professional societies, namely, the Black Hills Medical Society, the South Dakota State Medical Society, the American Medical Association, the Chicago & Northwestern Surgical Society, the Chicago, Burlington & Quincy Surgical Society, and the American Railway Surgeons Society. He is also a fellow of the American College of Surgeons, which indicates his high standing in the profession. In addition to being chief surgeon for the hospital, he has been health officer for the city for the past four years. Although his duties as a surgeon and physician are many and make heavy demands upon his energy, he has also found time to devote to other interests, having been a member of the board of education for ten years and having served as president of that body for part of that period. For thirty years he has been connected with the First National Bank of Lead and is now second vice president.

In 1885 Dr. Freeman was married in Lead to Miss Hattie V. Dickinson, of that city. To their union have been born four children: Ercel Dean; Marion E., the wife of S. G. Price, of Rapid City; John B., who is attending the State Agricultural College at Brookings; and Howard.

In politics Dr. Freeman is a republican and takes the interest of a good citizen in everything relating to the public welfare. Fraternally he belongs to Central City (S. D.) Lodge, No. 22, A. F. & A. M.; Golden Belt Chapter, No. 35, R. A. M., of Lead; Lead Commandery, No. 18, K. T.; Black Hills Consistory, No. 3, A. & A. S. R., of Deadwood; and Naja Temple, A. A. O. X. M. S., of Deadwood. He has held the principal offices in all of the above-mentioned bodies and is a prominent Mason of the state. He also belongs to Lead Lodge, No. 747, B. P. O. E. Dr. Freeman is one of the foremost citizens of Lead and the city has benefited by his labors in her behalf. His character is such as wins friendship and there are many who feel for him a warm personal regard as well as a deep respect for his undoubted ability.

LEVI B. FRENCH

Levi B. French, a Yankton attorney, member of the widely known law firm of French & Orvis, was born at Tekonsha, Michigan, October 24, 1845. His father, Willis French, was a native of New York and became a Michigan pioneer farmer and stock-raiser, having removed to that state in 1839 — the year in which it was admitted to the Union. Upon the farm where he first settled, he continued his residence to the time of his demise. He came of Holland descent. His wife bore the maiden name of Roxana Butler and they were the parents of seven children.

Levi B. French, the eldest of that family, was educated in the public schools of Michigan and in Hillsdale College, from which he was graduated in 1872 with the Bachelor of Arts degree. He read law in the office of John B. Shipman at Coldwater, Michigan, having determined to make the practice of law his life work, and when he had sufficiently mastered the principles of jurisprudence to pass the required examination he was admitted to the bar at Centerville, Michigan, in 1875. In the meantime, he had engaged in teaching in the high school at Cassopolis, Michigan, in 1873-74. Mr. French entered upon the active work of his chosen profession in Constantine, Michigan, where he practiced for about four years, or until 1878. On the 19th of June, of that year, he arrived in Yankton, where he has remained continuously since. He has engaged in the general practice of law and is now accorded a large and distinctively representative clientage. He was state's attorney of Yankton County for a number of years, and in 1879 he was appointed by Governor Howard to the office of district attorney, which he filled for some time. He has likewise been connected with the work of framing the laws of the state, having been a member of the territorial legislature in 1881 and afterward a member of the state senate during its first two sessions, from 1889 until 1891. He gave careful consideration to every question that came up for settlement and cast the weight of his influence upon the side of justice, progress and civic betterment. He served in 1881 as a member of the city council of Yankton and for many years has been a member of the school board, the cause of education finding in him a stalwart supporter who has done effective work to further and improve the interests of the schools. His political allegiance has always been given the republican party.

On the 20th of August, 1879, Mr. French was united in marriage to Miss Jeanette L. Wells, a daughter of Franklin and Helen (Barry) Wells, of Constantine, Michigan, and a niece of Governor Harry of that state. Mr. and Mrs. French are the parents of three children: Willis W.; Helen R., who is now the wife of Ernest Dowling, of Yankton; and Lucy H., at home.

In moments of leisure Mr. French enjoys shooting and fishing as a means of recreation from arduous professional cares and responsibilities. In Masonry he has attained high rank in both the Scottish and York Rites, being a member of the commandery and consistory. He has filled many of the chairs, has been high priest of the chapter and grand commander of the grand commandery of the territory of Dakota. The family attend the Congregational church and are connected with all those things which are of interest and benefit to the community. Mr. French is widely recognized as one of the state's prominent attorneys, his reputation being founded upon a thorough and comprehensive knowledge of the law and a high regard for the ethics and the dignity of the profession.

GEORGE HOWARD FULFORD, M. D.

Dr. George Howard Fulford, a practicing physician of Sioux Falls, whose efforts are attended with gratifying success, was born in Chittenango, New York, on the 18th of July, 1854, a son of the Rev. Daniel Fulford, who was a native of England. He came to the United States when a youth of fourteen years and, entering the ministry of the Methodist Episcopal church, devoted his entire life thereto. On coming to Dakota Territory in 1885, he settled in Sioux Falls and was active in revival work in the churches in that and neighboring towns to the time of his death, which occurred in 1889. His labors were an effective force for moral progress. He was not denied the full harvest nor the aftermath of his efforts and his teaching and his example proved a turning point in the lives of many. He married Clara A. Hamilton, a native of New York and a descendant of one of the old New England families.

Dr. Fulford is the youngest of their three children. He acquired a liberal education, for after passing through the public schools in his native county he pursued a course in the Ogdensburg (N. Y.) Business School. Later he entered Ives Seminary, from which in due time he was graduated, and subsequently he studied for a year in Syracuse University. His professional training was received at the Boston University School of Medicine, from which he was graduated with the class of 1880, winning his M. D. degree. He afterward took post-graduate work in the New York Polyclinic and throughout all the passing years he has remained a student of his profession, reading broadly, thinking deeply and keeping in touch with the advancement made by the members of the medical fraternity. He began active practice in New Haven, New York, where he remained for two years and later spent three years in Henderson, New York. In 1885 he arrived in Dakota, settling at Sioux Falls, where he has since remained in general practice, his efforts being attended with very substantial and desirable results. He is the originator of the modern "three days' cure" for alcoholism. He belongs to the Tri-State Medical Association and the South Dakota State Homeopathic Association and he is regarded as an able and conscientious practitioner, ever careful in the diagnosis of his cases.

On the 26th of November, 1881, Dr. Fulford was united in marriage to Miss Katie Thompson, a daughter of George and Harriet Thompson, of Henderson, New York, and they have two children, Allen F. and Ida Florence. In his political views Dr. Fulford is an earnest republican and for one term he served as coroner in Minnehaha County, while at the present writing he is county superintendent of the board of health, which position he is now filling for the second term. Fraternally he is connected with the Masons and religiously with the Methodists. For many years he has been a member of the board of stewards, has been president of the board of trustees and is chairman of the building committee, having charge of the erection of a new edifice for the Methodist church. His interests are broad, his ideals high, his activities resultant and he stands not only as one of the eminent physicians of his section of the state but also as one of its representative and valued citizens.

GEORGE C. FULLINWEIDER

During the entire period of his active life George C. Fullinweider has been connected with the banking business and in this field has risen to a place of prominence and importance, being today connected through official service with some of the leading banks of South Dakota. Since 1897 he has been identified with financial interests of Huron as an officer in the National Bank of Huron, an institution of which he is now president. Mr. Fullinweider understands the banking business in principle and detail and has built an unusual degree of success upon experience and knowledge. He was born in Crawford County, Indiana, November 11, 1872, and is a son of Clay and Amina Fullinweider, the former of whom passed away in 1872. In the following year the mother removed to Decorah, Iowa.

George C. Fullinweider was reared in Iowa and supplemented a public-school education by a course in Breckenridge Institute. After he laid aside his textbooks, he secured a position as bookkeeper in a bank at Estherville and was retained in this connection for seven years, after which he removed to Huron, South Dakota, where he has since resided. He has been connected with the National Bank of Huron for many years, serving in an efficient and capable manner as cashier for some time. Since January, 1911, he has been president of the institution and is recognized in financial circles as a man of executive ability, energy and power. The other officers are as follows: W. X. Farmer, vice president; H. C. Shober, vice president; and Camden Rayburn, cashier. The board of directors is composed of these officers and of the following additional members: B. E. Beach, A. A. Chamberlain, Neil McKay and F. R. Brumwell. The National Bank of Huron has a capital stock of fifty thousand dollars and the surplus and undivided profits amount to about fifteen thousand dollars. This institution was made a national bank in 1907, succeeding the Standard Savings Bank, a state institution, which was organized in 1896, following the discontinuance of the National Bank of Dakota. This in turn had been an outgrowth of the Traders Bank, a private institution. All of these banks have occupied the same building, at the corner of Dakota and Second streets, in Huron, and Mr. Fullinweider was connected with the Standard Savings Bank as cashier and vice president. The National Bank of Huron is conducted along modern lines and its policy of progressiveness is tempered by a safe conservatism, which has made it one of the solid and substantial moneyed institutions of the state. Mr. Fullinweider gives a great deal of his time to the affairs of this bank but his connection with it does not form by any means his only business affiliation, for his interests have extended over a wide territory and he is now well known in banking circles of the state. He was the organizer and is now vice president of the First National Bank at Miller and is president of the Hitchcock State Bank, another institution which he founded. The First State Bank of Cavour also owes its foundation to his initiative and enterprise and he has been president of that institution since it was established.

In 1894 Mr. Fullinweider married Miss Ruth Ballard, of Estherville, Iowa, and both are well known in social circles of Huron. Mr. Fullinweider is a member of the Masonic blue lodge, chapter and commandery and belongs to the Modern Woodmen of America, the Elks and the Knights of Pythias. He is a member of the Presbyterian church and gives his political allegiance to the republican party. For many years he has taken a prominent and active part in public affairs, serving in various positions of public trust and responsibility, acceptably filling the offices of alderman, school treasurer and city treasurer. All who have had business, official or social relations with him accord him their unqualified respect and esteem, while in financial circles he occupies a position of precedence, won through many years of capable and intelligent effort along this line.

RUTHERFORD H. FULTON

R. H. FULTON, late postmaster at Avon, Bon Homme County, was a native of the state of Illinois, having been born on a farm in Jo Daviess County on the 2d of May, 1877, and being a son of Peter and Caroline (Whitman) Fulton, the former of whom was born in Pennsylvania and the latter in Illinois. Of their twelve children six are living at the present time. Peter Fulton was reared on the homestead farm in the old Keystone state of the Union, where he remained until he had attained the age of eighteen years, when, in 1847, he came westward to Illinois, where he was employed on various farms for a number of years, carefully conserving his resources and thus being finally able to purchase a tract of land in Joe Daviess county, where he continued to be engaged in agricultural pursuits until the time of his death, which occurred in 1897, his devoted wife passing away in the same year. They were worthy church members, and the father was a stanch Republican in his political adherency.

Rutherford H. Fulton was reared on the homestead farm and acquired his educational discipline in the public schools of Jo Daviess County. In 1896 he went to Plymouth County, Iowa, where he secured employment in the office of the Akron Register, a weekly newspaper. In the following summer he returned to Illinois, where he remained about one year, at the expiration of which, in the summer of 1897, he returned to Akron, Iowa, and purchased a half interest in the publication in the office of which he had worked the preceding year, and there he continued to be actively engaged in the newspaper business until May, 1900, when he disposed of his interests and came to South Dakota, purchasing an interest in a newspaper at Alcester, Union county, and being identified with its publication about one year. He then came to Avon and here established the Avon Clarion, whose publication he continued until the 1st of February 1903, when he sold the plant and business to W. J. Robinson, having been appointed postmaster of the town in December, 1902. In that office he did much to improve the service and his administration met with unqualified approval while he enjoyed marked personal popularity in the village and surrounding country, his death, on July 17, 1903, being deeply regretted by all who knew him. He was a stalwart Republican in politics and was chairman of the first board of trustees of the village after its incorporation, while he served one term as justice of the peace of the village, and in 1902 was elected to the same office as a county official, but did not qualify, on account of his appointment as postmaster.

He was a member of the ancient-craft body of the Masonic fraternity; of Avon Camp, No. 8536, Modern Woodmen of America, and Avon Tent, No. 61, Knights of the Maccabees. On the 28th of September, 1898, Mr. Fulton was united in marriage to Miss Alice Myers, of Akron, Iowa. Two children have been born, Leon Ernest, born March 6, 1901, died July 10, 1901, and Ruth Hazel, born July 7, 1903.

HON. LORING ELLIS GAFFY

Hon. Loring Ellis Gaffy, lawyer, jurist and Dakota pioneer, now one of the leading citizens of Pierre, was born in Clinton County, New York, on the 12th of January, 1850, a son of James Gaffy, whose birth occurred in County Westmeath, Ireland, and who in the year 1834 crossed the Atlantic to the United States, settling in New York, where he remained until 1855. In that year he removed westward to Wisconsin with his family, settling near Fond du Lac, where he engaged in farming until his death, which occurred in 1886 when he was on a visit to North Dakota. He wedded Nancy Dale, a native of Vermont, and of their family of three children, Judge Gaffy is the second in order of birth. His sisters are Mrs. C. A. Walker, of Fond du Lac, Wisconsin; and Mrs. W. J. Young, of Seattle, Washington.

The public- school system of Fond du Lac afforded Judge Gaffy his early educational privileges, which were supplemented by study in De Lands Commercial College. His review of the broad opportunities of the business world led to his selection of the law as a life work and he began his preliminary reading in the office and under the direction of Judge Drury in his home city. In 1871 he went to Greeley County, Nebraska, where he remained until 1873, when he became compass man on the United States survey of western Nebraska. In 1874 he went to Grand Island, Nebraska, where he continued his studies in the office of George H. Thummel, and in 1876 was admitted to the Nebraska bar. The following year he came to Dakota territory, settling at Deadwood, where he continued in active practice until 1884. In the meantime, he had become recognized as one of the leaders of the republican party in that locality and was made the candidate for the territorial senate in his district in 1880.

Four years afterward Judge Gaffy removed to Pierre, where he has since resided, and throughout the intervening years he has been almost continuously in office, his official duties, however, always being in the strict path of his profession. He was elected states attorney of Hughes County in 1888 and was the incumbent in that office for four years, or until 1893. In 1894 he was appointed judge of the sixth judicial district and was thereafter elected and reelected to the bench until he had served continuously for twelve and a half years. His decisions were strictly fair and impartial and were characterized by a masterful grasp of every problem presented for solution. On his retirement from the bench, he resumed the private practice of law as a member of the firm of Gaffy & Stephens and is now senior partner in the well-known and leading law firm of Gaffy, Stephens & Fuller. He has always made the practice of law his real-life work and there is no one who more fully recognizes the necessity for a most thorough preparation or prepares his cases with greater care. In argument he is strong, logical and convincing and his utterances lead through the steps of orderly progression to the logical conclusion upon which the decision of every case finally turns. His interests outside of his profession are those which have to do with general business development as well as with individual success. In 1912 he was elected president of the First National Life & Accident Insurance Company and now largely devotes his time and energies to his important and responsible duties in that connection. He is also president of the Suburban Acreage Company and through that medium is largely interested in irrigated lands.

Judge Gaffy has been married twice. In March, 1878, he wedded Fannie B. Price, whose death occurred in Pierre in 1887. In February, 1900, he wedded Adelaide W. Warwick, of Mount Pleasant, Iowa, a daughter of Judge William I. Warwick, and again death entered his household on the 14th of February, 1913.

Judge Gaffy is prominently known as one of the foremost leaders of the republican party in South Dakota. He was among those most active in the spirited contest which finally resulted in the choice of Pierre as the state capital and he has always been found in the van of every movement of a progressive nature affecting his city or the state at large. His fraternal relations are with the Masons and Huron Lodge, No. 444, B. P. O. E., and along professional lines he is known as a member of the South Dakota Bar Association and the American Bar Association. He has broad insight into the basic principles of the law, supplemented by an intellect keen, discriminating and analytical. Moreover, he is a profound student along many lines and an omnivorous reader of the best English literature. Outside the diverse activities of an especially busy life, he has found time to devote to the many complex questions arising from the development of a new country from the condition when sod and claim shacks were prevailing features of the landscape to that of modern civilization. His influence has ever been a potent force for progress and development. For many years he has been deeply interested in prison labor reform and the general betterment of prison conditions and is a member of the Prison Labor Reform Society. In fact, he has studied deeply the grave political, sociological and economic questions of the day and at all times keeps abreast with the best thinking men of the age. He finds pleasure and recreation in hunting, fishing and horseback riding and through these means has maintained that even balance in life which is lacking when business cares monopolize attention. The state accords him position as one of its foremost lawyers and Pierre places him among its most prominent citizens.

LUTHER E. GAGE

L. E. GAGE, a representative citizen and business man of McCook County and vice-president of the Security State Bank of Montrose, was born in New York on the 27th of July, 1861, and is a son of Eugene S. and Elvira (Hazelton) Gage, representatives of old and honored families of the Empire state, where they were both born and reared. They now reside in Montrose, South Dakota, where they have made their home since 1880. The father of the subject was for many years engaged actively in farming and stock raising, but is now living practically retired. Of the eight children in the family all are living except one. the names, in order of birth, being as follows: Ellen, Luther E., Frank, Matilda, Gertrude, Earl, Orin and Smith, the last named being deceased. When the subject was yet a youth, his parents came to the west and located in Grundy County, Iowa, where his father was engaged in farming until his removal to South Dakota. The subject secured his educational discipline in the public schools of Iowa, and after leaving school he continued to give his attention to the great basic art of agriculture, to which he has ever since given his allegiance, appreciating the fact that it is a proud distinction to be termed a successful farmer. In the spring of 1879, at the age of eighteen years, Mr. Gage came to what is now the state of South Dakota and settled in Clear Lake township, Minnehaha county, where he entered claim to one hundred and sixty acres of government land, perfecting his title in due time and there continuing to reside until 1892, when he came to McCook county, where he engaged in farming and stock raising, eventually becoming the owner of a finely improved, landed estate of four hundred and eighty acres, which he still retains in his possession and to whose operations he still gives a general supervision. He has given special attention to the raising of high-grade cattle, and upon his ranch are usually to be found about five hundred head. In

1893, Mr. Gage engaged in the general merchandise business in Montrose, conducting this enterprise in addition to his ranching business, and he continued the same successfully for a period of two years, at the expiration of which he disposed of his interests in the line.

In March, 1897, Mr. Gage became associated with P. G. Williams, a leading business man of Montrose, in the conducting of an agricultural implement and real-estate business until the spring of 1902, when the Security State Bank was organized and opened for business on the 9th day of March of that year. They own the controlling stock in the bank, and the reputation which they bear in this section stands as ample voucher for the reliability and solidity of the institution and gives assurance of a representative popular support. Mr. Williams is president of the bank and the subject is vice-president, while L. S. Lillibridge is in active charge of the counting room in the capacity of cashier. Mr. Gage is, in politics, a stanch supporter of the principles of the Republican party, but has never sought or held public office of any description. His wife is a Baptist.

Fraternally, he is affiliated with the Masonic order, in which he has passed the degrees of the blue lodge, and is also affiliated with the Ancient Order of United Workmen. On the 23d of May, 1881, Mr. Gage was united in marriage to Miss Ana Williams, of this county. She was born and reared in Wisconsin and is a daughter of William and Mary Williams, who are now residents of Minnehaha County, this state. Mr. and Mrs. Gage have six children, namely: Roy, Nona, Allen, William, Irene and Clyde. Roy and Allen are students in the high school at Sioux Falls at the time of this writing, the former being a graduate of the class of 1903 and the latter will graduate with the class of 1904.

EDWARD GALVIN

Edward Galvin is the efficient manager of the Sturgis branch of the Bloom Shoe and Clothing Company. He is a native of LaSalle County, Illinois, born July 20, 1858, of the marriage of John and Mary Galvin. His parents were born, reared and married in Ireland, whence they came to the United States in 1852, making their way overland to LaSalle County, Illinois. The father was a bricklayer and continued to make his home in that county until his death in 1868. The mother died in 1881 at Council Bluffs, Iowa. Seven children were born to their union, of whom Edward is the fourth in order of birth.

The last named acquired his primary education in the schools of Peru, Illinois, and at the age of ten years was employed as an errand boy in Des Moines, Iowa, later working and attending night schools in Council Bluffs, that state. While still under fourteen years of age he was employed as clerk in the S. Bloom Company's clothing store of that city. In 1876 Mr. Bloom removed to the Black Hills but Mr. Galvin remained with the new proprietor of the Council Bluffs establishment until 1881, when he went to Deadwood and again entered the employ of Mr. Bloom. Two years later, when the branch store of the Bloom Shoe and Clothing Company was opened at Sturgis, he went there in the capacity of manager of the business. He is still directing the policy of that store, which carries a full line of shoes and clothing and is patronized by the best citizens of Sturgis and vicinity. He is financially interested in the Bloom Shoe and Clothing Company and is treasurer of that concern, which operates four stores besides the one in Sturgis, one in Deadwood, one in Red Lodge, Montana, one in Sheridan and one in Casper, Wyoming. Mr. Galvin is vice president of the Commercial National Bank of Sturgis, which opened its doors for business in 1902 and is president of the Sturgis Improvement Company, which owns a cattle ranch south of Tilford, South Dakota.

The marriage of Mr. Galvin and Miss Hattie May Jewett was solemnized January 25, 1889. Mrs. Galvin was born in Lowell, Indiana, near Crown Point, that state, and is a daughter of Orin W. and Delilah (Drake) Jewett, natives of Portland, New York, and Lowell, Indiana, respectively. Her father, who was a practicing attorney, removed with his family to Illinois and still later, in 1879, came to the Black Hills, locating in Sturgis. He served as the first county judge of Meade County and maintained the dignity and impartiality of the bench. In 1903 he went to Sawtelle, California, where he engaged in the real-estate business until his death in 1908. In the spring of 1861, he answered President Lincoln's first call for troops and served in the Union Army until the close of the war. After the death of his first wife, he was again married and his widow still lives in California.

Mr. and Mrs. Galvin have one child, a daughter, Delilah Margaret, who gave her hand in marriage to Wallace A. Trumbull, a resident of Sturgis and chief clerk of the quartermaster's department, United States army, at Fort Meade. They have one child, Margaret Galvin.

Mr. Galvin is a democrat and represented the fortieth senatorial district in the first state legislative body of South Dakota with honor to himself and to the satisfaction of his constituents. In 1889 and 1890 he was a member of the city council and in 1898 and 1899 was president of that body. He is well known in Masonic circles throughout the state, belonging to all of the bodies in that order and having taken ail of the degrees therein with the exception of the last and honorary degree. For ten years he was master of Olive Branch Lodge, No. 47, of Sturgis. His other fraternal connections are with the Elks and the Ancient Order of United Workmen. His knowledge of the conditions and happenings of the early days of the statehood of South Dakota is valuable to the present generation, as the work of the pioneers is too apt to be forgotten by those who reap the benefit of their labor.

HARRY L. GANDY

Harry L. Gandy, of Rapid City, member of congress from the third district of South Dakota, was born in Churubusco, Indiana, on the 13th of August, 1881, a son of W. S. and Ellen J. (Matthews) Gandy. His mother died when he was but seven years old and his father was subsequently married to Emily J. Donaldson, who is still living. W. S. Gandy was a lawyer by profession and was highly esteemed by his colleagues and the general public. He has passed to his reward.

Harry L. Gandy is the third in order of birth in a family of four children. After passing through the grammar and high schools of Churubusco he taught school for a while and then entered the Tri-State College at Angola, Indiana, from which he was graduated with the Bachelor of Science degree with the class of 1901. He resumed teaching but did not continue in that profession long, as he decided to engage in the newspaper business and entered that field at La Grange, Indiana, where he continued until 1907, when he sold out and came to South Dakota, locating at Rapid City. He was made a night editor of the Rapid City Journal and held that position for a year and a half and subsequently served as manager of the Gate City Guide. He next purchased the Wasta Gazette, of which he is still the owner and which is a progressive, reliable and prosperous paper.

On the 14th of March, 1910, Mr. Gandy was appointed United States commissioner and continued in that connection until he resigned on the 1st of July, 1913. During his incumbency he received public land applications and heard the final proofs in that section and proved very efficient in the discharge of his duties. At the general election of 1910 he was elected to the state senate from Pennington County by a majority of eighty-five on the democratic ticket, although at that time the county was normally republican by a majority of about six hundred. In 1912 he was the democratic candidate for congress from his district and, while he was defeated, succeeded in reducing the usual republican majority by about seven thousand. On the 21st of June, 1913, he was appointed receiver of public moneys of the United States land office, his being the first land office appointment in the state under the Wilson administration. His appointment was confirmed by the senate five days later without an objection. On the 16th of July, 1913, he took charge of the office and while serving therein instituted a number of reforms that greatly promoted the efficiency of the office and benefited the homesteaders. A homesteader himself, he understood the ways in which the land office could increase its service to those who take up public lands and his previous experience as commissioner gave him an unusual grasp upon the duties of the position of receiver. At the primary election in March, 1914, he was again nominated by the democratic party for congressman from his district and in the following November was elected by a majority of sixteen hundred and thirty-two. He has the distinction of being the first democratic congressman ever elected in the state. Those who have followed his career so far have no hesitancy in predicting for him achievement in congress that will reflect honor upon himself and credit upon his district and state.

Mr. Gandy was married on the 30th of October, 1909, to Miss Frances Reiser, a daughter of James and Anna (Williamson) Reiser, of Wasta, South Dakota. Fraternally he is a member of the Masons, the Independent Order of Odd Fellows and the Knights of Pythias, and in his daily life he recognizes the claims of his fellowmen upon him, thus practicing the basic teaching of those orders. He has an enviable record as a public official and his political success has come as the merited reward for the efficient and conscientious discharge of his duties and a recognition of his grasp of the political problems of the time. His campaign was made upon a straightforward presentation of issues that left no doubt in the minds of his constituents as to his position upon the political questions of the day.

FRANK B. GANNON

Frank B. Gannon, president of the First National Bank of Aberdeen, was born in Genoa, Ottawa county, Ohio, on the 21st of October, 1851, being a son of William and Sarah A. (Compton) Gannon. The mother died in 1893. The father is a farmer by occupation, and still resides at Genoa, Ottawa county, Ohio. The subject secured his early educational training in the common schools, and when but fifteen years of age began to depend upon his own exertions in defraying the expenses of his school work. He continued to attend the public schools two and one-half years and also was for a short time a student in the Lebanon Normal School at Lebanon, Ohio. At the age of nineteen he began teaching in the district schools of Ohio, and through this means accumulated two hundred dollars, which practically served as the nucleus of his present fortune. In 1874 Mr. Gannon engaged in the meat-market business in Eaton Rapids, Michigan, continuing this enterprise five years, and being thereafter engaged in the boot and shoe business in the same town, for three years, at the expiration of which, in November, 1882, he came to Jamestown, Dakota territory, and shortly afterward located in Ellendale, both places being now in the state of North Dakota. In the latter village he engaged in the banking business under the title of Gannon, Smith & Company. In 1801 the institution was reorganized as a state bank, and was thereafter conducted under the firm name of F. B. Gannon & Company, until November, 1902, when it was reorganized as the First National Bank of Ellendale, our subject being elected president at the time and still being incumbent of this position. On the 7th of March, 1899, he became associated with J. H. Stuttle in purchasing a controlling stock in the First National Bank of Aberdeen, and of its institution he has since been president, having been a resident of Aberdeen since 1899.

In 1902 Mr. Gannon was one of the organizers of the Aberdeen Wholesale Grocery Company, of which he is treasurer, and this has become one of the leading commercial enterprises of this thriving city. Mr. Gannon has also been for a number of years prominently interested in the cattle business in North Dakota, and in company with his brother, W. H., he is the owner of one of the finest herds of full-blooded Herefords to be found in this section of the northwest. In politics he has ever maintained an independent attitude, giving his support to the men and measures meeting the approval of his judgment, but having no political ambition in a personal way.

Mr. Gannon is a Mason, belonging to the blue lodge, the chapter, commandery, consistory and the Shrine. He is also a member of the Odd Fellows fraternity, holding membership at Ellendale. South Dakota. On July 2, 1873, Mr. Gannon married Sarah Cook, of Sandusky County, Ohio. They became the parents of two sons: Deak, who died aged four years and eight months; and Ralph, who died aged eight months.

JACOB S. GANTZ

Jacob S. Gantz, of Rapid City, has for twelve years been clerk of the courts and for a quarter of a century has held public office, his unusual record being proof of his ability and public-spirited service. He was born in Hagerstown, Maryland, on the 23d of September, 1850, a son of Henry and Catherine (Shoop) Gantz. His father was a contractor of public works and was seventy years old at the time that he retired. He passed away on the 28th of November, 1908, when eighty years of age, his demise being much regretted by all who had come into contact with him. He belonged to one of the old families of Maryland. His widow is still living at the advanced age of eighty-eight years and makes her home with her sons in Deadwood and Rapid City.

Jacob S. Gantz is the oldest in a family of three children. He received his preparatory education at Lawrenceville, New Jersey, and took his college course at Lafayette College, Pennsylvania, from which he was graduated with the class of 1872. Four years later he removed to Sidney, Nebraska, and in 1877 he arrived in the Black Hills and located at Rapid City. From 1879 until 1882 he served as clerk of courts and in 1882 was elected register of deeds and served three terms, until January 1, 1889. He served as deputy county auditor in 1899 and 1900, and in November, 1902, was elected clerk of courts. He has served continuously since, his record being again indorsed by reelection in 1914. He is naturally systematic and methodical and has so arranged the work of his office as to secure the greatest efficiency with the least waste of time and effort.

Mr. Gantz was married on the 4th of May, 1882, to Miss Mary Addie Soule, a native of Maine and a representative of one of New England's oldest families. On the 20th of October, 1911, she passed away and interment was made at her old home in Maine. Mr. and Mrs. Gantz became the parents of six children: Katherine Von der Lieth, deceased; Saxe P., a graduate of the South Dakota State School of Mines; Mrs. Frederick H. Clarkson, who is a graduate of the New England Conservatory of Music; Ben Soule, who is an alumnus of Harvard University; Gardner, who is a student in Lafayette College of Easton, Pennsylvania; and Frank E., who is now attending a preparatory school at Stamford, Connecticut.

Mr. Gantz is a democrat and is one of the leaders of his party in the Black Hills district. He has been a loyal member of the Masonic order since September 26, 1871, and since the organization of the Knights of Pythias in South Dakota in 1882 he has belonged to that order. He is also a charter member of the Rapid City Lodge of the Benevolent Protective Order of Elks. His religious affiliation is with the Christian Science church. Mr. Gantz has seen a great deal of the development that has changed South Dakota from a pioneer section into a prosperous commonwealth and has worked constantly and willingly to further the progress of his own section of the state. He is held in the highest esteem, in Pennington County and is respected as a man and as a public official, his record being without a shadow of suspicion. Personally, he is genial, courteous and kindly, and few men have a larger circle of sincere friends than he.

MILTON D. GARDNER

Milton D. GARDNER, one of the leading farmers and stock raisers of Bon Homme County, is a native of Oneida county, New York, and dates his birth from April 30, 1837. His grandfather, Benjamin Gardner, moved to that county in an early day from Rhode Island and was one of the leading citizens of the community in which he spent the remainder of his life. He was a farmer by occupation, took an active part in the affairs of Oneida county and died there many years ago, leaving a family of six children, viz: Daniel, Frederick, David, Mary, Harriet and Narcissus, all deceased except Harriet, who still lives in the state of New York.

Frederick Gardner, the second son, was born September 23, 1811, married Sarah Wiggin, whose birth occurred in the year 1816, and departed this life in Oneida county, January 16, 1870, his wife dying seven years after that date. Mr. Gardner followed tilling the soil for a livelihood and was a man of sterling worth. He was a Democrat in politics, a Baptist in his religious belief and as a neighbor and citizen bore an excellent reputation. Frederick and Sarah Gardner reared a family of seven children, whose names are as follows: Joanna, born January 10, 1835, married Alexander Bowers, and died in Dubuque, Iowa, October 10, 1900; Milton D., the subject of this review, is the second in order of birth: Anna Eliza was born June 28, 1839: Harriet, wife of William Bowers, was born February 24, 1842, and died in 1898; George W., whose birth occurred on the 17th of September, 1846, died in childhood: Henry J., born March 23, 1849, is living a retired life with the subject: A. W. was born March 22, 1835, and makes his home in Maquoketa, Iowa.

Milton D. Gardner was educated in the public schools of his native county, grew to manhood on the farm and remained with his parents until twenty-seven years of age. In 1864 he severed home ties and went to Minneapolis, Minnesota, but after spending a short time at that place changed his abode to Waseca, in the same state, where he clerked for two years in a mercantile house. Resigning his position at the end of that time he became bookkeeper for a firm in Dubuque, Iowa, where he remained until 1873, the meanwhile becoming familiar with business and well qualified to enter upon the duties of the active career which awaited him in the west. In the above year Mr. Gardner came to South Dakota and with his brother engaged in the implement business at Yankton, where the two conducted a large establishment until 1883, building up a lucrative trade during that time and becoming widely and favorably known in commercial circles. Disposing of his interest at the time noted, the subject came to Bon Homme County and purchased his present farm of one hundred and sixty acres in the township of Bon Homme, which he at once began to improve and which he has since converted into one of the best farms as well as one of the most beautiful and attractive country homes in this part of the state. Since moving to this place, he has devoted his attention to agriculture and stock raising and that his success has been most flattering is attested by his steady advancement in material affairs, being at this time the owner of eleven hundred acres of valuable land in Bon Homme County, four hundred of which are in cultivation and otherwise highly improved. He devotes especial attention to corn, millet, alfalfa and hay, which he raises in abundance and feeds to his live stock. Mr. Gardner has achieved enviable repute as a raiser of fine blooded cattle and has on his farm at this time thirty-five registered shorthorns, also a large herd of other superior breeds, besides owning two hundred Poland-China hogs, and a number of fine horses, for both draft and road purposes. He exhibits his livestock and the products of his farms have taken a number of premiums awarded by the state fairs, all of which he attends and in the deliberations of which he takes an active interest and prominent part. In addition to his general agricultural and large live-stock interests, Mr. Gardner has a wide reputation as a grower of fine varieties of corn. So great has been the demand for this product of his farm that in the year 1903 he shipped more than a thousand bushels to different parts of the state and yet was unable to fill all orders that came to him. He has given close and critical study to corn culture and his efforts have resulted in the improvement of standard varieties and the development of new and highly productive kinds, for all of which he receives fancy prices.

Fraternally, Mr. Gardner is a Mason, belonging to the blue lodge at Tyndall and the chapter at Scotland and he is also identified with the Pythian order, holding membership with the lodge which meets at Springfield. While not a politician in the strict sense of the word, he keeps well informed on the leading public questions of the day, and gives his support to the Democratic party, though in local affairs frequently voting for the best qualified candidate, regardless of political ties.

Mr. Gardner, on May 1, 1861, was united in marriage with Miss Ophelia Brewer, of Oneida county, New York, the union resulting in the birth of three children, the oldest of whom, Asa, was born on May 8, 1866. This son is now a prosperous stock dealer and lives at New England, North Dakota, where he has a family of five children, his wife having formerly been Miss Emma Harrison, of Bon Homme county; Isabella S., the second of the subject's children, was born March 12, 1868, and married Herbert Silverwood, a farmer of Bon Homme county, this state: the youngest of the family, a son by the name of Clarence E., was born on May 24, 1879, and is his father's able assistant on the farm.

HERMAN H. GAREY

Herman H. GAREY, of Mount Vernon, Davison County, was born in Oswego County, New York, on the 6th of December, 1859, being a son of James W. and Susanna (Griffin) Garey, of whose three children he was the first in order of birth. He received his rudimentary education in the public schools of his native state, and when he was about ten years of age his parents removed to Iowa, where he continued to attend the district schools until he had attained the age of twenty years. He then learned the art of telegraphy, and for three years was employed as telegraph operator and station agent by the Chicago & Northwestern Railroad, at various points in Iowa. In the autumn of 1888 he came to South Dakota, having previously been employed in a banking institution in the state of Nebraska for about three and one-half years. Upon coming to the present state of South Dakota he located in Mount Vernon, where he established the Davison County Bank, of which he became one of the principal stockholders, while he served as cashier of the institution until 1900, when he resigned his executive office, though still retaining his capitalistic interest in the bank. In 1892 Mr. Garey organized the Mount Vernon Milling Company and in 1896 he further manifested his progressive spirit by effecting the organization of the Mount Vernon Co-operative Creamery Company, while he was also actively identified with the organization of the Mount Vernon

Merchandise Company, in all of which concerns he still retains a financial interest, while all have exercised important functions in connection with the industrial advancement of this section of the state.

Mr. Garey established himself in the real-estate business, and in the line, he has built up an extensive and prosperous enterprise, to which he devotes much of his time and attention. In politics he is a stanch advocate of the principles of the Republican party, but his many business interests are so insistent in their demands that he takes no active part in political affairs.

He is a member of the Masonic fraternity, in which he has attained the thirty-second degree of the Scottish Rite, while he is also affiliated with the Benevolent and Protective Order of Elks. On the 24th of February, 1889, Mr. Garey was united in marriage to Miss Mary Samuels, of Mount Vernon, South Dakota, she being a daughter of John and Sarah Samuels.

C. R. GARNER

C. R. Garner, who is successfully engaged in the real-estate, loan and abstract business in Onida, was born in Douglas County, Illinois, on the 15th of December, 1872, a son of William E. and Hester A. (Turner) Garner, both natives of Clinton County, Ohio. They removed from the Buckeye state to Illinois shortly after their marriage and resided in the Prairie state until 1883, when they came to South Dakota and located on a farm near Onida. The father gave his time and energies to the improvement of that place until 1910, when he and his wife removed to California. They now reside in Banning, Riverside County, that state, and he is living practically retired although he engages in the growing of fruits and nuts to some extent. He still owns land in Souths Dakota and has many friends here. He was one of the early settlers of Sully County and erected the first residence in Garner township. Although never an office seeker he was elected to a number of township offices. To him and his wife were born two children: Camillus R.; and John Newton, who resides in Banning, California, and who is an important official in the government forestry service, having charge of a large district.

C. R. Garner received his early education in the public schools of Onida and Pierre and later attended the State Normal School at Madison and Huron College. A number of years before completing his education, however, he helped provide for his own support, as when about sixteen years of age he was employed by others. When twenty-two years old he began teaching school in Sully County and for two terms taught the Onida school and for seven terms the Waterford school. During vacations he farmed and thus added to his income. In 1901, however, he became a resident of Onida and engaged in the real-estate, abstract and loan business, with which he is still connected. He deals in South Dakota lands and also handles real estate in other states and has negotiated many important transactions. He also has a gratifying patronage in the other branches of his business. He is a stockholder and a director in the Mexican Oil Company, whose well at the time it was sunk, in 1913, was the second largest in the world; and in the Idol Island Oil Company of the same place, which now has three wells. He owns farm lands in South Dakota and is one of the substantial citizens of Sully County. He devotes practically his entire time to his real-estate, loan and insurance business and has demonstrated his acumen and sound judgment.

Mr. Garner was married on the 12th of October, 1914, to Miss Maud Cole, a daughter of John F. Cole, a sketch of whom appears elsewhere in this work. To this union has been born a daughter, Audrey Belle, who is attending school.

Mr. Garner is a republican and is now serving his second year as mayor of Onida. He is a very able official and his conduct of the affairs of the office has gained him the commendation of his fellow citizens. His religious faith is that of the Presbyterian church, and fraternally he is identified with the Masonic order, belonging to the blue lodge of Onida, in which he is senior warden, and the chapter of Pierre, and to the Ancient Order of United Workmen. He has gained the friendship of many and the respect of all with whom he has been brought in contact.

JAMES C. GARRICK

James C. Garrick, of Webster, filling the office of sheriff of Day County, was born in Delhi, New York, December 20, 1872, a son of Alex and Elizabeth (Cowan) Garrick, who were natives of Delaware County, New York, born in 1845 and 1843 respectively. The father is still living but the mother passed away in 1909. They were married in the Empire state and in 1880 removed to Iowa, where the father secured a farm and in 1883, they became residents of Faulk County, South Dakota, where he took up land from the government. After cultivating that tract for a time, he removed to the vicinity of Faulkton and at the present time is living retired, making his home with his children. His business affairs were carefully and wisely conducted, bringing him success. His family numbered five children, of whom four are living: Isabella, the wife of William Plants, a merchant and farmer living near Faulkton; W. R., who is sheriff of Faulk County; A. A., manager for the Day County Garage Company; and James C. The father is a member of the Congregational church and an active representative of the Independent Order of Odd Fellows. In politics he is a republican and for several years served as county commissioner of Faulk County. His father, Alex Garrick, Sr., was born in Scotland and at the age of seventeen years came to the United States. He followed the occupation of farming and died in the state of New York. The maternal grandfather of James C. Garrick was Andrew Cowan, who was born in Scotland, and also engaged in agricultural pursuits to the time of his demise, which occurred in New York.

James C. Garrick after acquiring a common-school education turned his attention to farming and to the grain business and since starting out independently has made steady progress. He has an interest in the firm of Potter, Garrick & Potter, which controls a line of nine elevators at various points in this state and they handle an extensive amount of grain, their business furnishing an excellent market for the grain raisers, while at the same time it is a source of profitable income to the partners. Believing in South Dakota and its future, Mr. Garrick has invested to a large extent in land in this state and is also the owner of land in North Dakota.

In 1902 occurred the marriage of Mr. Garrick and Miss Evelyn Potter, a daughter of S. L. Potter, of Webster, South Dakota, and they have one child, Carlyle, born in 1906. The parents occupy an enviable social position and are regarded as devout members of the Congregational church.

In Masonry Mr. Garrick has taken the degrees of the Scottish Rite and of the Mystic Shrine. His political allegiance is given to the republican party and he has served as alderman of Webster, while in 1912 he was elected to the office of sheriff of Day County, in which he is making a most creditable record by the prompt, fearless and faithful discharge of his duties. He represents one of the old pioneer families of his section of the state and has for about a third of a century been identified with the progress and development of this part of South Dakota.

OTTO HENRY GERDES, M. D.

DR. O. H. GERDES.

O. H. Gerdes, an able representative of the medical profession in Eureka, McPherson county, is a native of Hanover, Germany, where he was born on the 25th of January, 1868, coming of sterling old German lineage and being a son of Henry and Margaret (Heiken) Gerdes, who were likewise born in Hanover, in which province the former was identified with agricultural pursuits until his death, which occurred in 1873. In the family were five children, and in 1885 the widowed mother with two of sons came to America and located in Manson, Iowa, where another one of his sons took up his residence two years previously. Mrs. Gerdes returned to Germany in 1895, and still remains there, while the three sons continue to reside in America. Dr. Gerdes secured his early educational discipline in the excellent national schools of the fatherland, completing a course in the gymnasium, which is analogous in its provisions and functions to the high school of the United States. A few months after coming to America with his mother, being seventeen years of age at the time, he secured a position in the drug store of Foley Brothers, at Manson, Calhoun county, Iowa, and was thus employed until 1888, when he began reading medicine under the efficient direction of Dr. D. T. Martin, of the town mentioned, continuing his technical studies under this preceptor until the autumn of 1889, when he was matriculated in the celebrated Rush Medical College, in the city of Chicago, Illinois, where he completed the prescribed course and was graduated as a member of the class of 1892, receiving his coveted degree on the 29th of March of that year. A few months later he came to Hutchinson County, South Dakota, and in March, 1893, established himself in the practice of his profession in Eureka, McPherson County, where he has since remained and where he has been most successful in the work of his profession, having gained distinctive prestige as a physician and surgeon and being known as a close student and one who keeps in close touch with the advances made in both sciences involved, while his personality is such that he has gained the high esteem of the people of the community. He is a member of the American Medical Association and the South Dakota State Medical Society.

The Doctor is a member of the Ancient Order of United Workmen, and is local medical examiner for the same, as well as for several of the leading life insurance companies having agencies here, notably the New York Mutual Life. He is also a thirty-second-degree Mason. Religiously he is a Lutheran and politically a Republican. On the 22d of October, 1894, the Doctor was united in marriage to Miss Bertha Bryan, who was born and reared in Woodstock, Illinois, being a daughter of Thomas and Susan Bryan. Dr. and Mrs. Gerdes have three daughters, — Irene, Lillian and Maude.

In a supplemental way it may be stated that the Doctor's grandfather, Henry H. Gerdes, was the owner of three excellent farms in Hanover, Germany, where he died in 1888, at the venerable age of ninety-three years. He left a large and valuable estate, and the properties mentioned still remain in the possession of his descendants. He was a soldier under the renowned General Blucher, and was in that officer's command at the memorable battle of Waterloo.

OSCAR SHERMAN GIFFORD *

OSCAR S. GIFFORD, superintendent of the Hiawatha Insane Asylum, at Canton, South Dakota, was born October 20, 1842, at Watertown, New York. While yet young he accompanied his parents upon their removal to Rock County, Wisconsin, but subsequently lived with his maternal grandfather, David Resseguie, in the Adirondack mountains in New York. In 1853 he removed with his parents to Boone County, Illinois, and in October, 1871, he settled in Lincoln County, Dakota, where he has since resided.

Mr. Gifford received a common school education, which was supplemented by attendance at the Beloit (Wisconsin) Academy. During the war of the Rebellion the subject evinced his patriotism by the service of his country, serving one and a half years in the engineer corps and one year in the Elgin Battery, Illinois Light Artillery. After his discharge from military service, Mr. Gifford entered upon the study of law and in 1871 he was admitted to the bar. In 1874 he was elected county judge of Lincoln County, but declined to serve, and in June of the following year he formed a law partnership with Mark W. Bailey, since which time he has continuously been actively engaged in the practice of his profession.

Mr. Gifford has several times been engaged in public service and has always acquitted himself creditably. He was a member of the constitutional convention which convened at Sioux Falls in September, 1883, and had been mayor of the city of Canton during 1881 and 1882. In November, 1884, he was elected a delegate to congress from Dakota territory, being re-elected a delegate in November, 1886, and in 1889 he was elected a member of congress from South Dakota, serving in the forty-ninth, fiftieth and fifty-first congresses as a Republican. While a member of that body Mr. Gifford served as a member of the committees on agriculture, Indian affairs and public buildings, which committees had charge of the more important matters in which the people of Dakota were interested. It was largely through the subject's efforts that the Crow, Sisseton, Sioux and Wahpeton Indian reservations were opened for settlement and Indian industrial schools were established at Pierre and Flandreau and a large number of day schools opened in the Indian country. The question concerning the division of Dakota and the admission of North Dakota and South Dakota as states was the most important measure before congress while Mr. Gifford was a member thereof and it was largely through his efforts, aided by the sentiments of his constituents, that Dakota was divided and two states formed from the immense territory. The measures known as the "omnibus bill," by which North and South Dakota, Montana and Washington became states, was approved by the President and became a law February 22, 1889, and, as before stated, at the first election thereafter, in October, 1889, Mr. Gifford was elected a representative from this state. Mr. Gifford reported to the house and had full charge of the measure for the construction of a public building in Sioux Falls. In November, 1901, Mr. Gifford received the appointment as superintendent of the Hiawatha Asylum, at Canton, a United States Indian insane asylum. He entered upon the discharge of his duties with an intelligent appreciation of its responsibilities and has discharged the same to the full satisfaction of every one.

In May, 1874, the subject was united in marriage with Miss Phoebe M. Fuller. Fraternally, Mr. Gifford has long been actively and prominently identified with the time-honored order of Ancient Free and Accepted Masons. He was initiated, passed and raised as a Master Mason in 1877, and in 1879 he was elected worshipful master of Silver Star Lodge at Canton. He was elected grand treasurer of the grand lodge of Dakota in 1881, was elected grand master of the grand lodge in June, 1882, and was re-elected to that position in June, 1883. In politics he has always been an earnest and active Republican.

ANDREW DONALD GILLIES

Since 1906 Andrew Donald Gillies has been engaged in general merchandising in Florence. His birth occurred in Stormont County, Ontario, on the 15th of September, 1876, his parents being Donald and Helen Gillies, who were of Highland Scotch descent. The father was a master mechanic and ship carpenter and devoted his life to industrial activity. Both he and his wife have now passed away.

At the usual age Andrew D. Gillies entered the public schools of his native county and pursued his studies until he had taken the high-school course. When his school days were over, he became an apprentice to the butter and cheese making trades and at the Columbian Exposition held in Chicago in 1893 the cheese which he made was awarded ninety-nine and a half per cent out of a possible one hundred per cent. He is a graduate of the Guelph Dairy School and the Kingston Dairy School and he was with the Lovell Christmas Cheese Exporting Company for six years, during which time he had charge of their factories. In 1899 he arrived in South Dakota and engaged in the manufacture of cheese about six miles west of Florence through three summers, while in the winter seasons he worked as a farm hand. He afterward spent six months in the employ of F. M. Stewart, a hardware merchant at Bradley, and then went to Clark, where he spent six months in the largest creamery in the state making butter. He afterward worked on a thresher as engineer and also engaged in farming, but in the fall of 1906 turned his attention to commercial pursuits, erecting the first general store building in Florence. He started in a small way, but has seen the business increase each year and his trade become equal to any in his line in his section. He employs five salesmen, carries an attractive line of goods and is accorded a gratifying and constantly increasing patronage.

On the 15th of September, 1906, Mr. Gillies was united in marriage to Miss Minnie Best, a daughter of John and Delia Best, representatives of one of the old-time pioneer families of this section. Both parents are yet living and Mrs. Gillies is a native daughter of the state, having been born on the old family homestead at Florence. The only child of this marriage is Kenneth Donald John, aged seven years.

The parents are members of the Presbyterian church, to the teachings of which they are faithful, while in furthering the work of moral progress they take an active part. Mr. Gillies enjoys hunting and fishing and all outdoor exercises and in such finds his recreation.

His political allegiance is given to the republican party. Fraternally he is connected with the Masons, his membership being in a lodge in Ontario. He is also a member of the Elks lodge No. 838, at Watertown;

the Woodmen of the World; and the Sons of Scotland. For six terms he has filled the office of school treasurer and he is devoted to the best interests of South Dakota, cooperating in all measures and movements for the public good. While actuated by high ideals, his methods are practical and the result of his labors is seen in the furtherance of those interests which have been potent factors in upbuilding his town and county.

WILLIAM WALLACE GIRTON

W. W. GIRTON, secretary of the State Normal School, at Madison, was born in Lincolnshire, England, on the loth of April, 1850, being a son of John and Mary (Hubbard) Girton, both of whom were likewise born in England, of stanch old English lineage. The father of the subject there devoted his attention to farming until 1850, when he came with his family to America, locating in Florence, Michigan, where he engaged in fanning, and in that state, he passed the remainder of his life, his death occurring in 1851, while his wife moved to Wisconsin with her two orphan boys, both of whom are living, the subject of this sketch being the younger in order of birth. The mother died at the home of her eldest son in Winchester, Tennessee, November 3, 1893, at the age of seventy-one years.

William W. Girton received his rudimentary education in the public schools of Wisconsin, attending the district schools of Sauk county during the winter terms until he had attained the age of eighteen years, when, in 1868, he entered an academy at Spring Green, that state, where he continued his studies for two terms, while during the winter of 1869 he was a student in the academy at Sextonville, Wisconsin. That he had duly profited by the advantages thus afforded him is evident when we revert to the fact that in the fall of 1870 he initiated his career as a teacher, having charge of a district school near Reedsburg, Sauk county, and being thus employed during the winter of 1870-71. In April, 1871, he entered the State Normal School at Platteville, Wisconsin, where he completed a thorough course, being there graduated in June 1874. In 1875-6 he was incumbent of the position of principal of the graded schools at Muscoda, Wisconsin, and then went to Vinton, Iowa, where he held the office of assistant superintendent of the State School for the Blind for one year, at the expiration of which he became principal of the public schools at Harlan, that state, where he rendered most effective service until November, 1880, when he entered upon his duties as superintendent of the schools of Shelby County, Iowa, to which office he had been elected to fill a vacancy, while he remained incumbent of the same for four years, proving a most able and discriminating executive and showing great facility in organization and systemization. In 1883 he founded the Shelby County Republican, at Harlan, Iowa, and continued as editor and publisher of the same until 1886, in September of which year he came to South Dakota, having disposed of his newspaper property. In December, 1886, Mr. Girton organized the Vilas Banking Company, at Vilas, Miner County, South Dakota, and was president of the same for the ensuing three years, while he also established the Miner County Farmer, which he conducted simultaneously during the period mentioned. In 1892 he was elected county superintendent of schools for Miner County, in which capacity he served two terms, doing much to forward educational interests in that section of the state. In 1889 he served as deputy territorial auditor, and in the same year was chief clerk of the joint commission which had in charge the settlement of accounts between the new states of North and South Dakota. In 1896 he was elected to the chair of geography and civics in the State Normal School, at Madison, of which office he has since remained incumbent, while he has served as secretary of the institution for the regents of education, during the same time, enjoying the respect and esteem of his confreres and also of the students of the school, while he has here added materially to his prestige as a capable and enthusiastic worker in the field of education. He has been particularly successful and prominent in normal institute work in the state during the past fifteen years, and it may be said without fear of contradiction that he has conducted more teachers' institutes in that period than has any other man in the state, while in the connection he has accomplished a work of unequivocal value and one of which he may justly be proud. In the year 1901-2, in the absence of the president, Mr. Girton was appointed acting president of the State Normal School, which position he filled to the entire satisfaction of the regents. It may be farther noted that he served as chief engrossing clerk of the last territorial legislature, in 1889, and while clerk of the joint commission of North and South Dakota shipped the territorial library, records and other property, having an aggregate weight of nearly sixty tons, down the Missouri river from Bismarck to Pierre, the new capital of South Dakota, while he also made copies of the territorial records for this commonwealth, a work of no little magnitude and difficulty.

In politics Mr. Girton has ever given a stanch allegiance to the Republican party in the promotion of whose cause he has taken an active interest, while as candidate on its ticket he was elected to the office of county superintendent of schools in Shelby county, Iowa, and later in Miner county, South Dakota. In 1878 he became a member of the First Baptist church at Harlan, Iowa, and holds a letter from the same at the present time. He has advanced to high degree in the Masonic fraternity, of which noble order he is an appreciative member, having reached the Royal Arch degree of the York Rite bodies, while he is now serving his fifth consecutive year as master of Evergreen Lodge, No. 17, Ancient Free and Accepted Masons, at Madison, South Dakota, and he has attained the thirty-second degree in the Ancient Accepted Scottish Rite, being affiliated with Yankton Consistory, Sublime Princes of the Royal Secret, in the city of Yankton. He also holds membership in Madison Lodge, No. 20, Independent Order of Odd Fellows, and Howard Lodge, No. 62, Ancient Order of United Workmen.

On the 1st of August, 1877, Mr. Girton was united in marriage to Miss Frances Richmond, who was born in Belturbel, County Cavan, Ireland, on the loth of May, 1851, being a daughter of Francis and Susan (Moore) Richmond, who came to America in 1860 and located in Green County, Wisconsin, where Mrs. Girton was reared and educated. The subject and his wife have six children, whose names are here entered, with respective dates of birth: Lee Richmond, August 13, 1878: Daisy M., April 8, 1880; Susan M., May 17, 1882; Edith A., January 27, 1884; William T., July 6, 1886, and John F., September 21, 1891.

The State Normal School at Madison was established by act of the territorial legislature in March, 1881, and commenced its work in December, 1883. It is situated on elevated-ground in the north part of the city of Madison on a nearly level campus of twenty acres, which has been artistically laid out and set with trees. The main school building was erected in 1886. It is constructed of red quartzite, obtained at Dell Rapids, South Dakota, and trimmed with white cut stone from La Crosse and with Milwaukee pressed brick. This building is seventy-six by eighty-four feet, four stories in height, the lower one being half basement. It is finished throughout with oak and Georgia pine. It cost thirty-five thousand dollars. It is situated near the center of the campus. The oldest dormitory, called West Hall, situated near the southwest corner of the campus, is a frame brick-veneered building, thirty-six by eighty-six feet, four stories in height and contains rooms for the accommodation of sixty-five students. It is occupied by the young men. This building cost eleven thousand dollars.

East Hall is a four-story, massive structure, built of Sioux Falls stone and trimmed with the same. It is ninety by one hundred and ten feet and was erected in 1900, at a cost of twenty-two thousand dollars. Eighty young women make their home in this building and more than one hundred assemble in the spacious dining room in the basement for meals. The faculty is at present composed of twelve members as follows: W. W. Girton, acting president, psychology, book keeping; J. W. Goff, English, rhetoric, literature; W. H. Dempster, mathematics, physical geography; Cora M. Rawlins, Latin, English grammar; Mirza French, drawing, arithmetic, librarian; Louise A. Wilkinson, elocution, physical culture; Olga B.

Forsyth, history, vocal music, elementary algebra; Isabel Larsen, zoology, botany, physiology, general history; Winifred K. Buck, elementary English, geography, civil government; Anna B. Herrig, principal training department, methods; Susan W. Norton, grammar critic; Nellie Collins, primary critic.

WALTON S. GIVEN

Walton S. Given, cashier of the First National Bank of Britton, was born in Woodstock, Illinois, February 4, 1879, and is descended from early American ancestry represented in the Revolutionary war among the Virginian troops with Pitkin and Sumter. His parents, C. A. and Elizabeth (Ryder) Given, were both natives of Woodstock, Illinois, although their parents were Virginians. C. A. Given made farming his life work and thus provided a comfortable living for his family. He was a well read and broad-minded man and the salient traits of his character were such as commended him to the confidence and high regard of all. His early political support was given to the democratic party but later he joined the ranks of the republican party. Fraternally he was connected with the Masons and religiously with the Presbyterian church, while his wife was a member of the Methodist Episcopal church.

Walton S. Given completed a high-school course in Elgin, Illinois, by graduation with the class of 1897, being then a youth of eighteen years. Soon afterward he made his way to Watertown, South Dakota, and for two years engaged in teaching in the country schools near that place. He afterward attended the State Normal School at Madison, from which he was graduated in 1900, and then accepted the position of principal of the schools of South Shore, South Dakota. A year later he removed to Britton, where he was city superintendent of schools from 1901 until 1910, and from 1905 until 1910 he spent his summers in teachers' institute work all over Dakota. He was particularly able in that field, as well as in the regular work of the schoolroom, where his ability to impart clearly and readily to others the knowledge that he had acquired made him a most valued educator. His efforts have been an important force in the development of the school system of his part of the state, for he was largely instrumental in advancing the standards of the schools. He promoted his own knowledge through attendance for several seasons at the University of Chicago, and broad reading, study and investigation have continually augmented his intellectual force. In 1910 he was elected assistant cashier of the First National Bank of Britton, of which he was made cashier in January, 1911, and has since been identified with this institution, to which he gives his undivided attention.

In 1906 Mr. Given was united in marriage to Miss Annie Sheridan, a native of Madison, South Dakota, and a daughter of Elmer Sheridan, who is engaged in the abstract and insurance business. They have one child, Elmer S. Mrs. Given belongs to the Presbyterian church, while Mr. Given is a member of the Masonic fraternity. In politics he is a republican but has never sought nor desired office, preferring to concentrate his energies upon his business duties. He is now making good in the position of cashier of the First National Bank of Britton and is accorded the high regard and confidence of his colleagues and contemporaries.

WILLIAM H. GLYNN

William H. Glynn, a prominent young lawyer of Parkston, where he has practiced his profession continuously since 1909, is now serving a two-year term as states attorney, having been elected to that office on the republican ticket in 1914. His birth occurred in Clayton, Iowa, on the 3d of April, 1880, his parents being Alfred and Lena (Lape) Glynn, who still reside in the Hawkeye state. By profession the father is a mechanical engineer.

William H. Glynn acquired his general education in the graded and high schools and subsequently entered the law department of the University of South Dakota at Vermillion, from which he was graduated in 1909. He at once located for practice in Parkston and has there remained to the present time, having built up an extensive and profitable clientage. In 1914 he was honored by election to the office of states attorney, in which he is now serving and has already made a very creditable record.

On the 1st of September, 1909, Mr. Glynn was united in marriage to Miss Amelia Becker, a daughter of John Becker. He gives his political allegiance to the republican party and has ably served as city attorney of Parkston. His religious faith is that of the Presbyterian church, while fraternally he is identified with the Masons. He delights in outdoor recreation of all kinds and in his home community is popular and esteemed as an able attorney and progressive young citizen.

P. S. GORDON

P. S. Gordon, the president of the Home National Bank of Dell Rapids, which he assisted in organizing in the spring of 1910 and of which institution he has been at the head since January, 1912, has for about three decades been a dominant factor in the business and financial circles of Minnehaha County. His birth occurred in Lisbon, New Hampshire, on the 22d of March, 1852, his parents being George W. and Elvira R. (Hodge) Gordon, who came of Scotch ancestry and spent their entire lives in the Granite state. Both the Gordons and Hodges represented old New England families. George W. Gordon was considered one of the wealthy and influential agriculturists of his section.

P. S. Gordon was reared at home and in the acquirement of an education attended the Lisbon public schools. When a young man of twenty he left the parental roof and started out independently, spending a number of years in journeying over the United States and covering about forty states in his travels. In 1879 he was united in marriage to Miss Flora E. Wells, of Lisbon, New Hampshire, an old schoolmate and sweetheart, for whom he returned to the place of his nativity. He remained in New Hampshire for about five years after his marriage and in 1885 came to South Dakota, locating in Dell Rapids. Throughout the intervening three decades he has been a leading factor in the business and financial life of the community. For about sixteen years he was successfully engaged in farming and in the raising of thoroughbred stock, breeding Hereford cattle and Shropshire sheep. In 1902 he disposed of his stock and farm holdings, being the first man in his section of the state to sell a farm for as high as fifty dollars per acre, which at that time was considered an exorbitant price. Subsequently Mr. Gordon took up his abode in Dell Rapids, where he has since resided. In the spring of 1910, he was one of the dominant factors in the organization of the Home National Bank and was chosen vice president of the institution. In January, 1912, he was elected to the presidency of the bank and in that important position has since demonstrated his capability as an executive and his wisdom in affairs of finance. During the past ten years he has also served as president of the Dell Rapids Cooperative Lumber Company and, with the aid of an able board of directors, has developed the business to a remarkable extent, stock shares which were quoted as low as fifteen cents having risen in value to two dollars and a quarter. Mr. Gordon lost his wife in 1910, her demise occurring on the 13th of June of that year.

In fraternal circles he is known as an exemplary Mason, belonging to Dell Rapids Lodge, No. 40, A. F. & A. M., and Flandreau Chapter, R. A. M., of Flandreau, South Dakota A man of exceptional executive talent, of great activity and energy and with ability to make and keep friends, his name is inseparably associated with business and social life as one of the most valued citizens of Dell Rapids and Minnehaha County.

IVAN WILBUR GOODNER *

Ivan W. GOODNER, of Pierre, a representative member of the bar of the state and president of the state board of regents of education, is a native of the state of Illinois, having been born in Washington County, on the 24th of July, 1858, and being a son of Rev. William Milton and Margaret Nancy (Edmiston) Goodner, natives respectively of the states of Tennessee and Kentucky, the former being of Holland Dutch lineage and the latter of English. Rev. William M. Goodner was a clergyman of the Methodist church for many years, and later was a Swedenborgian missionary in the western states, being a man of ripe scholarship and exalted integrity of character. The subject of this review received his early educational training in the public schools of the states of Illinois and Michigan, later attended Graham's Academy, in New York City, while he completed his technical law course in the law department of the University of Nebraska, at Lincoln, where he was graduated, with the degree of Bachelor of Laws, in 1897. He had previously become an expert shorthand reporter, and to this vocation devoted his attention for a number of years. He came to what is now the state of South Dakota in 1884, and from 1880 to 1889 he followed the vocation noted. He was the first clerk of the supreme court of the state, resigning the office in 1896 to enter the practice of law. He was the official reporter of debates in the South Dakota constitutional conventions of 1885 and 1889, in 1898-9 was city attorney of Pierre, while he rendered most efficient service as state's attorney for Hughes County from 1900 to 1904. In 1901 he was appointed, by Governor Charles N. Herreid, a member of the state board of regents of education, being elected president of the board in 1903 and being still incumbent of that important office, in which connection his efforts have proved of great value in forwarding and conserving the educational interests of the state. He was admitted to the bar in 1885 and has won marked distinction both as a trial lawyer and a counsellor, having been identified with a large amount of important litigation, notably the long line of bond litigations in which the city of Pierre was involved. He carried these cases through the federal courts and to the supreme court of the United States, before which he was admitted to practice in April, 1901. In politics Mr. Goodner has ever been stanchly aligned as a radical Republican and has been an active worker in its cause in South Dakota.

In the Masonic fraternity he has attained to the degrees of the commandery, was deputy grand master of the Masonic grand lodge of the state, and this year (1904) was elected grand master. He is also past grandmaster of the Independent Order of Odd Fellows in South Dakota and is also identified with the Modern Woodmen of America. On the 16th of September, 1880, Mr. Goodner was united in marriage to Miss Minnie Ada Perry, who was born in Bolton, Vermont, on the 24th of May, 1860, being a daughter of David and Emma (LeGro) Perry. Of their six children four are living, namely: Ivan E., Milton P., Grace E. and Ernest F. Those deceased are Mabel and Ruth.

FRANK E. GRANGER

Frank E. Granger, of Aberdeen, the oldest court reporter in South Dakota, in point of continuous service in that capacity, was born in Chicago, Illinois, and there acquired his early education, afterward reading law and winning admission to the bar of Illinois. In 1883 he located in Aberdeen, South Dakota, where he proved up on some government land. Jive years later he was made court reporter and for more than a quarter of a century has held that position, discharging his duties in a capable, prompt and able manner.

Mr. Granger is also well known in Aberdeen as the founder of the Granger Business School, which he established in 1900 as a school of stenography. Later he installed a complete business course, buying out the Aberdeen Commercial College. In 1906 he established a branch at Big Stone City, South Dakota, later moving this to Ortonville, Minnesota, and selling it in 1913 to C. J. Stark. In 1908 Mr. Granger established another branch school, buying the Watertown Business School, which he sold two years later. In 1913 he sold the Aberdeen school to George L. Kemper, its present owner, who has placed M. B. Dewey in charge. In November, 1883, Mr. Granger was united in marriage to Miss Fannie Roe, of Chicago, and they have become the parents of three children. Mr. Granger is connected fraternally with the Masonic lodge and he gives his political allegiance to the republican party. In 1893 he served as a member of the school board and did capable and intelligent work in that office. He has lived in Aberdeen for many years and is held in high regard there as a progressive and useful citizen.

OTTO PETER THEODORE GRANTZ

Otto P. T. Grantz is a native of Germany, born November 9, 1835, in Tonning, duchy of Schleswig, the son of Jurgen and Amalia Grantz, the former coming to America in 1849, and settled in California, his wife having died in Germany in 1840. Jurgen Grantz was one of the first to arrive in the gold fields of the Pacific coast and he continued mining in California and other western states and territories until his death, which occurred in Idaho, when he was sixty-eight years old. Mrs. Grantz died when the subject was five years old and another son, who came to the United States, departed this life in the latter part of the fifth decade.

Otto P. T. Grantz was reared in his native land and received a good education in the schools of Tonning, which he attended at intervals during his childhood and youth, finishing his intellectual training at the age of fifteen. Later he entered a mercantile establishment and after becoming familiar with the business, became manager of stores, in which capacity he continued in Germany until the year 1858, when he came to the United States.

In coming to this country Mr. Grantz settled in Iowa, where he engaged in agricultural pursuits, but after spending one year in that state removed to Illinois, where he, during the ensuing three years, also devoted his attention to tilling the soil. Severing his connection with farming in 1862, he crossed the plains and on August 24th reached Oregon, where he engaged in mining for several months, when he left that state for Boise Basin, Idaho, arriving at the latter place in January, 1863. During the thirteen years following he devoted his time and energies to mining in various parts of Idaho, but in November, 1876, left that country and came to the Black Hills, which has since been his field of action, making his home the greater part of the time at Deadwood, of which city he has long been an honored resident.

Mr. Grantz has devoted nearly forty-two years to mining and it goes without saying that during this long period he has become thoroughly familiar with every phase of the important industry which is so intimately associated with the developments and prosperity of the great west. In the main his undertakings have prospered, success has characterized his career and today he occupies a conspicuous place in business and industrial circles, besides being identified with j enterprises and measures having for their object the advancement of the city and state and the promotion of the general welfare. In the spring of 1863, while a resident of Idaho, Mr. Grantz volunteered to fight the Indians, who were then on the war path and causing the settlers much trouble, and he experienced considerable active service before the hostiles were repulsed and peace was restored. He has ever been ready to respond when duty calls, his services at all times are at the disposal of his I adopted country and as a citizen he is as loyal to the government and its institutions as any American-born reared under the protecting folds of the stars and stripes. In state and national affairs, he is a Republican, but in local matters cares little for party ties, giving his support to the candidates who in his judgment are best qualified for the positions to which they aspire.

Mr. Grantz stands high in Masonic circles and is identified with a number of the most important branches of the order, being a member of Deadwood Lodge, No. 7; Dakota Chapter, No. 3, Royal Arch Masons; Golden Belt Lodge of Perfection, No. 3; Rose Bruce Chapter, Rose Croix, No. 3; Council Knights of Kadish, No. 3: Black Hills Consistory, No. 3, thirty-second degree K. C. O. H.; Naja Temple, Deadwood, and Deadwood Chapter, No. 23, Order of Eastern Star. These different relations with the ancient and honorable order have brought him into close contact with the leading members of the brotherhood throughout the state, among whom he is held in the highest personal esteem. He has also been elected at different times to important official stations in the order, in all of which he discharged his duties ably and consistently, proving worthy the confidence reposed in him and a credit to the organization by which the honors were conferred. On February 3, 1877, Mr. Grantz was united in the bonds of wedlock with Miss Christina Johnson, the ceremony being solemnized in the city of Deadwood. Mrs. Grantz was born in Sweden, and is a daughter of John and Johanna Johnson, who were also natives of Sweden. This marriage has been blessed with four children, Theoline, Otto, Lillie and Lillie, the second of whom died in infancy.

JOHN GRAY

John GRAY, one of the sterling pioneers of the Black Hills, was born in Durham. England, on the 28th of February, 1846, and is a son of Henry and Elizabeth (Nelson) Gray, both of whom were born in Cumberland, England, as was also his grandfather, Henry Gray, who was there identified with mining during his entire business career. The father of the subject was reared in Cumberland and there followed the same vocation as did his honored sire. In 1840 he removed to Durham, where he continued the mining operations until his death, his wife also passing the closing years of her life there. Of their nine children six are living, while but one of the number is a resident of the United States.

The subject received somewhat limited educational advantages, since, as was customary with the majority of miners' sons in the locality, he early went to work in the mines. At the age of eight years, he began work as a trapper in the Durham mines, and gradually rose step by step until he had attained the dignity of a full-fledged miner. He continued to be employed in the mines of his native county until he had attained the age of twenty-three years, when, in March, 1869, he came to America. He first located in Steubenville, Ohio, where he was engaged in mining for nine months, after which he went to the city of Pittsburg and there secured a position in the mines at Saw Mill run, on the Monongahela River, where he was employed until 1870, when he removed to the Scranton district and worked in the Dunmore mine for several months, after which he passed about six months in the Pittsburg district, where he had previously been employed. He then went to the Sugar Creek mines, in Ohio, and three months later went to Brazil, Clay County, Indiana, where the work of opening the first block-coal mines in this district was in progress, Mr. Gray being one of the first miners to be employed there. He remained until September, 1872, when he came west to Rock Springs, Wyoming, being one of the pioneer miners in that locality, and there organizing the first miners' union. In January of the following year he left for French Guiana, being one of a party of fifty-two men, recruited from Wyoming, Utah and Montana. They proceeded to Salem, Massachusetts, and there embarked on a sailing vessel, which in due time bore them to their destination. There they engaged in prospecting for gold, but owing to the peculiar laws in force in the country they found it practically impossible to secure title to any ground. John Murphy, with his wife and son, were the first to strike the pay streak, but conditions were such that they could not work the property to any profit, owing to the legal restrictions. Nine of the party died of yellow fever, and twenty-two were sent back to New York through the kindly interposition of the British consul, nineteen others scattered about in various localities and the four Wyoming men, John Hartler, John Brunskill, Edward Jeffries and Mr. Gray, sailed to Georgetown, British Guiana, where they remained four months and then set sail for New York, having been absent about nine months from the time of leaving Salem.

From the national capital the subject went into the Cumberland mountains in Tennessee, where he was employed for a while, and then he returned to Rock Springs, Wyoming, where he entered the employ of the Rock Spring Mining Company, by which he was sent to the mine in Carbon, that state. There he shortly afterward organized a company to start for the Black Hills, the intention being to make the trip under the guidance of "Tom's Son," a well-known stock man of Wyoming, but this individual received an offer of two thousand dollars from another party to compensate him for his services as guide, and as. he accepted the proposition the other company abandoned the expedition. In the fall of 1875 Mr. Gray went to Des Moines, Iowa, where he remained until February of the following year, when he returned west to Cheyenne. In June following he started for the Black Hills with what was known as the Colorado Charlie and Wild Bill train, the first named being captain of the expedition, while Wild Bill and the husband of Madame Mustachio were his two lieutenants, the three being well-known characters on the frontier. They found a number of dead men at Indian creek and Red Canon, showing that the hostile Indians were in the proximity, but as their party was a large one, comprising one hundred and ninety persons, they were not molested by the savages while enroute, and arrived in Custer on the 14th of July. Among the women in the party were Calamity Jane (whose death occurred about a year ago), Madame Mustachio and Dirty Em., each of whom will be remembered by the old timers. Mr. Gray went to work in mine No. 79, below the smelter, on Whitewood creek, and Jack McCall was working on the next claim. On the 2d of August, 1876, McCall killed the man known as Wild Bill, the subject being at work at the time. He was intimately acquainted with the victim, and speaks of him as having been a square man, generous to a fault and possessed of many other admirable qualities. In April, 1877, Mr. Gray returned to Cheyenne for his wife, and they had a pleasant trip on the way back. After his return to the hills Mr. Gray purchased claim No. 2 above discovery in Deadwood gulch, and continued to work the same until November of the following year, when he found it unprofitable to continue operations, as it was virtually worked out. He realized a large sum from this claim. In December, 1878, he removed to Terraville, where he purchased what was then known as the Caledonia boarding house, which historic building he still occupies as his home, having modernized and otherwise improved the property. He continued to be identified with mining enterprises, having been for a time in the Carbonate camp in the Bald mountains, and in January, 1884, he left for the Coeur d'Alene mining district of Idaho, being one of the first in that now famous district. He bought the discovery claim on Pritchard creek, and there sunk what is known as the Combination shaft, this being the first sunk and drifted upon up to that time. The venture proved a distinctive failure and he sunk twenty thousand dollars as well as his unprofitable shaft, having remained there for a period of thirteen months.

He then returned to the Carbonate camp, where he had heavy interests, and there remained until the enterprise went down. He then went on with his mining in the Ruby basin, and still owns valuable interests in that section. In 1896 Mr. Gray, in company with John Blatchford, D. A. McPherson and W. L. McLaughlin, purchased what was known as the McShane property, in the Yellow Creek or Flatiron district, and this was operated thereafter under the general management of Mr. Blatchford, as a shipping proposition— that is, the ore was shipped out instead of being treated on the ground. In 1898 Mr. Gray became general manager and work was continued as before until 1900, when the company built a fifty-ton cyanide plant, whose capacity was doubled five months later, and since that time the property has been working only quartzite, as a coarse-crushing proposition, quarter mesh. In 1900 the work was carried to a depth of only five feet into the quartzite ledge, and during the last year the company have penetrated to a depth of twenty feet, with a width of three hundred feet. The development is giving good returns and the subject is the largest individual stockholder, as well as general manager of the company, which is incorporated as the Wasp No. 2 Mining Company. Mr. Gray has maintained his home in Terraville since 1878 and is one of the honored and public-spirited citizens of the town and county.

In politics he is found arrayed as a stanch advocate of the principles of the Republican party, and fraternally he has attained the thirty-second degree of Scottish Rite Masonry, being also a member of the Ancient Arabic Order of the Nobles of the Mystic Shrine and the Order of the Eastern Star, while aside from the Masonic affiliations he has been identified with the Independent Order of Odd Fellows since 1870 and with the Knights of Pythias since 1871; while he also enjoys the good fellowship implied in his membership in the Benevolent and Protective Order of Elks. He is a member of the American Mining Congress and a director of the Mining Men's Association of the Black Hills. He is also an ex-president of the Black Hills Pioneer Association. In 1875 Mr. Gray was united in matrimony to Miss Ellen Chamberlain, who was born in St. Ellens, Lancastershire, England, while her marriage to the subject was solemnized in the city of Chicago, she was summoned into eternal rest on the 13th of March, 1898, and is held in loving memory by all who knew her. No children were born of this union.

WASHINGTON C. GRAYBILL

W. C. GRAYBILL, one of the highly honored citizens of Chamberlain, was born in Fairfield county, Ohio, on the 24th of January, 1851, being a son of Samuel R. and Sarah A. (Carlisle) Graybill, of whose children live are living, namely: Henry Clay, who is traffic manager of the Belt Railroad & Stock Yards Company in the city of Indianapolis, Indiana; George R., who is traveling emigrant agent for the Frisco Railroad Company, at Shelbyville, Illinois; Frank C, who is engaged in the commission trade in Kansas City, Missouri; Washington C, who is the immediate subject of this sketch; and Sarah O., who is the wife of Charles McLeod, of Portland, Oregon. The father was likewise born in Fairfield County, Ohio, whither his parents removed from Pennsylvania in the pioneer days, both having been native of Germany. Samuel R. Graybill was reared on the pioneer farmstead and as a young man prepared himself for the legal profession, being duly admitted to the bar of his native state. About 1859 he removed to Shelby County, Illinois, where he engaged in farming and stock growing, having been led to devote his attention to the great basic art of agriculture from the fact that he had married the daughter of a prosperous farmer. His own parents were well-to-do and had given him a liberal education, but he never had cause to regret his final choice of vocation. He was originally an old-line Whig, but eventually arrayed himself with the Democracy, having held various local offices. His death occurred in 1895, while his wife passed away in 1871.

The honored subject of this sketch was reared on the homestead farm and after duly attending the public schools continued his studies in the Shelbyville College, in Shelbyville, Illinois. At the age of nineteen he began teaching in the district schools, and for thirteen years thereafter was successfully engaged in pedagogic work. In 1883 he came to Dakota and located in Chamberlain, where he was soon afterward admitted to the bar of the territory, having previously given careful attention to the study of law while engaged in teaching. He opened a law office here and also established himself in the real-estate business, while he soon gained a strong hold on the confidence and regard of the community. In 1886 he was elected county judge of Brule County, and was chosen as his own successor two years later, giving a most able and discriminating service on the bench and showing himself well informed in the minutiae of the law. In 1890 Judge Graybill was elected register of deeds of the county, serving one term, and in 1894 he was appointed receiver of the United States land office at this place, retaining this position until 1898. In the fall of 1902, he was elected to represent his district in the lower house of the state legislature, being also the minority candidate for speaker, and here he has shown himself once more the loyal citizen and one deeply interested in the welfare and progress of his state, serving on several important committees. He has ever been a stalwart Democrat and has been an active worker in the party cause.

He is a prominent member of the Masonic fraternity, being affiliated with Chamberlain, Lodge, No. 56, Free and Accepted Masons; Pilgrim Chapter, No. 10, Royal Arch Masons; St. Bernard Commandery, No. 11, Knights Templar, at Mitchell; and El Riad Temple, Ancient Arabic Order of the Nobles of the Mystic Shrine, at Sioux Falls; while he has been also a prominent figure in the Knights of Pythias, having served as grand chancellor of the grand lodge of the state in 1890, and being a member of Castle Lodge, No. 10, in his home city. On the 30th of January, 1895, Judge Graybill was united in marriage to Miss Marion W. Perry, of Saratoga Springs, New York, no children having been born of this union. Mrs. Graybill's only brother, Dr. John L. Perry, is one of the proprietors of the United States Hotel at Saratoga, New York, and it is worthy of mention that the family is related to Commodore Perry, of Lake Erie fame.

ORLANDO T. GRATTAN

Orlando T. Grattan, was born in [Mount Carroll, Carroll County, Illinois, on the 8th of May, 1853, being a son of H. G. and Phoebe (Tisdell) Grattan, the former of whom was born in Connecticut. The paternal grandfather of the subject was Amos Grattan, who was a blacksmith by trade and who came of stanch old New England stock. As a young man H. G. Grattan learned the printer's trade, becoming one of the pioneer newspaper men of Illinois, and having been identified with the publication of papers at Mount Carroll, Freeport and Sterling. He later became general agent for the McCormick Harvesting Machine Company, and finally removed to Waukon, Allamakee County, Iowa, where he died in 1896, his wife having passed away in 1866, at Sterling, Illinois. The subject attended the schools of Sterling, Illinois, until he had attained the age of thirteen years, and then accompanied his father on his removal to Waukon, Iowa, where he worked on his father's farm until he had attained the age of eighteen years, in the meanwhile attending school as opportunity afforded. He then entered the employ of the McCormick Harvesting Machine Company as traveling salesman, and was thus engaged about seven years. In December, 1880, he came to Elkton, South Dakota, and here engaged in the hardware business, beginning operations with a capital of only two hundred dollars of his own. Upon coming to the state, it was his intention to locate in Pierre, but at Tracy he met a traveling salesman for the house of Hibbard, Spencer, Bartlett & Company, of Chicago, who advised him to look over the field at Elkton, which was then known as Ivanhoe. He arrived in the embryonic village at ten o'clock at night, and his first impression could not have been very favorable, for he found entertainment, so called, in the only hotel, which was connected with the local blacksmith shop. The interior was not plastered, and the second story had a floor of looseboards, while the roof was of most flimsy construction. There were five, beds in the room which was assigned to him, and during the early days of his sojourn in the town blizzards raged every day, while he states that the snow was drifted so deep in some places that one might, if desired, sit on top of the telegraph poles and view the prospect over. This memorable winter of 1880-1 was one of the worst ever experienced since the settlement of this section, but the subject was not dismayed by the outlook and determined to establish a business here.

About the middle of January, he began the erection of his two-story "business block," the same being a most primitive structure. He secured a portion of the lumber from Flandreau, eighteen miles distant, and the remainder from Lake Benton. Twice within that winter he made his way on foot to and from Flandreau, and when the roof was placed on his building those engaged in shingling the same could walk about on the snow drifts and prosecute their work, though the building was of two stories. On the 15th of April, 1881, Mr. Grattan equipped himself with snow-shoes, on which he started for Gary, thirty-five miles distant, to meet a friend. The journey required two days. The first night he stopped at the home of Henry Kienast, ten miles out, and there found that the only supply of food was that secured by grinding wheat in an ordinary coffee-mill and then baking the same into bread. He finally had to hire a team to take him to his destination, having become snow-blind, so that it was unsafe for him to continue alone. He then returned to Waukon, Iowa, where his wife and two children had remained in the meanwhile, and as soon as the railroad was opened in the spring, he brought his family to the new home, and for the first week after their arrival they slept on improvised beds laid on the floor of the local railway station, a small and rude building. Thereafter the family resided in the rooms over the store for seven years, when they took possession of the present attractive and commodious modem residence, which is valued at about five thousand dollars, and which is one of the best in the town.

During the first year of business in Elkton, Mr. Grattan made expenses and cleared sixteen dollars, and from this nucleus he has built up his present extensive and flourishing enterprise and has gained precedence as one of the leading business men and capitalists of the town. In 1897 his place of business was destroyed by fire, entailing a loss of four thousand dollars, but he promptly erected his present substantial brick and stone block, of two stories, which is one of the best in the town, being valued at ten thousand dollars, while his stock of hardware reaches a valuation of four thousand dollars. He formerly handled farm machinery, but has now dropped this branch of his enterprise. He controls a large and representative trade, and in addition to his hardware business does a large loan and insurance business. In politics he supported the Republican party until 1896, when he became convinced of the legitimacy of the financial policy adopted by the Democratic party in its platform, and showed the courage of his convictions by transferring his allegiance to the latter, whose principles he has since advocated. He is not formally identified with any religious organization, but gives his support to the Baptist church, of which his wife is a devoted member.

He is identified with the lodge and chapter of the Masonic fraternity in Elkton, with the commandery of Knights Templar at Brookings, and with the temple of the Ancient Arabic Order of the Nobles of the Mystic Shrine at Sioux Falls. On the 18th of May, 1874, Mr. Grattan was united in marriage to Miss Eva Hersey, who was born and reared in Waukon, Iowa, being a daughter of Adaniram J. and Mary (Reed) Hersey, who came to that state from Massachusetts. Mr. and Mrs. Grattan have three children, concerning whom we offer the following data: Paul H., who was graduated in the South Dakota State Agricultural College in 1896, and in the law department of the Iowa State University in 1899, is now a traveling salesman; Ray J., is associated with his father in the conducting of the store; and Edna G., who is now prosecuting her musical studies in the city of Buffalo, New York, where she will complete a two-years course in 1903, was previously a student in the Francis Shirmer Musical Academy of the University of Chicago, and is a specially skilled pianist, having gained a high reputation in Buffalo, where she is now studying.

CHARLEY F. GRAVES

C. F. Graves owns and operates a fine farm of four hundred and eighty acres situated on sections 19 and 20, Clifton township, Spink County, and has been a resident of South Dakota for over thirty years. He was born near Chicago, Illinois, on the 26th of April, 1861, a son of Daniel P. and Leonora (Diggins) Graves. The family is of Scotch descent, but was established in this country before the war of the Revolution. Daniel P. Graves was a farmer of Champaign County, Illinois, where he had removed in 1865 and where he remained until 1882, when he came to this state and homesteaded a part of the farm now belonging to C. A. Graves. The land was raw prairie when it came into his possession, but he brought it to a high state of cultivation and gathered therefrom abundant harvests. He died in October, 1908, at the age of seventy-eight years, having survived his wife since 1889. She was sixty-nine years of age when she passed away and both she and her husband are buried in the Ashton cemetery.

Charley F. Graves was educated in Champaign County and left high school when a youth of nineteen years. He then assumed the management of his father's farm, but when twenty-one years of age came to South Dakota and filed on a preemption claim which he improved. In 1899 he purchased his father's property and that farm and his claim, making four hundred and eighty acres in all, are both well improved and highly cultivated. He follows mixed farming, but is giving added attention to the raising of stock. He is a man of untiring industry and, as his crops are planted in good season and well cared for according to the most approved methods, he almost invariably has a high average per acre of grain. His stock is of good grade, bringing a high price upon the market.

Mr. Graves was married in Ashton, this state, on the 3d of December, 1888, to Miss Esther Roberts, a daughter of John T. and Ellen (Davis) Roberts, the former a pioneer farmer and carpenter of that district. He died in 1904 and was buried in the cemetery at Ashton. His wife survives and makes her home at Ashton. Mr. and Mrs. Graves have one daughter, Nellie, the wife of Erwin Bloomhall, who is residing upon the homestead, and they have a little daughter, Edna. Mr. Graves is a republican and has taken an active part in local public affairs, serving as county treasurer for two years and in a number of town offices. Fraternally he is a chapter Mason and also holds membership in the Independent Order of Odd Fellows, the Benevolent Protective Order of Elks and the Ancient Order of United Workmen. He likewise belongs to the Eastern Star. For over three decades Mr. Graves has been actively connected with the agricultural interests of the county and has been one of those progressive farmers who have made Spink County one of the prosperous sections of the state. He has made many improvements upon his farm, erecting all of the buildings, and has kept everything in splendid condition, and the success which he now enjoys is but the merited and natural reward of his enterprise and ability.

ARTHUR A. GRAY

Arthur A. Gray is a member of the Gray Construction Company, prominently associated with the improvement of Watertown. In fact, many of the most important buildings of the city have been erected by this company and Mr. Gray is therefore ranked with the leading and successful business men of the eastern part of the state. He was born in Brooklyn, Green County, Wisconsin, October 29, 1864, and is a son of Alhanon and Janet Gray. The father, who was a farmer by occupation, died when his son Arthur was but seven years of age but the mother is still living, making her home at Oregon, Wisconsin.

In the acquirement of his education Arthur A. Gray attended the public schools and high school and also a select school at Dayton, Wisconsin. When his textbooks were put aside, he entered upon an apprenticeship to the carpenter's trade under Robert Hankinson, of Brooklyn, with whom he remained for four years. He then began contracting on his own account, in Brooklyn. In 1887 he removed to Plankinton, South Dakota, where he remained for one season. Returning to Wisconsin he settled at Belleville, where he carried on business for a number of years, and in June, 1897, he came to Watertown. A list of the buildings with which he has been connected in his business capacity indicates his high standing as a contractor and builder. He erected the Kampeska Hotel, the J. J. Case building, the high school, the northwest and the southeast ward schools, the Elks Club and the Commercial Bank, all of Watertown. He also does a large amount of work in Montana and Minnesota. He was the builder of the courthouse in Walworth County, South Dakota, also in Hyde County and Sully County, South Dakota, the high school at Pierre, the high school at Redfield, the courthouse in Faulk County and the courthouse at Rosebud, Montana. He is thoroughly acquainted with every phase of building — the scientific principles as well as the practical features of the work — and his understanding of architectural laws is evidenced in the fine appearance of many of the buildings which he has erected. He is also the owner of a farm of five hundred and sixty acres in Codington County.

On the 18th of March, 1886, Mr. Gray was married to Miss Julia F. Southwick, a daughter of Marshall Southwick, who removed from Rutland, Wisconsin, to Plankinton, South Dakota, in 1881. To Mr. and Mrs. Gray have been born seven children: Gladys, now the wife of Roy L. Rose, of Watertown; Earl, a postal clerk, living in Watertown; Vernice, the wife of Roy Klinge; Lucille, now Mrs. Rudolph Martin, of Watson, Minnesota; Lucien, a brick mason; and Nettie and Mortis, both at home. The religious faith of the family is that of the Episcopal church.

In politics Mr. Gray is an independent republican and fraternally he is connected with the blue lodge and chapter of Masons at Watertown, the Benevolent Protective Order of Elks, the Modern Woodmen of America and the Independent Order of Odd Fellows. When there is a leisure moment in his busy life, he enjoys a fishing or hunting trip and he also finds rest and recreation in motoring. He is interested in everything pertaining to South Dakota and believes firmly that there is opportunity for great empire building in this state, for its natural resources have scarcely been touched, much less exhausted, and it remains to the prosperous and progressive citizens to make of the state what they will Mr. Gray cooperates in every movement for the public good and while he is guided in his business career by the laudable ambition to attain success, at the same time he never loses sight of his opportunity to further the public welfare by advocating a class of buildings that will add to the beauty, adornment and attractiveness of the city.

THEODORE FREDERICK GREFE

Theodore Frederick Grefe, secretary of the Queen City Insurance Company, has been a resident of Sioux Falls only since 1910, but within this comparatively brief period he has gained many friends and made for himself a creditable position in business circles. He was born in Brownsville, Pennsylvania, July 31, 1856, and is a son of Albert and Wilhelmina (Appenrodt) Grefe, both of whom were natives of Germany. In the year 1857 they removed with their family to Des Moines and there Theodore Frederick Grefe was reared. He attended the common schools and afterward pursued a course in the business college at Davenport, Iowa. His first work was in a machine shop at Des Moines, where he sought and secured employment when seventeen years of age. He afterward entered his father's grocery store in Des Moines, where he continued until he reached the age of twenty-two years. He next became connected with the State Insurance Company in that city and was in its service for about thirty-five years, or until 1910, when he removed to Sioux Falls as secretary of the Queen City Insurance Company. He is a director in the State Insurance Company of Des Moines and there is probably no man in South Dakota who is more thoroughly versed concerning insurance than Mr. Grefe.

Mr. Grefe has been married twice. In Des Moines he wedded Melissa Miller, who died in 1900, leaving four children: Wilma, the wife of A. J. Mehlin; Fred; Letha, the wife of J. C. Westerfield; and Beatrice, the wife of J. P. Haworth. In 1906 Mr. Grefe was again married, his second union being with Miss Ella J. Cummins, a sister of Senator Cummins. They hold membership in the Christian church and are prominent socially, the hospitality of their home being greatly enjoyed by all who know them.

Mr. Grefe is a republican in his political views, but has never sought nor desired office. He served, however, as school director in Des Moines for twenty years and the cause of education has ever found in him a stalwart friend. He is a Mason of high rank, having attained the thirty-second degree of the Scottish Rite, while he is also a member of the Mystic Shrine. He likewise belongs to the Knights of Pythias lodge and is a member of the Dacotah and Country clubs. He possesses the enterprise characteristic of the northwest and Sioux Falls numbers him among her representative and worthy citizens.

THOMAS JOHNSTON GRIER

Thomas Johnston Grier, whom the Daily Call characterized as "Lead's best friend and her people's," was the superintendent of the Homestake Mining Company for thirty years, or until death called him on the 22d of September, 1914. In the famous Black Hills district of South Dakota, the Homestake Mining Company developed its interests with such signal success that the region is today second to no other mining district in the world. The business management of the company, which has for more than a generation never failed to declare a liberal dividend annually, creates admiration among miners and mining experts of the world as well as among the captains of industry and finance. Wide experience and sound practical judgment are evident in every feature of the control of this colossal enterprise. The man who was responsible for the uniform advancement and to whom more than to any other is due the high reputation and wide prestige which the Homestake mines enjoy is Thomas Johnston Grier, the late efficient superintendent, a man not only familiar with every detail of the mining industry, but also the possessor of business tact and executive ability of high order, as his thirty years of successful management attest. The manner in which this gigantic enterprise is conducted led someone to remark, "It is a huge and highly efficient manufacturing plant with gold as its product." Back of every such mammoth concern is a strong personality and, in this instance, it was that of Thomas Johnston Grier, a man whose business ability and executive force were equaled by his keen sagacity and his broad humanitarianism.

Mr. Grier was born at Pakenham, Ontario, Canada, May 18, 1850, and was the fourth in a family of ten children, six sons and four daughters the others being: J. R. H., who died in Montreal in 1911; George E., now a resident of Iroquois; Annie M., the wife of Gilbert Fell, of Ogden, Utah; William John, who died at San Francisco in 1909; Elizabeth V., the wife of Arthur Williams, of Montreal; Margaret A., who died at Anaheim, California, in 1883; Albert E., who died in Denver, Colorado, in 1907; Charles Allen, who died in Iroquois in 1882; and Georgetta Clara, now the wife of Charles Withycomb, of Montreal.

Thomas Johnston Grier spent his youth largely in Iroquois, Ontario, Canada, where, in the acquirement of his education, he passed through consecutive grades to the high school. His first practical business training and experience came to him as a clerk under his father in the post office and while thus engaged he devoted his leisure moments to the study of telegraphy. At the age of seventeen he went to Montreal and became an employee in the mail office of the Montreal Telegraph Company, with which he was connected until 1871. He then crossed the border into the United States and made his way to Corinne, Utah, where he was employed as an operator by the Western Union Telegraph Company for about two and a half years. He was then placed in charge of the operating room at Salt Lake City, where he continued for four years.

The year 1878 witnessed Mr. Grier's arrival in the Black Hills, at which time he entered the employ of the Homestake Company as bookkeeper. Six years later, or in 1884, following the demise of Samuel McMaster, he was appointed to the vacant position of superintendent of the company and so remained for three decades, honored and respected alike by stockholders and employes. Under his direction was developed the largest gold mine in the world, but Mr. Grier, although he had every opportunity to do so, never became a stockholder, feeling that he could serve the interests of both employers and employes with greater fairness and justice if he was not financially connected with the corporation. He was, however, president of the First National Bank of Lead. Working his own way upward, Mr. Grier never forgot the fact that he won his advancement and was therefore in sympathy with the humblest employe. Any man with a just grievance was sure to obtain an audience and recognized the fact that fairness would be meted out to him. It is probable that no other superintendent of a like corporation in the United States ever enjoyed so fully the respect of the employes — respect which he won by reason of his great consideration and fairness to the man who earns his bread by honest toil. As manager and superintendent, he was also ever looking out for the welfare of the corporation which he represented. He was given carte blanche in regard to the control of affairs and he continually studied out methods to promote efficiency and produce more substantial results. Under his direction many millions of dollars were expended in improvements which have added to the value of the plant and promoted its efficiency. In this connection the Daily Call wrote:

"Under his regime was built the great water system which supplies the company's works, the city of Lead and other towns. The Spearfish, hydro-electric plant was completed during his term of office, the great Ellison hoist, the viaduct connecting the mills with the railway system of the company, the Star and Amicus mills, adding to the capacity of the company's milling plants, and other works which, while adding to the efficiency and the output of the company, have given employment to hundreds of people. Under him the work of building the new B. & M. hoist, the power plant and boiler plant, which is now under way, was started. The Recreation building was conceived by Mr. Grier, and the plans for its completion carried out by Chief Engineer and Assistant Superintendent Richard Blackstone. It is one thing that will stand as a monument to Mr. Grier, and a reminder of the thought and care which he gave to the interests of those who worked under him." As manager for the Homestake Company Mr. Grier superintended the efforts of twenty-five hundred people with a payroll of two hundred and twenty-five thousand dollars per month, the mines turning out over six million dollars in gold and owning over sixteen million dollars' worth of property. The business was largely developed through the efforts of Mr. Grier. Labor troubles in 1908, when the company was obliged to take issue with the Western Federation of Labor, were finally settled after Mr. Grier had put into effect a card system, by which all employes declared they would not become affiliated with the union. This has since been in effect and the soundness of his judgment in the matter is indicated in the fact that neither riot nor murder accompanied the labor trouble and there were few arrests for disturbances, so perfectly were his orders executed by his subordinates.

Perhaps one of the greatest public testimonials of the business worth and ability of Mr. Grier was given at the time when the United States Industrial Commission made its recent investigation of the Homestake Company, going carefully into all details with the result that the commission made the public statement that they had never found any corporation so equitably managed or so perfectly systematized as the Homestake under what they termed, "Mr. Crier's benevolent despotism."

On the 8th of August, 1896, Mr. Grier wedded Mary Jane Palethorpe, of Glasgow, Scotland, and they became parents of four children, Thomas Johnston, Evangeline Victoria, Lisgar Patterson and Ormonde Palethorpe. Mr. Grier also had two stepchildren, whom he regarded with the same love and affection that he entertained for his own. These are James and Madge Ferrie. His home was his recreation.

A little more than two weeks prior to his death Mr. Grier, accompanied by his wife and two sons, went to California and at Los Angeles, on the 22d of September, 1914, he passed away. He was a life member of the Benevolent Protective Order of Elks, a member of several of the Masonic bodies and also of the organization known as the Homestake Veterans. His religious faith was evidenced by his membership in and regular attendance at the services of the Episcopal church. When the news of his death was received in the city in which he had so long lived it was said that old men that had been in the employ of the company for over thirty years could be seen on the street crying like children over the loss which they regarded as personal. Every form of public amusement or entertainment was cancelled or postponed from the time the news was received until after the funeral, and not only in Lead but in every portion of the country public tribute was paid to the memory of the man who was so highly revered where he was best known. Perhaps something of the nature of Mr. Grier's splendid life work can best be gleaned from the remarks made by Professor Commons, of the industrial commission, after his investigation of the Homestake properties and their management. He said:

"I would like on this question of the underlying causes that you have brought out, I would like for my personal use, not as stating any idea of my colleagues, to state to you what seems to me to be our purpose and line of suggestions which, from my standpoint, would be of use in the work that we have to do. As I stated at the beginning, we are required by congress to investigate the underlying causes of industrial unrest, and to make recommendations for legislation to congress and, naturally, to the states. If we find unrest, what are its causes and what legislation we should recommend as a remedy.

"Now, I might state what seems to me to be the summing up of this testimony, that is, the way it strikes me from my own point of view, not representing either the employer or the employes, but simply as a looker-on, you might say: You have here the most remarkable business organization that I have come across in the country. You have developed welfare features which are beyond anything that I know of, and they are given with a liberal hand. You have a high scale of wages, reasonable hours — very fair hours. There has been evidently great progress made in taking care of the employes in the hospital service, and you have taken care of the cost of living, have kept it down below what employes in other communities have been forced to pay. You have practically been able by your great strength here as a huge corporation, dominating the whole community, to look out for the welfare of your employes, and to bring in an admirable class of citizens. It seems also that you are influential in politics, that you secure a good class of officials, and that you have secured the enforcement of law, the reduction of immorality. It seems also that you make an effort to build up the religious life of the community and that your policy is broad and liberal in all respects. I take it also that this policy depends solely upon your personality. Such inquiries as I have made here indicate that in all cases the stockholders leave all these matters to you personally and that this broad policy has been carried out by you on your own initiative; and that you have felt that it was necessary, for the good of the community, the securing a fine class of labor here, which you have undoubtedly done, that you should hold the reins pretty tight on this community."

Adding that he had visited business men and talked with individuals in the camp, the chairman stated that from all he could see or hear the Homestake management had wielded its power with the utmost fairness, had encouraged the religious life and educational life of the community, and asked suggestions from Mr. Grier as to recommendations to be made congress as a basis for legislation, pointing out in the course of his remarks the fact that another man in Mr. Grier's place might not exercise his power with the same fairness, justice and generosity that have characterized Mr. Grier's administration.

Splendid and well merited tribute to Mr. Grier was paid by one of the local papers which said:

"It was not his great executive genius alone, his ability for the management of a great property involving countless details and unlimited capacity for work, that Mr. Grier in his superintendency of the Homestake Mine made Lead unique in the industrial world. It was by the high character of the man — the honor, courage, justice and generosity. It was not merely a working policy that gave to Homestake employes and to Lead people in general whatever of good it lay in his great power to bestow — it was the big, fatherly heart that made it possible for every man to look to Mr. Grier for justice and generous treatment and never to look in vain. In the management of Homestake affairs Mr. Grier was given all power. It rested with him to institute and carry out policies and plans for the control of an industry upon whose successful working Lead and her people depend absolutely while all the Hills is to a great degree dependent upon it. How many men would have been able to lay aside every consideration of personal aggrandizement or personal ambition and think only of the interests of the employes of the company and the rights of the stockholders? There was no reason why Mr. Grier should not have been a heavy stockholder. No reason why he should not have been a millionaire many times over without in any way breaking the requirements of law and of honesty. There was no reason, that is, except the fine sense of of honor that prompted him, feeling that not being a stockholder would place him in better attitude toward the company and its operatives, to refuse to profit himself by the increase in values brought about largely through him. That unselfishness showed itself in many ways. Mr. Grier could have spared himself much of anxiety and of effort had he been less concerned for the welfare of others and more for his own. But in all things the well-being and happiness of those under him and the interests of the company whose property he controlled came before any personal consideration."

A modern statesman and philosopher has said: "In all this world the thing supremely worth having is the opportunity, coupled with the capacity, to do well and worthily a piece of work, the doing of which shall be of vital significance to mankind." Such an opportunity came to Mr. Grier and well did he improve it and his career illustrates the saying of another eminent American statesman, "There is something better than making a living — making a life."

FRED DE KRAFFT GRIFFIN

Fred de Krafft GRIFFIN, the able editor and publisher of the Walworth County Record, at Selby, has the distinction of being a native of the national capital, having been born in the city of Washington, D. C, on the 16th of January, 1862, and being a son of Robert C. and S. Adelaide Griffin, both of whom were likewise born and reared in that city. The lineage on the paternal side is traced back to Lawrence Griffin, who settled near Leonardtown, Maryland, in 1742, having emigrated from England, his native land.

Baron J. C. P. de Krafft, the maternal great-grandfather of the subject, assisted L'Enfant in laying out the city of Washington, and his son, Lieutenant de Krafft, was with Decatur at Tripoli, as a member of the United States navy. The Baron's grandson, Rear Admiral de Krafft, of the United States Navy, died within recent years, having well upheld the prestige of the honored name which he bore.

The subject was reared in his native city, in whose public schools he received his early educational discipline, having been graduated in the high school as a member of the class of 1878. He initiated his association with the "art preservative of all arts" on the 1st of January, 1881, when he secured a position in the office of the Evening Critic, of Washington, while from 1884 to 1887 he was employed in the treasury branch of the government printing office. In July of the latter year, he came to the present state of South Dakota and located in Bangor, Walworth County, and on the 18th of the following September he became the editor and publisher of the Central Dakotan, the name of which was changed to the Walworth County Record in 1890, since which time he has continued the publication under that title, while the office and general headquarters of the paper were removed from Bangor to Selby in 1900. In his political proclivities Mr. Griffin is a stalwart supporter of the Republican party, and personally and through the columns of his paper he has done much to further its success in the state, being one of the party leaders in his section and having served for several terms as chairman of the Walworth County central committee, while for six terms he was a member of the Republican state central committee.

Fraternally he is identified with the Masonic order, the Modern Woodmen of America and the Knights of the Maccabees, and both he and his wife are communicants of the Protestant Episcopal church. On the loth of February, 1882, was solemnized the marriage of Mr. Griffin to Miss Emma B. McNelly, who likewise was born and reared in Washington, D. C, being a daughter of Arthur and Mary McNelly. Mr. and Mrs. Griffin has seven children, the first two having been born in the capital city and the others in Walworth County. South Dakota, their names, in order of birth, being as follows: Charles, Evelyn, Fred, Arthur, Elton, Clifford and Edwin.

ABRAHAM D. GRIFFEE

A. D. GRIFFEE, register of deeds of Potter County, is a native of the state of Iowa, having been born in the city of Oskaloosa, on the 21st of September, 1861, and being a son of Abraham and Nancy (Higgenbotham) Griffee, the former of whom was born in Virginia and the latter in Ohio, while their marriage was solemnized in the state of Ohio. The Griffee family is of German extraction and was founded in the old and patrician state of Virginia in the early colonial era, with whose history the name has been prominently identified. The father of the subject was reared and educated in Virginia, and as a young man removed thence to Ohio, where he maintained his residence for a few years, and then about 1840, made the long overland journey to Iowa with team and wagon, being accompanied by his wife and their three children, the other four of the children in the family having been born in the Hawkeye state. He became one of the pioneers of Mahaska County, where he reclaimed and improved a valuable farm, and there he continued to reside until his death, which occurred in 1886. He became a man of prominence and distinctive influence in the community and passed away in the fullness of years and well-earned honors. His devoted wife was summoned into eternal rest in 1899, and of their children all are still living, the subject of this review having been the sixth in order of birth.

Abraham D. Griffee was born in the town of Oskaloosa, Iowa, and from his sixth year was reared on the farm and in his youth was accorded the advantages of the excellent public schools of his native state, completing a course in the high school at Oskaloosa. He continued to be associated in the work and management of the home farm until 1884, when he came to South Dakota and took up land in Faulk County, whose organization had been effected about a year previously. Upon this pre-emption claim he made good improvements, the place being eligibly located near the village of Seneca, and there he continued to be engaged in farming and stock growing until 1893, while he still retains possession of the property, which has greatly appreciated in value in the intervening years. In the year mentioned he came to Gettysburg, the official center of Potter County, and here engaged in the grain business, owning an interest in the elevator here, and he continued to be identified with this line of enterprise for the ensuing five years, at the expiration of which he disposed of his interests in the same and turned his attention to the lumber business, at which he was engaged until 1900. In 1900 he was elected to the office of register of deeds of Potter County. He gave an able and systematic administration of the office and was chosen as his own successor in the fall of 1902, for a second term of two years. He manifests a lively interest in public affairs and is an uncompromising Democrat in his political adherency, having been an active worker in the party cause. Mr. Griffee is a man of ability and has been successful in his business affairs since casting in his lot with the people of South Dakota. In addition to his landed interests in Faulk County he is also the owner of valuable realty in Potter County.

Fraternally he is identified with the Masonic order. Knights of Pythias, Ancient Order of United Workmen, Modern Woodman of America and Independent Order of Odd Fellows. On the 2d of February, 1886, was solemnized the marriage of Mr. Griffee to Miss Mary E. Douglas, who was born and reared in Lonaconing, Maryland, being a daughter of Capt. John W. and Ellen Douglas, and a sister of Herbert Douglas, who is now an official of the Crow Creek Indian reservation. Mr. and Mrs. Griffee have one daughter, Rhea, who was born on the 19th of July, 1887.

GEORGE C. GRIFFIN

George C. Griffin is cashier of the Ware & Griffin Bank at Clark and in his business, career has made wise use of his time and his opportunities. He was born in Chicago, Illinois, on the 5th of August, 1861, and is a son of Stephen B. and Fanny A. (Brown) Griffin, both of whom are deceased. The father was for many years engaged in railroad work.

At the usual age George C. Griffin became a public-school pupil, passing through consecutive grades until he was prepared for the high school. When he had completed his more advanced studies, he secured employment in an insurance office and later in a bank at Morris, Illinois. The fall of 1882 witnessed his arrival in South Dakota, at which time he came to Clark, where he engaged in the loan and real-estate business. He secured a fair clientage in that connection and won a substantial measure of success. At length, however, he entered the banking business, with which he first became connected in the '80s. Subsequently he again, took up the real-estate business but in 1900 he renewed his connection with banking and in 1904 he organized the Ware & Griffin Bank, entering upon the duties of cashier, with. Fred Ware as the president. The business has doubled since the opening of the bank, which, is now in a prosperous condition. It follows a safe, conservative yet progressive policy and the number of its depositors and the amount of its business along general lines is constantly increasing.

Mr. Griffin has been married twice. In 1884 he wedded Adeline McSpadden of Clark, and unto them were born three children: Emma, now the wife of R. J. Hart, of Watertown; Helen; and Elizabeth. In 1910 Mr. Griffin was again married, his second union being with Nina B. Brown of Clark, and they have one son, George C, Jr.

Mr. Griffin gives his political indorsement to the men and measures of the republican party, but has no aspiration for office. Fraternally he is connected with the Masons, having taken the degrees of both the lodge and chapter. He also has membership with the Elks, the Knights of Pythias, the Woodmen, the Workmen and the Modern Brotherhood of America. He is now president of the council and of the Commercial Club and his efforts have been a salient force in promoting public progress, in extending business connections and in advancing the general welfare along many lines. His religious faith is that of the Congregational church and his well spent life has won for him the high regard of all with whom he has come in contact, gaining for him a circle of friends almost coextensive with the circle of his acquaintance.

AUGUST F. GRIMM

August F. Grimm, who has lived in South Dakota for about three decades, is the pioneer merchant of Parkston and has long been recognized as an influential, prosperous and leading citizen of his community. He carries an extensive stock of general merchandise and his establishment is regarded as one of the finest of its kind in the state. His birth occurred in Wisconsin on the 9th of February, 1861, his parents being Henry and Carrie Grimm, the former a merchant. He attended the public schools in the acquirement of an education and when sixteen years of age left the parental roof and became connected with mercantile interests.

In 1885, when twenty-four years of age, Mr. Grimm came to South Dakota, first locating about three miles southeast of Parkston, in which town he took up his abode at the end of a year and a half, when the railroad was built through. Here he embarked in business as a merchant and his was the first store of the locality. The enterprise was necessarily a modest one in the beginning, but with the settlement and development of the community his patronage has steadily grown until his is now one of the most extensive and best equipped establishments of the character in the entire state. Other business interests have also claimed his attention to a considerable extent, for he is at the head of the Parkston Canning Factory, is the proprietor of the well-known St. Charles Hotel of Parkston and also organized the creamery, of which he served as manager for seven years. His connection with any undertaking ensures a prosperous outcome of the same, for it is in his nature to carry forward to successful completion whatever he is associated with. He has earned for himself an enviable reputation as a careful man of business and in his dealings is known for his prompt and honorable methods, which have won him the deserved and unbounded confidence of his fellowmen.

On the 26th of January, 1888, Mr. Grimm was united in marriage to Miss Clara Bell Emery, her father being James Emery, a homesteader of this state. Their children are two in number, namely: Dacotah Bell, now the wife of Edward B. Lucius of Chicago; and Emery L., a merchant of Iowa.

Mr. Grimm is a republican in politics and has been a prominent figure in the local ranks of the party, having served for six years as mayor of Parkston, for a number of years as a member of the city council, and also on the school board. He is likewise the president of the Commercial Club and a recognized leader in all movements instituted for the benefit and upbuilding of the community and the promotion of its best interests. Fraternally he is identified with the Masons, belonging to the commandery at Mitchell and the Mystic Shrine at Sioux Falls. Mr. Grimm is regarded as one of the wealthiest men of his section, and his career has ever been such that he enjoys the unqualified confidence and high esteem of all with whom he has been associated.

MARTIN M. GROVE, M. D.

The reputation of Dr. Martin M. Grove in the field of surgical practice extends far beyond the limits of Minnehaha County, in which he makes his home. He maintains his office in Dell Rapids, where he located in 1905. Through the intervening period he has demonstrated his marked ability in successful private practice and in hospital work as well, for he was the founder and has been the promoter of the Dell Rapids Hospital, now widely recognized as one of the most valuable institutions of the southeastern part of the state. Dr. Grove is a western man by birth, training and preference. He was born in Plainview, Minnesota, on the 18th of September, 1879, and is a son of Martin A. and Mary A. (Christopher) Grove, both of whom were natives of Norway, but came to the United States in childhood with their respective parents, the two families settling in Wabasha County, Minnesota. There Martin A. Grove and Mary A. Christopher were reared and married, following which they began their domestic life upon a farm in Wabasha County, where they have since made their home. For many years Mr. Grove continued in active connection with general agricultural pursuits, but is now living retired, making his home in Plainview.

Dr. Grove was reared upon the old home farm in Wabasha County and the district schools afforded him his early educational privileges. Later he attended the Plainview high school, from which he was graduated with the class of 1899. He afterward entered the University of Minnesota and in 1901 took up the study of medicine, matriculating in the College of Physicians and Surgeons of the University of Illinois at Chicago. In due time he was graduated with the class of 1905. During the last year of his college course, he took up hospital work and filled the position of interne in St. Mary's, following his graduation until the fall of 1905, when he removed to Dell Rapids and opened an office for the private practice of medicine. There he has since remained, covering a period of ten years, and as time has passed his practice has constantly grown in volume and importance. In 1908 he established a hospital with four beds and since that time his hospital practice has grown to such an extent that he now has thirty beds. For the conduct of the institution, he organized the Dell Rapids Hospital Company and, in the summer of 1914, a modern hospital building, equipped with thirty beds, was built. It is supplied with every modern facility for the care of the sick and for surgical work and, in fact, is a model institution of its kind. In 1911 Dr. Grove was joined in practice by Dr. J. B. Eagan and in February, 1914, they admitted a third partner, Dr. Arthur F. Grove, a brother of the senior member of the firm. These three are today practicing under the style of Grove, Eagan & Grove and they are the only ones doing major surgery in Dell Rapids. They have a well merited reputation as expert surgeons of eastern South Dakota and do a vast amount of work along that line.

In January, 1906, Dr. Martin M. Grove was married to Miss Grace Fisk, of Plainview, Minnesota, and they have become parents of four sons, Martin Stewart, Raymond Fisk, Donald B. and Harold. Dr. and Mrs. Grove are members of the Methodist Episcopal church and take an active and helpful interest in its work. Their home is a hospitable one, whose good cheer is greatly enjoyed by many friends.

Dr. Grove is identified with several fraternal organizations. In Masonry he has attained high rank, belonging to Dell Rapids Lodge, No. 40, F. & A. M.; Occidental Consistory, No. 2, A. & A. S. R.; and El Riad Temple, A. A. O. N. M. S., of Sioux Falls. He is a member of both the subordinate lodge and encampment of Odd Fellows at Dell Rapids, of Dell Rapids Lodge, K. P., and of Sioux Falls Lodge, No. 262, B. P. O. E. He likewise belongs to the Dell Rapids Commercial Club and is in sympathy with all of its movements and purposes for the progress and upbuilding of the city. Dr. Grove belongs to the Seventh District Medical Society, in which he has been honored with the presidency, and he is also a member of the South Dakota Medical Society and a fellow of the American Medical Association. He is likewise connected with the Clinical Congress of Surgeons of North America and thus he keeps in touch with the advanced thought of the profession in all its scientific researches and investigations.

GEORGE GROVER

George Grover, one of the representative citizens and prominent merchants of Hartford, Minnehaha County, is a native of the state of Michigan, having been born on a farm in Pulaski township, Jackson County, on the 3d of June, 1859, and being a son of Allen W. and Jane E.

(Phipps) Grover, natives of New York state. The father was one of the representative farmers of that county and a man of prominence in his section. He died in 1902, while the mother is still living at the old homestead. The subject was reared to the sturdy and invigorating discipline of the homestead farm and was afforded excellent educational advantages. After completing the curriculum of the public schools he was matriculated in the Michigan State Agricultural College, at Lansing, where he completed the prescribed four-years course and was graduated as a member of the class of 1881, receiving the degree of Bachelor of Science. After leaving college Mr. Grover was for two years a successful teacher in the public schools of his native county and he then, in 1882, purchased the Concord Enterprise, at Concord, that county, continuing as editor and publisher of the same for two years, after which he was there engaged in the general merchandise business until 1889, when he removed to Janesville, Wisconsin, where he learned the art of telegraphy, at which he was there employed for some time, as was he later in Hamilton, Minnesota. He was thus employed in the service of the Chicago, St. Paul, Minneapolis & Omaha Railroad for nearly a decade, in Minnesota and South Dakota, having been station agent and operator at Hartford, this state, from 1891 until 1898. He thereafter passed a year in looking for an eligible location in the southern states, but became convinced that South Dakota offered superior attractions, and in 1899 he returned to Hartford, where he entered into partnership with Herman C. Robsahm, under the firm name of Robsahm & Grover, and engaged in the general merchandise business, with which enterprise he has since been successfully identified, having purchased the interests of his partner on the 1st of May, 1903, and being now the sole proprietor of the business, which is one of the most important of the sort in this section, his store being well stocked in its various departments and controlling a trade which extends throughout the wide radius of country normally tributary to Hartford. Mr. Grover has ever believed in the principles of the Democratic party as exemplified in the teachings of Jefferson and Jackson, but the heretical tendencies in the party ranks in later years have caused him to withdraw his allegiance and he is now an out-and-out supporter of the policies of President Roosevelt.

Fraternally he is identified with Hartford Lodge, U. D., Ancient Free and Accepted Masons, at Hartford; and Sioux Falls Lodge, No. 262, Benevolent and Protective Order of Elks, at Sioux Falls, South Dakota. On the 4th of August, 1891, was solemnized the marriage of Mr. Grover to Miss Hattie B. Smith, daughter of Isaac F. and Mary A. (Earl) Smith, of Jackson County, Michigan, and of this union have been born three children: Allen S., who was born on the 16th of September, 1894; Raymond, who was born on the 21st of July, 1899; and Theodore, who was born on the 28th day of October, 1903.

H. H. GUERNSEY

For over a third of a century H. H. Guernsey has been postmaster of Altamont and has a record that is probably not equaled in the state for length of service. For about the same length of time he has held a license as notary public and in both capacities has proved able, accurate and efficient. He was born in Lisbon, New Hampshire, on the 5th of July, 1842, a son of Orin and Sarah (Cooley) Guernsey, both natives of New Hampshire and descended from old New England stock. The father was a man of more than local prominence both in New Hampshire and Wisconsin, to which state he removed in 1843. He served in both state legislatures and was also a member of the National Peace Commission, which negotiated a treaty with the Indians in 1866 or 1867. He was appointed to that position by Hon. D. M. Cooley, then commissioner of Indian affairs, and he located at Dubuque, Iowa, in order to facilitate the transaction of his official duties. For the last twenty years of his life, he was engaged in the insurance business in Janesville, Wisconsin, and both he and his wife passed away in that city. He was a man of large mental caliber and a conspicuous figure in the public affairs of the early days of Wisconsin. Besides taking part in the affairs of civil government in New Hampshire, he was colonel of the state militia for several years.

H. H. Guernsey was reared under the parental roof and acquired his education in the public schools. After completing the elementary course, he entered Janesville high school, but in his senior year enlisted in the northern army for service in the defense of the Union. On the 15th of August, 1861, he became a member of Company E, Twenty-second Wisconsin Volunteers, and after serving for two years with this command he passed an examination before the government board of examiners at Nashville and was commissioned first lieutenant of Company D, Fourteenth United States Colored Infantry, Colonel Thomas J. Morgan commanding. Colonel Morgan was later commissioner of Indian affairs under Governor Hayes. On the 29th of March, 1866, Mr. Guernsey was mustered out of the Federal military service, having been reserved for garrison duty for some time following the close of the war between the north and south. He returned to Janesville and there engaged in the insurance business until 1879, in which year he came to South Dakota, locating in Deuel County. He entered a homestead and tree claim two miles southwest of the present town of Altamont. In August, 1880, just after the town site had been surveyed and platted Mr. Guernsey purchased the first town lot sold and built the first residence and store in Altamont, where he engaged in general merchandising for twenty-one years, being the pioneer trader in that part of the county. In December, 1880, he was appointed postmaster and has served continuously in that capacity since, excepting three years under a democratic administration when he served as deputy postmaster. He is one of the oldest postmasters in the state and his record is one of conscientious and capable performance of the work devolving upon him and reflects great credit upon him. For a quarter of a century, he has also been notary public; served as county judge in the '80s and was a member of the board of county commissioners from 1903 to 1907.

In 1866 Mr. Guernsey was married to Miss Sophia Naomi Hoisington, of Jefferson, Wisconsin, and of the five children born to them four survive, namely: Clarence C, who is agent for the Chicago, Milwaukee & St. Paul Railroad Company at Shakopee, Minnesota; Ardelle, now the wife of John Knuckey, postmaster of Clear Lake, this state; Harry Summer, agent of the Chicago, Milwaukee & St. Paul Railroad Company at Edgeley, North Dakota; and Laura May, now Mrs. Chester E. Courtney, of Pomeroy, Washington.

Mr. Guernsey is a republican in politics and is much interested in everything pertaining to the public welfare. Fraternally he belongs to Phoenix Lodge, No. 129, A. F. & A. M., at Clear Lake, and to Freeman Thayer Post, G. A. R., of Watertown. He is entitled to honor as one of that fast-diminishing band who are the survivors of the brave men to whom we owe the unity and greatness of our country today. He has always borne in mind the fact that the pursuits of peace also offer opportunities for the exercise of patriotism and in placing the public good above individual interests he has throughout his life served well his country.

FRED W. GUNKLE

Fred W. GUNKLE, who is numbered among the successful and popular business men of Sioux Falls, was born in the city of Reading, Pennsylvania, on the 26th of October, 1857, and is a son of Fred and Elizabeth (Kalkhofl) Gunkle, both of whom were born and reared in Germany, and both of whom are now deceased, the father having been a roadmaster for the Philadelphia & Reading Railroad. The subject received his early educational discipline in the public schools of his native city, and in his early youth entered upon an apprenticeship at the machinist's trade in one of the extensive concerns oi Reading. He became a skilled artisan in the line and continued his residence in the old Keystone state until 1876, when he located in the city of Chicago, where he was for the ensuing three years employed in the works of the Crane Brothers' Manufacturing Company. In 1879 he located in Dubuque, Iowa, where he held a responsible position with the Iowa Iron Works for the following two years, at the expiration of which he returned to Chicago and accepted a position as traveling representative for Samuel Bliss & Company, with whom he remained until 1884, having established headquarters in Sioux Falls in 1881, at the time of entering the employ of the concern. In 1884 he became a traveling salesman for the Sioux City Steam Engine Works, of Sioux City, Iowa, retaining this incumbency four years. In 1891 he was appointed deputy United States marshal for western division, northern district of Iowa, with headquarters at Sioux City, Iowa, holding office until 1895, and being thereafter traveling representative for the Andrew Kuehn Company, of Sioux Falls, South Dakota, in the meanwhile maintaining his home in Sioux Falls during the greater portion of the interval. In 1896 he "quit the road" and engaged in the wholesale cigar and tobacco business in this city, and he has reason to be satisfied with the results which have been attained, for his trade is of the best order and covers a good territory, normally tributary to the city as a jobbing center. In politics he is stalwart Republican and ever shown a deep interest in the promotion of the party cause, though he has never been a seeker of official preferment.

In a fraternal way Mr. Gunkle is identified with Unity Lodge, No. 130, Ancient Free and Accepted Masons; Sioux Falls Chapter, No. 2, Royal Arch Masons; Sioux Falls Commandery, No. 2, Knights Templar; and El Riad Temple of the Ancient Arabic Order of the Nobles of the Mystic Shrine, while he is also a prominent and popular affiliate of the Sioux Falls Lodge, No. 262, Benevolent and Protective Order of Elks, of which he is past exalted ruler, while he has also represented the same in the grand lodge of the state. On the 13th of June, 1888, Mr. Gunkle was united in marriage to Miss Emma J. Carter, who was born in the state of Illinois, and who was a resident of Sioux Falls at the time of her marriage. They have no children.

EDGAR M. HALL

Edgar M. Hall, who has resided in South Dakota continuously for the past twenty-six years, was elected mayor of Aberdeen in May, 1911, and has ably served in that important office to the present time. His birth occurred in Sparta, Wisconsin, on the 10th of February, 1868, his parents being George B. and Hattie M. (Morrison) Hall. He attended the public schools in the acquirement of an education and subsequently worked at the barber's trade for a period of twenty years. In 1887 he came to South Dakota, locating first in Watertown, while on the 1st of August of that year he took up his abode in Aberdeen. In 1906 he purchased a farm, the operation of which claimed his time and energies for a period of three years. Mr. Hall was elected alderman on the republican ticket in 1905 and in May, 1911, was made mayor of Aberdeen, being the first executive chosen under the commission form of government. He has given the city & progressive and businesslike administration, instituting many measures of reform and improvement which have promoted its welfare along various lines.

In November, 1890, Mr. Hall was united in marriage to Miss Belle B. Bailey, of Watertown, South Dakota, by whom he has one son. In Masonry, he has attained the thirty-second degree of the Scottish Rite and also belongs to the Mystic Shrine, while his other fraternal connections are with the Benevolent Protective Order of Elks and the Knights of Pythias. His genuine worth and his devotion to all that is right, just and elevating, make him a man whom to know is to respect and honor.

PHILO HALL

The legal affairs of the great state of South Dakota at the present time are placed in able hands, and as attorney general of the state the subject of this sketch is giving an administration which is creditable to the commonwealth and to himself professionally and officially. Mr. Hall is a native of the state of Minnesota, having been born in Wilton, Waseca County on the 31st of December, 1865, a son of Philo and Mary E. Greenel Hall. Philo Hall, Sr., was born in Caledonia Springs, Canada, being the son of Philo and Susana Hall, both of whom were born in the state of Vermont. When about fifteen years of age the father of the subject left his native town in Canada and went to Kenosha, Wisconsin, his father having died when Philo was a mere child. He attended school in Kenosha and Racine, Wisconsin, continuing his studies until he was about nineteen years of age, and he then removed to Waseca County, Minnesota, where he turned his attention to teaching school, gaining distinctive prestige in this profession. In April, 1861, in response to the President's first call for volunteers, he enlisted as a member of the First Minnesota Volunteer Infantry, with which he served three years, making the record of a valiant and faithful soldier of the republic. He then returned to his home in Minnesota and engaged in the hotel business in Wilton, having married Miss Mary E. Greene, daughter of William and Mary Greene, of New York City. The father of the subject died on the 30th of April, 1883, and he is survived by his wife and their four children, the mother being now a resident of Brookings, South Dakota, which is likewise the home of her son, the attorney general, who is the eldest of the four children, the others being as follows: Mary E., who is the wife of Arthur Alton, of Brookings; George P., who is likewise a resident of this place: and Nellie, who remains with her mother. After the death of his father in 1883, the family removed to Brookings, and here the subject of this review took up the study of law in the office of Judge J. O. Andrews, under whose direction he prosecuted his technical reading until 1886, and was admitted to the bar of the territory of Dakota in 1887. Shortly afterward Mr. Hall entered into partnership with his former preceptor. Judge Andrews, this association continuing until 1889, when Judge Andrews was elected to the circuit bench, and since that time Mr. Hall has been actively engaged in the practice of his profession in Brookings, and is now the senior member of the present firm of Hall, Lawrence & Roddle. Mr. Hall has ever been a stanch advocate of the principles of the Republican party and has been a valued and able worker in the cause of the same. In 1894 he was elected state's attorney of Brookings County, and was chosen as his own successor in 1896, while in 1895 and was elected mayor of the city of Brookings, serving one term and giving a most able administration of municipal affairs. He has also served as city attorney and in 1901 he represented his district in the state senate. In the autumn election of 1902, he was elected to his present distinguished office of attorney general of the state, assuming the duties of the position in January, 1903, and was unanimously renominated to that office at the Republican state convention at Sioux Falls, May 4, 1904.

He is a member of the Masonic fraternity, the Independent Order of Odd Fellows and the Ancient Order of United Workmen. On the 27th of April, 1890, Mr. Hall married Mrs. Mary A. Cooke, and of this union have been born three children, namely: Vivian, who was born on the 25th of September, 1891; Philo, Jr., who was born on the 8th of August, 1895, and Morrell, who was born on the 26th of March, 1898.

CHARLES HAMILTON

The business interests of Britton find an active representative in Charles Hamilton, who is proprietor of a lumberyard and the vice president of the First National Bank. He is wide-awake, alert, energetic and resourceful and carries forward to successful completion whatever he undertakes. He is a typical western man in spirit and interests, ever manifesting that progressiveness which has been the dominant factor in the development of this section of the country. He was born at Winona, Minnesota, March 1, 1863, a son of Andrew and Mary (Whitten) Hamilton, natives of Ireland, the former born in 1828 and the latter in 1832. When a young man Andrew Hamilton crossed the Atlantic, and Mary Whitten came with her mother to the new world. They were married in Albany, New York, and remained in that state for some time, Mr. Hamilton working as a silversmith. In 1850 he removed to Winona, Minnesota, where he established a lumberyard and in the conduct of his business met with substantial success, becoming one of the well-to-do citizens of that place. He was also prominent and influential in public affairs and was three times elected mayor of the city on the democratic ticket, his reelection being proof of his capability, his fidelity in office and the confidence reposed in him. He died in the year 1898, while his wife passed away in 1907, in the faith of the Methodist Episcopal church, in which she held membership. Of their family of eight children only two are now living, the daughter being Mrs. A. H. Reed, a widow.

Charles Hamilton was educated in the Winona high school and the Winona Normal School and when seventeen years of age became the active associate of his father in the lumber business, in which he has since continued. Removing to Dakota territory in 1886, he established the Dakota Lumber Company of

Britton, conducting business under that style until 1913, when he purchased his partner's interest and changed the name to the Hamilton Lumber Company. This business is incorporated with a capital stock of one hundred thousand dollars and Mr. Hamilton, as president and chief stockholder of the company, is operating six yards in South Dakota and one in North Dakota. His trade has now reached extensive proportions, marking him as one of the most active and representative business men of his section. He is also the vice president of the First National Bank and has extensive landed interests, having made judicious investment in real estate.

Mr. Hamilton has been married twice. In 1889 he wedded Miss Maude Aplin, a native of Iowa, and to them were born four children, as follows: Shepard, a practicing attorney who received his education in Cornell University of Ithaca, New York; and Marion, Gail and S. W., all at home. The wife and mother passed away in 1900 and in the year 1902 Mr. Hamilton was again married, his second union being with Miss Glendora M. Davidson, who was born at Reeds Landing, Minnesota, and by whom he has a daughter, Lucile, now eight years of age. Mrs. Hamilton and the children are members of the Presbyterian church.

Mr. Hamilton is an exemplary representative of the Masonic fraternity, belonging to the lodge, chapter and consistory, and is also connected with the Workmen, the Woodmen and the Royal Neighbors. In politics he is a republican, well versed on the questions and issues of the day but never an office seeker. He is not remiss in the duties of citizenship, however, and cooperates in many plans and projects for the general good, while for fifteen years he has served on the school board, the cause of education finding in him a stalwart champion. The major part of his attention has naturally been concentrated upon his business affairs and he has ever displayed marked ability in discriminating between the essential and the nonessential. His plans are ever carefully formulated, and while he has never been actuated by the spirit of vaulting ambition, he has never feared to venture where favoring opportunity has led the way. Moreover, his success has never been won at the sacrifice of others' interests, for he has always followed constructive methods, winning his prosperity through close application, careful management and indefatigable energy.

PETER A. HAMMERQUIST

P. A. Hammerquist who is pleasantly located on a fine ranch twenty miles from Rapid City on Rapid creek, his land being redeemed from the wilderness by his own industry and skill, was born on March 12, 1848, in Sweden and remained there until he was nineteen, receiving a good common-school education and working in stores after leaving school. In 1867 he came to the United States, and after passing some time at Chicago and Calumet, Indiana, having a brother living at the latter place, he moved to Lee County, Illinois, where for two years he carried on barbering in small towns. At the end of this period, he moved to Boone, Iowa, and after barbering in that town, Marshalltown and State Center for some time, went to Sioux City in the early part of 1873, and soon afterward came to South Dakota, locating in Clay County, where he took up land and turned his attention to farming. The grasshoppers devoured his crops and he was forced to return to Sioux City and work at his trade. He then passed a year at Davenport in the same employment and another in the coal fields south of there. In 1875 he returned to South Dakota, crossing the river on ice and found that his homestead had been jumped. He then went to Vermillion and opened a barber shop which he conducted until February, 1877. At that time, in company with three other men, he came to the Black Hills. The party had one wagon which was heavily laden with goods and they were obliged to walk most of the way. Their route was by way of Pierre and they were compelled to cross the Missouri on ice and had great difficulty in doing so. The ice broke under the wagon and it went to the bottom of the river, but they succeeded by great effort in getting it out and across without material loss in their supplies. They joined the first train that reached Rapid City by way of Pierre. They had no armed guards for protection, but nearly all the members of the party, consisting of sixty-five men, were armed. Arriving at Rapid City on March 19th, and having his barbering outfit with him, Mr. Hammerquist determined to remain there and for employment opened a shop, a much-needed enterprise in the small town as it was then. He witnessed all the exciting events of its early history and took his part like a man in every movement for the general weal. In 1878 he went east for a short visit and on his return found his town property jumped. He recovered this, however, and in it opened a small drug store which he profitably conducted for a few years. In the fall of 1881, he purchased the claim to the ranch he now occupies and moved his family there the next spring, this being the second family to settle at this end of the creek. Since then, this has been his home and here he has been actively engaged in the stock industry. After moving to the ranch, he went east and bought a small herd of cattle which was the nucleus of his present holdings in this line, and by vigorous management of his business he has steadily expanded it until he has become one of the leading stock growers in this part of the county. He has also pushed forward the improvement of his ranch from year to year, and thus made it one of the most attractive rural homes in the neighborhood. The land is nearly all under irrigation and is very productive, yielding abundant returns for his labor and a generous support to his stock. In the local affairs of the county Mr. Hammerquist has ever been energetic and serviceable, and having displayed more than ordinary capacity for administrative duties, has been chosen by his fellow citizens to places of trust and importance in the public service. He has been postmaster at Farmingdale since 1890 and was county assessor from 1890 to 1894, two terms. He is an ardent worker in the Republican party and has commanding influence in its councils. He has also been zealous and helpful in school affairs and prominent in every movement for the advancement of the county.

He belongs to the Masonic order, with membership in the lodge at Rapid City. On October 12, 1879, Mr. Hammerquist was married at Comstad, in Clay County, to Miss Mary E. Anderson, a native of Norway, who came to America in childhood and to Vermillion in 1873, when she was sixteen. They have eight children, Ida F., Harry E., Fred A., Anton W., Earl N., Erma M., Charles L. and Helen C.

EDWARD O. HANSCHKA

Edward O. HANSCHKA, of Deadwood, was born on March 7, 1863, in Germany, and is the son of Frederick and Caroline Hanschka, also natives of the fatherland, where the father was an industrious and well-to-do blacksmith. Edward remained at home until he reached the age of seventeen, receiving a common-school education and serving an apprenticeship at the trade of his father. In 1880 he came to the United States and, passing by the allurements of the cultivated east, made his way direct to the Black Hills, locating at Central City, where he secured employment from the Homestake Mining Company at its Terry mine near that town, he to do blacksmithing there for the company. After five years' service to this company, he bought a shop of his own at Central City and began business for himself. The shop he purchased had an interesting history. It was originally owned by John Belt, one of the pioneers of the Hills, and many important events in the early history of this section were started, discussed and planned under its rude roof. He was in business at this stand two years, then when the town of Carbonate was located, he moved the shop to that point, being one of the founders and locators of the town. There he remained two years, and during this time was busily employed running his shop, supplying timber and limestone for the Iron Hill Mining Company, and hauling its ore from the mines to the smelter by contract. In the spring of 1888, he moved to Deadwood and went into the employ of the Golden Reward Mining Company as master mechanic, especially for the purpose of erecting for that company the first mill put up in the Hills except the Homestake stamp mills. He remained with this company a year, the mill being destroyed by fire at the end of that time; and as it was impossible for the company to rebuild it until the next year, he again accepted a berth in the blacksmithing department of the Terry mines of the Homestake Company, at Deadwood. As soon as the Golden Reward Company was ready to rebuild its mill he returned to its aid and constructed the plant, after which he worked for the company until 1892. He then took an engagement to build the Little B smelter for the Deadwood & Delaware Smelting & Refining Company, and when this was finished, he built for the same company its Big B smelter, being master mechanic in the erection of both. After the completion of the Big B, he took charge of its blacksmithing department, of which he had the management two years. In 1895 he entered into a contract with the company to supply it with limestone and do all its hauling. Since then, he has continued to furnish the limestone needed in the operations of the company, which has averaged nine thousand tons a month. In 1900 he first became interested in mining for himself, and the next year, he bought one thousand acres of mining land. That same year he organized the Standard Mining Company of Deadwood, of which he is the principal stockholder and the vice-president and manager: The company at once erected a mill on its property, which is located in the Ragged Top district, and its operations have been active and eminently successful, it being beyond doubt one of the best mining properties in the Hills at this time. In 1903 Mr. Hanschka bought other large tracts of mining land on Elk creek seven miles south of the Homestake properties. These were known as the Hogan & Anderson and the Scandinavian properties, but he has rechristened them, calling them together the New Bonanza, and it is his intention to work them separately from his other enterprises. In the same summer he built a mill on them, and the results so far obtained justify him in the belief that they will be as rich in yield as the Standard. He has in addition several small mining interests and is a stockholder in some of the larger companies. In 1898 he started an industry in raising and handling cattle, running his stock on the Grand River north of this locality where he bought ranch land. In this venture he has been successful and is continually enlarging his business.

On January 1, 1889, Mr. Hanschka was married at Deadwood, to Miss Minnie Walking, a native of Germany. They have one daughter, Emma C. Since his marriage the subject has made his home at Deadwood, where he has a fine residence. He belongs to the Modern Woodmen of America here, and also to the Masonic order, having solved the mysteries of the York Rite through the commandery and those of the Scottish Rite to and through the thirty-second degree.

F. J. HANSEN

F. J. Hansen, founder of the Dakota Produce Company of Aberdeen, was born and educated in Denmark. He came to the United States in 1903 and settled in Nebraska, whence he removed to San Francisco, California. With that city as his headquarters, he traveled in the interests of a produce concern for a number of years. In 1910 he came to Aberdeen and commenced business under the firm name of The Dakota Produce Company. Two years later he incorporated the Dakota Produce Company and bought the M. E. Gibson Creamery and has since given his entire time to the affairs of this concern. The company operates a creamery with a capacity of one and a half million pounds of butter a year. It owns a cold storage plant with a capacity of fifteen cars of eggs and an equal amount of butter and a freezing plant which is one of the largest of its kind in the state, and it does a large business in butter, eggs, poultry and ice cream. The growth of the business has necessitated larger quarters and the company will in the near future move into its new plant, which is modern, sanitary, and complete in every particular.

Mr. Hansen is a member of the Masonic lodge, chapter, commandery and Shrine and is affiliated also with the Benevolent Protective Order of Elks.

NIELS EBBESEN HANSEN

Niels E. HANSEN, professor of horticulture in the South Dakota Agricultural College, at Brookings, and horticulturist at the government experiment station, was born near Ribe, Denmark, on the 4th of January, 1866, being the youngest child and only son of Andrew and Bodil (Midtgaardt) Hansen. The family came to America in the autumn of 1873, and the first three years were passed in the states of New York and New Jersey. The father was a fresco artist, of sturdy Danish farmer ancestry. In 1876 they removed to Des Moines, Iowa, in whose public schools the subject prosecuted his educational work, having entered the high school in East Des Moines in 1879 and having there been a student for two years. Something over two and one-half years were spent as assistant in the office of the secretary of state under appointment of Hon. J. A. T. Hull, of Des Moines, while secretary, beginning in the fall of 1881, which helped in preparations for college. In 1887 he was graduated in the Iowa Agricultural College, at Ames, and during his collegiate course he made a specialty of study and investigation and experimentation in horticulture, under Professor J. L. Budd, who attained national distinction and reputation through his effective efforts in introducing Russian fruits, trees and shrubs and in originating new varieties of fruit. The four years immediately succeeding his graduation Professor Hansen spent in practical work in two of the leading commercial nurseries of Iowa, at Atlantic and Des Moines, respectively, and he resigned his position in this connection in the autumn of 1891, when he returned to his alma mater, the Iowa Agricultural College, where he became assistant professor of horticulture under Professor Budd, remaining thus engaged for four years and then resigning to accept his present position, in September, 1895. Four months of the summer and autumn of 1894 were devoted to a study of horticulture in eight countries of Europe, including Germany, Russia, England, Denmark, Sweden, Austria, France and Belgium, while for four years he served as assistant secretary of the Iowa State Horticultural Society. Lender commission from Hon. James Wilson, secretary of agriculture of the United States, Professor Hansen was absent from June, 1897, to March, 1898, on a ten-months tour of exploration, securing new seeds and plants for the said department, and in this connection, he visited Russia, Siberia, the Crimea, Transcaucasia, Turcomania and other parts of Russian Turkestan and western China. About five carloads of products were obtained, and some of the new seeds thus introduced by the subject have proved so valuable that larger lots have since been imported to meet the demands, notably the Turkestan alfalfa. The two-thousand-mile overland journey made in Asia by the Professor included a trip of thirteen hundred miles in a wagon and seven hundred in a sleigh, and in the connection, he encountered several tussels with the strenuous and turbulent Siberian blizzards, in his endeavor to return home by way of Omsk, on the Siberian Railway. At one time he was fully one thousand miles from the nearest railroad, while Kuldja, in western China, was the most eastern point reached. This adventuresome journey showed the remarkable powers of endurance of the young explorer, while the danger involved was the last thing considered by him.

Professor Hansen is an honorary life member of the Minnesota State Horticultural Society and of many other associations in the line of his profession, and he frequently attends their sessions. He is secretary of the plant section of the American Breeders' Association and secretary of the South Dakota State Horticultural Society. He has written many bulletins and papers and contributes much to the agricultural press. In 1890 he wrote and published a "Handbook of Fruit Culture and Tree Planting for the Northwestern States," the same being published in the Danish Norwegian language. In 1902-3 he assisted

Professor Budd in preparing the "American Horticultural Manual," published by John Wiley & Sons, of New York.

The present collection of trees and shrubs at the South Dakota Agricultural College grounds is very extensive and is constantly being enlarged by importations and exchanges, many novelties are propagated and sent out for trial. The chief feature of the experimental work is the originating of new varieties of fruit, especially from the native Dakota species by hybridizing and by selection from large numbers. At present the one quarter of a million fruit seedlings on the station grounds is second in number only to that grown by Luther Burbank, of California, who has the largest fruit-breeding establishment in the world. The object of Professor Hansen's work in this direction is to obtain hardy and choice fruits for the northwest, better adapted to this region than any now in cultivation. Already many valuable varieties have been bred up from the native species. In short, the work means the creation of a new pomology.

At La Crosse, Wisconsin, on the 16th of November, 1898, was solemnized the marriage of Professor Hansen to Miss Emma Elise Pammel, who is likewise a graduate of the Iowa Agricultural College. Two children, Eva and Carl, have come to bless their home. Mrs. Hansen was born in La Crosse, Wisconsin, and is a daughter of Louis and Sophia (Freise) Pammel.

Professor Hansen is a Lutheran in his religious faith, and fraternally is a Royal Arch Mason, while both he and his wife are affiliated with the adjunct organization, the Order of the Eastern Star. In politics he gives his allegiance to the Republican party.

MAJOR JOSEPH R. HANSON

Major Joseph R. Hanson, of Yankton, is one of South Dakota's earliest pioneers and his name is indelibly inscribed upon the pages of its history. He aided in shaping events which figure prominently in its annals along both military and legislative lines, and for an extended period of about three decades has been a factor in the agricultural progress of his county and state. He was born in Lancaster, New Hampshire, a son of Joseph Hanson, who was likewise born in that state, and a grandson of Isaac Hanson, who came from England and was one of the first settlers of the White Mountain district. He is also a descendant of John Hanson, who was a delegate to congress under the Articles of Confederation from 1781 to 1783, and served as president of that congress in 1781-2. The father, Joseph Hanson, was united in marriage to Ann Pinkham, a daughter of Daniel Pinkham, builder of the Mount Washington turnpike, for which he received a grant of land, and a part of that grant became the homestead property upon which Major Hanson was born.

The last named attended the grammar and high schools of his native city and also pursued a short course of study in the academy at Salem, Massachusetts. In 1856, thinking to find better business opportunities in the middle west, he made his way to Illinois, settling for a time in Chicago, where he was in the employ of his brother, who was engaged in the furniture business. In 1857 he removed to Winona, Minnesota, where he continued in active connection with the furniture trade, but the following year he and three companions started with ox teams for the territory of Dakota. They arrived at the present site of Sioux City, Iowa, and there crossed the Missouri river into Nebraska, finally reaching a point in the Missouri directly opposite Yankton, where they prepared their camp for the winter. During that season Major Hanson crossed the river and located a piece of land adjoining the present corporate limits of the city and that tract is still in his possession. He located permanently in Yankton in 1858, and at that time there were but four white people in the settlement, all employed at the trading post of Frost Todd & Company. The following year, however, emigration having begun, Mr. Hanson embarked in the real-estate business and has been so engaged from that date to the present. Of the actual settlers of Yankton, Mr. Hanson was the second, having been preceded only by John C. Holman, who had built his cabin about a month prior to Major Hanson's arrival.

From the time that Yankton numbered him among its citizens to the present, Mr. Hanson has borne an active and helpful part in the work of general improvement and development and his name is indelibly inscribed upon the pages of Yankton's history. In 1862 he became chief clerk of the territorial legislature and served for two years. He was then chosen to represent his county in the fourth session of the territorial council and was also appointed territorial auditor and judge advocate. In military circles his name became well known, for in the Home Guards, organized for protection against the Indian raids, he served with the rank of colonel. He was also made a member of the commission formed to adjust claims for Indian depredations and took charge of building of fortifications known as the Yankton stockade in 1862. The survey of the government road from the Minnesota state line to Old Fort Pierre was made under his direction in 1865 and the same year he was appointed by President Lincoln as Indian agent for the upper Missouri region, and as such had supervision over all the various branches of the Sioux nation, there being more than twenty thousand Indians under his charge. Before his appointment was confirmed by the senate President Lincoln was assassinated and he was reappointed by President Johnson, continuing to fill that important position until 1870, with headquarters at Crow Creek Agency and with sub-agencies at Fort Sully and Fort Rice. His administration covered a period when the Indians were in constant revolt against the army and the white settlers and it was members of these same tribes who later perpetrated the historic Custer massacre.

Mr. Hanson was a member of the first constitutional convention held at Sioux Falls m 1885 and the code, with slight modifications, as ratified by the second convention, was adopted by the people and is the present organic law of South Dakota. Important and numerous as have been the connections of Mr. Hanson already mentioned, he has figured actively in other pursuits. He was secretary and member of the board of directors of the first railway, known as the Dakota Southern, built within Dakota territory. He has lived to see the state covered by a great network of railway lines, bringing it into close connection with north, south, east and west.

In October, 1872, Mr. Hanson was united in marriage to Miss Annie M. G. Mills, a daughter of Abraham Mills, a member of the Long Island family of that name, and they had one son, Joseph Mills Hanson, who is widely known as a writer and magazine contributor. Soon after coming to this territory Major Hanson secured a farm of two hundred acres two miles from Yankton and thereon later established the homestead upon which he has lived for more than thirty years, being now most comfortably situated in life.

In politics Mr. Hanson has been consistently a republican from the birth of the party, and in 1859 organized the first republican caucus held in Dakota territory. Few men among Dakota's pioneers are more widely and favorably known and there are few chapters of Yankton county's early annals but contain his name as one of the active participants in events recorded. He is able, genial and kindly, is prosperous and is rightly numbered among the sterling characters who have shaped the destinies of the vast country embraced in Dakota territory. His has been an active life and his is the satisfaction of having done a man's work in the transformation of the wilderness as he found it into one of the fairest states in the Union. Hanson County is named in his honor.

Fraternally he is connected with the Masons and in his life has exemplified the beneficent spirit of the craft, which is based upon mutual helpfulness and brotherly kindness. His memory forms a connecting link between the primitive past and the progressive present and he relates many interesting incidents concerning the early days when only here and there had the seeds of civilization been planted and the work of development begun. He has lived to see this become a prosperous state, enjoying all of the opportunities and equipped with all of the conveniences of the older east and his influence and his labors have been potent elements in bringing it to its present condition.

CALVIN J. B. HARRIS

Practicing at the bar of Yankton, Calvin J. B. Harris has gained a good clientage, the result of his recognized ability to successfully solve intricate and involved legal problems. In other directions, too, he has left his impress upon the history of the state, notably as a member of the constitutional convention of 1889. He was born in Danville, Vermont, on the 2d of February, 1844, and has, therefore, completed the Psalmist's allotted span of three score years and ten, but in spirit and interests he seems yet in his prime and his activity as a member of the bar is undiminished. His father, William H. Harris, was likewise a native of the Green Mountain state. The earlier members of the family came from Massachusetts, where the first American ancestor settled on emigrating from England about 1630. William H. Harris was united in marriage to Louisa Dan forth, a daughter of Leonard and Betsy (Henry) Danforth, the former a relative of the Patrick Henry family of Virginia. Mrs. Harris was a native of Vermont, to which state her parents removed from New Hampshire soon after the Revolutionary war. The maternal great-grandfather of C. J. B. Harris was Henry Little, who valiantly served in defense of the cause of liberty in the Revolutionary war. His great-granduncle, Henry Marchant, was the first United States judge of Rhode Island, a position to which he was appointed by President Washington, choosing that office in preference to a place in Washington's cabinet. He was also a member of the convention which framed the United States constitution.

In the public schools of Danville, Vermont, Calvin J. B. Harris acquired his early education, which was supplemented by study in the Phillips Academy of Danville, Vermont, and in the Burlington high school, in which he pursued his preparatory course. War drove all other thoughts from his mind, however, and with patriotic spirit aroused he offered his services to the government on the 30th of September, 1861, enlisting in the Sixth Vermont Infantry, with which he served until July 1, 1865, being first sergeant at the time of his discharge. He participated in the battles of Lees Mills, Williamsburg, the seven days' engagement in front of Richmond, the second battle of Bull Run, South Mountain, Antietam, Fredericksburg, Chancellorsville, the third battle of Fredericksburg, Gettysburg, the Wilderness and Petersburg and, though often in the thickest of the fight in many of the most hotly contested engagements of the war, he was never wounded. He has maintained pleasant relations with his old army comrades as a member of Phil Kearny Post, No. 7, G. A. R., of Yankton, of which he has served as commander and has been the official delegate to many national encampments.

Following the close of the war Mr. Harris began reading law, pursuing his studies in Danville, in St. Johnsbury and in Montpelier, Vermont. He was admitted to practice at the bar of his native state in December, 1867, and there followed his profession through the ensuing two years. In 1870 he came to Yankton and has since been a representative of the bar of that city. In the early days he practiced all over the settled portions of Dakota territory, but with the rapid growth of his district his efforts have naturally been more and more closely confined to Yankton and he has appeared in connection with much important litigation tried in the courts of his district.

Mr. Harris has been a recognized leader in political circles as a supporter of the democratic party. While in his native city he was for two years superintendent of schools and since coming to Yankton has been honored with various public offices, serving as a member of the city council for two years and for two terms as mayor. He was for eleven years city attorney, comprising eleven separate terms, and his election to the office indicated the public confidence in his professional ability and in his devotion to the public good. In 1883 he became a member of the volunteer constitutional convention and in 1889 was chosen a member of the permanent constitutional convention, which framed the present organic law of the state. He took an active part in its deliberations and thus left the impress of his individuality upon the history of South Dakota.

In January, 1881, Mr. Harris was united in marriage to Miss Mary Noon an, a daughter of John Noonan, of Yankton, and to them have been born four children: C. J. B., of Chicago, who is engaged in the engraving business; Mrs. Alice Ladd, of Omaha: Josephine, living in Omaha, Nebraska; and William S., of Chicago. The family attend the Catholic church and Mr. Harris is a thirty-second degree Mason. Aside from his membership in the Grand Army of the Republic he is connected with the Union Veterans Union. He stands today as one of the foremost citizens of Yankton, well fitted for leadership and active in advancing all those interests which are vital forces in civic betterment and public improvement.

CHARLES N. HARRIS

The subject of this sketch, who is engaged in the active practice of his profession in Aberdeen, South Dakota, is one of the pioneer members of the bar of Brown County. Charles Nelson Harris was born in Readstown, Vernon County, Wisconsin, on the 1st of September, 1856, and is a son of Joseph and Sarah E. Harris, the former of whom was born in Pennsylvania and the latter in Ohio, while both trace their genealogical lines back to English origin. The Harris family settled near Chambersburg, Pennsylvania, at an early epoch in the history of the old Keystone state, and John Harris, who laid out that town and who was captured and tortured by the Indians, was an uncle of the grandfather of the subject. As a young man Joseph Harris removed to Ohio, where he was married, and he and his wife thereafter became numbered among the pioneers of Vernon County, Wisconsin, where he was engaged in farming, becoming one of the prominent and influential citizens of that locality. The father still resides in Wisconsin. The mother died in 1880, at the age of forty-six years.

Charles N. Harris received his early scholastic discipline in the public schools of his native state, and in 1879 was matriculated in the law department of the celebrated University of Wisconsin, at Madison, where he was graduated as a member of the class of 1879, receiving the degree of Bachelor of Laws and being admitted to the bar of the state in that year. He initiated the practice of his profession in Viroqua, the county seat of Vernon County, in the same year, and there remained until January, 1882, when he came to the territory of Dakota and established himself in practice in Aberdeen, which was then a small village. Here he has ever since engaged in the work of his profession and with the rapid settling of the country and magnificent advancement of the city, which is now one of the most progressive and attractive in the state, he has found his legal business constantly cumulative and has been concerned in much of the important litigation in the courts of this section, retaining a large and representative clientage, and being held in high regard in business, professional and social circles. He is a stanch Democrat of the Jeffersonian type, and, as he personally states the case, has not become imbued with any of the "new-fangled" notions which have drifted the party from its firm moorings and caused its success to wane in recent years.

He is a thirty-second-degree Mason, being affiliated with Aberdeen Consistory, No. 4, of the Ancient Accepted Scottish Rite. He and his wife attend the Presbyterian church, of which the latter is a member. On the 1st of October, 1879, Mr. Harris was united in marriage to Miss Dora E. Bouffleur, who was born in Springville, Wisconsin, in June, 1858, being a daughter of Philip and Mary Bouffleur, and of French extraction in the paternal line. She died in August, 1888, leaving three daughters: Edna S., Minnie M. and Genevieve L.. In November, 1892, Mr. Harris was married to Jessie G. Campbell, of Aberdeen, a sister of Judge Campbell, of that place.

CHARLES M. HARRISON

In business circles of Sioux Falls Charles M. Harrison has won a creditable and enviable position. He successfully practices law and is also conducting a real-estate, loan and insurance business which is bringing him substantial success.

The birth of Mr. Harrison occurred in Springfield, Ohio, June 22, 1851, his parents being Thomas and Michael (Morris) Harrison, who were natives of England and of Ohio respectively. The father came to the United States in 1836. He was a journeyman printer and upon his arrival in the new world began preaching as a local minister, exerting a strong and wide-felt influence through his efforts to advance moral progress. He became very well known in educational as well as religious circles and was called to the editorship of the Western Christian Advocate at Cincinnati. He was likewise president of a Methodist college and of various other schools. Gifted by nature with strong mentality, he used his talents wisely and well and made for himself an enviable name in those circles where mental force wisely directed by a sense of moral obligation is doing effective work for the uplift of mankind. He achieved much more than local prominence as a man of letters and contributed several valuable volumes to the literature of the country. He was always a champion of the cause of education, which became his life work. He taught through the press, in the schoolroom and from the pulpit, ever bearing a message that carried with it a recognition of the true meaning of life and its obligations. His death occurred after he had retired from active labor in Shelbyville, Indiana, when he had attained the venerable age of ninety years but his memory still remains as an inspiration and a blessed benediction to all who knew him. His widow survived him for but thirty days. In their family were three sons: Charles M.; Robert, a resident of Shelbyville, Indiana; and Thomas, who resides in Cincinnati.

In the public schools of Springfield, Ohio, Charles M. Harrison pursued his education to the age of thirteen years and then entered the preparatory department of Moore's Hill College at Moore's Hill, Indiana, when his father became president of that institution. He continued his studies there for six years, or until he reached the age of nineteen, and was graduated in 1870 with the Bachelor of Arts degree. In the course of time his alma mater conferred upon him the Master of Arts degree. After leaving college he became an instructor in high schools, devoting four years to that profession. He regarded this, however, as an initial step to further professional activity and began reading law in Shelbyville, Indiana, devoting three years to law reading in that city and in Indianapolis. He was admitted to practice in 1878 and entered upon the active work of his profession in Lebanon, Indiana, where he remained until 1883, winning a creditable name and place for himself in legal circles of that section.

Attracted by the opportunities of the northwest, Mr. Harrison came to South Dakota in 1883, settling in Huron, where he concentrated his efforts upon commercial law practice, remaining in that city for a decade. He has never carried on a general law practice but has always adhered to commercial law and has attained marked skill and distinction in the field of his specialty. In 1891 he was elected a member of the second state legislature as representative from Beadle County. In 1893 he removed to Sioux Falls, where he has since maintained his home, continuing in the practice of commercial law and also extending the scope of his activities to include a real-estate, loan and insurance business. Substantial success has crowned his efforts. His wise judgment has enabled him to carefully direct his own interests and those of others entrusted to his care. He is now secretary and manager of the Realty Company, which has played an important part in the development of Sioux Falls in laying out and improving subdivisions and additions to the city. It is still an active corporation and Mr. Harrison devotes much time to the business of that company, also to the conduct of the loan agency and to individual operations in the field of real estate.

In 1880 Charles M. Harrison was married to Miss Anna R. Shirk, a native of Newcastle, Indiana, and they have become the parents of three children: Ruth, now the wife of Fred I. Powers, of Bozeman, Montana; Ben Tom, a resident of Dallas, Texas; and Florence, the wife of Sam L. Stutes, of Sioux Falls.

Mr. Harrison is a member of Minnehaha Lodge, No. 2, A. F. & A. M.; Sioux Falls Chapter, R. A. M.; Lafayette Commandery, K. T.; and El Riad Temple, A. A. O. N. M. S. His political faith throughout his entire life has been that of the republican party and he has long been active in its councils. In 1912 he was an alternate national delegate from South Dakota to the republican convention in Chicago and his opinions have done much in shaping the policy of the party in his state. For thirty-two years he has been a member of the Congregational church and in its teachings have been found the motive springs of his conduct, making him in every relation of life a man worthy of the esteem and confidence of his fellowmen. Life has ever meant to him opportunity — opportunity for advancement along the lines of legitimate business, for cooperation in all those movements which promote the political, educational, social and moral interests of the race.

JOHN S. HART

Among the leading commercial enterprises represented in the thriving city of Aberdeen is that conducted under the title of the J. S. Hart Lumber Company, and of this important concern, which operates a chain of several retail lumber yards throughout the state, the subject of this sketch is the executive head, while he is known as one of the representative business men of Aberdeen, in which city he has made his home and headquarters since 1898. In 1898 Mr. Hart engaged in the retail lumber business in Aberdeen, and the enterprise so rapidly increased in scope and importance that in 1900 it was found expedient to increase its facilities, and Mr. Hart then associated himself with George H. Hollandsworth, of Sioux City, Iowa, and effected the incorporation of the business under the present title, while the company is capitalized for one hundred thousand dollars. Since the incorporation retail yards have also been established in Ipswich, Faulkton, Mellette, Wanier, James, Columbia, Houghton and Plana, while the main offices of the company are in Aberdeen. It is scarcely needless to state that full and complete lines of lumber and builders' material are kept in stock at all times and in each of the several yards, while the concern has grown to be one of the largest and most important of the sort in the state. The company gives employment to a corps of about twenty-five men and the business is conducted with that progressive and alert spirit so characteristic of the west.

John S. Hart, who has been mainly instrumental in the building up of this enterprise, is a native of the state of Iowa, having been born in Clinton County, on the loth of December, 1863, and having passed his boyhood days on the farm, while, his educational training was secured in the public schools of his native state. He is a son of H. A. and Mary Jane Hart, the former of whom was born in the state of Ohio and the latter in Indiana. In early days the father was a trader on the Ohio and Mississippi rivers. He removed to Iowa in 1847, purchasing a large tract of land near Camanche, in Clinton County. He then returned to Indiana, but in 1859 he came back to Iowa and built on his land, at the same time building a flouring mill, which he operated for several years, carrying on farming operations at the same time on a large scale. He raised a family of four sons and four daughters, of whom seven are still living. He died in 1885, aged seventy-seven years. His widow survived until 1902, when she died, aged seventy-three years.

In his political proclivities, though never ambitious for any official preferment, Mr. Hart is a Democrat, and fraternally he has attained the thirty-second degree in the Masonic order, having completed the round of the York and Scottish rites so far as conferring of degrees in America is possible. He is an enthusiastic sportsman and finds recreation afield and afloat during his vacations, while he is one of the prominent and popular members of the Aberdeen Gun Club. At Charter Oak, Iowa, on the 12th of August, 1889, Mr. Hart was united in marriage to Miss Celia M. Marshall, who was born and reared in that state, being a daughter of Clark T. and Dora Marshall. Of this union have been born three children, Harry, Maud and Cloe M.

JAMES HARTGERING

James Hartgering has had wide experience as a civil and mining engineer and has gained a reputation in those lines that is statewide. He was born in Ottawa county, Michigan, on the 22d of September, 1852, the third in a family of six children, whose parents were Alexander and Josephine Hartgering. The father was a teacher by profession and was a veteran of the Mexican war.

James Hartgering entered the public schools of his native county at the usual age and after completing the course offered there attended the Grand Rapids Business College. Some years later he attended the engineering school of the South Dakota School of Mines. Before entering that institution, he had worked for a time at the carpenter's trade. In 1877 he came to the Black Hills, where he engaged in placer mining to some extent, but later followed the trade of a millwright and built or installed many of the early stamp and other mills of that section. Since taking up the work of engineering he has completed many important government contracts and in 1897 did much of the work connected with the official geological survey of the Black Hills district. For three years he was city engineer of Rapid City and for two years was county surveyor of Custer County. He is counted among the leading engineers of the state and one of the ablest authorities on civil and mining engineering in western South Dakota. He has made a thorough study of geology, natural science and astronomy and is one of the best-informed men on geological formation of the Black Hills. For many years he was an active member of the American Society for the Advancement o! Science; is a member of the American Geographic Society; and a member and director of the South Dakota Engineering Society.

Mr. Hartgering has a number of valuable mining interests, a fine ranch in Custer County, is a stockholder in the Security Savings Bank of Rapid City and a stockholder and director of the Ranchman's State Bank of Fair burn, South Dakota.

On the 21st of March, 1883, Mr. Hartgering was united in marriage to Miss Jennie M. McRae, a daughter of John McRae, who was a native of Scotland but a resident of Ottawa, Canada. To this union five children have been born, namely: Constance M., a graduate of the University of Minnesota, who is now teaching in a high school at Pittsburgh, Pennsylvania; James F., deceased; Genevieve, also a graduate of the University of Minnesota and now instructor in domestic arts at the State Agricultural College at Brookings; John McRae, who graduated from the South Dakota State School of Mines and the Iowa State College of Agriculture and Mechanic Arts and who is now mechanical engineer for the city of Detroit, Michigan; and Francis B., a graduate of the South Dakota State College and now assistant principal of the schools of Hecla, South Dakota, and teacher of chemistry, domestic science and German.

Mr. Hartgering is a republican with independent tendencies and fraternally is a Mason, having taken the third degree in the Scottish Rite, and belonging also to the commandery, the Shrine and the Eastern Star. In attaining prominence in his chosen profession, he has not forgotten the duty that he owes to his community and has always been found ready to aid in furthering the public welfare.

J. A. HAWKINS

J. A. Hawkins, one of the interested principals in the Bank of Pierpont, Day County, is a native of the state of Minnesota, having been born in the village of Frankfort, Mower County. He received his preliminary educational discipline in the public schools of his native town, and thereafter completed a course of study in the Minnesota State High School, at Spring Valley. In 1892 he came west with a carload of horses, intending to return to Minnesota. He visited Montana, Idaho and North and South Dakota, and became impressed with the attractions offered to a young man in the new commonwealth last mentioned, and finally decided to cast in his lot with its people. He first located in Waubay, Day County, where he maintained his home for five years, being engaged in various pursuits, including teaching, surveying and the operation of a meat market. He then removed to Pierpont, where he was employed as a teacher in the village schools for a short interval, at the expiration of which he established himself in the grain business, becoming associated with the late C. C. Dart, under the firm name of Dart & Hawkins. They built up a prosperous and important enterprise in the line and continued operations until the death of Mr. Dart, when it devolved upon the surviving partner to settle up the business, and he became associated with Mrs. W. M. Hart, in establishing the Bank of Pierpont, in the ownership of which institution they have since continued, the bank now controlling an excellent business and being one of the solid financial concerns of this section of the state. In politics the subject gives an uncompromising allegiance to the Republican party, and served for many years as treasurer of the village and also as treasurer of the school district.

He and his wife are active and valued members of the Baptist church, and fraternally he is identified with the Masonic order, while he is also affiliated with the Order of the Eastern Star, the Independent Order of Odd Fellows and its auxiliary, the Daughters of Rebekah; the Ancient Order of United Workmen and its Degree of Honor; the Modern Woodmen of America, the Royal Neighbors and the Knights of the Maccabees. Mr. Hawkins was married to Miss Ethel M. Dart, who was born in the state of Illinois, and they have three children.

JOHN R. HAWKINS, M. D.

J. R. HAWKINS, who was summoned to the life eternal on the 3d of May, 1904, in the very flower of his manhood, was a native of Sioux Falls and a son of one of its honored pioneers, Robert C. Hawkins, to whom a memorial tribute is accorded on other pages of this volume. Dr. Hawkins was born in Sioux Falls, on the loth of July, 1874, and was a son of Robert C. and Harriett (Albertson) Hawkins. He secured his early education in the public schools and manifested from his boyhood a distinctive predilection for study. After completing a course in the local high school, he entered the University of Chicago, where he continued his studies for four years, at the expiration of which he was matriculated in Rush Medical College, in Chicago, where he completed the prescribed technical course and was graduated as a member of the class of 1900, receiving his degree of Doctor of Medicine. Through his own efforts he, to a large extent, paid the expenses of his higher education, and in the few years of his active professional work he had gained marked prestige and distinction. Soon after his graduation he engaged in active practice in his native city, making a specialty of the diseases of children, and he gained a representative support and a stronghold upon popular confidence and esteem, as well as upon the high regard of his professional confreres. He was made major surgeon of the Second Regiment of the South Dakota National Guard, and recently promoted to surgeon general with the rank of colonel, and held this office at the time of his demise, while he was a member of the State Medical Society and secretary of the Minnehaha County Medical Society, as well as county coroner and medical counselor of the ninth district when summoned from the sphere of life's activities, having been incumbent of the office of county coroner for three years. He was deeply devoted to his profession and took a great interest in all that tended to conserve its advancement. He was practically the originator of the present medical laws of the state, having expended much time, effort and money in preparing the measure and urging its passage, the enactment of the law having been made by the last legislature.

He was a Master Mason, being identified with Minnehaha Lodge, No. 5, and was a consistent and valued member of the Methodist Episcopal church. On the 19th of June, 1900, was solemnized the marriage of Dr. Hawkins to Miss Minnie Edna Dull, of Freeport, Illinois, who survives him.

ROBERT C. HAWKINS

ROBERT C. HAWKINS, who stood as an honored citizen of Sioux Falls from practically the time of its inception to that of his death, and who passed to his reward on the 16th of September, 1903, was born in Plattsburg, Clinton County, New York, on the 23d of July, 1825, and was a scion of colonial stock, while his parents were numbered among the pioneers of the Empire state, where he was reared to manhood and where he received a common-school education which he later effectively supplemented through personal application and the valuable lessons of experience. He acquired the trade of mason, to which he gave his attention in his native state until 1844, when he removed to Illinois, and thence, a few years later, to Richland Center, Richland County, Wisconsin, where he followed his trade and also engaged in farming. He was chairman of the township board of supervisors, township clerk and treasurer, chairman of the county board and justice of the peace, while he was sheriff of the county for one term. A man of broad mental ken and decided views, it was but natural that his intrinsic patriotism and loyalty should manifest themselves in a definite way when the thundering of rebel guns against the ramparts of old Fort Sumter heralded the opening of the Civil War. He raised the first company of volunteers in Richland

County, being made captain of the same, which became Company H, Fifth Wisconsin Volunteer Infantry. He continued in active service with his command for nearly two years when he received his honorable discharge, owing to disabilities resulting from his service in the field.

Soon after the close of the war Mr. Hawkins removed to Woodstock, in the same county of Richland, and was there engaged in the mercantile business until September, 1872, when he came to the territory of Dakota and located in Sioux Falls, where he was engaged in the work of his trade for two or three months. In the early winter he started to return to his home in Wisconsin by way of St. Paul, and so severe were the snowstorms and so many the other obstacles encountered that an entire week elapsed before he reached the city mentioned. In the spring of the following year, in company with his family, he returned to Sioux Falls, where he ever afterward made his home. In the early days he took up a homestead claim in Wayne township, the same comprising the south half of the southeast quarter of section 33, and the south half of the southwest quarter of section 34, and this property he improved and retained in his possession until his death. He followed contracting in the line of his trade about two years after his return to Sioux Falls. He soon gained the confidence and esteem of the people of the city, and became influential in public affairs, having ever given a stanch allegiance to the Republican party and having been for a number of years an active political worker in a local way. In 1874 he was elected justice of the peace and continued incumbent of that office, with the exception of one term, until he was elected police justice of the city, upon its incorporation, in 1883. In the latter office he served consecutively until April, 1894, representing a full decade. He also held the office of probate judge of Minnehaha County for eight years, and in every office of trust to which he was called, he manifested the utmost fidelity, honor and zeal, while his mature judgment and strong individuality made him a power for good in whatever work he undertook. He was one of the prominent representatives of the Masonic fraternity in the state and one of the charter members of Minnehaha Lodge, No. 328 on June 10th 1870, and he did much to forward the interests of the order in his home city.

In 1843, Mr. Hawkins was united in marriage to Miss Ada Monroe, of Plattsburg, New York, and they became the parents of three children, Frederick B., who is now a resident of Sioux Falls; Albert, who resides in Sioux City, Iowa; and Isabel, who is the wife of George W. Clark, of Pasco, Washington. Mrs. Hawkins was summoned into eternal rest in 1869, and on the 23d of December, 1872, at Alma, Wisconsin, was solemnized his marriage to Miss Harriet Albertson, who was born in Stroudsburg, Monroe County, Pennsylvania, and she survives him and still retains her residence in Sioux Falls, as did also their only son, the late Dr. John R., of whom individual mention is made elsewhere in this work. In religion Mr. Hawkins was a Methodist.

Mr. Hawkins was the architect of his own fortune, and upon his life rested no shadow of wrong or injustice while his kindly and genial nature won him firm and abiding friendship, his memory resting as a benediction upon all who came within the immediate sphere of his influence.

CHARLES A. HECKMASTER

Charles A. Heckmaster is conducting a wholesale produce and creamery business at Canton, where he has made his home continuously since 1890. He has not always been, however, the successful merchant which he is today, for he has attained this position through untiring effort and energy, having started out in business life in a humble capacity. He was born in Madison, Wisconsin, on the 13th of November, 1864, and is a son of Henry and Wilhelmina (Schmidt) Heckmaster, both of whom have passed away.

The father was a stonemason and plasterer. The son pursued his education in the public schools of Iowa and after his textbooks were put aside engaged in the creamery business, having learned the trade of butter making in 1881. In 1883 he returned to his native state, where he engaged in business until 1890. That year witnessed his arrival in South Dakota, at which time he took up his abode in Canton. When he first came, he worked with threshers and afterward bought out the retail oil business in Canton, which he conducted in connection with the street lighting of the city until 1904. He and Charles A. Reynolds then purchased the old bottling plant from the Northwest Land Company and after continuing successfully in that line in connection with the produce business for several years they extended the scope of their activities by adding the creamery business in 1908. Their trade in that line has increased rapidly and substantially until they now employ fifteen men and do a volume of business amounting to about seventy-five thousand dollars annually. The firm erected a new concrete plant in 1914, sixty-six by one hundred feet, with all modern improvements for the most sanitary care of produce and creamery supplies. Familiar with every phase of the business and holding to high standards in the character of service rendered their patrons, they have built up a splendid trade and are today at the head of one of the important commercial enterprises of the city.

On the 12th of February, 1889, Mr. Heckmaster was united in marriage to Miss Nora Alice Engle, a daughter of Charles and Jemima Engle. To them has been born a daughter, Edith, who acts as her father's bookkeeper and who is quite talented in music. The family hold membership in the Congregational church and their influence is always on the side of right, truth and progress.

In politics Mr. Heckmaster is a democrat and fraternally he is connected with Silver Star Lodge, No. 4, F. & A. M.. He holds membership in the Canton Commercial Club and is now president of that body which is a potent force in promoting the advancement of the city. He has served on the school board, as city commissioner and as commissioner of waterworks and sewers and is interested in the public welfare of his community, giving active and earnest support to various projects which have been instituted for the benefit and upbuilding of Canton. However, he is not particularly ambitious along the line of office holding, for he is devoted to business and his close application and well formulated plans constitute the foundation upon which he has builded his success.

SAMUEL C. HEDGER

Samuel C. HEDGER, one of the representative business men of the city of Aberdeen, is a native of Michigan, having been born on a farm in Monroe County, on the 15th of March, 1853, a son of B. H. and Mary A. Hedger, both of whom died in this state. He received his early educational training in the common schools and supplemented this by a course of study in that celebrated institution, the Michigan State Agricultural College, near Lansing, this having been the first college of the sort established in the Union and one which has ever remained a model for all others. After leaving college he was variously engaged for a time and finally engaged in the general merchandise business in South Lyon, Oakland County, Michigan, where he remained until 1882, having been successful in his operations. In March of that year he came to Brown County, South Dakota, and located in Columbia, this county, but shortly afterward took up a homestead near the present village of Detroit. He was the founder of this village, having platted the town on his land and having named the same in honor of the metropolis of his native state. In 1885 Mr. Hedger was elected auditor of Brown County, and this caused him to take up his residence in Aberdeen. He was twice re-elected to this responsible office, thus serving for six consecutive years and gaining unqualified popular commendation. After retiring from office, he was for eight years employed as traveling salesman for George D. Barnard & Company in South Dakota, still retaining his residence in Aberdeen, and since that time he has here been established in the real-estate and insurance business, receiving a large and representative support in both departments of his enterprise, while he is also one of the stockholders in the Aberdeen Gas and Electric Light Company and other local enterprises.

In politics he is stanchly arrayed in support of the principles and policies advanced by the Republican party, and fraternally he has attained the Knights Templar degrees in the Masonic order, thus completing the York rite. On the 22d of February, 1878, in Oakland County, Michigan, Mr. Hedger was united in marriage to Miss Mary Bullock, who was born and reared in the state of Michigan, and who was summoned into eternal rest in Columbia, South Dakota, August 16, 1888. Her only child, Ivy, is now the wife of Frederick Bartholomew, of San Francisco, California. On the 28th of April, 1896, Mr. Hedger wedded Miss Elizabeth Chalmers, who was born in Illinois, where she was reared and educated, and they have one child, Jeanette.

PETER J. HEGEMAN

Peter J. Hegeman, is the father of the South Dakota lineage of the Hegeman family, and grew to manhood in the state of New York, where he married Miss Catharine Allen, who was a daughter of Daniel Allen, a native of Scotland. Catharine Allen's mother, Magadaline Houghtaling, was what was known as Mowhawk Dutch, of New York, and her mother was a daughter of Lord Etherington.

The Aliens came as early settlers into the state of New York and were of Scotch descent. Daniel Allen was one of seven sons, and the Houghtaling's are still residents of New York state, and are a thrifty and well-to-do people.

Peter J. Hegeman was married in Perth, New York, and afterwards settled in Gloversville, the same state, engaging actively in the occupations of farming and manufacturing, in which city he lived until 1864. when he moved to Sparta, Wisconsin, and there again engaged in manufacturing until the year 1878, when he moved to Brookings County. South Dakota, and settled eight miles east of where the town of White is now located, taking up one hundred and sixty acres of land as a homestead, and also a tree claim, remaining upon said land and cultivating it for eight and one-half years, after which time he moved to White and there lived a retired life until the year 1892, in which year his wife Catharine passed away upon the 27th day of May. His home having been broken by the hand of death, he then removed to the town of Brookings and made his home with his daughter, Mrs. Eva A. Wright, where he died, October 16, 1900.

Peter J. Hegeman was a man who lived an upright, honorable life, and was well spoken of by his fellow citizens, thus going down to his grave in peace, and showing, that the ancestral teaching of the Hegeman family, which tenaciously clung to the religion of the Methodist Episcopal church, had not been taught to him in early childhood in vain. The above statements will, however, only appear too modest when we state that under urgent and peculiar circumstances Peter Hegeman walked to Brookings, twenty-three miles, in order to be present and to aid in the organization of a Masonic lodge in that place, he having previously became a member of the above order in Gloversville, New York, in the year 1860.

E. E. HEMINGWAY

Some wise man has well said that "A country is largely measured by the kind of men it turns out"; another has said that "Some men are born great, some achieve greatness, and that some have greatness thrust upon them". The subject of this sketch, Hon. E. E. Hemingway, has come to his present eminence by worthy achievement and the nobility of hard and persistent labor. He was born in the township of Marathon, in Lapeer County, Michigan, on the 16th day of December, 1861. His father was Hon. H. L. Hemingway, who was a son of Needham Hemingway, a native of Canandaigua, New York. The Hemingway family came to this county originally from Wales. The grandfather, Needham Hemingway, was a contractor of mills, and at the same time was also engaged to a considerable extent in farming. He came to the state of Michigan m an early day, braving the rigors of a new country, and there spent the remainder of his sturdy life in the above occupation.

Hon. H. L. Hemingway first saw the light of day on a farm where he was afterward reared, having received by nature and hard manual labor a strong constitution. He early in life became engaged in the lumber business and the fruitful occupation of farming. While thus gaining an honorable livelihood, he was chosen by the people of Lapeer County, Michigan, to fill many important offices in the township and county.

He was united in marriage to Lydia E. Tower, whose family came from the state of New York, from the same vicinity that the Hemingway family had previously emigrated. Mrs. Lydia Hemingway departed this life March 31, 1876. In the course of time H. L. Hemingway was again united in marriage, this time to Susan C. Tower. He was the father of nine children, four of whom still survive him. Sarah (deceased) was the wife of William Larkin, of Otter Lake, Michigan. Ernest is a resident of Otter Lake, Michigan. Laura (deceased) was the wife of James A. Tompkins, of Oxford, Michigan. Ella J. is the wife of W. S. Cook, of Pontiac, Michigan. Eugene died in young manhood. Ida, the sixth child of the family, died in infancy. E. E., the subject, was the seventh child of this excellent family. The eighth child, Ada, died at the tender age of thirteen years. The ninth child, Bruce W., now resides at Otter Lake, Michigan, on the old Hemingway homestead. Hon. H. L. Hemingway passed away upon the 11th day of April, 1903.

While the subject of this interesting sketch applied himself industriously in the mill and on the farm, he managed to receive his primary schooling in Marathon township, Lapeer County, Michigan, until he was fifteen years of age, at which time he entered college at Oxford, Michigan, and there spent three years, from which institution he graduated. He afterward took a commercial course in the Pontiac International Business College, which is situated in the same state. Thus, amply fitted, he was called to take a position in the bank of William Peter, of Columbiaville. Michigan, which position he ably filled for five years. Upon August 17, 1887, he removed to Watertown, South Dakota, where he at once engaged with the Dakota Loan and Trust Company, and at the same time he assisted the Watertown National Bank, filled the office of city clerk of Watertown for three years and for two years was the manager of the electric light plant. Mr. Hemingway continued actively in business in Watertown for five years. During the last half of 1892 he was employed by the W. H. Stokes Milling Company, of Watertown, as collector and salesman, making extensive trips into South Dakota, Minnesota, Towa, Illinois and Missouri. In October, 1892, he removed to Brookings, South Dakota, and engaged in the retail boot and shoe trade, and continued successfully in this business until December, 1894. In 1895 he was appointed public examiner of South Dakota, by Governor Sheldon, in which position he ably and efficiently served his term of two years, which expired March 6, 1897, He then engaged with the Minneapolis Journal until May, 1898. After the expiration of this work he engaged with the George D. Barnard Company, of St. Louis, Missouri, as traveling salesman for the space of two years. On May 1, 1900, he engaged with the C. Ross Coal Company, of Sheboygan, Wisconsin, and traveled for them in North and South Dakota, Minnesota and Iowa. Upon December 15, 1902, he was again appointed public examiner for the state of South Dakota, to fill an unexpired term, and was again reappointed in January, 1903, to hold until March, 1905.

Believing that it was not good for man to be alone, Mr. Hemingway was married on the 29th day of June, 1892, to Miss Jennie E. Wing, of Brookings, who was a daughter of O. C. and Elizabeth Wing, who came to Brookings in 1882. Her father still resides there, the mother having passed away on May 14, 1900. These sturdy people were of English descent. Mr. Hemingway's family consists of four children, three sons and one daughter: Charles, ten years of age; Robert, aged eight years; Grace, aged five, and Frank, but five months old. Mr. Hemingway has always been to an eminent degree a public-spirited man, actively engaged in the promotion of any and all worthy causes.

He is a member of the Masonic order, and has attained the degree of the Royal Arch and Temple. He also belongs to the Eastern Star, of Brookings, and El Riad Temple, of the Mystic Shrine, at Sioux Falls. He is a charter member of the Woodmen at Brookings, and was the first worthy advisor. The Watertown Knights of Pythias lodge still claims him as a member in good and regular standing, as also does the lodge of Royal Neighbors, to which Mrs. Hemingway belongs. In politics he is a stanch Republican and his family are members of the Methodist Episcopal church.

MARTIN R. HENINGER

M.R. Heninger conies of stanch old Virginia stock and is himself a native of the state of Missouri, having been born on the homestead farm, in Monroe County, on the 29th of November, 1851, and being a son of William W. and Eliza J. (Stalcup) Heninger, both of whom were born in the Old Dominion state, whence they came westward as pioneers of the state of Missouri, where the father devoted the remainder of his life to agricultural pursuits. The subject of this sketch was reared to the sturdy discipline of the farm and after completing the curriculum of the common schools, took a course of study in Central College, at Fayette, Missouri. When he was seventeen years of age his father died and he then left school to assist in caring for the widowed mother and the seven other children of the family. He remained on the old farm until 1882, when he came to South Dakota and located in the village of Ordway, Brown County, where he followed the lumber trade for one season and then, in February, 1883, removed to Westport, where he was successfully engaged in the lumber business until July, 1902, since which time he has maintained his home in Aberdeen. While a resident of Westport he did the banking exchange business of the town, affording accommodations that were duly appreciated by its business men, while in the vicinity of the town he also owned a fine farm of four hundred and fifty acres. He disposed of his interests in Westport in January, 1902, and came to Aberdeen, where he purchased an interest in the Aberdeen Gas and Electric Light Company, of which he has since been vice-president, and to this important enterprise he has since devoted the major portion of his time and attention, while he also has other capitalistic interests.

The father of the subject was a stanch Union man during the war of the Rebellion, and thus the son was reared in the faith of the Republican party, to which he has ever continued to give an unfaltering allegiance, while he has taken an active interest in its cause and been prominent in public affairs of a local nature. He was a delegate from Brown County to the state constitutional convention in 1889, held in the city of Sioux Falls, and was appointed by Governor Sheldon a member of the state board of regents of education, but he resigned the position shortly afterward, feeling that the demands of his private business would not permit him to give the requisite attention to official duties. He was elected clerk of Brown County in 1895 and served for two years, giving a most able and satisfactory administration. He has been frequently a delegate to the county, state and district conventions of his party and been an active factor in its councils.

He is identified with the Masonic fraternity, in which he has attained the Knights Templar degrees and also with the Ancient Order of United Workmen and the Modern Woodmen of America. On the 9th of July, 1882, Mr. Heninger was united in marriage to Miss Mary A. Way, who, like himself, was born and reared in Monroe County, Missouri, and they have three children, Nora L., Mabel H. and Mildred D., all of whom still remain beneath the home roof and lend cheer and brightness to the family circle.

A. H. HENNEOUS

A. H. Henneous is one of the honored and representative business men of White Lake, while he has also served as state's attorney of Aurora County and as county judge, being held in the highest esteem in the community, in which he has maintained his home for more than a score of years, while he is now engaged successfully in the lumber business here. Mr. Henneons is a native of Erie County, Pennsylvania, where he was born on the 13th of November, 1859, being a son of Frederick and Carrie (Sanders) Henneous. the former of whom has long been one of the prominent farmers and honored citizens of Erie County, where he still resides, being eighty-three years of age. His devoted wife passed away in 1900, at the age of seventy years, having been a zealous member of the Presbyterian church, with which he also has been prominently identified for many years, while he is a stanch Republican in politics.

Judge A. H. Henneous was reared on the homestead farm and after completing the curriculum of the public schools became a student in Allegheny College, where he remained five years, thereafter taking a course in the Pennsylvania State Normal School, at Edinboro, Pennsylvania. He thereafter devoted his attention for a full decade to teaching in the public schools of Pennsylvania and Iowa, to which latter state he removed in 1880. In the spring of 1882, he came to White Lake, where he has ever since resided. For a short time after his arrival, he was engaged in the sale of agricultural implements. In 1890 he was elected state's attorney for this county, and after the expiration of his term served three successive terms as county judge. He was not then permitted to retire from public office, since he was again elected to the position of state's attorney, in which he served one term. He had given considerable attention to the study of law and was eminently qualified for the duties devolving upon him in each of these responsible offices. He was admitted to the bar January 5, 1891. In 1898 Judge Henneous opened a lumber yard in White Lake, and in this line of enterprise he has built up a large and successful business. He has ever given a stanch allegiance to the Republican party and has wielded no little influence in promoting its cause.

He is a member of White Lake Lodge, No. 85, Free and Accepted Masons, and both he and his wife are valued members of the Presbyterian church in White Lake, our subject being a member of its board of trustees. On the 27th of August, 1887, Judge Henneous was united in marriage to Aliss Minnie M. Ponto, of Floyd County, Iowa, and they have three children, Agnes, Ralph and Fern.

GEORGE H. HENRY

George H. Henry, of Platte, deputy state fire marshal, is one of the prominent citizens of his city and is a leader in movements seeking the public welfare. He was born in Mineral Point, Wisconsin, on the 8th of

July, 1870, a son of George and Nettie (McHugh) Henry, the former a native of that place, and the latter of New York state. At the age of eight years Mr. Henry of this review was brought to South Dakota by his parents, the family home being established at Oakwood Lakes, Brookings County, in 1878. The father subsequently started a bank at Volga, Brookings County, which is still conducted by two of his sons and is known as the First State Bank. He was actively identified with the early development of Brookings County and left his impress upon its history and his demise, which occurred in 1889, was sincerely mourned.

George H. Henry was educated in the country schools of Brookings County and in 1887, when a youth of seventeen, was apprenticed to the Volga Tribune at Volga and there learned the printer's trade. He was later employed upon the Argus Leader of Sioux Falls, the Brookings Press and the Dell Rapids Tribune. In 1900 he purchased the Parker Leader and conducted it for two years, after which he removed to Platte and bought what is now the Platte Tribune. He successfully published that journal until 1915, when he sold it to a Mr. Pruner, and maintained its high standing as one of the best weeklies of the state, its news columns giving clearly written and reliable accounts of happenings both of local and general interest and its wide circulation among the representative people of Charles Mix County making it an excellent advertising medium. On the 15th of December, 1913, Mr. Henry was appointed deputy state fire marshal and is at present serving ably in that capacity.

In 1902 Mr. Henry was married to Miss May Tolles, a native of Minnesota, and they have three children: May Bell, Lois and Howard. Mr. Henry is a republican and has always been a leader in local political affairs. He has held a number of positions of trust and honor and in the years 1910 and 1911 was mayor of Platte, giving the city a businesslike and progressive administration. His interest in educational matters was recognized when he was chosen as a member of the board of education, in which capacity he served for two years, while for six years he was clerk of the board, resigning that office in July, 1914. For a number of years he was secretary of the Charles Mix County Fair Association and the success of the fairs was due in no small measure to his unremitting efforts. Fraternally he belongs to Doric Lodge, No. 93, A. F. & A. M.; Yankton Consistory, No. 1, A. & A. S. R; El Riad Temple, A. A. O. N. M. S., of Sioux Falls; the subordinate lodge of the Independent Order of Odd Fellows of Platte; and the Blue Goose, an insurance association. Under his management the Platte Tribune was recognized not only as an excellent means for the dissemination of news but also as a powerful factor in the formation of an intelligent public opinion that has demanded and secured a number of improvements and reforms in various phases of the community life. Even those who differ from him as to matters of policy respect his sincerity and honor his integrity.

BIRTRUM F. HERINGTON

Birtrum F. Herington, engaged in the banking business at Waubay, was born in Jackson, Michigan, December 7, 1859, a son of Pulaski N. and Elizabeth (Brewer) Herington. The paternal grandfather, Irwin Herington, was a native of New York, devoted his entire life to farming and passed away in Michigan. The maternal grandfather, Samuel Brewer, was born in England, came to the United States in 1847 and settled in Jackson County, Michigan, where he carried on general agricultural pursuits, living on the old homestead to the time of his death, which occurred when he had reached the venerable age of ninety-two years. The father was born in the state of New York in 1834 and his life record covered the intervening years to 1904. His wife, who was born in England in 1839, passed away in the year 1902. They were married in Jackson, Michigan, where Mr. Herington had located when twenty years of age, accompanying his parents to that place. He had acquired a district school education and he turned his attention to farming, purchasing land which he occupied and cultivated until 1858. He then purchased other land, on which his remaining days were spent. He was a self-made man, enterprise and industry constituting his salient characteristics. In politics he was active as a supporter of the democratic party but never held nor desired office. He belonged to the Independent Order of Odd Fellows and to the Methodist Episcopal church. In the family of Mr. and Mrs. P. N. Herington were six children, of whom four are living, namely: D. P., a hardware merchant residing in Waubay, this state; S. O., a retired agriculturist who makes his home in Moscow, Idaho; Birtrum F., of this review; and William, a farmer residing in Jackson, Michigan.

In the public schools of his native city B. F. Herington acquired his preliminary education and afterward pursued a business course. He started out in life as a salesman for a grain company in South Dakota, to which state he came in 1883, and subsequently engaged in the grain business on his own account at Waubay, where he located in 1889. For fifteen years he was active in the grain trade, meeting with substantial success, after which he turned his attention to banking, purchasing the controlling interest in the First National Bank of Waubay in 1904, in which year he became president. It is capitalized for twenty-five thousand dollars, has surplus and undivided profits of fifteen thousand and average deposits of two hundred and twenty- five thousand. The bank has enjoyed a healthful growth and is in excellent condition, a general banking business being conducted, while a liberal patronage is accorded the institution. Mr. Herington's high standing in banking circles is indicated by the fact that in 1914 he was elected president of group five of the National Bankers of the State of South Dakota. In addition to his activities as a banker he handles real estate and farm loans and is himself the owner of one thousand acres of fine land. The proud American title of a self-made man is his by right of his industry, determination and perseverance, for those qualities have advanced him from a humble financial position to a place of prominence in the business circles of his adopted county.

Mr. Herington has been married twice. In 1892 he wedded Miss Mary Fitzpatrick, by whom he had three children, as follows: Guy, who is employed in his father's bank; Hazel, who has completed her education; and Harold, who is attending school. The wife and mother died in 1902, passing away in the faith of the Methodist Episcopal church, of which she was a devoted member. In 1905 Mr. Herington was again married, his second union being with Miss Dina Arntz, a native of Cochrane, Wisconsin, by whom he has two children, Alberta and Donald.

Mr. and Mrs. Herington attend the Methodist Episcopal church and he is a prominent Mason, belonging to the lodge, chapter, consistory and Mystic Shrine. He also has membership with the Odd Fellows, the Woodmen and the Workmen and believes in the principle of fraternity which underlies these organizations. In politics he is a democrat and has the distinction of being the only democrat ever elected from his county to the state legislature, to which he was sent as a representative in 1897. He has served on the town board and for eight years filled the office of mayor, carefully directing municipal affairs with the same thoroughness and capability that have marked his business career. That he is interested in the cause of education has been shown by his effective work as a member of the school board. Progress has ever been his watchword and he seeks for the public good with the same eagerness and enthusiasm that he displays in advancing his individual interests.

CHARLES N. HERREID

CHARLES N. HERREID.

If some philosopher like Herbert Spencer would write a treatise on the "Philosophy of Popularity," it might be of vast service to the army of ambitious statesmen struggling for public favors. popularity is the one thing most desired by this class of men. They pursue it as ardently as the old alchemist sought the philosopher's stone which would transmute all things into gold, and with the same success. The elements of one are as elusive as those of the other. The Scriptural injunction, "Seek and ye shall find," seems to be inapplicable to the search for popularity, for the more it is sought after the less it is realized. The qualities which win it cannot be acquired. They must be spontaneous in the soul. The personal magnetism — whatever that may be — which produces popularity, is like genius. It refuses to be weighed, measured or analyzed. It is an endowment, and blessed is the man who possesses the gracious gift.

Charles N. Herreid, the present governor of South Dakota, is one of these favored sons. If any demonstration of the fact were needed, the state Republican convention of South Dakota, in 1900, would be ample proof, for he was nominated for governor unanimously in the convention of 1,052 delegates, without even the suggestion of opposition. This is a characteristic example.

He was born In Wisconsin, in 1857. His father was a farmer and one of the pioneers of the state. Young Herreid, after receiving a common school education, attended the Galesville University and took a three years' course. Determining to be a lawyer, he read law one year before entering the law department of the Wisconsin state university, from which, after a two years' course, he graduated in 1882. The same year he was married to Miss Jeannette Slye, and in 1888 went to establish his home in the territory of Dakota, which then embraced the states of both North and South Dakota. He settled at Eureka, McPherson County, where he has since lived. Eureka has earned the reputation of being the largest primary wheat market in the world, and Mr. Herreid's law practice partook of the prosperity of the town. He also held successively the offices of judge and state's attorney. He was made a trustee of the state university, and, later, a member of the board of regents, having charge of all the educational institutions of the state. The duties on these boards, although not particularly ostentatious, made Mr. Herreid known throughout the commonwealth, and through them he became distinguished for his sound judgment, strict impartiality, and discretion. Though factional strife's concerning the institutions were rife at times, Mr. Herreid's character of fairness and honesty of purpose shielded him from the taint of partisanship and injustice.

In 1892 he was elected lieutenant governor of the state, and was re-elected to the same position in 1894. This office is frequently regarded as a political tomb, or a sort of retiring room for the politician. But Mr. Herreid so discharged the duties as to increase his reputation and enhance his popularity. During the two terms that he was president of the senate he more fully demonstrated his capacity for public affairs; he showed thorough knowledge of parliamentary practice; displayed remarkable tact in forming the committees of the senate — a duty which is often a stumbling-block to presiding officers; he exhibited patience and skill in unraveling the intricacies of debate and decided points of order with such a clear comprehension of questions involved and with such fairness as to win, not only the respect, but the admiration of opponents as well as friends. It is well worthy of remark that during the whole of his administration no appeal from his ruling was ever taken. It is said that no similar record was ever made by the president of the senate of any other state. Therefore, the unanimous vote of thanks at the close of the term was not a mere perfunctory matter of form, but a genuine expression of sincere regard.

Mr. Herreid has always been a Republican. He was chairman of the state Republican committee in the campaign of 1898 and acted as a member of the national Republican committee and has exhibited a more than common executive ability in every position occupied. His activity, however, has not been confined to politics. He is a Knight of Pythias and has been grand chancellor of the domain of South Dakota.

He is a member of the A. O. U. W., and was chairman of the committee to revise the constitution and statutes of the grand lodge of that order, and has held other important and prominent positions in the organization. He is also a thirty-second degree Mason and a deputy inspector general for South Dakota, and has held high offices in the consistory.

In manners, Mr. Herreid is modest and unassuming almost to the verge of timidity, being also rather reticent and not given to flattery. Although firm in his opinions, he does not assert them with arrogance. He conveys the impression of being sincere and straightforward, and, even when in opposition, his manner of putting his side of the question inspires confidence rather than antagonism. His home life at Eureka is almost ideal. He has two children, a girl just budding into womanhood, and a boy twelve years old. He attends the Presbyterian church, of which his family are members. No man in the state is held in higher respect, and it is doubtful if another equals him in popularity in public and private life.

FRANK GABRIEL HERRON

Frank G. Herron, one of the successful business men of Sioux Falls, where he conducts a well-equipped grocery establishment, was born on a farm in Vernon County, Wisconsin, on the 16th of August, 1857, and is a son of William A. and Mira Herron, both of whom are now living in Sioux Falls, while both were natives of Athens County, Ohio, and representatives of pioneer families of the old Buckeye state. When the subject was about twelve years of age his parents removed to Warren County, Iowa, and in the public schools of Indianola, the county seat, he received his early educational training. In 1875 he entered upon an apprenticeship to the printer's trade, in the office of the Indianola Herald, becoming a skilled workman and being engaged in the work of his trade for several years. In 1883 he came to South Dakota and took up his residence in Huron and was in business there for five years. In 1888 he removed to Sioux Falls and until March, 1902, he was employed as foreman in the Brown & Saenger printing establishment, but gave up that position and, with his son, Bert, established his present prosperous business enterprise, and they, under the firm name of Herron & Son, have gained a place of prominence in the commercial life of the city. In politics Mr. Herron is a stanch Republican but has never sought official preferment, and fraternally he is identified with the local organization of the Masonic order and its adjunct, the Order of the Eastern Star, and also with the Royal Arcanum, the Ancient Order of United Workmen and the Fraternal Order of Eagles.

On the 28th of November, 1883, Mr. Herron was united in marriage to Miss Ida A. Tisdale, who was born and reared in Lake City, Minnesota, being a daughter of Luther J. and Adaline Tisdale, and of this union have been born four children, of whom three are living: Bert F. was born October 11, 1884; Roy was born January 11, 1888, and died on the 7th of February of the following year; Mabel R. was born January 2, 1889; and Charles L., March 6, 1890.

JOHN WILLIAM HESTON

John William Heston, president of the State Normal School at Madison, South Dakota. has long been a recognized leader in educational circles and has done particularly notable work in the northwest in the upbuilding of the South Dakota Agricultural College, with which he was connected before coming to his present position. A native of Bellefonte, Center County, Pennsylvania, he is a son of Elisha B. and Catherine (Echel) Heston. His father, who was a coach manufacturer, served in the Fifty-fourth Regiment of Pennsylvania Volunteers during the Civil war.

After attending the public schools of his native state John William Heston continued his studies in the Center Hall Normal and in the Pennsylvania State College, from which he was graduated with the class of 1879, winning the Bachelor of Arts degree. Two years later his alma mater conferred upon him the Master of Arts degree and in 1894 he received the honorary degree of Ph. D. from the University of Seattle. Practically his entire life has been devoted to educational work. In early manhood he took up the profession of teaching, which he followed for three years in the country schools of Pennsylvania before entering the Pennsylvania State College. He taught in the preparatory department there during his college course and was afterward elected principal of the preparatory department, remaining in that position for six years, on the termination of which period he was elected professor of the science and art of teaching, which was the first chair of the kind in any college in Pennsylvania. He likewise taught agriculture in the Pennsylvania State College. In the meantime, he studied history and constitutional law under Dr. H. B. Adams of the Johns Hopkins University and after passing a most rigid examination was admitted to the Pennsylvania bar as an attorney in 1890. He then left the Keystone state to practice law in Seattle, but soon tired of that and reentered the profession of teaching, spending three years as principal of the Seattle high school. Later he organized the Washington Agricultural College, but resigned its presidency to accept the presidency of the South Dakota Agricultural College, in which position he was retained for seven years, or from 1896 until 1903, when it became necessary either to retire or become a figurehead and see unfit and incompetent men placed in important positions and the authority of the executive dissipated, for at that period political intrigue became dominant in the affairs of the school. When those conditions were forced upon Mr. Heston he preferred to retire and for two years was entirely out of school work. At the end of that time, he was chosen president of the Madison State Normal School, which position he still holds. Though connected no longer with an agricultural college, he is an enthusiastic advocate of vocational education and is especially interested in securing the introduction of agriculture in all public schools and the increased adoption of science in the school curriculum. His chief work has been done perhaps in two important educational institutions – the Pennsylvania State College and the South Dakota Agricultural College. The latter he transformed into a modern school in four years. His high professional standing can be best shown perhaps in quoting from those who have been his colleagues and contemporaries in the educational field or who have watched his work because of a keen interest along those lines. Dr. William Frear of the Pennsylvania experiment station said: "Dr. Heston has shown in his work here a remarkable understanding of human nature which has enabled him to deal with students in a manner preeminently successful. The same trait has enabled him to a degree greater than in any other case in my acquaintance to win the confidence of men of influence in various classes of society: an ability which would find large scope in the organization and management of a state university. Dr. Heston stood high as a scholar, but even higher as an energetic, whole-souled upright Christian gentleman; always ready to give the larger share of the glory to his coadjutors and subordinates."

Harry J. Patterson, director of the Maryland experiment station, wrote of Mr. Heston as follows: "I regard President Heston as one of the best teachers I was ever under and he has always been able to get his students enthusiastic in their work. As a college president he has proven his ability to place the work on a high plane, to procure and hold students, and has been popular with his coworkers. He is a good forceful speaker, a ripe scholar, a deep thinker and a man of affairs."

Mr. Aldrich, secretary of the regents of education in South Dakota, said: "Our college was in bad condition from internal troubles when Dr. Heston became president. The attendance was small and it did not have the confidence and support of the people of the state. During Dr. Heston's administration the attendance has grown remarkably, being now second or third in the United States. The people of the state have changed their opinion of the institution and have built, through legislative appropriations, five good sized buildings on the campus and authorized two more last winter. The Doctor is a genial gentleman, always very popular with students and patrons. His influence in educational circles is large and his acquaintance over the country quite extensive. His policies are broad and far-reaching and based on sound and civic principles. He is in full sympathy with industrial ideas."

The foregoing have been the opinions of people specially interested in education and the views of the public are perhaps even better expressed by quoting from an editorial in the Argus-Leader, the largest daily published in the state, relative to his work as head of the South Dakota Agricultural College: "The Agricultural College is not only one of the most flourishing educational institutions in the northwest, not only has experienced a most surprising growth and achieved a most flattering reputation, but it is an institution of especial interest and value to a state whose chief industry is agriculture. The Argus Leader desires to testify to the remarkable efficiency with which President Heston has managed the institution during his six years' incumbency, to the powerful stimulus which he has exerted among students and faculty, to the great growth in attendance, a growth which has quadrupled the number of students during six years and to the farsightedness, energy, persistence and high executive ability with which he has built up each department and strengthened the course of study. Dr. Heston has achieved a most flattering success and the people of the state have reason to congratulate the board of regents who secured him and the boards who have retained him and held up his hands. He is not only an educator of high culture and broad learning, but an executive officer who has produced results of far-reaching value to the state. Dr. Heston has made a hobby of agricultural education, not only of the close study of cattle and crops, but of all that goes to enlarge the farmer's mind, to fill it with the ideas and the culture required to secure the highest and broadest results from the cultivation of the soil and the rearing of cattle. Realizing that the first interest of South Dakota lies in successful agriculture, he has conceived that the educational forces of the state should be wielded so far as possible to raise agricultural education to a higher plane, to broaden it and deepen it and to send forth upon the farms and ranges and throughout the state, hundreds of young men and women who will regard agriculture not as a common trade to be pursued indolently, indifferently and with little thought of methods and results, but as a profession requiring keen thought, thorough intellectual development and careful and complete training in all the history and philosophy designed to produce the highest results. Dr. Heston advocates that the rudiments of an agricultural education should be taught in the grade schools of the state, as it is beginning to be taught in the schools of Wisconsin, and that the more thorough education along this line should be given in the agricultural college."

At Harrisburg, Pennsylvania, on the 16th of August, 1881, Mr. Heston was married to Miss Mary Ellen Calder, a daughter of Rev. James Calder, D. D., of Harrisburg, Pennsylvania, who for twelve years or more was president of the Pennsylvania State College. He was also active in the missionary field, serving the Methodist church in that capacity for seven years in China. His son was later a missionary in India for about seven years. Mr. and Mrs. Heston have two sons. Charles Ellis, the elder, married Miss Jane Bechtle, of Le Mars, Iowa, and they have one child, Elizabeth. He is an electrical engineer and is now general manager for the Mathews Brothers Electrical Company of St. Louis. For seven years he was with the United States government as special electrician and as such traveled all over the world on federal business, wiring all United States forts throughout the Philippines and in the other foreign possessions. The younger son, Edward Heston, is now a successful physician of Seattle, Washington. He was graduated from the Northwestern University at Chicago, where he took high rank as a student and as instructor in histological laboratory work.

Mr. and Mrs. Heston are members of the Baptist church and he belongs to the Elks lodge and has taken high ranks in Masonry, being affiliated with the lodge, chapter, commandery and the Mystic Shrine. He holds pronounced views on education, claiming that the vocational or practical plan is by far the best for the average citizen; that one may acquire culture, power and correct habits of work better from a study of the modern sciences than from the study of ancient languages. He has continued his advocacy of this idea until he has won over the strongest men in the state and the public-school curriculum is slowly but surely being changed to conform to this. In administrative affairs Mr. Heston holds that presidents and city superintendents should have their power granted by law. His views upon any vital question are not hastily formed or ill-advised, but are the result of close and discriminating study of every fact that bears upon the point at issue, and he is ever looking for broader and more effective methods of teaching, with full realization of the fact that education should be a preparation for life's practical duties and responsibilities.

JAY RUSSELL HICKOX

Jay R. Hickox, of Deadwood, is a scion of stanch old colonial stock, and is himself a native of New England, where was cradled so much of our national history. He was born in South Britain, New Haven County, Connecticut, on the 3d of April, 1865, and is a son of Henry P. and Julia E. (Bradley) Hickox, both of whom were likewise born and reared in that state, being of English lineage, and there they still retain their residence, the father being a farmer by vocation. The subject secured his preliminary educational discipline in the public schools and then entered Yale College, where he was graduated in 1886, with the degree of Ph. B. Thoroughly equipped in scientific knowledge of a general order and with practical skill in a technical way, in the year of his graduation Mr. Hickox became identified with the engineering department of the Burlington & Missouri River Railroad, and first came to the Black Hills in 1889, to take charge of the construction of the northern end of the Deadwood branch of the line of that road, from Edgemont to Deadwood. After the completion of this work, he was prominently identified with extensive operations in connection with the development of the irrigation systems of the state as well as of Nebraska, until 1899, when he took up his residence in Deadwood and opened a general engineering office. His services have been in requisition in connection with much important work in the line of his profession, while from the time of locating in Deadwood he has held the office of United States deputy mineral surveyor, and has done all of the engineering work for the city.

In politics Mr. Hickox is a stanch supporter of the principles and policies of the Republican party, and fraternally is identified with Deadwood Lodge, No. 7, Ancient Free and Accepted Masons, of which he served as worshipful master in 1902. On the 28th of November, 1805, Mr. Hickox was united in marriage to Miss Minnie Harding, who was born in Diamond City, Montana, on the 16th of November, 1869, being a daughter of John A. and Matilda (Kline) Harding.

HERMAN A. HILDEBRANDT

Herman A. Hildebrandt, of Watertown, is filling the position of county treasurer of Codington County and has at other times held public office, the duties of which have ever been discharged with credit to himself and satisfaction to his constituents. He was born in Germany on the 26th of May, 1848, his parents being Peter and Johanna Hildebrandt, who in 1850 came with their family to the United States, settling first in Washington county, Wisconsin, where the father followed the occupation of farming. Both he and his wife are now deceased.

Herman A. Hildebrandt was but two years of age when the family came to the new world and in the public schools of Wisconsin, he pursued his education and afterward entered upon railroad work as a telegraph operator, being thus engaged until 1886. Three years before that time, or in 1883, he came to South Dakota, spending three years as an operator. At the end of that time, he became head bookkeeper for Stokes Brothers of Watertown, in which capacity he continued for twelve years, a fact indicative of his thorough reliability and efficiency. His fellow townsmen, appreciative of his worth, then asked that he serve them in public office and in 1898 he was elected sheriff, to which position he was reelected in 1900, thus serving for two terms of two years each. In 1903 and 1904 he represented his district in the state legislature and in 1906-7 was registrar of the United States land office. On his retirement from that position, he went upon the road as a traveling salesman, spending three years in that way, and in 1911 he was elected county treasurer, which position he has now filled for four years, being a most able, faithful and conscientious custodian of the public funds. Mr. Hildebrandt has ever regarded a public office as a public trust and it is well known that no trust reposed in him is ever betrayed in the slightest degree.

On the 12th of December, 1869, Mr. Hildebrandt was united in marriage to Miss Henrietta Schultz, a daughter of Christian Schultz, and they have become parents of a daughter and two sons: Ida, now the wife of F. Harraden, of Watertown; Henry J., who is living in Portland, Oregon; and Edward F. W., upon a farm in Codington County.

In politics Mr. Hildebrandt has ever been a stalwart republican and keeps well informed on the questions and issues of the day, so that he is able to support his position by intelligent argument. He stands for progress and improvement along every line that affects the welfare and upbuilding of his city, county and state. For twenty-three years he has been a member of the school board and has constantly advocated the adoption of progressive methods in relation to the work of the schools. Fraternally he is connected with the Masons both in the lodge and chapter and with the Elks and his religious faith is that of the Lutheran church. While born across the water, he is thoroughly American in spirit and interests, for, in fact, practically his entire life has been spent in the United States. He is, indeed, a public-spirited citizen and one to whom the state can ever look for practical assistance along the lines of general improvement.

IRA C. HILL

Ira C. HILL, county treasurer of Roberts County and a gentleman of high standing in the business and social circles of Sisseton. is a native of New York, born in the city of Elmira, on March 9, 1848. His father, Felix Hill, was also a New Yorker by birth, being descended from one of the old families of that commonwealth, and his mother, who bore the maiden name of Julia Hoover, came of old New England stock, her father having served with distinction in the war of 1812, Felix and Julia Hill were the parents of eight children, five sons and three daughters, all living, the majority well settled in life and greatly esteemed in their respective places of residence.

Ira C. Hill spent the first eight years of his life in the state of his birth and in 1856 accompanied his parents on their removal to Wisconsin, where he lived until 1863. He was reared on a farm, with the rugged duties and wholesome discipline of which he early became familiar, and when old enough he entered the district schools which he attended of winter seasons until a youth in his teens. In 1863 he went with the family to Minnesota, where a little later lie tendered his services to the government to help put down the rebellion, enlisting in Company D. Ninth Minnesota Infantry, with which he shared the fortunes and vicissitudes of war for a period of eighteen months, the meanwhile taking part in several campaigns and in a number of hard-fought battles. At the expiration of his period of service he returned to Minnesota, where he followed agricultural pursuits until 1892, when he disposed of his interests in that state and came to Roberts County, South Dakota, where he purchased land and engaged in farming. Later, 1897, he moved to Sisseton, and started a hardware store, to which line of business he devoted his attention until 1900, when he was elected treasurer of Roberts County, which position he still holds, having been re-elected in 1902. Mr. Hill's career has been eminently satisfactory and it is universally conceded that the county has never been served by a more capable or obliging official. He has handled the public funds judiciously, and as a custodian of one of the people's most important trusts has so deported himself as to gain the confidence of his fellow citizens of all parties and shades of political opinion. He has also served two terms as county commissioner and during his incumbency in that office was untiring in his efforts to promote public improvements, but at all times careful and even conservative in the matter of expenditures.

Mr. Hill is still engaged in agriculture on an extensive scale, owning a finely improved farm of four hundred acres in the northern part of Roberts County, all under cultivation, in addition to which he has various other interests, being a heavy stockholder in the First National Bank of Sisseton and in the Citizens' State Bank at White Rock. He has been quite successful in all of his enterprises and is now regarded as one of the financially strong and reliable men of his city and county.

He is a member of Sisseton Lodge, No. 31. Free and Accepted Masons, and his name is also found on the records of Reservation Lodge, No. 66, Knights of Pythias, being a zealous worker in both orders, besides at all times exemplifying their principles and precepts in his relations with his fellow men. Mr. Hill was married in Minnesota, May 27, 1878, to Miss Jennie Rhodes, daughter of Elica Rhodes, of New York, the union resulting in the birth of a daughter. Susie J., at home, and Felix, who is married and lives on the home farm.

ROBERT HILL, M. D.

Robert HILL, a leading physician of Ipswich, South Dakota, was born in the north of Ireland (County Antrim), April 10, 1865, and is the son of Joseph and Harriett (Collins) Hill. The father was also a native of North Ireland, is a farmer by occupation, and still resides in Ireland, being now in his seventy-sixth year. The mother died in 1892.

Doctor Hill was reared in County Antrim, and during the period of his youth, between the age of eleven and fourteen years, he attended the Lesburn Academy. From this institution he matriculated into the Queen's University, Belfast, where he partially completed the medical course, spending about three years at the university. In 1885 he came to the United States and joined his brother in McPherson County, South Dakota, with whom he remained a few years, and then went to Keokuk, Iowa, and entered the College of Physicians and Surgeons in that city, where he was graduated in 1894. He began the practice of medicine at Leola, McPherson County, South Dakota, during the summer of 1894, following which he visited his old home in Ireland, where he spent most of that winter. In the spring of 1895, he returned to the United States and, stopping in New York and Chicago, spent some time in hospital work. He then located at Ipswich. The Doctor is a member of the Aberdeen District Medical Society, the South Dakota Medical Society and the American Medical Association.

He is a thirty-second-degree Mason, and also belongs to the Modern Woodmen of America, the Knights of the Maccabees and the Ancient Order of United Workmen, being medical examiner for the three orders. He has served as coroner of McPherson County for the past eight years. He is a Republican in politics and in religion is a member of the Congregational church. Dr. Hill was married, September 18, 1895, to Bird R. Roe. who was born in Michigan, and to them have been born three children. Helen Harriett, Ruth Elizabeth and Robert Roe.

W. S. HILL

W. S. Hill, one of the representative business men of Hanson County and an influential citizen of Alexandria, was born in Edgar County, Illinois, on the 3d of June, 1863, being a son of Joseph and Rebecca (Braden) Hill, of whose four children three are living at the present time, namely: Elizabeth, wife of William Hillyard, of Wayne County, Iowa; Albert, a resident of Alexandria, South Dakota; and W. S., the immediate subject of this sketch. Joseph Hill was born in Washington county, Pennsylvania, and his wife in Greene County, that state, both being of Scotch-Irish lineage, and both having removed to the state of Illinois when young, their marriage having been there solemnized a few years later. The father of the subject was reared on a farm but as a young man learned the trade of carpenter, becoming a skilled artisan. He followed his trade for a time in Iowa, having resided in Keokuk, and then returned to Illinois, settling in Edgar County after his marriage and there engaging in agricultural pursuits. He tendered his services in defense of the union at the time of the Civil war, enlisting as a member of Company E, Twelfth Illinois Volunteer Infantry, with which he served eighteen months, — until the close of the war, when he received his honorable discharge. In 1869 he removed to Iowa and located in Wayne County, where he became a prominent and prosperous farmer, there continuing his residence until his death, in 1897, at the age of sixty years. He was a Republican in politics from the time of the organization of the party, and was originally a member of the Presbyterian church, later embracing the faith of the Methodist Episcopal church. His widow is still living, making her home in Wayne County.

The subject of this sketch completed the curriculum of the common schools and was graduated in the high school at Allerton, Iowa, as a member of the class of 1884, while two years prior to this he had completed a course in the Pierce Business College, in Keokuk, Iowa, being duly graduated in 1882. At the age of twenty-one years, he secured a position with a firm of wholesale dealers in farming machinery and implements in the city of Des Moines, remaining thus engaged for a short time and then accepting a position with the McCormick Harvesting Machine Company, while a year later he entered the employ of a wholesale grocery house in Des Moines. In the spring of 1887, Mr. Hill came to South Dakota and located in Alexandria, where he purchased an interest in the business of Lanz & Jacobs, securing the interest of the junior member of the firm, while operations were continued under the title of Lanz & Hill, the enterprise involving the handling of agricultural implements and machinery and varied allied lines of goods. In 1893 the subject's brother, Albert, purchased Mr. Lanz's interest in the business, which was conducted for the ensuing six years under the firm name of Hill Brothers. In 1899 our subject purchased his brother's interest and has since been in entire control of the extensive business which has been built up through energy, enterprise and honorable methods. He handles a complete assortment of agricultural implements, vehicles of all kinds, harness and saddlery goods and also coal, and the enterprise ranks as one of the foremost of the sort in this section of the state.

In 1897 Mr. Hill became identified with the cattle business, making his first purchase of ranch land in that year, and from time to time he has made additional purchases until he now has a fine landed estate of fifteen hundred and twenty acres, all being located in Hanson County and being known as the Riverview ranch, while it is recognized as one of the finest stock farms in this section, having the best of modern improvements and facilities. Mr. Hill makes a specialty of the breeding of registered red polled cattle, and in this line, he has attained a high reputation throughout the state and has done much to improve the grade of cattle raised here. In politics he is a stanch Republican, and he is now serving his third term as mayor of Alexandria. He is secretary of the Retail Implement Dealers' Association of South Dakota, Southwestern Minnesota and Northwestern Iowa, having held this office from the time of the organization of the association, in 1899. He and his wife are prominent members of the Presbyterian church, in which he is an elder, taking a deep interest in all departments of church work.

He is affiliated with Celestial Lodge, No. 37, Free and Accepted Masons, at Alexandria; Mitchell Chapter, No. 16, Royal Arch Masons, in Mitchell: St. Bernard Commandery, No. II, Knights Templar, in this city; Oriental Consistory, No. I, Ancient Accepted Scottish Rite, in Yankton; and El Riad Temple of the Mystic Shrine, in Sioux Falls, while he is also identified with Alexandria Lodge, No. II, Ancient Order of United Workmen. On the 3d of September, 1890, was solemnized the manager of Mr. Hill to Miss Ida Kellogg, of Wayne County, Iowa, and they are the parents of five sons, Joseph L., W. Braden, Emory K., Lawrence M. and Robert D.

HENRY W. HINRICHS

Henry W. Hinrichs is a banker occupying an important place in the financial circles of Rapid City, and is connected with a number of the leading enterprises in the Black Hills region. His birth occurred in Charles City, Iowa, May 19, 1874. His father, William Hinrichs, was a native of Germany and emigrated to the United States in 1867. Although a miller by trade, he engaged in farming after coming to the United States, purchasing land near Rockford, Iowa. In 1884 he removed to Dakota territory with his family and settled upon a homestead near Kimball. He became one of the most prosperous men of his community and was particularly interested in the cattle business, doing much to demonstrate the adaptability of South Dakota lands to profitable stock-raising. In many ways he contributed to the advancement of agricultural interests in his locality, but a number of years ago he retired from active life and now resides at Albany, Oregon. His wife was in her maidenhood Miss Minnie Friesmann, was also born in Germany and was a passenger on the same vessel in which Mr. Hinrichs crossed the Atlantic to America, their acquaintance beginning upon that voyage.

Henry W. Hinrichs is the oldest in a family of eight children and received his education in the country schools and in the State Agricultural College at Brookings. At the age of seventeen years, he was placed in the Kimball State Bank, where he worked for a year and a half for his board. He next served for a similar period as deputy postmaster at Chamberlain, South Dakota, and then spent a year in special study at the State Agricultural College at Brookings. A part of the following year was devoted to work upon the home farm, but in the spring of 1897, he returned to the Kimball State Bank, accepting a position as bookkeeper at thirty dollars per month. He also bought an interest in the institution and after three years purchased the stock of W. H. Wyant, who had served as cashier, and was himself appointed to that position. He remained with that bank until January, 1904, and then removed to Chamberlain, purchasing a half interest in the Chamberlain State Bank and becoming its cashier. A short time afterward he organized the First National Bank of White Lake, South Dakota, and was chosen its president. Subsequently he was made president of the Kimball State Bank. In addition to the concerns already mentioned he organized the Chamberlain Wholesale Grocery Company and the Farmers State Bank of Pukwana, South Dakota, and became one of the owners of the Bank of Bijou Hills, South Dakota. In 1907 he disposed of his interests in Chamberlain and removed to Rapid City, where soon afterward he organized the Security Savings Bank and erected the Security Savings Bank building, being the majority owner in both. Subsequently he sold part of his holdings, but still retains the vice presidency of the bank. He was one of the organizers of the Lamphere-Hinrichs Lumber Company, which was later known as the Warren-Lamb Lumber Company, but in 1912 he disposed of his interests in that concern. He is at present one of the owners and treasurer of the Dakota Plaster Company, which has its works at Black Hawk, South Dakota, and he was one of those who organized the Midwest Coal & Lumber Company, of which he is still one of the chief owners and also the president. He is responsible for the erection of the new buildings of the Kimball State Bank and the First National Bank of White Lake, two of the finest structures of the kind in the state. He has invested quite heavily in farm lands and is much interested in stock-raising, and particularly in the breeding of blooded shorthorn cattle.

Mr. Hinrichs was married on the 25th of September, 1901, to Miss Kate M. Brchan, a daughter of Thomas Brchan, whose farm adjoins the Hinrichs homestead. Four children have been born to this union, namely: Floyd, Grace Anna, Frederick William and Ada Louise.

Mr. Hinrichs is quite prominent in the counsels of the democratic party and has been a candidate upon that ticket for county treasurer and also for state senator. He realizes the great importance of an adequate system of public schools and as a member of the Rapid City school board has for several years done much to maintain the schools of that city at a high standard. His religious faith is indicated by his membership in the Presbyterian church, of which he is a trustee. Fraternally he is a thirty-second degree Mason, belonging to Yankton Consistory, No. 1, and is also a Woodman. His initiative, executive ability and sound judgment as to financial matters have been of great value to the Black Hills country, as he has been instrumental in founding a number of banks and industrial concerns that have aided materially in the development of that part of the state. He has also contributed to the general welfare along other lines, as he is a man of many interests and of broad-minded views and is ever ready to aid in the accomplishment of any worthy public work.

WILLIAM HOESE

William HOESE, one of the honored and influential citizens of Spencer, McCook County, was born in the village of Hinton. Plymouth county, Iowa, on the 28th of March, 1868, a son of William and Henrietta (Bandt) Hoese, of whose four living children he is the youngest, the others being as follows: Clara, who is the wife of William Lerch, of Sioux City, Iowa; Louisa, who is the wife of John Gudekenst, of State Center, Iowa; and Frank, who is a resident of Merrill, that state. William Hoese, Sr., was born in Launsberg, Germany, in 1822, and the wife was born in the same place, in 1832. There he was reared to maturity, learning the trade of miller, eventually becoming the owner and operator of an old-style mill in his native land, the motive power being furnished by a windwheel. He was married in his native town and there two of his children were born. In 1857 he emigrated with his family to America, landing in New York City and thence coming west to Iowa City, Iowa, where he remained a short time and then removed to Ponka, Nebraska, being the first white settler in that place, being engaged in farming in that locality for the ensuing five years, having purchased government land. In 1862 he passed through Sioux City, searching for an eligible location in Iowa, and though there was no flouring mill in the little village of Sioux City at the time, he decided to locate in Hinton, Plymouth County, where he erected the first grist mill in western Iowa, being one of the first settlers in that locality and anticipating the tide, of immigration by several years. Six years later he disposed of his milling property and removed to Merrill, Plymouth County, in which locality he acquired extensive farming interests, eventually becoming one of the most influential agriculturists and stock growers in that section, where he continued to reside until his death, which occurred in 1894, his devoted wife having preceded him into eternal rest by about four months. He was a stalwart Republican in his political views, and while wielding distinctive influence in his party councils, he has never been an aspirant for public office.

William Hoese, the immediate subject of this sketch, secured his early educational training in the public schools, and at the age of fourteen was sent to the Northwestern Business College, in Sioux City, Iowa, where he was graduated in 1884. He then held a clerical position in a mercantile establishment in that city for one year, at the expiration of which, at the age of seventeen years, he came to Bridgewater, South Dakota, and engaged in the hardware business, in partnership with Theodore Montague. Three years later he disposed of his interests in this line and went to Sioux Center, Iowa, where he organized the bank of

Sioux Center, of which he was made president, being at the time the youngest bank president in the state, as he had not yet attained his twenty-first year. In 1890 Mr. Hoese disposed of his banking interests and came to Spencer, South Dakota, where he effected the organization of the State Bank at Spencer, of which he was sole owner and officially cashier, his father and brothers permitting the use of their names on the corps of officials in order to comply with the technical provisions of the law. Mr. Hoese successfully conducted this enterprise until the 1st of January, 1903, when he sold the business, since which time he has not actively identified himself with any other enterprise, giving his attention to his various capitalistic interests. He has ever given an unequivocal allegiance to the Republican party and has shown a zealous interest in its cause, having been a member of the county central committee ever since taking up his residence in Spencer. While in no wise ambitious for political preferment, he was nominated for the state senate in 1898 and was elected, though the normal Democratic majority in the district was three hundred and sixty-one at that time. He gave a most creditable and satisfactory service in the upper house during the ensuing general assembly and fully justified the popular confidence reposed in him. He has also served in various local offices of trust, having been mayor of Spencer in 1894, and also serving as a member of the town council, as village treasurer and as a member of the school board.

He is a member of Spencer Lodge, No. 147, Ancient Free and Accepted Masons; Salem Chapter, No. 34, Royal Arch Masons; Constantine Commandery, No. 17, Knights Templar, of Salem; and El Riad Temple of the Mystic Shrine, in Sioux Falls, while he is also affiliated with the local lodges of the Modern Woodmen of America and the Ancient Order of United Workmen. On the 3d of September, 1895, Mr. Hoese was married to Miss Ida T. Janke, of Spencer, and they are the parents of two sons and one daughter, namely: William R., Frank H. and Clara T.

SILAS MATTHEW HOHF, M. D.

Dr. Silas Matthew Hohf, successfully engaged in the practice of medicine and surgery in Yankton, specializes in the latter field and has won recognition as one of the ablest surgeons of the city. He has offices at the corner of Fourth street and Douglas Avenue and the demand made upon him is almost continuous. He was born at Hopkins Station, Allegan County, Michigan, August 30, 1872, and is a son of John and Barbara (Katz) Hohf, both of whom were natives of Germany. They went to Michigan at an early day, the father becoming one of the pioneers in the section of the state in which he settled. There he followed farming and saw the early development of the district in which he lived. In 1882 he removed to South Dakota and purchased one hundred and sixty acres of land. Again, he bent his energies to the cultivation of the soil and followed farming until a substantial measure of success rewarded his efforts. He afterward sold the old homestead about 1899 and, removing westward to the coast, took up his abode in Salem, Oregon, where he lived retired until his death, which occurred in 1905. For more than fifteen years he had survived his wife, who passed away in 1889. They're a family of ten children, seven sons and three daughters: Anna, the wife of W. M. Garnjobst, a resident of Salem, Oregon; George, who is now a contractor of Florida; Bernard, who is engaged in the lumber business in Beresford, South Dakota; Arnold, who is a lumber merchant located at Worthing, South Dakota; S. M., of this review; J. A., a physician of Yankton, who is specializing in his practice in the treatment of diseases of the eye, ear, nose and throat; Lena B., the wife of Walter H. Noble, of Chehalis, Washington; John G., a mining engineer living at Everett, Washington; Sarah M., the wife of Ed Seeger, a traveling salesman of Topeka, Kansas; and Emanuel, who is a student in the Northwestern University Dental College in Chicago. The father was a pioneer of two states, Michigan and South Dakota, and contributed to their early substantial development.

Dr. Silas M. Hohf was a lad of about ten years when brought by his parents to South Dakota and upon the old homestead farm in Clay County was reared, sharing with the family in all the hardships and experiences incident to farm life in a new country. He attended the district schools until he reached the age of sixteen and afterward had the benefit of instruction in the Normal School at Grand Island, Nebraska. He next engaged in teaching in South Dakota, where he remained for three years in order to obtain funds which would enable him to continue his studies. He later entered the Illinois Medical College of Chicago, where he won his M. D. degree in 1897, and thus qualified for practice he returned to Yankton, where he opened an office. He was in active practice until 1901, when he again went to Chicago and took up the further study of medicine in the North-Western University Medical College, winning his degree of M. D. in that institution in 1903. During that period, he served as an interne in Mercy Hospital of Chicago and gained that broad knowledge and experience which only hospital practice can bring. He then returned to Yankton and again took up the work of his profession, in which he has since continued. He has made a specialty of surgery and ranks with the foremost surgeons of the state He spent six weeks in the Post-Graduate College of New York in 1908 and devoted on month to study in the Johns Hopkins Medical College at Baltimore, giving special attention to surgery in both instances. He belongs to the District Medical Society, the South Dakota Medical Association, the American Medical Association, the Chicago Medical Society and the Sioux Valley Medical Association, and through his identification with all these keeps in close touch with the advanced work that is being done by the profession and the most modern scientific investigations along the lines of both medical and surgical practice. Moreover, Dr. Hohf has business connections of importance, being now a director of the Dakota National Bank of Yankton and a director of the Yankton Brick & Tile Company, and he and his brother, Dr. J. A. Hohf, are now erecting an office building at Fourth street and Douglas Avenue.

On the 12th of October, 1898, was celebrated the marriage of Dr. Hohf and Carrie Elizabeth Sniffin, a native of New York city. Their children, Lillian and Florence, are both now in school. Dr. Hohf has been a member of the board of education of Yankton since 1911 and believes thoroughly in the employment of good teachers and the adoption of progressive educational methods, realizing that in the school system of the country is laid the strength of the nation. He belongs to the Yankton Commercial Association, of which he is a director, and at all times manifests a public-spirited devotion in his relation to county and state. Fraternally he is connected with St. Johns Lodge, No. I, A. F. & A. M.; with Mackay Chapter, R. A. M.; De Molay Commandery, No. 3, K. T.; Oriental Consistory, No. I, A. A. S. R. F., in which he has attained the thirty-second degree of the Scottish Rite; and Yelduz Temple, A. A. O. N. M. S. He is now serving as master of his lodge and he ranks high among his brethren of the fraternity as one who is an exemplary representative of the craft. His political allegiance is given to the republican party, his support being a matter of personal conviction upon political questions and not given with any desire for office. He regards his professional pursuits as abundantly worthy of his best efforts and his close and discriminating study, his persistency and his conscientious work have done much to bring him to the goal of success and gain him prominence in his chosen calling.

DWIGHT GERARD HOLBROOK

Dwight G. Holbrook, of Sioux Falls, who is manager for South Dakota for the Mutual Life Insurance Company, of New York, is a native of Windsor Locks, Hartford County, Connecticut, where he was born on the 27th of July, 1867, being a son of Dwight and Kalista (Thayer) Holbrook, both scions of prominent families of New England, where the father was an inventor and a manufacturer of scientific and school apparatus, his birth having occurred in Derby, Connecticut. He died in 1891, and his wife resides in New York state. The subject of this sketch is of the seventh generation in direct line of descent from John Holbrook, who immigrated from Derby, England, and settled at Oyster Bay, Long Island, in the early part of the seventeenth century. His son Abel was the first white child born at Oyster Bay, the date of his nativity having been 1653. Several of the descendants of the original American ancestors were valiant soldiers in the Continental line during the war of the Revolution. On the maternal side the subject is descended from Richard Thayer, who settled in Braintree, Massachusetts, in 1640; Henry Adams, who was born in 1626; John Alden and his wife, Priscilla; William White, of the "Mayflower" and in the fourth generation from Rev. Joseph Thaxter who was commissioned by the "council of the Colony of the Massachusetts Bay," on the 23d of January, 1776, as "chaplain of the regiment whereof John Robertson, Esq., is colonel," and who carried a musket at the battles of Concord Bridge, Lexington and Bunker Hill. In 1825 Rev. Joseph Thaxter conducted the religious service at the laying of the corner-stone of Bunker Hill monument. His commission as chaplain is now in the possession of his great-granddaughter, the mother of him whose name initiates this resume. As to the genealogy of the Holbrook family specific reference is made in the following named historical publications: American Ancestry, volume I, page 38, and volume VII, page 6; Austin's Ancestral Dictionary, page 27, also allied families, pages 131-3; Dodd's History of East Haven, Connecticut, page 129; Orcutt's History of Derby, pages 729-31; and Vinton's Genealogy, pages 185-8 and 330-40. Of the Thayer and Thaxter families mention is made in detail in Massachusetts Historical Society, volume XVII, page 280; in the Records of the Town of Braintree, 1640-73; and in East Anglia, volume III, page 35; while of the Adams, Alden and White families, record appears in Savage's Genealogical Dictionary.

Dwight G. Holbrook received his early educational discipline principally in private schools in his native state, where he was prepared for college. He, however, decided to enter business life, in 1884, rather than to continue a burden upon a mother whose courage, business sagacity, self-abnegation and unqualified devotion had hitherto given him ample opportunities. After nine months of clerical service in the passenger department of the New York Central Railroad, he resigned, in October, 1884, to become a clerk in the actuary's department of the Mutual Life Insurance Company of New York, winning advancement through his fidelity, discrimination and marked executive ability, and being made private secretary to the vice-president of the company in 1889, while in 1893 he was given his present important preferment as general agent for the Dakotas, in which capacity he has accomplished a great work in the interests of a great company, maneuvering his forces with consummate skill and distinctive initiative and administrative force, and thus bringing much prestige to this old, reliable and well-known insurance corporation. He is a Republican in his political proclivities, but has never desired office.

Fraternally he is identified with the Knights of Pythias, and the Masonic order, in which latter he is affiliated with Minnehaha Lodge, No. I, Free and Accepted Masons; Sioux Falls Chapter, No. 2, Royal Arch Masons; Cyrene Commandery. No. 2, Knights Templar; and Oriental Consistory, No. I, Ancient Accepted Scottish Rite. In the city of Minneapolis, Minnesota, on the 14th of July, 1898, Mr. Holbrook was united in marriage to Miss Charlotte B. Long, daughter of Joseph D. Long, and of this union have been born two children, namely: Robert Dwight, June 7, 1899, and Darwin Long, July 5, 1903.

FRED HOLCOMB

F. Holcomb was born in Jefferson County, New York, at the town of Carthage, on July 2, 1851, and is the son of William and Maria (Fanning) Holcomb. who were also natives of New York. The father was a prosperous and energetic farmer in Jefferson County, and in 1855 the family moved to Dubuque County, Iowa, four miles from the city of Dubuque, where they followed dairying for a time, then farming. In this county Mr. Holcomb grew to manhood and was educated. In 1869 he moved to Abilene, Kansas, where, with his brother, he was occupied in the cattle business until 1872. He then took a band of cattle to Des Moines, Iowa, and sold them, and with the proceeds paid his tuition for a term at a business college in Dubuque. In April, 1873, he came to South Dakota with a herd of cows which he left at Yankton while he went back to Dubuque and got married. Returning to Yankton with his bride, he settled there and started a dairy business on a small scale, carrying the milk about in cans on foot. A year later he had two wagons and his business continued to increase. In the spring of 1879, he came to Rapid City in company with his father to look over the country with a view to settling here. The father remained, but Mr. Holcomb returned to Yankton, making the trip on the only stage that was ever held up on the line between Rapid City and Pierre, this event occurring before the stage reached the Cheyenne river. In July of 1877, he made a visit to Rapid City for his health, and, determining to make this his future home, he went back to Yankton and disposed of his interests there, and in the spring of 1881 brought his family and cattle to this section, settling the family at Rapid City and placing the cattle on the range along the Cheyenne, removing them later to the White River. His cattle are now mostly to the north, on Sulphur and Morrow creeks. He has made a great success of his business by keeping steadily at it and applying the wisdom gained in experience and observation, ever increasing its magnitude and conducting it along the lines of the most wholesome progress and development. His acreage in both ranch and grazing lands is very large and his stock industry is the leading one belonging to an individual citizen in this part of the state. The Holcomb home has been at Rapid City ever since the family settled here, and is one of the most elegant and attractive in the town.

The head of the house is an active and devoted member of the Masonic fraternity, with membership in the lodge at Rapid City. On June 4, 1873, Mr. Holcomb was married in Dubuque County, Iowa, to Miss Minnie V. Miller, a native of that county. They have one child, May, the wife of George H. White, of Rapid City. Mrs. Holcomb's parents came to Rapid City in 1880 and remained there until death, the father dying in 1886 and the mother in 1891. The father was prominent as a stockman and also conducted one of the first hotels at Rapid City.

R. H. HOLDEN

R. H. Holden, of White, Brookings County, is a native of the Badger state, having been born in Sparta, Monroe County, Wisconsin, on the 26th of November, 1874, and being a son of Nelson H. and Nettie H. (Stewart) Holden, both of whom were born and reared in the state of New York, where their marriage was solemnized. The father of the subject read law for some time and continued to make his home in the old Empire state until the latter part of 1860, when he removed to Sparta, Wisconsin, where he was for some time a popular teacher in the public schools, eventually becoming superintendent of schools in Monroe County. In the spring of 1879, he came with his family to South Dakota and located on a homestead claim, in Sherman township, Brookings County, being numbered among the first settlers in this section. He continued to reside on this farm for eight years, in the meanwhile accumulating other tracts of land and becoming one of the prosperous farmers of the county. In 1886 he established himself in the banking business in White, opening what was known as the Citizens' Exchange Bank, of whose stock he was the sole owner. In 1898 he reorganized the institution under the name of the Bank of White, and in 1901 it was incorporated as the Farmers' State Bank of White, and converted into the Fanners' National Bank of White, in 1904, he being one of the largest stockholders. He is now a director of the bank and is one of the town's most influential and honored citizens. Of his eight children we enter the following brief record: Almond N. is a teacher in the state school for the deaf and dumb of San Francisco; Mabel is the wife of Arthur H. Kenyon, a successful lawyer of Spokane, Washington; Nellie is the wife of Dr. Henry H. Clark, who is engaged in the practice of his profession in Watertown, South Dakota; Ralph H. is the immediate subject of this sketch; Florence is the wife of Delbert E. Wood, assistant postmaster at Pipestone, Minnesota; and Pearl, Patience and Netta still remain at the parental home.

The subject of this sketch was a lad of five years at the time of his parents' removal to South Dakota, and he was reared to the age of fourteen years on the homestead farm in Brookings County, in the meanwhile attending the district schools. After the family located in White he entered the public schools, being graduated in the high school as a member of the class of 1892. In the following spring he entered the Northern Indiana Normal School and Business University, at Valparaiso, Indiana, where he was graduated in 1895, with the degree of Bachelor of Arts. He then went to the city of Spokane, Washington, where he began reading law in the office of his brother-in-law, Mr. Kenyon. In October of the following year, he returned to White and entered his father's bank, being made cashier at the time of the first reorganization, in 1898, while upon the second reorganization, under the present title, he became a stockholder in the institution, in which he acted as assistant cashier until April, 1902, when he was elected to his present office of cashier. He has shown marked discrimination and administrative ability and has handled executive duties to the full satisfaction of all concerned. He is the owner of a section of valuable land, located in Oaklake and Sherman townships and also of two or three residence properties in White, having accumulated about fifteen thousand dollars since leaving school and being one of the progressive and public-spirited young business men of the state which has been his home from his boyhood days. In politics Mr. Holden gives an uncompromising allegiance to the Republican party, in whose local ranks he has been an active and valued worker, having been a member of the county central committee since 1898 and having been a delegate to several of the state conventions of his party, as well as to the minor conventions.

Fraternally he is affiliated with Washington Lodge, No. 3, Ancient Free and Accepted Masons, of which he is master at the time of this writing. On the 3d of July, 1902, was solemnized the marriage of Mr. Holden to Miss Grace A. West, a daughter of Frank H. West, a prominent citizen of White, and she was summoned into eternal rest only a few months later, her death occurring on the 20th of the following November.

FRED H. HOLLISTER

Among the men who have during the past quarter of a century aided in developing and shaping the business history of Sioux Falls is Fred H. Hollister, who since 1887 has been Identified with various important business interests here. Since the organization of the Brown Drug Company, he has been its secretary and treasurer and he is connected with financial interests as a member of the board of directors of the State Bank & Trust Company. He was born in Rockton, Illinois, August 21, 1865, and is a son of

George H. and Fanny E. (Hooker) Hollister. He acquired his education in the public schools of Rockton and Rockford, Illinois, and in 1887 moved to Sioux Falls, South Dakota, where he engaged in real estate and banking, later adding fire insurance to the list of his activities. Upon the organization of the Brown Drug Company, he was made secretary and treasurer, offices which he has filled with credit and ability since that time. His work has been one of the important factors in the rapid success of this enterprise and through his connection with it he has added to his reputation as a farsighted and progressive business man. In addition to his position with the Brown Drug Company Mr. Hollister is also a member of the board of directors of the State Bank & Trust Company. As a financier he stands high in the public esteem and his business probity is beyond question.

On the 21st of December, 1893, at Dell Rapids, South Dakota, Mr. Hollister was united in marriage to Miss Belle L. Gifford, and they have become the parents of three children, Helen Hooker, Mary Gifford and Frances. Mr. Hollister is a member of the Episcopal church and belongs to the Country and Dacotah Clubs. He is connected fraternally with the Masonic order, holding membership in the Knights Templar commandery and in the Shrine. His political allegiance is given to the republican party. Mr. Hollister has been a resident of Sioux Falls for over twenty-five years and all with whom he has come in contact have recognized his sterling qualities and have accorded to him their respect and goodwill.

JOHN HOLMAN

J. Holman, of the law firm of Gamble, Tripp & Holman, and distinctively one of the leading attorneys of the Yankton bar, is a native of Wisconsin and the son of Sjur and Ragrilda Holman, both parents born in Norway. Sjur Holman came to the United States in 1849, and settled near Deerfield, Wisconsin, where he shortly afterward married Ragrilda Aase, who was brought to this country by her parents in 1845, when about thirteen years of age. After his marriage, Mr. Holman turned his attention to agricultural pursuits and, though beginning in a modest way with but limited capital, he succeeded by good management and consecutive industry in accumulating a handsome competence, so that he is now enabled to spend the closing years of his life in comfortable and honorable retirement in the town of Deerfield. Of the children born to this estimable couple, eight are living at the present time, namely: Mrs. Martha Sterricker, of Omaha, Nebraska: Andrew, who lives in Copper Center, Alaska, of which place he was the first settler and founder: Nel, a graduate of the law department of Wisconsin University, but now publishing a paper in Deerfield, that state; Lewis, who is stationed at the Oknago Indian Mission in British Columbia; John, of this review; Gerina, at home; Edwin, editor and proprietor of a newspaper in Minnesota, and Ella, who is still with her parents.

John Holman was born February 10, 1867, in the town of Deerfield, Wisconsin, and grew up at home, attending for some years the common schools and later taking a full course in the seminary at Red Wing, Minnesota, from which institution he was graduated in the spring of 1887. In the following fall he entered the law department of the University of Wisconsin, and after prosecuting his legal studies for the greater part of two years, was graduated with the class of 1889, immediately after which he accepted a clerkship in the office of one of the leading attorneys of Madison. Young Holman spent about one and a half years in clerical work at the nominal salary of fifteen dollars per month and board, but becoming restive under such manner of living he resigned his position at the expiration of the time noted, and in January, 1891, came to Yankton, South Dakota, where, with something like fifty dollars saved from his meager earnings and about two hundred and forty dollars of borrowed capital, he opened an office and entered upon his career as a lawyer. His first year in this city was one of struggle and self-denial, clients being few and expenses by no means light. By husbanding his resources, however, he managed to acquire sufficient business to keep his bark afloat until the fall of the following year, at which time he was induced by his Republican friends to announce himself a candidate for the office of state's attorney. Arrayed against the candidate for the Republican ticket in that campaign were the combined forces of Democracy and Populism, a fusion which its members confidently believed would sweep the country and capture every office, state, district and county. Notwithstanding the strong opposition, Mr. Holman accepted the nomination and, entering upon the campaign with the determination of doing his best, made a thorough, systematic and brilliant canvass, the result of which was his election by a very handsome majority over a popular competitor. During his first term as prosecutor, he formed a law partnership with L. L. F. Cleeger, and opened a branch office at Centerville, Mr. Cleeger looking after the business at the latter place, the subject taking charge of the office in Yankton. At the expiration of his term Mr. Holman was chosen his own successor and at the same time his associate was elected state's attorney of Turner County, in consequence of which their partnership was dissolved, the subject shortly thereafter becoming a member of the law firm of Cramer & Holman, which continued for a period of two years.

After practicing alone for one year, Mr. Holman entered into a partnership with Robert E. McDowell, present private secretary of Senator Gamble, which lasted until the formation of the present legal firm of Gamble, Tripp & Holman in the year 1901. Actuated by a spirit of intense patriotism, Mr. Holman, in May, 1898, sacrificed his law practice, which in the meantime had become large, far-reaching and lucrative, to enter the service of his country in its war with Spain. Enlisting in Company C, First South Dakota Volunteer Infantry, he was soon on his way to the Philippines, where he experienced the vicissitudes and hardships peculiar to warfare with a barbarous foe in a hot and trying climate. Soon after joining the army, he was made corporal, subsequently was promoted quartermaster sergeant and still later rose to the rank of lieutenant, which position he held until his discharge, in October, 1899. Returning home, he assumed his law practice, which soon regained its former magnitude, and from that time to the present he has devoted his attention closely to his profession, with the result that he today commands an extensive business and occupies a conspicuous place among the leading members of the Yankton bar.

In the spring of 1900 Mr. Holman was elected mayor of Yankton, and the ensuing fall he was further honored by a third election to the office of state's attorney, in which position he is now serving his fourth term, having been re-elected in the fall of 1902. Mr. Holman's frequent election to important official station demonstrates not only superior professional ability, but a trustworthiness and popularity with members of all political parties such as few attain. In December, 1900, Mr. Holman was married, in Yankton, to Miss Alice Flanagan, of this city, the union being blessed with two children, a daughter by the name of Susan R. and a son named Bartlett.

Mr. Holman is a member of the Masonic order, in which he has risen to a high degree, and he is also identified with the Knights of Pythias and the Ancient Order of United Workmen. He was reared a Lutheran and, though still adhering to that faith, he has attended of recent years the Episcopal church of Yankton, to which his wife belongs. He contributes liberally to the support of both these religions, is also alive to all kinds of charitable and benevolent work, and assists to the extent of his ability any laudable enterprise having for its object the social advancement of the community or the moral good of his fellow men.

CHARLES MARVIN HOLLISTER, M. D.

Dr. Charles Marvin Hollister is a prominent representative of the medical profession, practicing in Pierre, where he represents the Chicago Northwestern Railroad as district surgeon, and is also physician to the Pierre Indian School. He has ever held to high professional standards and continuous reading and investigation have constantly broadened his knowledge and promoted his efficiency. He keeps in touch with the onward march of the profession nor lacks the discrimination that enables him to readily determine between the worthless and the valuable in the ideas that are advanced in relation to medical practice. Mr. Hollister is a native of Pawlet, Vermont, born September 1, 1867. His parents are Francis S. and Julia L. Hollister, the former a veteran of the Civil war. The family was represented in the Revolutionary war by Captain Asbel Hollister, who valiantly fought for the independence of the nation. In the maternal line the ancestry can be traced back to the duke of York.

Liberal educational advantages were afforded Charles Marvin Hollister, who supplemented his public-school training by a course in Williams College of Massachusetts, in which he was graduated with the class of 1892, the Bachelor of Arts degree being then conferred upon him. For his professional training he entered the University of Pennsylvania and won his M. D. degree as a member of the class of 1895. He immediately entered upon practice and his professional career has been one of growing success. He was physician and surgeon and also athletic director at Beloit College in Beloit, Wisconsin, for three years. Subsequently he became athletic director and lecturer on physical culture and hygiene at the Northwestern University at Evanston, Illinois, where he remained for four years. He has been a resident of Pierre since 1905 and at the present time is district surgeon for the Chicago & Northwestern Railroad, is physician and surgeon to the Pierre Indian School and was formerly president of the pension examining board. While at Beloit he served as superintendent of the board of health and also filled that office in Pierre, but retired. He is likewise a member of the board of education and is the present county coroner of Hughes County. His political allegiance has always been given to the republican party.

On the 4th of September, 1895, at Cooperstown, New York, Dr. Hollister was united in marriage to Miss Regina S. Reustle, a daughter of J. F. Reustle, a veteran of the Civil war. Dr. and Mrs. Hollister have one child, Regina. The parents are communicants of the Trinity Episcopal church, in which Dr. Hollister is serving as warden. He has held various offices in different fraternities and is now worshipful master of Pierre Lodge, No. 22, A. F. & A. M. He also belongs to Pierre Chapter, No. 22, R. A. M., and Pierre Commandery, K. T., and is likewise a member of the Knights of Pythias Lodge at Blunt, the Maccabees, the Mutual Benefit Association and the Fraternal Order of Eagles. He is also connected with the Commercial Club, the Tennis Club and the Golf Club, and holds membership in Alpha Tau Omega, a college fraternity, and in the Pepper Society, a medical fraternity. Along strictly professional lines he is identified with the Fourth District Medical, the State Medical and the Tri-State Medical Associations and the American Association of Railway Surgeons. He holds to high professional standards, is most careful in the diagnosis of his cases and in matters of professional judgment is seldom, if ever, at fault.

WILLIAM C. HOLLISTER

The name of William C. Hollister has come to be regarded as synonymous with business development and progress in Sioux Falls, for he is not only one of the largest real-estate dealers in the city but is also prominently known in financial circles as founder and president of the Dakota Trust & Savings Bank. He was born in Rockton, Illinois, November 18, 1862, and is a son of George H. and Fannie E. (Hooker) Hollister, the former a native of Vermont.

William C. Hollister acquired his early education in the public schools of Rockton, Illinois, and later attended high school at Beloit, Wisconsin, supplementing this by a course in a business college at Milwaukee, from which he was graduated in 1881. Following this he located in Sioux Falls and entered the First National Bank as assistant bookkeeper, rising in five years to be assistant cashier. Mr. Hollister resigned this position in 1886 and formed a partnership with John S. Lewis under the name of Lewis & Hollister, dealers in real estate and fire insurance. This partnership existed for one year, after which Mr. Hollister continued alone in the real-estate and loan business until 1890. He then resumed his identification with financial interests, organizing the State Bank & Trust Company, of which he was made president. In July, 1906, he disposed of his interests in that concern and organized the firm of Hollister Brothers, dealers in real estate, loans and insurance. They today control one of the leading enterprises of that character in the city and have a large, representative and growing trade. In December, 1912, Mr. Hollister extended the field of his business activities, organizing the Dakota Trust & Savings Bank with a capital stock of one hundred thousand dollars. He has since been president of this concern and under his able management it has become in a short time one of the leading banks in Sioux Fails. Mr. Hollister is a resourceful, capable and farsighted financier and has made the policy of his institution one of progressiveness, tempered by a safe conservatism. He has met with a gratifying degree of success and occupies a position of precedence in financial circles of the city.

In Rockton, Illinois, October 12, 1886, Mr. Hollister married Miss Caroline H. Coller and they have become the parents of three children, William G., Louise and Eugenie. Mr. Hollister is a member of the Episcopal church, and his political allegiance is given to the republican party. He is well known in the Masonic order, holding membership in the commandery and Shrine, and he belongs to the Elks, the Country and the Dacotah Clubs. He keeps in close touch with financial interests and his ability in his chosen field is known and recognized.

ALBE HOLMES

A. HOLMES, superintendent of the Two Johns mine, located at Crow Hill, Lawrence county, comes of stanch old colonial stock, and is himself a native of the far-distant Pine Tree state, having been born in Belfast, Waldo County, Maine, on the 13th of June, 1848, and being a son of James and Hannah H. (Ward) Holmes, who were likewise born and reared in that county, both passing their entire lives in Maine, where the father devoted his attention to lumbering during his active business career. The subject secured his early educational training in the common schools of his native place and early began to assist his father in his lumbering operations. In 1869, upon attaining his legal majority, he came west as a youthful pioneer. He made his way to Nevada, where he was for a number of years employed in the great Comstock mine. In 1876 he came to the Black Hills, making the trip to Cheyenne, Wyoming, from which point he came overland in a stage coach, in company with ten other men, hiring a team from one of the old-time pioneers,

Tim Dyer. This was the second stage to enter the hills, and while the party were enroute a band of one hundred and fifty Indians passed their camp but gave them no trouble. They arrived in what is now the town of Custer on the 24th of March, and after devoting a few weeks to quartz prospecting Mr. Holmes started the first express line between Gayville and Deadwood, operating the same about six months, when he sold out. He then resumed prospecting, in which line he met with varying success during the following years. In 1896 he located the property now worked by the Spearfish Mining Company, and he still retains an interest in this property, which is a most promising one. In 1897 he was appointed superintendent of the Two Johns mine, named in honor of two well-known individuals of national reputation, John W. Gates and John A. Drake, the property being situated at Crow Hill, nine miles distant from Deadwood.

In politics Mr. Holmes gives a stanch support to the Republican party, and he is a member of the Business Men's Club, of Deadwood, being also a member of its house committee, while he also holds membership in the Mining Men's Association of the United States and the South Dakota Pioneer Society, as well as the time-honored Masonic fraternity, in which he has risen to the thirty-second degree of the Ancient Accepted Scottish Rite, while he also holds membership in the adjunct organization, the Ancient Arabic Order of the Nobles of the Mystic Shrine. On the 3d of April, 1886, Mr. Holmes was united in marriage to Miss Ellen V. Himes, who was born and reared in Pennsylvania.

WILLIAM HENRY HOLT

William H. Holt was born in Willington, Tolland County, Connecticut, on the 13th of July, 1846, and is a son of William Holt, who was likewise a native of the Nutmeg state and a scion of a family long identified with the annals of New England, whither the original progenitors in America came from England in the colonial days. When he was ten years of age his parents came to the west and were numbered among the pioneers of Delaware county, Iowa, where they passed the remainder of their lives, the father having been in the hotel business. In 1863 he moved to Lama County, Iowa, where he was in the drug business. Later he moved to Cherokee County, Iowa, where he died in 1883. The subject's mother died in 1861. The subject completed the curriculum of the public schools and then continued his studies for some time in the Bowen Collegiate Institute, now known as Lenox College, in Hopkinton, that state. He initiated his independent career in 1865 and continued to be engaged in the drug business in Iowa until 1869. In that year he located at Cherokee, Iowa, and was employed in the merchandise business. Two days after his twenty-fifth birthday anniversary he came to Sioux Falls, where he has ever since maintained his home and where he has been successfully engaged in the real-estate business, handling both farm and town property and being the owner of valuable realty in a personal way. He is a liberal and progressive citizen and has ever done his part in furthering enterprises tending to enhance the general welfare and advancement. In politics he gave his allegiance to the Republican party until 1896, when he exercised his franchise in support of Hon. William J. Bryan for the presidency.

He is a prominent and appreciative member of the time-honored Masonic fraternity, in which he has not only completed the circle of the York Rite bodies but has also attained to the thirty-second degree of the Scottish Rite, being affiliated with the consistory at Yankton, while he is also identified with the auxiliary organizations, the Order of the Eastern Star and the Ancient Arabic Order of the Nobles of the Mystic Shrine. For a number of years, he was the recorder and secretary of all the subordinate Masonic orders in Sioux Falls, and in 1884 was grand recorder of the grand commandery.

In politics Mr. Holt is a Republican and was deputy register of deeds for about two years. In 1873 he was appointed sheriff of Minnehaha County to fill an unexpired term, filling the position for two years, while at the same time he was deputy United States marshal. In 1881 he was elected city auditor of Sioux Falls and held the office for thirteen years.

In 1886 Mr. Holt commenced the collection of Masonic publications in the United States and over the entire world, having now one of the best collections in the Union. He also commenced, in 1894, a collection of the literature and publications of the Dakotas, intending to make of it a historical library for the state.

On the 15th of July, 1873, Mr. Holt was united in marriage to Miss Martha Helen Raymond, who was born in the city of Milwaukee, Wisconsin, on the 26th of November, 1847, being a daughter of Frank and Martha Raymond, who were early settlers in the "Cream City." Mr. and Mrs. Holt have two children, Martha Etta, wife of Lieutenant E. E. Hawkins, of Seattle; and Edmund R.

BEN P. HOOVER

Ben P. Hoover was born in Wayne, Wisconsin, in 1854; came to Dakota territory in 1871; and located permanently at Fort Bennett, in 1876. He engaged in stock-raising and government contracts until 1879, when he moved to Fort Sully and was in charge of a post trader's store until 1883. He held the office of county commissioner of Sully County from 1883, until January 1, 1885; was a member of the constitutional convention held at Huron in 1883; was appointed United States court commissioner by Judge A. J. Edgerton and held the office until Cleveland was inaugurated in 1885. He continued in stock-raising until 1893, located in Gettysburg, was reappointed United States court commissioner by Judge Edgerton and resigned when John E. Carland (democrat) was appointed United States circuit judge for South Dakota.

After the defalcation of W. W. Taylor in 1885, Mr. Hoover was appointed receiver of the Gettysburg State Bank. From 1891 to 1910 he was employed as legislative representative for the Chicago, Milwaukee & St. Paul and the Chicago & Northwestern Railway Companies; and the American and United States Express Companies and the Western Union Telegraph Company. He was presented with a gold watch by the members of the legislature at the close of the session in 1901, and a diamond ring at the close of the session of 1903.

Of his legislative work the correspondent of the St. Paul Dispatch has the following to say:

"His effectiveness is in his ability to pick up the strings from other men's broken packages, restore the wreckage to the hand of its owner and in some way to weave into the meshes of the string the ties of a common interest. Ben Hoover knows the purposes of the most secretive men by knowing the humblest of men, bell boys, hack drivers, janitors, clerks and chief clerks, senators and representatives, boards and state officers are all alike to him, and from each he learns something about the other fellow.

"A word uttered here has a bearing on something there, and Ben Hoover gets that word, associates it with another word or an idea or a desire some other place; he pieces the segments of string together; it finally becomes the one important string, it touches all interests.

"Knowledge, not force, is power, and that is where Ben Hoover is more powerful than some men in the vocation of a professional lobbyist which he has reduced to a science. By his method of picking up here a little and there a little he knows more of the characteristics of the membership of the legislature on the opening day than any other man, and he has probably saved more new and untried members from embarrassment through their own inexperience, than has any other man.

"More than this, he protects the men who favor his interests as well as those of the corporation which he represents. It is claimed that no one ever heard a threat pass Ben Hoover's lips. He is not a destroyer, but a builder. There is scarcely an educational or other institution, or an important act of legislature, or a public policy in the realm of the state that does not bear some mark of his indefatigable labor, his effort as a builder. Ben Hoover is a lobbyist, perhaps the most effective legislative agent now or ever in the state, but among 133 members of the legislature, and seventy-five elective and appointive officers, clerks and chaplains there is no personal enemy."

He is a member of the Masonic blue lodge and Eastern Star Chapter at Gettysburg, South Dakota; the Royal Arch Chapter at Faulkton, South Dakota; the Knights of Pythias, the Independent Order of Odd Fellows and Rebekah and the Woodmen Lodges at Gettysburg. From 1907 until the present date, 1915, he has been engaged in the mercantile business at Gettysburg.

GEORGE STEPHEN HOPKINS

George S. Hopkins was born in the city of Lockport, Niagara County, New York, on the 28th of August, 1852, and is a son of Stephen Hopkins, a great-grandson of Stephen Hopkins, one of the signers of that immortal document, the Declaration of Independence, and a lineal descendant of Stephen Hopkins, one of the Puritans who came over in the "Mayflower" in 1620 and landed on Plymouth Rock. The family name was long and conspicuously identified with the annals of New England history, whence representatives finally went into the state of New York, as pioneers, while scions of the sturdy stock are now to be found in the most diverse sections of the Union. The subject was reared in his native state and after completing the curriculum of the common schools took a thorough course in surveying and engineering in the city of Brooklyn, while he has attained a high reputation n in the northwest as a civil and mining engineer. He followed his profession in the east and in the western states until 1875, when, as a young man of twenty-three years, he came to what is now South Dakota and became one of the pioneers of the Black Hills, having arrived in this district in July of the year mentioned and having ever since followed his profession as a surveyor and civil and mining engineer, while he has also been interested in the development of a number of important mining properties. He holds high prestige in his chosen vocation and has been identified with much important work in the line, while he is at the present time serving as United States deputy mineral surveyor. He is one of the popular and highly esteemed residents of Deadwood, having the confidence and regard of all who know him and being prominent in both business and social circles. He is one of the most prominent and valued members of the Black Hills Pioneer Association, of which he is historian, having been elected to this office for life.

In politics he accords a stanch allegiance to the Republican party, and fraternally he is identified with the Independent Order of Odd Fellows, being past grand of his lodge and also past district deputy grand master, while he has attained the thirty-second degree in Scottish Rite Masonry, and is affiliated with Naja Temple of the Ancient Arabi: Order of the Nobles of the Mystic Shrine. On the 16th of September, 1888, Mr. Hopkins was united in marriage, at Spearfish, this state, to Miss Jessie O. Robinson, and they have three children, namely: Georgiana C, who was born in Spearfish, on the 18th of September, 1889; William Stephen, who was born in Deadwood, on the 31st of May, 1891: and Florence Ruth, who was born in Spearfish on the 26th of October, 1892.

CHARLES ALLEN HOWARD

Charles A. HOWARD, who is successfully engaged in the real-estate business in the city of Aberdeen, was born in Frontier, Clinton County, New York, on the 16th of July, 1865, being a son of Charles Adams Howard, who was a farmer by vocation, while the maiden name of the subject's mother was Nancy Patterson. Charles Adams Howard was likewise born in Frontier, being a son of Junio Howard, whose father, Antipas Howard, was numbered among the early settlers in that section of the old Empire state. Antipas Howard was born in Andover, Vermont, and was a son of James Hayward, who was born in Mendon, Massachusetts, on the 18th of February, 1724. The latter was a son of Jonathan Flayward, who was the third of the name in America, being a son of Jonathan 2d, who was a son of Jonathan 1st, born in Ashford, Connecticut, in 1692. The last mentioned was a son of John Hayward, who was with Miles Standish in 1643. Martha, the wife of John Hayward, was a daughter of Thomas Hayward, who came from England prior to 1638 and settled Duxbury, Plymouths County, Massachusetts. This data is derived from Volume XI American Ancestry, published in 1898. The subject is also a grandson of Rebecca J. Spaulding, also representing one of the old and prominent families of New England, the ancestry being fully traced in the Spalding Memorial, published in 1897.

Charles A. Howard, the immediate subject of this review, was reared on the old homestead farm and his educational advantages were such as were afforded in the public schools of his native county. By the death of his father, in 1877, he was thrown upon his own resources, and went to Ontario, Canada, in the following year, at the age of thirteen. In 1879 he took up his residence in Port Huron, Michigan, entering the employ of the Grand Trunk Railroad and continuing in the service until 1883. In May of that year, he came to Columbia, Brown County, Dakota. In January, 1884, he secured a position as clerk in the office of the register of deeds of Brown County, and in January of the following year was appointed deputy register. He resigned this position in November, 1885, and engaged in the abstract business, in which he has ever since continued, in connection with his extensive real-estate enterprise.

In November, 1887, Mr. Howard enlisted as a private in Company F, National Guard of Dakota, in Aberdeen. He became corporal on the 3d of June, 1889: second lieutenant January 23, 1892: first lieutenant October 2, 1893; and captain May 7, 1894. He held this position in Company F, First Regiment, South Dakota National Guard, until the outbreak of the Spanish-American war. He then took his company to Sioux Falls, the state rendezvous, arriving there on the 1st of May, 1898, where four days later he was mustered into the United States service as captain of Company F, First South Dakota Infantry, United States Volunteers, enjoying the distinction of being the first South Dakota soldier to be mustered into the service of the United States. On the same day he was promoted to major of his regiment and assigned to the command of the Second Battalion, consisting of Companies D, M, F and E. He proceeded with his regiment to the Philippines and took part in every march, skirmish and battle in which any of this valiant regiment was engaged during the war. He was mustered out of the service, in San Francisco, California, in October, 1899, with the other members of his regiment, which had made a gallant record in the Orient. Major Howard has ever been a stanch supporter of the Republican party and has been an active worker for the promotion of its interests. He served as a member of the board of aldermen of Aberdeen in 1890, and was a member of the state senate during the general assembly of 1895.

Fraternally the subject is affiliated with the following named bodies: Aberdeen Lodge, No. 38, Ancient Free and Accepted Masons ; Aberdeen Chapter, No. 14, Royal Arch Masons; Damascus Commandery, No. 10, Knights Templar; El Riad Temple, Ancient Arabic Order of the Nobles of the Mystic Shrine; Aberdeen Lodge, No. 49, Independent Order of Odd Fellows; Aberdeen Lodge, No. 55, Knights of

Pythias; Bab-el-Wed Temple, No. 17, Dramatic Order Knights of Khorassan, and Aberdeen Lodge, No. 30, Ancient Order of United Workmen. Of the last mentioned he has served as master workman, while in 1900 he was eminent commander of Damascus Commandery, Knights Templar, being now the grand generalissimo of the grand commandery of the state, and has held other official chairs in the various bodies noted. He has been a member of the Theosophical Society since 1898.

In Aberdeen, on the loth of December, 1902, Major Howard was united in marriage to Miss Grace E. Brown, who was born in Maquoketa, Iowa, October 5, 1874, being a daughter of Ebenezer C. and Emma H. (Smith) Brown.

We cannot more consistently close this sketch than by quoting the following words uttered by its genial and popular subject; "I have been since coming to Dakota an ardent believer in the grand future of the territory now embraced in the states of North and South Dakota, and this confidence has never wavered, while to this individual faith I attribute my success in business."

HERBERT LINN HOWARD

Herbert Linn Howard, mayor of Lead, is giving to the administration of the affairs of the municipality the same undivided attention and careful consideration that a business man gives to the management of his private interests. He devotes his entire time to his official duties and has succeeded in introducing a number of improvements and reforms. He was elected mayor at the time the commission form of government was introduced in Lead and was reelected under the new government for a term of five years.

Mr. Howard was born in Clinton, Illinois, on the 29th of October, 1867, a son of William R. and Ellen (Short) Howard. The father, who was born in Kentucky, was a farmer by occupation and in 1836 removed to Illinois, where he continued to reside until his death, which occurred in 1907. He was prominent in his locality and noted for his unswerving integrity and scrupulous honesty. He occupied many positions of trust and his demise was deeply regretted. His wife passed away many years ago. The paternal grandfather of our subject was Joseph Howard, a native of Kentucky and a man of influence in his community. He eventually removed to central Illinois and was well known there in political and military circles.

Herbert L. Howard was reared and educated in Clinton, Illinois, and upon starting out in life for himself was employed for a number of years in railroad work. He later entered the commercial world as a traveling salesman, being so employed in various parts of the United States. In 1891 he made his way to Lead and became the traveling representative of a local concern. In 1910 he was elected mayor for a term of two years, and in 1912, after the city adopted the commission form of government, he was reelected mayor for a term of five years, being the present incumbent in that office. Under the commission form of government Lead has shown a marked improvement in health conditions and now has practically an ideal building code. It also has an unusually fine engineering department and the fire department is the best in the state. The achievements of the present administration are many and reflect great credit upon Mr. Howard.

In 1891 he was married to Miss Alice Atherton, of Jacksonville, Illinois. In his political belief he is a progressive republican and for many years he has been identified with the republican party in county and state politics and held various appointive positions in city and state government. He is a member of the South Dakota Panama-Pacific Exposition commission and has been active in the work of securing an adequate representation of the state at the exposition in San Francisco. Fraternally he belongs to Golden Star Lodge. No. 9, A. F. & A. M.; Golden Belt Chapter, No. 35, R. A. M.; and Lead Commandery, No. 18, K. T., all of Lead; Black Hills Council, No. I, R. & S. M.; Naja Temple, A. A. O. N. M. S., of Deadwood; and the Modern Woodmen of America. His interest in the material upbuilding of the city is evident from his membership in the Commercial Club, with whose spirit and aims he is thoroughly in harmony. He was formerly a member of the Illinois National Guard and is now a member of the South Dakota National Guard, in which he holds the rank of captain. His religious faith is indicated by his membership in the Methodist church and he is serving on its board of trustees. He has always been deeply interested in everything that pertains to the educational system of the city and has championed all proposed improvements in the public schools. His recreations are hunting and fishing, and he finds therein the strength of body and vigor of mind that enable him to perform more easily and more efficiently the many duties devolving upon him as chief executive of the municipality.

SAMUEL P. HOWELL

Samuel P. Howell of Frederick, Brown County, is a native of the old Buckeye state, having been born on a farm in Licking County, Ohio, on the 23d of December, 1837, and being a son of George P. and Matilda (Preston) Howell, the former of whom was born in New Jersey and the latter in Pennsylvania. Elias Howell, grandfather of the subject, was likewise a native of New Jersey, where the family was early established, and he removed thence to Ohio, in the pioneer epoch in that great commonwealth, becoming a man of prominence and influence in public affairs and having represented his district in congress for two terms. He passed the closing years of life in that state. George P. Howell was reared to manhood in Ohio and was there married. He continued to be identified with agricultural pursuits in Licking County until 1852, when he removed with his family to McLean County, Illinois, where both he and his wife passed the remainder of their lives. They became the parents of six sons and three daughters, the subject of this sketch having been the third in order of birth, while of the number five are living. Captain Howell received his early educational training in the common schools of his native state and later prosecuted his studies in the schools of Illinois. With the outbreak of the war of the Rebellion his patriotism was roused to responsive protest, and on the 25th of August, 1862, he enlisted as a private in Company I, Ninety-fourth Illinois Volunteer Infantry, commanded by Colonel W. W. Orm. His command was assigned to duty on the frontier and there remained during a considerable portion of its service. The regiment was in active service in the various operations in Missouri and Arkansas, later took part in the siege of Vicksburg and was present at the capitulation of Mobile and Spanish Fort. The Captain continued with his command until the close of the war, receiving his honorable discharge in August, 1865. Immediately after the organization of his company he was chosen second lieutenant, later was promoted first lieutenant and finally became captain of his company, over which he was in command at the time of the close of the great conflict, while he was discharged with the brevet rank of major.

After having thus proved by faithful service his loyalty to the Union, Captain Howell returned to the old homestead in McLean County, Illinois, where he remained until 1869, when he removed to the eastern part of the county and engaged in farming on an extensive scale, opening up a farm of two thousand acres. He improved a most valuable property and there continued operations until the spring of 1883, when he located in McPherson county, South Dakota, having made an investigating trip through this section the preceding autumn. He became the owner of twenty-four hundred acres, twelve miles north of Leola, and there gave his attention principally to the raising of cattle and horses, while three hundred acres of the property were placed under effective cultivation. He maintained an average of seven hundred head of cattle on the ranch, which he still owns and operates, the property having been well improved and having greatly appreciated in value during the intervening years, which have witnessed the settling of the country and the rapid development of all resources and industries.

The Captain has retained his residence in the village of Frederick in the winters, living on the McPherson county farm of summers, since 1898, and was one of the owners of the Bank of Frederick, of which he has been president since January, 1894, while he is also part owner of the Frederick flouring mill, which is equipped with the most modern machinery and has a capacity for the output of two hundred barrels daily. He also has other capitalistic interests of importance, owning controlling interests in sixty-seven hundred acres of Brown County farms, and is known as one of the public-spirited men of this section of the state, being at all times ready to lend his aid and influence in the support of enterprises and measures which inure to the general good. In politics he gives an unwavering allegiance to the Republican party, having cast his first vote for Lincoln in 1860. Though he has never been ambitious for political preferment he has served in various local offices, having held the office of county commissioner for McPherson County for an entire decade, and having been a member of the first board of commissioners of the county.

He has attained to the thirty-second degree in the Ancient Accepted Scottish Rite of Freemasonry and is also identified with the Independent Order of Odd Fellows. On the 8th of February, 1872, Captain Howell was united in marriage to Miss Mary Brooke, who was born in Media, Pennsylvania, being a representative of old colonial stock. They have six children, namely: Helen, who is now the widow of Bertine D. Gamble, of Milbank, and George Brooke, Mamie F., William E., Margaret and Jessie, who remain at the parental home, the elder son being the manager of the Frederick flouring mill.

OSMOND N. HOYT, M. D.

Dr. Osmond N. Hoyt has been prominently identified with questions of public education and of public health for more than a third of a century and has been honored with the presidency of the state board of health of South Dakota. He makes his home in Pierre, where he is successfully engaged in the practice of medicine and surgery, having made his home in that city during the greater part of the time since 1889. He was born May 2, 1843, at Magog, in the province of Quebec, Canada, a son of Nason Hoyt, who was born in Magog in 1812. The paternal grandfather, however, was American born and lived in Grafton, New Hampshire, until about 1800, when he removed to Canada. The mother of our subject bore the maiden name of Miriam Harriman and was born in Frankfort, Maine, in the year 1813.

Dr. Hoyt pursued his more specifically literary education in the common and select schools and received his professional training in Hahnemann Medical College of Chicago, from which he was graduated with the class of March, 1879. In the meantime, he had been actively connected with the profession of teaching. He taught his first school, a winter term, in Dover township, Fayette County, Iowa, in 1862 and devoted most of his time to teaching in Howard County, Iowa, through the succeeding decade. He was elected county superintendent of schools in that county to serve from January, 1874, until January, 1878, and when he retired from that position, he became a medical student at Hahnemann. Following his graduation, he located for practice at Cresco, Howard County, Iowa, on the 1st of April, 1879, and there remained until 1883, when he removed to Duluth, Minnesota, where he continued for six years.

Since that time — 1889 — he has practiced almost continuously in Pierre and is widely known as a successful physician and surgeon whose reading has been broad and whose knowledge is comprehensive and exact, so that he is seldom, if ever, at fault in diagnosing a case and determining the outcome of disease. His work, too, has been of a broad character far beyond that of the private practitioner in his deep concern for the public welfare and his interest in the vital questions affecting sanitary and health conditions.

He has held various offices along the line of his profession. He was county coroner and county physician in Howard County, Iowa, in 1881-2. He was also county coroner for one term in Pierre, South Dakota, and county superintendent of health for a number of terms in the same county. He became a member of the pension examining board and served as its secretary for a number of years and in 1908 he became a member of the state board of health on which he served until 1913. He was secretary and superintendent of the board for two years and through the succeeding two years was its president, in which connection he did important public service for the benefit of humanity in abolishing conditions detrimental to health and in disseminating knowledge of vital worth concerning sanitary and preventive measures.

Dr. Hoyt has been married twice. On the 24th of January, 1871, he wedded Amelia Laskey and following her demise he was married in September, 1887, to Cassie R. Rozelle, a daughter of Colonel N. W. Rozelle of Des Moines, Iowa. Mrs. Hoyt was a nurse at the Battle Creek Sanatorium at Battle Creek, Michigan, and was the first surgical nurse in Des Moines, Iowa. Dr. and Mrs. Hoyt have two children: Jessie E. and Alonzo, and have two adopted sons, Harry H., who married Lucy M. Millett and Fred F., who married Emma Millett.

Dr. Hoyt was formerly a member of the Congregational church and his name is now on the membership roll of the Baptist church. He does not believe, however, in denominationalism that separates Christian people into various sects. He does not believe in tearing down the old barriers but in rising above them, knowing that in all the major things of religion Christian people are united. Dr. Hoyt is a Master Mason and for about forty years has been a member of the Independent Order of Odd Fellows. He also belongs to the Ancient Order of United Workmen and is now serving his second term as grand medical examiner of South Dakota, having held that office since 1913. Since attaining his majority, he has been a republican and is now affiliated with the progressive wing of the party. His life has been one of activity and usefulness and he enjoys the high and well merited regard of many friends.

DANIEL NEWCOMB HUNT

DANIEL N. HUNT.

D. N. HUNT, one of the earliest settlers in Spink County, and the first mayor of the present attractive little city of Redfield, was born in Mansfield, Tioga County, Pennsylvania, on the 28th of January, 1843, and is a son of Dr. Daniel Newcomb Hunt and Miranda B. (Allen) Hunt, the former of whom was born in Rutland, Vermont, and the latter in Massachusetts. From a carefully compiled record of the genealogy of the Newcomb family the following data is obtained: Captain Charles Hunt, grandfather of the subject, married, in 1788, Jerusha Newcomb, a daughter of Lieutenant Daniel Newcomb, who was in the sixth generation in descent from Andrew Newcomb, who came from England to the New England colonies about 1650. Family tradition farther states, in connection with the maternal ancestry of the subject, that his grandfather Allen was a relative of Ethan Allen, of Ticonderoga fame, and also a descendant of Priscilla Alden, whose gentle virtues are so pleasingly recorded in the poem of "Miles Standish." by Longfellow. Both grand-fathers were valiant soldiers of the Continental line during the war of the Revolution.

In 1853 Dr. Daniel N. Hunt, father of the subject, removed with his family from Pennsylvania to Reedsburg, Sauk county, Wisconsin, where he was engaged in the practice of his profession about five years, at the expiration of which time he removed to Granger, Fillmore County, Minnesota, where the mother died in 1864, at the age of fifty-five years. The father was born in 1799. He lived through every administration of the United States government until his death. In 1880 he came to Spink County, South Dakota, where he died in 1884. The subject was about ten years of age at the time of the family's removal to Wisconsin, and from 1853 to 1858 he was a student in the public schools of Reedsburg, and from 1859 to 1861 he continued his educational work in the schools at Decorah, Iowa. After the close of his service in the Civil war he entered the Eastman Business College, in the city of Chicago, where he was graduated in the spring of 1866.

On the 15th of March, 1862, Mr. Hunt enlisted as a private in Company C, Fifth Minnesota Volunteer Infantry, and re-enlisted as a veteran in the same company and regiment in 1864, with which he served until the close of the war, having been mustered out on the 6th of September, 1865. He was with his regiment in thirteen campaigns, five sieges and thirty-four battles and minor engagements, among which was the siege of Fort Ridgely, during the Indian massacre in Minnesota, in 1862. Mr. Hunt's name appears upon a monument erected by the state of Minnesota in commemoration of this massacre. He also holds a medal presented to him by the same state, one of which was given to each soldier present at the memorable tragedy. After receiving his honorable discharge Mr. Hunt returned to Granger, Minnesota, and thereafter was engaged in farming and teaching school in that state until April, 1879, when he came to what is now Spink County, South Dakota, being one of the first citizens of the city of Redfield, he being here when the town was founded and surveyed. Here he established himself in the real-estate business, in which line he has ever since continued operations, being one of the leading dealers in this section of the state. He was register of deeds of the county, by appointment, from 1880 to January 1, 1881, and was secretary of the first Republican convention called in the county to elect delegates to the territorial convention. He was a member of the first constitutional convention of the territory, at Sioux Falls, in 1884. In May, 1883, he was elected the first mayor of Redfield, receiving a silver dollar as his salary, the facts in the case having been engraved on the coin by Order of the council, and it is needless to say that Mr. Hunt places a high valuation on this unique and historic souvenir. He has been four times re-elected to the office of mayor, having been re-elected the last time on May 1, 1904. He called and was chairman of the first school meeting held in the county, and from the early days to the present he has always been found at the front in lending his aid and influence in support of measures and enterprises tending to promote the general welfare and progress. He has given his efforts in furtherance of the cause of the Republican party, of whose principles he is a stanch advocate.

He was initiated in the Masonic fraternity in 1865 and is still actively affiliated with the same. He has been identified with the Grand Army of the Republic from the time of its organization in the territory of Dakota, having held office in his post and being at the present writing quartermaster of George H. Thomas Post, No. 5, in his; home city. On the 15th of February, 1873, Mr. Hunt was married to Miss Adalynn J. Ellis, who was born in the state of Vermont, on the 2d of October, 1849, and is a descendant of the Chase family who came from England to the Massachusetts colony in the early colonial epoch. Mr. and Mrs. Hunt have three children, Arlington Chase, who was born on the 2d of January, 1877; Georgie Mae, born August 15, 1881, and Ray Nelson, born February 8, 1887.

EUGENE HUNTINGTON

It is signally consistent that in a contemporary way shall be perpetuated the records of those who have aided in the development of a splendid civilization in the great northwest, for in the future years this data can not but prove of inestimable historic value. The subject of this sketch is to be noted as one of the early pioneers of the present state of South Dakota and as one who has done his part in advancing its material and civic progress. He has served in various positions of public trust, under both the territorial and state regimes, and is at the time of this writing incumbent of the office of deputy collector of internal revenue for the north half of the state, retaining his residence in Webster, Day County.

The name borne by the subject is one which has long been identified with the annals of American history. The original progenitor in the new world was Simon Huntington, who emigrated from Norwich, England, in 1633, but who died oil the voyage, his family settling in Roxbury, Massachusetts. His son Christopher was one of the founders of Norwich, Connecticut, being one of the twelve patentees of that place and one of its prominent and influential citizens. The subject is of the eighth generation in descent from Simon Huntington. the head of the original family in America.

Eugene Huntington was born in Norwich, Connecticut, on the 18th of April, 1844, being a son of Horatio and Julia (Horton) Huntington. His parents removed to New Jersey when he was a child, later to the state of New York, and in 1856 became pioneer settlers in Mitchell County, Iowa, where they passed the remainder of their lives. The father there gave his attention to agricultural pursuits and became a prosperous and highly honored citizen of the state. The subject of this review received a common-school education, having been a lad of about twelve years at the time of the family removal to Iowa, so that he has had his full quota of experience in connection with pioneer life. In 1896, shortly after the outbreak of the war of the Rebellion, he enlisted as a private in the Fourth Iowa Volunteer Cavalry, with which he served until the expiration of his term, in 1863, when he re-enlisted as a member of the same regiment and remained in active service therewith until the close of the great internecine conflict through which was perpetuated the integrity of the Union. He received his honorable discharge, as sergeant of his company, in August, 1865, and then returned to his home in Iowa. In 1867-8 Mr. Huntington was employed in the engineering department of the Union Pacific Railroad, and in 1869 held the position of construction engineer on the Illinois Central Railroad, while in 1872 he was similarly engaged in connection with the construction of the Iowa Pacific Railroad, which is now a portion of the system of the Chicago & Great Western Railroad.

In 1878 Mr. Huntington came to South Dakota, locating in Flandreau, Moody County, where he established himself in the real-estate and loan business, being one of the pioneers in the line in the state, which was then a portion of the great undivided territory of Dakota. In 1883 he removed to Webster, Day County, where he has since maintained his home, and where he continued in the same line of enterprise for a number of years, doing much to secure to this section a desirable class of settlers and also to further the upbuilding and advancement of the town.

In politics Mr. Huntington has ever given an unqualified allegiance to the Republican party, in whose cause he has been an active and efficient worker. He cast his first presidential vote for General Ulysses S. Grant, and has ever since been an uncompromising advocate of the principles of the "grand old party." In 1884-5 he was a member of the legislature of Dakota territory, and introduced the bill creating Marshall County, said bill being duly enacted. In 1888 he was appointed adjutant general by Governor Mellette, and held that office during the term of that honored and able chief executive of the state of South Dakota. He was the first president of the board of trustees of Webster after its incorporation as a village, and as an official and a private citizen he has ever shown a deep and loyal interest in all that pertains to the welfare of his home town, county and state. In 1899 he was appointed to his present office of deputy collector of internal revenue, and its duties demand practically his undivided attention.

In a fraternal way Mr. Huntington is identified with the Grand Army of the Republic, has attained the thirty-third and highest degree in Ancient Accepted Scottish Rite Masonry, and is also affiliated with the Ancient Order of United Workmen. On the 29th of December, 1867, Mr. Huntington was united in marriage to Miss Artemicia Button, who was born in the state of New York, and who was a resident of Iowa at the time of their marriage. They have four children, namely: Marcia, Richard, Grace and Gertrude.

GEORGE SMITH HUTCHINSON

G. S. HUTCHINSON, president of the James Valley Bank, at Huron, is a native of the old Empire state, having been born in Pike, Wyoming County, New York, on the 5th of December, 1853, and being a son of George and Angeline A. (Smith) Hutchinson, who removed to the state of Wisconsin when he was about nine years of age, locating in Manitowoc, where he secured his early educational training in the public schools, later continuing his studies in Milwaukee, Madison and Durand, that state, and receiving good advantages in the line. On the 1st of November, 1872, Mr. Hutchinson located in West Depere, Brown County, Wisconsin, where he secured a position as clerk in a general merchandise establishment, eventually securing an interest in the business, with which he continued to be identified until 1887, when he sold out his interest. In November of that year, he entered the employ of the extensive wholesale grocery house of Reid, Murdoch & Company, of Chicago, in the capacity of traveling salesman, and on the 16th of July, 1889, he came to South Dakota as representative of this concern in the state, with headquarters in Huron. He continued with the firm until May 1, 1902, when he resigned his position and forthwith effected the organization of the James Valley Bank, which was incorporated under the laws of the state on the 15th of that month, with a capital stock of thirty thousand dollars. He has been president of the institution from the time of its organization and has directed its affairs with consummate judgment and ability.

Mr. Hutchinson is a stanch Republican in his political proclivities and has been an active worker in its cause, in a local way. The hold which Mr. Hutchinson has upon the esteem and regard of the people of Huron has been given significant evidence, since in 1896 he was chosen mayor of the same, serving two years and giving a clean, capable and business-like administration of municipal affairs. He has been a member of the board of education since 1898 and in the connection his interest has been far removed from the apathetic and perfunctory. In 1902 still higher official preferment was conferred upon our subject, who was then elected to represent his district in the lower house of the state legislature, where he made an enviable record during the 1902-3 general assembly, while he is a candidate for state senatorial honors in the forthcoming election of November, 1904.

He is a Knight-Templar Mason and is also affiliated with the Ancient Arabic Order of the Nobles of the Mystic Shrine. On the 23d of July, 1884, Mr. Hutchinson was united in marriage to Miss Agnes J. Persons, of Brodhead, Wisconsin, and they have three children, Harry T., Augusta Jean and George.

I

DARWIN M. INMAN

DARWIN M. INMAN

"He did not proclaim his goodness but he lived it, which is the vital thing," wrote a close personal friend of Darwin M. Inman, and in this is summed up the strongest characteristic of his life. He was a believer in all those things which make for upright manhood in every relation and his belief found embodiment in his daily conduct. He did not seek to be a teacher, but the influence of his life was as a radiating force. He was perhaps best known to the public as banker, as legislator and as one of the founders and champions of the State University at Vermillion, and yet it was not his public career but the innate nature of the man that so endeared him to all with whom he came in contact, causing his memory to be revered and cherished by all who knew him. He was born March 14, 1838, in Clarendon, Orleans County, New York, and it was in his native city that he passed away on the 14th of January, 1913, while visiting his brother. In the family of his parents, Phillip and Anna (Thompson) Inman, were seven children. His ancestors were among the colonial residents of America and one family with which he was connected was represented in the Revolutionary war by father and six sons.

After attending the public schools of his native county, Darwin M. Inman continued his education at Holley and Albion Academies and completed a classical course in Rochester University, from which he was graduated with high honors. He took up the profession of teaching when but fourteen years of age and followed it for a number of terms, and his deep and helpful interest in educational affairs was ever one of the salient traits of his character. That he was a man of influence even in early life is shown by the fact that Clarendon elected him one of its supervisors when he was yet a young man and for two terms, he filled that position.

On the 28th of December, 1874, Mr. Inman was united in marriage to Miss Adele Lewis, of Columbus, Wisconsin. She was born in New York, a daughter of William L. and Eliza A. Lewis, both natives of Orleans County. New York, whence they removed to Wisconsin in 1856. They afterward came to South Dakota, settling in Vermillion, where Mr. Lewis lived retired until called to his final rest. In their family were five children, of whom three daughters survive: Mrs. M. D. Thompson, of Vermillion; Mrs. R. A. Morgan, also of Vermillion; and Mrs. Inman. Those who have passed away are M. J. Lewis and Jennie, who died at the age of twenty-three years. Mrs. Inman acquired her literary education in Wisconsin and received musical instruction in Madison and Milwaukee, Wisconsin, and in Chicago, and in early womanhood she engaged in teaching music. The wedding journey of Mr. and Mrs. Inman consisted of a trip to Vermillion, where they arrived on the 30th of December, 1874, thereafter continuing residents of that city, where Mrs. Inman still makes her home. Early in the following year Mr. Inman was instrumental in organizing a bank in connection with M. J. Lewis and M. D. Thompson. This was operated for some years as a private bank under the name of D. M. Inman & Company and was later converted into the First National Bank of Vermillion, Mr. Inman remaining at the head of that institution for thirty-eight years. This business brought him into close connection with many of his fellow townsmen and there are scores who attest his helpfulness in business relations and his ready assistance when financial aid was needed. Above all desire for success was ever found that broad spirit of humanitarian ism which he continually expressed in a helping hand extended to one in need of assistance.

It was but natural that a man of Mr. Inman's well-known ability and public spirit should have been called to office. In the fall of 1876, he was elected a member of the territorial legislature and was twice reelected, serving in all for three terms. He was also elected a member of the first state legislature and he left the impress of his individuality upon important laws enacted. He also served for four terms as a trustee of the State University, which institution he aided in founding and of which he was ever a stalwart champion, doing everything in his power to further its interests. While thus actively engaged in public affairs Mr. Inman continued in business and his efforts in that direction were attended with growing success. He was associated with M. J. Lewis and M. D. Thompson in the grain and elevator trade, in the lumber business and in other enterprises, all of which were carried forward to successful completion. In business affairs Mr. Inman's judgment was sound, his enterprise keen and his energy unfaltering.

In his political views Mr. Inman was ever a stalwart democrat. He kept well informed on the questions and issues of the day and was ever ready to support his position by intelligent argument. Fraternally he was a very active and prominent Mason. He held membership in Incense Lodge, No. II, A. F. & A. M.; Vermillion Chapter, No. 21, R. A. M., both of Vermillion; and also became a member of DeMolay Commandery, K. T., of Yankton. Later he demitted therefrom when Vermillion Commandery, No. 16, was organized. He was also a member of El Riad Temple, A. A. O. N. M. S., of Sioux Falls. He affiliated with the Baptist church, to which Mrs. Inman still belongs, and he was most active and helpful in church work. The Dakota Republican, in speaking of his religious life, said: "Mr. Inman affiliated with the Baptist church. He was a Bible student, and we doubt if there was another layman that could quote Scripture as readily as he. He was always a liberal supporter of the church. He lived a practical Christian life. His motto was the golden rule. His charities were boundless, helping where help was needed, and in all this he fulfilled the scriptural injunction of never letting his left hand know what his right hand was doing. Many were his acts of kindness, and many were the homes helped by his generosity that the world at large knew nothing of."

G. B. IRVIN

G. B. Irvin, a progressive, enterprising and respected young citizen of Iroquois, is actively engaged in business as a member of the firm of Irvin Brothers, dealers in farm implements. His birth occurred in Kentucky on the 9th of February, 1879, his parents being Gideon and Eliza Irvin, both of whom are deceased. Throughout his active business career, the father devoted his attention to general agricultural pursuits.

G. B. Irvin acquired a public-school education in his youth, and after putting aside his textbooks secured employment as a farm hand. Later he started out as an agriculturist on his own account and for a number of years gave his time and energies to the work of the fields with excellent results. In the spring of 1908 he came to South Dakota, settling at Osceola, where he embarked in the implement business and there conducted an enterprise of that character for two years. In 1911 he removed his stock to Iroquois, where he has remained to the present time and has been accorded an extensive and profitable patronage, being widely recognized as one of the promising and prosperous young business men of his adopted state.

On the 30th of January, 1901, Mr. Irvin was united in marriage to Miss Chloe Downs, a daughter of G. W. Downs, of Illinois. To them have been born two children, Gladys and Eunice. Mr. Irvin is a republican in politics. His religious faith is that of the Congregational church, while fraternally he is identified with the Masons, being a member of York Lodge, No. 53, A. F. & A. M., the Independent Order of Odd Fellows and the Ancient Order of United Workmen. He also belongs to the Commercial Club and is a public-spirited and loyal citizen whose deep interest in the development of South Dakota is manifest in his able support of many measures instituted to promote the advancement and upbuilding of the commonwealth.

EUGENE F. IRWIN

Eugene F. IRWIN, timekeeper for the Homestake Mining Company, Lead City, South Dakota, was born in Clinton, DeWitt County, Illinois, on June 27, 1865. On the maternal side he is a direct descendant of General Putnam, of Revolutionary fame, and his great-grandfather, Hiram Smith, was an aide-de-camp on the staff of General William Henry Harrison during the war of 1812. William R. Irwin, the subject's father, is a native of Ohio, and for a number of years resided in Illinois, but in 1881 removed to Missouri, where he has since been practicing law. He served five and a half years in the United States army, participated in many of the noted campaigns of the great rebellion, and after the close of the war was stationed for some time at Ft. Laramie, Wyoming, retiring from the service with the rank of captain. Mattie M., wife of William R. Irwin, and mother of the subject, is at the present time actively engaged in Grand Army and Woman's Relief Corps circles and for the past thirty years has been prominently identified with the mission work of the Presbyterian church.

Eugene F. Irwin was reared in his native state, received his education in the public schools of Clinton and remained in Illinois until 1881, when he accompanied his parents upon their removal to Nebraska. From 1881 to 1883 he worked as an apprentice on the Waterloo Gazette, but the latter year quit the office and entered the railway service with headquarters at Blair, Nebraska. After spending a. short time railroading, he resigned his position and in 1884 resumed newspaper work as compositor on the Blair Pilot, in which capacity he continued about one year. Severing his connection with the Pilot office, he worked for some time with the Cromwell Lumber and Grain Company, at Craig, Nebraska, and on quitting that firm returned to railroading, which he followed at various places and in various capacities until 1893. While thus engaged, he filled the position of bill clerk in the Omaha freight office, was station agent at different points, ticket agent and train dispatcher, quitting the same at Chadron, Nebraska, on April 26th of the year noted to enter the employ of the Homestake Mining Company at Lead, South Dakota, with which large and wealthy enterprise he has since been identified as timekeeper.

Mr. Irwin's career has been varied and active and, in the main, financially successful. He has the unbounded confidence of the wealthy corporation with which he is connected and discharges the duty of his responsible post with credit to himself and to the satisfaction of all concerned, enjoying not only the high esteem of his superiors, but the kindest regard of his associates and fellow workmen as well. Mr. Irwin is a Republican in politics and ever since old enough to exercise the right of franchise has been an active worker for the success of his party. In April, 1902, he was elected mayor of Lead City and his administration of the municipal government has been satisfactory in every way to Democrats as well as Republicans.

Mr. Irwin is a zealous Mason and enjoys worthy prestige in the fraternity, having been honored with a number of important official positions. He joined the blue lodge in October, 1886; the Royal Arch degree, February, 1890; Knights Templar, July, 1890: thirty-second or Scottish Rite degree, April, 1893; Shrine, August, 1892; Order of the Eastern Star, 1891, and Royal and Select Masters, August, 1895. He has served as worshipful master of Golden Star Lodge, No. 9; high priest of Golden Belt Chapter, No. 35, Royal Arch Masons; eminent commander of Dakota Commandery, No. I, Knights Templar; grand junior warden and grand senior warden of the grand commandery of Knights Templar, of South Dakota; grand junior warden and grand master of the first veil, grand chapter, Royal Arch Masons, of South Dakota; grand royal arch captain and grand principal sojourner of the same chapter, and grand junior deacon of the grand lodge, Free and Accepted Masons. By the foregoing list it will be seen that Mr. Irwin has held many of the most prominent positions within the power of the brotherhood to bestow, his elevation to the same attesting his capability and high standing in an order where merit and not prestige is the pathway to honorable station. Mr. Irwin was married, in Waterloo, Nebraska, July 29, 1886, to Miss Lucy M. Royce, whose ancestors were among the early settlers of northern Vermont, and whose family has long lived in that state. Three children have been born of this union, namely: Georgie D., Helen F. and Edith F., all living.

J

FRANKLIN T. JACKSON

F. T. Jackson, the immediate subject of this sketch, remained at the parental home until the time of his marriage, in 1883, having received his educational training in the public schools and the Curtis Business College, in Minneapolis. After his marriage he removed to Redwood County, Minnesota, where he engaged in farming and stock growing, in which line of enterprise he there continued until 1886, when he came to South Dakota, arriving in McCook County, on the 22d of January, in company with his wife and child, while his equipment for the winning of success and independence in the new home was summed up in his energy, integrity and determination, his visible accessories being represented in a span of mules and a lumber wagon. He took up a pre-emption claim of one hundred and sixty acres and there engaged in farming and stock raising. In the fall of 1886, Mr. Jackson took up his residence in the village of Montrose, where he devoted his attention to the buying and shipping of stock for the ensuing eight years. In 1894 he took up his residence in Salem, where he has since been successfully engaged in the same line of enterprise, being one of the leading stock buyers of this section of the state. He also owns and superintends the operation of more than a thousand acres of farming land in this county, and he is known as one of McCook county's most progressive and alert business men. In politics Mr. Jackson is a stanch Republican, and for a number of years past has been a prominent figure in local affairs of a public nature. In the fall of 1902, he was elected to represent his district in the state legislature, and his course has been such as to amply justify the choice of the voters of the district.

He is affiliated with Fortitude Lodge, No. 73, Free and Accepted Masons; Salem Chapter, No. 34, Royal Arch Masons; Oriental Consistory, No. I, Ancient Accepted Scottish Rite, in Yankton; Salem Lodge, No. 106, Independent Order of Odd Fellows; Sioux Falls Lodge, No. 262, Benevolent and Protective Order of Elks; Salem Lodge, No. 60, Knights of Pythias; Salem Lodge, Ancient Order of United Workmen; and Ramsey Camp, No. 5634, Modern Woodmen of America, of which he served two terms as consul. On the 19th of July, 1883, Mr. Jackson was united in marriage to Miss Nettie M. Gibbs, of Lake City, Minnesota, and they are the parents of four children, namely: John A., Fay F., Carol F. and Helen H.

GEORGE S. JACKSON

George S. Jackson, a prominent and honored citizen of Deadwood, comes of stanch old New England stock, and is himself a native of Vermont having been born in Bartonsville, that state, on the 2d of August, 1859, and being a son of Samuel and Harriet (Brought Billings) Jackson, both of whom were born and reared in Bellows Falls, Vermont. In 1861 the subject accompanied his parents on their removal to the city of Chicago, Illinois, where his father continued to be engaged in the wholesale coffee and spice business until his death, which occurred in 1864, while the devoted wife and mother was summoned into eternal rest in 1902. They became the parents of four children, of whom the subject of this review was the second in order of birth, while all are living.

Mr. Jackson received his early educational training in the public schools of the western metropolis and later completed a course of study in the Goddard Seminary, at Barre, Vermont. He then returned to Chicago, where he held a clerical position in the wholesale furniture house of C. C. Holton & Company until 1877, when, at the age of eighteen years, he came west to Leadville, Colorado, arriving on the 26th of February, a number of years prior to the great stampede of mining prospectors to that section. At the time of his arrival the town had a population of about two thousand persons, and he there engaged in mining enterprises and also in the mercantile business, meeting with excellent success. In 1884 he left Leadville and came to Deadwood, South Dakota, where he forthwith became identified with mining, his prime object in coming here having been to give his attention to the mining of tin ore and shipping the same to Europe, for the purpose of enlightening the persons there interested as to the possibilities offered in connection with the development of this industry in America. He successfully proved that his position was well taken, and at the present time he is personally interested in fully thirteen hundred acres patented tin-mining ground in this district, while he was also the promoter of the Victoria Gold Mining and Milling Company, which is to be listed as the third largest producer of the Ragged Top district. He is the principal stockholder of the company and its general manager. Mr. Jackson is also extensively interested in real estate in this locality, owning about four hundred acres of land adjacent to the city of Deadwood, while he devotes no little attention to the raising of cattle, giving; preference to the thoroughbred Hereford type. In addition to the mining properties mentioned it should be noted that he is also a member of the directorate of the Pluma Gold Mining and Milling Company and the Golden Empire Mining Company, both representing important enterprises. He was the originator and promoter of the Black Hills Mining Men's Association, which has accomplished much in connection with the mining interests of this section and which is mentioned in detail in the general historical division of this publication.

He is also a valued member of the Deadwood Business Men's Club, the American Mining Congress and the Olympic Association, while he has attained the thirty-second degree in the Masonic fraternity, being identified with the consistory, Ancient Accepted Scottish Rite, at Deadwood, as well as with Naja Temple, Ancient Arabic Order of the Nobles of the Mystic Shrine, at Deadwood. In politics he gives a stanch allegiance to the Republican party, but has never sought the honors or emoluments of public office, though he takes a deep interest in all that tends to conserve the best interests of his home city and state. On the 10th of October, 1888, Mr. Jackson was united in marriage to Miss Mary J. Power, who was born and reared in the city of Chicago, Illinois, and who is a daughter of Thomas Power, now a member of the Fish-Hunter Company, of Deadwood and Lead, South Dakota. Mr. and Mrs. Jackson have one son, George L., who was born on the 5th of October, 1889.

JOHN H. JACKSON

J. H. JACKSON, president of the Jackson Hardware Company, of Aberdeen, is known as one of the representative business men of the city. In 1888 Mr. Jackson established himself in the retail hardware business in Aberdeen, and soon gained a wide reputation as a progressive and able business man. The location of Aberdeen is such that from the start there came a demand for the accommodations afforded by a wholesale establishment in the line, and within three years after the inception of the enterprise fully seventy-five percent, of his business was of the wholesale nature. In 1900 he found it expedient to turn his entire attention to the jobbing trade, and the business has been that of a distinctively jobbing house since the year mentioned. The business has doubled in extent within three years, the annual sales having reached an average aggregate of a quarter of a million dollars. In 1903 the fine modern building now used was completed, which has an aggregate floor space of twenty-six thousand square feet. The Jackson Hardware Company was incorporated in 1902, with a capital stock of one hundred and fifty thousand dollars. Three traveling salesmen are employed by the house, who represent its interests throughout its extended trade territory.

J. H. Jackson was born in the province of Quebec, Canada, on the 22d of May, 1853, being a son of Alonzo and Mary J. Jackson. He was reared in his native province to the age of twenty-four years, and there received excellent educational advantages. In 1877 he removed to Marshall, Lyon County, Minnesota, where he gave his attention to farming until 1881, when he came to what is now the state of South Dakota and opened a hardware store in Ordway, Brown County, this being prior to the time of the completion of the line of the Chicago, Minneapolis & St. Paul Railroad to Aberdeen. In 1883 he also opened a store in Columbia, where he continued to be actively engaged in business until coming to Aberdeen, in 1888, since which time his business career has already been outlined in this article. In politics Mr. Jackson is a member of the Republican party, and takes an active interest in its cause. He was elected the first mayor of Columbia, South Dakota. During territorial days he served on the staff of Governor Church as commissary of supply, with the rank of major.

He is a member of the Masonic fraternity, having attained the Knight Templar, Scottish Rite and Mystic Shrine degrees. On the 20th of February, 1889, Mr. Jackson was united in marriage to Miss Nora Ringrose, who was born and reared in Wisconsin, and who was a resident of Aberdeen at the time of their marriage. They are the parents of five children, namely: Helen M., John H., Genevieve, Alice and Edward.

ROBERT JAMES JACKSON, M. D.

Dr. Robert James Jackson, engaged in the practice of medicine in Rapid City, was born at Forest, Ontario, Canada, August 10, 1874, a son of John and Joan (Elliott) Jackson. The former, who was a native of Scotland, crossed the Atlantic to Canada when seventeen years of age and during the period of his manhood engaged in farming there. He died at the age of fifty-six years, passing away in 1893.

Robert James Jackson, who is one of a family of eight children and the fifth in order of birth, was educated in the public schools of his native town and in the normal school at Brandon, Manitoba. Following his graduation from the normal school as a member of the class of 1895 he devoted three years to teaching, but regarded this merely as an initial step to other professional labor, for it was his desire to become a member of the medical profession. Accordingly, he entered the Michigan School of Medicine and was graduated with the class of 1902, at which time his professional degree was conferred upon him. He then came to South Dakota, settling at Yankton, where he remained for six months, and on the expiration of that period removed to Rapid City, where he has resided continuously since with the exception of extended visits to the central American republics, where he has important interests in coffee plantations. In addition to an extensive general practice, he serves as surgeon for the Chicago & Northwestern Railroad. He was also for four years coroner of Pennington County and for eight years was physician for the United States Indian school at Rapid City.

On the 14th of September, 1903, Dr. Jackson was united in marriage to Miss Jua B. Goodwin, of Boston, Massachusetts. He belongs to the Knights of Pythias fraternity, the Elks lodge and the Masons. In politics he is a republican where national issues are involved but casts an independent local ballot. He was chosen the first mayor of Rapid City under the commission form of government, serving for two years, at the end of which time he resigned because of the demands which were made upon him in that connection and which he felt caused his professional work to suffer. His principal out-of-door recreation is trout fishing, but he never allows this to interfere with his professional duties. He has gained an enviable reputation as a physician and has also found time to cooperate in every movement looking to the advancement of the city and surrounding territory. Thus, it is that he is not only regarded as one of the leading physicians but also as one of the valued and useful residents of western South Dakota.

JAMES L. JARVIS

Business enterprise finds a worthy, alert and energetic representative in James L. Jarvis, a hardware dealer of Brookings, who is also chairman of the board of county commissioners of Brookings County. He recognizes the duties and obligations as well as the privileges of citizenship and thus can find time from a growing business to devote to public service. He was born in South Bend, Indiana, on the 7th of January, 1860, a son of Eli and Lovina (Wyland) Jarvis, the former a native of Virginia and the latter of the Hoosier state. The father has been a lifelong farmer. After leaving the south he removed to Indiana and in 1860 went to Kansas but in 1862 took up his abode in Shelby County, Iowa, where he and his wife still make their home.

James L. Jarvis was educated in the public schools of Harlan, Iowa, and in the high school there and remained upon the home farm until he reached his twenty-first year. He then went to Wauseca, Minnesota, and a year later removed to Winona, Minnesota, where he worked at the carpenter's trade through the summer months, while in the winter he taught school. In 1881 he took up railroading and was employed by the Northwestern Railroad Company until 1883. In the fall of 1886 he came to South Dakota, settling at Langford, where he entered the service of the Dakota Lumber Company as manager of the yards, remaining in that position of trust and responsibility for five years. In 1891 he resigned his position and entered into partnership with J. C. Bassett of Aberdeen, South Dakota, opening a hardware store at Langford. Mr. Bassett, recognizing the ability of Mr. Jarvis, furnished him the requisite capital and for ten years the firm of Jarvis & Company did a prosperous business at that point. In 1901 Mr. Jarvis disposed of his interests there and removed to Brookings, where he established his present business, which has since been developed into one of the leading hardware houses of Brookings. He carries a large line of both shelf and heavy hardware and his patronage has grown from the beginning until his business has now reached large and gratifying proportions.

In the spring of 1883 Mr. Jarvis was united in marriage to Miss Vesta V. Sanford, of Winona, Minnesota, by whom he has one child, Ruth, now a high-school pupil of Brookings. Politically Mr. Jarvis is a republican, stanch in his advocacy of the principles of the party, and in 1908 he was elected to the board of county commissioners, where he made a creditable record, so that he was reelected to the board in 1912 and was made its chairman in 1913. Mr. Jarvis is well known in fraternal circles, holding membership in Brookings Lodge, No. 34, F. & A. M., while he and his wife are members of Brookings Chapter, No. 15, O. E. S., of which he is the present patron. He likewise belongs to Brookings Lodge, No. 40, I. O. O. F., and has membership with the Ancient Order of United Workmen and the Modern Woodmen. He is likewise a member of the Brookings Commercial Club and is in full sympathy with its purposes to further the business interests of the city, extend its trade relations and uphold its municipal honor. He and his wife have been members of the First Presbyterian church for many years and Mr. Jarvis is serving as one of its elders. His life has been characterized by high and honorable principles and the record which he has made in every relation marks him as a man who never lowers his standards and one who pursues a course not because it is policy to do so, but because he believes in the value and efficacy of the path that he has marked out.

ROBERT JASMANN, D. D. S.

Dr. Robert Jasmann is a well-known dentist residing in Scotland, South Dakota, where his birth occurred July 17, 1880. He has the distinction of being the first white child born in that town and is a son of Christian and Katherine (Vatz) Jasmann, who were natives of Russia, although of German descent. They came to this country with eighteen other families who sailed for America from Hamburg on the ship Cecelia in October, 1872. On the 24th of that month they landed in New York after a stormy voyage of twenty-one days. They passed the first winter with friends at Sandusky, Ohio, but the following spring continued their journey westward, arriving at Yankton, South Dakota, on the 13th of April. They located ten miles southeast of Scotland, forming what was known as the Odessa settlement. They were of deep religious convictions and in 1875 built a church. The parents of our subject took up their residence upon a half section of land in the Odessa settlement and followed farming until 1879. In that year a removal was made to Scotland and the father entered the mercantile business, conducting a general store. Later he sold out and engaged in raising high grade cattle until his death. Five children were born to him and his wife: Amelia, now Mrs. E. Geist, of Faulkton, this state; Emilie, who married Harry Wright, of Spokane, Washington; Robert, of this review; Wilhelmina, now Mrs. William Griess, of Shockham, Nebraska; and Elsie, a teacher in Aberdeen, Washington.

Dr. Jasmann entered the Scotland schools at the usual age and continued his education at the Wartburg Academy at Clinton, Iowa, for two years. Subsequently he took a three years' course in the Chicago College of Dental Surgery, being graduated therefrom in the spring of 1902. Not long afterward he opened an office in Scotland and has since remained there. He has built up a fine practice and is considered one of the best dentists in the state. A vacancy occurring on the board of dental examiners, Governor Byrne appointed Dr. Jasmann to the place, and upon the expiration of that term he was appointed for the full term of five years, which expires in 1919.

Dr. Jasmann was married November 26, 1908, to Miss Nina Wallace, a native of Monticello, Wisconsin, and a daughter of William and Elizabeth (Moore) Wallace. Mrs. Jasmann attended the South Dakota University at Vermillion, and subsequently engaged in teaching school there.

Dr. Jasmann is a Mason, belonging to the blue lodge and chapter at Scotland, the commandery and consistory at Yankton. He is a member of the International Dental Congress and the South Dakota State Dental Society. His wife belongs to the Presbyterian church and he attends its services. He finds needed rest and recreation in hunting and fishing and spent his vacation in the fall of 1913 hunting in the Black Hills. Although he is still a young man, he remembers the memorable blizzard of January 12, 1888, as he was in school at the time and his father sent a man to the schoolhouse to take him home. He has inherited the courage and determination of his pioneer parents and under changed conditions is working with equal loyalty for the best interests of his community and state. He has won not only a high place in his profession but has also gained the esteem and goodwill of all who know him.

GEORGE A. JEFFERS

Among the successful members of the bar of Rapid City is numbered George A. Jeffers, who was born in Jo Daviess County, Illinois, October 13, 1871, a son of Benjamin and Margaret (Ruble) Jeffers. The father was a native of Wisconsin and a son of Alba Jeffers, who was one of the earliest pioneers of that state, having settled there in 1840, in which year he emigrated from Watertown, New York. Benjamin Jeffers was a contractor and builder and won an honorable place in the estimation of his fellowmen. His widow, who is a native of Lewistown, Pennsylvania, survives, and is now a resident of Phoenix, Arizona. To them were born four children, all of whom are living.

George A. Jeffers, the second child in order of birth, was about a year old when the family removed to Iowa and as he grew to manhood there, he was a witness of much of the early development of that state. His general education was acquired in the grammar and high schools of Akron, Iowa, and at the Northwestern Normal School of Le Mars, Iowa. As he had decided to make the practice of law his life work, he entered the law school of the University of Michigan and was graduated therefrom with the class of 1892. In that year he located at Sioux Falls, South Dakota, and for the succeeding three years was a resident of that place. He then returned to Akron, Iowa, and in 1898 was elected county attorney and removed to Le Mars, which remained his place of residence until 1902, when he returned to South Dakota and located at Bonesteel, where he spent five years, but in 1907 he went to Dallas. He lived in the Rosebud country until 1914, and in the intervening seven years was almost constantly employed in a professional capacity in connection with the department of the interior and federal courts in the handling of litigation that arose out of the opening up of the Indian reservation to white settlers. During that time, he maintained offices both at Dallas and Washington, D. C, and the ability which he displayed in thus solving intricate legal tangles gained him a wide and enviable reputation as a lawyer. In 1914 he removed to Rapid City and joined Robert Burton in the formation of the firm of Jeffers & Burton, which has already taken rank as one of the leading legal firms of that city. He is the owner of valuable lands in the Rosebud country and is financially interested in the Black Hills Marble & Granite Company and the legal representative of that corporation.

On the 30th of June, 1913, Mr. Jeffers was united in marriage with Miss Ethel van Sant, a native of Westmoreland County, Virginia, and a descendant of one of the old colonial families of that state. Mr. Jeffers is a republican and takes a citizen's interest in everything pertaining to the public welfare, although he has never found time to actively participate in politics. His fraternal connections are with the Masons and the Elks, and he finds his chief recreation in hunting and fishing. The large measure of success that he has achieved is due to his fine mental powers and his thorough legal training and habit of making a careful study of both sides of any litigated subject and of so thoroughly preparing his cases that he is ready to take the offensive or defensive as the exigencies of the case may require. His zeal for his clients' interests never causes him to forget for a moment the highest standard of professional ethics and the demands of even-handed justice, and the bar and the general public alike have the greatest confidence in his integrity. His work in connection with the department of the interior in adjusting disputes that came up at the time of the settlement of the Rosebud reservation was of a particularly high order and many of his contentions were confirmed by the highest courts in the land.

DAVID H. JENKINS

David H. Jenkins is the president of the Garden City State Bank at Garden City, Clark County. He is yet a young man and few of his years have attained to the position of business importance and distinction which he now occupies. His birth occurred in Williamsburg, Iowa, on the 23d of December, 1888, his parents being William D. and Kate J. (Jones) Jenkins, both of whom survive. In early life the father learned the blacksmith's trade, which he followed until 1903, when he embarked in the lumber business at Sibley, Iowa. He later disposed of his business there and established a yard at Cedar Rapids.

In the acquirement of his education David H. Jenkins attended the public schools and was graduated from the high school of Sibley, Iowa, with the class of 1906. He afterward entered Grinnell College, in which he spent three years as a student, but before his college days he had had about two years' business experience in a bank and was also engaged in real-estate operations in Canada. After leaving college he returned to the First National Bank at Sibley, Iowa, and spent altogether about six years in connection with that institution, during which period he gained thorough, comprehensive and accurate knowledge of the various phases of the banking business.

Mr. Jenkins left Sibley to come to Garden City, where he located in June, 1912. Here he purchased the controlling interest in the Garden City State Bank and was elected its president. He has brought to bear in its conduct the most progressive ideas, and that his plans are practical and resultant is shown in the fact that when he became interested in the bank its deposits were fifty thousand dollars, and today they are double that amount. In 1912 the company erected a new bank building, so that the institution is situated in a pleasant home, splendidly equipped and appointed for the purposes intended. Mr. Jenkins has already gained for himself a most creditable position among the financiers of his section of the state and is also prominently known in other business connections, being treasurer of the Farmers Elevator Company and treasurer of the Garden City Telephone Company.

On the 3d of October, 1911, Mr. Jenkins was married to Miss Marie Hahne, a daughter of Fred and Sophia M. Hahne. Her father was one of the early settlers of Iowa, and was engaged in the grain and banking business at Schaller, Iowa, where his demise occurred in 1900. Mr. and Mrs. Jenkins have two daughters: Mary Louise, born July 9, 1912; and Elizabeth, born October 4, 1914. The parents are members of the Methodist church, and Mr. Jenkins belongs to Garden City Lodge, A. F. & A. M. He gives his political support to the republican party, which has elected him a member of the town board, while his wife is serving as a member of the school board. They are interested in everything pertaining to the welfare and progress of this section, and their influence is far-reaching and beneficial. Mr. Jenkins is alert, energetic and wide-awake. He understands thoroughly the conditions of trade, so that he is able to carry on his banking business in a manner that will result beneficially for the institution and at the same time will prove a help in promoting the business growth of town and county.

RUDOLPH D. JENNINGS, M. D.

Rudolph D. JENNINGS, of Hot Springs, has not only achieved worthy prestige in the line of his profession, but for many years has been prominent in the business circles of his adopted state, being one of the founders and chief promoters of the thriving city in which he now resides. Dr. Jennings was born November 21, 1853, in Fremont, Ohio, and grew to young manhood and received his literary education in Mt. Vernon, Iowa, to which place his parents removed when he was a mere youth. His father being a physician, he early took up the study of medicine and continued to prosecute the same in Mt. Vernon until 1872, when he came to Bismarck, Dakota territory.

Shortly after locating at Bismarck, Dr. Jennings entered the employ of the Puget Sound Land Company, and later was appointed deputy collector of internal revenue, in which capacity he served for a number of years, the meanwhile becoming identified with various enterprises for the development of Dakota and the opening of its resources. After remaining at Bismarck until 1876, he went to the Black Hills, locating first at Crook City, subsequently removing to Deadwood, with the growth and development of which he soon became actively interested. While a resident of Crook City he served as deputy collector of internal revenue for the Black Hills country, and to him also belongs the unique honor of being the first judge before whom a murder case was tried in the city, having been chosen to the position by practically the unanimous voice of the citizens of the place. In addition to his duties as collector, he also dealt quite extensively in real estate and as opportunities afforded continued the study of medicine with the object in view of ultimately making the profession his life work.

Dr. Jennings remained at Deadwood until the year 1881, when he came to the present site of Hot Springs for the purpose of looking over the country, having heard many favorable reports of the locality and of the advantages it possessed for becoming, under judicious management, the center of a thriving populace. Realizing these advantages he at once purchased a squatter right from a "squaw man" and took up a homestead where the city of Hot Springs was afterwards located, taking possession of the same in the summer of 1882. The same year he was instrumental in organizing the Dakota Hot Springs Company, with the object in view of developing this highly favored section and attracting attention to the springs, which already had become widely known for the purity and wonderful curative properties of their waters. Later Fred T. Evans, E. G. Dudley, L. R. Graves and Dr. Stewart, all of Deadwood, took stock in the company and under their joint management the town of Hot Springs was in due time laid out and a number of substantial buildings erected, among them being the Evans Hotel and Bath House, the Mankate House, the Big Plunge, besides several business blocks, and not a few private residences. The city thus founded soon met the high expectations of the proprietors, for it was not long until a thrifty class of people was attracted to the place and within a comparatively brief period Hot Springs not only became a favorite watering place and pleasure resort, but the center of population and the chief trading point for a large area of territory.

Dr. Jennings was untiring in his efforts to promote the varied interests of the town, took an active part in pushing its different enterprises to successful completion and to him more perhaps than to any one individual is due the credit of inducing the Burlington and Elkhorn railroad companies to extend their respective lines to the city. He was an influential factor in the Hot Springs Company as long as it existed, served for several years as its secretary, also as a director, and when it had accomplished its purposes, assisted to wind up its affairs to the satisfaction of all concerned.

Actuated by a laudable desire to finish his medical education and engage in the practice of medicine, Dr. Jennings, in 1885, entered a medical college at Chicago, and after his graduation, two years later, opened an office in Hot Springs, where in due time he built up a large and lucrative professional business. He was medical director of the Hot Springs Company for a period of ten years and his private practice during that time and since assumed large proportions and won for him much more than local reputation as an able physician and skillful surgeon.

Believing in taking advantage of every opportunity to add to his professional knowledge and efficiency, the Doctor, in 1890, went to London, England, where he took special courses under some of the most distinguished medical men of the age, thus by careful study and thorough research fitting himself for the most exacting duties of his chosen calling.

Dr. Jennings has not only been highly successful in his profession, but in business matters his advancement has also been rapid, being at this time one of the largest real-estate holders in Hot Springs, besides owning other valuable property in the city and elsewhere, all of which came to him through legitimate means and superior business management. He is a public-spirited citizen, deeply interested in the development of this thriving city, with the founding and growth of which he has had so much to do. and his influence and material support are also given to all progressive measures for the social, educational and moral advancement of the community. He served five years as a member of the state board of health, during three of which he was its chairman, and his labors in that capacity were productive of great and lasting results to every part of the commonwealth. In politics the Doctor is a Republican, but he has always declined public position, the claims of his profession and his large business interests having more attraction for him than the honors or emoluments of office.

Dr. Jennings is a thirty-second-degree Scottish Rite Mason, also a member of the Mystic Shrine, and is prominent in all branches of the ancient and honorable fraternity to which he belongs. He is also identified with the Independent Order of Odd Fellows, Master Workmen of America, Ancient Order of United Workmen and Improved Order of Red Men, in all of which he has not only been an active and influential worker, but an honored official, whose untiring efforts have made the organization realize the objects for which intended.

JAMES P. JENSEN

James P. Jensen is actively and successfully engaged in business as a general merchant at Erwin, having built up an extensive and well merited patronage. His birth occurred in Fillmore County, Minnesota, on the 1st of November, 1872, his parents being P. K. and Anna Jensen. He attended the public schools in the acquirement of an education and after putting aside his textbooks assisted his father for a time. Subsequently he spent a year as an employe in a shoe store at Austin and then resided during one summer at Minneapolis, while later he entered the service of the Milwaukee Railroad. In 1897 he removed to Bryant, South Dakota, and there first secured a position in a hotel, afterward turning his attention to farm work. In 1899 he located in Erwin and entered the general store and post office of J. R. Wills, remaining with him for one year. At the end of that time, he secured a position with A. J. Hilton, whose establishment he purchased in association with a Mr. Peterson in 1904. Subsequently he bought the interest of his partner and has conducted business independently during the past few years. An extensive and profitable patronage is accorded him, for he carries a large and well selected stock of goods at reasonable prices and has won an unassailable reputation for reliability and integrity. His record as a business man is one well worthy of emulation and commendation, as he started out empty-handed and has worked his way steadily upward unaided to a position among the prosperous and representative merchants of his adopted state.

On the 9th of July, 1902, Mr. Jensen was united in marriage to Miss Ellen Johnson, by whom he has three children, namely: Verna B., Orville H. and Curtis L. He gives his political allegiance to the democracy and has served as a member of the school board for six years, the cause of education ever finding in him a stanch champion. His religious faith is that of the Lutheran church and fraternally he is identified with the Masons, being a worthy exemplar of the craft. He finds recreation in fishing and motoring and also enjoys the companionship of friends, of whom he has made many during the period of his residence in this state.

CHARLES A. JOHNSON

Enterprise and laudable ambition have brought Charles A. Johnson to an enviable position in business circles, he being now president of the First National Bank of Fairfax. His birth occurred in Springville, Erie County, New York, September 11, 1857, his parents being David and Nancy (Quinn) Johnson, who

DR. JESSE E. BROSSEAU

came of English and Irish ancestry respectively. The Johnson family was founded in Massachusetts in 1766 — ten years before the Declaration of Independence was written. David Johnson was a farmer by occupation and also engaged extensively in manufacturing cheese. At the time of the Civil War, he attempted to enlist but was rejected on account of the condition of his health. His grandfather had been a soldier of the Revolutionary war, enlisting three times under General Washington. He was at Valley Forge and at Princeton and participated in a number of the important engagements that brought independence to the nation. Both Mn and Mrs. David Johnson have now passed away, the latter having died at the advanced age of eighty-seven years. In the family were eight children, five sons and three daughters.

Charles A. Johnson, the fifth in order of birth, supplemented his public-school education by study in the Elroy Seminary of Wisconsin, his people having removed to that state when he was a lad of nine years. Owing to illness, however, he was not able to complete his course in the seminary. For five years he engaged in teaching school in Wisconsin and in 1884 went to Nebraska, settling at Wood Lake, where he engaged in general merchandising, in the lumber business, in the live-stock business and in banking for twenty-one years, his activities contributing in large measure to the business development of the town.

The story of how Mr. Johnson became a banker, which he told twenty-five years ago to a number of his old-time friends, and since then it has been told many thousand times as a joke, is as follows:

"In 1885 I had an inspiration that I wanted to become a banker. I wrote a letter to Mr. Ben Woods, who was vice president of the Merchants National Bank of Omaha, who was acquainted with my father in their boyhood days in Erie County, New York. I asked him to write me a receipt telling me how to become a banker. He replied by saying there was no set rule, and that a knowledge of banking could only be gained by actual contact with the business.

"My desire was so great that I decided at once to apply myself to the contact. I had a fair sized safe which I moved into an empty building, and had the name 'Wood Lake Bank' printed across the front of the building in large red letters. Having procured eleven dollars' worth of check books and deposit slips I was open for business. This was before the days of all your foolish banking laws that so aggravate our present-day banker. No capital was required and the only law that governed your business was your conscience.

"The first day's existence of the Wood Lake Bank David Hanna came in and deposited five hundred dollars and secured a check book. The next day Alf Morris deposited two hundred and fifty dollars and Mel Hanna deposited four hundred dollars and Wash Honey deposited one thousand dollars. Sundry other men made deposits that week of various amounts and by Saturday night I had gained sufficient confidence in the institution to deposit my own money from my store and lumberyard.

"The banking business is done largely on confidence of which I have always had a large stock on hand. The ruling rate that small banks charged in those days was twenty-four to thirty-six percent, but I deny the charge of ever taking an unlawful interest. I figured that if the public were kind enough to furnish us the money to loan, we should be satisfied with ten percent interest.

"Having learned the lesson of strict economy which is taught in the 'University of Hard Knocks' of which I was a graduate, I was able to save enough money in two years to capitalize the Wood Lake Bank at ten thousand dollars. This was prior to the passage of a banking law in Nebraska.

"I have often thought the simple laws on banking of Confucius, the famous sage of China, written over five hundred years before Christ and still in force, are superior to our own. When a banker of China goes wrong and embezzles the people's money, they chop his head off with an ax."

Since that time Mr. Johnson has established and been president of six different banks, all now in flourishing condition. He gained from each day's experiences the lessons therein contained. He studied every phase of the business from a practical standpoint and as the years passed on broadened his interests and connections until he is today the foremost capitalist of his section of the state. While engaged in the banking business in Nebraska he there acquired many thousands of acres of land. In 1892 he came to South Dakota, at once recognized the possibilities for development in the western part of the state and established a line of stores and lumberyards. He also organized the Fairfax State Bank, the only bank in the Rosebud until the railroad was built through. He established and is president of the Citizens Bank of Bonesteel and the St. Charles State Bank of St. Charles, which he visits once a week, giving careful supervision to the conduct of the business. He is also president of The Johnson Farm Loan Company of Fairfax and his financial connections are now extensive and of an important character. Moreover, he is a resourceful business man and his efforts and activities have been by no means confined to one line. He sees and utilizes opportunities that others pass heedlessly by and when once he has determined upon a course he perseveres therein until he has reached a successful conclusion. He is called the alfalfa man of his part of the state, for he planted the first alfalfa in Gregory County, proved that it could be profitably cultivated and has since encouraged its planting. He is now cutting six tons to the acre in the year 1915. His landed possessions embrace several thousand acres in South Dakota and in other states. He has made very judicious investments in property and he is an enthusiastic farmer, doing everything in his power to produce better farming conditions. He started the movement that has put in the Rosebud one hundred silos and has introduced dairy cows there, claiming that the final conquest of the Rosebud will be by the dairy cow, for he believes that district to be a splendid region for dairy purposes. He was individually instrumental in securing the present railway facilities of Gregory County. When he thought the time was ripe, he went to Chicago to take the matter up and "dirt was flying" inside of ninety days, securing and donating seventy miles of right of way.

On the 27th of June, 1886, Mr. Johnson was united in marriage to Miss Matie M. Chandler, a daughter of Philander and Miranda Chandler, of Ohio. To them have been born three children, namely: Chester A., who is engaged in the cattle business and farming in Gregory County; Ava Nancy, at home; and Ina, who died at the age of four years.

Mr. Johnson and his family are Protestants in religious belief. He has attained the thirty-second degree in Masonry, belonging to the consistory at Yankton. He is also a Noble of the Mystic Shrine and a member of various other orders and fraternal societies. In politics he is a republican and is a believer in prohibition. Ever a close personal adherent of the temperance cause, he does all in his power to further its adoption and he cooperate in every plan and measure that he believes will prove of benefit in the upbuilding of city, county and state. He has given to Fairfax a library building and many of the books which it contains. He also donated the ground for the city park and planted the trees. He has long been an advocate of good roads and is now grand consul of the Washington Memorial Highway Association. His life record, if given in detail, would present a picture of every public project of the community in which he lives, for he has been identified with all that pertains to progress and upbuilding here. No man in his section of the state is more widely known or deserves in larger measure the gratitude and goodwill of the public. He came to the Rosebud when pioneer conditions existed here, saw its opportunities and has worked for public advantage as well as for private advancement. His fellow townsmen believe that he would ever sacrifice the latter before he would the former and attest that his patriotism is ever shown in actual practical work for the public good.

CHARLES E. JOHNSON

C. E. JOHNSON, postmaster of the city of Bridgewater, is the son of Joseph and Louise Johnson, and was born in Byron, Ogle County, Illinois, on the 27th day of August, 1856. His father was a native of Sweden, and when a young man married, in Europe, Miss Louise Daniels, who was born and reared in Scotland. Shortly after his marriage he came to the United States and settled in Ogle County, Illinois, where he spent the remainder of his life as a prosperous and contented tiller of the soil. Seven children were born to Joseph and Louise Johnson, five of whom survive, namely: John, of Winnebago county, Illinois; August, a business man of Chicago; Charles E., of this review; Mrs. Minnie Osborn and Laura, the last two living in the city of Chicago.

Charles E. Johnson grew up under the healthful influence of farm life, and remained at home until twenty years old, obtaining the meanwhile a fair educational training in the public schools of his native place. Leaving home at the age noted, he went to Chicago and after working about two years on the street cars of that city, spent one year with a civil engineering corps surveying a line of the Milwaukee Railroad, between the towns of Savannah and Elgin. In 1879 he went to Nebraska, where he purchased land and for two years was engaged in agricultural pursuits, disposing of his real estate at the expiration of that time and in 1881 locating at Bridgewater, South Dakota. Mr. Johnson came to McCook County when the country was new, consequently enjoyed exceptional advantages in the way of making a judicious selection of land. Purchasing a half section about four miles north of the town, he at once addressed himself to the task of its improvement and in due time had a good farm under successful cultivation, from which he soon began to realize a comfortable income. He continued agriculture and stock raising with success and profit until the spring of 1903, when he retired from farm life to enjoy the fruits of his many years of well-directed labor.

Mr. Johnson has been quite prominent in the affairs of McCook County ever since becoming a resident of the same and at different times he has been honored with important official positions, one of the first being that of township treasurer, in which he served for a period of eighteen consecutive years. A stanch Republican, he early became one of the party leaders in this county and in recognition of his valuable political services, as well as by reason of his peculiar fitness for the position, he was elected in 1893 to the upper house of the general assembly. His career as a legislator proving eminently satisfactory to his constituency, he was re-elected in 1897, being the only man in McCook County chosen the second time to the senate. Mr. Johnson was an indefatigable worker while in the legislature, served on several important committees, was influential in the general deliberations of the body, and as one of the Republican leaders succeeded in bringing about the enactment of a number of laws which have had important bearing upon the interests of the state. He is now a member of the Republican state central committee, in which capacity he has rendered valuable service to his party. He has also served on the central committee of McCook County, and as further evidence of his faithful and efficient service he was appointed by President McKinley, in 1897, postmaster of Bridgewater, which position he still holds, having been re-appointed in February, 1902, by President Roosevelt. In addition to the offices referred to, Mr. Johnson was for nineteen years a member of the Emery township school board, during which time he labored earnestly to advance educational interests, making the schools among the best in the state; he was president of the board, during the greater part of his incumbency and in that capacity succeeded in introducing a number of reforms, erected several fine modern buildings, and brought the educational system up to its present high standard of efficiency.

Mr. Johnson was married, in 1884, to Miss Jennie Campbell, of Byron, Illinois, and is the father of two children, Margaret, a graduate of the normal department of Huron College, and Mary, who is also an educated and cultured young lady, both daughters living at home with their parents.

Fraternally Mr. Johnson is a Mason of high degree, belonging to Eureka Lodge, No. 71, at Bridgewater; Salem Chapter, No. 34, Royal Arch Masons, and Salem Commandery, Knights Templar. He is also identified with the Modern Woodmen of America and the Ancient Order of United Workmen, in both of which organizations he has held important positions.

E. A. JOHNSON, D. D. S.

Dr. E. A. Johnson has a well-appointed dental office in Viborg and is accorded a liberal practice. He is in touch with the most modern and progressive methods and his work is proving highly satisfactory to his many patrons. South Dakota numbers him among her native sons, his birth having occurred in Clay County on the 5th of April, 1884, his parents being John and Lena Johnson, who came to this state at an early period in its development.

The father homesteaded in Clay County and there engaged in farming for a number of years. He passed away in 1886 but his widow survives and resides on the home farm.

After attending the district schools near his father's home Dr. Johnson became a pupil in a high school at Denver, Colorado, and continued his education in the University of Southern California, from which he was graduated on the completion of a course in dentistry with the class of 1908. Having thus qualified for the profession, he first practiced in the Lake Andes district for three years and then removed to Viborg, where he opened his office in 1912. He is the only dentist there and has a large practice drawn from the town and the surrounding country. He possesses the mechanical skill and ingenuity which is an essential element in the work of dentistry and he has, too, a broad scientific knowledge to which he is continually adding by reading and research.

On the 30th of June, 1914, Dr. Johnson was united in marriage to Miss Katherine Bacon, a daughter of Alonzo Bacon, of Hurley, this state. Dr. Johnson belongs to District Dental Society No. 1 and to the South Dakota Dental Association. He is also a member of the Alpha chapter of the Xi Psi Phi Society at the University of Southern California. His religious belief is that of the Baptist church, which finds in him a loyal member. His political indorsement is given to the democratic party and fraternally he is connected with the Masonic lodge at Hurley and with the Odd Fellows society. Recognizing the possibilities of South Dakota and its chances for development, he aids in many well-defined plans for the public good and seeks to benefit his community in every possible way. His strong and salient characteristics commend him to the confidence and regard of those with whom he has been brought in contact and he has a growing circle of friends.

GEORGE F. JOHNSON

G. F. Johnson is a prominent business man of Redfield, Spink County, and is now serving as register of deeds of said county. The original progenitor of the Johnson family in America immigrated hither in the early colonial period and located in New England, representatives of the name being found in various sections thereof at the present time. Franklin Johnson, the father of the subject, was a native of the state of Vermont, where he was reared to maturity. As a young man he removed thence to New Jersey, and there he married Miss Rispah Compton, who was born and reared in that state, and they became the parents of five children, of whom three are now living, the subject of this review having been the second in order of birth. He was born in this historic old town of Perth Amboy, Middlesex County, New Jersey, on the 5th of June, 1843, his father having been there engaged in the manufacturing of locks for a number of years. George F., received his early educational training in the schools of his native town and was about fifteen years of age when, in 1858, his parents removed to the west and settled in Waseca, Minnesota, as pioneers of the state. There the father engaged in the milling business, in which he continued during the remainder of his active career, and there his death occurred in 1893, at the venerable age of eighty-seven years, while his devoted wife died at the age of sixty-seven years.

The subject was associated with his father in the work of the mill at the time of the outbreak of the Civil war, and in March, 1863, at the age of twenty years, he enlisted as a private in Company A, First Minnesota Volunteer Infantry, which was commanded by Colonel Sully, who later became a general and distinguished himself in the Indian warfare of the west and northwest. The regiment proceeded to the national capital and shortly afterward Colonel Colvin assumed command. The regiment was assigned to the Army of the Potomac, and thereafter took part in every engagement in which this notable division of the Union forces was concerned until the close of the war, Mr. Johnson having received his honorable discharge, at St. Paul, Minnesota, in July, 1865, while the history of his regiment is the history of his record as a leal and loyal soldier of the republic.

After the close of the war Mr. Johnson returned to Minnesota, and in 1871 he engaged in the hotel business at Janesville, that state, continuing to be identified with this enterprise until 1881, when he came to Redfield, South Dakota, and became the pioneer hardware merchant of the town. He has ever since continued to be identified with this important branch of trade, has built up a large and profitable enterprise and is one of the influential and honored business men of the county. The business is now conducted under the firm name of G. F. Johnson & Son, his only son having been admitted to partnership in 1890. In politics Mr. Johnson is a stalwart Republican, taking a lively interest in the party cause. He served as the first city recorder and treasurer of Redfield, and is incumbent of these positions at the present time, while in November, 1902, he was elected register of deeds of the county, in which office he is giving a most systematic and able administration of the important affairs entrusted to his charge.

He is a member of George H. Thomas Post, No. 5, Grand Army of the Republic, and also of the Masonic fraternity, in which he is affiliated with Redfield Lodge, No. 34, Ancient Free and Accepted Masons, and Redfield Chapter, No. 20, Royal Arch Masons. On the 19th of May, 1869, Mr. Johnson was united in marriage to Miss Laura E. Storrs, who was born in Maples, New York, being a daughter of John and Sarah Storrs. The subject and his estimable wife are the parents of two children, Grace F., who is now the wife of Hubert W. Bartlett, of Lead, Lawrence County, this state, and Harry E., who is now associated with his father in the hardware business.

PROFESSOR HENRY CHARLES JOHNSON

Professor Henry Charles Johnson, since 1909 city superintendent of schools at Aberdeen, has devoted his life largely to educational work and, ever laboring for the attainment of high ideals, he has made his service a potent and helpful influence in promoting intellectual advancement in the various localities in which he has made his home. In his present position his record has been one of well-directed service and important accomplishment and stands as a credit to his belief in education, his sincerity of purpose and his public spirit. Professor Johnson was born at Mount Sterling, Wisconsin, October 11, 1876, and is a son of Erick and Mattie Johnson, who removed to South Dakota in 1909. The father is now engaged in farming near Greene, Iowa.

Professor Johnson acquired his high-school education in Mount Sterling, Wisconsin, and afterward attended a normal school in Charles City, Iowa. He received the degree of B. A. from the Iowa State University in 1902 and the degree of M. A. from the same institution in 1907. Following the completion of his studies he turned his attention to teaching and engaged in that occupation in the country schools of Iowa and Wisconsin, later becoming connected with the Keswick (Iowa) high school. He rose rapidly in his chosen profession, being appointed principal of the high school at Decorah, Iowa, and serving in that capacity for two years and for a similar period of time as superintendent of schools of that city.

Professor Johnson came to Aberdeen in 1909 and in the same year was appointed city superintendent of schools here, an office which he has filled with honor and credit since that time. He has become a recognized leader in the field of education and personally superintends every detail of the work entrusted to him. He planned the high school building which was erected in 1911 and ordered the equipment, which is modern, up-to-date and sanitary in every particular, making this one of the best and most modern school buildings in the state. The high school has four hundred and fifty pupils and the entire enrollment of the city schools is eighteen hundred, under charge of seventy-four teachers. Professor Johnson is one of the most progressive educators in the state and has inaugurated important departments in the school system of Aberdeen, providing for the medical examination of every pupil and for the promotion of physical efficiency and health by courses in physical culture. This department is in the hands of a physical director employed by the year and there is a trained nurse in constant attendance. In the new high school, there is a fine gymnasium and the playground is equipped with two thousand dollars' worth of apparatus, a visible evidence of the superintendent's belief in outdoor exercise as an aid to health. Professor Johnson has introduced into the schools of Aberdeen courses in manual training, printing and domestic science and these have already become popular departments. His entire life since attaining his majority has been given over to educational work and he is a recognized leader in this field. He is zealous and discriminating and studies each child from the standpoint of the individual, providing for his or her development along the most practical lines.

In 1905 Professor Johnson married Miss Marie Whitwell, of Decorah, Iowa, and they have become the parents of four children, one of whom has passed away. The Professor is a member of the Congregational church and gives his political allegiance to the republican party. He is connected fraternally with the Knights of Pythias and the Masonic lodge. Educational interests of Aberdeen owe to him a great and lasting debt, and his influence has been a tangible force for good in other fields.

JAMES W. JOHNSTON

James W. JOHNSTON, secretary and general manager of the Faulk County Land and Title Company, is a well-known citizen of Faulkton. He was born in Center County, Pennsylvania, on the 4th of October, 1854, being a son of William and Agnes (Watson) Johnston, both of whom were likewise born and reared in Pennsylvania. The father of the subject was a successful farmer of Center County, where he continued to reside until 1869, when he removed with his family to Lee County, where he and his wife resided until their deaths.

James W. Johnston passed his youth on the family homestead farm in Pennsylvania, and received a common-school education. He accompanied his parents on their removal to Iowa. In 1879 he came to South Dakota, so that he may be consistently termed a pioneer of the state, and shortly after his arrival he entered claim to one hundred and sixty acres of government land ten miles north of Watertown, which he proved up. He then assisted on the government surveys of the territory until January, 1883, when he removed to Faulk County, which was then unorganized, and filed a pre-emption on one hundred and sixty acres of land joining the town site of La Foon, which afterwards became the first county seat of Faulk County. At the first general election held in Faulk County, November 8, 1894, he was elected to the office of I register of deeds, being the first chosen to this position by popular vote. He served one term, while subsequently he was again elected to this office, serving one term. His long experience in the office has made him thoroughly familiar with land values in this section and this knowledge has been of great benefit to him in his real-estate operations. In 1886, when the railroad was completed to Faulkton, the present county seat, he removed to. the new town, with whose interests and upbuilding he has since been identified. He continued his business individually until 1893, when he effected the organization of the Faulk County Land and Title Company, of which he has been secretary and general manager from the start. The company own a complete set of abstracts of. land titles of Faulk County. Mr. Johnston is a member of the Republican party, and for the past eight years has served as chairman of the Republican County central committee. He served two terms as a member of the city council, and for three years as a member of the board of education.

Fraternally he is identified with Faulkton Lodge, No. 95, Ancient Free and Accepted Masons; Faulkton Chapter, No. 30, Royal Arch Masons, of which he is high priest at the time of this writing; the order of Knights of the Maccabees and Modern Woodmen of America. On the 5th of November, 1885, Mr. Johnston was united in marriage to Miss Lizzie M. Cochrane, of Des Moines, Iowa, who was born and reared in that state, being a daughter of J. C. Cochrane. In the spring of 1883 Mrs. Johnston came to South Dakota with her uncle, Joseph Cochrane, and filed a pre-emption claim. She may be termed a pioneer of Faulk County, having settled on her land prior to the time it came into the market. In December, 1884, Judge Seward Smith appointed her clerk of the district court, in which office she served about two years, having been the first woman to hold the office in the state. She resigned the position at the time of her marriage. Mr. and Mrs. Johnson have had born to them ten children, of whom but four are living: Belle, Lloyd, Laura and Ralph. Mr. and Mrs. Johnston are members of the Congregational church.

JULIUS H. JOHNSON

The student of history does not have to carry his investigations far before he learns that the northwest owes its development, progress and upbuilding to the Scandinavian race. The strong and sterling characteristics of those who claim their nativity in, or trace their ancestry to Norway, Sweden, or Denmark have been continuously manifest as factors in the material progress and the political and moral welfare of this section of the country. While a native of Iowa, Julius H. Johnson is descended from Scandinavian ancestry, his record being a proof of the facts stated above. He ranks today among the able lawyers of South Dakota, possessing comprehensive knowledge of the law with ability to accurately apply its principles. He is, moreover, an orator of considerable power and a deep and logical thinker, not only upon legal problems but also concerning the great vital principles affecting the welfare of state and nation. He practices law at

Fort Pierre but has been heard many times upon the lecture and political platforms and thus has become widely known throughout the state.

A native of Humboldt, Iowa, Mr. Johnson was born July 13, 1872. His parents were pioneers in Wisconsin and moved to Iowa in 1871. The father, Ole Johnson, was a successful farmer, but died in 1874 leaving the mother, Mrs. Anna Johnson, whose first husband had died in the Civil war, with a family of small children to raise. She is now past eighty and is making her home with her son Julius at Fort Pierre.

Julius H. Johnson spent his early youth on the farm where he worked early and late in addition to attending school, later continuing his education at the Red Wing Seminary at Red Wing, Minnesota, where he was graduated with the class of 1894. In 1900 he was graduated from the University of Minnesota with the degree of Bachelor of Literature, and the following year he received the degree of Bachelor of Laws from the University of Iowa. For three years Mr. Johnson was engaged in the practice of law in Clinton, Iowa. Then he removed to South Dakota, where he has since won distinction as an able and learned member of the bar. He was appointed city attorney of Fort Pierre and served for six years. In 1908 and 1910 inclusive he served Stanley County as states attorney. In this time, he secured fifty-nine convictions of criminals in the circuit court and also fifty-four convictions in justice court. The thoroughness and care with which he prepares his cases, combined with clear and cogent reasoning have been the salient features of his success.

On the 19th of June, 1901, in Milwaukee, Wisconsin, Julius H. Johnson and Lydia B. Carlsson were married. Their only child, Charlotte Amelia Johnson, was born at Clinton, Iowa, May 6, 1902. Extended mention is made of Mrs. Johnson elsewhere in this work in connection with her club work and her efforts in behalf of equal suffrage.

Mr. Johnson is a progressive republican and secured the endorsement of the conservation and irrigation plank in the republican platform of 1912. He has lectured extensively on political economy and few men have as comprehensive and accurate knowledge of the subject. Fraternally he is a Master Mason, and in 1913 he filled the office of noble grand in the Odd Fellows lodge at Fort Pierre. He has likewise been master workman in the Ancient Order of United Workmen and belongs to the Modern Woodmen of America. He is secretary of the Commercial Club of Fort Pierre and is deeply interested in every vital problem affecting the welfare, upbuilding and progress of the municipality and of the commonwealth. He has traveled extensively in Europe and while abroad studied governmental questions in England, Norway, Sweden and Germany. His views are comprehensive, his reasoning clear and his decisions are logical.

ELBERT ORLANDO JONES

Elbert Orlando Jones, a well-known representative of the legal profession in Sioux Falls, engaged in the general practice of law in partnership with Benoni C. Matthews, was born on a farm in Allamakee County, Iowa, June 9, 1872. He is a son of William J. and Susan R. (Smith) Jones, and is of Welsh and Yankee stock. His father, William Jones, was born on a farm near Brecon in Breconshire, Wales, December 14, 1838, and emigrated with his parents to the United States in 1842, making the passage of the Atlantic by sail boat, requiring six weeks in crossing to New York. From New York the family proceeded up the Hudson by boat, through the Hudson canal into the Great Lakes and thence by boat to Kenosha, Wisconsin, where they settled on a farm about ten miles southwest of Kenosha, at a place called Pleasant Prairie.

The father of our subject lived with his parents and attended the common schools until the spring of 1856, when he left home and started out to make his own way in the world. He worked on a farm in the summer and in the winter, he went into the pine forest near Green Bay, Wisconsin, and did logging. In the summer of 1856, he removed to Allamakee County, Iowa, where he worked on a farm until the spring of 1859, when he went with the early rush of gold seekers to Pike's Peak, Colorado, making the entire trip on foot. He returned in the fall of the same year to Allamakee County, Iowa. In the spring of 1860, he worked his way down the Mississippi river on a raft as far as Clarinda, Page County, Iowa, where he spent his time working on a farm until the spring of 1861, when he engaged to drive an ox team to Denver, Colorado, and return. On his return from this trip, he enlisted in Company I, First Nebraska Volunteer Infantry. His regiment did service in Missouri, Arkansas, Tennessee and Kentucky until the close of the war, when they were transferred to the plains of Kansas and Nebraska as a part of the cavalry branch of the service to fight against the Indians until July 1, 1866, when he was mustered out with the regiment as commissary sergeant at Omaha. He then went back to Allamakee County, Iowa, bought a farm and married Susan R. Smith. He commenced farming operations for himself in the fall of 1866, which he continued until 1873. In 1873 Mr. Jones came to Minnehaha County, South Dakota, and filed upon a homestead in Brandon township, and in the spring of 1875, he brought his family to the homestead, which was then fifty miles beyond the railway. His wife, Susan R. (Smith) Jones, was born on a farm in Indiana, September 26, 1842, of Revolutionary stock, which had led in the westward march of civilization over the Daniel Boone trail through Kentucky.

In the acquirement of an education Elbert Orlando Jones attended country schools in Minnehaha County, this state, and afterward was a student in the Normal School at Madison, South Dakota. He later entered the University of South Dakota at Vermillion and was graduated from the University of Nebraska in 1897, with the degree of B. L. Following the completion of his studies he returned to Sioux Falls and in August, 1897, engaged in the general practice of his profession in partnership with Benoni C. Matthews, with whom he graduated and is still associated. This is one of the prominent law firms of the city and it controls a large and growing patronage, for both partners are able, resourceful, vigorous and capable attorneys.

In Fremont, Nebraska, September 27, 1899, Mr. Jones was united in marriage to Miss Marietta Gray, a daughter of Mr. and Mrs. Enos F. Gray, of that city, and they have become the parents of a son, Enos Gray, born July 3, 1900.

Mr. Jones is interested in farming lands in Minnehaha County and elsewhere and has valuable holdings. He is well known in the Masonic order, holding membership in all the various bodies, including the Shrine. He gives his political allegiance to the republican party and is interested in public affairs without being active as an office seeker. He is numbered among the leading representatives of the bar in Sioux Falls and holds a high place in professional and social circles.

JAMES GURNAL JONES

James G. Jones, one of the pioneers of Charles Mix County, is a native of the old Empire state of the Union, having been born on a farm in Oneida County, New York, on the 21st of April, 1851, a son of William J. and Ann (Wheldon) Jones. The grandparents of the subject were born in Wales, whence they emigrated to the United States about the year 1812, locating in the state of New York, where they passed the remainder of their lives. The father of our subject was born in Oneida County, New York, and became a prominent farmer near Utica, Oneida county, where he died in 1877. James G. Jones received his early educational discipline in the common schools and in an academy at Rome, New York, while he has ever been a wide reader and student of affairs, and is a man of broad and exact information, having supplemented his early training by systematic personal application. He continued to assist in the work of the home farm until he had attained the age of sixteen years, when, in 1867, he gave rein to his spirit of adventure and came to the west, passing five years in Texas and the Indian territory and gaining much experience in regard to life on the frontier. In 1873 he came to what is now the state of South Dakota and settled in Charles Mix County. In 1879, when the county was organized, Governor Howard appointed Mr. Jones County commissioner, while in the first popular election, in the fall of the same year, he was elected register of deeds of the county. He was re-elected in 1880, serving for a total of three years, as the first incumbent of this office. Four years later he was chosen representative of his county in the first constitutional convention of the south half of the territory of Dakota, but declined to serve, said convention having been held at Sioux Falls. In 1887 he was elected a member of the territorial legislature, serving with marked ability and being chosen as his own successor two years later. Prior to the organization of Charles Mix County Mr. Jones and Major Thad S. Clarkson, ex-commander-in-chief of the Grand Army of the Republic, were rival candidates for the territorial legislature, and the vote proved to be a tie. Under these conditions Brule County, which gave Mr. Jones a majority, was conveniently thrown out on a technical pretext and his defeat was thus compassed, this being in the year 1876.

The subject was a stanch supporter of the Republican party until the organization of the Populist party, when he transferred his allegiance to the same, and he has ever since been one of the ablest and most enthusiastic advocates of its cause in the state, while he has been an effective worker in the promotion of its interests. In 1893 Mr. Jones was the nominee of his party for the state senate, but met defeat by a narrow margin. In 1896 he was elected enrolling and engrossing clerk of the house of representatives. In 1898 he was again the nominee of his party for the state senate, and at this time a gratifying majority was rolled up in his favor, and he proved an able and valued member of this body. In 1900 he was one of the delegates-at-large from this state to the People's party national convention, at Sioux Falls, which nominated Bryan for the presidency and Towne for the vice-presidency. Mr. Jones is a man of strong individuality and marked intellectuality, being a close student of the political and economic questions of the hour and being ever fortified in his convictions. He is the owner of a fine landed estate of three hundred and twenty acres, in the Missouri valley district of the county, and is one of the successful farmers and stock growers of this section.

Fraternally he is identified with Doric Lodge, No. 93, Free and Accepted Masons, at Platte, which village is fourteen miles distant from his fine farm home. On the 15th of July, 1877, Mr. Jones was united in marriage to Miss Winifred Mulleague, who was born in County Roscommon, Ireland, whence she came to America at the age of thirteen years and established her home with her brothers and sisters in Bon Homme County, South Dakota, where she was reared to maturity. As before noted, she was the first white woman to settle in Charles Mix County, where she resided almost two years with her husband without seeing a person of her sex and race, and her eldest child was the first white child born in the county. Mr. and Mrs. Jones are the parents of eight children, all of whom have been accorded the best possible educational advantages, their names, in order of birth, being as follows: Whitfield, William James, Mary Laura, Gordon Gurnal, Winifred Ann, Roscoe Conkling, Francis, Wheldon and Emma Lela. Four of the children are successful and popular teachers in the public schools of the county, namely: Whitfield, Mary L., Gordon G. and William J.

HON. JOSEPH WARREN JONES

Judge Jones was born on a farm in Fountain County, Indiana, and is a son of John T. and Indiana (Guthrie) Jones, the former a native of Kentucky. He received his education in the common schools of that county, and in Asbury (now De Pauw) University, at Greencastle, Indiana, from which institution he was graduated in 1870. He entered upon the active practice of law in Danville, Illinois, where he was admitted to the bar, and remained in that city from November, 1870, until April, 1883. From 1877 until 1881 he was states attorney of Vermillion County, Illinois, proving himself to be an able lawyer and official in this position.

In 1883 Mr. Jones came to Sioux Falls, South Dakota, and here established himself in practice. In 1893 he was elected judge of the circuit court of the second judicial circuit for four years and has been reelected ever since, being today one of the oldest jurists in the state in point of service. He entered upon his duties on the 2d of January, 1894, and for more than twenty years has rendered decisions from the circuit bench. He is deeply read in the law and as the presiding officer of his court has ever upheld dignity and justice.

On March 27, 1879, at Bloomington, Illinois, Judge Jones married Miss Luella Campbell. He is a republican in politics, and fraternally is a member of the Masonic order, having reached the thirty-second degree in the Scottish Rite. He is a Knight Templar and Shriner, a member of the Elks, of the Dacotah and Country Clubs of Sioux Falls. The name of Judge Jones stands for the highest expression of judicial fairness, and his long and distinguished record is an honor to the state which has honored him.

R. R. JONES, M. D.

Dr. R. R. Jones, engaged in the practice of medicine and surgery at Britton, was born at Cambria, Wisconsin, September 19, 1862. His father, Hugh R. Jones, a native of Wales, was born in 1837 and about 1850 became a resident of Cambria, settling on a farm in that locality on which he lived for a number of years. Later he removed to Colorado but died in 1913, at Britton, while visiting his son. In Cambria he had married Laura Williams, who was born in Wales in 1840 and survives. His religious belief was that of the Presbyterian church, to which his widow also belongs. Fraternally he was connected with the Woodmen and in political faith was a republican. To him and his wife were born three children, namely: R. R., of this review; Emma, who is married and resides in Denver, Colorado; and Mary Jane, deceased.

R. R. Jones supplemented his early education by study in Downer College at Milwaukee, Wisconsin, in which he pursued his academic course. Later he entered Rush Medical College of Chicago, from which he was graduated with the class of 1888, after which he returned to Cambria, Wisconsin, but in the fall of that year he removed to Britton, where he has since remained, being now the oldest practitioner in the county. From the beginning a liberal patronage has been accorded him and at all points in his professional career he has demonstrated his ability to cope with the intricate problems that continually confront the physician. He is careful in diagnosing his cases and is continually promoting his knowledge by further reading and study. His property holdings include farm lands and he is today in very comfortable circumstances as the result of his judicious investments and the success he has won in his profession.

In 1890 Dr. Jones was united in marriage to Miss Florence Thayer, a daughter of Alonzo Thayer, who was born in New York and on coming to this state purchased a farm in Marshall County, where the remainder of his life was spent. The Doctor and his wife have two children, Gracene and Marion, both high-school students.

The religious faith of the family is that of the Presbyterian church and in social circles the members of the household occupy an enviable position. Fraternally Dr. Jones is a Royal Arch and Scottish Rite Mason and is also identified with the Mystic Shrine at Aberdeen. He is likewise connected with the Odd Fellows, the United Workmen and the Maccabees and is medical examiner for a number of fraternal orders. Politically an earnest republican, he was elected on that ticket to the office of mayor in 1909 and has since been the chief executive of the city, covering a period of six years, during which time his activities have largely furthered the public welfare because his administration has been both businesslike and progressive. For twenty years he has been president of the school board and is ever seeking to advance the best interests of education in his city. He has served on the county central committee, but while active in political circles and public affairs, his interest chiefly centers in his profession, in which he meets every duty with a sense of conscientious obligation. He is now a member of both the district and state medical societies and thus keeps in touch with the progressive thought of the medical fraternity.

STEPHEN V. JONES

Stephen V. JONES, one of the honored pioneer members of the bar of Turner County, was born in the township of Union, Rock County, Wisconsin, and is a son of Ira and Sarah J. (Lemon) Jones, both of whom were born and reared in Ohio. The Jones family came originally from Wales, the progenitors in the new world locating in Pennsylvania prior to the war of the Revolution, in which representatives of the name were active participants, aiding in the securing of the independence of the colonies, while those of later generations showed their patriotism by taking part in the war of 1812, the Mexican war and that of the Rebellion, while members also served in connection with the early Indian wars in Ohio, being contemporaries and companions of Allen Poe and other noted Indian fighters. The Lemon family came from England to Virginia and became prominently identified with the early history of the patrician Old Dominion, where the name stood for loyalty and patriotism, members of the family taking part in the early French and Indian wars and also in the Revolution, one, at least, of the name having been a member of Harry Lee's famous light horse cavalry. The Lemons became numbered among the early pioneers of Ohio, and were associated with Simon Kenton and other celebrated Indian fighters. Representatives of this stanch old stock have been found in every war in which the nation has been involved, from the revolution up to and including that with Spain.

Immediately after their marriage Ira and Sarah J. Jones removed from Ohio to central Illinois, where they located about 1835, thus becoming pioneers of the state. They later removed to the northern part of the state and then to Rock County, Wisconsin, where they settled upon a pioneer farmstead in 1840, there being but few white settlers in that section at the time, while the Indians were much in evidence. There the honored parents of the subject passed the remainder of their lives, being persons of sterling character and ever commanding the unqualified esteem of all who knew them.

The subject of this review was reared to the sturdy discipline of the home farm, and his early educational training was secured in the public schools and under the direction of private tutors. He early put his scholastic acquirements to practical use by engaging in teaching, through which means and through soliciting for insurance companies he obtained the funds which enabled him to further prosecute his studies. He was ever ready to turn himself to any honest labor which presented and has retained the most wholesome respect for the dignity of honest toil and endeavor. He studied surveying, and for a time followed work along this line, in 1870, 1871 and 1872. He was a member of what was known as the Colorado river exploring expedition, under command of Major J. W. Powell, and in this connection has the distinction of being one of the seven men who have ever gone through the magnificent canons of the Green and Colorado rivers. The trip was made in open boats and was attended with much peril. The party started at Green River Station, in southeastern Wyoming, and after a year and a half left the Colorado river near the southeastern line of Nevada.

Mr. Jones was admitted to the bar of the state of Illinois, after careful preliminary study, and he was for a short time engaged in practice in Wichita, Kansas, coming to the present state of South Dakota, arriving at his present home town of Parker, on the 19th of September, 1883, and having ever since been actively and successfully established in the practice of his profession here. He has served several terms as state's attorney of Turner County, and in 1896 was the Republican candidate for attorney general of the state, but met the defeat which attended the party ticket in general in the state election of that year. He has ever been an uncompromising and ardent advocate of the principles and policies for which the "grand old party" stands sponsor and has been an active worker in its cause.

He has been for many years identified with the Masonic fraternity and the Independent Order of Odd Fellows, while his two elder sons are likewise Freemasons, his wife a member of the Woman's Relief Corps and the Daughters of Rebekah, and his daughter is affiliated with the Royal Neighbors. Mrs. Jones is a communicant of the Methodist Episcopal church, and all the other members of the family incline toward the faith of the same.

On the 22d of January, 1883, Mr. Jones was united in marriage to Miss Jennie R. Boys, who was born in Stroudsburg, Pennsylvania, being a daughter of Samuel and Catherine (Andre) Boys, who removed to central Illinois when she was young, her educational training having been secured in the public schools of Pennsylvania and Illinois, including a course in the high school at Lacon, latter state, and in Quincy College, Illinois. Concerning the children of Mr. and Mrs. Jones we incorporate the following brief record: Claude L. was graduated in the Parker high school and the Iowa College of Law, at Des Moines. In October, 1897, he was admitted to practice in the supreme court of South Dakota and in May, 1899, to that of Iowa. Since June 1, 1899, he has been associated with his father in practice, under the firm name of Jones & Jones. In November, 1902, he was elected state's attorney of Turner County, just sixteen years after his father's first election to that office, and had the distinction of receiving the largest majority ever given any candidate in the county, Ethel, the only daughter of the subject, is a graduate of the Parker high school and the Northwestern University, at Evanston, Illinois. Carl R., is a graduate of the home high school and the Iowa College of Law, having been admitted to the bar in 1902, and is now engaged in the practice of his profession. Ira A., was graduated in the Parker high school as a member of the class of 1904.

WILLIAM J. JONES

William J. Jones is the secretary of the Spink County Farmers Mutual Insurance Company of Frankfort, which position he has occupied since 1908. He was a young man in the twenties when he arrived in South Dakota, establishing his home within the borders of the territory in 1885. He came from Sandwich, Illinois, his native city, his birth having there occurred on the 7th of February, 1857, his parents being John and Johanna (Sly) Jones. The father, who followed the occupation of farming, was a native of Wales and came to the new world in 1844. He settled in Illinois in 1845 and in 1850 traveled on foot across the country to California, returning in 1854. He purchased one hundred and sixty acres of government land at a dollar and a quarter per acre and sold that property in 1898 for one hundred and fifty dollars per acre.

His death occurred in the same year when he had reached the age of seventy-one, and he was laid to rest in the Millington (Ill.) cemetery. His widow still resides at Sandwich, Illinois, and has reached the very advanced age of eighty-eight years.

William J. Jones obtained his primary education in his native town, pursuing his studies to the age of twenty years, while in the summer months he worked on his father's farm. He then attended the Bryant & Stratton Business College in Chicago and afterward became a clerk in a drug store in that city. About 1879 he became connected with railway interests, to which he devoted his attention until 1882. In that year he went to Storm Lake, Iowa, where he ran an engine until 1885, when he came to South Dakota and entered into partnership with A. M. Costello in the purchase of a drug store at Frankfort. That business was conducted by the firm for three years, at the end of which time Mr. Jones purchased his partner's interest and remained as sole proprietor for eleven years, winning substantial success during that period. He then sold out and invested in two hundred and twenty-three acres of land and afterward bought additional land, so that he now owns six hundred and sixty-three acres, the development and improvement of which he personally manages. He has become recognized as one of the foremost agriculturists of his county and he also has other important business connections, being president of the James River Bank, president of the Frankfort Elevator Company, director of the Citizens Lumber Company, and secretary of the Spink County Farmers Mutual Insurance Company, all of which are important business enterprises, contributing to the material development of his section of the state. He has also erected various buildings and his business interests have ever been of a character to further public progress.

On the 4th of November, 1888, at Lake Byron, Mr. Jones was united in marriage to Miss Grace Underhill, a daughter of Mr. and Mrs. Alfred Underhill. The father, a pioneer agriculturist of South Dakota, passed away in 1913 and lies buried at Ponca, Nebraska. His widow now makes her home in Tilden, that state. Our subject and his wife have one son, Otho J., who is attending school.

Mr. Jones exercises his right of franchise in support of the men and measures of the republican party and is a local leader in its ranks. He has served as mayor of the city for six years past, and has given to Frankfort a businesslike administration that has been productive of various needed reforms and improvements in municipal management. He has attained the Knight Templar degree in Masonry as a member of the commandery at Redfield and he also belongs to the Elks lodge, the Ancient Order of United Workmen and the Modern Woodmen of America. In his business career he has advanced steadily step by step, gaining at all times a broader outlook and wider opportunities, which he has improved to the benefit of the community as well as to the advancement of his individual interests. His life record should serve to encourage and inspire others, showing what may be accomplished when determination and energy point out the way.

ARTHUR J. JORDAN

Arthur J. Jordan, prominently connected with business interests of Sioux Falls as the proprietor of a planing mill and sash and door factory, operated under the name of Jordan Brothers, is a native son of the city, born September 19, 1881. His parents were Charles E. and Rose Mary (Austin) Jordan, the former of whom was born in Rye, England, and came to America in his infancy with his father, William Henry Jordan. Charles E. Jordan was a carpenter and contractor by trade and came to Sioux Falls in 1878. He was the founder of the firm of Jordan Brothers and continued active in its conduct until his death, February 20, 1910.

Arthur J. Jordan acquired his education in the public schools of Sioux Falls and the Sioux Falls Baptist University, graduating from the latter institution in 1901. Two years later he formed a partnership with his father and they established a planing mill which they operated under the name of Jordan Brothers. This name it still retains, although Arthur J. Jordan has been the sole proprietor since the death of his father. He has built up a large and profitable business and is held in high respect in business circles.

On the 10th of August, 1905, at Milwaukee, Wisconsin, Mr. Jordan was united in marriage to Miss Grace A. Fischer, who passed away March 8, 1911, leaving three children: Martin Fischer, Arthur J., Jr., and William Henry. Mr. Jordan belongs to the Dacotah and the Elks Clubs. He is identified with the blue lodge in Masonry, belongs to the Knights of Pythias and gives his political allegiance to the republican party. He is a young man of ability, ambition and enterprise, qualities which form an excellent foundation upon which to build success.

REX A. JOYCE

Rex A. Joyce, who is engaged in the undertaking and embalming business at Hot Springs, was born in St. Louis, Missouri, November 21, 1889, a son of James W. and Mary E. (Adams) Joyce. The father's birth occurred at Brownley, Kent County, England, and the mother was born in New York state at Dexter, near Watertown. When about fourteen years of age James W. Joyce came to the United States. He first settled in New York, but soon afterward went to St. Louis, Missouri, and in 1890 removed to Hot Springs, establishing what is now the Joyce Undertaking Parlors. He continued in the business until his death, which occurred July 1, 1911. After locating in Hot Springs, however, he conducted a furniture business in connection with the undertaking establishment for a number of years. He filled the office of county coroner for a number of terms and was a well-known and highly respected citizen of his community. His widow still makes her home in Hot Springs. In the family were two children, but the elder died in infancy.

Rex A. Joyce attended the public schools of Hot Springs and the Boyles Business College at Omaha, Nebraska. After studying embalming at the Williams Institute at Kansas City he assisted his father in the business until the latter's death and then took charge of the business, which he has since successfully conducted. He is accorded a liberal patronage and he devotes his entire time thereto. The business is conducted in buildings which were erected by the father and the equipment is complete and modern. He carries a large line of caskets and undertakers supplies and in all of his dealings is thoroughly reliable. He is also a landowner in the county and state and owns city property in Hot Springs.

On the 8th of June, 1912, Mr. Joyce was married to Miss Merial M. Chappell, who was born in South Dakota near Pierre, a daughter of Rev. E. S. Chappell, a Methodist Episcopal minister now located in Bellingham, Washington, being manager for the Bellingham district of the Washington Children's Home. His wife is a native of England.

Mr. Joyce gives his political allegiance to the democratic party but has never sought nor desired public office. He is well known in fraternal circles, belonging to the Masonic lodge at Hot Springs, of which he is the secretary, the Independent Order of Odd Fellows, the Modern Woodmen of America and the Yeomen. He is likewise a member of the South Dakota Undertakers' Association and thus keeps in touch with everything that is of interest or value to his line of business. He is likewise a member of the Commercial Club of Hot Springs and gives a helpful cooperation to plans and measures for the general good. His fellow townsmen recognize in him an enterprising young business man and his social qualities have made him popular with many friends.

ELMER R. JUDY

Among those who are active in controlling and directing financial interests in South Dakota is E. R. Judy, president of the Forestburg State Bank. In the town where he now resides, he is widely known, for it was there that he was born on the 8th of August, 1885, representing one of its old families. His father, Morris K. Judy, was a native of Ohio, born near Washington Court House, that state. He became one of the pioneers of Sanborn County, South Dakota, where he settled on a homestead claim in 1881, eight years before the admission of the state into the Union. He became one of the county's most highly respected and prosperous citizens. Coming to the state with scarcely a dollar and walking from Yankton to what is now Forestburg, he advanced steadily in a financial way until he was recognized as one of South Dakota's foremost farmers and stockmen, owning a splendidly improved tract of land of fourteen hundred acres, equipped with all modern accessories and conveniences. His death occurred September 22, 1909, when he was fifty years of age, while his wife, who bore the maiden name of Isabel M. McGillvray, and is a native of Vermont, still resides in Forestburg.

Elmer R. Judy supplemented his public-school training by study in the Dakota Wesleyan University and such was his early experience and such the standing that he gained, that he was appointed assistant superintendent of the South Dakota Agricultural Exhibits at the Louisiana Purchase Exposition in St. Louis in 1904. He was with his father upon the home farm until 1907, when he became one of the organizers of the State Bank of Forestburg and in 1913 was elected to the presidency. He has contributed much to the successful conduct of this institution, making it one of the important and indispensable business features of the town. Aside from this he is still largely interested in farming lands and in the breeding of registered cattle and his broad experience and progressive methods enable him to speak with authority concerning the best methods of developing land and caring for livestock. He also served as treasurer of the first Farnsworth Cooperative Telephone Company.

On the 2d of June, 1909, Mr. Judy was joined in wedlock to Miss Clarinda A. Jeffery, of Miller, South Dakota, a daughter of William H. and Mary (Richards) Jeffery. Mr. Judy greatly enjoys touring with his motor car and also takes delight in travel by train. He is fond of outdoor sports and is an advocate of good roads. Fraternally he is a chapter Mason and an Odd Fellow and he has long been a recognized leader in republican circles in his part of the state, serving as a member of the state central committee in 1914. He believes in advancement and is actuated by the spirit of progress and enterprise along all those lines which affect the general interests of society. He is recognized as a young man of unusual promise and his record is already adding new luster to the honored name of his father. He is exceedingly active in the live-stock business and has done much to promote an interest in live-stock exhibits at the state fairs. He is also secretary of the Sanborn County Fair Association, of which he was one of the chief promoters.

OHN HERNDON JULIAN

John Herndon Julian, secretary and registrar of the University of South Dakota, was born in Warsaw, Indiana, May 19, 1886, a son of Paph and Felicia (Herndon) Julian, both of whom were born in Frankfort, Kentucky. The father is a minister of the Christian church. The mother passed away January 19, 1915. They had two children, the sister of our subject being Margaret, the wife of William E. Lattin, of Davenport, Iowa, head of the department of mathematics in the Davenport high school.

John H. Julian grew to manhood in the mountains of Kentucky, in the vicinity of Morehead and Corbin, and there attended the public schools until he was thirteen years of age. He then entered the high school of Frankfort, Kentucky, and in 1901 came to South Dakota. His parents preceded him here a year. He remained upon the Pine Ridge Indian reservation for one year and then entered the University of South Dakota at Vermillion as a student in the arts and science department, being graduated therefrom in June, 1907. During the summers of 1907, 1908 and 1909 he was a graduate student in the department of physics in the University of Chicago and was engaged during the winters of those years in teaching physics in the University of South Dakota, as immediately after graduation he was appointed instructor in that institution. He held that position for five years and in 1912 was made secretary and registrar of the State University of South Dakota, in which capacity he is now serving. He is systematic and methodical in his work and makes a study of the best methods to be pursued, seeking always the maximum efficiency.

Mr. Julian was married on the 24th of August, 1910, to Miss Elsie Sargent, a native of Akron, Iowa, and a daughter of E. W. and Abbie (Haskell) Sargent. Her father is a retired farmer living in Vermillion, South Dakota. While a resident of the Hawkeye state he founded the town of Akron. He is the owner of considerable farming land and is an esteemed citizen of Vermillion.

Mr. Julian is liberal in his political views and watches with great interest the events and developments that affect our civic life. He is active in church work, is a loyal member of the local Baptist church and for four years was superintendent of its Sunday school. His fraternal associations are with the Masonic order and he has been junior deacon in the blue lodge. While a student in the university he was popular among his fellows and honored by them with election to a number of offices. The same qualities of character that won him the liking and respect of his fellow students have gained for him the warm regard and esteem of those who are associated with him in his work as an official of the university.

GENERAL S. H. JUMPER

The name of General S. H. Jumper is inseparably interwoven with the history of Aberdeen. He was the first man who slept upon the townsite of the city and was the first actual settler there. From that day to this he has taken an active part in many projects and business enterprises which have had to do with the development and upbuilding of the city, with its adornment, its prosperity and its happiness. He is far separated from his birthplace — New Gloucester, Maine. His natal day was October 24, 1844, and his parents were John and Mary Jumper. His youthful days were spent in New England, where he acquired a public-school education. He was a youth of less than seventeen years at the time of the outbreak of the Civil war, and in 1861 he enlisted, his response to the country's call making him a member of Company K, Tenth Maine Infantry, with which he served until July, 1866, or for fifty-six months. Four of his brothers were also soldiers of the Civil war and their combined service covered twenty-one years. Three are still living. Three of the brothers enlisted at the first call for men to serve for three months, which time, it was then believed, would see an end of the war. They after reenlisted at the reorganization of regiments, and three of the brothers remained in the service for a year or more after the actual close of hostilities, being stationed in South Carolina during the troublesome reconstruction days. All participated in some of the most important and sanguinary engagements that marked the Civil strife. George Jumper, now of San Francisco, was a captain of cavalry in the First Maine Regiment and was twice in Libby prison. After his first incarceration he managed to escape, but was afterward again taken prisoner and remained until exchanged. General Jumper was advanced from one rank to another until at the time of his discharge he was serving as sergeant major of the Twenty-ninth Maine Regiment. He was on active duty throughout the entire period of the war.

After the close of hostilities S. H. Jumper turned to the west, making his way to Minneapolis, Minnesota, where he acted as manager of the Nicollet House for about fourteen years, or from 1867 until 1881. In the latter year he removed to Aberdeen and has since been identified with the city. Dakota territory, as it then was, was a largely unsettled and undeveloped district, and General Jumper was the first man to spend a night upon the present site of Aberdeen and the first to take up a permanent residence there. He also established the first general store and was in the mercantile business for two years, but on the expiration of that period he turned his attention to financial interests and in 1883 established the Farmers and Merchants Bank. In 1884 he organized the First National Bank, and was president of both institutions. Under President McKinley he became postmaster of Aberdeen and sold his banking business. He remained as postmaster for one term, was afterward assistant postmaster for a term, was then again appointed acting postmaster and is now once more serving as assistant postmaster. The growth of a city is no where more plainly indicated than in the increased business of the post office, and the business of the Aberdeen post office grew greatly during the years that General Jumper was connected with the position. On May 1, 1915, he resigned his position in the postal service after exactly seventeen years as postmaster and assistant and retired to private life. Aside from his official interests he has been president of the Home Building & Loan Association since its organization and he has filled several local offices. He was alderman of the city, and in 1890 was elected mayor of Aberdeen for a two years' term, during which he gave to the city a businesslike and progressive administration. The title by which he is generally known came to him as the result of his service as brigadier general of the state militia from 1889 until 1893.

General Jumper was united in marriage in 1875 to Miss Ella M. Hilt, of Maine, and they have an extensive acquaintance in Aberdeen, their friends being numbered by the score. General Jumper is well known in connection with fraternal organizations. He belongs to the Masonic lodge, to the chapter and commandery and upon him have been conferred some of the highest offices within the gift of the state organizations of the order. He has been grand high priest of the grand chapter and eminent grand commander of the grand commandery, and he has a very extensive acquaintance among the craft of South Dakota. He has likewise crossed the sands of the desert with the nobles of the Mystic Shrine and now belongs to Yelduz Temple, A. A. O. N. M. S. He belongs to Robert Anderson Post, No. 38, G. A. R., of which he has been commander several times, and he also holds membership with the Benevolent and Protective Order of Elks and the Knights of Pythias. His political allegiance is given to the republican party and his loyalty and citizenship none question, for his public spirit has been again and again demonstrated in many connections and his efforts have been of essential value and benefit to city and state.

OTTO L. KAAS

Otto L. Kaas, actively engaged in the practice of law at Britton, his ability having gained for him a large and distinctively representative clientage, was born at Grand Meadow, in Mower County, Minnesota, February 14, 1877, a son of Johannes J. and Christine (Lundberg) Kaas. The father was born near Christiania, Norway, in 1835, and in Stockholm, Sweden, in 1864, was married, the lady of his choice being a native of that city, born in 1844. Six years after their marriage, or in 1870, they came to the United States, settling at Grand Meadow, Minnesota, where Mr. Kaas was employed as a clerk and bookkeeper. In his native country he had been an army officer. In 1883 he removed to Dakota territory and secured a homestead claim in Marshall County in 1884, after which he gave his attention to general agricultural pursuits for a number of years but retired from that life twenty-two years ago. In politics he was always a republican until 1892, when he was elected, county auditor of Marshall County on the populist ticket. He belonged to the Lutheran church and in that faith passed away in 1904. To him and his wife, who is still living, were born sixteen children, of whom four survive, as follows: Otto L., of this review; Therese, who gave her hand in marriage to Ole J. Johnson, a farmer residing at Staples, Minnesota; Elmer who was the first white child born in Marshall County, this state, and is employed in a bank in Stanley County; and Emily, who is employed as clerk in a store at Veblen, South Dakota.

After acquiring a common-school education Otto L. Kaas became a student in the St. Paul College of Law. He was elected register of deeds of Marshall County in 1898, serving for four years, and while acting in that capacity he devoted the hours which are usually termed leisure to preparation for the bar, being admitted to practice in 1905, in which year he immediately entered upon the active work of the profession. In 1906 he was elected states attorney and filled that position for four years. In 1910 still higher political honors came to him in his election as representative to the state legislature, in which he served for one term. Upon his retirement from that office, he resumed the practice of law, in which he has since continued actively, and his ability to handle intricate legal problems has brought to him a large and growing clientage. He also has extensive landed interests, having made judicious investments in property which now return to him a gratifying annual income.

On the 13th of June, 1900, Mr. Kaas was united in marriage to Miss Mildred E. Miller, her father being James E. Miller, a retired agriculturist. To them has been born a son, Durward O., whose natal day was June 11, 1907.

Mr. Kaas has always been a republican in his political views and has taken an active interest in political work throughout his entire life. As a Mason he is connected with the blue lodge, the chapter, the consistory and with the Mystic Shrine at Aberdeen, and he is now serving for the second term as master of the lodge at Britton. He also belongs to the Elks Lodge No. 1046 at Aberdeen. His religious belief is that of the Lutheran church, while his wife holds membership in the Presbyterian church. They are highly esteemed as people of sterling worth, their many good traits of heart and mind establishing them in a high position in social circles where character and intelligence constitute the passports to good society.

RALPH F. KAMMAN

Ralph F. Kamman, cashier of the Bank of Spearfish, has been identified with that institution for a number of years, entering the bank as messenger and working his way tidily upward to his present position of responsibility. He was born at Central City, South Dakota, August 15, 1888, and is a son of Chris H. and Eleanor M. (Kleine) Kamman, who were natives of Germany and Kankakee, Illinois, respectively. The father was brought to the new world when two years of age and was reared to manhood in Kankakee, Illinois. He thence went to Minneapolis, where he was employed in the Washburn Crosby flour mills. Removing still farther west, he engaged in mining in the Black Hills. He afterward became foreman in the De Smet mill at Central City, now a part of the Homestake properties, and continued in that connection for about twelve years. He then removed to a farm near Sundance, Wyoming, and remained there for nine years, after which he arrived in Spearfish in the fall of 1900, taking up his abode there in order that his children might enjoy the benefit of education in the schools of that place. The mother and the family resided in Spearfish, making their home there while the father engaged in mining. He is now superintendent of the Pahasa Mining Company at Hill City. He served as clerk of the courts in Crook County, Wyoming, and as assessor for two terms and made a most creditable record in office by his prompt and faithful discharge of the duties devolving upon him. In the family were two children, the daughter being Mildred E., who is a graduate of the State Normal School at Spearfish and is now attending the University of Colorado at Boulder, specializing in library work.

The son, Ralph F. Kamman, attended the public schools at Sundance, Wyoming, for three years and afterward spent a year in the public schools of Spearfish and two years in the Normal Training School. He was then a student in the Normal School at Spearfish for three years and for four months attended the School of Mines at Rapid City. At the age of eighteen years, he was employed in a drug store at Spearfish, devoting his vacation periods to that work for about two years. It was later that he attended school at Rapid City for four months and at the end of that time he entered the Bank of Spearfish as messenger and general assistant. His fidelity and capability won him promotion and he was made bookkeeper and was promoted to the cashiership of the bank on the 13th of June, 1911, since which time he has served in that capacity. He has likewise been treasurer of the Lawrence County Fair Association for three years and is president of the Business Men's Club of Spearfish, serving for a second term. He is a most progressive and enterprising young man and his efforts as president of the club are contributing to the development and improvement of business conditions in his city.

Fraternally Mr. Kamman is connected with the Masonic lodge, in which he is serving as senior warden; with the Royal Arch Chapter as high priest; with the commandery, in which he is recorder; and with the Mystic Shrine. He is a member of the First Congregational church of Spearfish and in these associations are found the principles which guide his life and govern his conduct. In his political views he is a republican, but while he keeps well informed on the questions and issues of the day, he has never sought nor desired public office.

JOHN T. KEAN

J. T. KEAN, of Woonsocket, Sanborn County, one of the able and prominent members of the bar of South Dakota, has been an important factor in public affairs, having served as lieutenant governor of the state and in other offices of trust and responsibility, and being particularly deserving of representation in this history of the commonwealth with whose affairs he has been so intimately identified.

John Taylor Kean is a native of the Badger state, having been born in Whitewater, Wisconsin, on the 11th of March, 1857, a son of John V. and Phoebe S. (Taylor) Kean, the former of whom was a carpenter by trade and vocation, having been one of the pioneers of Wisconsin, where he took up his residence in the territorial epoch, having removed thither from the state of Pennsylvania. Both he and his wife are now deceased, and of their six children two are living at the present time. The subject completed his preliminary educational discipline in the public schools of Monroe, Wisconsin, and early manifested a strong predilection for literary pursuits and public speaking, while his ambition to acquire a thorough education led him to put forth every effort to secure the funds with which to pursue his professional studies. In 1876 he entered the law department of the University of Wisconsin at Madison, where he was graduated as a member of the class of 1877, and thereafter he completed a post-graduate course in the National Law School in Washington, D. C, this being in 1883. Owing to his financial position he was compelled to seek other employment for a time before entering upon the practice of law, and thus worked in the sawmills and shingle mills of Wisconsin and at whatever else came to hand, ever having a high appreciation of the ability of honest toil, in whatever field of endeavor. In 1880 Judge Kean located at Lake Mills, Iowa, where be initiated his independent professional career. From 1882 to 1884, inclusive, he was employed in the offices of the war department in Washington, and in the spring of 1884, he came to South Dakota and took up his residence in Woonsocket, where he resumed the practice of law, soon gaining distinctive prestige through his ability and ambitious effort in his chosen profession. He is well grounded in the science of jurisprudence, familiar with the minutiae of the law in its various branches and over showing facility in his recourse to precedents, while he is known as a strong advocate and conservative counsel, invariably giving careful preparation to every case and having exceptional strength as an advocate before a jury. He has a large and important practice and is one of the leading members of the bar of the state, while he also has extensive and valuable real-estate interests. He is an able public speaker, graceful in diction and pleasing in address, and he has taken a prominent part in the various political campaigns, in which he has proved an able exponent of the principles and policies of the Republican party, while he is also frequently called upon to deliver public addresses in other lines, his services being thus in requisition almost invariably on the occasion of public observances of the Fourth of July and Memorial Day. In 1890 he was elected county judge of Sanborn County, and remained in tenure of this office for two years, his rulings being wise and impartial and never meeting with reversal in the higher tribunals. He was the candidate of his party for the office of lieutenant governor in the election of 1898, was elected by a gratifying majority and was incumbent of the office for the two ensuing years. He was elected chief executive of the municipal government of Woonsocket in 1902 and guided its affairs with marked discrimination and genuine public spirit.

Fraternally he is identified with the Masonic order and the Society of the Sons of the American Revolution. On the 3d of April, 1884, Judge Kean was united in marriage to Miss Ressie F. Perry, daughter of Waldo G. Perry, of Vermont, who was for many years superintendent of the dead letter office in the national capital, in which city the marriage of the subject was solemnized. Mrs. Kean died April 17, 1903, at Palo Alto, California.

MAURICE KELIHER

Maurice Keliher, one of the prominent and enterprising stock growers and highly esteemed residents of Pennington County, was born on July 20, 1849, at Bangor, Maine, and while he was yet a child the family moved to near Harvard, Illinois, where the father took up land and engaged in farming. The old homestead now belongs to Mr. Keliher and is one of his most cherished possessions. On it he was reared to the age of eighteen, and near it in the little country schoolhouse he received his education. In 1867 he left the scenes and associations of his childhood and youth, and moved to Denver, Colorado, then a small place in a new country, but with the promise of its mighty growth and enterprise already showing plainly. After a short residence there he went to Montana and for a short time was engaged in freighting in that state, after which he returned to Denver and again followed freighting in partnership with his brother Michael, who was afterward killed by outlaws in Texas. They had a number of bull teams and carried on an extensive and profitable business, freighting between Denver and the Indian reservations and also between that town and Cheyenne. In 1877 Mr. Keliher went east to visit his parents and on his return to Cheyenne was married. He remained in that city until the fall of 1878. At that time freighting became unprofitable owing to the completion of the railroad, and Mr. Keliher determined to come to the Black Hills and turn his attention to raising cattle. He brought cattle with him and, locating on Spring creek, gave his whole time and energy to building up and expanding his business. To this enterprise he has adhered steadfastly ever since, and has made a decided success of it, becoming one of the most extensive stock growers in this part of the country, and producing stock of high grades. His home is at Rapid City where he has a handsome residence of modern style and furnished with every consideration for the comfort and enjoyment of its inmates.

On November 24, 1877, Mr. Keliher was married, at Cheyenne, Wyoming, to Miss Eleanora Walsh, a native of Ireland who came to the United States with her parents in her childhood. They have five children, Frank, Eleanora, Margaret, Morse and Miriam. Mr. Keliher belongs to the Masonic order and the United Workmen, holding his membership in both at Rapid City. In politics he is an unwavering and active Republican, but has always declined public office.

WILLIAM FRANKLIN KELLER, M. D.

Dr. William Franklin Keller, a leading and successful representative of the medical fraternity of South Dakota, has practiced continuously for many years in Sioux Falls, and has also acted in the capacity of city health officer since 1908. His birth occurred in Reimersburg, Pennsylvania, in 1866, his parents being William and Catharine Keller. In the acquirement of an education, he attended the public schools of his native town and also Rimersburg College.

After completing his education in Pennsylvania, he came west, locating in Nebraska, where hf followed the drug business until 1891 when he came to South Dakota, making his home in Sioux Falls. In 1893 he entered the University of Illinois and received the degree of M. D. from the University of Nashville, Tennessee, in 1897. Since that time, he has followed the practice of general medicine in Minnehaha County, South Dakota, his practice having become extensive and highly successful. He has served two years, 1912-1914, as physician of Minnehaha County and for a similar period has been physician of the state penal and deaf-mute institutions. In 1908 he was made city health officer of Sioux Falls, which position he still holds, and in which connection his labors have been of far-reaching benefit and recognized value. Dr. Keller is a member of the Missouri Valley Medical Association, also the South Dakota Medical Association and the Seventh District, represents several of the old-line insurance companies, and is also United States pension examiner at Sioux Falls. In 1906, at Sioux Falls, Dr. Keller was united in marriage to Miss Bertha Stringham, a daughter of N. E. Stringham. His political allegiance has always been given to the democratic party, and his religious faith is that of the Episcopal church.

Fraternally he is identified with the Masons, having attained the thirty-second degree of the Scottish Rite and also belonging to the Mystic Shrine. He is popular in fraternal, social and professional circles of his adopted city and has gained recognition as one of its leading and representative residents.

CHARLES M. KEELING, M. D.

The attractive town of Springfield, Bon Homme County, has in Dr. Keeling an able physician and surgeon and one whose prestige and success place him among the representative members of the medical profession in the state. The Doctor was born in Bartholomew county, Indiana, on the 16th of February, 1863, being a son of William W. and Mary R. (Speirs) Keeling, all of whose five children are yet living, namely: John R., who is a merchant at Shelbyville, Indiana; William F., who is engaged in the drug business at Nemaha, Nebraska; Charles M., who is the subject of this sketch; Dr. James E., who is a practicing physician at Sulphur Hill, Indiana; and Marian R., who is the wife of Edward L. Culver, of Omaha, Nebraska.

The father of the subject is a representative of one of the pioneer families of Indiana, having been born in that state in the year 1830, and being there reared to maturity. As a young man he prepared himself for the practice of medicine, entering the Eclectic Medical College of Cincinnati, Ohio, and being there graduated about 1858. He entered upon the practice of his profession in Indiana, where he remained until 1863, when he went to Nemaha, Nebraska, where he continued the work of his noble profession very successfully, becoming one of the leading citizens of that section. In 1863 he was elected a member of the Nebraska legislature, and shortly after the expiration of his term of office he returned to Indiana, locating at Sulphur Hill, where he continued in the active practice of medicine about a quarter of a century, being recognized as one of the leading physicians of that section. About 1890, he returned to Nemaha, Nebraska, where he has since maintained his home and where he still devotes more or less attention to his profession, though well advanced in years. He is a Democrat in his political proclivities, and his religious faith is that of the Methodist Episcopal church. Mary R. Speirs was born in Indiana in 1840 of Scotch parents.

Dr. Charles M. Keeling was an infant at the time of his parents' removal to Nemaha, Nebraska, and was about three years of age when they returned to Indiana, and thus he secured his early educational training in the public schools of Sulphur Hill, that state. At the age of sixteen years, he was matriculated in Hartsville College, at Hartsville, Indiana, where he continued his literary studies for some time. He was thereafter engaged in teaching in the public schools for five years and then began reading medicine under the effective direction of his honored father, thus continuing until 1885, when he entered the Medical College of Indiana, at Indianapolis, where he was graduated as a member of the class of 1887, receiving his coveted degree of Doctor of Medicine. Soon after his graduation he came to South Dakota and took up his abode in Springfield, where he has since continued in the practice of his profession, being known as a skilled physician and surgeon and having a large and constantly increasing business. In 1899 he completed a postgraduate course in Chicago, while in 1901 he took another post-graduate course in New York City, ever aiming to keep in touch with the advances made in the sciences of medicine and surgery and thus the more thoroughly fortifying himself for his practical work in connection with the same. He is a member of the State Medical Society, of which he was president in 1901, and is also identified with the American Medical Association.

In politics he gives his allegiance to the Democratic party and fraternally he holds membership in the lodge and chapter of the Masonic order and in the adjunct order of the Eastern Star; also, the lodge and Daughters of Rebekah. Independent Order of Odd Fellows, the Modern Brotherhood, and the Knights of the Maccabees, and the Modern Woodmen of America.

On the 22d of March, 1882, Dr. Keeling was united in marriage to Miss Viola E. Osborn, of Sulphur Hill, Indiana, and they have one child. Era. Mrs. Keeling's father, John C. Osborn, was born in 1840, in Ohio, and was a school teacher. He died in 1866. The mother, whose maiden name was Roanna Hawkins, was born in Indiana in 1841.

WILLARD N. KEEN

Business enterprise at Garden City finds a worthy representative in Willard N. Keen, who is proprietor of a general store, occupying a modern building, which he erected in 1910. Probably every state in the Union has furnished. its quota of citizenship to South Dakota and among those who have come from Pennsylvania is Willard N. Keen, who was born in the Keystone state on the 15th of November, 1863, his parents being George M. and Mary J. (Jenkins) Keen. The family arrived in South Dakota in 1882, settling in Clark County, where the father secured a homestead on section 29, Eden township. He at once began to clear and develop the land and for nineteen years carried on general farming there. His efforts were attended with good success, for his methods were practical, his enterprise unfaltering. The years brought him the prosperity which is the merited reward of persistent and honorable labor and he and his wife are now living retired in Garden City, having a competence sufficient to supply them with all of the comforts and some of the luxuries of life.

In the public schools of Pennsylvania Willard N. Keen pursued his studies and afterward assisted his father. Later he engaged in railroad work until he came to the west with the others of the family when a young man of nineteen years. He also took up a preemption claim, covering the southwest quarter of section 32, township 117, range 56, in Clark County and a tree claim, covering the northwest quarter of section 30, township 117, range 56. In accordance with the property laws, he at once began to develop his land and remained thereon for nineteen years, at the end of which time the property bore no resemblance to the wild and undeveloped tracts which came into his possession when the government gave over the title to him. At the end of that period, he rented his farm and opened his present place of business at Garden City, but since that time he has disposed of his lands. He embarked in general merchandising with but a small stock, but with the settlement of the county and the increasing popularity of his establishment his trade has steadily grown and he has been forced to add to his stock to meet the demands of the increased patronage. Today he carries one of the largest lines of general merchandise in his part of the state and in 1910 he erected his present substantial business block in Garden City, of which he occupies the first floor and basement and also a large wareroom containing the reserve stock. His trade is now extensive and is growing year by year. He has ever realized the fact that satisfied patrons are the best advertisement and he has made earnest effort to please his customers, giving them the quality of goods desired at reasonable prices. His cooperation has been sought along other lines and he is now a stockholder in the Opera House, in the Garden City Telephone Company, in the Garden City State Bank and in the County Fair.

On the 24th of November, 1886, Mr. Keen was joined in wedlock to Miss Ella B. Spencer, a native of New York state and a daughter of A. A. and Eleanora Spencer. Her father was also one of the old-time settlers of Clark County, arriving in this part of the state in 1883, but both he and his wife are deceased. Mr. Keen is a democrat in his political views, but without ambition for office. Fraternally he is connected with the Masons and he enjoys a game of baseball, finding interest and recreation therein. He may well be called one of South Dakota's promising business men. He recognizes the opportunities and the possibilities of the northwest and works for the benefit of his community as well as for the advancement of his individual interests. His plans meet the existing conditions in a way that utilizes them to the best advantage and his work has, indeed, been a potent force in public progress.

HENRY KEETS

Henry Keets is the president of the American National Bank at Spearfish and has other business interests which to some degree claim his time and attention. His activities have always been directed along lines in which the public has been the beneficiary, while he has promoted his individual success. He has passed the seventy-fifth milestone on life's journey but still remains active in business and his sound judgment and experience are proving elements in the success of his different interests. He was born in New York City, December 30, 1839, a son of John and Mary (Kada) Keets, the former a native of England, while the latter was born in the state of New York, of German parentage. When a young man John Keets came to the United States and when in New York was a skipper on an old-time sailing vessel. After many years devoted to that life he was lost at sea. His wife passed away in New York City.

Henry Keets, their only child, attended the public schools of the eastern metropolis and at the age of fifteen years began working for others on farms. He went to Kentucky and in that state enlisted as a private in the First Kentucky Cavalry, in which he served for two years and eleven months, becoming a noncommissioned officer. He was mustered out at Lebanon, Kentucky, after rendering valuable and loyal service to the Union. He was never wounded nor confined in a hospital and yet he was often in the thickest of the fight. When the war was over, he enlisted in the regular army, becoming a member of the Fifth United States Cavalry, with which he served for nearly four years.

When his military experience was over Mr. Keets engaged in the stock business in Wyoming, near Cheyenne, continuing in that business until 1904. At about that time he became connected with an electric plant at Redwater, South Dakota, where he built a hydraulic plant and transmitted power to Deadwood and Lead. He sold the plant to the General Electric Company about 1909 and since that time has been occupied with his duties as president of the American National Bank. He is the owner of stock farms and fruit farms in South Dakota and from his property interests derives a substantial annual income but devotes the greater part of his attention to his banking interests.

In September, 1877, Mr. Keets was united in marriage to Miss Emma Leppla, who was born in Boone County, Iowa, a daughter of Jacob and Mary (Zella) Leppla, both of whom were natives of Bavaria, Germany. They became early residents of Iowa and afterward removed to Spearfish, South Dakota, where the father lived in practical retirement from business, both he and his wife spending their remaining days in Spearfish. To Mr. and Mrs. Keets were born six children: Florence, the wife of Dr. Bernard Bettelheim, who is engaged in sheep growing near Spearfish; Charles, who married Miss Maud Bell and resides in Arizona, where he is engaged in mining; and four children who have passed away.

Mr. Keets is a Mason and has advanced from the blue lodge to the Shrine. He attends the Congregational church and in politics is a democrat. He has held various local offices, including that of mayor of the city of Spearfish, and his efforts have been a potent element in advancing those interests which are a matter of civic virtue and civic pride. He stands for progress at all times and in every connection, and his life work has been an element of advancement in the various localities in which he has made his home.

ALBERT JACKSON KEITH

Albert Jackson Keith, a successful representative of the legal fraternity in Sioux Falls, has here practiced his profession continuously since 1900. His birth occurred in Hamilton, New York, on the 5th of June, 1877, his parents being Hosmer Hale and Mary (Spear) Keith. The first representative of the family in this country came from Scotland on the Mayflower. Albert J. Keith, who was a little lad of six years when his parents took up their abode in Sioux Falls, South Dakota, in 1883, acquired his education in this city and was graduated from Sioux Falls College in 1894. Subsequently he pursued a classical course in the University of Chicago and then prepared for a professional career in the University of Minnesota, being graduated from the law department of that institution in 1900. He was admitted to the bar in the same year and opened an office in Sioux Falls, having since practiced in the United States and state courts. His practice is extensive and of an important character. He is remarkable among lawyers for the wide research and provident care with which he prepares his cases. At no time has his reading ever been confined to the limitation of the questions at issue. It has gone beyond and compassed every contingency and provided not alone for the expected but for the unexpected, which happens in the courts quite as frequently as out of them. On the 28th of June, 1900, at Sleepy Eye, Minnesota, Mr. Keith was united in marriage to Miss Iva Gress, a daughter of G. M. Gress. Their children are three in number, namely: Hale Gress, Granville Spear and Katharine.

In his political views Mr. Keith is an unfaltering republican, and fraternally he is identified with the Masons, belonging to the Knights Templar commandery and the Mystic Shrine, and holding the office of illustrious potentate. He has also attained the thirty-second degree of the Scottish Rite and likewise belongs to the Elks, the Country Club and the Dacotah Club, while his religious faith is that of the Baptist church. Mr. Keith is interested in all matters of progressive citizenship to the extent of giving his cooperation wherever his aid can be of avail, but he has little time for work outside of his profession, his practice having constantly grown in volume and importance. He is also the founder and president of the Credit Reference Company, of Sioux Falls, which is the credit rating guide for the merchants and professional men of the county, and is likewise president of a similar company at Sioux City, Iowa.

HOSMER H. KEITH

H. H. Keith, was born at North Brookfield, Madison County, New York, July 12, 1846, his father having been a farmer and of Scotch ancestry. Besides receiving instruction in the common schools, Mr. Keith was graduated at Whitestown Seminary and afterwards received the honorary degree of Master of Arts from Colgate University at Hamilton, New York. During his young manhood he not only worked on the farm, but, like many other energetic young men of his time, he also engaged in school teaching. He studied law for two years, and then entered the Law School at Albany, New York, graduating in 1870. He was admitted to the bar at a general term of the supreme court in New York in June, 1870, and has since then, first in New York and subsequently in South Dakota, been in the active practice of his profession. He came to Sioux Falls in the spring of 1883. At the election of officers for the proposed state of South Dakota, under the Sioux Falls constitution, he was elected judge of the circuit court of the second district. At the election in the fall of 1888, he was elected a member of the territorial legislature from the counties of Hanson, McCook and Minnehaha, receiving a majority of four hundred and ninety-eight votes over his competitor, J. T. Gilbert, who had been elected to the previous term by a majority of one hundred and sixty-five votes. Mr. Keith was elected speaker of the house of representatives and filled the position with marked ability. He took a prominent part in the division of the territory and the admission of the southern half as a state. He stands high as a public speaker and is always listened to with marked attention. As a lawyer he ranks among the best in the state. When he is employed in a case, his opponents know there is to be a contest from the beginning to the end. He is a sagacious trier of cases, a good advocate and when summoned to a court of last resort he is well equipped and able to make the best presentation of his case. As a citizen he is independent and enterprising and takes an active part in all public matters. For several years he was president of the Commercial Club and Business Men's League of his city.

Mr. Keith is a prominent member of the Baptist church, and is also well known in fraternal circles, belonging to Masonic blue lodge No. 5, the Scottish Rite consistory, the Mystic Shrine and the Benevolent and Protective Order of Elks, all at Sioux Falls. In politics he has always actively supported the Republican party. He was elected city attorney of Sioux Falls in 1901 and has since been retained in that office. On the 9th of August, 1870, he was united in marriage to Mary Katherine Spear, the daughter of Philitus B. Spear, D. D., of Hamilton, New York, and to them have been born three children, namely; Flora Belle, who was graduated from a ladies' seminary at Hamilton, New York; Edwin Spear, who graduated from Pillsbury Academy, Owatonna, Minnesota, and took two years in Chicago University, is now a successful merchant in Bremerton, Washington; Albert Jackson, who was graduated from Sioux Falls College and the law department of the University of Minnesota, is now practicing law with his father at Sioux Falls.

I. A. KEITH

I. A. Keith, the leading druggist of Lake Preston and a man of state reputation by reason of his connection with important public enterprises, was born in Rock County, Wisconsin, on September 20, 1847. His parents, Alonzo A. and Julia M. (McFarland) Keith, were natives of New York, and there lived until about the year 1845, when they moved to Rock County, Wisconsin, where the father entered land, developed a farm and became successful in agricultural pursuits. In 1882 he disposed of his interests in that state and came to South Dakota, locating at Lake Preston, near which place he took up a homestead and retired from active life. He died at his home in Lake Preston in the year 1895, leaving a widow and three children, the former still living at the advanced age of eighty-one. Alonzo Keith was a man of strict integrity and high repute, popular with all who knew him and for many years lived an earnest, consistent Christian life, as a member of the Congregational church, to which denomination his good wife also belongs. Of the four children born to this excellent couple, three are living, Irwin A., the subject of this sketch, Edgar P., a prominent real-estate dealer and large landowner of Algonia, Iowa, and Charles W., who is connected with a Chicago business enterprise; Herbert, the third in order of birth, died at the age of fourteen years.

The subject of this review was reared in Rock County, Wisconsin, grew to manhood on his father's farm and attended the public schools until fifteen years old, the training thus received being supplemented by a course of study in an academy at Allen's Grove and a commercial college at Janesville, Wisconsin. At the age of twenty he entered a drug store in Janesville, and after remaining four years in that city and becoming a proficient pharmacist, came west, stopping one year in Iowa, and in 1882 settled with his family at Lake Preston, South Dakota. In March of the latter year, he purchased a small pioneer stock of drugs, representing a value of two hundred and sixty-five dollars, and soon built up a lucrative business. Meanwhile, in 1882, Mr. Keith took up a tree claim, and later located a homestead, on both of which he proved up, and from which he has since received no small part of his income. He owns one tract of real estate, amounting to one hundred and sixty acres, adjoining Lake Preston, its proximity to the town adding greatly to its value, and he now has a beautiful and, in every respect, desirable home on this property.

Mr. Keith devoted his attention very closely to the drug trade until recently, since which time his son Herbert, a professional pharmacist and a graduate from the pharmaceutical department of State Agricultural College of South Dakota, has managed the business. Mr. Keith has been officially identified with the South Dakota Pharmaceutical Association since its organization, in 1886, and for ten years served as secretary of that organization and the state board of pharmacy, and for six years he has been a member of the state board of pharmacy, being at this time its president. In 1895 he assisted in organizing the Druggists' Mutual Fire Insurance Company of South Dakota, and has served as secretary of the same since that date, the success of the enterprise being largely attributable to his interest and able management. This company was organized by the leading druggists of the state and has its headquarters at Lake Preston, and carries all classes of commercial risks, having a large and well-distributed business in nearly every city and town in the state. It has saved its policy holders approximately seventy-five thousand dollars in premiums refunded, and has paid fire losses amounting to thirty thousand dollars. The cost to its members has been about fifty per cent, of existing insurance schedules.

The domestic life of Mr. Keith dates from 1872, on June 4th of which year he was wedded to Miss Addie C. Burke, of Rochester, New York, daughter of P. Y. and Miranda Burke, old and respected residents of that city. To Mr. and Mrs. Keith three children have been born, Minnie, Herbert, who has charge of his father's drug business, and Grace, all three at home.

Mr. Keith belongs to the Masonic fraternity and Ancient Order of United Workmen, and is a charter member of the Odd Fellows lodge at Lake Preston, which he has served in the highest official capacity within the gift of the organization. Religiously he is a Congregationalist, as is also his wife, both being members of the church at Lake Preston, besides being most liberal contributors. He has for many years been a member of the board of education and in 1897 represented the twenty-first senatorial district in the upper house of the state legislature, in which body he made an honorable record, serving as chairman of the senate appropriation committee and as a member of the committees on insurance and banking, education, cities and municipal corporations and public health, besides taking an active part in the general deliberations on the floor. In politics he is a Republican, casting his maiden vote for U. S. Grant in 1868. He was, however, identified with the Populist party for several years, being led to this action by reason of his views upon the financial question and other reform measures of that party. He is a political leader in Kingsbury County and is not only a power in local politics, but his influence as an organizer and campaigner is felt throughout a large section of the state.

MORRIS H. KELLY

Morris H. Kelly, who at the time of his death, which occurred on the 21st of December, 1904, was receiver of the land office at Aberdeen, was born in Indianapolis, Indiana, in the year 1849, of Quaker parentage. His father, John Kelly, was a farmer by occupation, making that pursuit his life work. He married Elizabeth Hunt and they became the parents of eight children. Good educational advantages were afforded the family and Morris H. Kelly, after attending the public schools, continued his studies in the Quaker Academy at Bloomingdale, Indiana. When a young man he left home and went to Farmer City, Illinois, where he engaged in the hardware business. Thinking that he would find still broader opportunities in the new but growing northwest, he came to South Dakota, moving a stock of goods to Ashton, where he arrived on the 3d of March, 1882. He opened the first hardware store in the town and conducted the business successfully until July, 1887, when he went to Aberdeen. There he joined the Western Farm Mortgage Company, of which he became treasurer. He was connected therewith for a number of years. Later he was made receiver of the land office and continued to acceptably fill that position to the time of his death.

Mr. Kelly was not only active in a business way, but also in connection with public affairs. He was interested in everything that pertained to civic progress and improvement and for several years did excellent service for the city as a member of the city council. He was also a member of the building committee at the time the Mitchell library was erected. He believed in the employment of each opportunity and in many ways, he demonstrated his devotion to the public good, even though he would derive no individual benefit therefrom.

In 1872 in Tuscola, Illinois, Mr. Kelly was united in marriage to Miss Bertha Glasgow, who was born in Charleston, Illinois, a daughter of Kimball Glasgow, a native of Hardin County, Kentucky, who removed to Charleston, Illinois, at an early period in the development of that place. He was extensively engaged in farming and stock-raising in that locality, being one of the leading representatives of agricultural interests there. He married Margaret Reat, of Ohio, and they were the parents of eight children. Mr. and Mrs. Kelly had a family of four children, namely: Mrs. A. W. Vodish; Margaret R.; John R., who is now a lieutenant in the United States army; and Herbert G., deceased.

Mr. Kelly voted with the republican party and was always ready to support his political position by intelligent argument. He stood very high in Masonic circles, was most active in the order and attained an honorary thirty-third degree, given only in recognition of valuable service to the craft. At one time he was grand commander of the grand commandery of the state. In his passing death removed one of the valued citizens of Aberdeen, for he was reliable and enterprising in business, loyal in citizenship, faithful in friendship and devoted to the welfare of his family.

HAMPTON RAY KENASTON, M. D.

Hampton R. KENASTON who is successfully engaged in the work of his profession in Bonesteel, Gregory County, was born near Elmwood, Cass County, Nebraska, on the 24th of March, 1870, and is a son of Dr. James and Caroline Kenaston, the latter being now deceased. They became the parents of twelve children, of whom eight were sons, and of the number ten are yet living. The ancestors of the Doctor in the agnatic line came from Scotland to America in the colonial epoch of our national history, the original orthography of the name having been McKenaston, and the prefix having been dropped by the American branch. At the outbreak of the war of the Revolution the grandfather of the subject was but eight years of age, his parents being at the time residents of Vershire, New Hampshire. His eldest brother was a member of the famous Boston "tea party," and, with others of the older brothers, rendered valiant service in the cause of independence, as a soldier in the Continental line. The Kenaston family followed the march of civilization westward through Ohio, Indiana, Illinois and Wisconsin, and the year 1855 found them in Warren County, Iowa, while the father of our subject served as a valiant soldier in the war of the Rebellion. He removed from Iowa into Nebraska, locating in Elmwood, Cass County, where he engaged in the practice of his profession, and where he passed the remainder of his life. The subject of this review secured his early educational discipline in the public schools of his home town and there remained until the death of his mother, in 1889, after which he accompanied two of his brothers to the Pacific coast, passing a year in Washington and Oregon, and returning home through the Canadian northwest. The Doctor then located in Butte, Boyd county, Nebraska, where, in the spring of 1891, he began the study of medicine under the able preceptorship of Dr. A. S. Warner, of that place: In 1893 he was matriculated in the Sioux City (Iowa) College of Medicine, where he continued his studies for one year, completing his technical course in the medical department of the U. S. Grant University, at Chattanooga, Tennessee, where he was graduated with honors, receiving his degree of Doctor of Medicine on the 22d of March, 1898. In the following month he came to South Dakota, and located in Bonesteel, Gregory County, where he at once began the practice of his chosen profession. He has been most successful as a general practitioner and has built up a large and representative professional business, while he has the confidence and high regard of the people of the community. In 1902 he received a certificate as a registered pharmacist, after examination before the state board of pharmacy, and has since conducted a drug store as a complement to and base of supplies for his professional work. When the Citizens' Bank of Bonesteel was incorporated in May, 1902, the Doctor was one of its incorporators and was chosen a member of its directorate, while in May of the following year he was elected vice-president of the institution. In 1902 he was appointed local surgeon for the Chicago & Northwestern Railroad. In the autumn of 1903, he took a postgraduate course in the New York Polyclinic medical school and hospital, in New York City. In 1900 Dr. Kenaston was appointed vice-president of the Gregory County board of health, and the following year was made superintendent of this board, which incumbency he still retains. He is a stanch advocate of the principles of the Republican party, and upon the organization of Gregory County was elected coroner, in which office he has ever since continued to serve efficiently. He is a member of the South Dakota State

Medical Society and of the American Medical Association, while on February 20, 1904, he was appointed a member of the national auxiliary congressional and legislative committee of the latter association.

He is identified with the Masonic fraternity. The Doctor has an especially well-equipped office, in which is found a fine sixteen-plate X-ray machine and several other electrical instruments. He is essentially a self-made man, having depended entirely upon his own efforts and resources in securing his education. He has ever been foremost in lending his support to those measures and enterprises which have for their object the enhancement of the material prosperity of the community and the bettering of humanity. He is imbued with distinctive literary taste and has a splendid library. On the 8th of November, 1899, Dr. Kenaston was united in marriage to Miss Jean May McKee, who was graduated in the State Normal School at Clarion, Pennsylvania, as a member of the class of 1892, and who was prior to her marriage a teacher in the public schools of Butler, that state. Dr. and Mrs. Kenaston have one son, Hampton Ray, Jr., who was born on the 13th of October, 1902.

MICHAEL R. KENEFICK

Honored and respected by all, there is no man who has occupied a more enviable position in the financial and business circles of the southeastern section of South Dakota than Michael R. Kenefick, who passed away on the 11th of February, 1906. The place which he occupied in public regard was due not alone to the success he achieved but to the straightforward and honorable policy which he ever followed, to his courteous manner, his cordial nature and his friendly spirit. He ever recognized the good in others and was continually extending a helping hand to assist a fellow traveler on life's journey, finding opportunity for this in business and in other connections. From the organization of the First National Bank of Dell Rapids under its present form until his death he occupied the position of cashier and was prominently identified with banking interests elsewhere.

Mr. Kenefick was a Canadian by birth, born in the province of Quebec, near Laubinerre, in 1853. He was but a year old, however, when his parents crossed the border into the United States, settling upon a farm in Wisconsin, and his youthful days were spent amid the usual experiences of the farm lad of the middle west. His education was acquired in the public schools and when his books were put aside, he concentrated his energies upon the occupation to which he had been reared, being thus identified with agricultural interests until the accidental discharge of a gun caused him the loss of his left hand in 1868.

It was about that time that the family removed to Iowa and Mr. Kenefick took up the profession of teaching, which he followed in both Butler and Grundy counties. While thus engaged he devoted the evening hours to reading law and after mastering many of the principles of jurisprudence was admitted to the bar in Franklin County, Iowa, in 1876. Almost immediately afterward he removed to South Dakota and secured a claim in Moody County, upon which he lived for two years. In 1878 he came to Dell Rapids and formed a law partnership with Albion Thorne, with whom he remained until the fall of 1880. On the dissolution, of that partnership he joined A. H. Hall and when later in the same year the partnership with

Mr. Hall was discontinued, he became the professional associate of Hon. Robert Robertson, with whom he remained until February, 1881, when Mr. Robertson died. Mr. Kenefick was then alone in practice until the spring of 1884, when he turned his attention to the banking business, aiding in the organization of the Peoples Bank of Dell Rapids, of which he was chosen vice president. At a later date that institution was converted into the First National Bank and Mr. Kenefick was elected cashier, holding the position uninterruptedly to the time of his death. He contributed in large measure to the success of the institution. He familiarized himself with every phase of the banking business and gave earnest attention to the wishes, wants and needs of its patrons, whose interests he most carefully safeguarded. He also extended his efforts to banking activity elsewhere. In 1889 he became one of the organizers of the Colman State Bank, of which he was chosen president. In the winter of 1903 that bank was reorganized and converted into a national bank under the name of the First National Bank of Colman and Mr. Kenefick remained as its president until his death. He was one of the heaviest stockholders in the First National Bank of Dell Rapids and he was also the owner of large property interests in the city and throughout the surrounding country, having made judicious investments in real estate from time to time. He started out in life practically empty-handed but worked his way upward, his life record proving the force of determination, perseverance and laudable ambition.

On the 4th of September, 1881, Mr. Kenefick was united in marriage to Mrs. Coralynn A. Codington, of Medary, South Dakota, who in her maidenhood was Coralynn Chamberlin, a daughter of Colonel Enoch Chamberlin, of Waterloo, New York, who was a colonel of the Fifteenth Regiment of the New York State Militia. He was a prominent farmer of Seneca county who occupied the old home farm of his father, Tenbrooke Chamberlin, located about seven miles from Seneca lake. He died at Syracuse, New York, whither he had removed after retiring from active business life in 1859. His death occurred in 1889, when he had reached the age of eighty-one years. His daughter Coralynn had become the wife of the Rev. George S. Codington, a Congregational minister, who was one of the pioneer preachers of the northwest and for a time followed his holy calling in Illinois. From Sioux City, Iowa, he started with his young wife for South Dakota in 1872, driving from the former place to Medary, this state, with a single horse. The roads were crude and the country wild and the settlement in which they took up their abode was largely inhabited by the foreign element, containing only seven American families. A few years later the Rev. Codington passed away, and his widow subsequently became the wife of Michael R. Kenefick. To them was born a son, Robert E. Kenefick, who is now married and makes his home in Dell Rapids. Mrs. Kenefick has been prominently and actively identified with fraternal organizations, being a charter member of the Dell Rapids Eastern Star and first worthy matron of the order. She was also the first noble grand of the Rebekahs, which lodge was named "The Coralynn" in her honor, thus conferring upon her a very unusual distinction. She is one of the well-known pioneer women of South Dakota and a lady of refinement and culture who has made many warm friends.

Mr. Kenefick was a prominent figure in fraternal circles. He held membership with the Masons, Odd Fellows, Modern Woodmen and Canton Militant lodges of Dell Rapids and with the Elks lodge at Sioux Falls. He was a charter member of the Knights of Pythias, the Eastern Star and the Rebekahs and an honorary member of Dahlgren Post of the Grand Army of the Republic. His life was ever honorable and upright, and he never deviated from a course which he believed to be right between himself and his fellowmen. He stood for progress and improvement in public affairs and at various times did effective work for the benefit of his city. For several years he served as president of the council, was at various times a member of the board of education and in 1890 was chosen mayor of Dell Rapids, in which capacity he was continued by reelection until the spring of 1894. He possessed a most generous disposition and there are various residents of South Dakota who owe their start in life to his assistance and friendly interest. No trust reposed in him was ever betrayed in the slightest degree and he held friendship inviolable. He was a man of mild disposition, yet lacked not that determination which enabled him to pursue a course that he believed to be right and to carry forward to successful completion whatever he undertook. When death called him, proof of the high regard in which he was held was indicated in the fact that his funeral was the largest ever seen in this community. Many resolutions of respect were passed by the organizations with which he was identified. The resolutions of the Odd Fellows spoke of him as "a stanch Odd Fellow, a true friend and benefactor to many, and a kind and affectionate husband and father, who exemplified the teachings of the order by his tenderness in sympathy and his kindness to others in their grief."

CHARLES B. KENNEDY

CHARLES B. KENNEDY

Charles B. Kennedy, capitalist of Madison, has left the impress of his individuality in large measure upon the history of his county and state. There is no feature of pioneer life in the county with which he is not familiar and from the period of early settlement he has borne an active and helpful part in the work of general progress and improvement.

A native of Maine, Mr. Kennedy was born March 28, 1850, a son of Bartholomew C. and Oliva S. Kennedy, both descended from old New England stock, their ancestors on both sides having participated in the Revolutionary war. Like all New England farmers of those days, his parents were not possessed of wealth but were honest, hardworking people and their greatest desire was that their children should enjoy better advantages than had fallen to their lot. In early manhood Bartholomew C. Kennedy became a member of the Masonic fraternity, as had his father before him, and to the teachings of that organization he was greatly devoted. His wife was a member of the Freewill Baptist church.

Charles B. Kennedy acquired his early education in a log school house near his father's farm. The building was seated with long wooden benches, one row on either side with an aisle in the center. He was fifteen years of age when his father sold the old home farm in New England and purchased another five miles from Bangor, Maine. While living on the latter place Charles B. Kennedy walked four miles to attend high school, doing the chores night and morning. He afterward worked in a sawmill and earned sufficient money to enable him to attend the Pittsfield (Me.) Institute for one term. He afterward kept up his studies and at the same time taught school and later spent one term as a student in the Maine State College at Orono, working on the college grounds to help defray expenses, but ill health prevented him from completing his course. Soon afterward he was elected district superintendent of schools and held that position until his removal to the west.

On the 20th of May, 1873, Mr. Kennedy wedded Miss May Ella Williamson, a daughter of Judge Henry Williamson, of Maine. Coming to the Mississippi valley, several years were spent in Le Roy, Minnesota, where Mr. Kennedy taught high school for a year and was also deputy county superintendent of schools of Mower County. He then established the first newspaper published at that point, calling it the Le Roy Independent. After editing and publishing that journal for four years he sold out and on the 18th of March,

1878, came to Dakota territory, ninety miles beyond an operating line of railway. He secured a homestead and tree claim of three hundred and twenty acres, at which time there were but nine families in the county, located around the two lakes, Madison and Herman. There was not a white person west of them, save a few scattered settlers along the James and Missouri rivers, and those who had recently located in the Black Hills on the western border of the territory. They were indeed on the frontier. Not an acre of improved land nor a tree, building or sign of human habitation was in sight from their locality, nothing but wild prairie as far as the eye could reach. Deep Indian and buffalo trails led from every direction to the permanent spring of water on the land in what is now Lake Park in Madison. It was this spring of water that led Mr. Kennedy to locate on that particular tract and also the fact that the claim was only a half mile from the center of the county at the junction of two valleys which would naturally be sought by any railroads penetrating the county. His prescience found fulfillment, for both valleys have since been occupied by railroads.

After building a temporary sod house Mr. Kennedy began breaking prairie with a four-ox team and a little later built a small frame house and frame and straw stable, the lumber being drawn with ox teams from the nearest railway point about sixty miles distant. After two years a survey was made for an extension of the southern Minnesota division of the Chicago, Milwaukee & St. Paul Railroad to near the center of Lake County, the survey crossing Mr. Kennedy's land. On the south shore of Lake Madison there had sprung up a little village of about a dozen little buildings, which was called Madison, and which was the county seat. The railway survey passed nearly three miles north of the village of Madison, but passed through the village of Herman on the north shore of Lake Herman. Bitter rivalry sprung up between the two towns for the county seat and also the village of Wentworth, which had just been platted on the new railway survey, ten miles east of Herman, was bidding for the honor. It was then that Mr. Kennedy saw his opportunity. His three hundred and twenty acres of land was within a half mile of the center of the county, between two large lakes in a well-drained valley with plenty of pure water — an ideal location for a town site. He had little difficulty in convincing the people of Madison that he had the place to which they should move and negotiations were soon completed to that end. He immediately platted a town, which he named New Madison, and before the platting was completed the first building to be moved from the old town was on its foundation in the new one. The rival town of Herman, however, did not give up the claim to the county seat without a struggle and the builders of the new town of Madison realized that two towns, only two and a half miles apart in a sparsely settled country, could not continue long to exist. The New Madison people, therefore, made a proposition to the townspeople of Herman that they would give them in New Madison an equal number of lots and as well located as they possessed in Herman if they would move their buildings to New Madison. The Herman townspeople made a similar proposition to the residents of the other town and so little progress was made in that direction. At length a committee of six, three from each town, met to arbitrate. An all-night session ensued, without result, and other meetings followed which were equally un resultant. Then two other members were added to the committee from each town, but still without result. About this time the people of New Madison learned that three different buildings at Herman could be bought, and in a quiet way Mr. Kennedy and two others purchased these buildings and proceeded to move them, one at a time to New Madison, taking the smallest first. When the people of Herman saw what was being done, they rose en-masse, many armed with weapons of warfare, but the foresight of Mr. Kennedy and his associates had provided for the situation and a sheriff and several deputies were on duty. The people of the rival town saw that opposition would be useless and felt that this was only one building. What was their consternation when they saw the second and then the third building going to New Madison. They did not know what the end would be, nor how much property the New Madison forces had acquired and soon the two committees again met and Herman agreed to move to New Madison on the original terms, since which time the growth of the county seat has been uninterrupted.

In the winter of 1880-81 Mr. Kennedy represented Lake and seven adjoining counties in the territorial legislature and at that session secured the passage of an act vacating the old site of Madison and changing the name of the new town to New Madison and also designating it as the county seat of Lake County. He was likewise instrumental in securing the passage of an act establishing the State Normal School at Madison and he donated a twenty-acre site for the school — the site being now occupied by four large stone buildings, while the campus is covered with fine shade trees. The winter of Mr. Kennedy's service in the legislature was a memorable one in the history of the state. The snow lay to such depth that no trains ran throughout the winter, and at the close of his service in the legislature it seemed impossible for him to return to his home, a distance of seventy-five miles in direct line and about one hundred and fifty miles by rail. Mr. Kennedy and three others of the legislators, however determined to brave conditions and hired a team and sled, starting upon the trip. There was not even a track through the drifted snow, which was three feet or more all over the ground and in some of the ravines was from fifteen to twenty feet deep, so that much of the way they had to shovel and tread a track to get the team through. They could only make from five to ten miles in a day and night found the team jaded and the men practically exhausted. The next day they would send home the team and driver of the day before and hire a fresh team and after eleven days of most terrible hardships, much of the way through blinding snow storms, they reached Madison, two of the party stopping at Sioux Falls and one of them dying in a few days from exhaustion on this trip.

In the spring of 1881 Mr. Kennedy opened a real-estate and private banking business in Madison and in 1884 became one of the organizers of the First National Bank and its first president. In 1885, in connection with his brother, William F. Kennedy, he organized the Kennedy Brothers banking, farm loan and real-estate business, which in 1889 they merged into the Northwestern Loan & Banking Company, of which Charles B. Kennedy was president and his brother cashier and secretary. The increase in business demanded that the banking department be conducted separate from the farm loan and real-estate departments and in 1891 they organized the Madison State Bank, with the same officers as the Northwestern Loan & Banking Company, and both continued to do business in their several departments in their office building at the northwest corner of Egan Avenue and Sixth street. In 1909, desiring to retire from the banking business, a consolidation of the Madison State Bank with the First National Bank was affected and the former merged into the latter. The Northwestern Loan & Banking Company, however, continues to conduct a general farm loan and real-estate business and as president Mr. Kennedy directs its interests.

His largest business concerns, however, are his farms, which he began to buy when the county was first settled. He now owns forty farms and much of the land is improved. In this process he has developed raw prairies, breaking the sod, fencing, tiling, constructing buildings, planting trees and doing other work that has transformed the unsettled prairies to a state of high cultivation. During the past six years he has erected nothing but solid concrete buildings, having many of them on different farms throughout the county at the present time. He derives his greatest pleasure from the development of his farms in a permanent manner and along scientific lines. He has always had the greatest faith in the future of farm lands in South Dakota and has utilized every opportunity for the advantageous purchase of such. All days in his career have not been equally bright. In fact, he has seen the storm clouds gather, but he has managed to turn threatened defeat into victory and has lived to see the prevailing prices of five and ten dollars per acre, which existed during the financial panic from 1893 to 1897, advance until improved farms in the county today are worth usually one hundred and fifty dollars per acre. At the present time Mr. Kennedy is largely turning over his business to his sons, C. Le Roy and Dean M., yet he still keeps supervision over his interests and, as indolence and idleness are utterly foreign to his nature, could not be content without some business interests. His notable success may be attributed largely to his unfaltering diligence and his temperate habits, and now he has opportunity to enjoy rest if he so desires. In fact, he spends the winter months and indeed about half of his time at Los Angeles, California. He was for many years interested quite extensively in the raising of livestock and during that time was a member of the Dakota Fine Stock Breeders Association, of which he served as president for one term. He has been the leader in the erection of concrete buildings in his section of the state, being the first to follow this plan in Lake County and thus setting an example for others. He recognized the value of such buildings, which are cool in summer and warm in winter. Improving farms makes stronger appeal to him than anything else, and he rejoices in the change from crude nature to highly improved land.

In politics Mr. Kennedy is a progressive republican and has ever manifested a public-spirited interest in the vital questions and issues of the day. He has membership with the Masons and the Odd Fellows, being a member of Evergreen Lodge, No. 17, A. F. & A. M.; Cyrus Chapter, No. 26, R. A. M.; Madison Chapter, No. 6, O. E. S.; and Madison Commandery No. 20, K. T., all of Madison, and Oriental Consistory, No. I, Yankton; and El Riad Shrine Temple of Sioux Falls.

He has lived to witness notable changes throughout this section of the country. There were just nine families in Lake County at the time of his arrival and he went through the period of hardships and privations incident to settlement upon the frontier. At that period the nearest railroad was ninety miles from his home and all lumber for building purposes had to be hauled the entire distance with ox teams. Notable has been the change in methods of travel since that time, today Mr. Kennedy speeds over the country in a motor car and his progressive spirit is indicated in the fact that he was the owner of the first automobile in his part of the state. Mr. Kennedy may truly be called a self-made man. He started out in life without a dollar and even earned the money to pay the expenses of his education after leaving the common schools. He has never received a dollar by gift or inheritance from any source whatever. While his early advantages were limited, he has learned many valuable lessons in the school of experience and is today a broad and liberal-minded man, in touch with the world's advancement and exemplifying in his own life the progressive spirit of the age. He has always taken an active part in the welfare of this city which he helped to build, serving for many years as a member of the city council and for two years as its mayor. He has also been active in territorial and state matters, having been one of twelve or more men from different parts of the territory to spend several months in Washington, D. C, in the interest of the fight to secure in congress an act dividing the territory and admitting the two states, North and South Dakota. He was for several years chairman of the republican central committee of Lake County and a member of the state central committee, but in later years has been too much engrossed in business to give political matters much attention. In both political and religious views, he has been quite liberal, being strenuously opposed to blindly following bosses and self-constituted leaders in either line. He has never adopted a belief simply because some one else advocated it or because his ancestors were devotees of it, but has always exercised his own judgment and rejected those ideas or theories which have not appealed to his reason. Such is the history of one of Lake county's foremost citizens and a man not unknown as a leader in the state. Great, indeed, are the changes which have been wrought since he came to Dakota. Advantages were few at the time of his arrival, but opportunities were many for the ambitious, industrious and energetic man, and these he utilized until he stands today as one of the most prosperous residents of South Dakota, strong in his ability to plan and to perform, strong in his honor and his good name.

ROBERT F. KERR

Robert F. Kerr, the able and popular librarian of the State Agricultural College of South Dakota, at Brookings, is a native of the state of Indiana, having been born at Sugar Grove, Tippecanoe County, on the 12th of April, 1850, a son of Andrew J. and Nancy (Sayers) Kerr. His father was born in Franklin County, Ohio, and was a son of Samuel Kerr, who was a native of Chambersburg, Pennsylvania, being the sixth son of John Kerr, who was born in Northern Ireland, whence he emigrated to the United States in the colonial epoch of our national history, while he was a valiant soldier in the Continental line during the war of the Revolution, and he was numbered among the sterling pioneers of the old Keystone state, the family having been principally engaged in agricultural pursuits during the various generations. Andrew J. Kerr removed from Ohio to Tippecanoe County, Indiana, in company with an elder brother, being a lad of eleven years at the time, and he forthwith initiated his independent career and began to depend union his own resources. He continued to work by the month until his marriage to Miss Eliza Ward, two children being born of this union, — Jesse, who is a resident of Sioux Falls, South Dakota; and Josephine, who became the wife of John Sprague, her death occurring in Tippecanoe County, Indiana. After the death of his first wife Andrew J. Kerr married Miss Nancy Sayers, whose father was Robert Sayers, while the maiden name of her mother was McMillan. Robert Sayers was a native of Virginia. and the family name has been identified with the history of Indiana from the early pioneer days. The McMillan family is of Scotch-Irish extraction, and representatives of the same were patriot soldiers in the war of the Revolution. The mother of the subject died in 1864, and his father subsequently consummated a third marriage, having devoted his active life to agricultural pursuits in Tippecanoe County, Indiana, while he is now living retired in New Richmond, that state, having attained the venerable age of eighty-four years, while he still retains possession of his old homestead farm, which he purchased in 1848. Of his second marriage were born six children, concerning whom we incorporate brief record, as follows: Robert F. is the immediate subject of this review; Clara is the wife of James D. Thomas, who resides near Wingate, Indiana; Martha is the wife of William Bennett, who resides near New Richmond, that state; Susan H., who is a maiden, resides in Wingate, Indiana: Mary E. is the wife of J. L. Hayes, of Newtown, Indiana; and Emma died in early childhood. Of the third marriage were born three children, namely: Thomas L., who resides near Otterbein, Indiana; Hattie F., who is the wife of Daniel E. Storms, now secretary of state of Indiana: and Nettie, who is the wife of John Rust, residing near Otterbein, that state.

Robert F. Kerr received his preliminary educational discipline in the public school in the vicinity of his home, continuing his studies in this way until he attained the age of nineteen years, while during the summer vacations he gave his attention to farm work. At the age noted he began teaching school in Warren County, Indiana, being thus engaged during one winter term and then entering Wabash College, at Crawfordsville, Indiana, where he continued his studies one term, after which he again taught a term in the same school as before. In the spring of 1872, he was matriculated in Asbury College, now known as DePauw University, at Greencastle, Indiana, while he thereafter continued to teach and attend college at intervening periods, depending upon his pedagogic efforts for the securing of the funds to defray his college expenses. He was a student in the college mentioned during the entire sessions of the years 1876-7, completing the classical course and being graduated as a member of the class of 1877, with the degree of Bachelor of Arts. He then secured a position as a teacher in the public schools at Kentland. Indiana, and in the spring of 1878 was chosen county superintendent of the schools of Newton County, that state. In April, 1878, he went to Japan, where he was for eighteen months employed as a teacher in the provincial school at Hirosaki, returning to the United States in October, 1880, and during the year 1881 and a part of 1882 he was an assistant in the surveying of the route of the Clover Leaf Railroad through Ohio, Indiana and Illinois, knowing nothing of the details of the business at the time he joined the surveying party, but so rapidly accumulating technical knowledge that within nine months he was placed in charge of a corps of men. Thereafter he was assistant principal in schools at Blair, Nebraska, until 1885, when he came to Brookings, South Dakota, as principal of the preparatory department and teacher of history in the State Agricultural College. The school had been organized but one year previously, and he has thus been intimately identified with the work and history of this now nourishing and important institution, having known in a personal way every student who has been graduated in the college. In 1892 he went out of the institution, which was placed under different executive control at the time, but in January, 1899, he was recalled, assuming the principalship of the preparatory department and also being placed in charge of the library of the college, while for the past year he has had the supervision of the library and the college extension work. After leaving the college in 1892 Professor Kerr was for one year traveling representative of a leading book-publishing concern, while in 1894 he was elected county superintendent of schools for Brookings County, of which position he continued incumbent until he was again called to official duty in the college as noted. He received the degree of Master of Arts from DePauw University in 1880. In politics he has always given an uncompromising allegiance to the I Republican party, in whose cause he has taken a lively interest. He is a member of the directorate of the State Historical Society of South Dakota, and has made valuable contributions to the literature pertaining to the annals of the state.

Professor Kerr is an appreciative member of the Masonic fraternity, with which he has been identified since 1874, being identified with the lodge, chapter and commandery in Brookings and also with the El Riad Temple, Ancient Arabic Order of the Nobles of the Mystic Shrine, in Sioux Falls. He also holds membership in the local chapter of the Order of the Eastern Star, of which he is the past grand patron of the grand chapter of the state, while at the present time he is worshipful master of Brookings Lodge, No. 24, Free and Accepted Masons. He is now preparing to follow through the circle of the Scottish Rite degrees of Masonry. He is identified with the Ancient Order of United Workmen and was also a member of the Knights of Pythias until the lapse of the lodge organization in Brookings, while he is affiliated with the Beta Theta Pi college fraternity. His religious faith is that of the Methodist Episcopal church, and he is a steward of the local congregation and also a member of the board of trustees, taking an active interest in the various departments of the church work.

HARRY N. C. KIMBLE

Harry N. C. Kimble, a representative citizen and well-known public official residing in Mitchell, Davison County, is now serving for the second term as registrar of deeds, having been first elected in 1911 and having been reelected to the position in the fall of 1914. His birth occurred in Aurora, Illinois, on the 11th of December, 1874, his parents being James and Minerva Kimble, who came to South Dakota in 1882, when he was a lad of eight years. The father took up a homestead claim in Sanborn County and there successfully carried on agricultural pursuits for about fourteen years, on the expiration of which period he retired to enjoy his remaining days in well-earned ease. His demise occurred in May, 1912, but his widow survives and is well known and highly esteemed in her home community.

Harry N. C. Kimble began his education in the district schools and subsequently attended the high school at Mitchell, while later he pursued a commercial course in the Dakota Wesleyan University, being graduated from that institution with the class of 1900. He then turned his attention to agricultural pursuits and was engaged in farming and the stock business until elected to the position of registrar of deeds. In that capacity he made such a creditable record that he was again chosen for the position in the fall of 1914 and is therefore the present incumbent, discharging the duties devolving upon him in a most commendable and efficient manner. He owns some valuable property and is widely recognized as one of the prosperous and esteemed citizens of his county.

On the 17th of January, 1902, Mr. Kimball was united in marriage to Miss Harriett Priest, a daughter of Charles and Evelyn (Burnside) Priest, both natives of Iowa, who removed to South Dakota in 1883 and are now residents of Mitchell. Mr. and Mrs. Kimble have two children, James Kenneth, born May 20, 1904, and Charles Kenton, born September 16, 1906. The family are Protestants in religious faith,

Mr. Kimble is identified fraternally with the Masons, belonging to the blue lodge and the chapter, and he also holds membership in the Knights of Pythias, the Benevolent Protective Order of Elks and the Independent Order of Odd Fellows, being connected with both the subordinate lodge and encampment of the last named. He finds needed recreation in fishing, hunting, tennis, football and other outdoor sports. The period of his residence in this state covers about a third of a century and he has been not only an interested witness of its development but also an active participant in the work of upbuilding and progress.

CHARLES C. KING

Charles C. KING, is one of the representative citizens and honored business men of Scotland, Bon Homme County, where he has maintained his home since 1890, being president of the First National Bank of Scotland, succeeding the Bank of Scotland in 1903, one of the solid and popular monetary institutions of the state.

Charles Clark King is a native of the state of Illinois. having been born in the town of La Harpe, Hancock County, on the 7th of July, 1863, and being a son of Luranus F. and Laura (Andrews) King, both of whom were born and reared in Ohio, whence they removed to Illinois in an early day. In 1866 they removed to Polo, Ogle County, Illinois, the father there turning his attention to banking. The subject of this sketch secured his educational discipline of a preliminary sort in the public schools, being graduated in the high school at Polo, Illinois, as a member of the class of 1883. He then devoted one year to the reading of law, after which he was employed as a stenographer until 1887, when he removed to Duluth, Minnesota, and there engaged in the real-estate and loan business. In the following year he went to the city of Boston, Massachusetts, where he remained for two years as representative of the American Loan & Trust Company, of Duluth, and at the expiration of this period, in May, 1890, he came to South Dakota and took up his residence in Scotland, where he has ever since maintained his home. He here purchased a controlling interest in the Bank of Scotland, of which institution he has ever since been president. He is known as a careful and conservative executive and able financier and has the confidence and esteem of those with whom he has come in contact in either business or social relations. In politics Mr. King is a stalwart advocate of the principles of the Republican party, in whose cause he has ever shown a zealous interest, though never a seeker of political preferment for himself. He served as a member of the state executive committee of his party during the campaign of 1900 and at the time of this writing he is chairman of the Republican central committee of his county. He has held no elective offices save that of treasurer of the school district, of which he is now incumbent.

He and his wife are prominent and valued members of the Methodist Episcopal church, and fraternally he is an appreciative member of the Masonic order, in which he has attained to the thirty-second degree in the Ancient and Accepted Scottish Rite, being affiliated with Oriental Consistory, No. I, at Yankton, while he is also a member of the El Riad Temple of the Ancient Arabic Order of the Nobles of the Mystic Shrine, in Sioux Falls. On the 19th of February, 1896, was solemnized the marriage of Mr. King to Miss

Delia Robinson, daughter of A. F. Robinson, a respected citizen of Dixon, Illinois. Mr. and Mrs. King have one son, Robert R., who was born on the 27th of October, 1900.

JOHN HEREFORD KING

John H. KING, who is engaged in the real-estate, loan and insurance business in the city of Huron, Beadle County, and who is a distinguished member of the legal profession, is distinctively a western man and imbued with its self-reliant and progressive spirit. He was born at Salem, Henry County, Iowa, on the 3d of October, 1845, and is a representative of one of the sterling pioneer families of that state. He is a son of Samuel and Content (Verion) King, both of whom were birthright members of that noble organization, the Society of Friends, to whose faith they adhered throughout life, the father being a native of Pennsylvania and the mother of Georgia. They removed, with their parents, to Ohio about 1815, and after their marriage removed to Iowa in 1844, settling in Henry County, at Salem, and later moving to Cedar County, Iowa, where the father entered the land whereon West Branch now stands. The subject was reared on the old homestead farm, early beginning to assist in its work, while he also learned the trade of broom making under the direction of his father. His early educational advantages were such as were afforded in the common schools of the locality, and was supplemented by a three-months course in an academy conducted by Joel Beans, at West Branch, that state. He left school at the age of eighteen years and continued to work on the home farm until his marriage, at the age of twenty-one. He then, in 1866, located on a tract of land in Hardin County, Iowa, and engaged in farming on his own responsibility, breaking the greater portion of the ground himself and fencing the property, which was virgin prairie at the time when it came into his possession. In the meanwhile, he was employed as teacher in an adjoining district school for three winter terms. In the spring of 1869 he began the careful study of law at his home, and completed his technical reading under the direction of an able preceptor, Hon. H. L. Huff, of Eldora, Iowa, being admitted to the bar of Iowa in the winter of 1870, and located in Eldora, the county seat of Hardin county, where he initiated the active practice of his profession, and two years later he removed to Hampton, Franklin county, where he rapidly gained prestige in his profession, building up a large and lucrative legal business and being one of the leading lawyers of that section for many years. In 1877 he was elected to represent his district in the state legislature, said district comprising the counties of Franklin and Cerro Gordo, and he was chosen as his own successor in 1879, receiving large and gratifying majorities on both occasions. He took a very prominent part in the legislative proceedings and held the important position of chairman of the house committee on railroads during the eighteenth general assembly. At the time of the Civil War, he was most desirous of enlisting in defense of the Union, but his parents, being of the Quaker faith and thus opposed to warfare by principle and training, refused to permit him to become a volunteer. In July, 1880, he came to South Dakota and in the fall of that year laid out Chamberlain and became president of the town-site company, and soon removed there with his family. He was appointed postmaster in 1882 and became editor of the Chamberlain Register and actively engaged in the many enterprises calculated to build up a town. Like many others in South Dakota, he lost his all in the hard times of the later 'eighties, but stuck to the state and with keen foresight later saw the great development that might come, and he believed would come, to this great artesian section of Central South Dakota. After a painstaking search he secured help from Dubuque capitalists and purchased a very large quantity of land, commencing in the latter part of 1899, in Beadle, Spink, Hand, Hyde, Hughes and Sully counties, fully eighty thousand acres, and nearly five years ago removed to Huron and commenced pushing and advocating the digging of artesian wells, and planting of trees, and bringing new settlers into the country, loaning money to help farmers and others who wished to build and buy more land. He improved a large number of farms, building good houses and barns, and infused new life and confidence in central South Dakota and built up a great business at Huron, in lands, loans and insurance.

In politics Mr. King has ever been an ardent Republican and has been a vigorous and effective worker in its cause. He made an uncompromising stand against the free-silver heresy in 1896, and in the presidential campaign of that year made a large number of strong speeches in advocacy of the single gold standard, the now established financial policy of his party.

Fraternally he is affiliated with the Masons and the Benevolent and Protective Order of Elks. He was reared in the faith of the society of Friends, of which he is a birthright member, but both he and his wife now hold membership in the Congregational church. On the 20th of September, 1866, was solemnized the marriage of Mr. King to Miss Permelia A. Andrews, who was born in Hamilton County, Indiana, being a daughter of William E. and Mary E. Andrews, who were early settlers in Iowa. Mr. and Mrs. King have four children, namely: Guneath D., now Mrs. Gilbert E. Roe, of New York City; Laona M., now Mrs. Walter Montgomery, of Chamberlain, South Dakota; Lorena C, a graduate of Chicago University, now at home in Huron, and Grace E., now Mrs. Fred J. Hutchins, of Chicago, all of whom share their father's loyalty in the belief in South Dakota's future greatness.

TAMES A. KISER

T. A. Kiser, a member of the well-known real-estate firm) of Kiser Brothers, of Redfield, Spink County, was born on a farm near Madison, Dane county, Wisconsin, on the 24th of February, 1865, and is a son of William C. and Lucy A. (Black) Kiser, the former of whom was born in Virginia and the latter in Ohio, where her father was a pioneer, the Black family having been founded in America in the colonial days. The father of the subject passed his early childhood in the Old Dominion state and was about two years of age at the time of his father's death. His mother later removed with her children to Ohio and located in Montgomery County, on the site of the present National Soldiers' Home, near the city of Dayton. While he was still a boy the family removed to Logan County, Ohio, where he remained until 1862, when he located in Dane county, Wisconsin, where he was engaged in farming until 1881, when he came as a pioneer to what is now the state of South Dakota, taking up government land ten miles east of the present village of Mellette, Spink County, where he developed a valuable ranch, upon which he still resides. In 1888 he was elected county treasurer of Spink County; of which office he was incumbent two years.

James Kiser, the immediate subject of this sketch, passed his youth in Dane County, Wisconsin, and received his educational training in the public schools of the city of Madison. He was sixteen years of age at the time of the family removal to Spink County, and here he assisted in the work and management of the home ranch until his father was elected county treasurer, when he served as a clerk in the office for two years. At the expiration of this period, in 1891, he purchased an interest in an abstract and real-estate business in Redfield, being identified with this enterprise until 1894, when he disposed of his interests and went to California, where he remained until 1899, when he returned to Redfield and became associated with his brother, William C. Jr., in the real-estate business, the enterprise having been established some time previously by his brother, and they have since continued the business under the firm name of Kiser Brothers. They have finely appointed offices in Redfield, and courteous attention is given to all who seek their aid or advice in connection with the sale or purchase of property.

The subject of this sketch is a staunch Democrat in politics, and fraternally he is a member of the order of Freemasons, being identified with Redfield Lodge, No. 34; Redfield Chapter, No. 20, Royal Arch

Masons; Huron Commandery, Knights Templar, and El Riad Temple, Ancient Arabic Order of the Nobles of the Mystic Shrine, at Sioux Falls. On the 20th of March, 1889, Mr. Kiser was united in marriage to Miss Lydia A. Markham, a daughter of Giles Markham, a prominent citizen of Markesan, Wisconsin, in which state she was born and reared.

RUSSELL DYER KITTREDGE

Russell Dyer Kittredge, one of the leading representatives of the younger members of the bar of South Dakota controlling an important and growing patronage in Sioux Falls, was born in Fitchburg, Massachusetts, October 12, 1886. He is a son of Herbert William and Marian (Thatcher) Kittredge, the former a native of New Hampshire. The parents removed to Westfield, Massachusetts, in 1890. Mr. Kittredge is a nephew of Alfred B. Kittredge, former United States senator from South Dakota, serving from 1901 to 1903 and from 1903 to 1909. Senator Kittredge died May 4, 1911.

Russell D. Kittredge acquired his early education in the public schools of Westfield, Massachusetts, which he left in 1904. He afterward entered Yale University and was graduated from the academic department in 1908 and from the law department in 1910. He was admitted to the bar in Massachusetts in February, 1911, and after residing in Westfield until August removed to Sioux Falls, South Dakota, where he has since engaged in general practice. He is known as a strong and forceful lawyer and in the four years of his residence here has become connected with a great deal of important litigation.

Mr. Kittredge belongs to the Country Club and the Elks and is a blue lodge Mason and a member of the Knights of Pythias. He gives his political allegiance to the republican party. He is well known in social circles of the city, while in his profession he has gained that success which always follows earnest and conscientious labor.

EIVIND KLAVENESS, M. D.

Dr. Eivind Klaveness, who since November, 1906, has engaged in the practice of medicine in Sioux Falls and is well known as an able physician and surgeon, specializing in dermatology and urology, and one who has made valuable contributions to the literature of the profession, was born in Sandefjord, Norway, a son of Anton Frederik and Birthe Marie (Anderson) Klaveness. The ancestral records can be traced back to 1590, the records of a prior time having been burned. These records are prepared by the government archivist and show an unbroken line.

In the public schools of his home town Dr. Klaveness pursued his early education and afterward attended the high school at Moss, Norway. Later he went to Drammen, where he was graduated in 1889, with the degree of Bachelor of Arts. He afterward entered the University of Christiania, Norway, and there in 1890 won the Doctor of Philosophy degree. He entered upon the study of medicine in the University of Christiania and on the 21st of December, 1897, was graduated, having completed the full course. In 1898 he was made assistant physician to Dr. Carlsen, government physician at Bodeo, Norway, where he remained from January to April. Through the following summer he served in the royal navy, ranking as second lieutenant and attaining the rank of first lieutenant in October, 1898. He continued in the navy until 1901, when he was honorably discharged, and in May, of the same year, he crossed the Atlantic to America, thinking to find better professional opportunities in the new world. Making his way to Chicago, he there pursued a three months' post-graduate course in the Chicago Clinical School and in September, 1901, he located in Brookings, South Dakota, where he practiced for five years. He afterward sold his practice and left that city in June, 1906. After a temporary sojourn at Bristol, South Dakota, he came to Sioux Falls in November, 1906, and has here since actively engaged in practice, winning success as his ability has become recognized by the general public. Since February, 1911, Dr. Klaveness has devoted all of his time to his specialties — dermatology and urology, which, with his extensive insurance business, take his entire attention. While studying in Europe he gave special attention to these branches of medicine and it was owing to the scarcity of population in South Dakota when he first located here that he engaged in general practice until 1911. His practice is now very extensive, extending not only over a wide district in South Dakota, but into northwestern Iowa and southwestern Minnesota as well.

His professional record is, indeed, creditable. He was county physician of Brookings County, South Dakota, for four years, and from 1907 until 1909 he was attending physician to the South Dakota School for Deaf and Mutes. Since 1909 he has been medical director for the Dakota Western Assurance Company. In addition to these duties of a semi-public character and in addition to an extensive and growing private practice he has become well known as the author of various valuable papers upon medical subjects.

On the 25th of August, 1903, in Brookings, South Dakota, Dr. Klaveness was united in marriage to Miss Edith W. Archer, daughter of Dr. F. B. Archer, of Bridgetown, Barbados, and their children are Francis Asthore and Helene Marie. Since becoming a naturalized American citizen Dr. Klaveness has given stanch support to the republican party, in years gone by having been one of the prominent leaders of the progressive faction, and fraternally he is connected with a number of organizations.

He is a thirty-second degree Mason and Mystic Shriner, an Odd Fellow and is likewise connected with the Sons of Norway, of which he has been chief medical examiner since 1907. He has held all of the chairs in the local organization of the Improved Order of Red Men and in the Great Council, at present he is the great prophet. Dr. Klaveness has been a member of the Southwestern Minnesota Medical Society since 1903; was president of the Seventh District Medical Society in 1910 and was a delegate from that society to the state association in 1911 and 1912. He is now secretary of that society. He recently received notice of his appointment as "honorable vice president of Norwegian-American Auxiliary for the Panama Pacific International Exposition in recognition of distinguished patriotic service as a citizen of the United States of America, particularly reflecting honor upon Norway, the land of our fathers." This appointment was dated December 21, 1914, and was given in response to recommendations of his fellow compatriots of South Dakota by officers of the exposition. He has never had occasion to regret his determination to come to the new world, for here he has found the opportunities which he sought and, in their improvement, has reached a prominent position in professional circles. He is a man of broad scholarly attainments and one with whom association means expansion and elevation.

JOHN C. KLEMME

For many years John C. Klemme figured as one of the most prominent insurance men of Huron and his section of the state, and the agency which he established is still conducted under his name, although he has retired from active connection therewith. He is a well-known figure in fraternal circles and is everywhere mentioned as one of the valued residents of Huron. His birth occurred in Franklin County, Indiana, in 1852, and in his youthful days he attended the country schools, but his education and training have been largely acquired in the school of experience. His father was Henry W. Klemme, a resident farmer of Indiana, who, in 1860, removed to Winneshiek County, Iowa, where he owned large tracts of land, being one of the leading farmers of that district. His last years were spent in Elma, Iowa, where he owned a fine residence. A native of Germany, he crossed the Atlantic in a sailing vessel, eight weeks being required in making the voyage. His wife, who bore the maiden name of Catherine Gasell, was also a native of Germany, having been born on the banks of the Rhine in Prussia. They became the parents of fourteen children, of whom thirteen, eleven sons and two daughters, are yet living.

John C. Klemme was a little lad of eight years when the family, removed to Iowa, and in the usual manner of farm lads his boyhood and youth were spent. In 1878, when twenty-six years of age, he came to South Dakota from Vinton, Iowa, for the purpose of looking over the country. He made his way to Springfield, this state, and was well pleased with its prospects. He returned to Vinton for the winter, but in the spring of 1879 again went to Springfield, where he established a real-estate and insurance office, conducting business there for eight years. In 1886 he located in Huron, having taken up a tree claim that included what is now the southern part of the city. For many years he conducted an extensive insurance, real-estate and loan business in that city, having a very large and gratifying clientage. For thirty-four years he represented the Phoenix Insurance Company and established the Calumet agency in South Dakota and in Iowa. For twenty-two years he was special agent and adjuster for the Phoenix Insurance Company in North and South Dakota, and there is no phase of the insurance business with which he is not familiar. His agency was known as the Klemme Agency, and the business is still carried on under that name, although he has retired. The name has become a synonym for the highest standard of service along insurance and real-estate lines.

While at Springfield, South Dakota, Mr. Klemme was united in marriage to Miss Florence Sandison, of Vinton, Iowa, who passed away thirteen years later. A few years subsequent to her death Mr. Klemme wedded Mrs. L. E. Choate, of Yankton, South Dakota, who in her maidenhood was Miss Annie E. Edwards. Her father was one of the pioneers of the state, settling at Elk Point, Dakota, in 1860. Subsequently he moved to Yankton, where he established a dray line. His first home was a log cabin and the family met the usual experiences and hardships of pioneer life, but his business grew with the settlement of this state.

Mr. Klemme has always taken a very active part in the affairs of the city, is a public-spirited man and one whose interest has been of a most helpful character. He is prominently known in fraternal circles, holding membership with the Knights of Pythias, the Benevolent and Protective Order of Elks, the Independent Order of Odd Fellows and the Masons. He was largely instrumental in building the Masonic Temple in Huron and became one of its largest stockholders. He is ever loyal and true to the teachings of these organizations, exemplifying in his life the spirit of fraternity. He belongs to the Episcopal church, and he gives his political allegiance to the republican party. For four years he filled the office of register of deeds in his county and for five or six years was city treasurer of Huron, discharging the duties of both offices with promptness and fidelity. In every relation of life, he has measured up to high standards of manhood and citizenship and in business his record is indeed an enviable one, winning for him the regard and confidence of colleagues and contemporaries. The rest which has come to him in his retirement from business is well merited, but, while he has put aside the more arduous cares of business life, he is by no means a recluse, for he takes a most active and helpful interest in the fraternal organizations with which he is connected and gives generous, hearty and helpful support to all those measures which are a matter of civic virtue and civic pride.

LESLIE C. KROH

Leslie C. Kroh, engaged in the lumber business in Yankton, is a native of Illinois. He was born in Albany, that state, on the 15th of November, 1862, and is a son of William G. Kroh, who was a native of Cincinnati, Ohio, while the grandfather was born in Germany. William G. Kroh conducted business as a hardware merchant and in 1882 removed to the far west, spending his last days in Idaho, where he passed away in 1894. His wife, who bore the maiden name of Alice Alvoid, was a native of Pennsylvania and in their family were five children

Leslie C. Kroh, the third in order of birth, was educated in the graded and high schools of Lyons, Iowa, and in a business college, becoming thus well qualified for entrance into commercial circles. He first became connected with the lumber trade at Clinton, Iowa, as an employe of the Clinton Lumber Company, with which he remained for three years. He afterward spent one year in the employ of J. H. Queal & Company at Des Moines, Iowa, and subsequently removed to Maurice, Iowa, where he remained for a year. He afterward spent a decade in Sutherland, Iowa, as manager of a lumberyard, and in 1897 the present business was established in Yankton with Mr. Kroh in charge. He also has supervision over fourteen other branch yards and the company with which he is connected is one of the most extensive lumber concerns of the state, their business constantly growing and expanding along substantial lines. Mr. Kroh is familiar with every phase of the lumber trade, knows the condition of the market and the demands of the public, and his readiness to serve the people in an honorable and efficient manner is a potent feature in his success. He is a stockholder in and superintendent of the Queal interests and is the auditor.

On the 3rd of April, 1887, Mr. Kroh was united in marriage to Miss Mollie E. Brown, a daughter of James Brown, a native of Maryland, and to them have been born two children: Mabel Alice, a graduate of the Maryland College for Women at Lutherville, Maryland; and William Leslie, who is a graduate of the high school at Yankton and is now with his father as assistant auditor of a system of lumberyards controlled by Mr. Kroh.

The family hold membership in the Congregational church and occupy a prominent social position. Mr. Kroh is a valuable representative of the Independent Order of Odd Fellows and of the Masonic fraternity, in which he has attained the thirty-second degree of the Scottish Rite in the consistory. He is a republican in his political views, but votes independently when there is no issue before the people. His strong and salient characteristics are such as have qualified him for leadership. He possesses much of the spirit of initiative and seems to readily recognize the various conditions which point out the path to success. His close application and indefatigable industry have continuously advanced him in his business career until he now ranks among the foremost lumber merchants of the northwest.

JOHN W. KRUEGER

John W. Krueger, residing in Erwin, Kingsbury County, is proving a popular and able official as cashier of the Bank of Erwin. His birth occurred in Wisconsin on the 15th of December, 1876, his parents being Carl and Genevieve Krueger, who came to South Dakota in 1884, the father purchasing land in Day County. Both Mr. and Mrs. Carl Krueger have passed away.

John W. Krueger attended the public schools in the acquirement of an education and also pursued a business course at Charles City, Iowa. Subsequently he was employed in a store at Andover, South Dakota, for eleven months and afterward was connected with a produce concern at Fargo, North Dakota, for a short time. He next became bookkeeper in the State Bank at Andover and was later promoted to the position of cashier, in which capacity he served for nine years. On the expiration of that period, he entered the service of the Day County Land Company, a real-estate concern, and subsequently embarked in the real-estate business on his own account at Blunt, Hughes County, being thus engaged for a year and a half. In 1912 he embarked in the hardware business but later sold out and entered the Bank of Erwin as cashier, in which capacity he has ably served to the present time, contributing to the continued growth and success of the institution in an appreciable degree.

On the 7th of January, 1908, Mr. Krueger was united in marriage to Miss Eva Hitchcock, a daughter of Gideon Hitchcock. He exercises his right of franchise in support of the men and measures of the republican party and in religious faith is a Congregationalist. Fraternally he is identified with the Masons, belonging to the lodge, chapter, commandery and the Mystic Shrine. He is fond of motoring and all outdoor sports and has won the high esteem and friendship of those with whom he has come in contact in both business and social relations.

GEORGE W. KRUM

George W. KRUM, a representative citizen and successful business man of Claremont, Brown County, is a native of the Wolverine state, having been born in Kent County, Michigan, on the 2d of August, 1844, and being a son of Abraham and Theresa (Holmes) Krum, both of whom were born in New York state, the former lacing of Holland Dutch extraction and the latter of English. Abraham Krum was born in Ulster County, New York, and removed to Kent County, Michigan, in 1837, being one of the very early settlers in that now populous and opulent section of the state. Grand Rapids, the second city of the commonwealth, being located in the county mentioned. In 1838 he returned to New York, where he married Miss Theresa Holmes, who returned with him to the pioneer farm in the midst of the primeval forests of Michigan, where they passed the remainder of their long and useful lives, retaining the uniform esteem of all who knew them. The subject was reared to the sturdy discipline of the homestead farm, in Vergennes township, and early began to aid in its work, while his educational advantages as a boy were those afforded in the common schools, while later he attended the high school in the city of Grand Rapids. He continued to reside on the old homestead until 1874, when he went to the couth, where he remained six years, passing the major portion of this time in Texas and the Indian territory. He then, in 1881, came to what is now Brown County, South Dakota, and settled on a homestead claim three miles west of Groton, where he developed a good farm and continued to be engaged in farming and stock growing until the autumn of 1886, when he located in Claremont and opened a real-estate and loan office. He has built up a most prosperous enterprise, is recognized as an able and straightforward business man, and through his well-directed operations has done much to forward the development of the section of the state in which he conducts his enterprise, while he commands the unequivocal confidence and esteem of all who know him. He still owns his original homestead, besides other valuable properties in the county.

In politics he gives his allegiance to the Prohibition party and fraternally he is a member of Cement Lodge, No. 103, Ancient Free and Accepted Masons, in Claremont, and of Aberdeen Chapter, No. 12, Royal Arch Masons, in Aberdeen.

JOSEPH KUBLER

J. Kubler is a native of the province of Alsace, Germany, where his birth occurred on August 23, 1854. He attended the schools of that country until his seventeenth year, after the Franco-Prussian war, when he left home and came to the United States, landing in New Orleans, thence after a short time went to Jackson, Mississippi, where he remained about two years, during which he was variously employed. From the latter place he went to St. Louis, Missouri, later to Kansas City, thence to Omaha, Nebraska, and finally, in 1873, made his way as far west as Denver, Colorado.

Shortly after reaching his objective point, he entered a newspaper office, to serve an apprenticeship at the printing business. It was while thus engaged that the Black Hills country was opened, and in the spring of 1876, he engaged with Mervick & Laughlin, who took a newspaper outfit to Custer City, to work in their office. Reaching their destination, these gentlemen while waiting for part of the material and stock of paper, issued a circular announcing to the people that their publication would appear in due time, but before the supplies arrived the gold excitement at Deadwood broke out, the effect of which was to cause a rush from Custer City, until the latter place was almost depopulated. Moving their plant to Deadwood, Messrs. Merrick & Laughlin, assisted by Mr. Kubler, issued, on June 8th of the above year, the first number of die Black Hills Pioneer, a sprightly, well edited local sheet, devoted to the mining and other interests of the town and surrounding country, and which under the original management was regularly issued for some years thereafter. Mr. Kubler severed his connection with the paper and returning to Custer City, purchased, in partnership with A. D. Clark, a newspaper plant, that had been brought to the place some time previously, and on September 4th of the same year the first number of the Custer Chronicle was issued under the new management. After publishing the paper jointly for a period of five years, Mr. Kubler purchased his partner's share, since which time he has been sole proprietor, the Chronicle under his able editorial and business management growing steadily in public favor the meanwhile, until it is now not only one of the oldest newspapers in the Black Hills, but also one of the most successful, as well as one of the ablest and most influential local sheets in the state. Mr. Kubler has a well-equipped office, supplied with all the latest and most approved machinery and appliances, and the Chronicle is not only well edited, but is neat in its mechanical makeup and a model of typographical art, ranking in every respect with larger and much more pretentious metropolitan papers. Strongly Republican in politics and a zealous partisan, Mr. Kubler has never sought office or public position of any kind, believing that he can better promote the interests of his party through the medium of his paper than in any other way. He has attended many of the county, district and state conventions since locating in Custer City, and has wielded a strong influence in these bodies, being recognized as a safe and judicious counsellor. In May, 1900, he was appointed postmaster of Custer City, and was reappointed in May, 1904, and has since discharged the duties of the position in a creditable and business-like manner.

Mr. Kubler is a thirty-second-degree Scottish Rite Mason, also belongs to the Mystic Shrine, and for a number of years has been a member of the blue lodge at Custer City, having served several terms as master of the same, besides holding various official positions in the other branches of the order with which he is identified; he also holds membership with the Pythian brotherhood, being one of the active workers in the lodge, which meets in the city of his residence. Mr. Kubler is one of the most enterprising men in the Black Hills, has always stood for progress and improvement and, although of foreign birth, he is intensely American in his inclination and tendencies, being a loyal supporter of the government under which he has achieved such marked prestige and success.

Mr. Kubler, in July, 1883, was united in marriage with Miss Louisa Katsch, of Germany, but at the date noted a resident of Custer City, the following children being the fruit of the union: Joseph W., William L., Carl H., Eva, Frank, Grace and Louisa.

HARRY KUNKLE

Harry Kunkle, who's well-earned recognition as an attorney has made him known throughout the state, maintains his office in Yankton, where he has remained continuously since 1904, although he resides in Nowlin, Stanley County, Pennsylvania claims him as a native son, his birth having occurred in Venango County, that state, on the 16th of October, 1865. His father, Joseph J. Kunkle, was born in Westmoreland County, Pennsylvania, and was a representative of one of the old pioneer families of that state, founded there in colonial days, in the year 1682. Several representatives of the name have attained fame and prominence in Pennsylvania. Joseph J. Kunkle was a printer by trade but after learning the business was engaged for a time in the oil business in Venango County, Pennsylvania, where he was living at the time of the birth of his son Harry. Soon afterward, however, he returned to Westmoreland County, where he took up the occupation of farming, which he followed for a long period. At the present writing, however, he is living retired, enjoying the fruits of his former toil. He married Hannah E. Stewart, a daughter of Joseph Stewart. She was born in Armstrong County, Pennsylvania, and also survives.

Harry Kunkle was the oldest in their family of eight children, having five brothers and two sisters. He was reared upon his father's farm with the usual experiences of the lad who divides his time between the work of the fields and the acquirement of a common school education. After leaving the district schools he attended Irwin Academy at Irwin, Pennsylvania, and later took up the profession of teaching, which he followed through seven winter seasons, while in the summer months he worked as a coal miner. He was thus engaged until 1888, when he made his way to the northwest, settling in Centreville, Turner County, South Dakota, where he secured work as a section hand. He was thus engaged for six months and on the expiration of that period he entered the employ of the Citizens Bank at Centreville, retaining that position for three years. He had the entire responsibility of the bank management, being made cashier. He became ill with typhoid fever about September, 1895, and did not return to the bank, his health being so greatly impaired that he felt it would be detrimental to enter upon the close confinement of his duties as cashier. Moreover, he had an ambition which he wished to satisfy and began the study of law, being admitted to the bar in April, 1896. He then began practice in Centerville, where he remained until 1904 and in addition to his law practice, he conducted a farm, loan and insurance business. He opened an office in Yankton in 1904 and has since met with great success. His practice extends over the entire state, from Rapid City to Yankton, and he has been connected with many important cases as attorney for the defense or prosecution. He is an able and learned lawyer, well versed in the principles of jurisprudence, and his analytical mind enables him to readily understand the strong and potent features of his cases and present them with clearness and cogency. The collection department of his business has likewise grown to gratifying proportions and in addition to these interests he has a farm of four hundred and eighty acres of good land near Nowlin, Stanley County, which has been brought to a high state of cultivation and is now a most valuable tract.

Mr. Kunkle was married, in Columbus, Ohio, in 1888 to Miss Estella L. Crawford, of that city, who died in April, 1889. In November, 1891, he married again, his second union being with Miss Maggie J. Oakland, a native of Turner County, South Dakota. His family numbers seven children: Percy, at home; Ruth, the wife of Ray Noble, of Albion, Michigan; Lilly, a graduate of the Yankton high school; Montrose, Taylor and George, all in school; and Bertie, at home.

Mr. Kunkle is a democrat but has never been active in politics nor has he sought office. He belongs to Myrtle Lodge, No. 91, A. F. & A. M., of Centerville, and in professional lines his membership is with the South Dakota State Bar Association and the Commercial Law League of America. He is a man of determination and strong will power and an earnest worker, so that his success is the logical and legitimate outcome of his efforts.

JOHN KNOX KUTNEWSKY, M. D.

Dr. John Knox Kutnewsky, superintendent and physician for the State School and Home for the Feeble Minded at Redfield, was born in Groveland, Illinois, April 20, 1858, his parents being John and Margaret (Knox) Kutnewsky. The former died in 1884 and the latter in 1903 and their remains were interred in the Redfield cemetery. The father was one of the pioneer settlers and business men of Spink County and in 1882 began the operation of the first mill of Redfield, which also still remains the only mill. He was quite prominent and active in local political circles in Illinois, where he filled the position of postmaster. To him and his wife were born five children: Martha, now residing in Maiden, Washington; John K., of this review; Benjamin H., who is engaged in general merchandising at Maiden, Washington; Charles F., who is state agent for the Equitable Life Insurance Company at Boise, Idaho; and Fred H., who is conducting a hardware store in Maiden, Washington.

In the district schools of his native state Dr. Kutnewsky began his education. He afterward attended the Illinois State University and then in preparation for a professional career entered Rush Medical College of Chicago, from which he was graduated at the age of twenty-three years. He then entered upon the active work of his profession at Groveland, Illinois, where he continued until February, 1884, when he came to South Dakota following his father's death. Opening an office in Redfield, he there remained in active practice until 1901, when he was appointed superintendent of the School for the Feeble Minded. Here he has since remained in charge, covering a period of fourteen years. He has closely studied modern methods of teaching and caring for this unfortunate class, has introduced new and improved ideas and has made the institution a creditable one to the humanitarian spirit which prompted its founding.

In 1882, at Athens, Illinois, Dr. Kutnewsky was united in marriage to Miss Etta Kincaid, a daughter of John K. and Vienna (Williams) Kincaid, both of whom are deceased and lie buried at Athens. Our subject and his wife have two children, namely: Walter Knox, of North Yakima, Washington, who is a land agent and also captain of Company C of the Washington National Guard; and Edna, who is still under the parental roof. Liberal educational advantages have been accorded the children, Walter K. being a graduate of the University of Minnesota, while Edna completed a domestic science course in Columbia University of New York City and is now dietitian of the Redfield institution.

Dr. Kutnewsky is a republican in his political views and for four years filled the office of alderman, during which period he put forth every effort in his power to advance the welfare of the city and uphold its civic interests. He is also a school trustee. Fraternally he is well known as a member of various organizations, including the Masonic lodge, the Elks, the Modern Woodmen of America, the Ancient Order of United Workmen and others. He has filled all of the chairs in the blue lodge and chapter of Masonry and at the present time is eminent commander of the commandery. In 1906 he was grand high priest of the Grand Chapter of South Dakota, and he is a past president of the Masonic Veterans Association. High and honorable are the principles which have actuated him in all life's relations. He has ever reached out a helping hand to the unfortunate and at the same time he is ever embracing his opportunities for advancement that his life work may be of greater usefulness and benefit to his fellowmen. The course which he has ever followed in his official connection with the School for the Feeble Minded has won high encomiums, and various plans and methods that he pursues might profitably be adopted by other institutions of similar character.

Finis